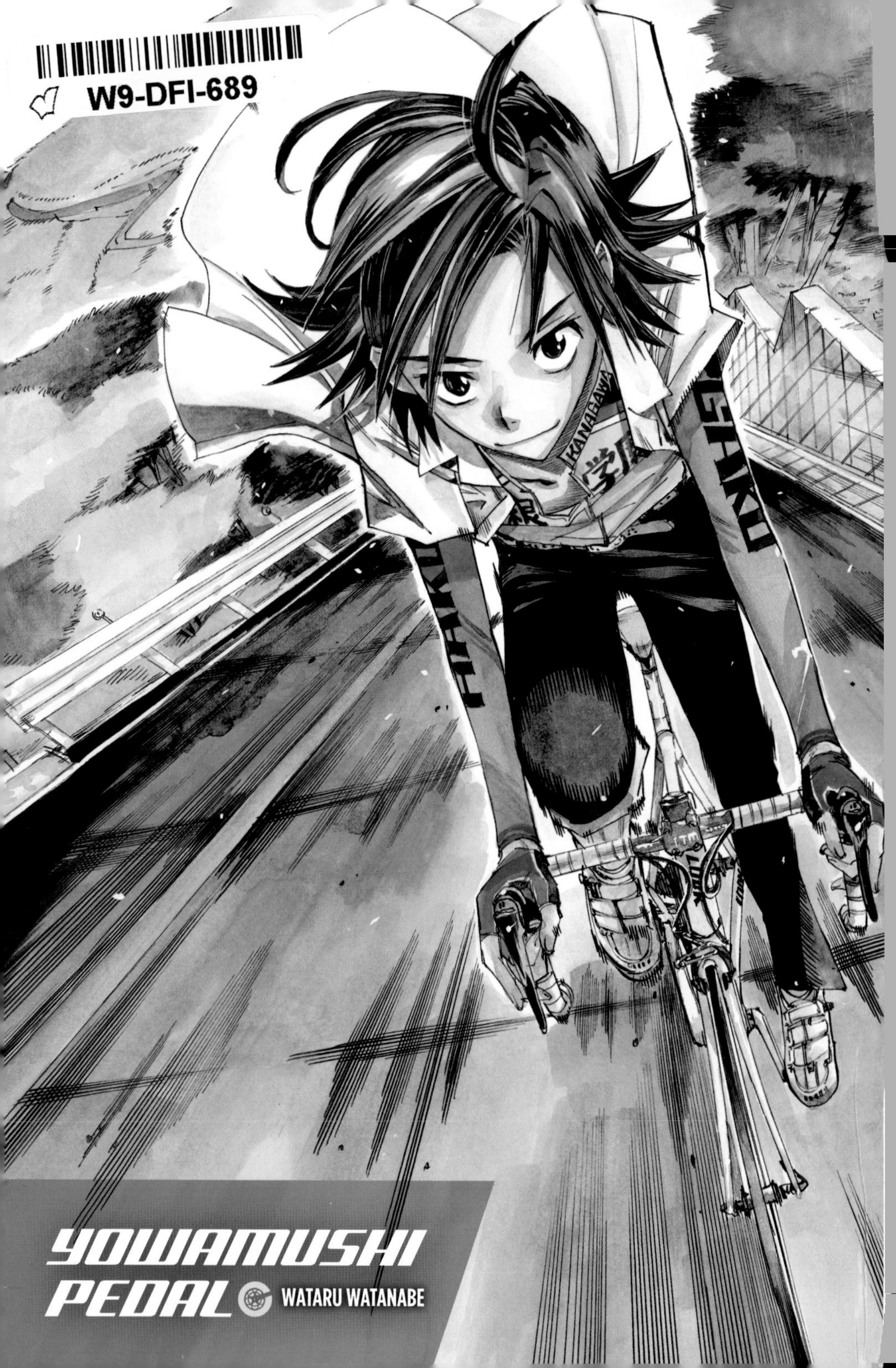
KANAGAWA

YOWAMUSHI PEDAL

WATARU WATANABE

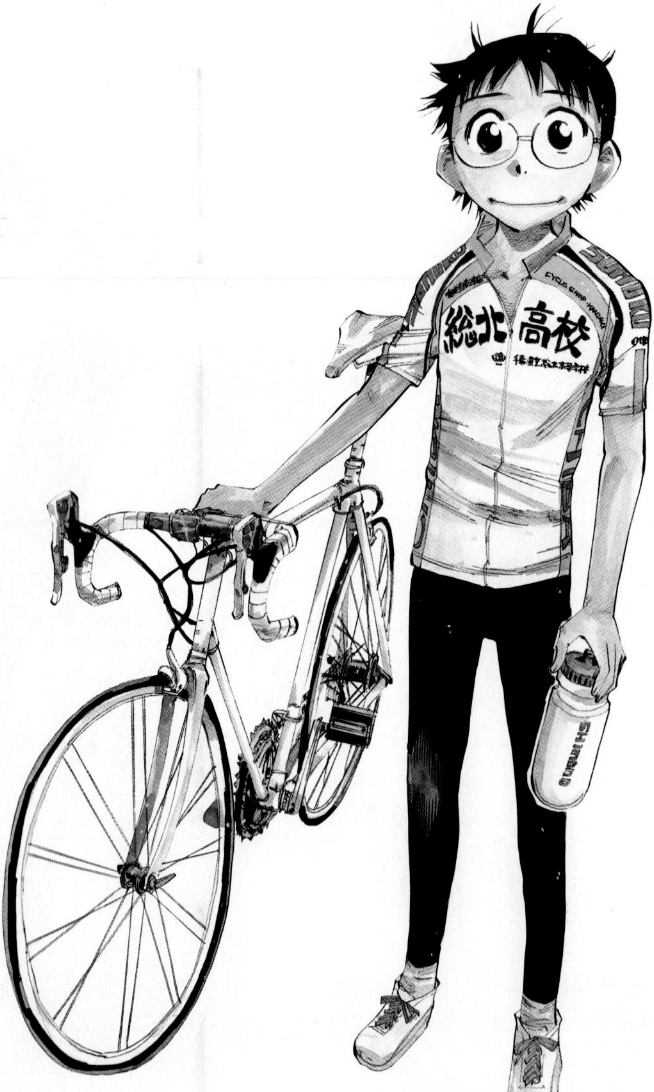
総北高校

YOWAMUSHI PEDAL

3

WATARU WATANABE

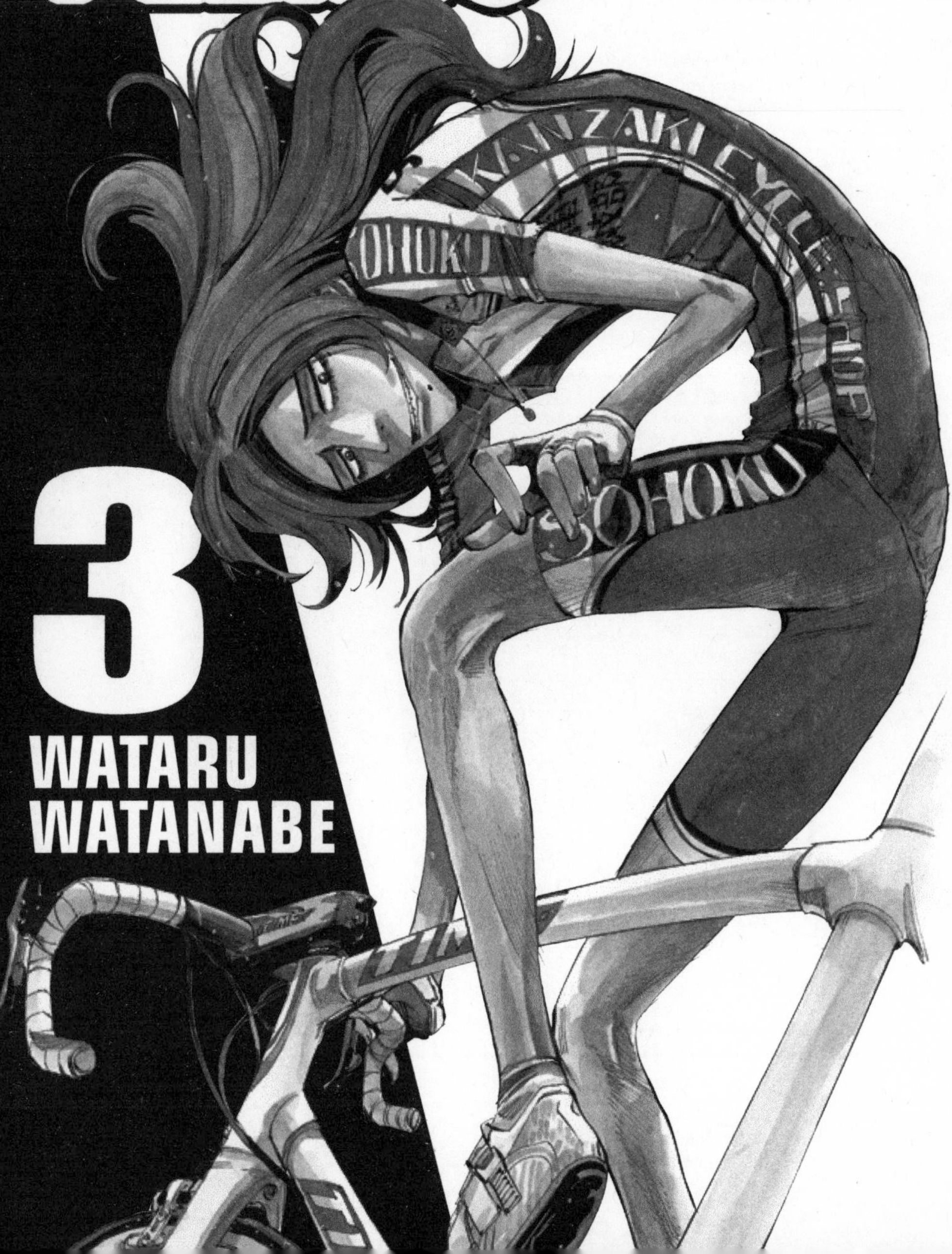
SOHOKU

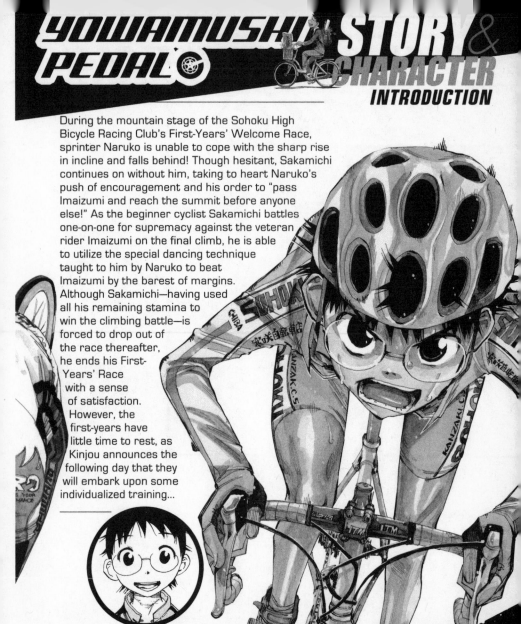

YOWAMUSHI PEDAL STORY & CHARACTER INTRODUCTION

During the mountain stage of the Sohoku High Bicycle Racing Club's First-Years' Welcome Race, sprinter Naruko is unable to cope with the sharp rise in incline and falls behind! Though hesitant, Sakamichi continues on without him, taking to heart Naruko's push of encouragement and his order to "pass Imaizumi and reach the summit before anyone else!" As the beginner cyclist Sakamichi battles one-on-one for supremacy against the veteran rider Imaizumi on the final climb, he is able to utilize the special dancing technique taught to him by Naruko to beat Imaizumi by the barest of margins. Although Sakamichi—having used all his remaining stamina to win the climbing battle—is forced to drop out of the race thereafter, he ends his First-Years' Race with a sense of satisfaction. However, the first-years have little time to rest, as Kinjou announces the following day that they will embark upon some individualized training...

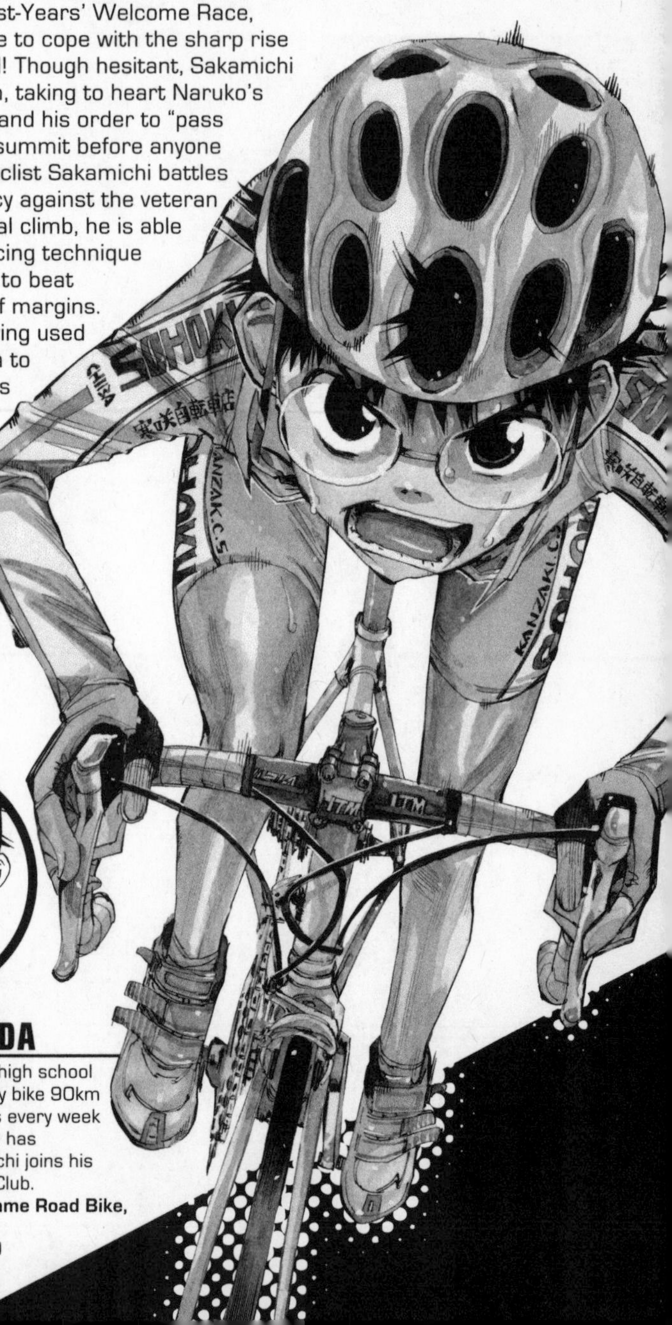

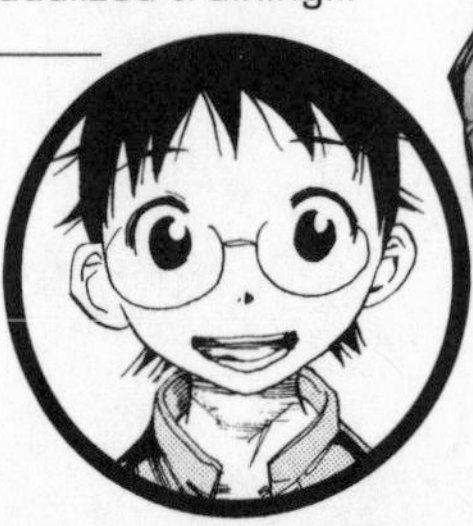

SAKAMICHI ONODA

Sakamichi is an anime-loving high school student who rides his mommy bike 90km round- trip up extreme slopes every week to visit Akiba. Hearing that he has potential as a cyclist, Sakamichi joins his high school's Bicycle Racing Club.

Preferred Bike: **Chromoly Frame Road Bike, Mommy Bike** (maker unknown)

Cycling Style: **High Cadence Climber**

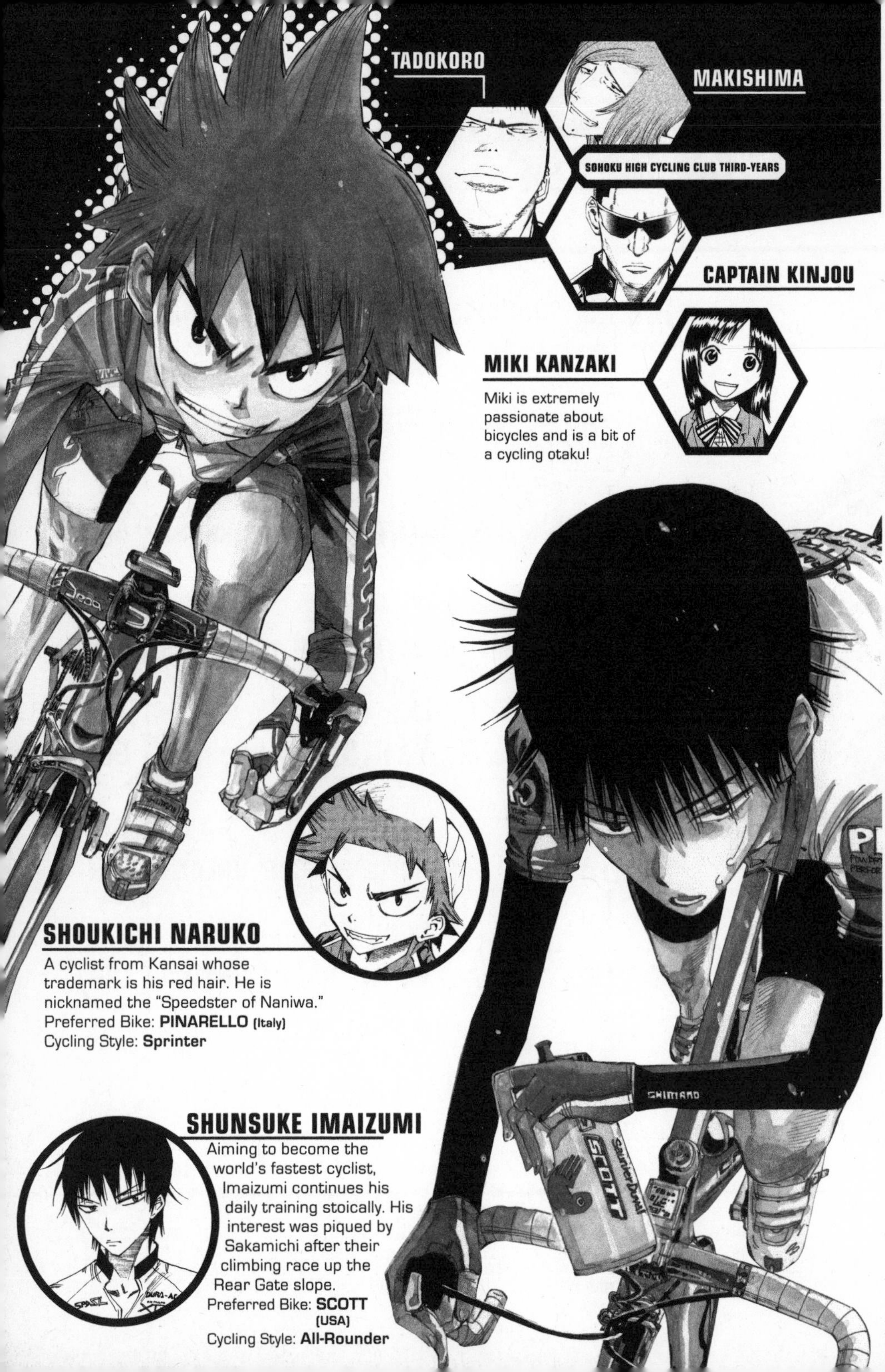

SOHOKU HIGH CYCLING CLUB THIRD-YEARS

MAKISHIMA

TADOKORO

CAPTAIN KINJOU

MIKI KANZAKI

Miki is extremely passionate about bicycles and is a bit of a cycling otaku!

SHOUKICHI NARUKO

A cyclist from Kansai whose trademark is his red hair. He is nicknamed the "Speedster of Naniwa."
Preferred Bike: **PINARELLO (Italy)**
Cycling Style: **Sprinter**

SHUNSUKE IMAIZUMI

Aiming to become the world's fastest cyclist, Imaizumi continues his daily training stoically. His interest was piqued by Sakamichi after their climbing race up the Rear Gate slope.
Preferred Bike: **SCOTT (USA)**
Cycling Style: **All-Rounder**

VOL.3

YOWAMUSHI PEDAL
CONTENTS

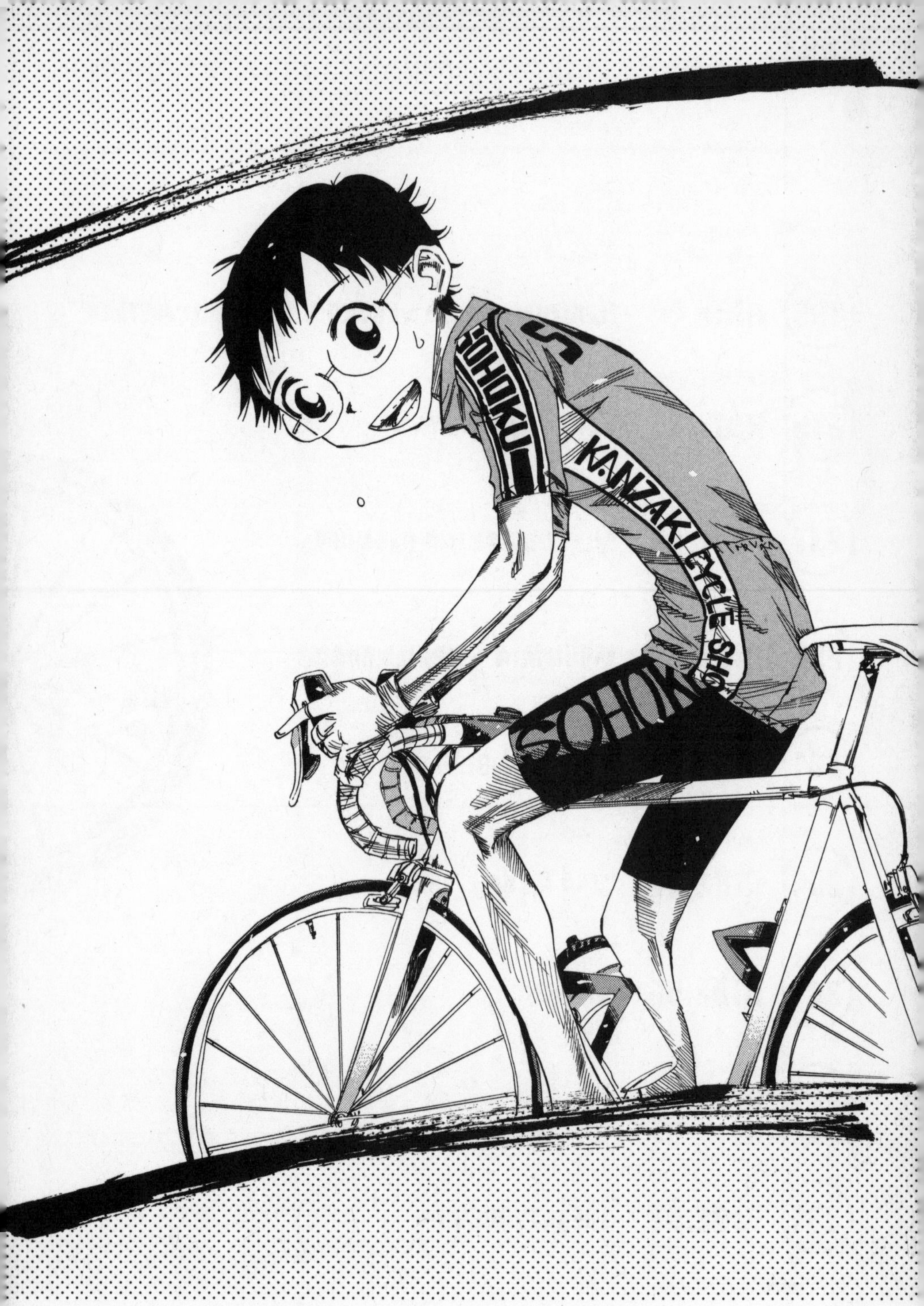
SOHOKU

RIDE.35 INDIVIDUALIZED TRAINING BEGINS

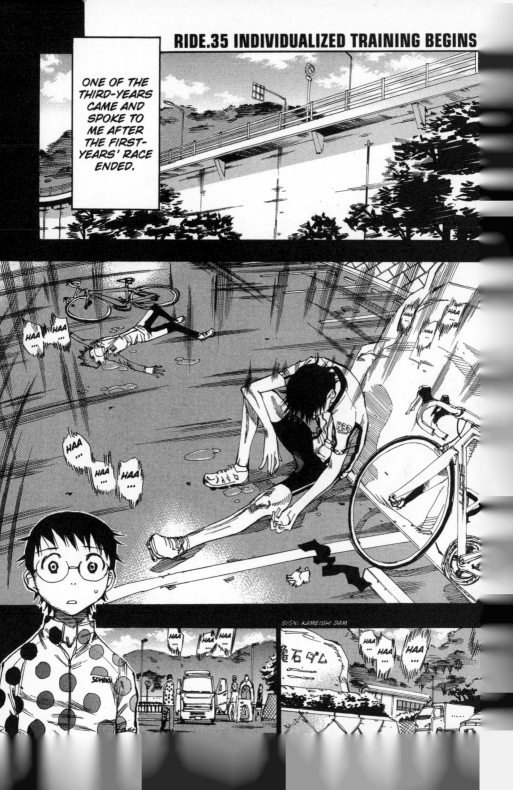

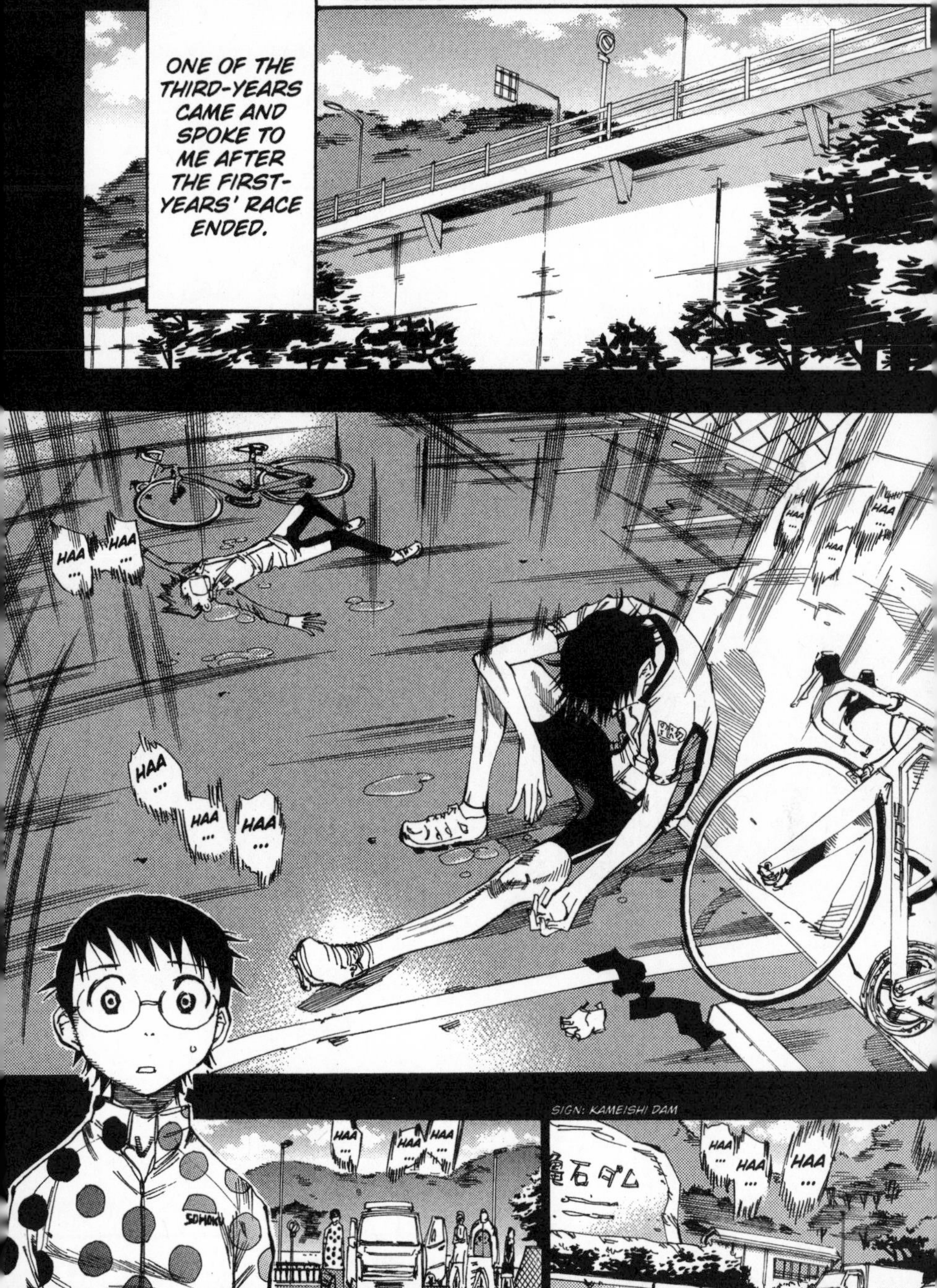
ONE OF THE THIRD-YEARS CAME AND SPOKE TO ME AFTER THE FIRST-YEARS' RACE ENDED.
HAA...
HAA...
HAA...
HAA...
HAA...
HAA...
HAA...
HAA...
SIGN: KAMEISHI DAM
亀石ダム
HAA...
HAA...
HAA...
HAA...
HAA...
HAA...
SOHOKU

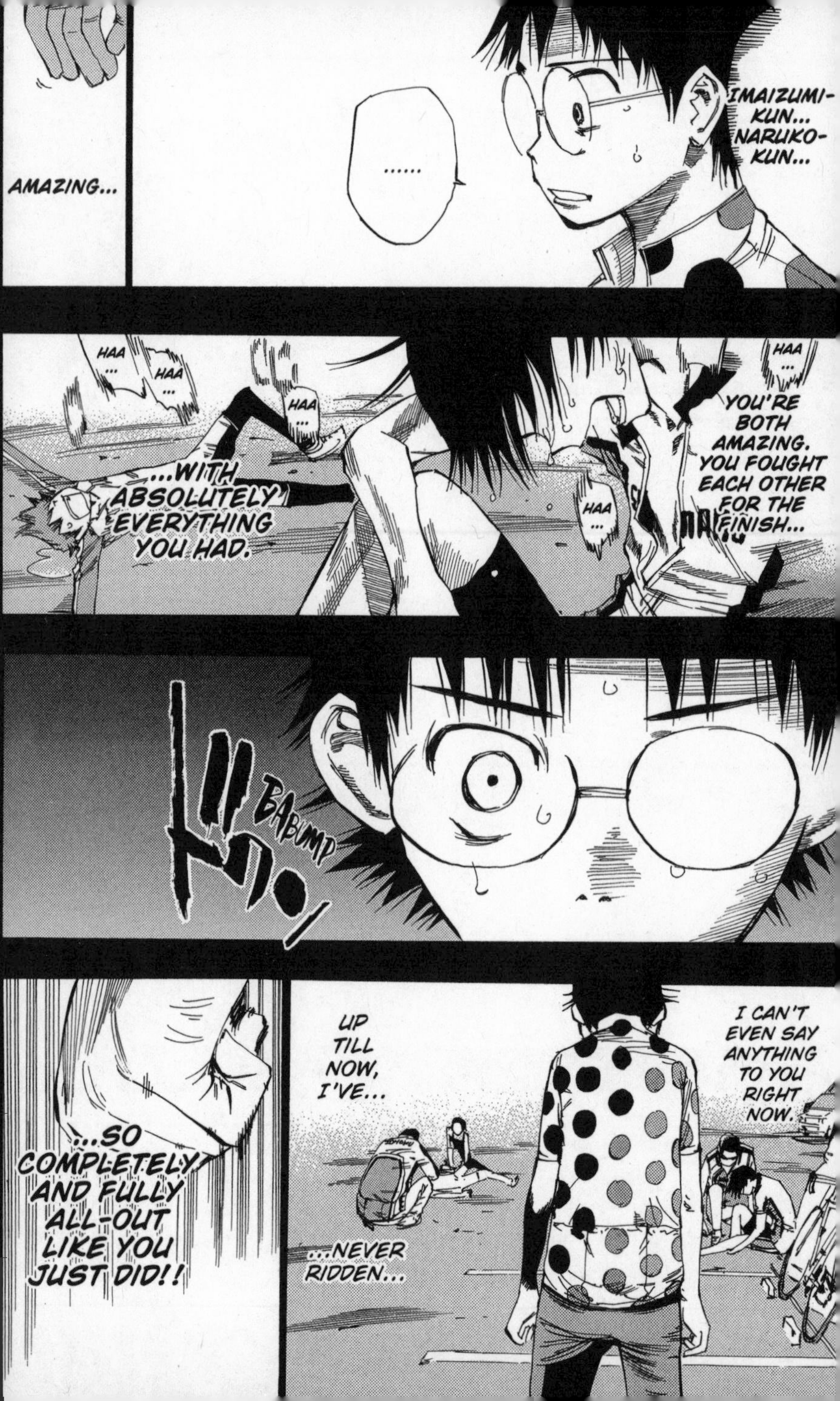
IMAIZUMI-KUN... NARUKO-KUN...
......
AMAZING...
HAA...
HAA...
YOU'RE BOTH AMAZING. YOU FOUGHT EACH OTHER FOR THE FINISH...
HAA...
HAA...
...WITH ABSOLUTELY EVERYTHING YOU HAD.
HAA...
BABUMP
I CAN'T EVEN SAY ANYTHING TO YOU RIGHT NOW.
UP TILL NOW, I'VE...
...NEVER RIDDEN...
...SO COMPLETELY AND FULLY ALL-OUT LIKE YOU JUST DID!!

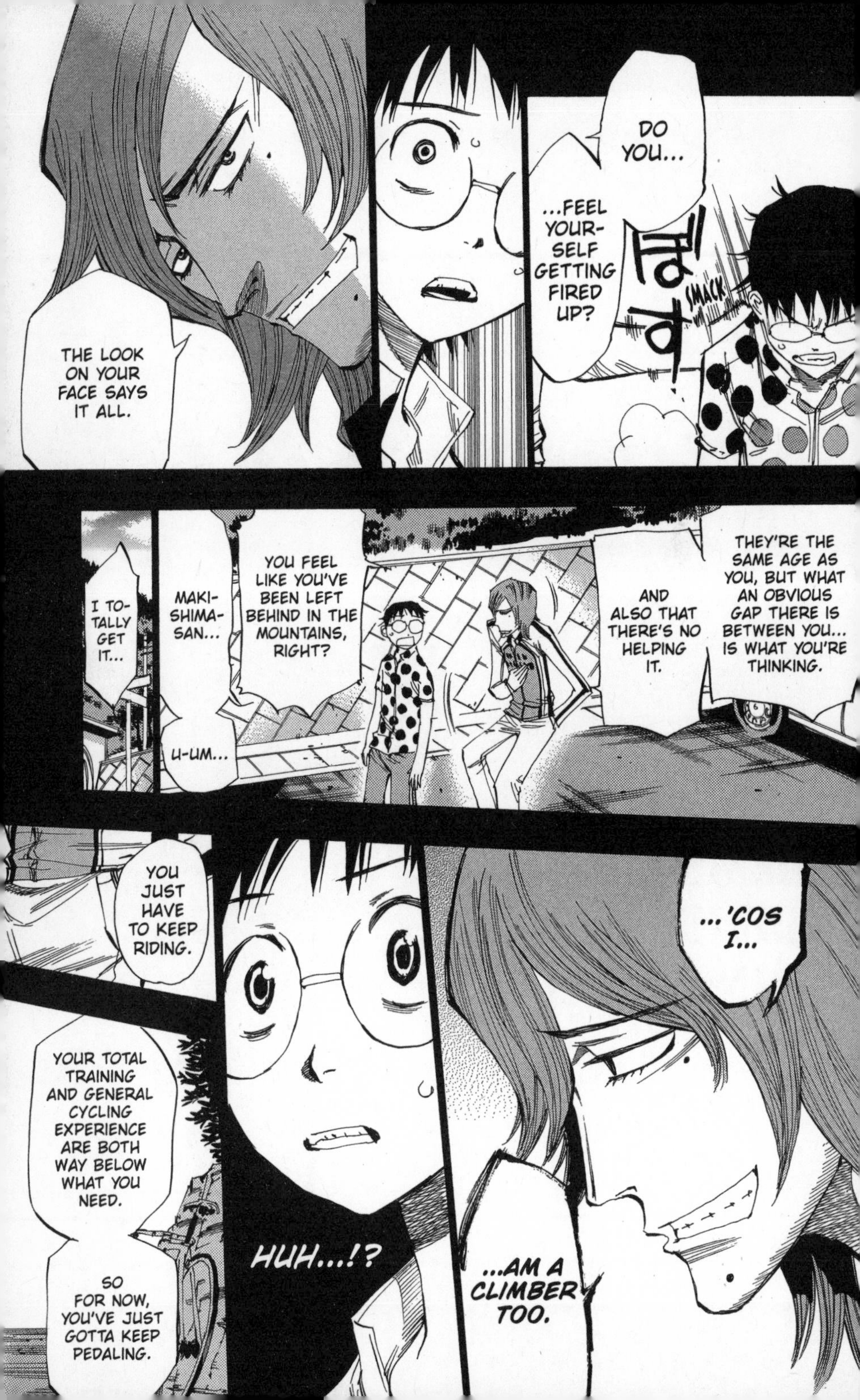
DO YOU...
...FEEL YOURSELF GETTING FIRED UP?
ぼす
SMACK
THE LOOK ON YOUR FACE SAYS IT ALL.
THEY'RE THE SAME AGE AS YOU, BUT WHAT AN OBVIOUS GAP THERE IS BETWEEN YOU... IS WHAT YOU'RE THINKING.
AND ALSO THAT THERE'S NO HELPING IT.
YOU FEEL LIKE YOU'VE BEEN LEFT BEHIND IN THE MOUNTAINS, RIGHT?
MAKISHIMA-SAN...
U-UM...
I TOTALLY GET IT...
...'COS I...
...AM A CLIMBER TOO.
HUH...!?
YOU JUST HAVE TO KEEP RIDING.
YOUR TOTAL TRAINING AND GENERAL CYCLING EXPERIENCE ARE BOTH WAY BELOW WHAT YOU NEED.
SO FOR NOW, YOU'VE JUST GOTTA KEEP PEDALING.

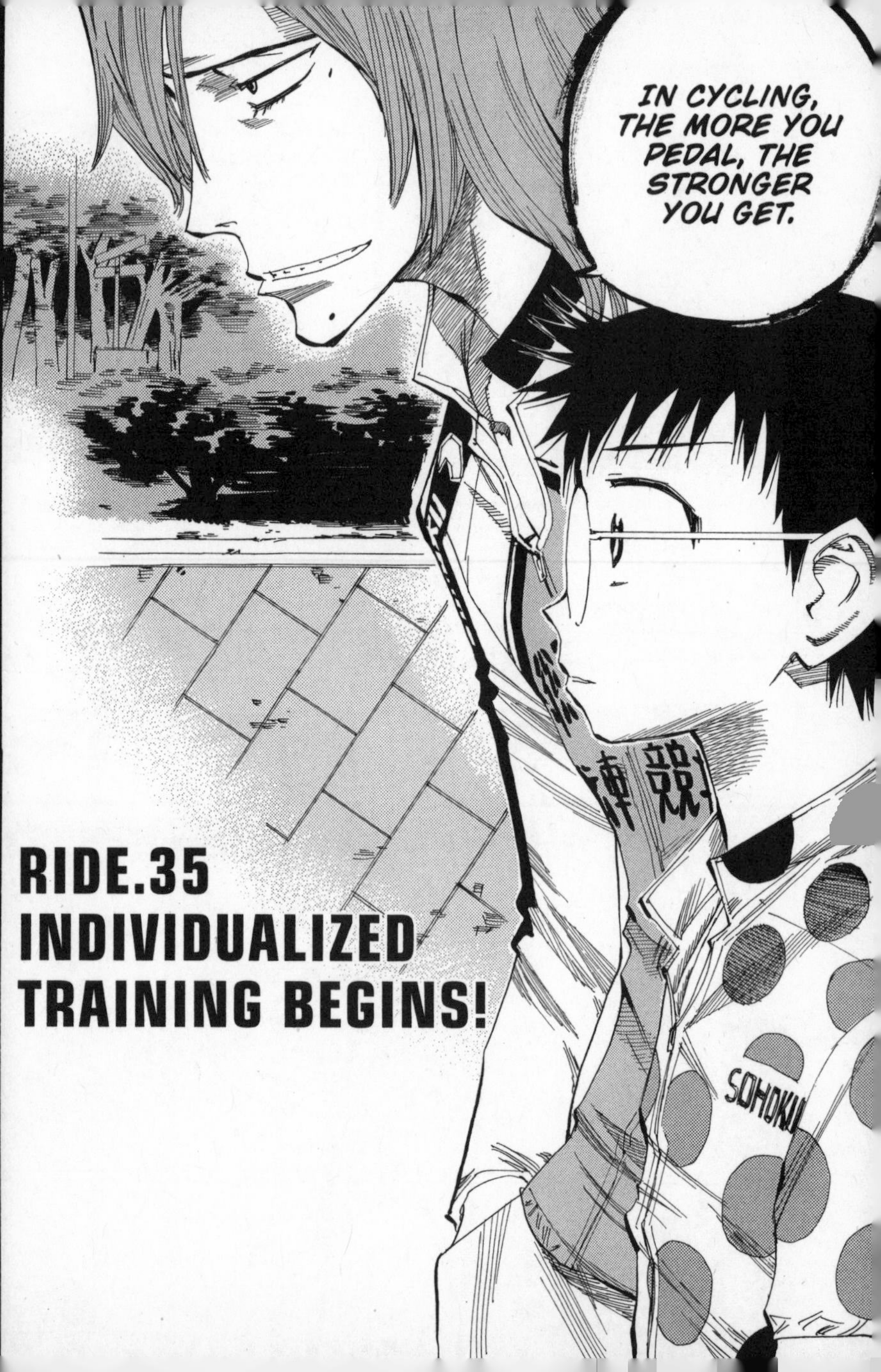
IN CYCLING, THE MORE YOU PEDAL, THE STRONGER YOU GET.
RIDE.35
INDIVIDUALIZED TRAINING BEGINS!
SOHOKU

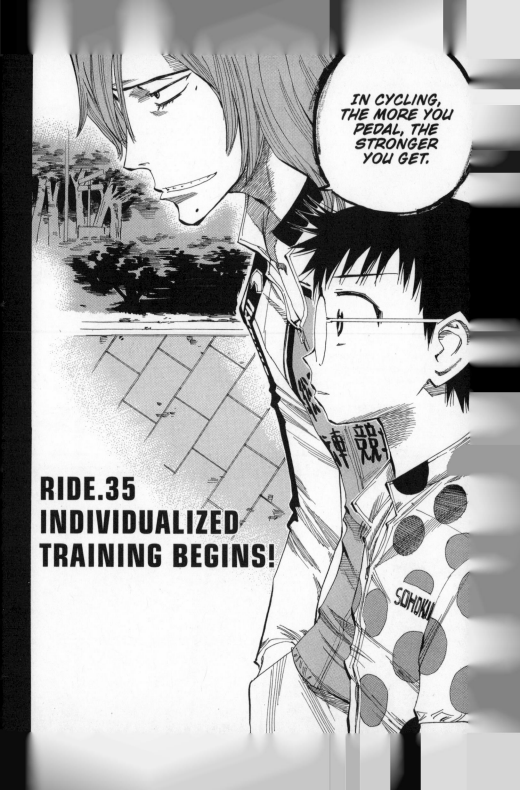

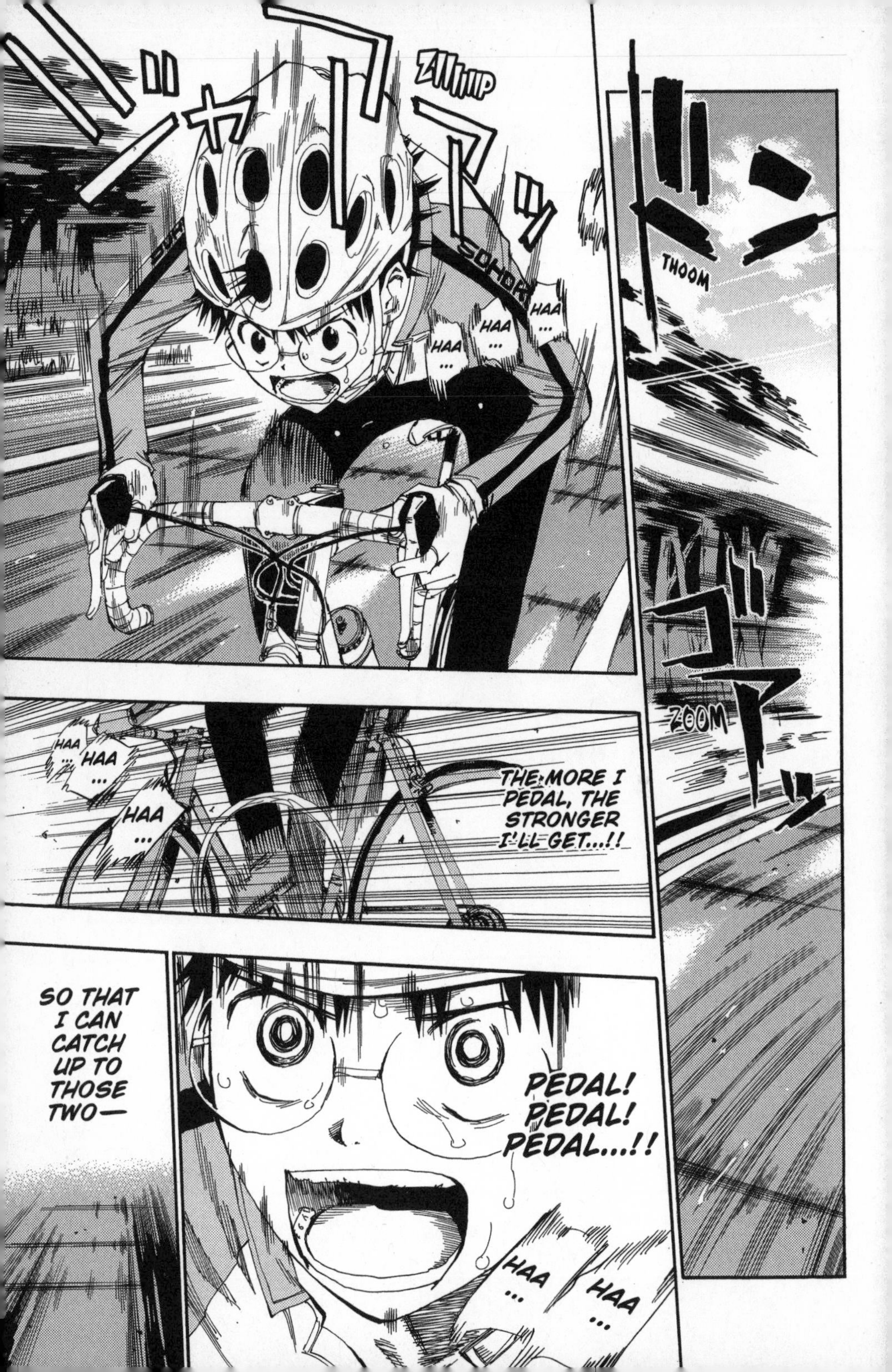

THOOM
ZOOM
ZIIIIP
HAA...
HAA...
HAA...
THE MORE I PEDAL, THE STRONGER I'LL GET...!!
HAA...
HAA...
HAA...
PEDAL! PEDAL! PEDAL...!!
SO THAT I CAN CATCH UP TO THOSE TWO—
HAA...
HAA...

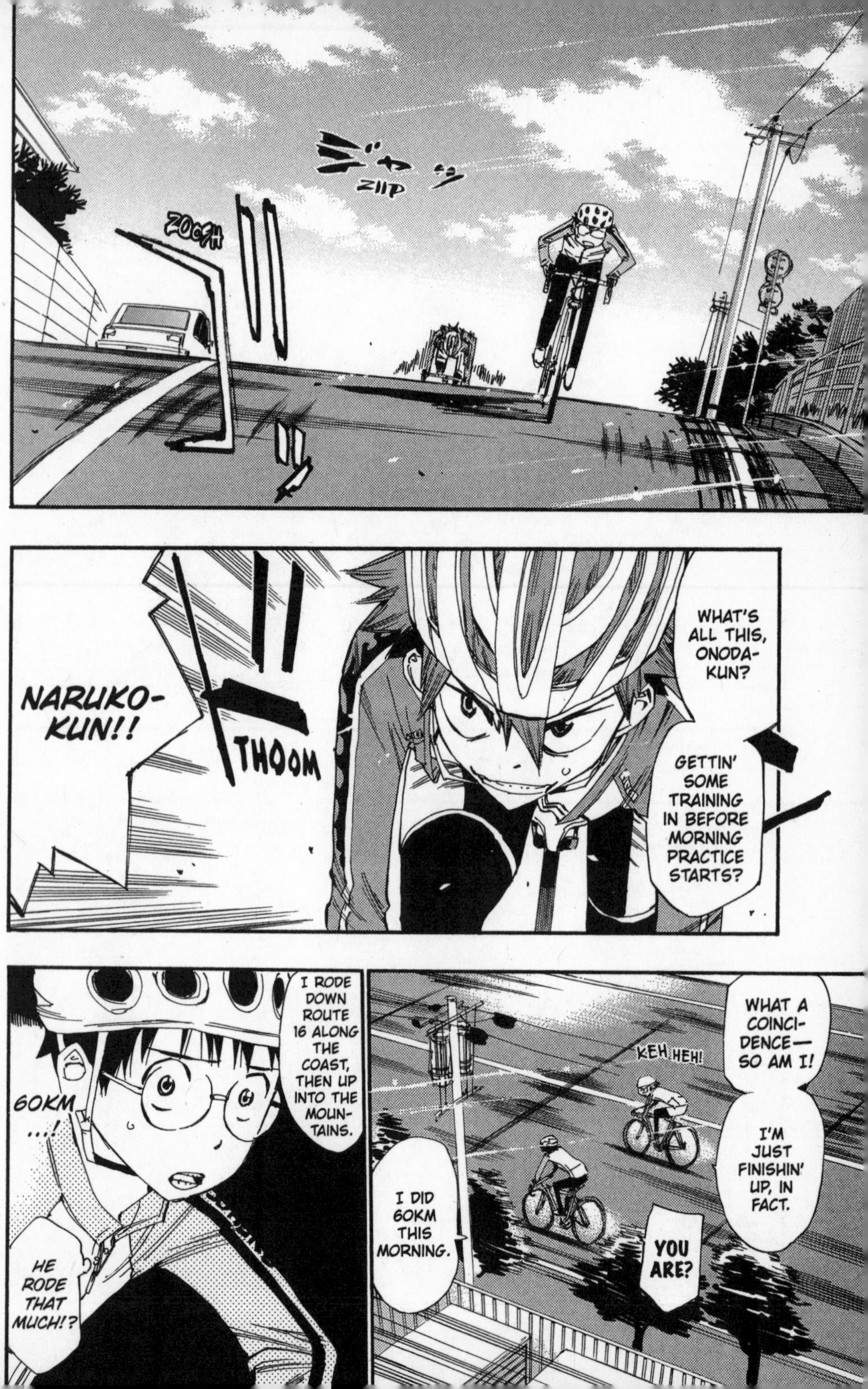
ZIIP
ZOOSH
WHAT'S ALL THIS, ONODA-KUN?
GETTIN' SOME TRAINING IN BEFORE MORNING PRACTICE STARTS?
THOOM
NARUKO-KUN!!
WHAT A COINCIDENCE—SO AM I!
KEH HEH!
I'M JUST FINISHIN' UP, IN FACT.
YOU ARE?
I DID 60KM THIS MORNING.
I RODE DOWN ROUTE 16 ALONG THE COAST, THEN UP INTO THE MOUNTAINS.
60KM ...!
HE RODE THAT MUCH!?

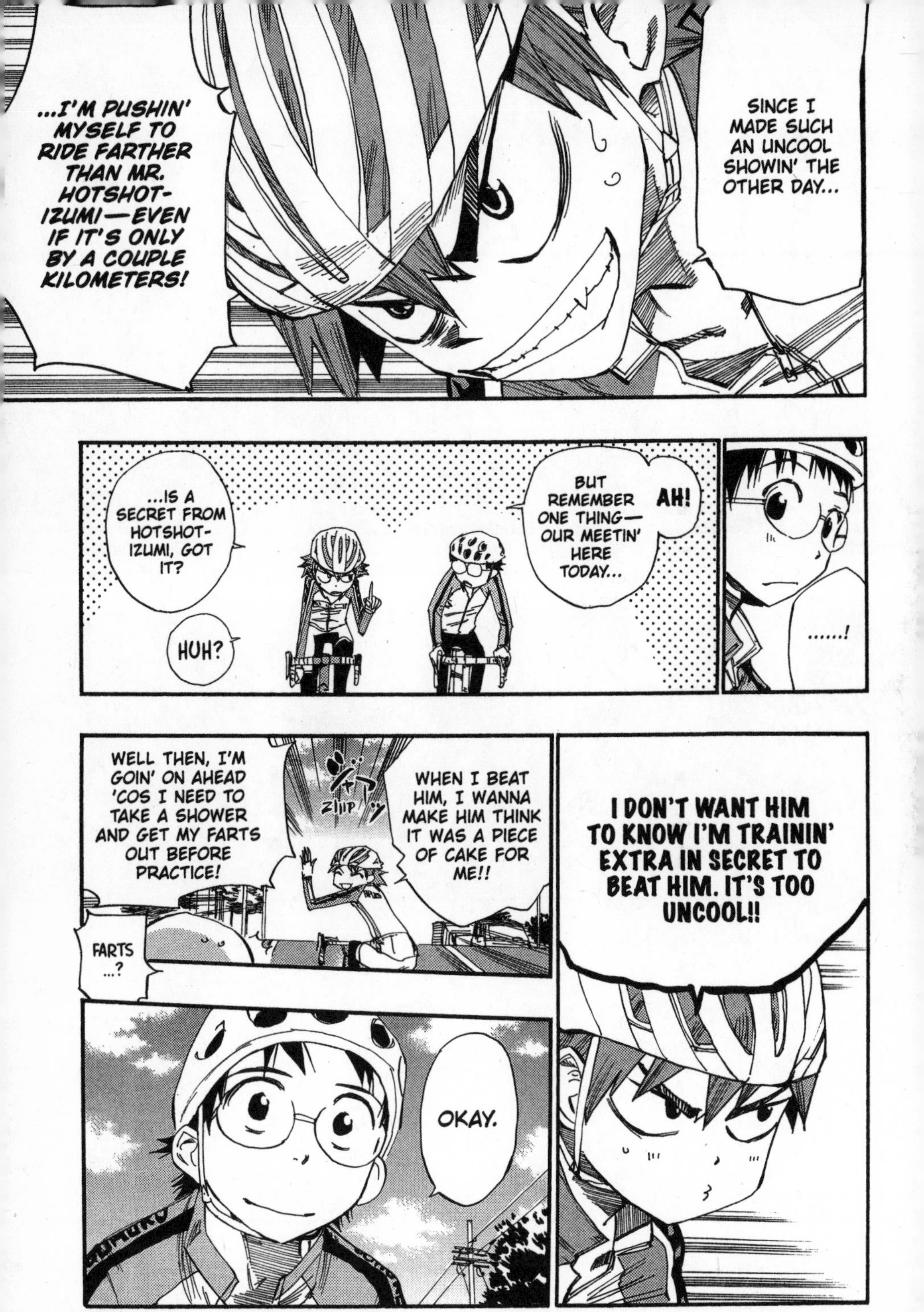

SINCE I MADE SUCH AN UNCOOL SHOWIN' THE OTHER DAY...
...I'M PUSHIN' MYSELF TO RIDE FARTHER THAN MR. HOTSHOT-IZUMI—EVEN IF IT'S ONLY BY A COUPLE KILOMETERS!
......!
AH!
BUT REMEMBER ONE THING—OUR MEETIN' HERE TODAY...
...IS A SECRET FROM HOTSHOT-IZUMI, GOT IT?
HUH?
I DON'T WANT HIM TO KNOW I'M TRAININ' EXTRA IN SECRET TO BEAT HIM. IT'S TOO UNCOOL!!
WHEN I BEAT HIM, I WANNA MAKE HIM THINK IT WAS A PIECE OF CAKE FOR ME!!
ZIIIP
WELL THEN, I'M GOIN' ON AHEAD 'COS I NEED TO TAKE A SHOWER AND GET MY FARTS OUT BEFORE PRACTICE!
FARTS ...?
OKAY.

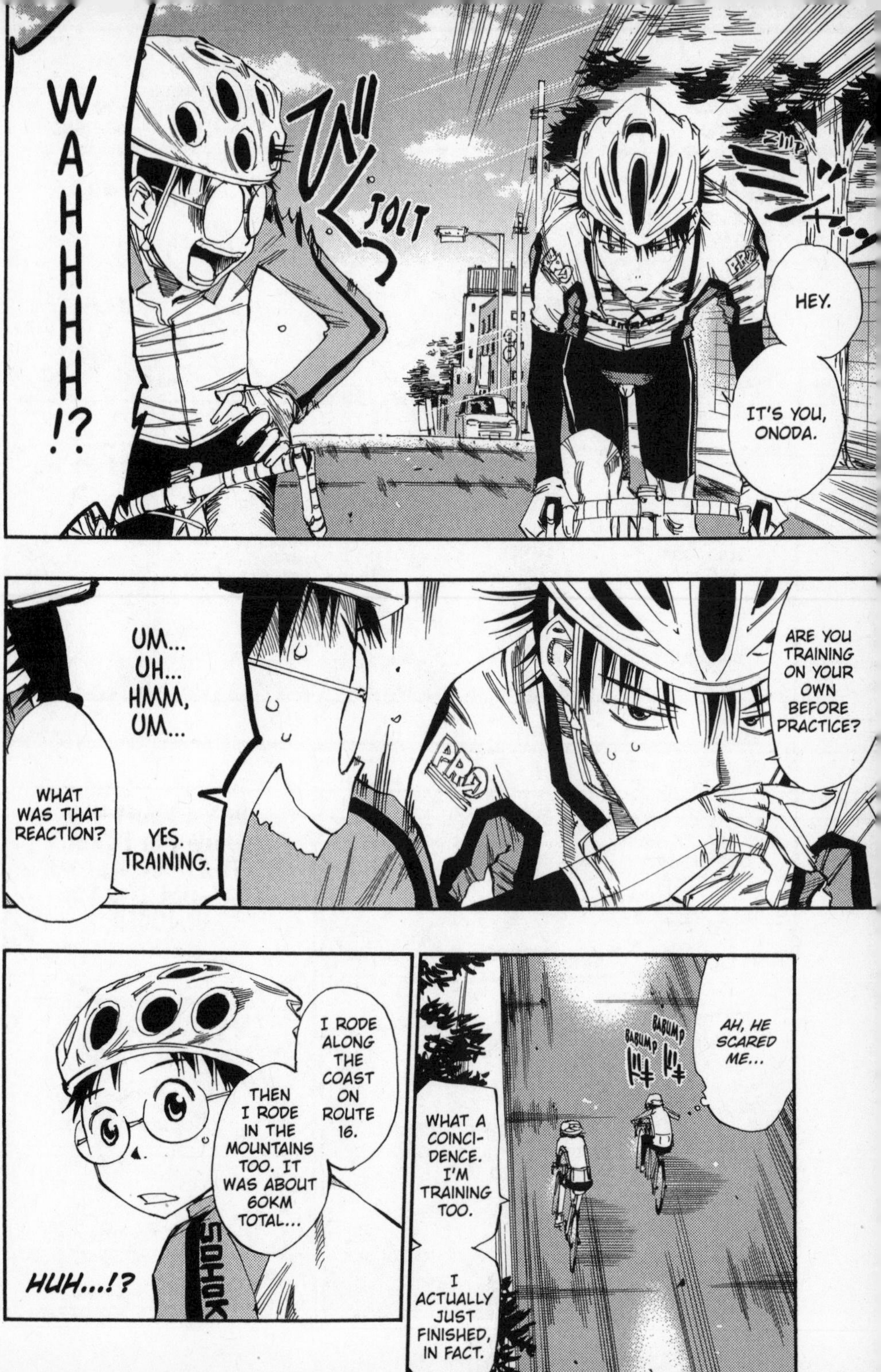
HEY.
IT'S YOU, ONODA.
JOLT
WAHHHHH!?
ARE YOU TRAINING ON YOUR OWN BEFORE PRACTICE?
UM... UH... HMM, UM...
YES. TRAINING.
WHAT WAS THAT REACTION?
AH, HE SCARED ME...
BABUMP
BABUMP
WHAT A COINCI-DENCE. I'M TRAINING TOO.
I ACTUALLY JUST FINISHED, IN FACT.
I RODE ALONG THE COAST ON ROUTE 16.
THEN I RODE IN THE MOUNTAINS TOO. IT WAS ABOUT 60KM TOTAL...
HUH...!?

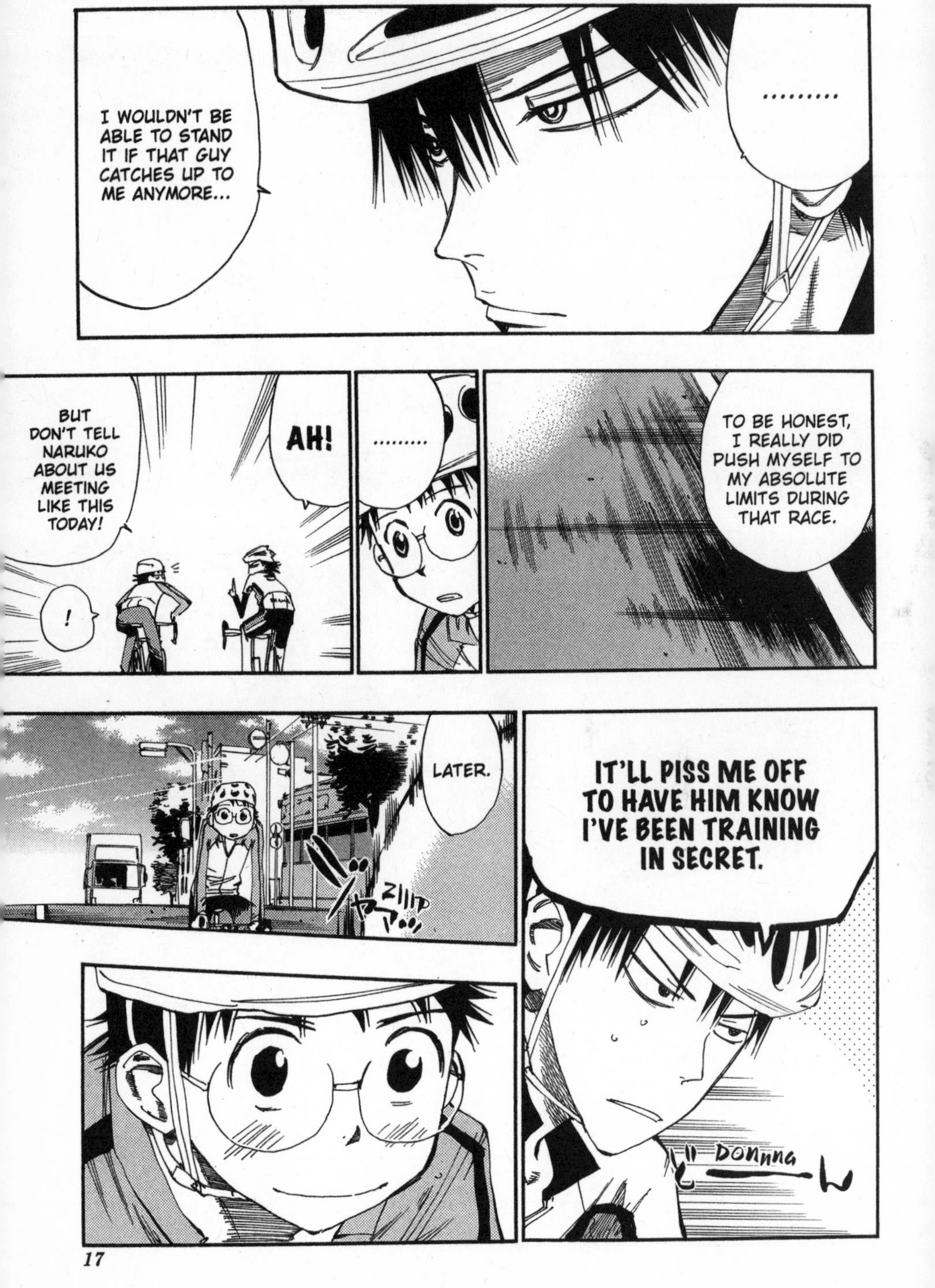
....
I WOULDN'T BE ABLE TO STAND IT IF THAT GUY CATCHES UP TO ME ANYMORE...
TO BE HONEST, I REALLY DID PUSH MYSELF TO MY ABSOLUTE LIMITS DURING THAT RACE.
....
AH!
BUT DON'T TELL NARUKO ABOUT US MEETING LIKE THIS TODAY!
!
IT'LL PISS ME OFF TO HAVE HIM KNOW I'VE BEEN TRAINING IN SECRET.
DONnnG
LATER.
ZIIIP

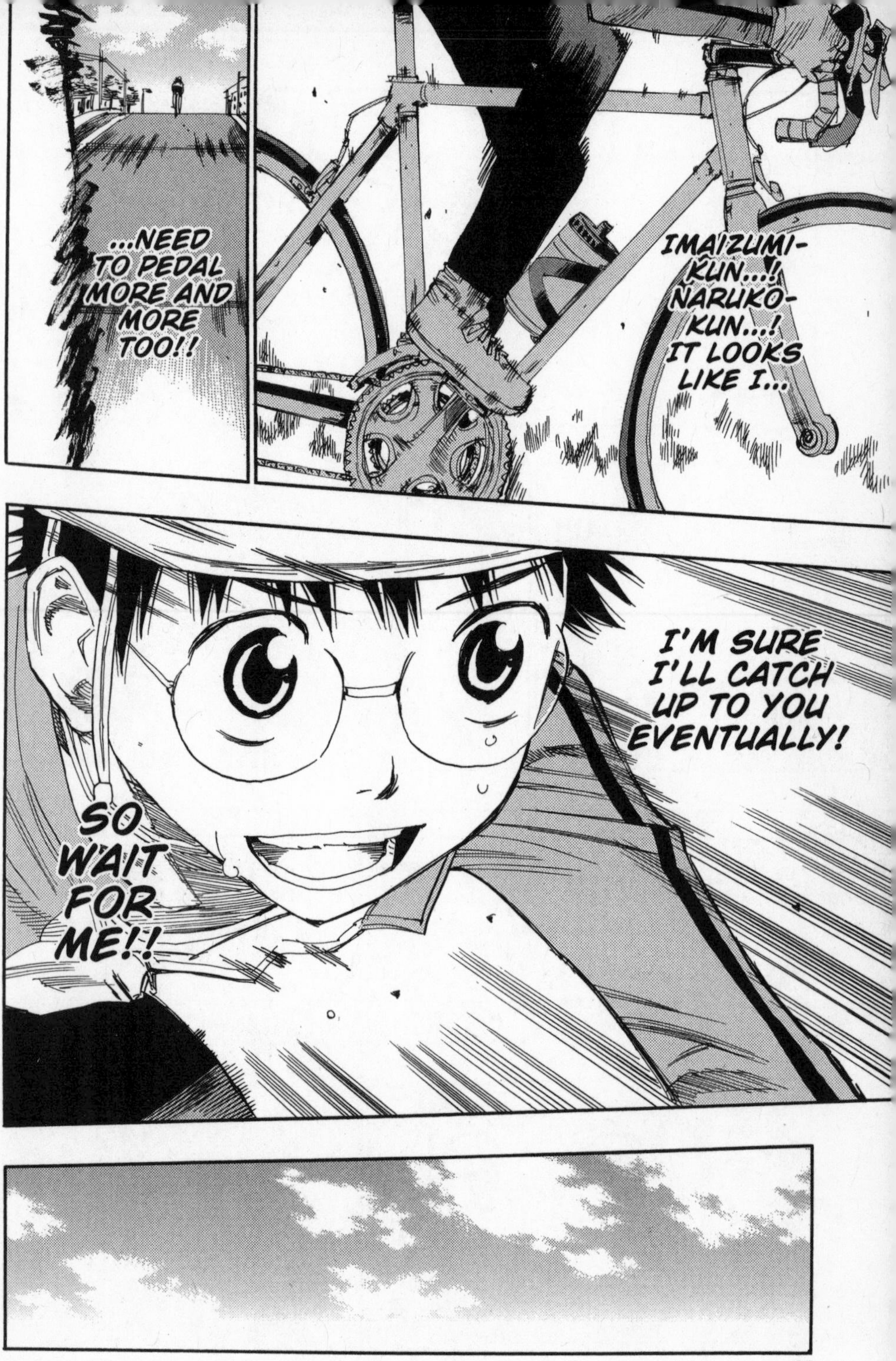
IMAIZUMI-KUN...! NARUKO-KUN...! IT LOOKS LIKE I...
...NEED TO PEDAL MORE AND MORE TOO!!
I'M SURE I'LL CATCH UP TO YOU EVENTUALLY!
SO WAIT FOR ME!!

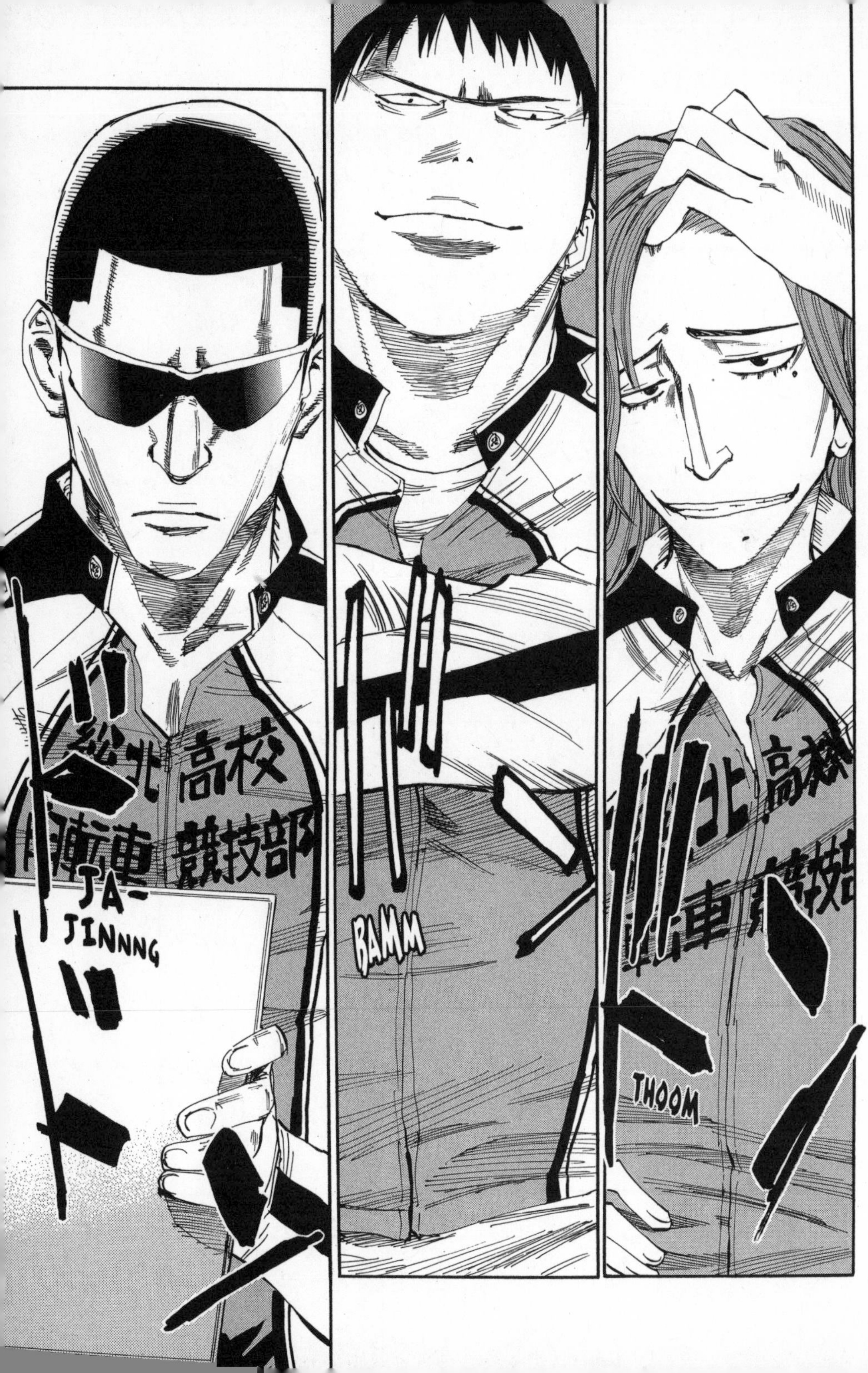
THOOM
BAMM
総北高校
自転車競技部
JA-JINNNG

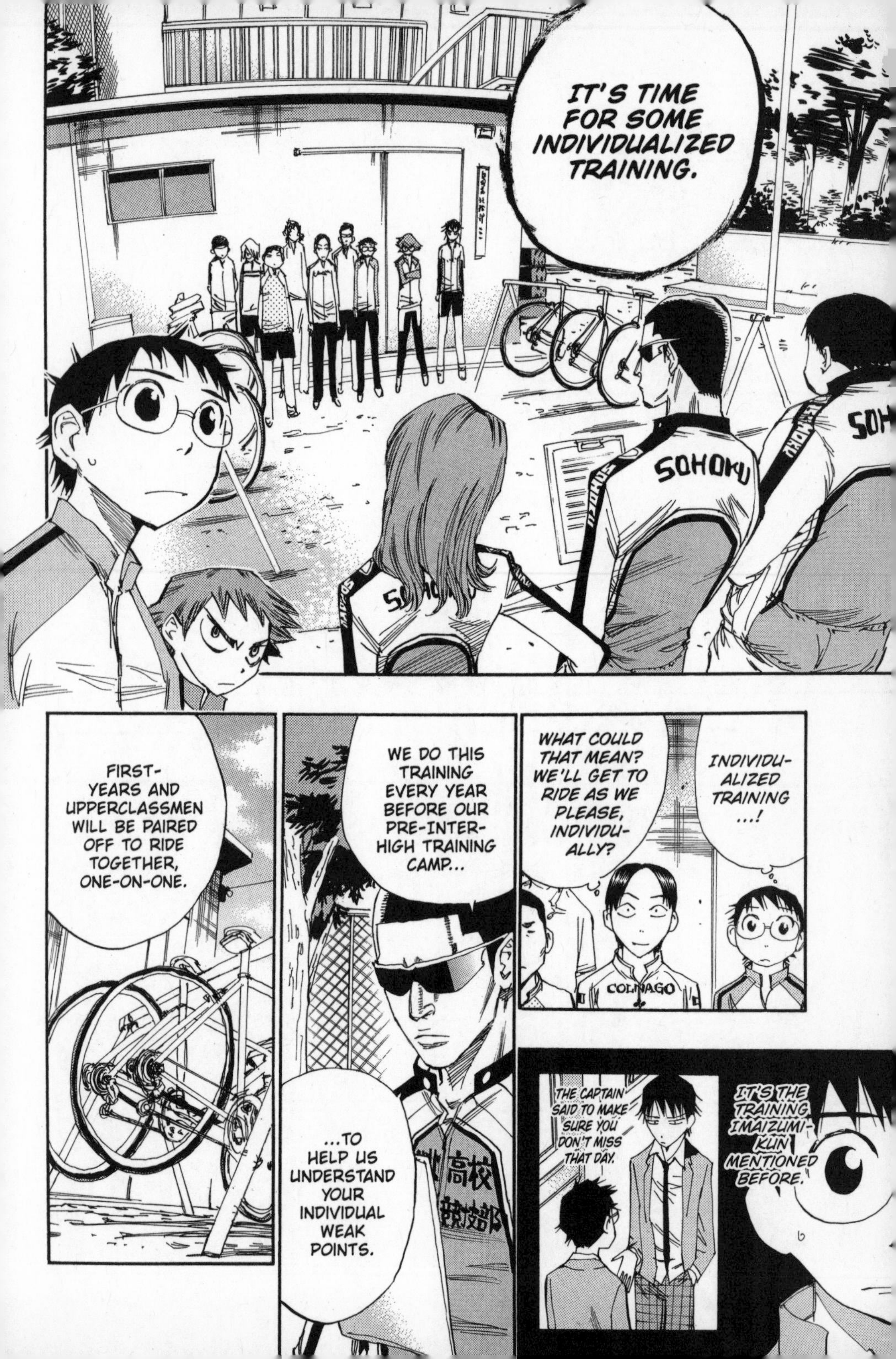
IT'S TIME FOR SOME INDIVIDUALIZED TRAINING.
INDIVIDU-ALIZED TRAINING ...!
WHAT COULD THAT MEAN? WE'LL GET TO RIDE AS WE PLEASE, INDIVIDU-ALLY?
IT'S THE TRAINING IMAIZUMI-KUN MENTIONED BEFORE.
THE CAPTAIN SAID TO MAKE SURE YOU DON'T MISS THAT DAY.
WE DO THIS TRAINING EVERY YEAR BEFORE OUR PRE-INTER-HIGH TRAINING CAMP...
...TO HELP US UNDERSTAND YOUR INDIVIDUAL WEAK POINTS.
FIRST-YEARS AND UPPERCLASSMEN WILL BE PAIRED OFF TO RIDE TOGETHER, ONE-ON-ONE.

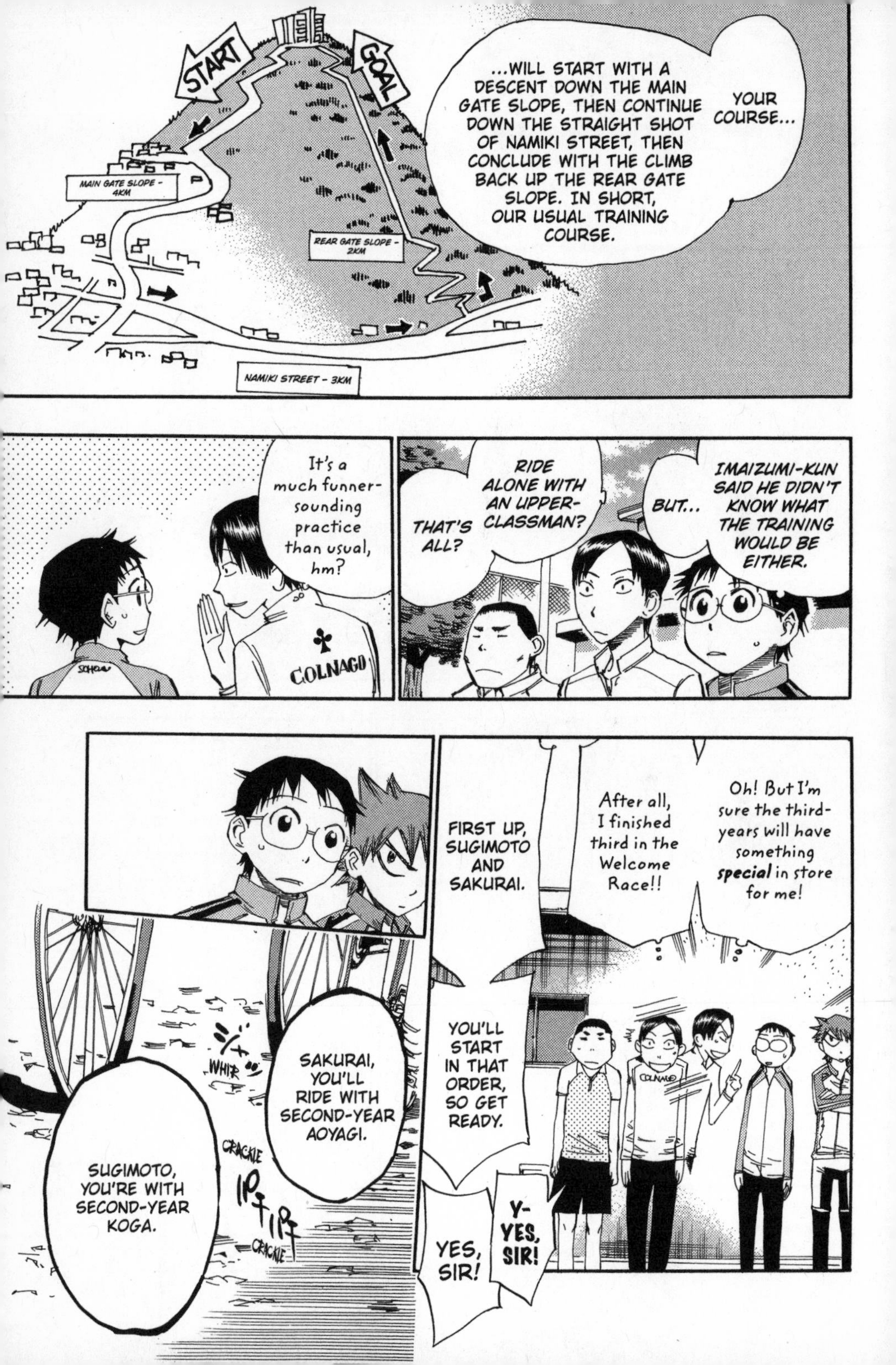
YOUR COURSE...
...WILL START WITH A DESCENT DOWN THE MAIN GATE SLOPE, THEN CONTINUE DOWN THE STRAIGHT SHOT OF NAMIKI STREET, THEN CONCLUDE WITH THE CLIMB BACK UP THE REAR GATE SLOPE. IN SHORT, OUR USUAL TRAINING COURSE.
START
GOAL
MAIN GATE SLOPE - 4KM
REAR GATE SLOPE - 2KM
NAMIKI STREET - 3KM
IMAIZUMI-KUN SAID HE DIDN'T KNOW WHAT THE TRAINING WOULD BE EITHER.
BUT...
RIDE ALONE WITH AN UPPER-CLASSMAN?
THAT'S ALL?
It's a much funner-sounding practice than usual, hm?
COLNAGO
Oh! But I'm sure the third-years will have something **special** in store for me!
After all, I finished third in the Welcome Race!!
FIRST UP, SUGIMOTO AND SAKURAI.
YOU'LL START IN THAT ORDER, SO GET READY.
Y-YES, SIR!
YES, SIR!
COLNAGO
SAKURAI, YOU'LL RIDE WITH SECOND-YEAR AOYAGI.
WHIR
SUGIMOTO, YOU'RE WITH SECOND-YEAR KOGA.
CRACKLE
CRACKLE

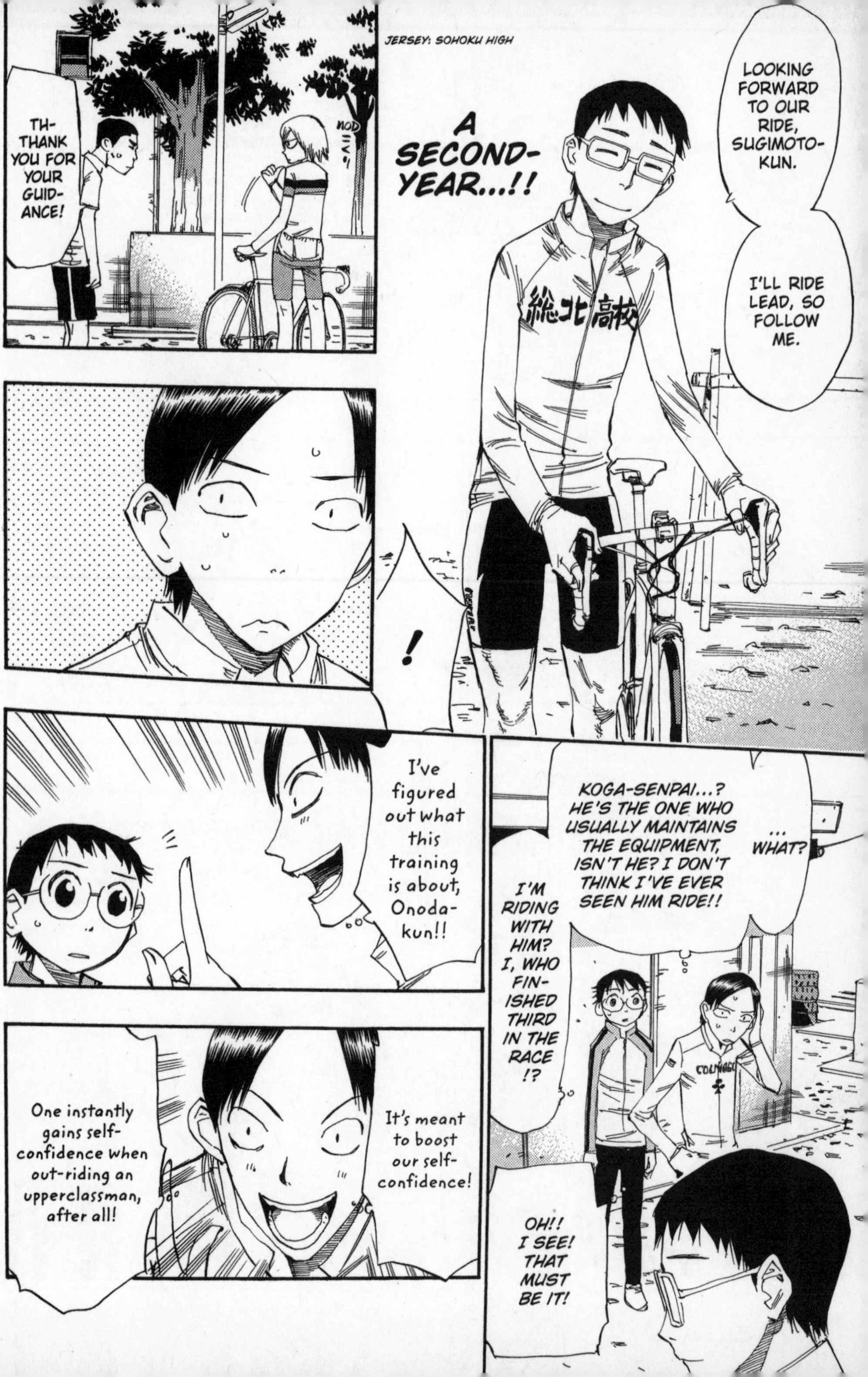

LOOKING FORWARD TO OUR RIDE, SUGIMOTO-KUN.
I'LL RIDE LEAD, SO FOLLOW ME.
A SECOND-YEAR...!!
JERSEY: SOHOKU HIGH
NOD
TH-THANK YOU FOR YOUR GUIDANCE!
!
...WHAT?
KOGA-SENPAI...? HE'S THE ONE WHO USUALLY MAINTAINS THE EQUIPMENT, ISN'T HE? I DON'T THINK I'VE EVER SEEN HIM RIDE!!
I'M RIDING WITH HIM? I, WHO FINISHED THIRD IN THE RACE!?
OH!! I SEE! THAT MUST BE IT!
I've figured out what this training is about, Onoda-kun!!
It's meant to boost our self-confidence!
One instantly gains self-confidence when out-riding an upperclassman, after all!

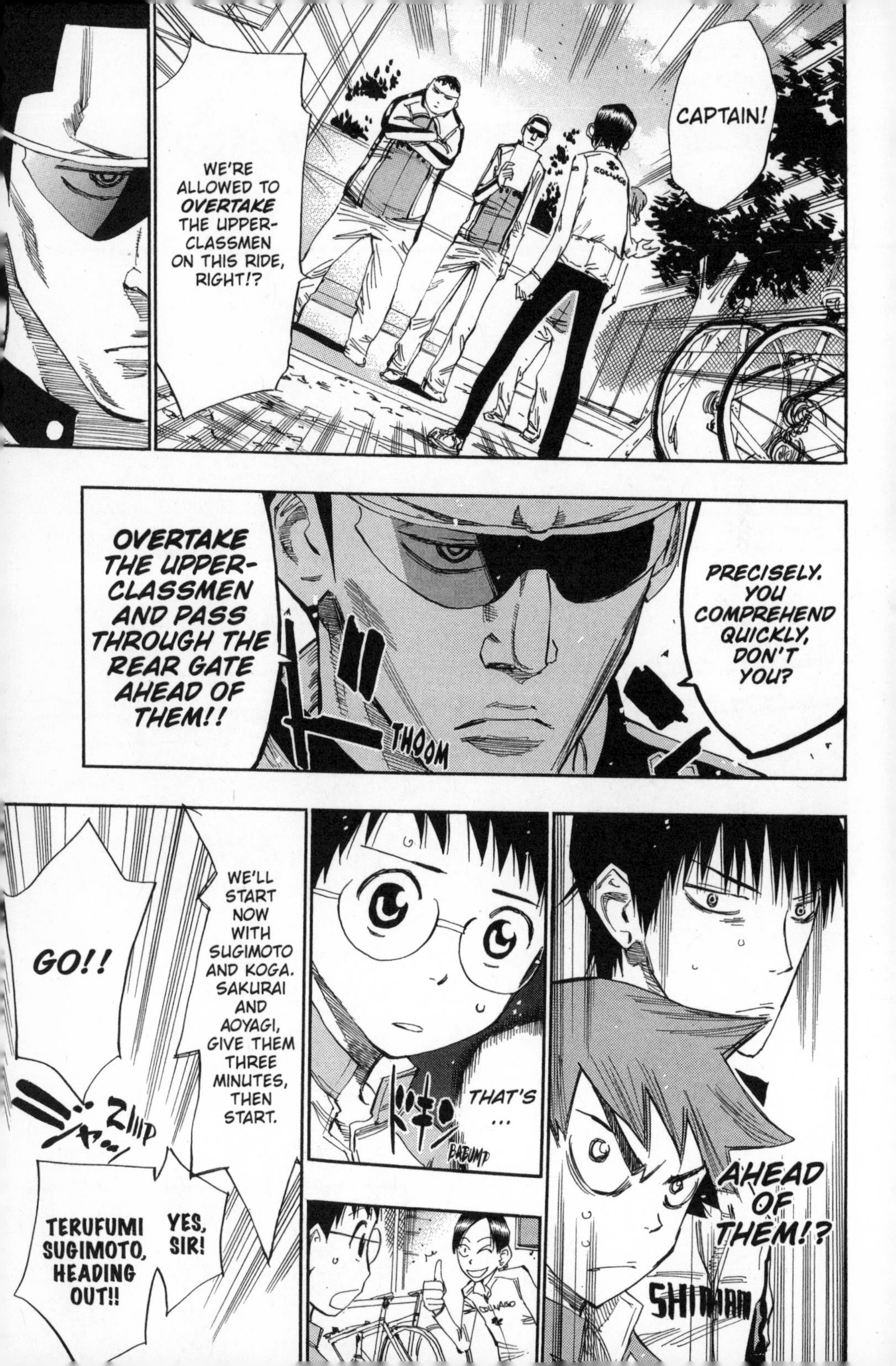
CAPTAIN!
WE'RE ALLOWED TO OVERTAKE THE UPPER-CLASSMEN ON THIS RIDE, RIGHT!?
PRECISELY. YOU COMPREHEND QUICKLY, DON'T YOU?
OVERTAKE THE UPPER-CLASSMEN AND PASS THROUGH THE REAR GATE AHEAD OF THEM!!
THOOM
AHEAD OF THEM!?
SHIMAN
THAT'S ...
BABUMP
WE'LL START NOW WITH SUGIMOTO AND KOGA. SAKURAI AND AOYAGI, GIVE THEM THREE MINUTES, THEN START.
GO!!
ZIIIP
YES, SIR!
TERUFUMI SUGIMOTO, HEADING OUT!!

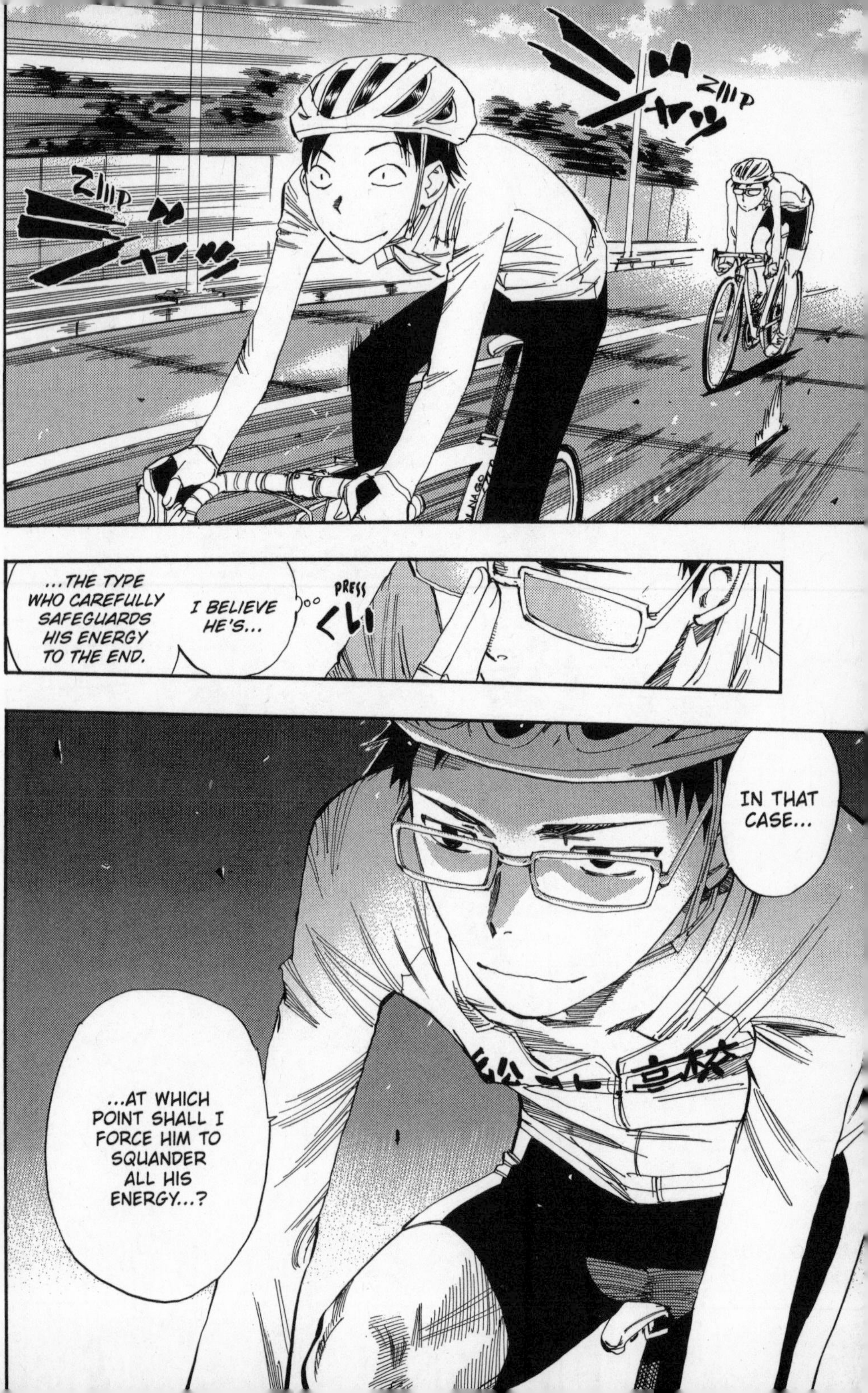

ZIIIP
ZIIIP
PRESS
I BELIEVE HE'S...
...THE TYPE WHO CAREFULLY SAFEGUARDS HIS ENERGY TO THE END.
IN THAT CASE...
...AT WHICH POINT SHALL I FORCE HIM TO SQUANDER ALL HIS ENERGY...?

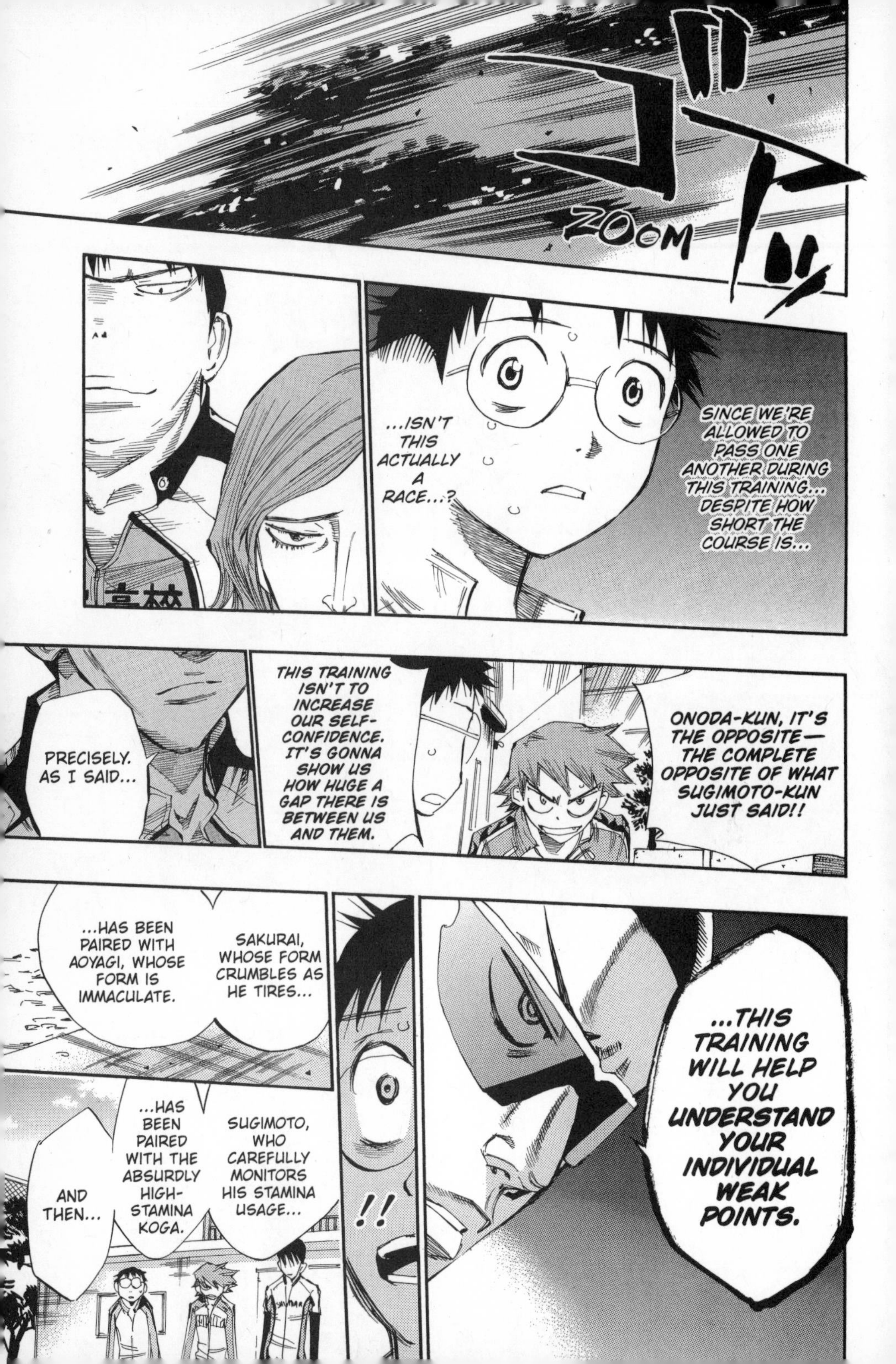
ZOOM
SINCE WE'RE ALLOWED TO PASS ONE ANOTHER DURING THIS TRAINING... DESPITE HOW SHORT THE COURSE IS...
...ISN'T THIS ACTUALLY A RACE...?
ONODA-KUN, IT'S THE OPPOSITE— THE COMPLETE OPPOSITE OF WHAT SUGIMOTO-KUN JUST SAID!!
THIS TRAINING ISN'T TO INCREASE OUR SELF-CONFIDENCE. IT'S GONNA SHOW US HOW HUGE A GAP THERE IS BETWEEN US AND THEM.
PRECISELY. AS I SAID...
...THIS TRAINING WILL HELP YOU UNDERSTAND YOUR INDIVIDUAL WEAK POINTS.
!!
SAKURAI, WHOSE FORM CRUMBLES AS HE TIRES...
...HAS BEEN PAIRED WITH AOYAGI, WHOSE FORM IS IMMACULATE.
SUGIMOTO, WHO CAREFULLY MONITORS HIS STAMINA USAGE...
...HAS BEEN PAIRED WITH THE ABSURDLY HIGH-STAMINA KOGA.
AND THEN...

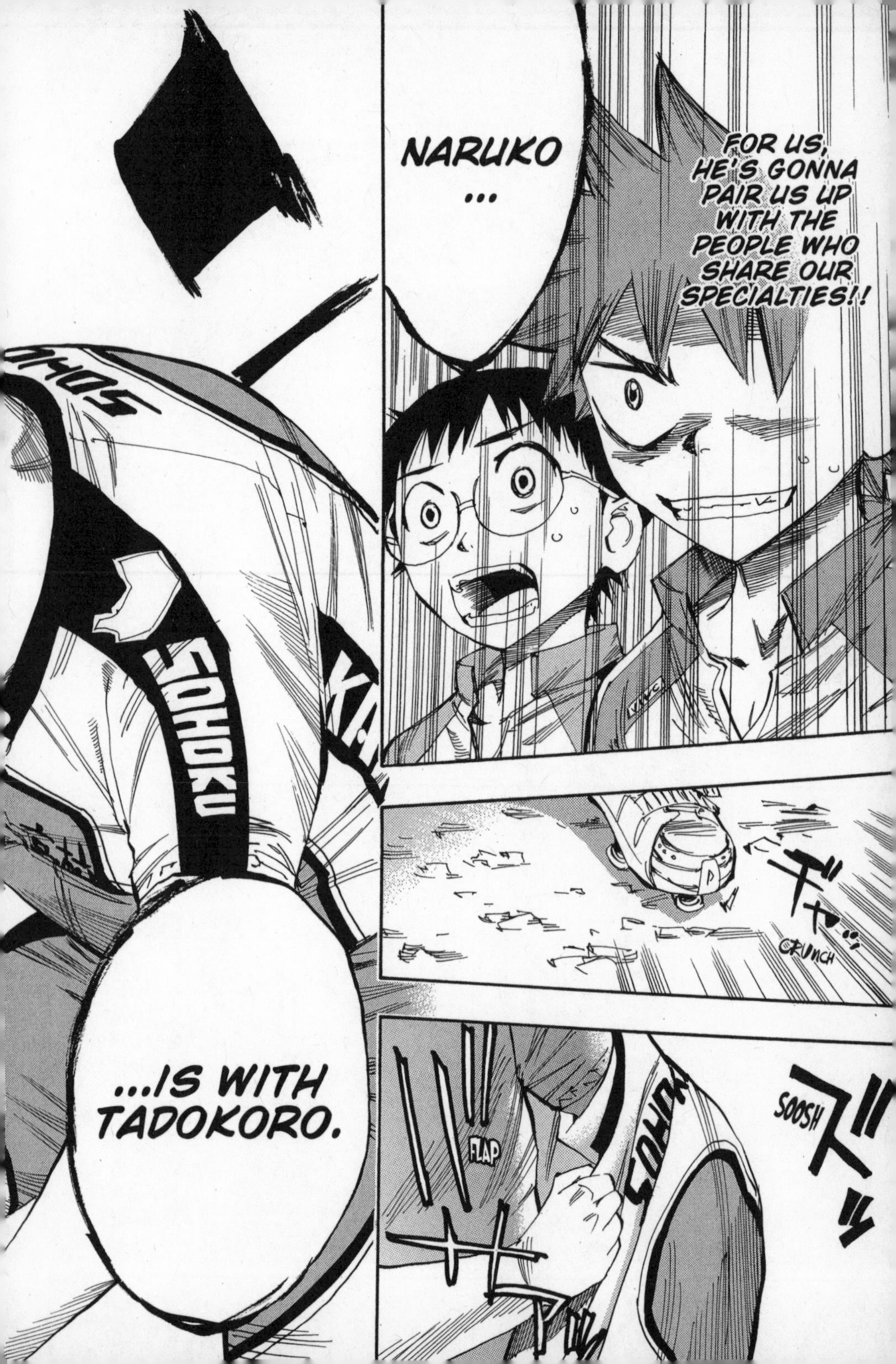
FOR US, HE'S GONNA PAIR US UP WITH THE PEOPLE WHO SHARE OUR SPECIALTIES!!
NARUKO ...
CRUNCH
SOOSH
FLAP
...IS WITH TADOKORO.

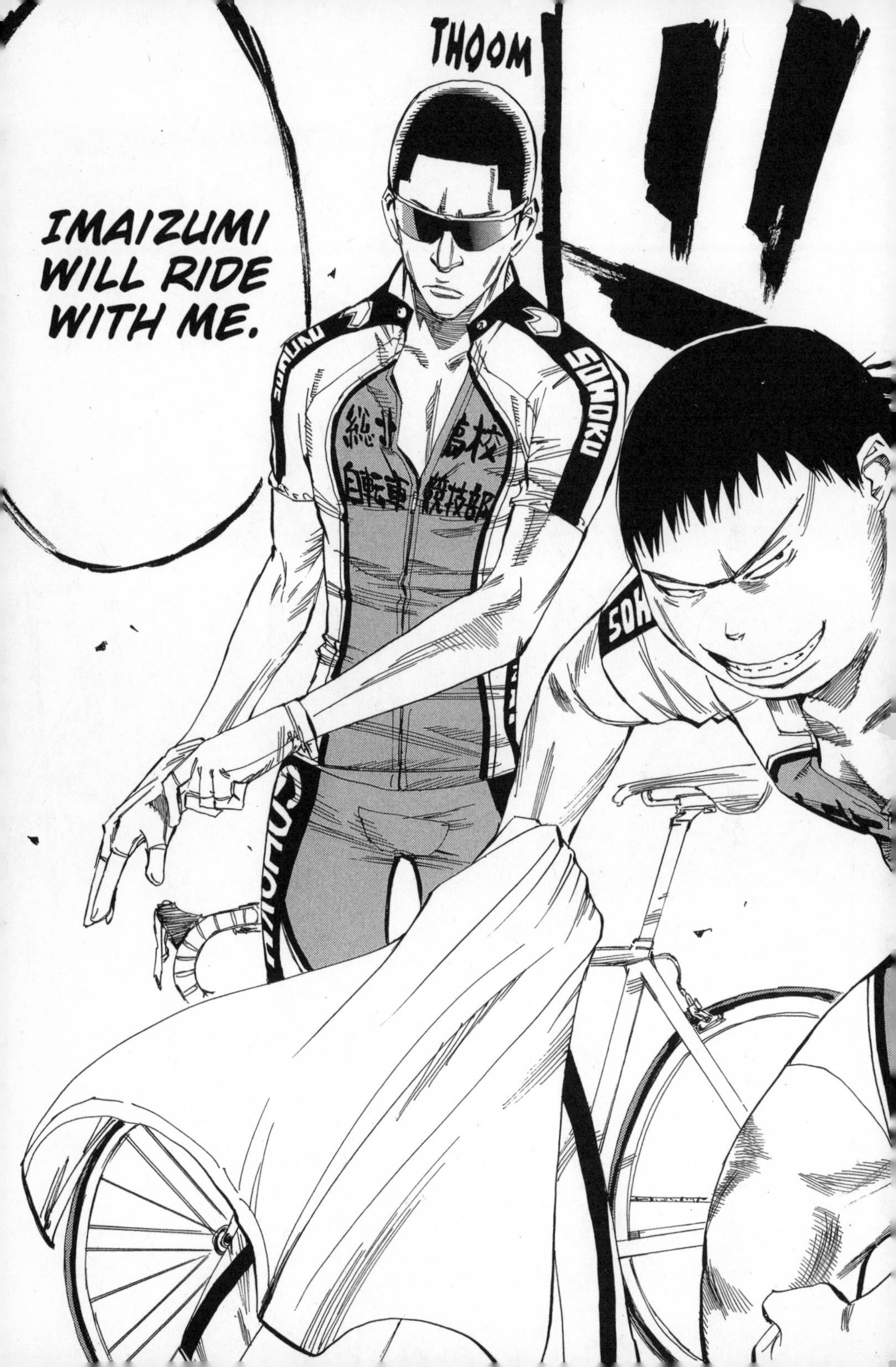
THOOM
IMAIZUMI WILL RIDE WITH ME.
総北 高校 自転車 競技部
SOHOKU
SOHOKU
SOHOKU
SOH

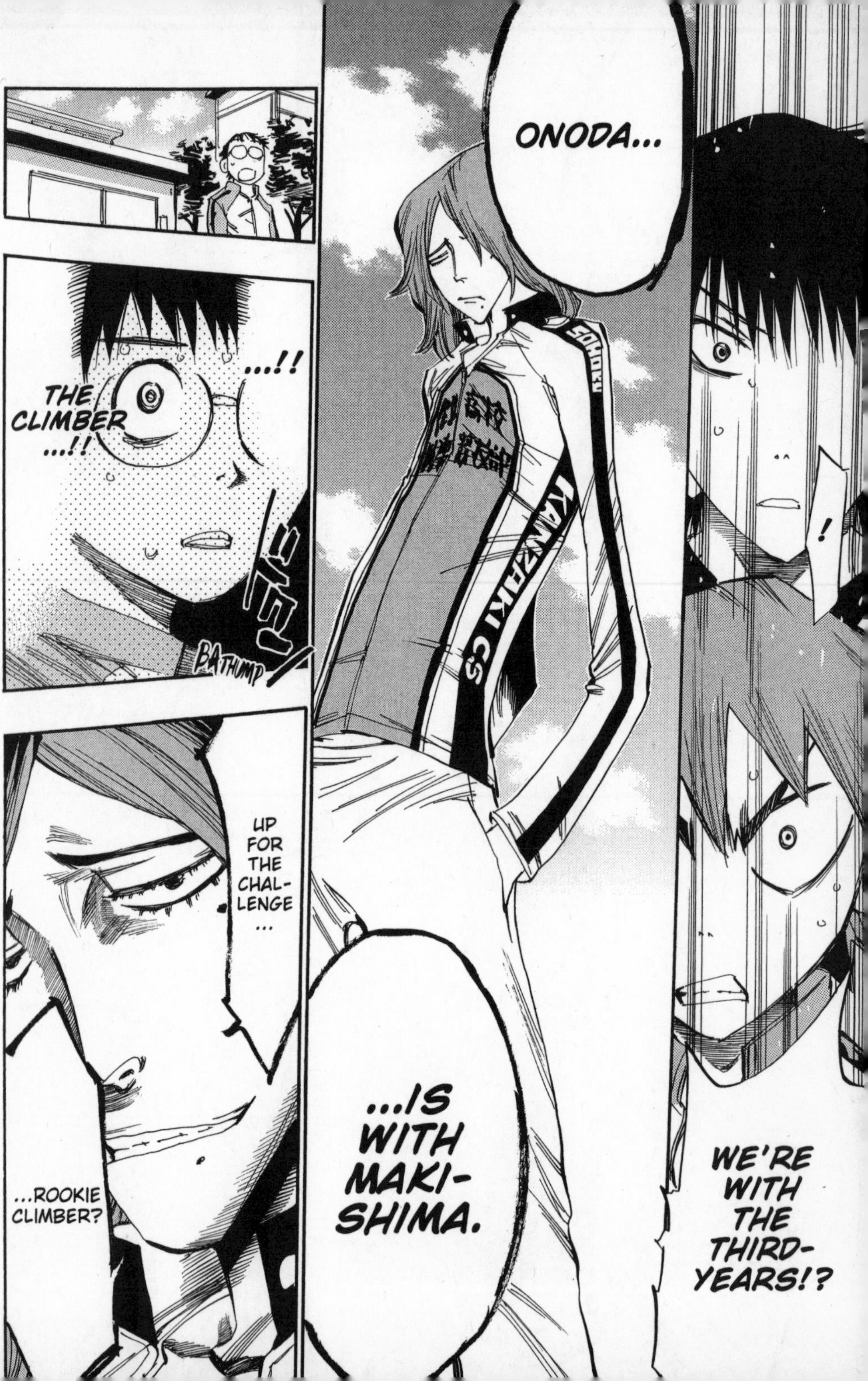
!
WE'RE WITH THE THIRD-YEARS!?
ONODA...
...IS WITH MAKISHIMA.
...!!
THE CLIMBER...!!
BATHUMP
UP FOR THE CHALLENGE...
...ROOKIE CLIMBER?

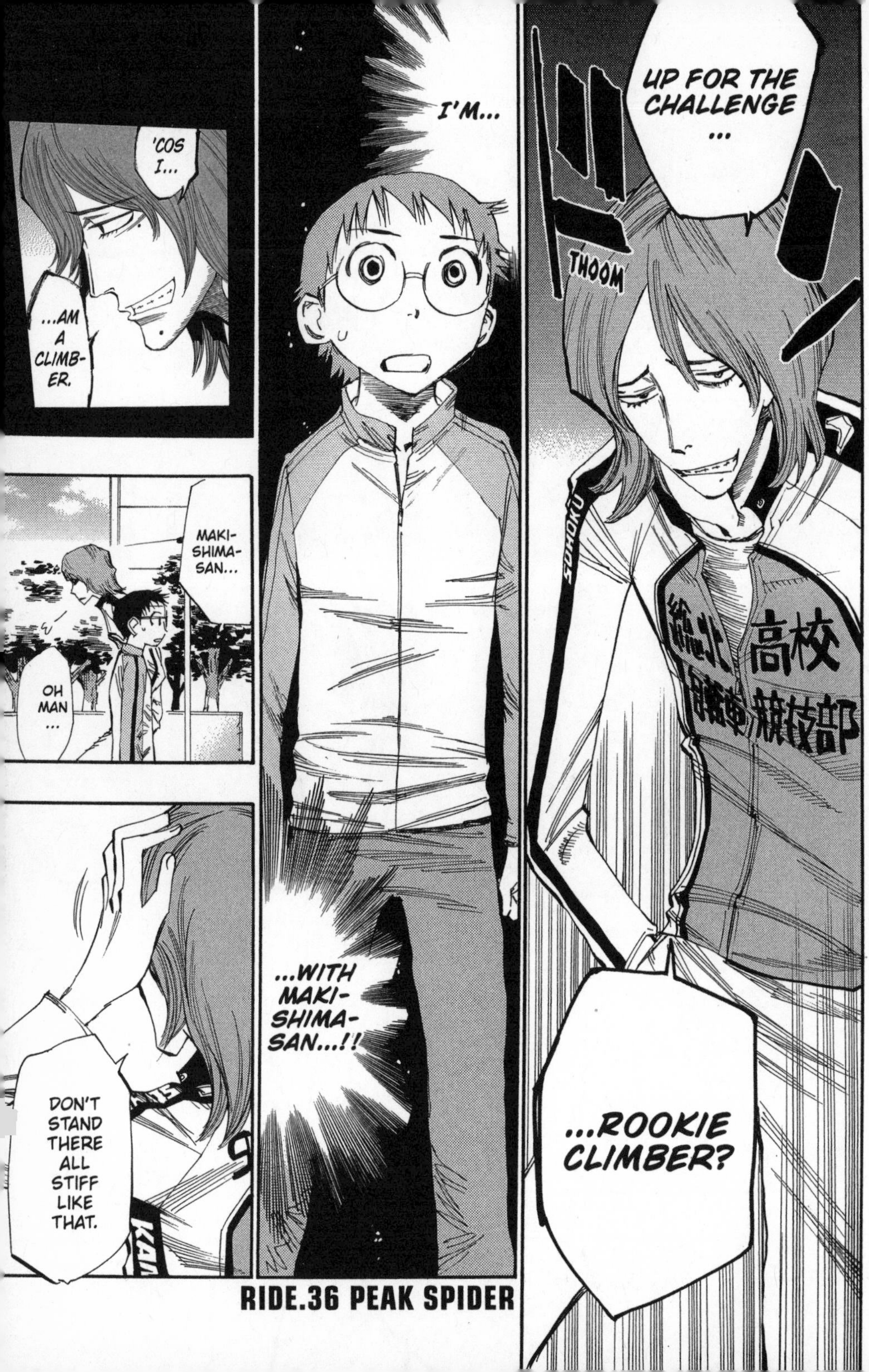
UP FOR THE CHALLENGE ...
THOOM
...ROOKIE CLIMBER?
I'M...
...WITH MAKI-SHIMA-SAN...!!
'COS I...
...AM A CLIMB-ER.
MAKI-SHIMA-SAN...
OH MAN ...
DON'T STAND THERE ALL STIFF LIKE THAT.

RIDE.36 PEAK SPIDER

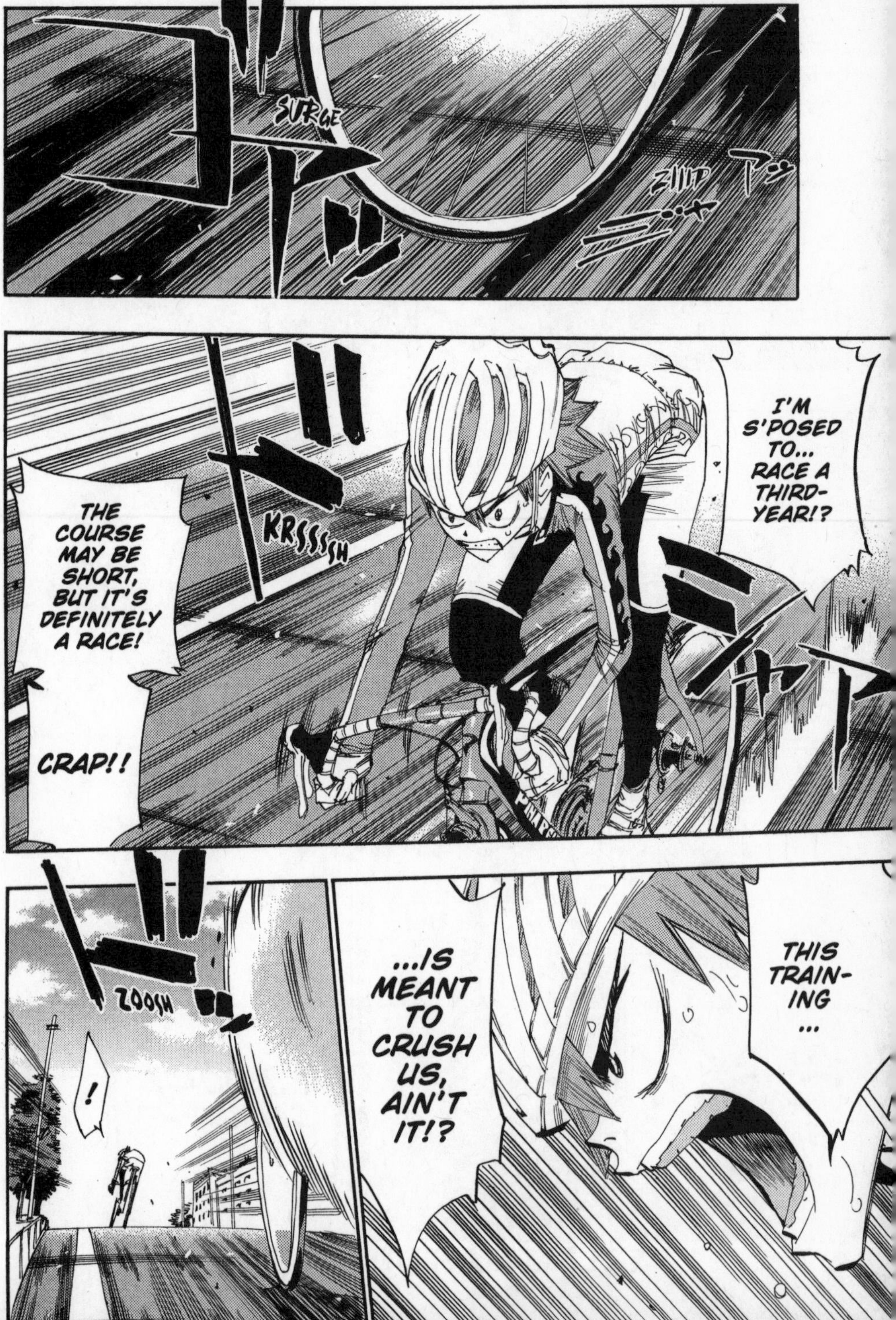
ZIIIP
SURGE
I'M S'POSED TO... RACE A THIRD-YEAR!?
KRSSSSSH
THE COURSE MAY BE SHORT, BUT IT'S DEFINITELY A RACE!
CRAP!!
THIS TRAIN-ING ...
...IS MEANT TO CRUSH US, AIN'T IT!?
ZOOSH
!

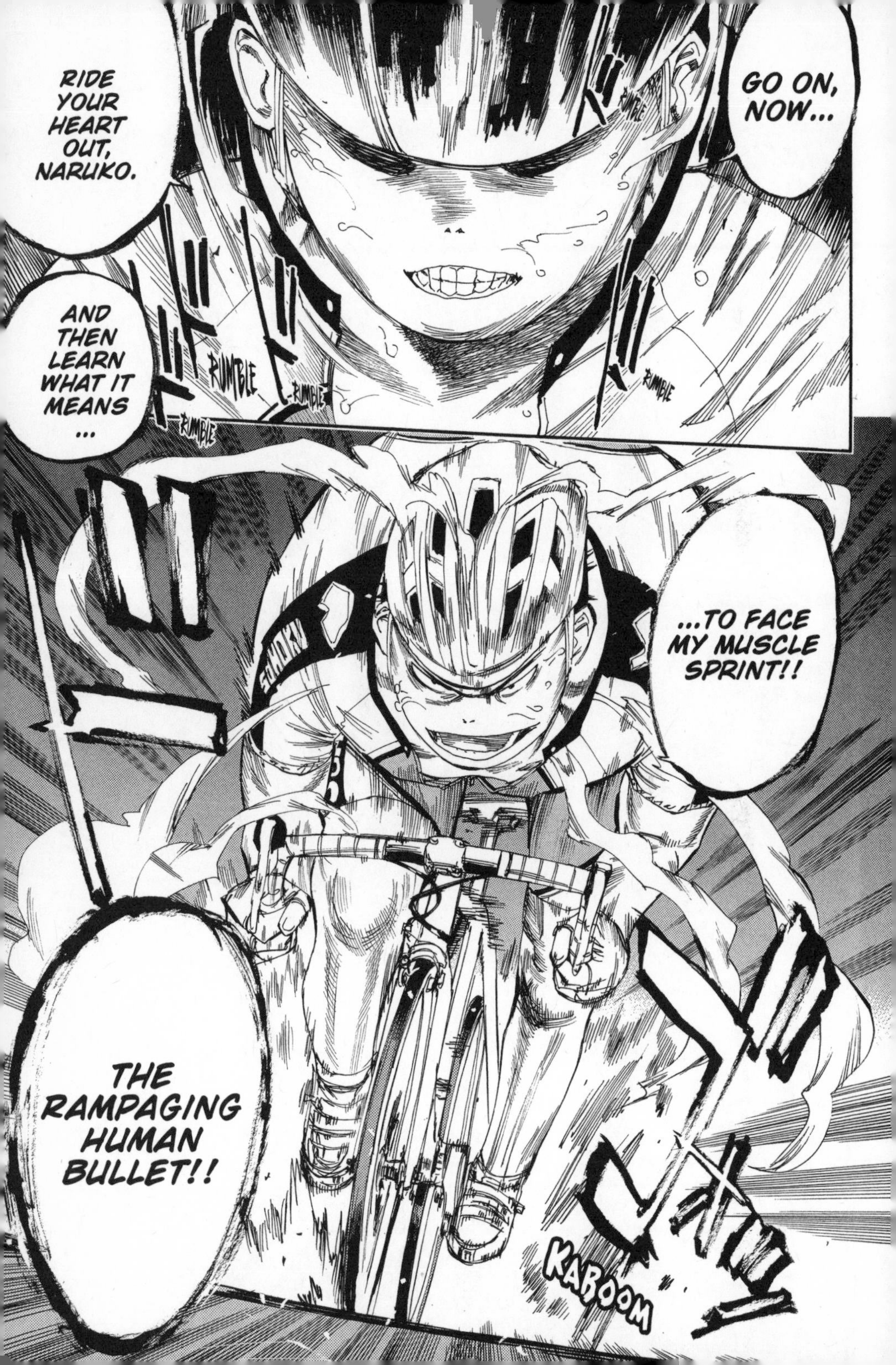
GO ON, NOW...
RIDE YOUR HEART OUT, NARUKO.
AND THEN LEARN WHAT IT MEANS ...
RUMBLE
RUMBLE
RUMBLE
RUMBLE
RUMBLE
...TO FACE MY MUSCLE SPRINT!!
THE RAMPAGING HUMAN BULLET!!
KABOOM

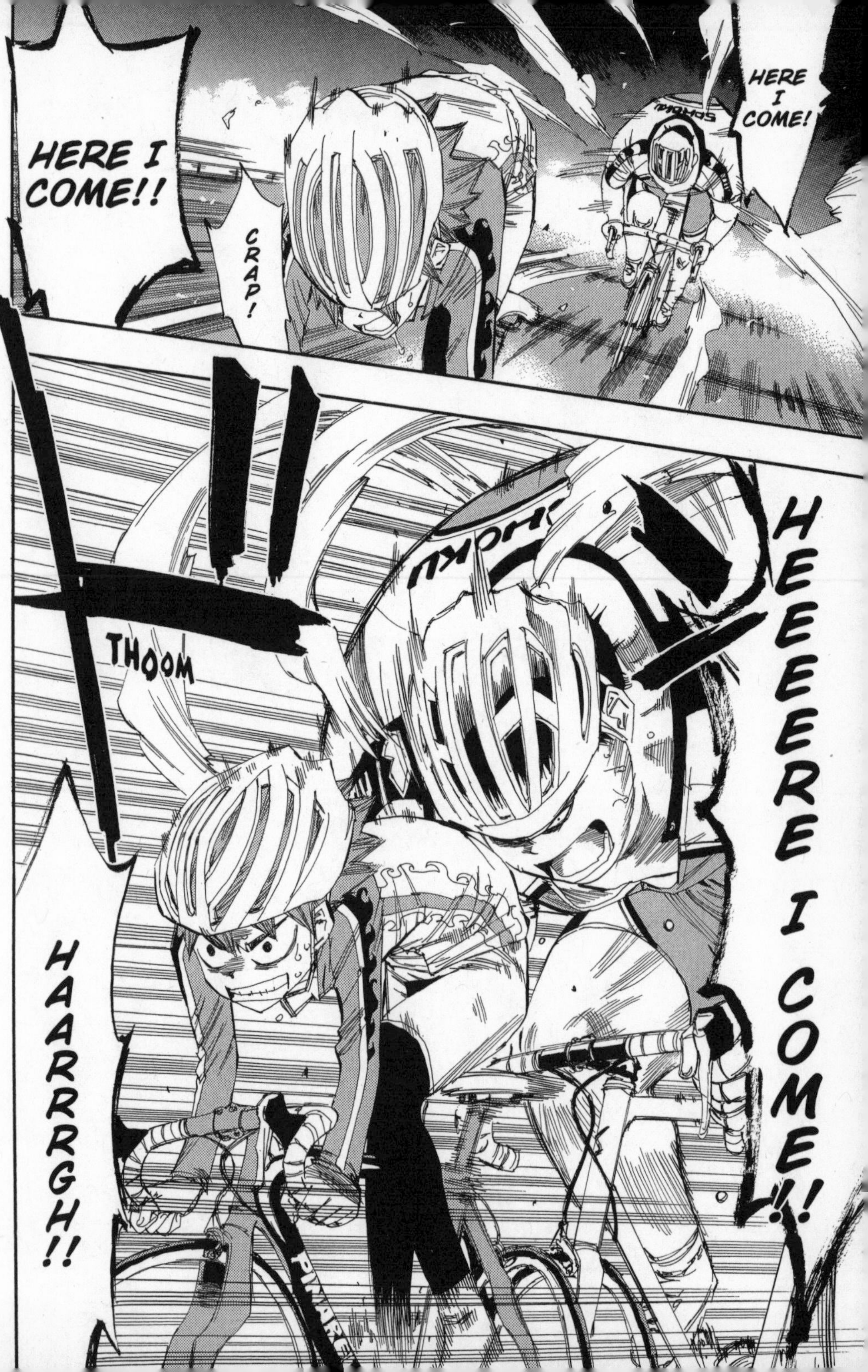
HERE I COME!
CRAP!
HERE I COME!!
HEEEERE I COME!!!
THOOM
HAARRRGH!!

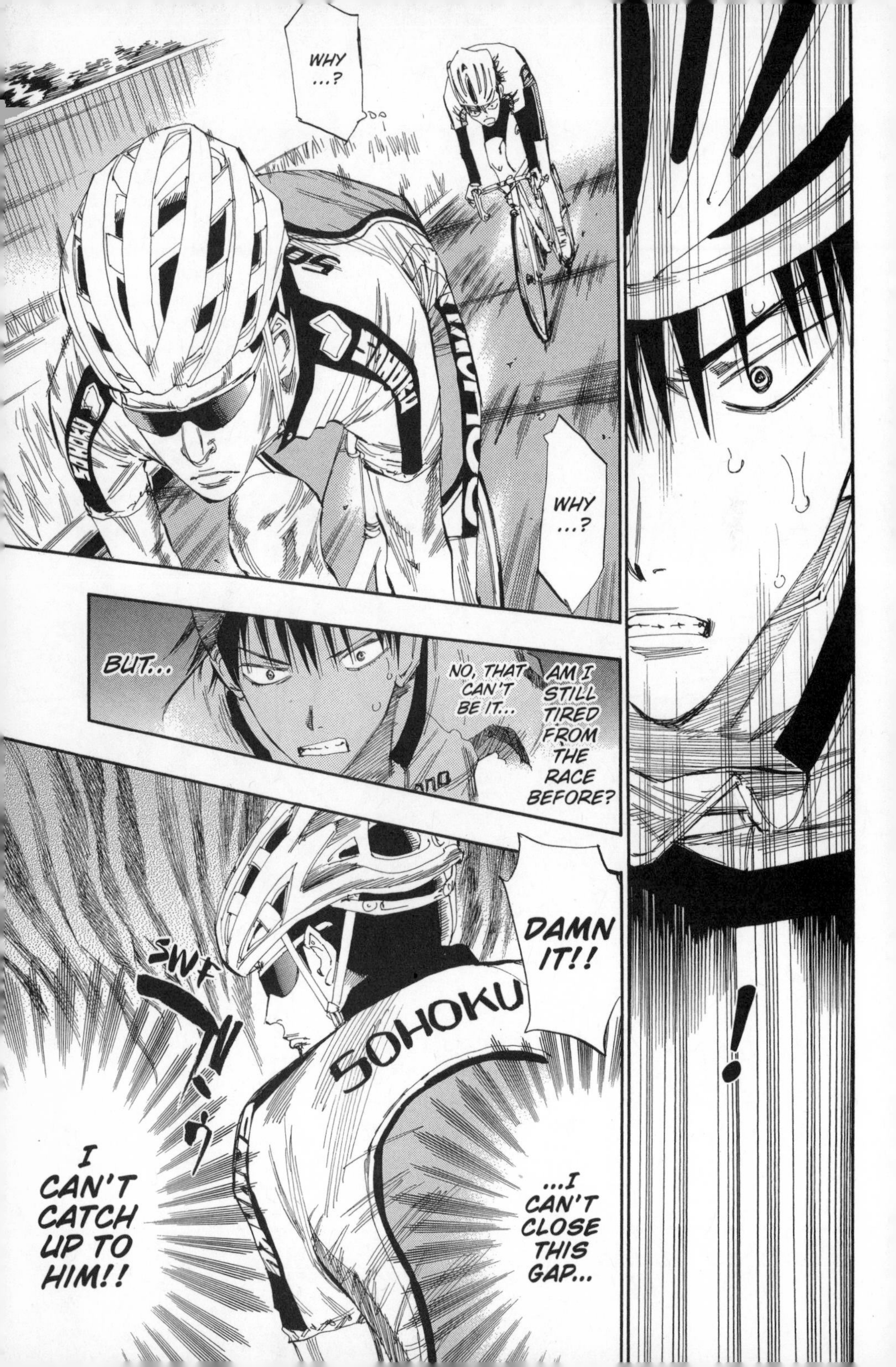
!
WHY ...?
WHY ...?
AM I STILL TIRED FROM THE RACE BEFORE?
NO, THAT CAN'T BE IT...
BUT...
DAMN IT!!
SWF
...I CAN'T CLOSE THIS GAP...
I CAN'T CATCH UP TO HIM!!

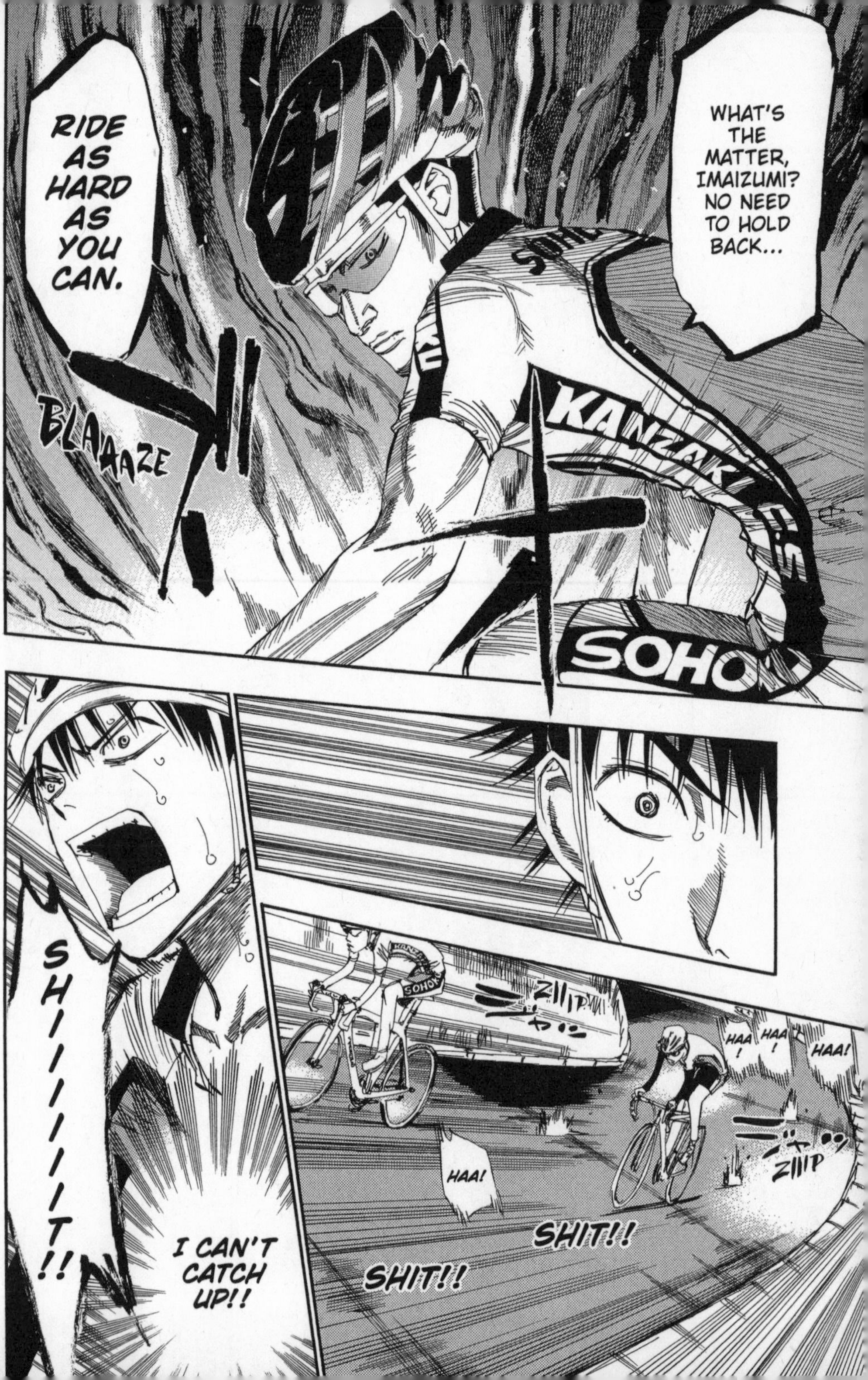
WHAT'S THE MATTER, IMAIZUMI? NO NEED TO HOLD BACK...
RIDE AS HARD AS YOU CAN.
BLAAAAZE
ZIIIP
HAA! HAA! HAA!
ZIIIP
HAA!
SHIT!!
SHIT!!
SHIIIIIIIT!!
I CAN'T CATCH UP!!

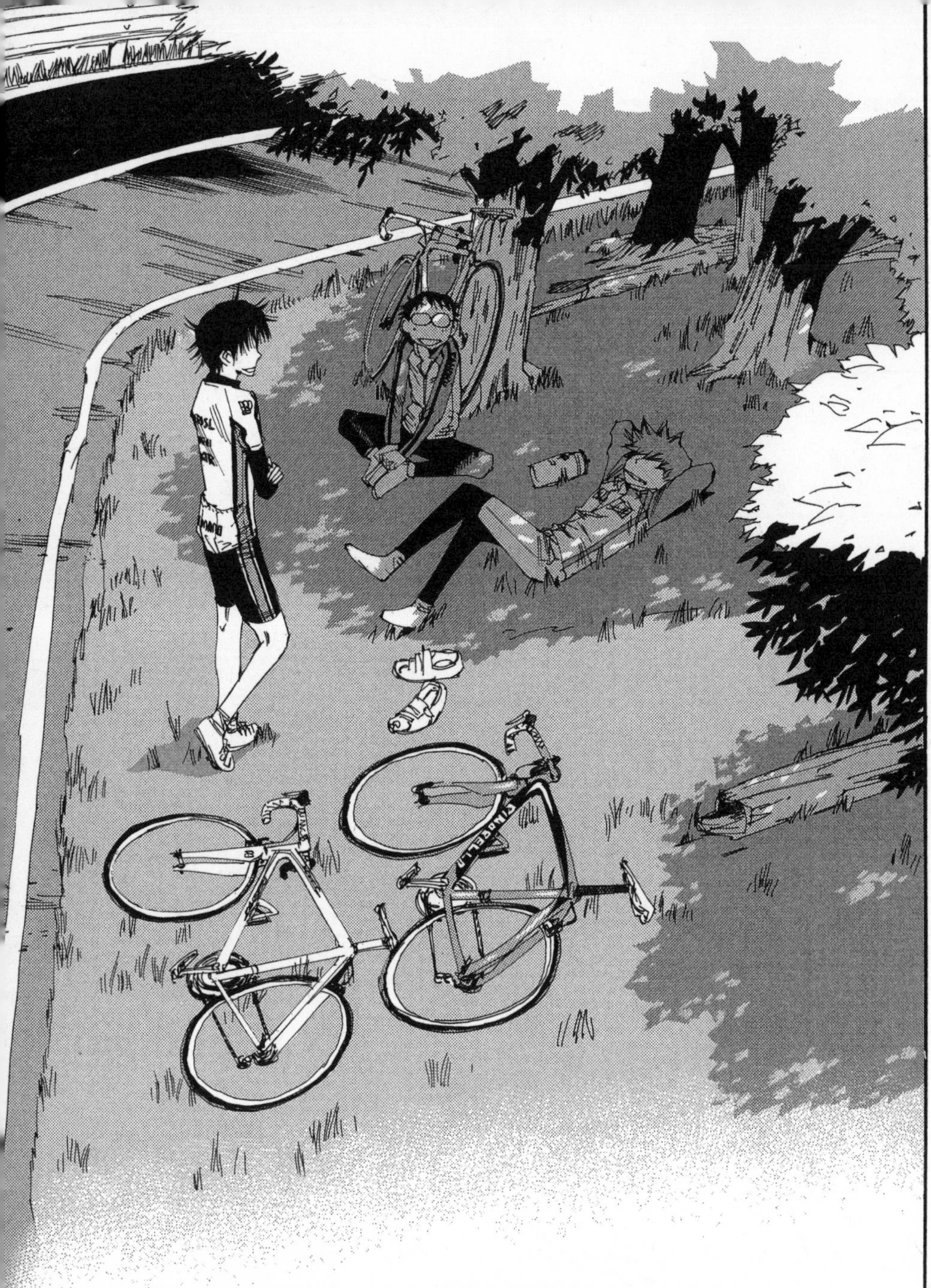

RIDE.36 PEAK SPIDER

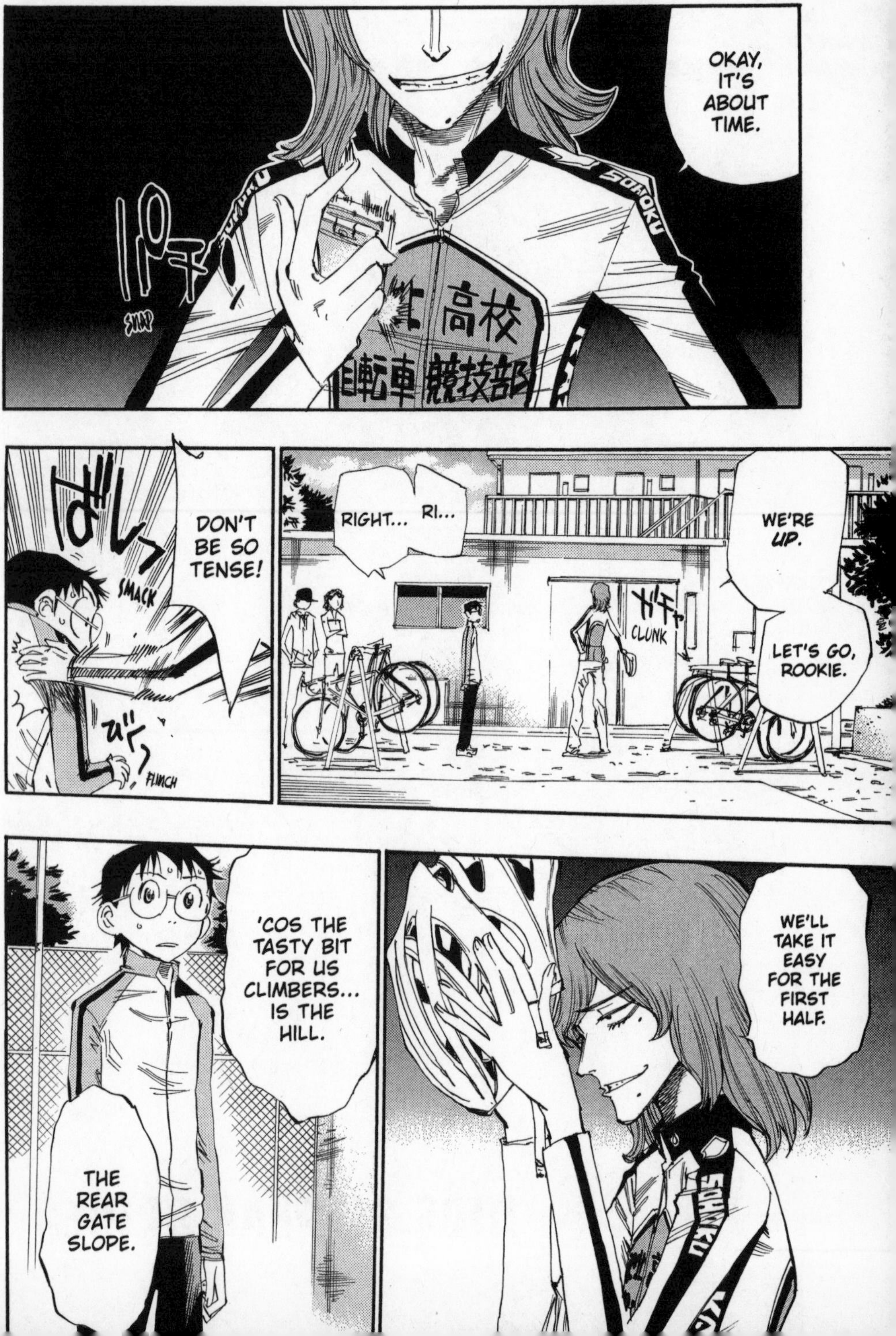
OKAY, IT'S ABOUT TIME.
パチ
SNAP
SOHOKU
高校
自転車競技部
WE'RE UP.
LET'S GO, ROOKIE.
ガチャ
CLUNK
RIGHT... RI...
DON'T BE SO TENSE!
ばしっ
SMACK
びくっ
FLINCH
WE'LL TAKE IT EASY FOR THE FIRST HALF.
SOHOKU
'COS THE TASTY BIT FOR US CLIMBERS... IS THE HILL.
THE REAR GATE SLOPE.

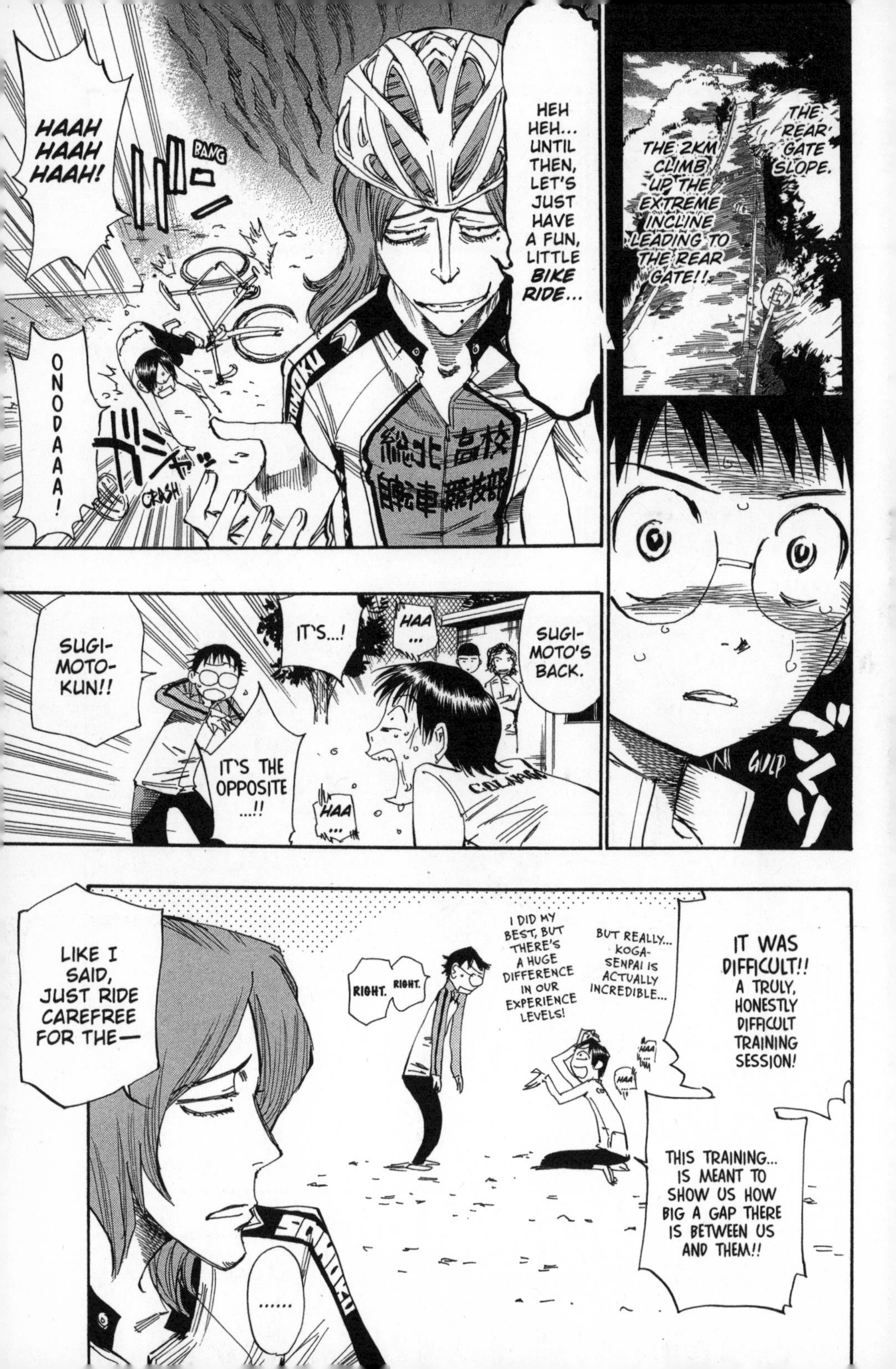
THE REAR GATE SLOPE.
THE 2KM CLIMB UP THE EXTREME INCLINE LEADING TO THE REAR GATE!!
GULP
HEH HEH... UNTIL THEN, LET'S JUST HAVE A FUN, LITTLE BIKE RIDE...
HAAH HAAH HAAH!
BANG
ONODAAAA!
CRASH
SUGI-MOTO'S BACK.
HAA...
IT'S...!
SUGI-MOTO-KUN!!
IT'S THE OPPOSITE...!!
HAA...
IT WAS DIFFICULT!! A TRULY, HONESTLY DIFFICULT TRAINING SESSION!
BUT REALLY... KOGA-SENPAI IS ACTUALLY INCREDIBLE...
I DID MY BEST, BUT THERE'S A HUGE DIFFERENCE IN OUR EXPERIENCE LEVELS!
RIGHT.
RIGHT.
THIS TRAINING... IS MEANT TO SHOW US HOW BIG A GAP THERE IS BETWEEN US AND THEM!!
LIKE I SAID, JUST RIDE CAREFREE FOR THE—
......

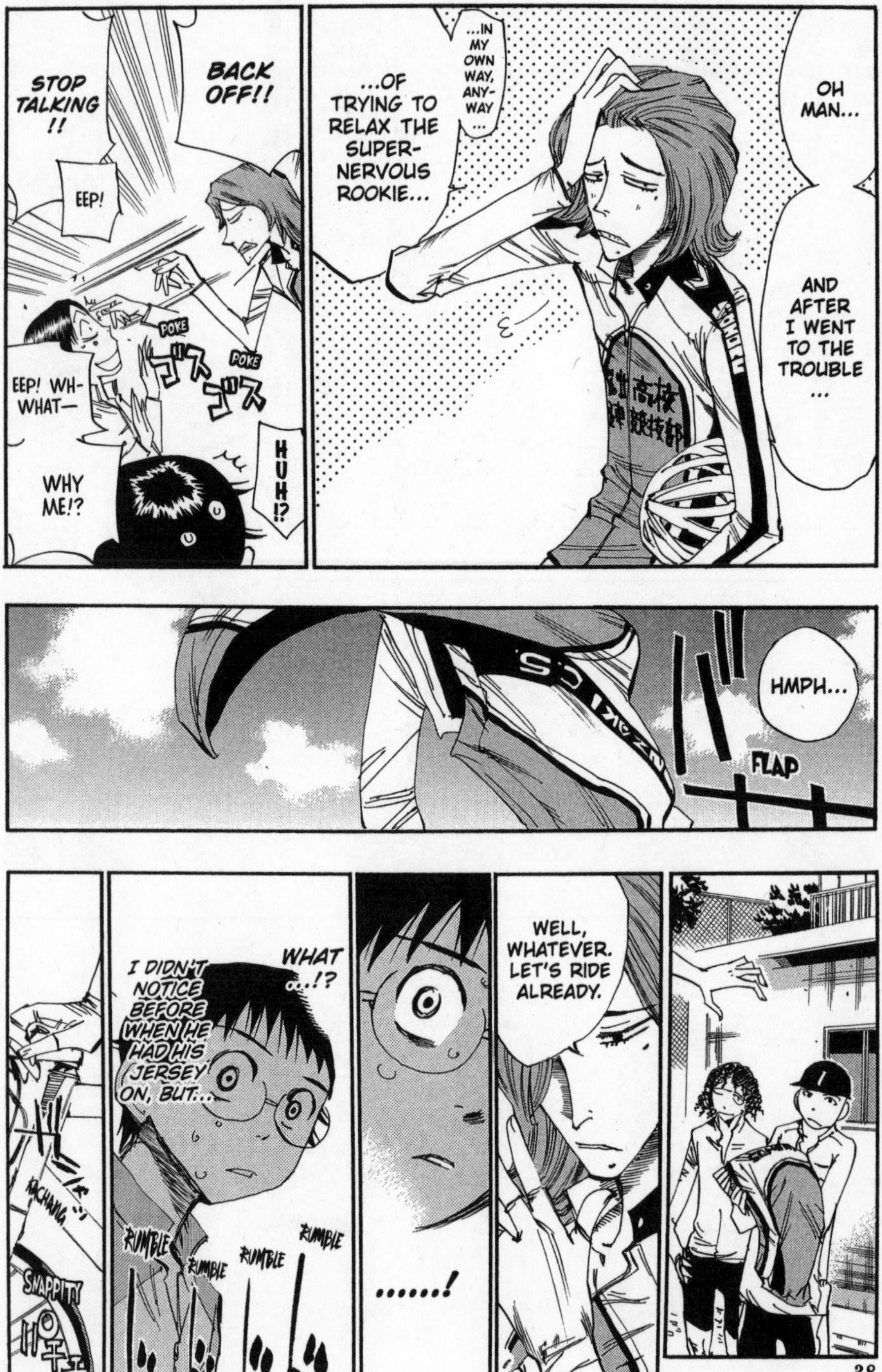
OH MAN...
AND AFTER I WENT TO THE TROUBLE...
...OF TRYING TO RELAX THE SUPER-NERVOUS ROOKIE...
...IN MY OWN WAY, ANYWAY...
BACK OFF!!
STOP TALKING!!
EEP!
POKE
POKE
ゴスゴス
EEP! WH-WHAT—
HUH!?
WHY ME!?
HMPH...
FLAP
WELL, WHATEVER. LET'S RIDE ALREADY.
......!
WHAT...!?
I DIDN'T NOTICE BEFORE WHEN HE HAD HIS JERSEY ON, BUT...
RUMBLE
RUMBLE
RUMBLE
RUMBLE
KACHANG
SNAPPITY

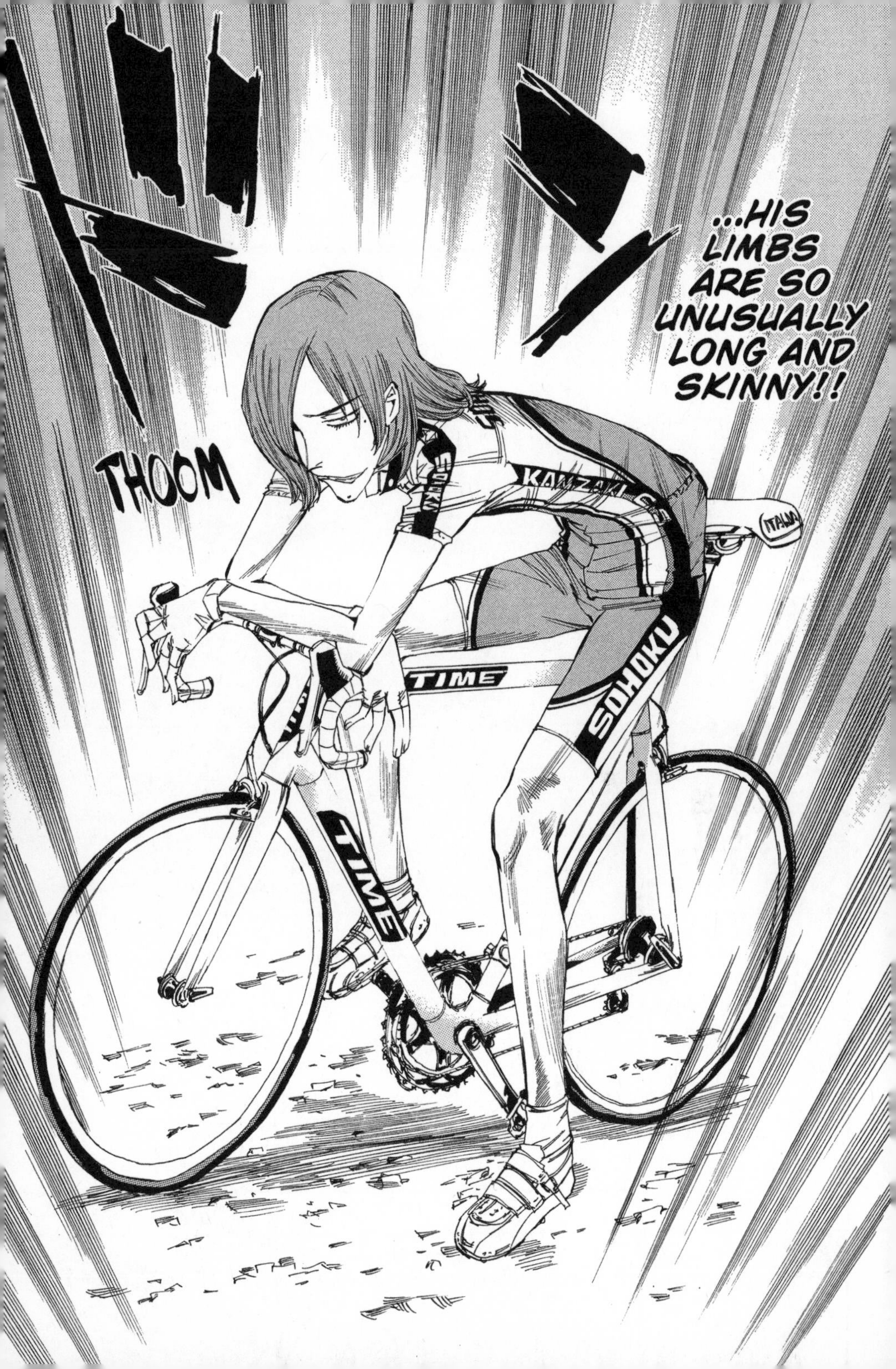
...HIS LIMBS ARE SO UNUSUALLY LONG AND SKINNY!!
THOOM
KANZAKI
SOHOKU
TIME
ITALIA

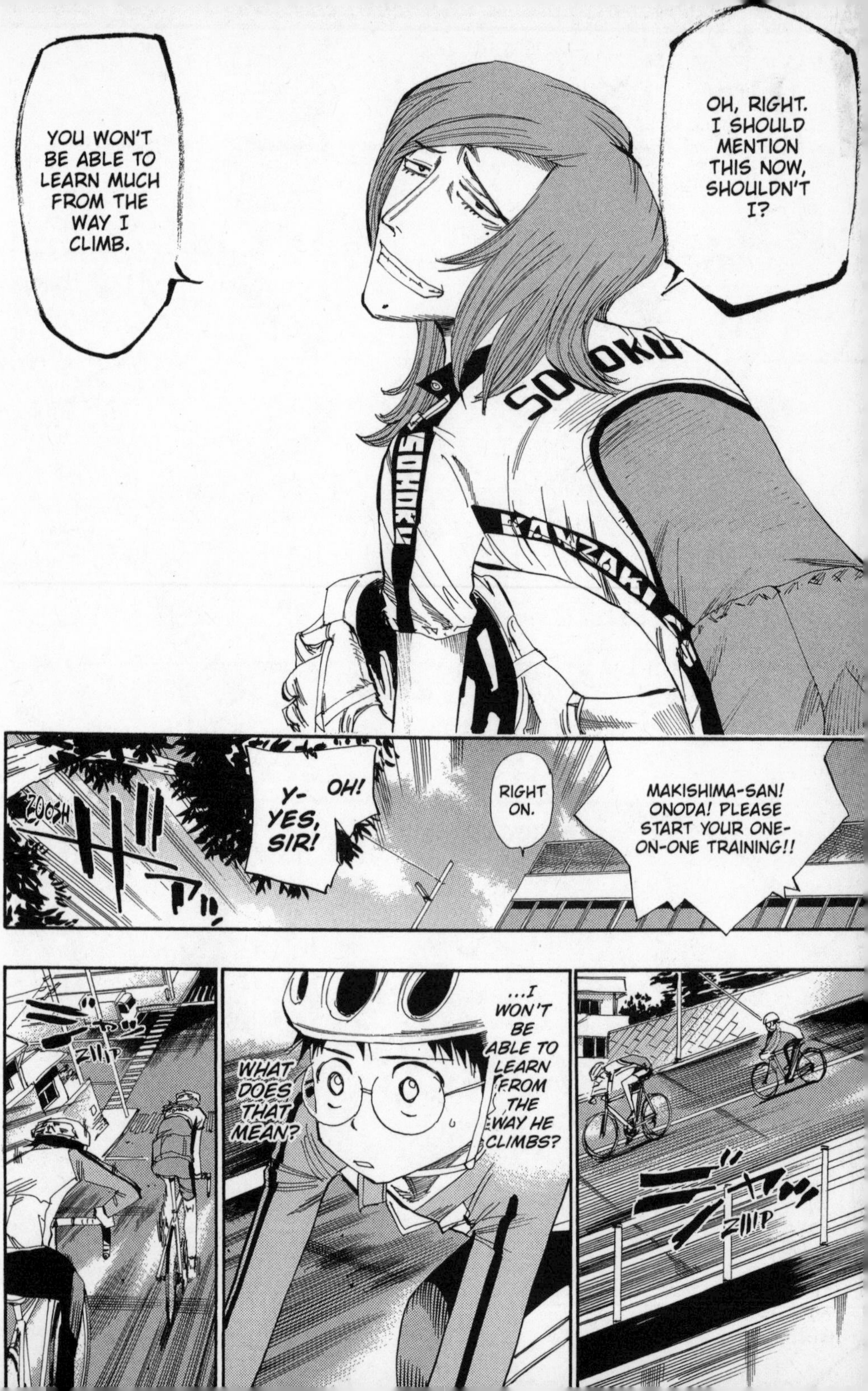
OH, RIGHT. I SHOULD MENTION THIS NOW, SHOULDN'T I?
YOU WON'T BE ABLE TO LEARN MUCH FROM THE WAY I CLIMB.
MAKISHIMA-SAN! ONODA! PLEASE START YOUR ONE-ON-ONE TRAINING!!
RIGHT ON.
OH!
Y- YES, SIR!
ZOOSH
ZIIIP
...I WON'T BE ABLE TO LEARN FROM THE WAY HE CLIMBS?
WHAT DOES THAT MEAN?
ZIIIP

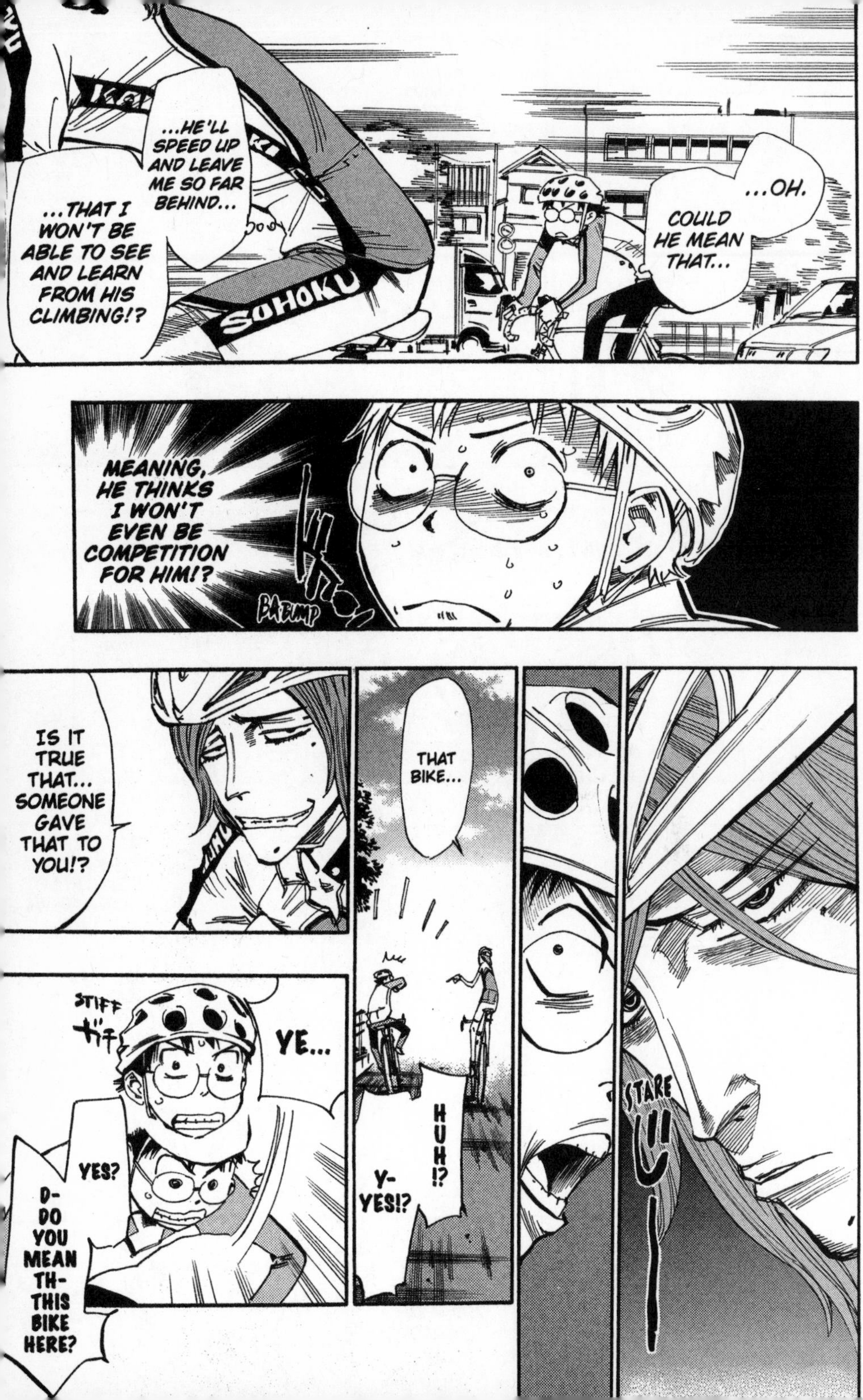
...OH.
COULD HE MEAN THAT...
...HE'LL SPEED UP AND LEAVE ME SO FAR BEHIND...
...THAT I WON'T BE ABLE TO SEE AND LEARN FROM HIS CLIMBING!?
MEANING, HE THINKS I WON'T EVEN BE COMPETITION FOR HIM!?
BA-BUMP
STARE
THAT BIKE...
HUH!?
Y-YES!?
IS IT TRUE THAT... SOMEONE GAVE THAT TO YOU!?
STIFF
YE...
YES?
D-DO YOU MEAN TH-THIS BIKE HERE?

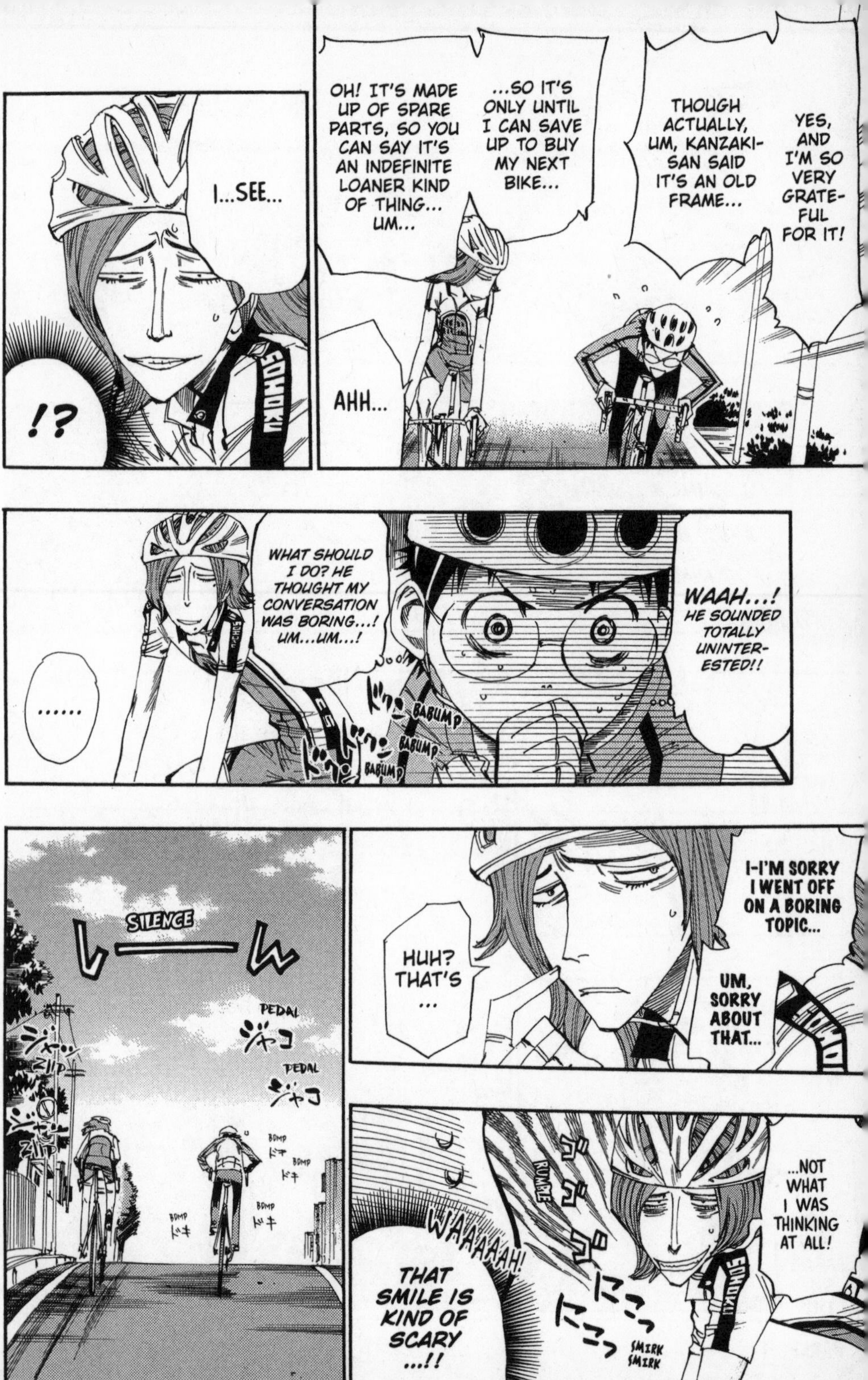
YES, AND I'M SO VERY GRATE-FUL FOR IT!
THOUGH ACTUALLY, UM, KANZAKI-SAN SAID IT'S AN OLD FRAME...
...SO IT'S ONLY UNTIL I CAN SAVE UP TO BUY MY NEXT BIKE...
OH! IT'S MADE UP OF SPARE PARTS, SO YOU CAN SAY IT'S AN INDEFINITE LOANER KIND OF THING... UM...
AHH...
I...SEE...
!?
WAAH...! HE SOUNDED TOTALLY UNINTER-ESTED!!
WHAT SHOULD I DO? HE THOUGHT MY CONVERSATION WAS BORING...! UM...UM...!
BABUMP
BABUMP
BABUMP
......
I-I'M SORRY I WENT OFF ON A BORING TOPIC...
UM, SORRY ABOUT THAT...
HUH? THAT'S ...
...NOT WHAT I WAS THINKING AT ALL!
RUMBLE
SMIRK SMIRK
WAAAAAAH!
THAT SMILE IS KIND OF SCARY ...!!
SILENCE
PEDAL
ジャコ
PEDAL
ジャコ
ZIP
ZIP
BDMP
ドキ
BDMP
ドキ
BDMP
ドキ

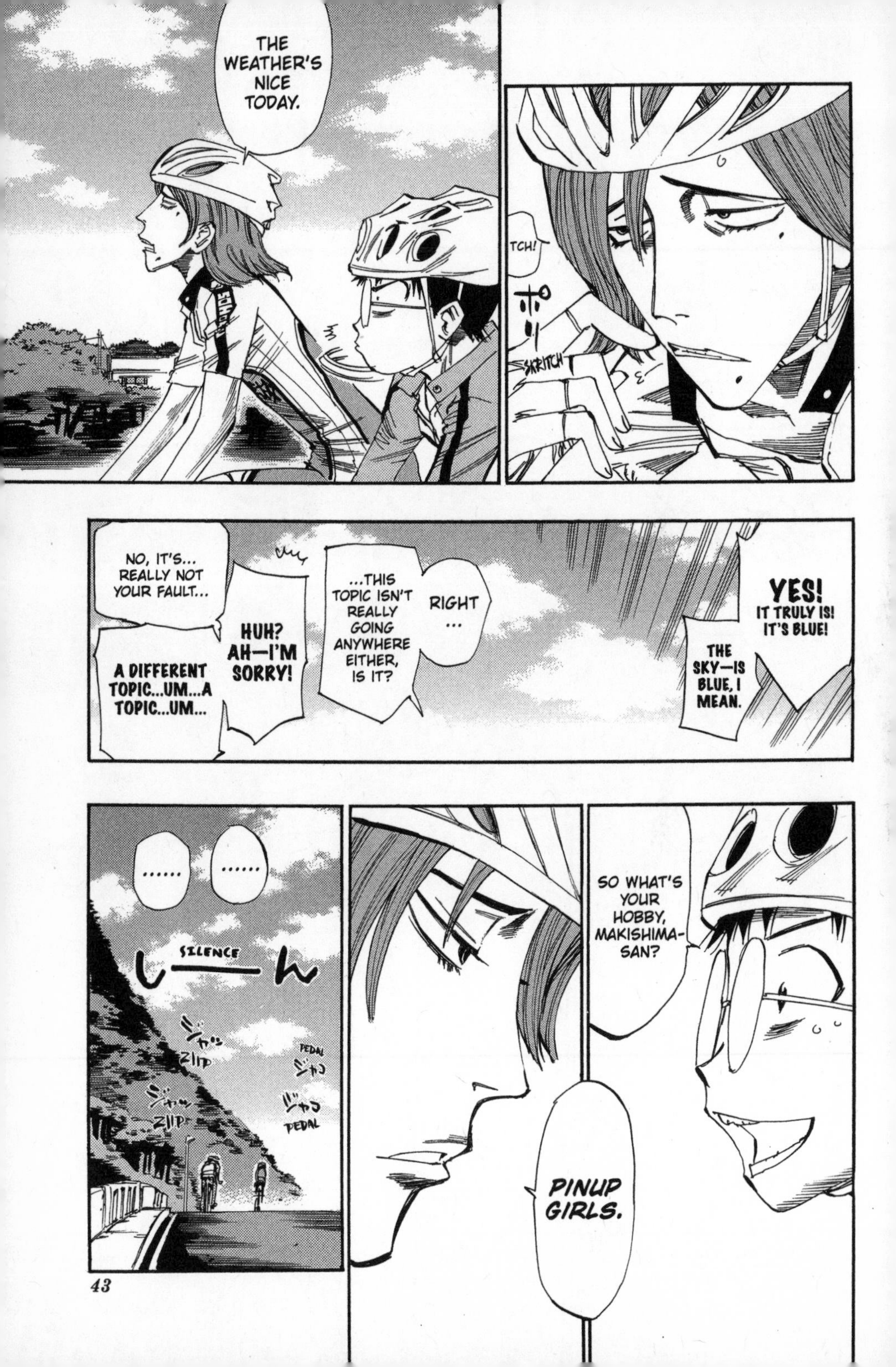
TCH!
SKRITCH
THE WEATHER'S NICE TODAY.
YES! IT TRULY IS! IT'S BLUE!
THE SKY—IS BLUE, I MEAN.
RIGHT...
...THIS TOPIC ISN'T REALLY GOING ANYWHERE EITHER, IS IT?
HUH? AH—I'M SORRY!
NO, IT'S... REALLY NOT YOUR FAULT...
A DIFFERENT TOPIC...UM...A TOPIC...UM...
SO WHAT'S YOUR HOBBY, MAKISHIMA-SAN?
PINUP GIRLS.
......
......
SILENCE
ZIP
PEDAL
ZIP
PEDAL

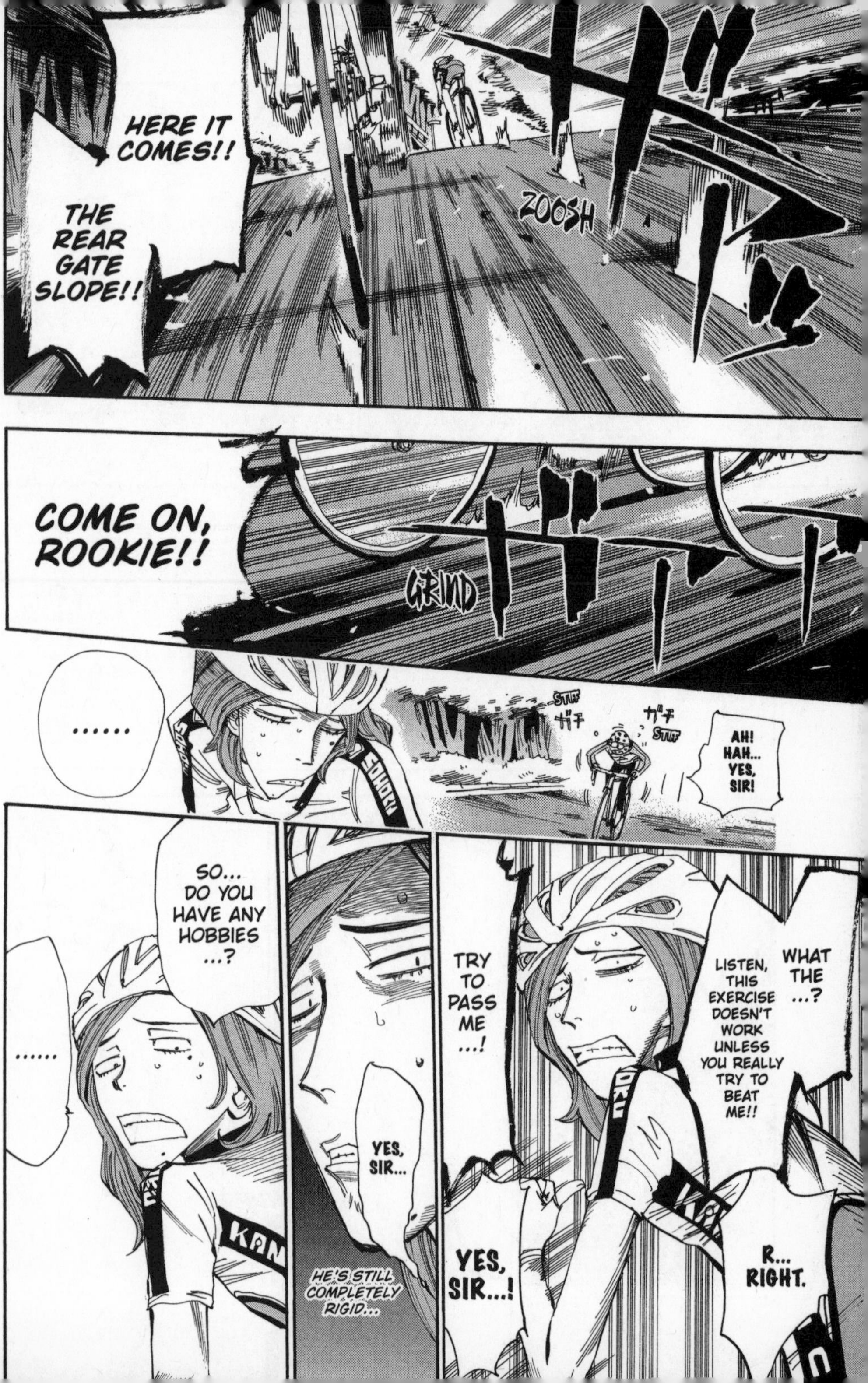
ZOOSH
HERE IT COMES!!
THE REAR GATE SLOPE!!
GRIND
COME ON, ROOKIE!!
AH! HAH... YES, SIR!
STIFF
STIFF
......
WHAT THE ...?
LISTEN, THIS EXERCISE DOESN'T WORK UNLESS YOU REALLY TRY TO BEAT ME!!
TRY TO PASS ME ...!
R... RIGHT.
YES, SIR...!
YES, SIR...
HE'S STILL COMPLETELY RIGID...
SO... DO YOU HAVE ANY HOBBIES ...?
......

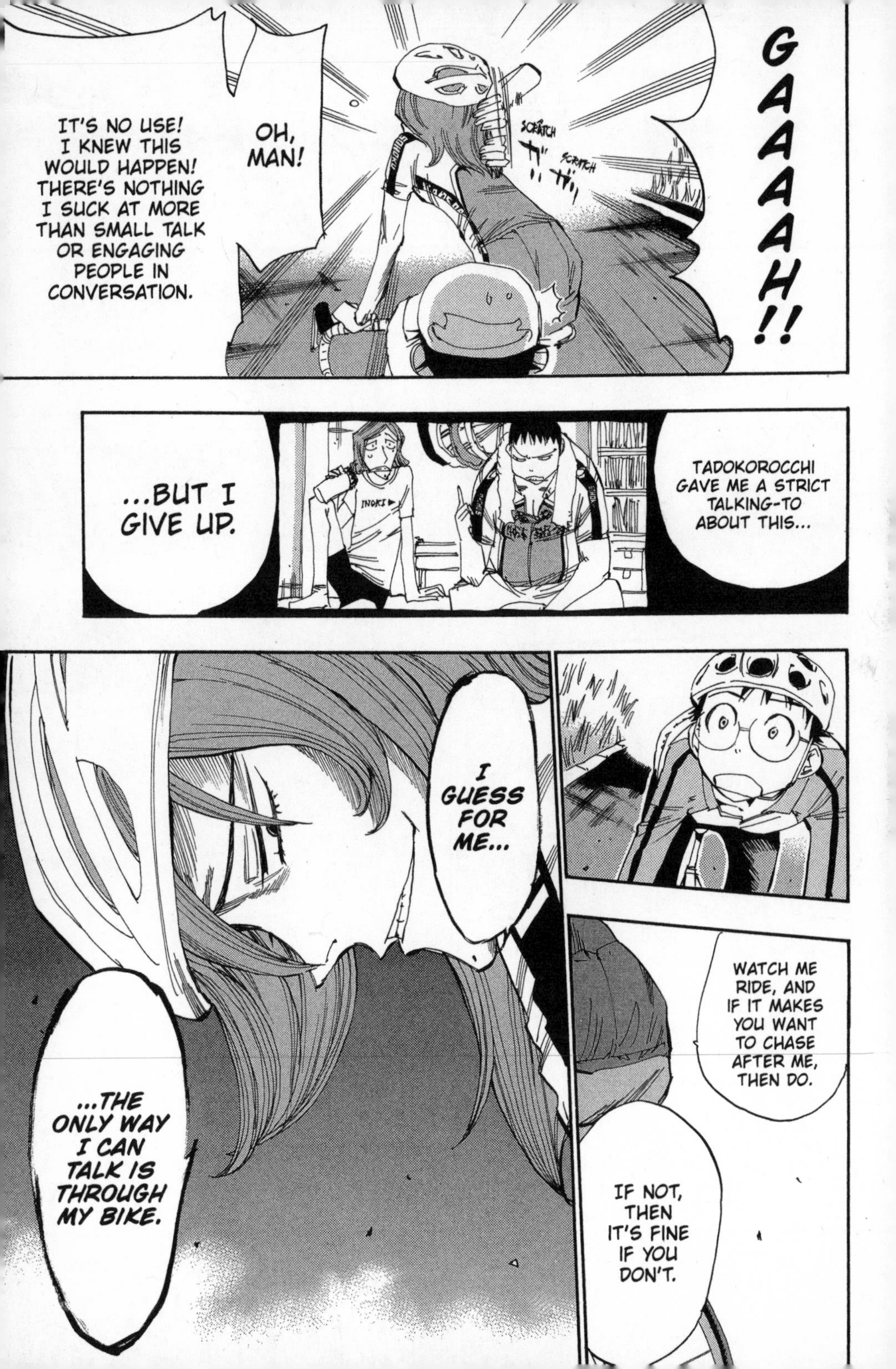
GAAAAAH!!
SCRATCH
SCRATCH
OH, MAN!
IT'S NO USE! I KNEW THIS WOULD HAPPEN! THERE'S NOTHING I SUCK AT MORE THAN SMALL TALK OR ENGAGING PEOPLE IN CONVERSATION.
TADOKOROCCHI GAVE ME A STRICT TALKING-TO ABOUT THIS...
...BUT I GIVE UP.
WATCH ME RIDE, AND IF IT MAKES YOU WANT TO CHASE AFTER ME, THEN DO.
IF NOT, THEN IT'S FINE IF YOU DON'T.
I GUESS FOR ME...
...THE ONLY WAY I CAN TALK IS THROUGH MY BIKE.

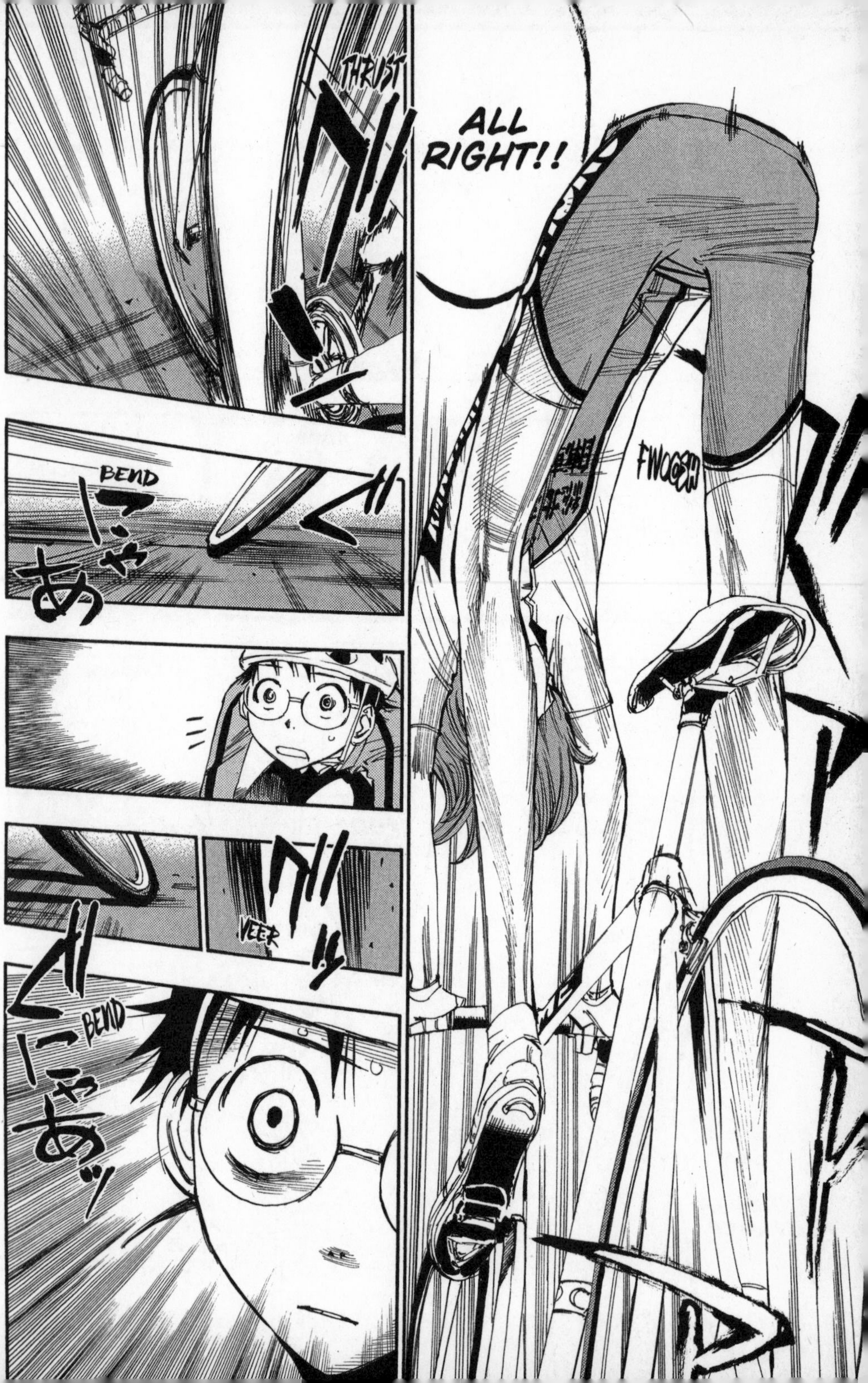
ALL RIGHT!!
FWOOSH
THRUST
BEND
VEER
BEND

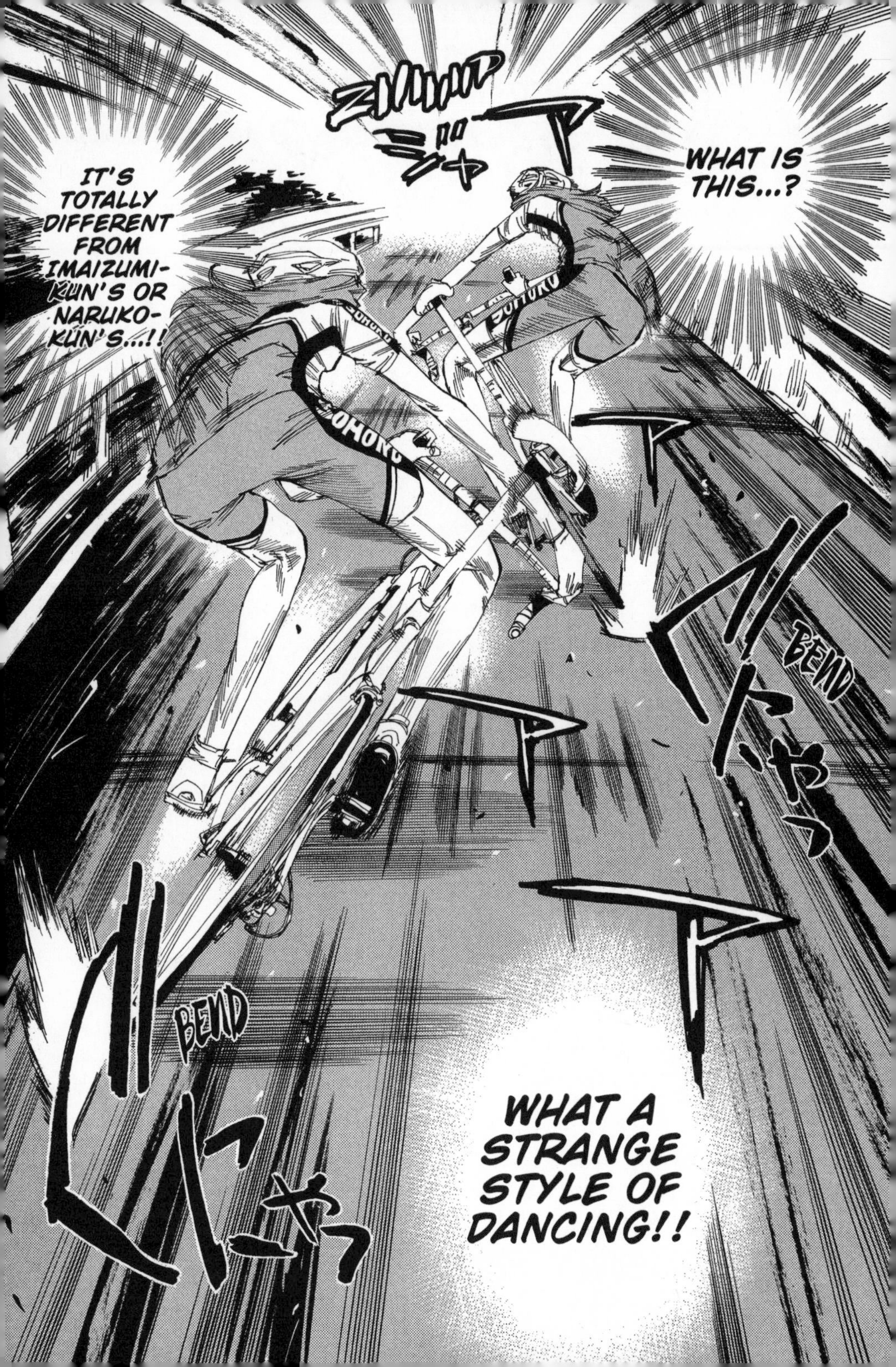
WHAT IS THIS...?
IT'S TOTALLY DIFFERENT FROM IMAIZUMI-KUN'S OR NARUKO-KUN'S...!!
BEND
BEND
WHAT A STRANGE STYLE OF DANCING!!

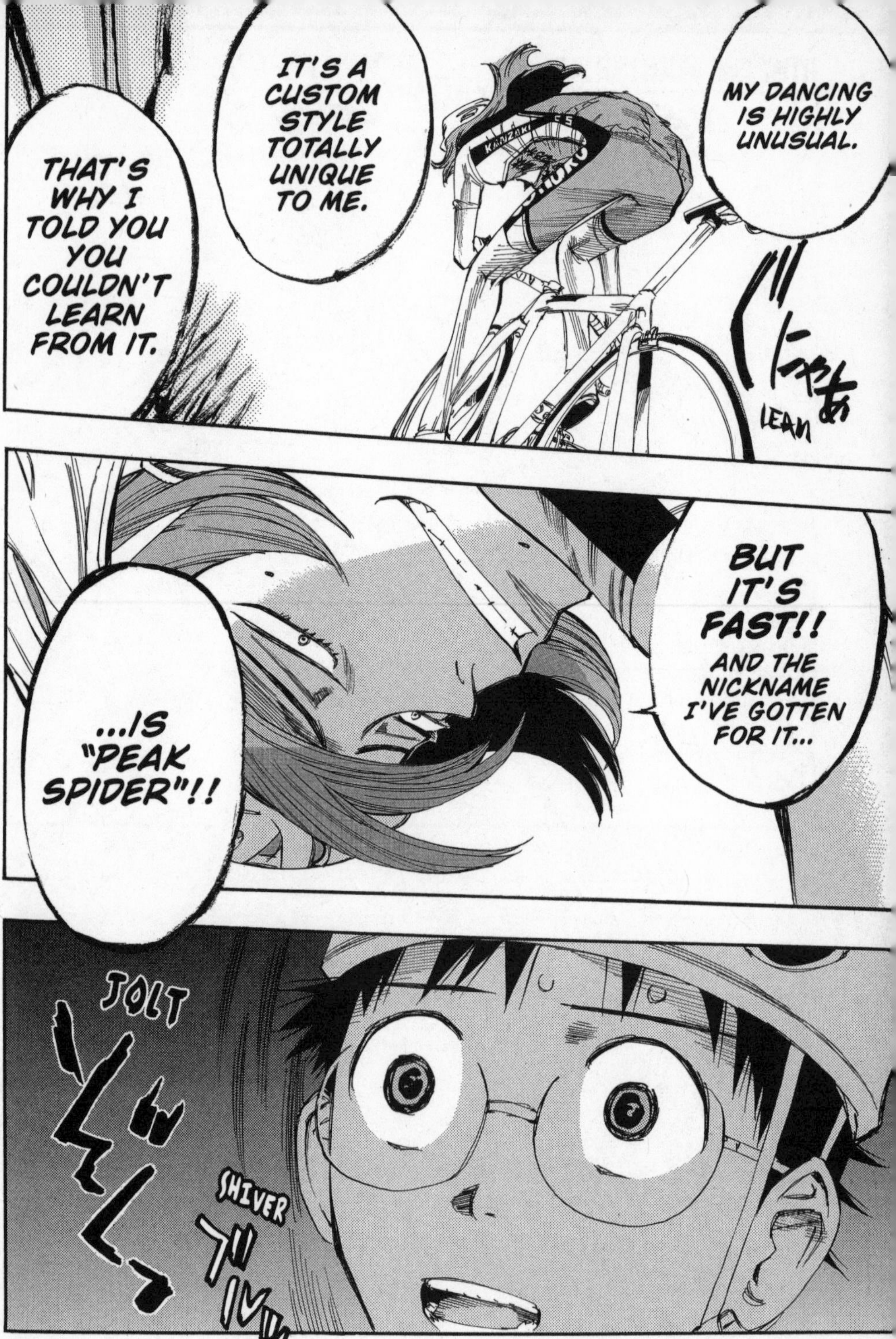
MY DANCING IS HIGHLY UNUSUAL.
IT'S A CUSTOM STYLE TOTALLY UNIQUE TO ME.
THAT'S WHY I TOLD YOU YOU COULDN'T LEARN FROM IT.
LEAN
BUT IT'S FAST!! AND THE NICKNAME I'VE GOTTEN FOR IT...
...IS "PEAK SPIDER"!!
SHIVER
JOLT

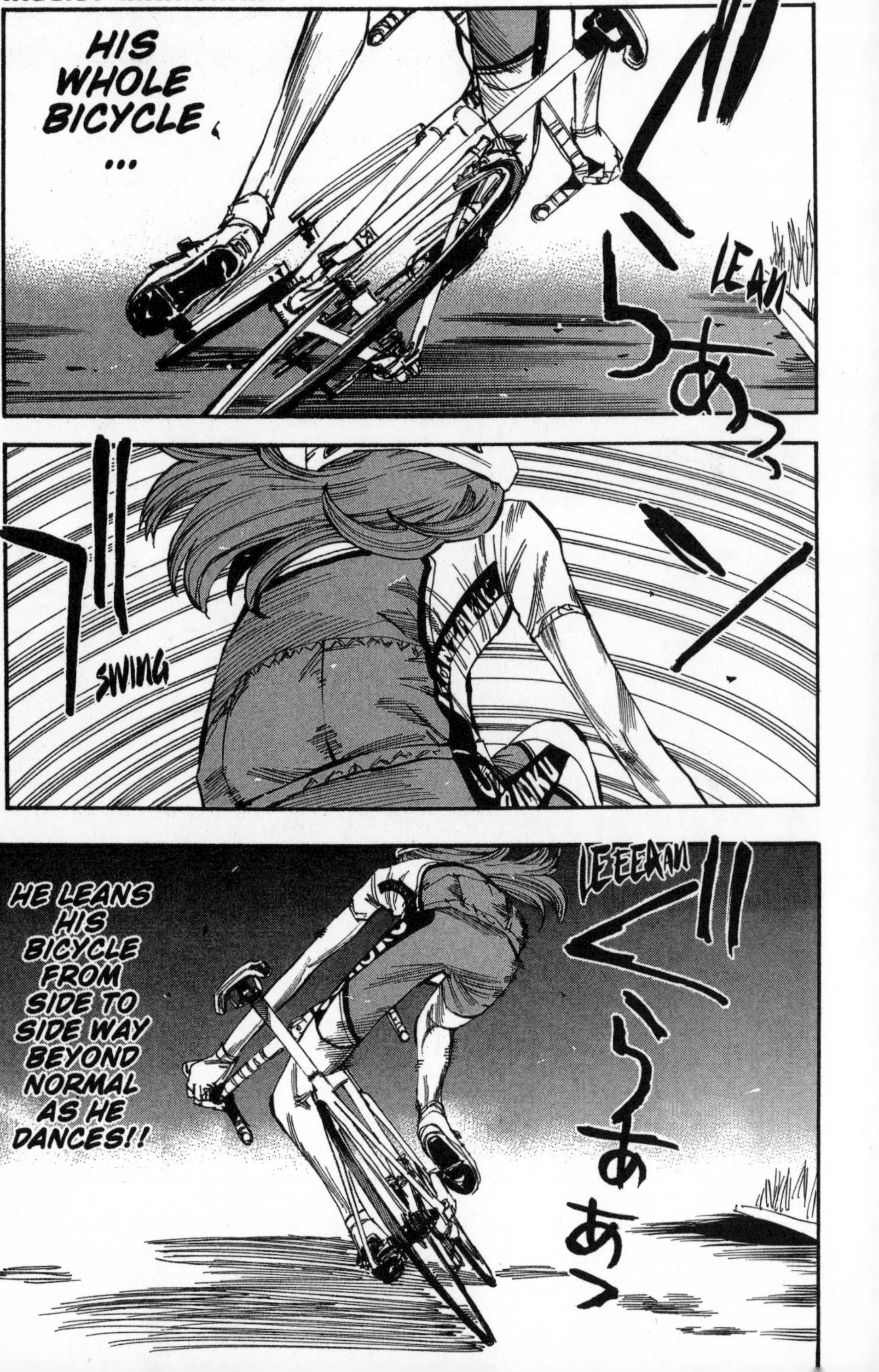
ぐらあっ
LEAN
HIS WHOLE BICYCLE...
SWING
ぐらああっ
LEEEEAAN
HE LEANS HIS BICYCLE FROM SIDE TO SIDE WAY BEYOND NORMAL AS HE DANCES!!

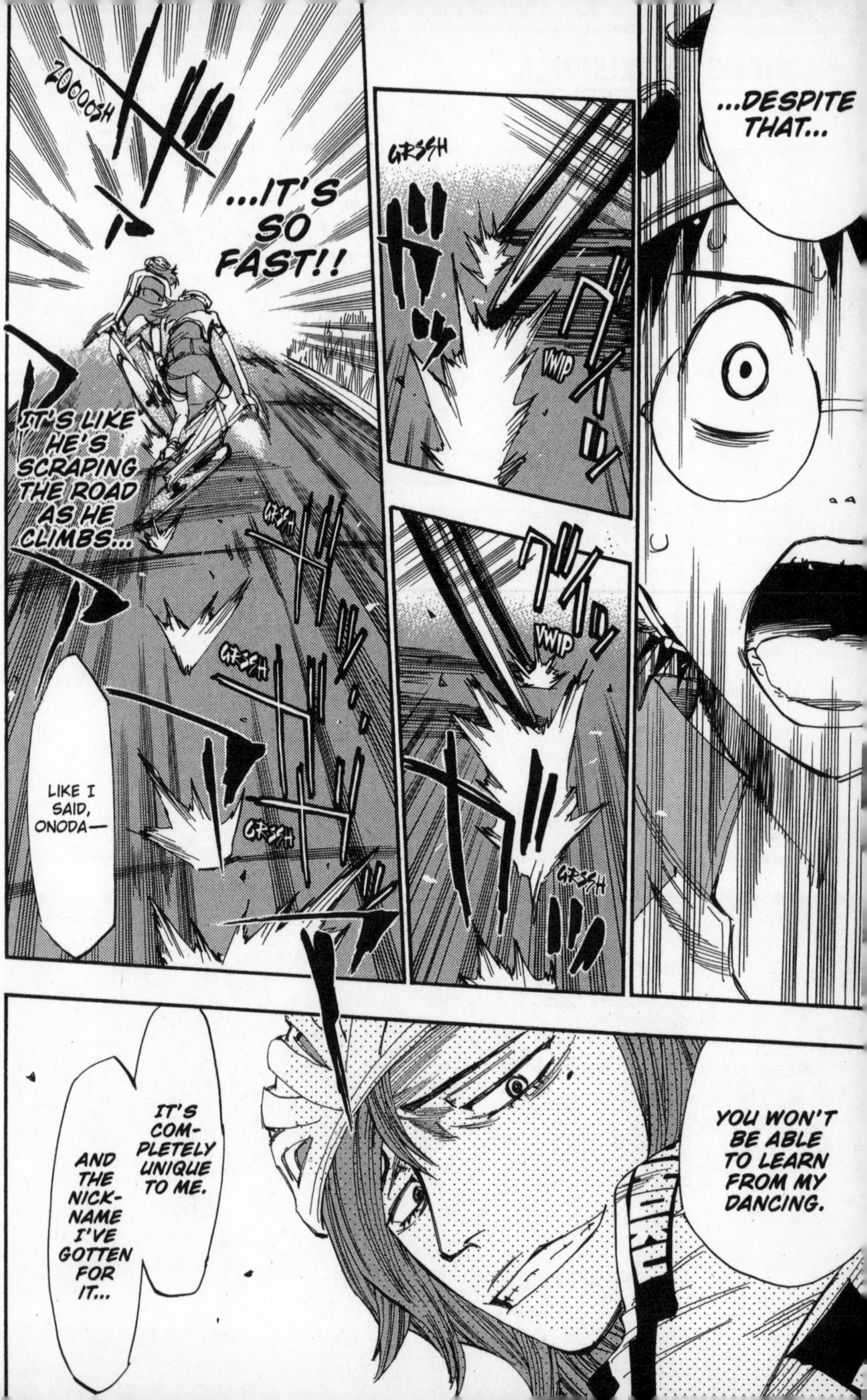
...DESPITE THAT...
GRSSH
VWIP
VWIP
GRSSH
ZOOOOSH
...IT'S SO FAST!!
IT'S LIKE HE'S SCRAPING THE ROAD AS HE CLIMBS...
GRSSH
GRSSH
GRSSH
LIKE I SAID, ONODA—
YOU WON'T BE ABLE TO LEARN FROM MY DANCING.
IT'S COM-PLETELY UNIQUE TO ME.
AND THE NICK-NAME I'VE GOTTEN FOR IT...

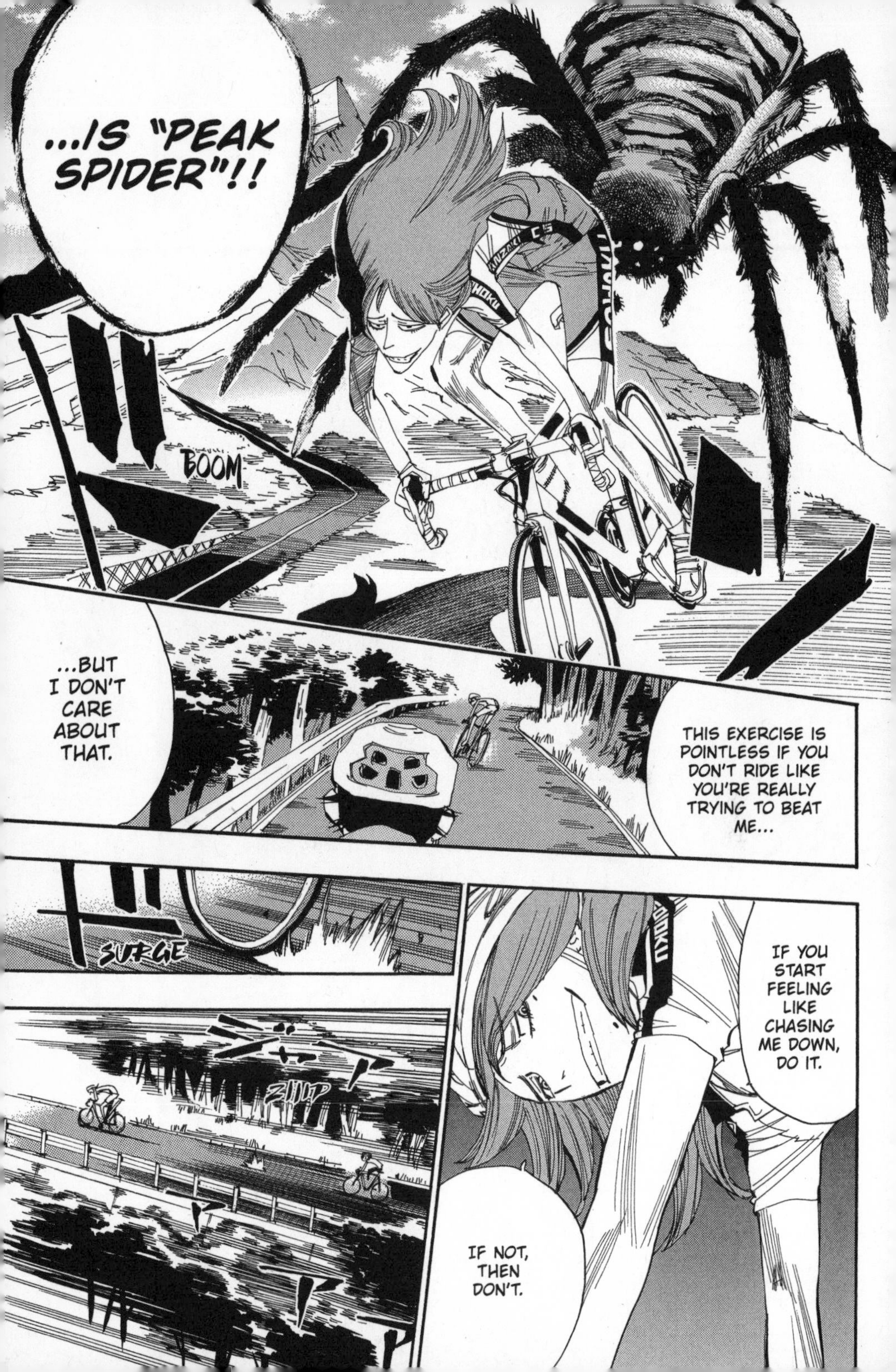

...IS "PEAK SPIDER"!!
BOOM
THIS EXERCISE IS POINTLESS IF YOU DON'T RIDE LIKE YOU'RE REALLY TRYING TO BEAT ME...
...BUT I DON'T CARE ABOUT THAT.
IF YOU START FEELING LIKE CHASING ME DOWN, DO IT.
IF NOT, THEN DON'T.
SURGE
ZIIIP

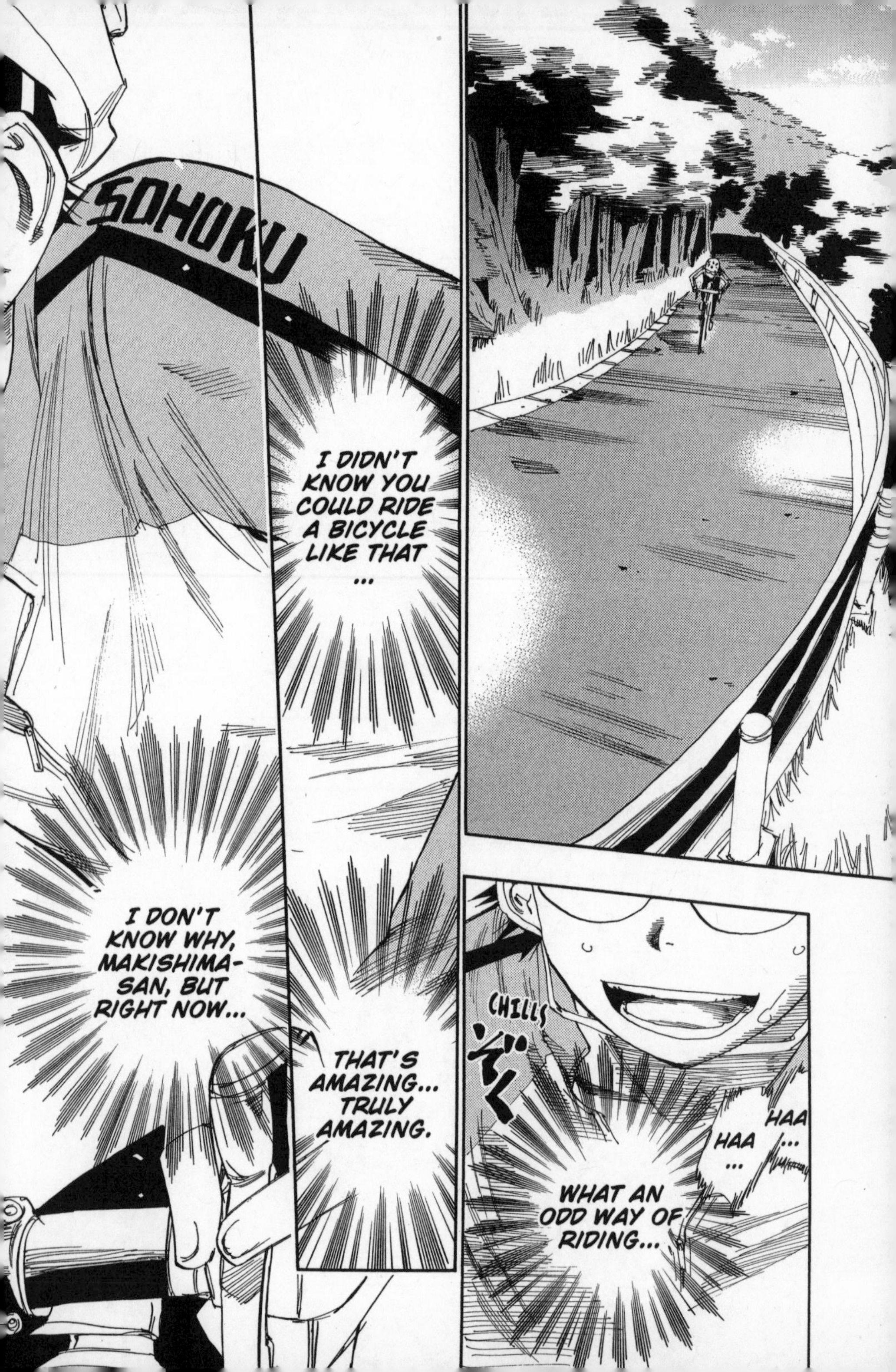
CHILLS
ゾく
HAA HAA...
HAA...
WHAT AN ODD WAY OF RIDING...
I DIDN'T KNOW YOU COULD RIDE A BICYCLE LIKE THAT...
THAT'S AMAZING... TRULY AMAZING.
SOHOKU
I DON'T KNOW WHY, MAKISHIMA-SAN, BUT RIGHT NOW...

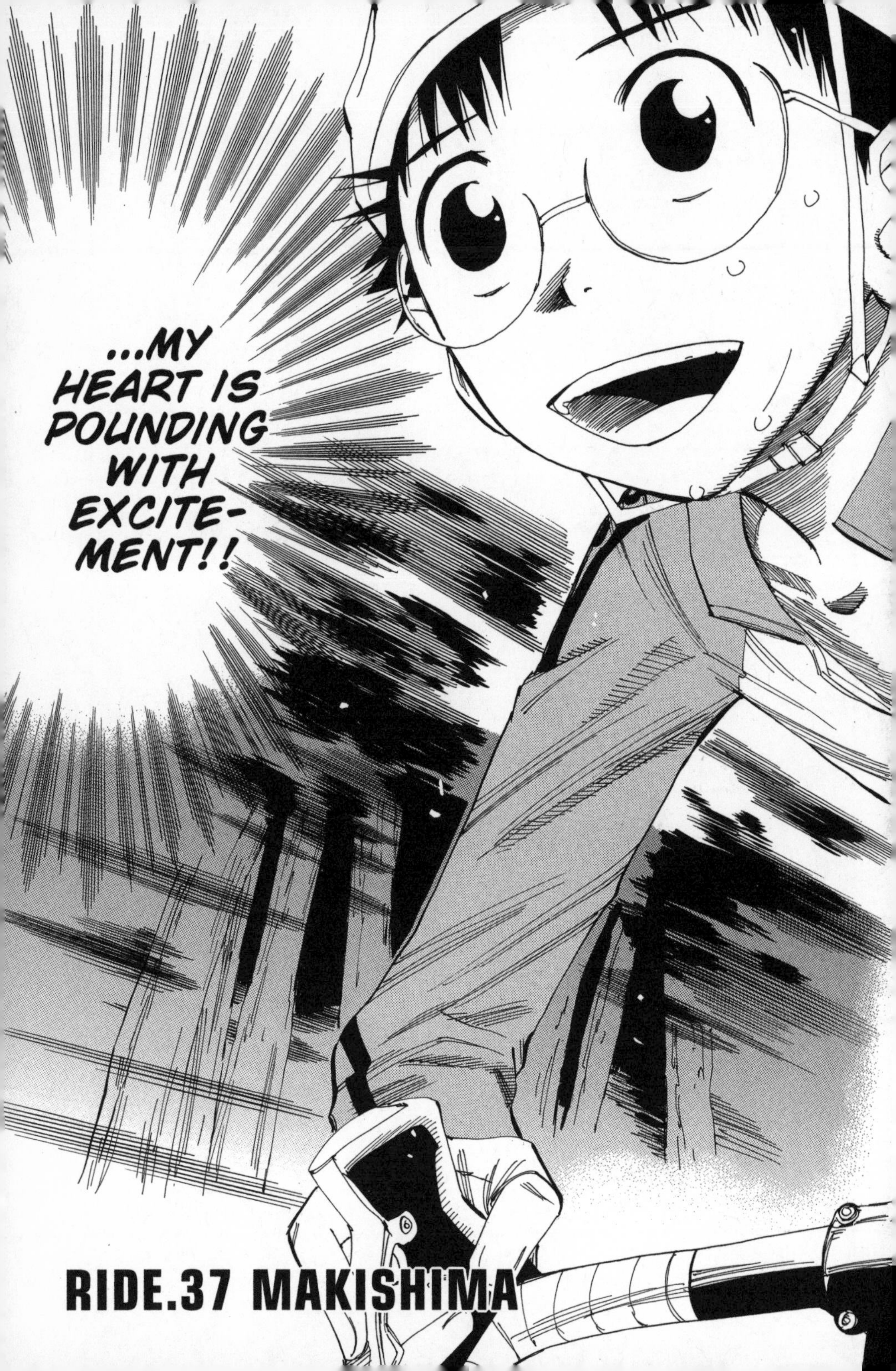
...MY HEART IS POUNDING WITH EXCITE-MENT!!
RIDE.37 MAKISHIMA

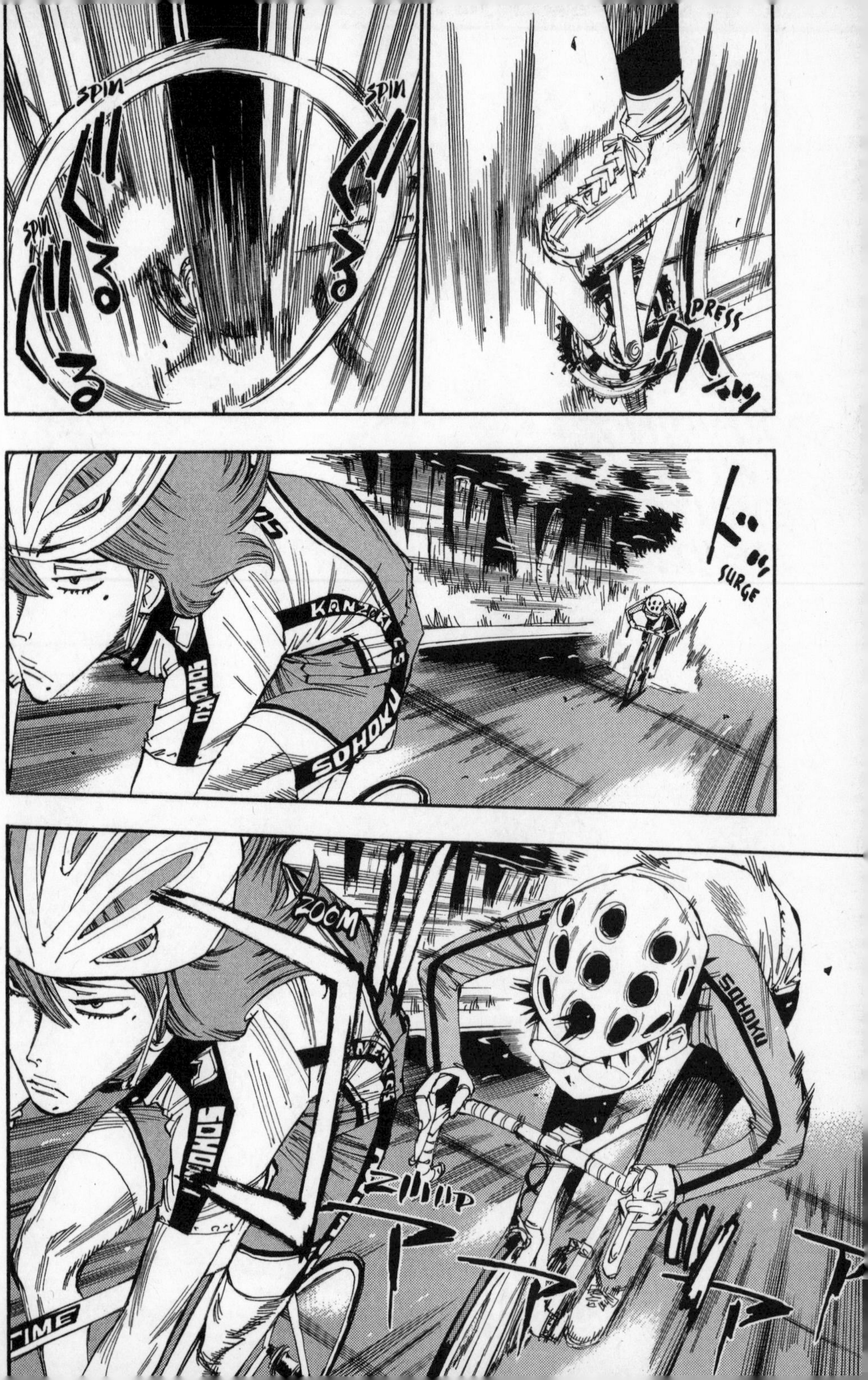
PRESS
SPIN
SPIN
SPIN
SURGE
ZOOM
ZIP

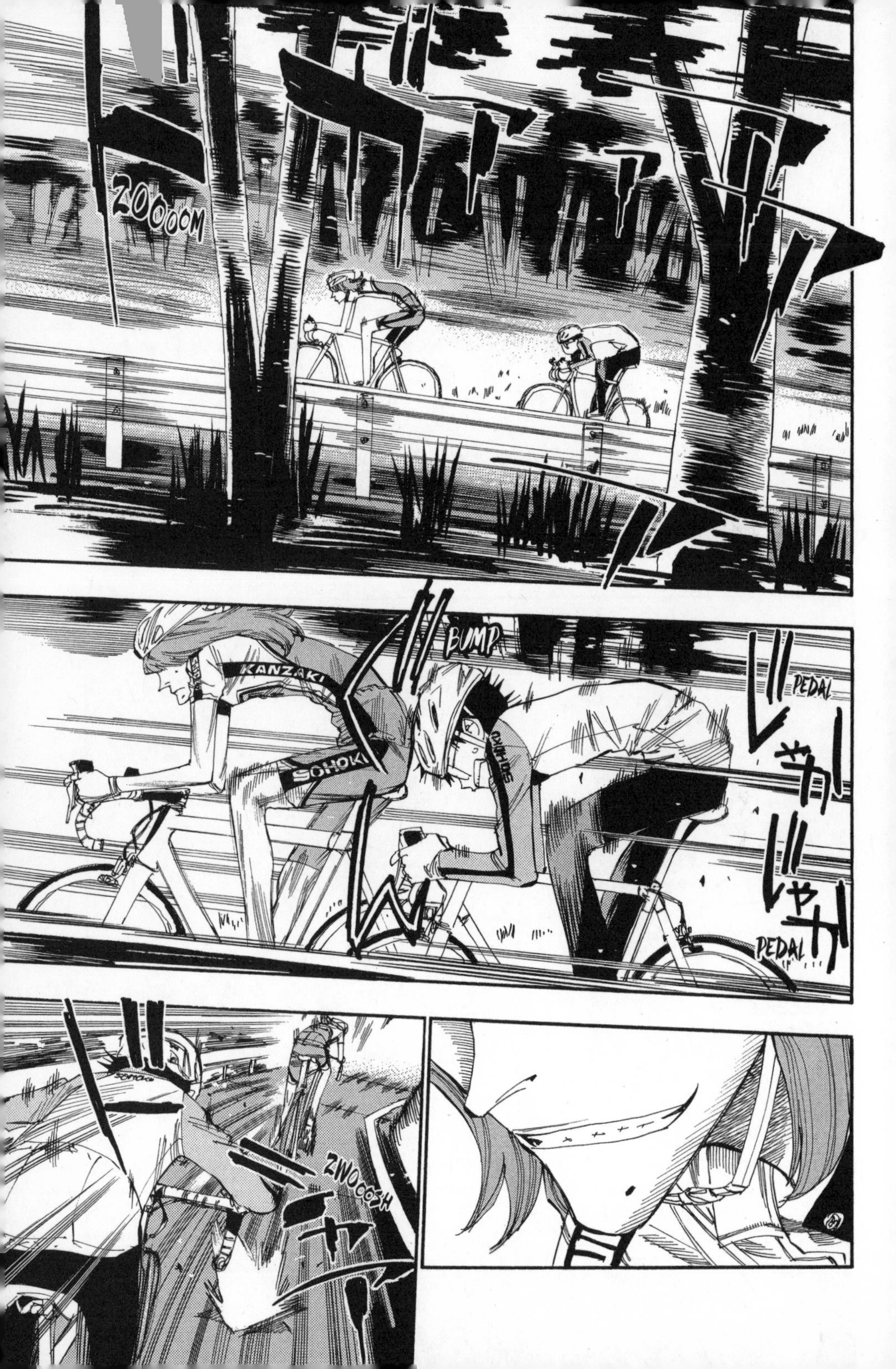

ZOOOOM
PEDAL
BUMP
KANZAKI
SOHOKU
PEDAL
ZWOOOSH

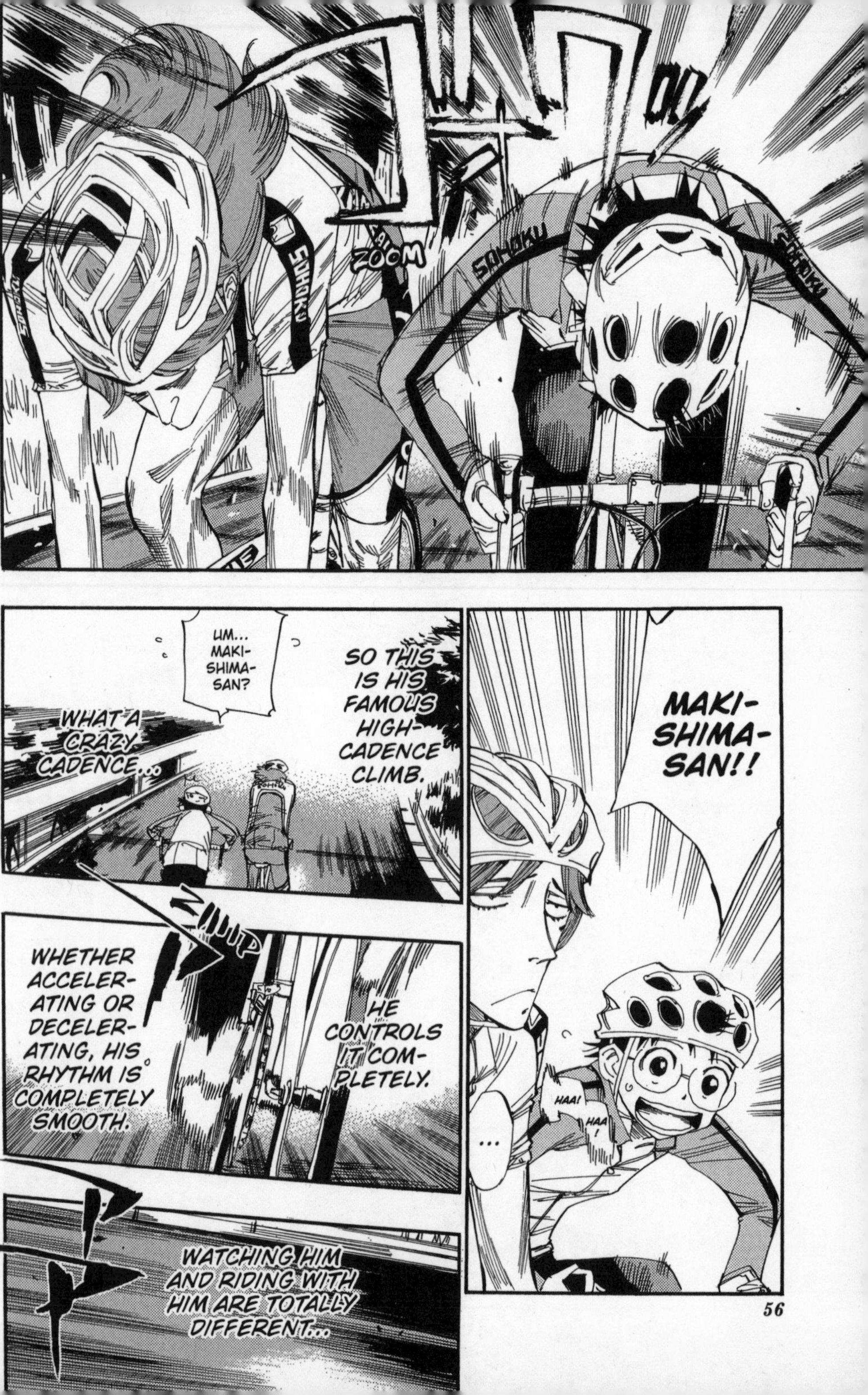
ZOOM
MAKI-SHIMA-SAN!!
HAA! HAA!
...
SO THIS IS HIS FAMOUS HIGH-CADENCE CLIMB.
UM... MAKI-SHIMA-SAN?
WHAT A CRAZY CADENCE...
ZIIIIP
HE CONTROLS IT COMPLETELY.
WHETHER ACCELERATING OR DECELERATING, HIS RHYTHM IS COMPLETELY SMOOTH.
WATCHING HIM AND RIDING WITH HIM ARE TOTALLY DIFFERENT...

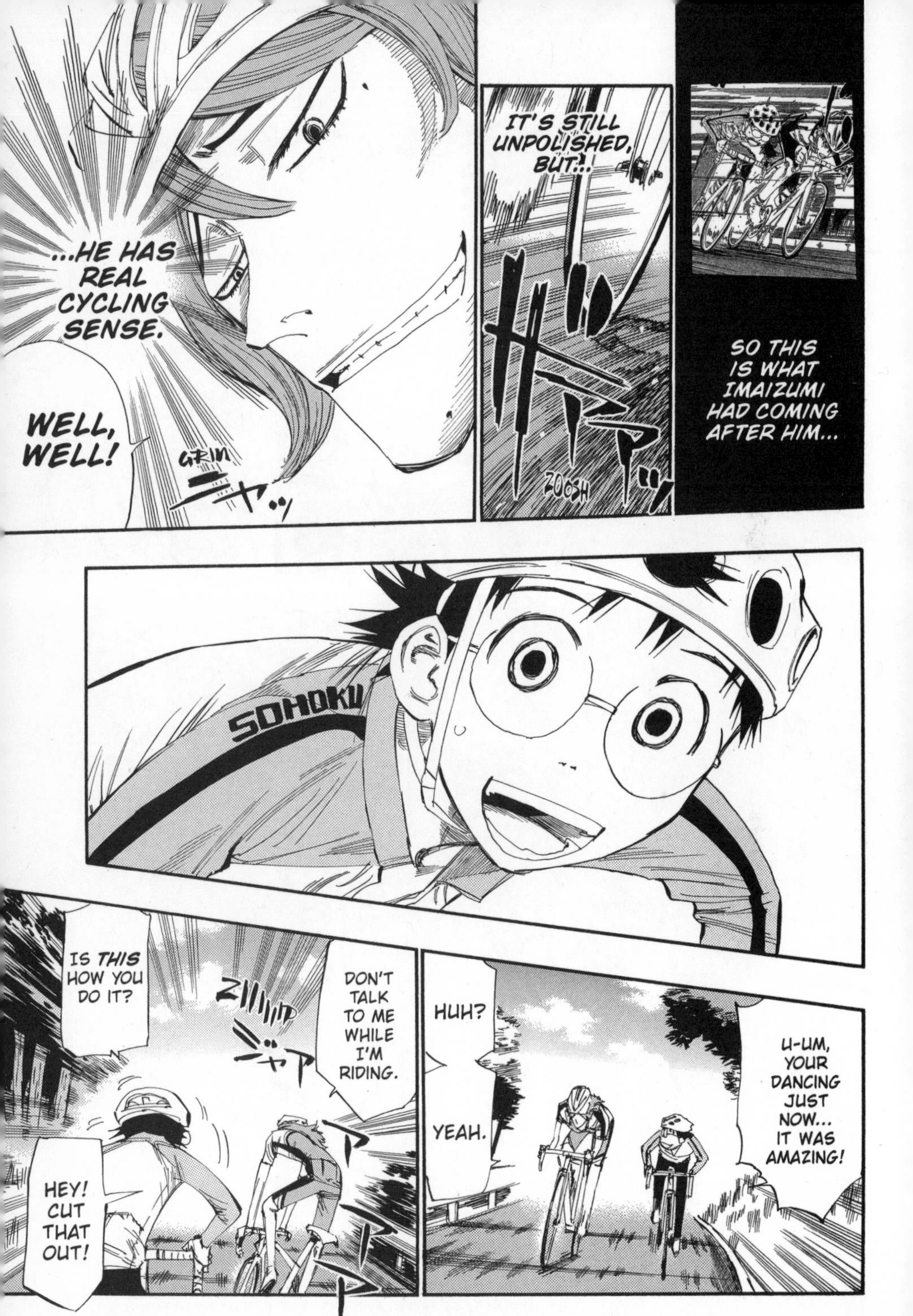
SO THIS IS WHAT IMAIZUMI HAD COMING AFTER HIM...
IT'S STILL UNPOLISHED, BUT...
ZOOSH
...HE HAS REAL CYCLING SENSE.
WELL, WELL!
GRIN
SOHOKU
U-UM, YOUR DANCING JUST NOW... IT WAS AMAZING!
HUH?
YEAH.
IS THIS HOW YOU DO IT?
DON'T TALK TO ME WHILE I'M RIDING.
ZIIIIP
HEY! CUT THAT OUT!

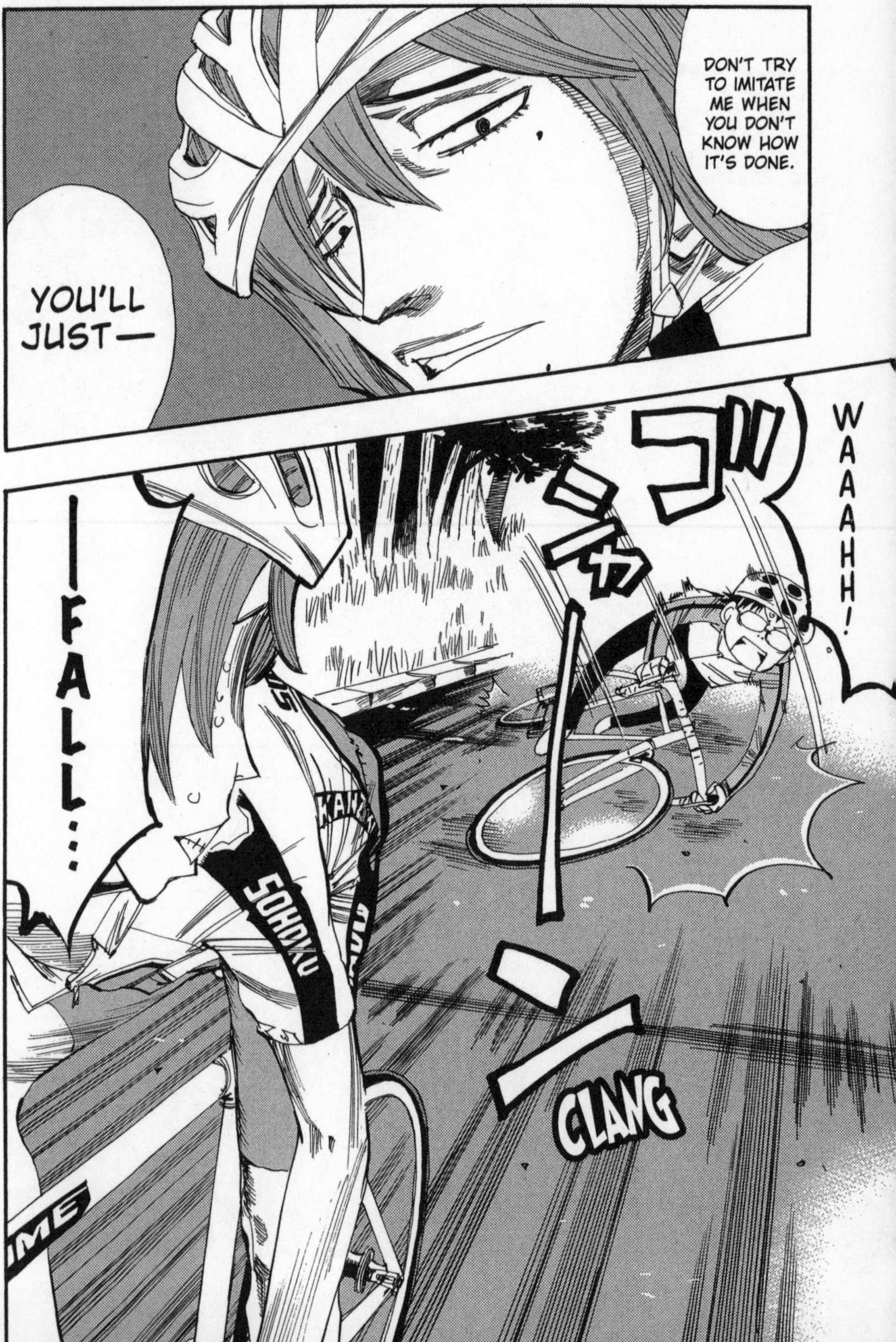
DON'T TRY TO IMITATE ME WHEN YOU DON'T KNOW HOW IT'S DONE.
YOU'LL JUST—
WAAAAHH!
CLANG
—FALL...

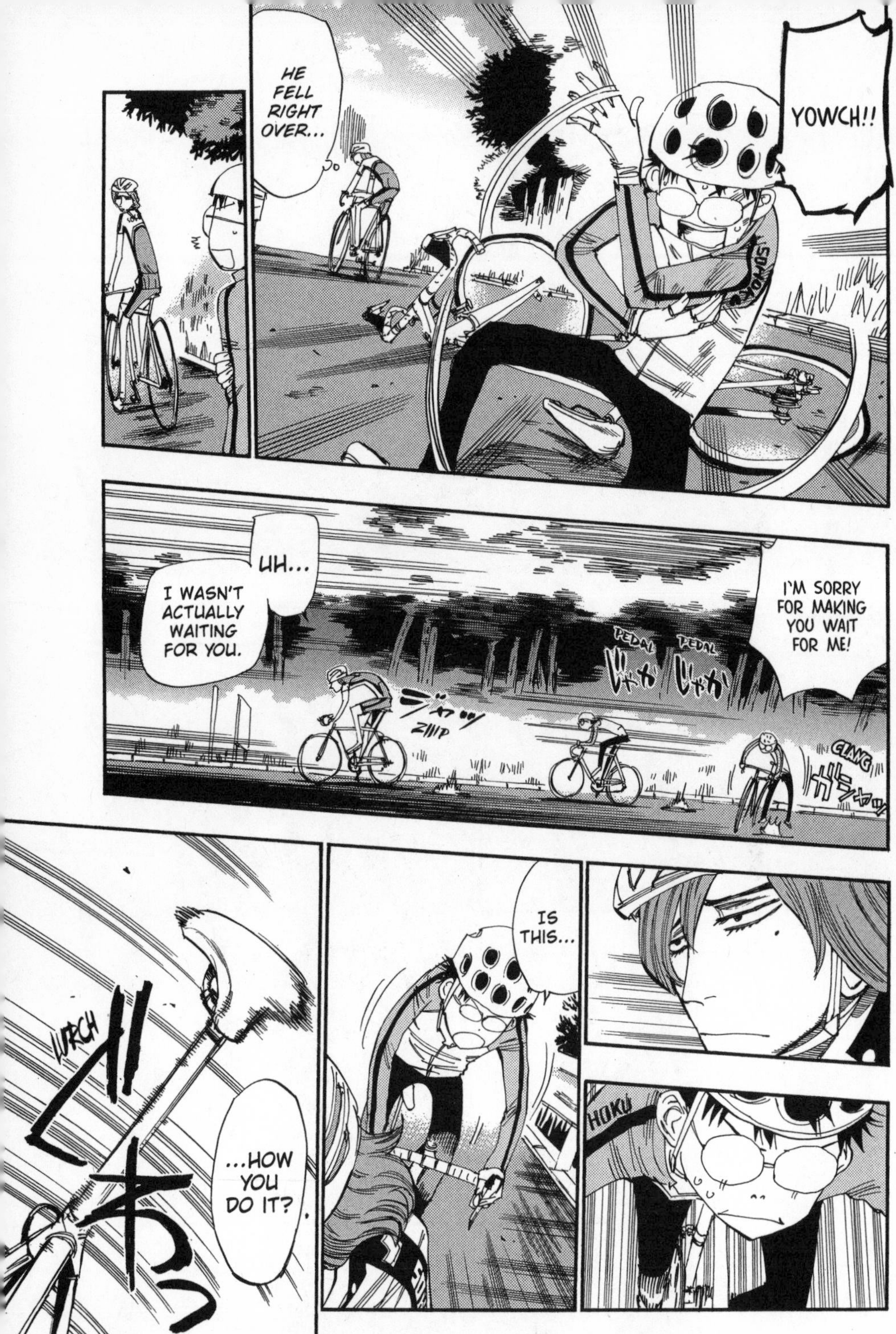
YOWCH!!
HE FELL RIGHT OVER...
I'M SORRY FOR MAKING YOU WAIT FOR ME!
CLANG
PEDAL PEDAL
じゃか じゃか
ZIIP
UH...
I WASN'T ACTUALLY WAITING FOR YOU.
HOKU
IS THIS...
...HOW YOU DO IT?
LURCH

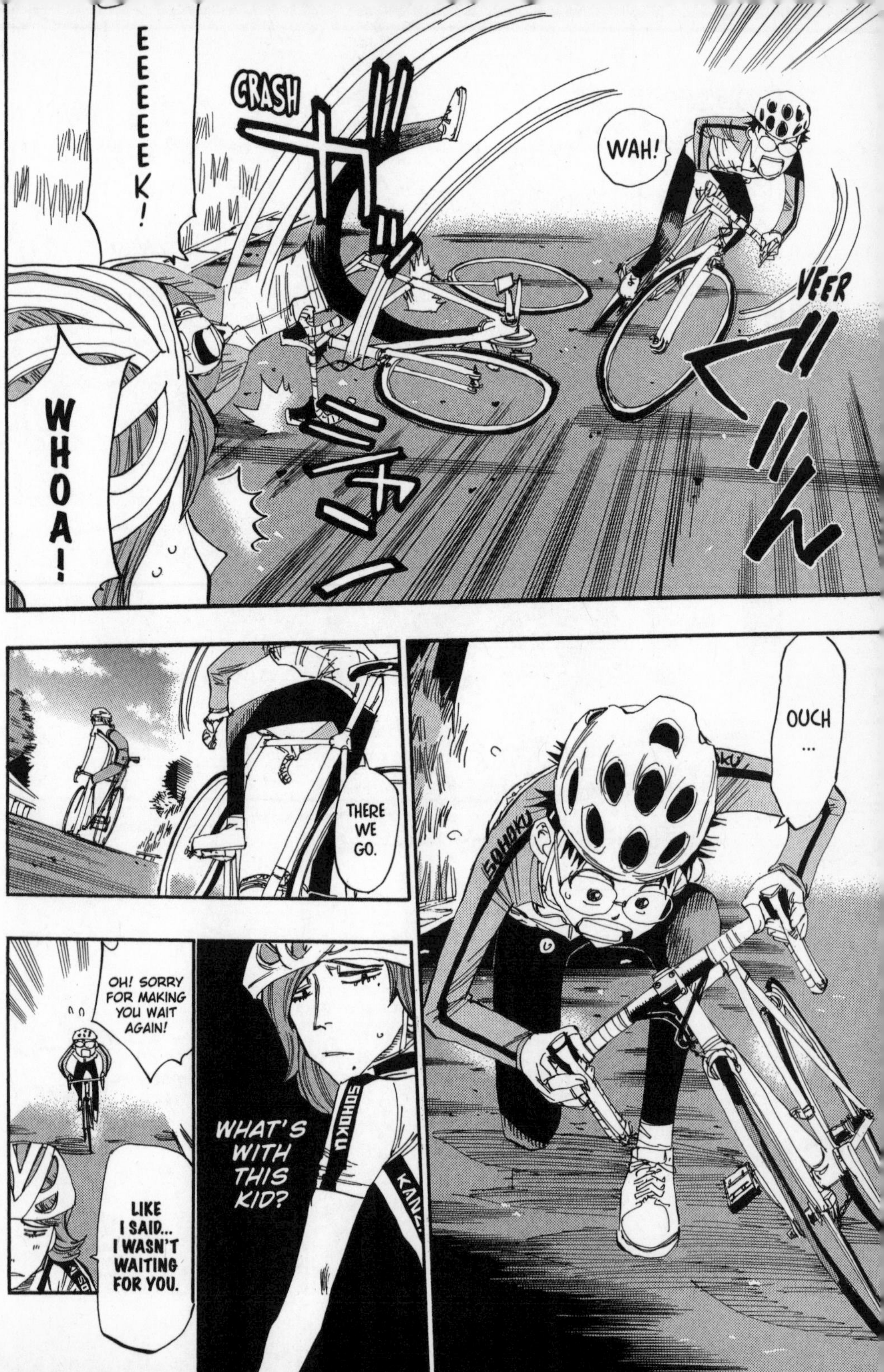
WAH!
VEER
CRASH
EEEEEK!
WHOA!
OUCH ...
THERE WE GO.
WHAT'S WITH THIS KID?
OH! SORRY FOR MAKING YOU WAIT AGAIN!
LIKE I SAID... I WASN'T WAITING FOR YOU.

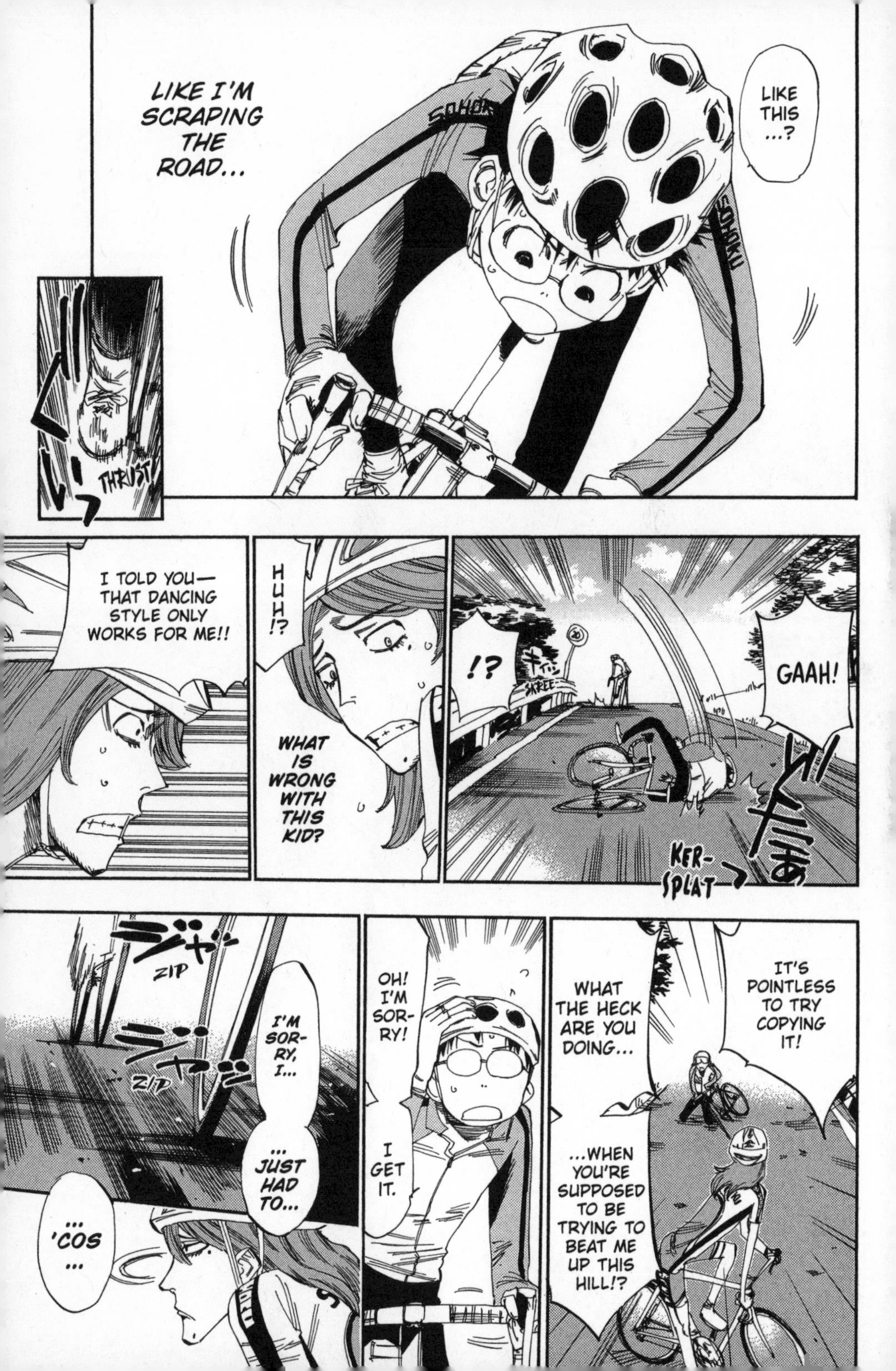
LIKE THIS ...?
LIKE I'M SCRAPING THE ROAD...
THRUST
GAAH!
!?
SKREE
KER-SPLAT
HUH!?
WHAT IS WRONG WITH THIS KID?
I TOLD YOU— THAT DANCING STYLE ONLY WORKS FOR ME!!
IT'S POINTLESS TO TRY COPYING IT!
WHAT THE HECK ARE YOU DOING...
...WHEN YOU'RE SUPPOSED TO BE TRYING TO BEAT ME UP THIS HILL!?
OH! I'M SORRY!
I GET IT.
I'M SORRY, I...
...JUST HAD TO...
ZIP
ZIP
...'COS...

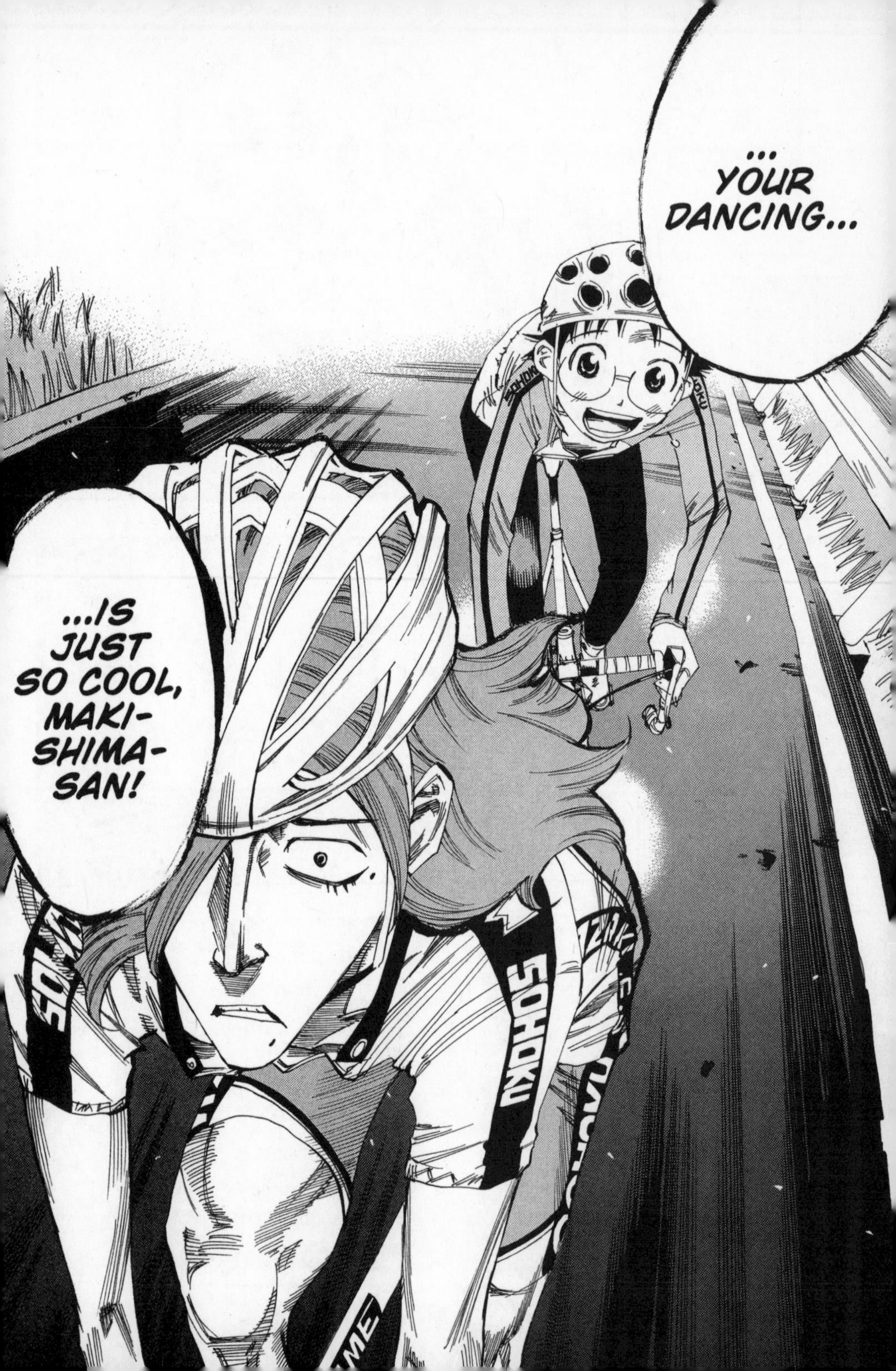
... YOUR DANCING...
...IS JUST SO COOL, MAKI-SHIMA-SAN!

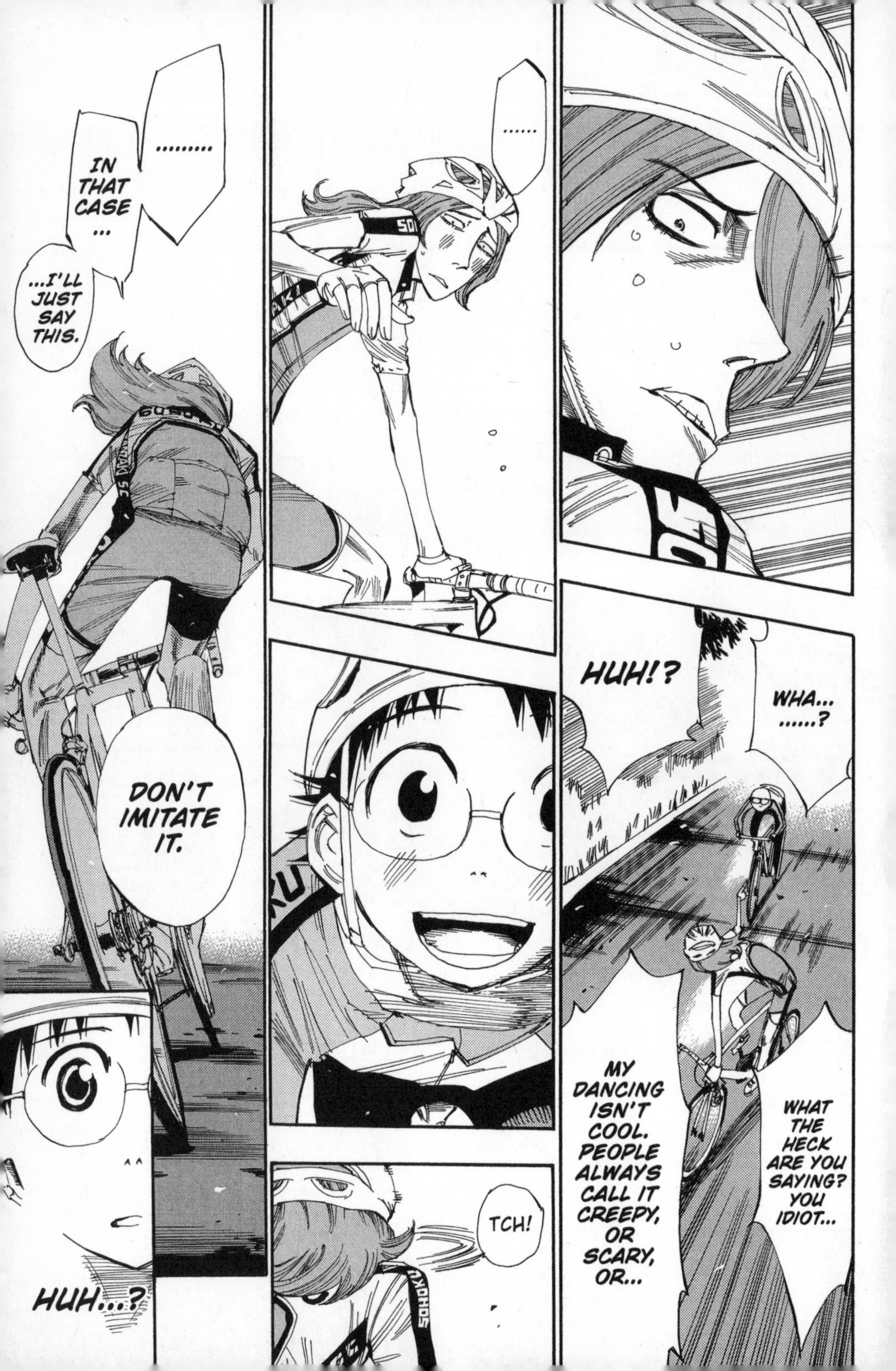

......
....
IN THAT CASE ...
...I'LL JUST SAY THIS.
DON'T IMITATE IT.
HUH!?
WHA... ......?
MY DANCING ISN'T COOL. PEOPLE ALWAYS CALL IT CREEPY, OR SCARY, OR...
WHAT THE HECK ARE YOU SAYING? YOU IDIOT...
HUH...?
TCH!

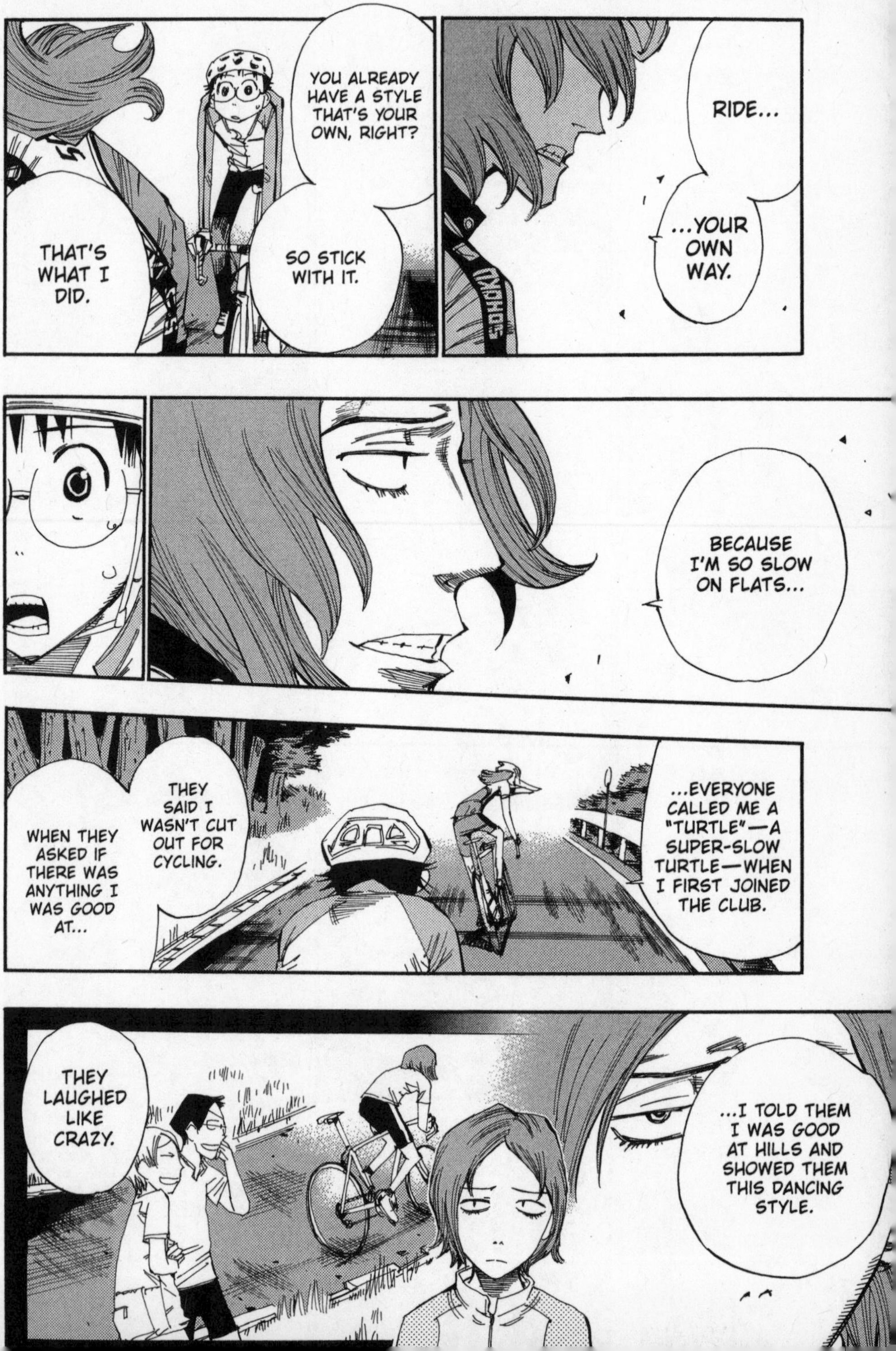
RIDE...
...YOUR OWN WAY.
YOU ALREADY HAVE A STYLE THAT'S YOUR OWN, RIGHT?
SO STICK WITH IT.
THAT'S WHAT I DID.
BECAUSE I'M SO SLOW ON FLATS...
...EVERYONE CALLED ME A "TURTLE"—A SUPER-SLOW TURTLE—WHEN I FIRST JOINED THE CLUB.
THEY SAID I WASN'T CUT OUT FOR CYCLING.
WHEN THEY ASKED IF THERE WAS ANYTHING I WAS GOOD AT...
...I TOLD THEM I WAS GOOD AT HILLS AND SHOWED THEM THIS DANCING STYLE.
THEY LAUGHED LIKE CRAZY.

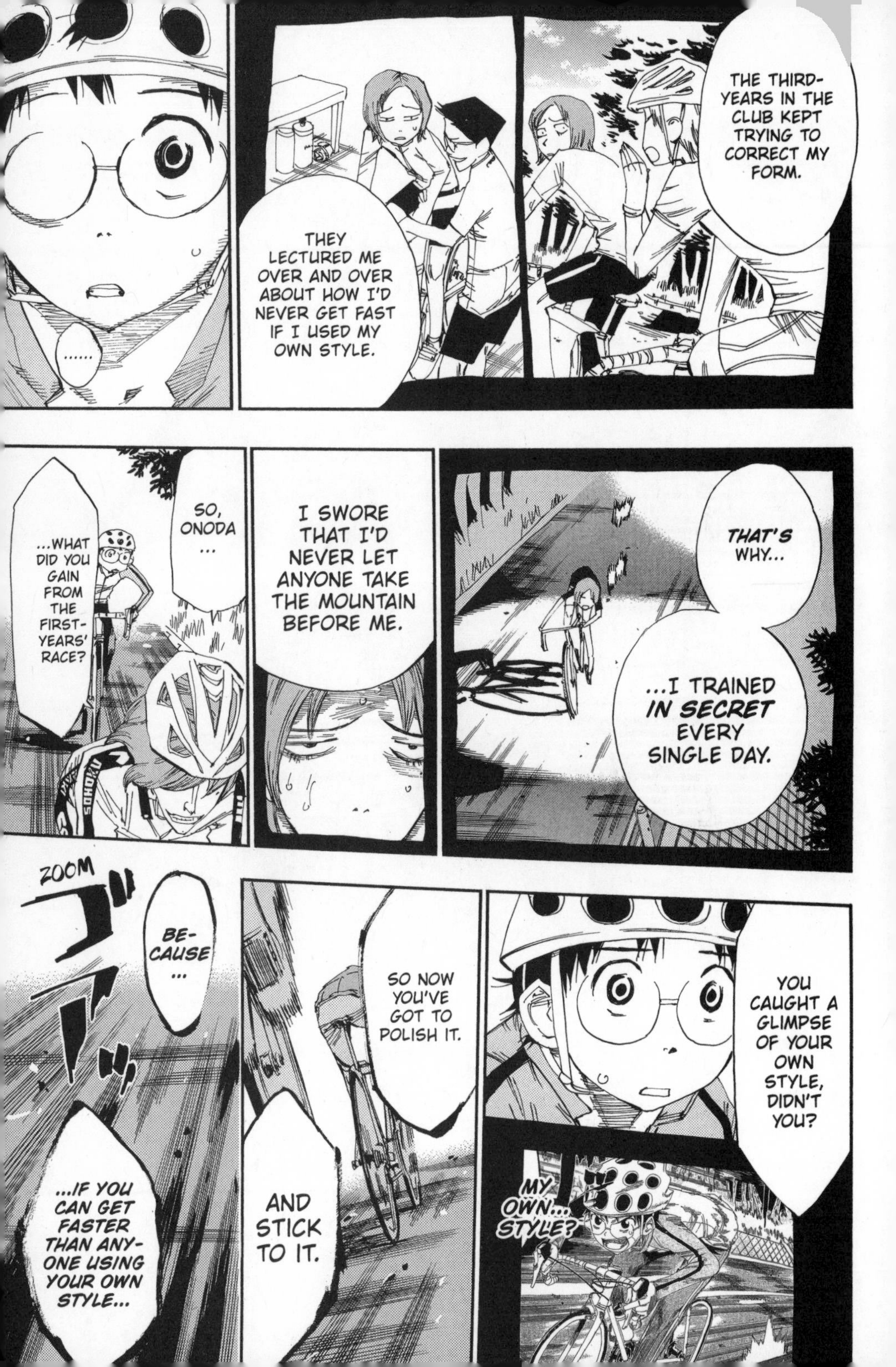
THE THIRD-YEARS IN THE CLUB KEPT TRYING TO CORRECT MY FORM.
THEY LECTURED ME OVER AND OVER ABOUT HOW I'D NEVER GET FAST IF I USED MY OWN STYLE.
......
THAT'S WHY...
...I TRAINED IN SECRET EVERY SINGLE DAY.
I SWORE THAT I'D NEVER LET ANYONE TAKE THE MOUNTAIN BEFORE ME.
SO, ONODA...
...WHAT DID YOU GAIN FROM THE FIRST-YEARS' RACE?
YOU CAUGHT A GLIMPSE OF YOUR OWN STYLE, DIDN'T YOU?
MY OWN... STYLE?
SO NOW YOU'VE GOT TO POLISH IT.
AND STICK TO IT.
ZOOM
BE-CAUSE...
...IF YOU CAN GET FASTER THAN ANY-ONE USING YOUR OWN STYLE...

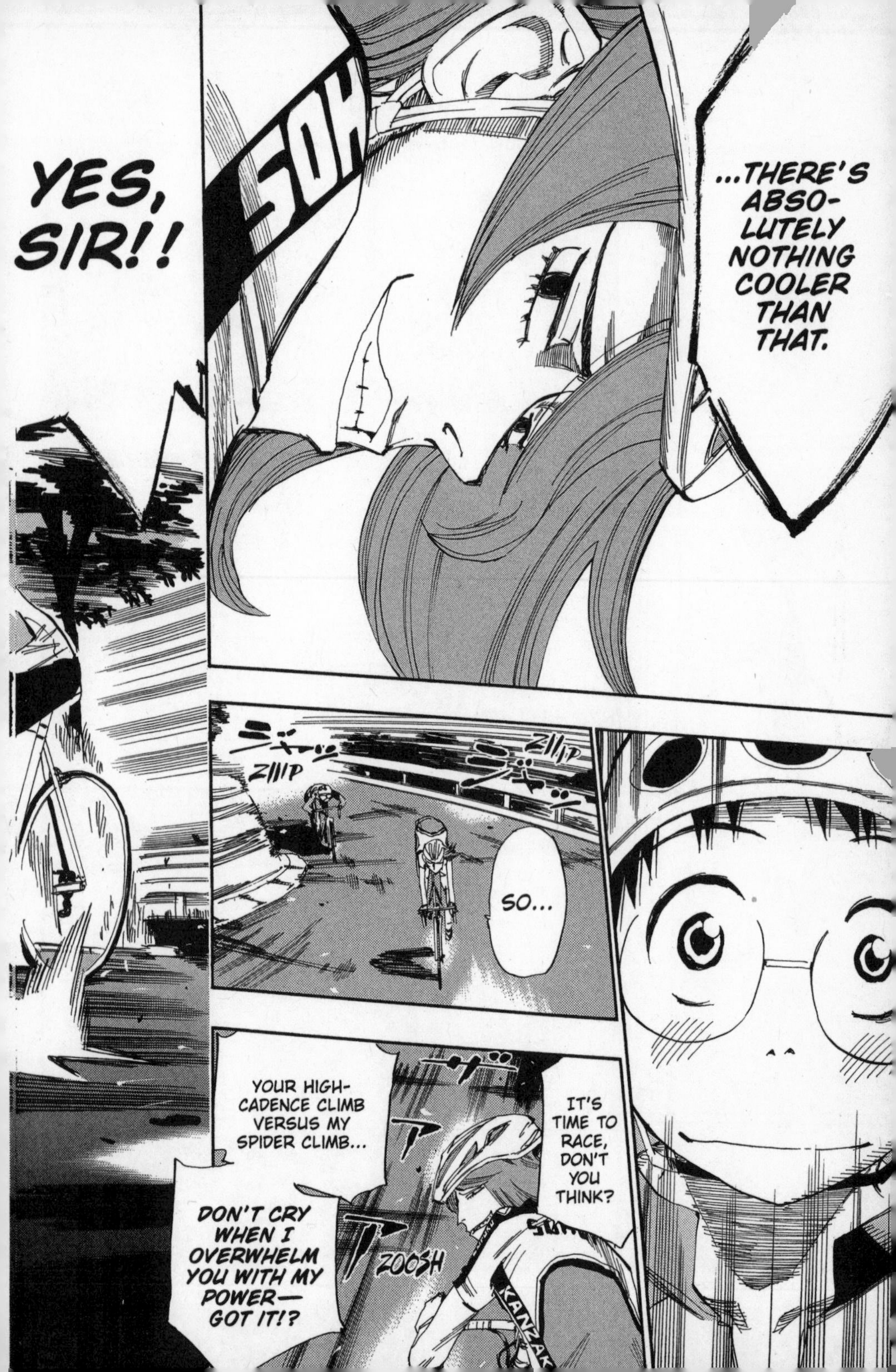

...THERE'S ABSO-LUTELY NOTHING COOLER THAN THAT.
ZIIP
ZIIP
SO...
IT'S TIME TO RACE, DON'T YOU THINK?
YOUR HIGH-CADENCE CLIMB VERSUS MY SPIDER CLIMB...
DON'T CRY WHEN I OVERWHELM YOU WITH MY POWER—GOT IT!?
ZOOSH
YES, SIR!!

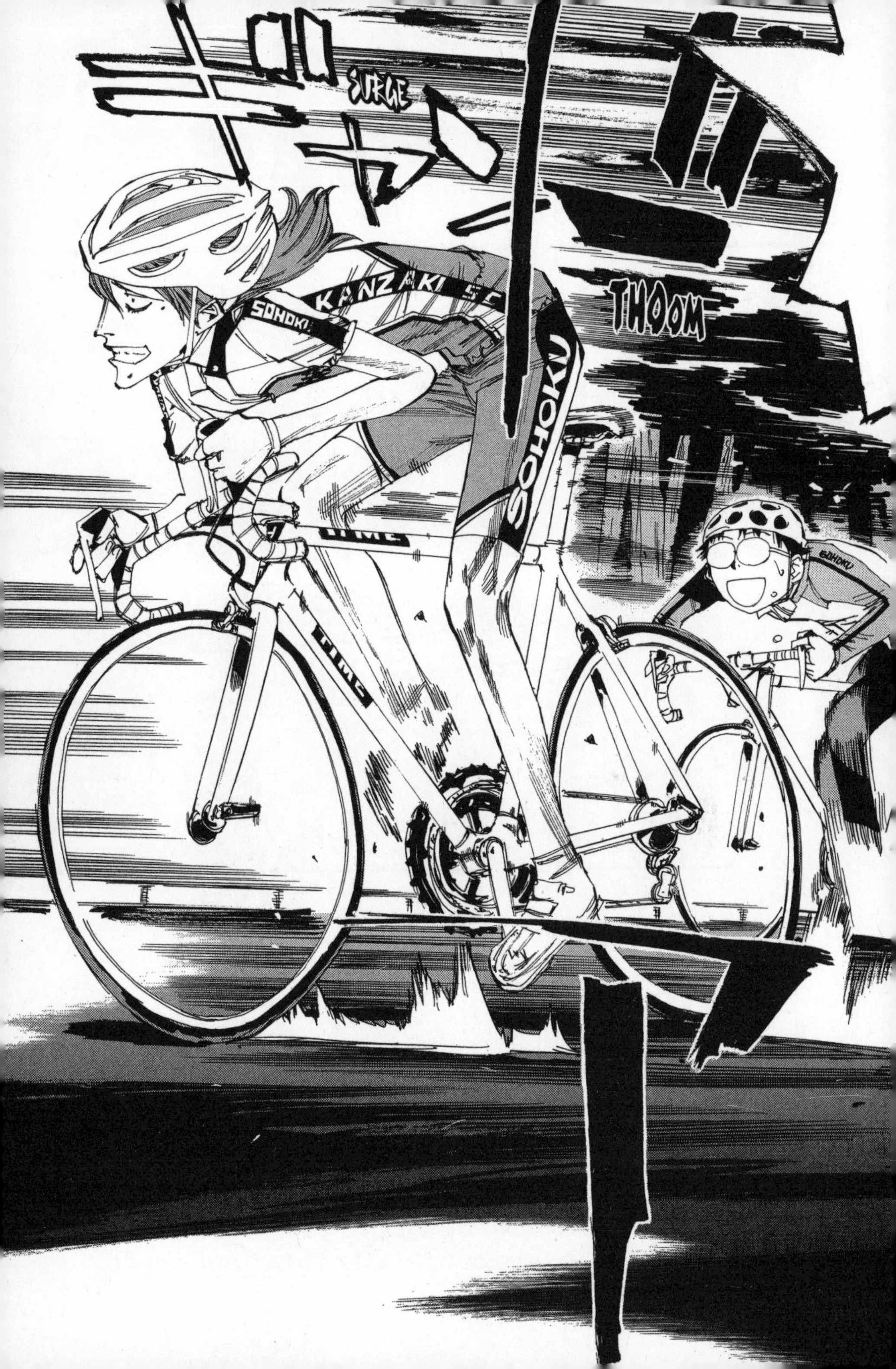
SURGE
THOOM

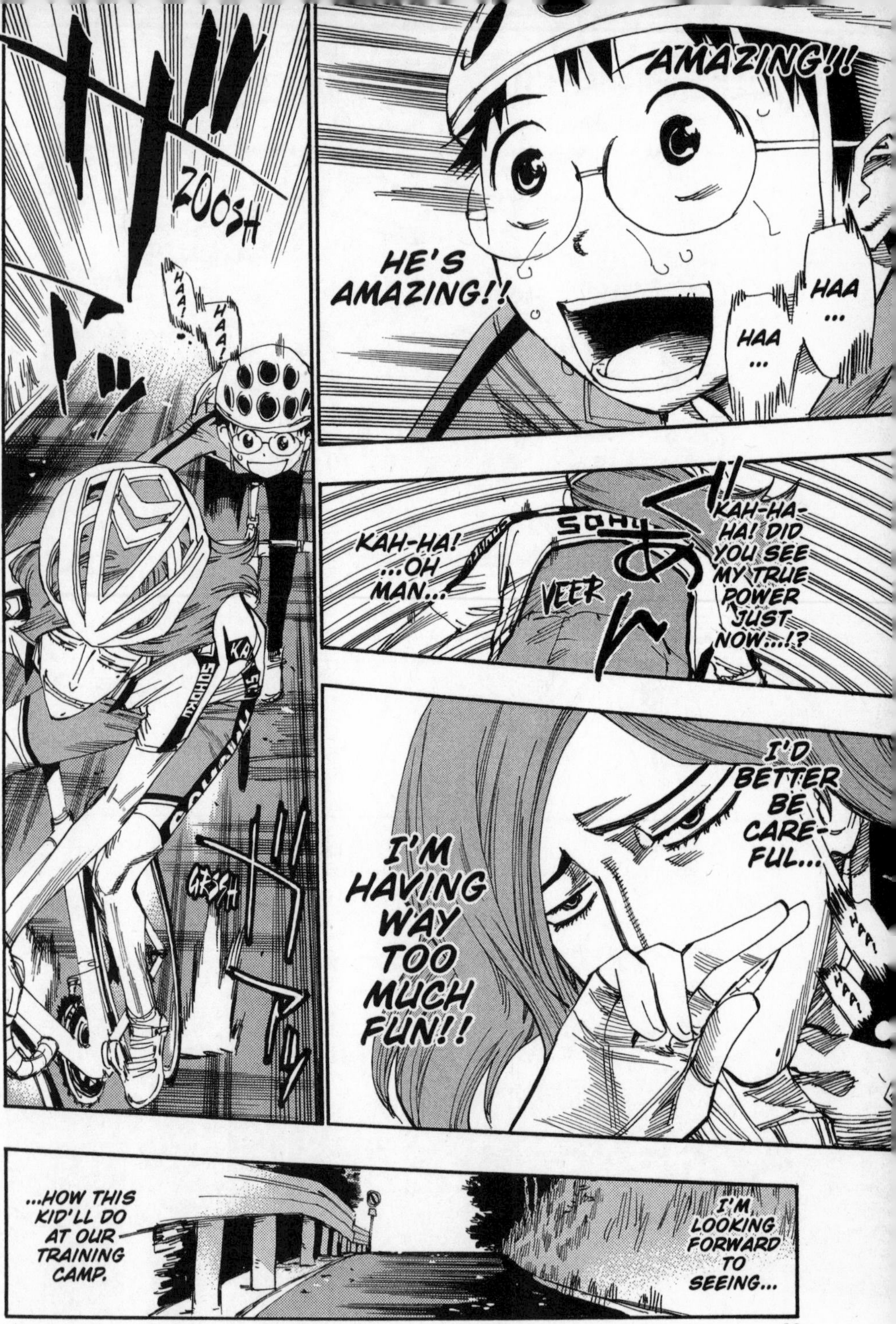
AMAZING!!
HE'S AMAZING!!
HAA ...
HAA ...
KAH-HA-HA! DID YOU SEE MY TRUE POWER JUST NOW...!?
VEER
KAH-HA! ...OH MAN...
I'D BETTER BE CARE-FUL...
HAA!
HAA!
I'M HAVING WAY TOO MUCH FUN!!
ZOOSH
HAA!
HAA!
GRSH
I'M LOOKING FORWARD TO SEEING...
...HOW THIS KID'LL DO AT OUR TRAINING CAMP.

RIDE.38
THE INTER-HIGH QUALIFIERS

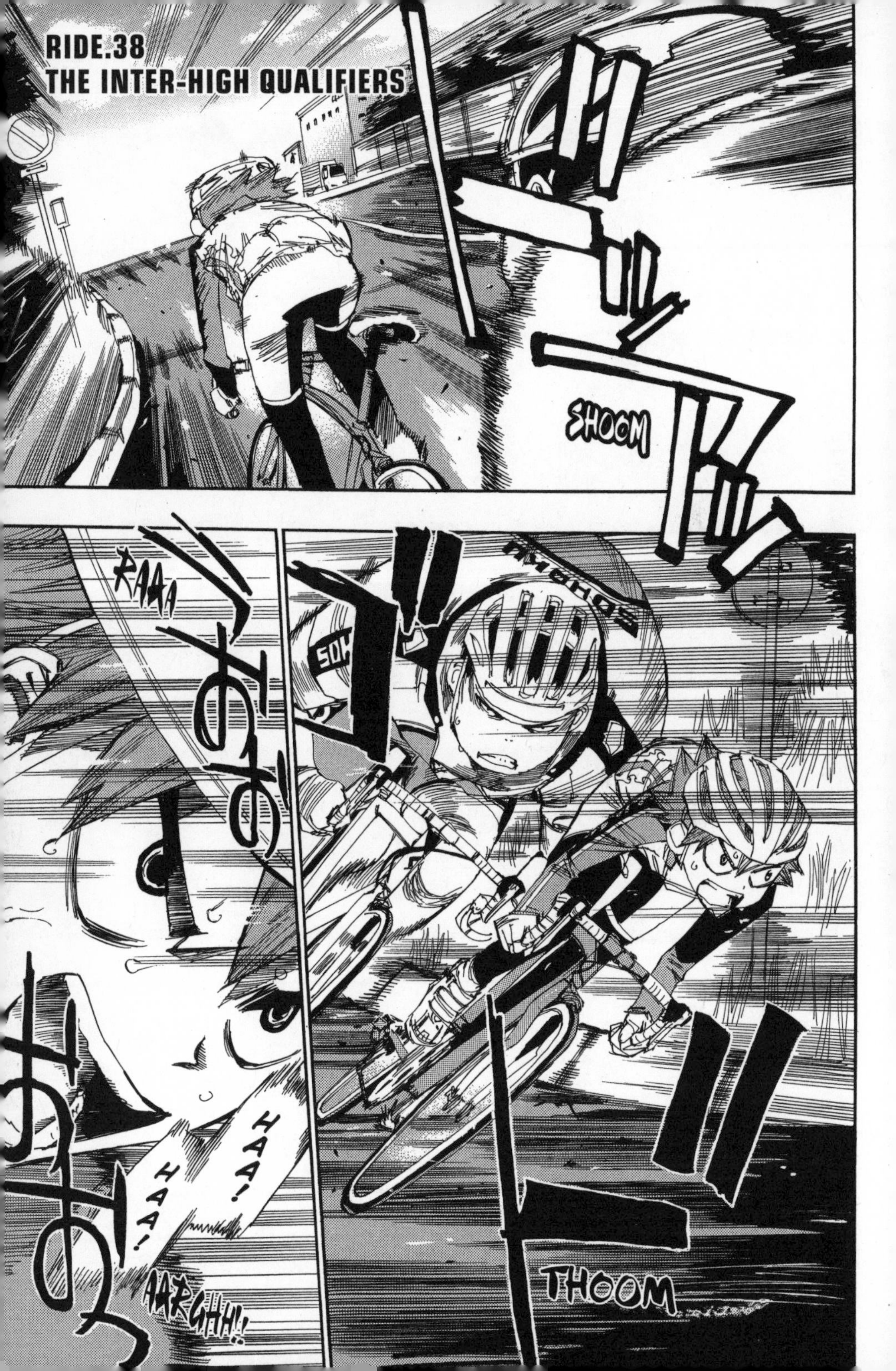
SHOOM
RAAA
HAAA!
HAAA!
AARGHH!!
THOOM

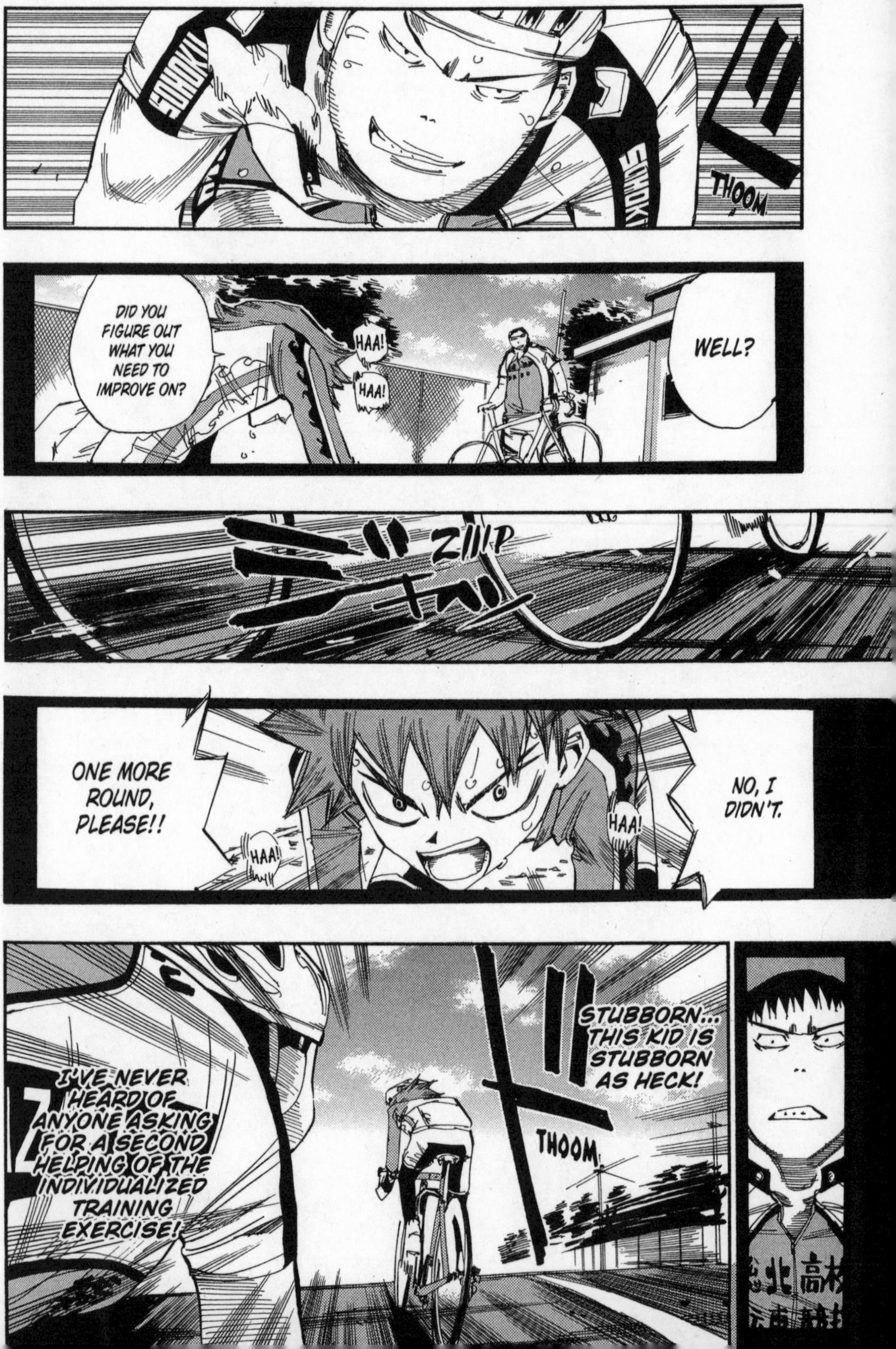
THOOM
WELL?
HAA!
HAA!
DID YOU FIGURE OUT WHAT YOU NEED TO IMPROVE ON?
ZIIIP
NO, I DIDN'T.
HAA!
HAA!
ONE MORE ROUND, PLEASE!!
STUBBORN... THIS KID IS STUBBORN AS HECK!
THOOM
I'VE NEVER HEARD OF ANYONE ASKING FOR A SECOND HELPING OF THE INDIVIDUALIZED TRAINING EXERCISE!

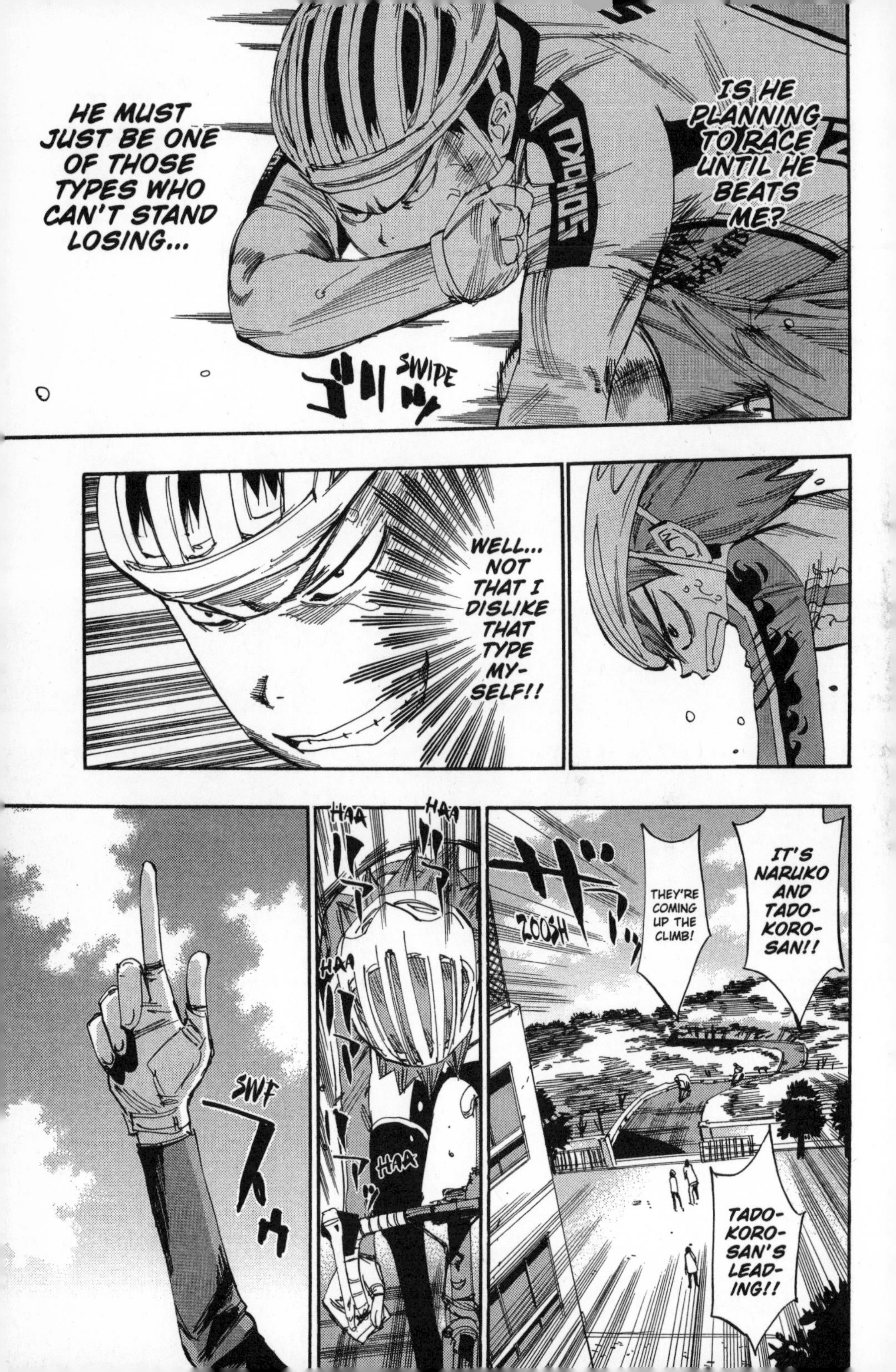
IS HE PLANNING TO RACE UNTIL HE BEATS ME?
HE MUST JUST BE ONE OF THOSE TYPES WHO CAN'T STAND LOSING...
SWIPE
WELL... NOT THAT I DISLIKE THAT TYPE MY-SELF!!
IT'S NARUKO AND TADO-KORO-SAN!!
THEY'RE COMING UP THE CLIMB!
ZOOSH
TADO-KORO-SAN'S LEAD-ING!!
HAA
HAA
HAA
HAA
SWF

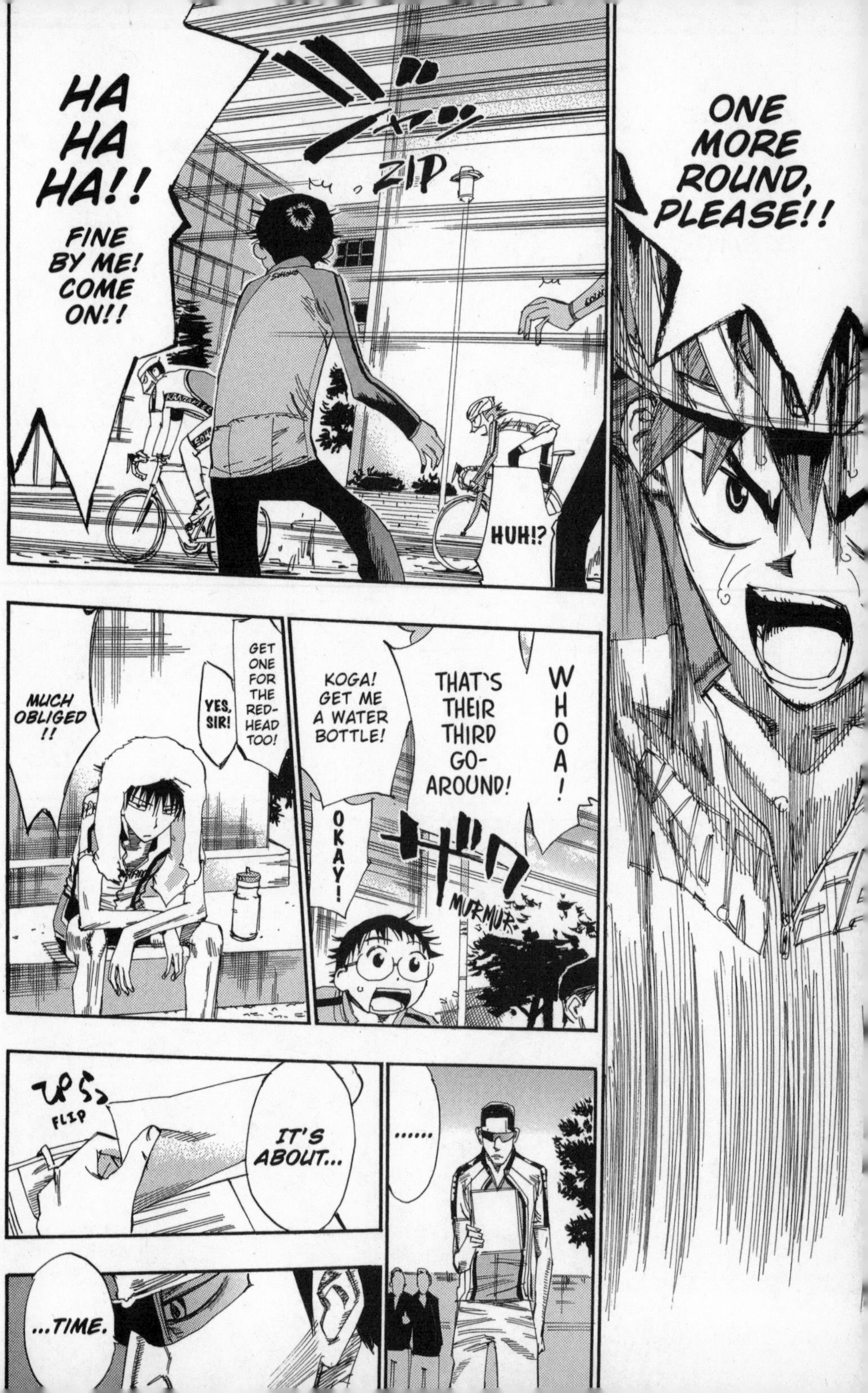
ONE MORE ROUND, PLEASE!!
ZIP
HA HA HA!!
FINE BY ME! COME ON!!
HUH!?
WHOA!
THAT'S THEIR THIRD GO-AROUND!
KOGA! GET ME A WATER BOTTLE!
OKAY!
MURMUR
GET ONE FOR THE RED-HEAD TOO!
YES, SIR!
MUCH OBLIGED!!
......
IT'S ABOUT...
FLIP
...TIME.

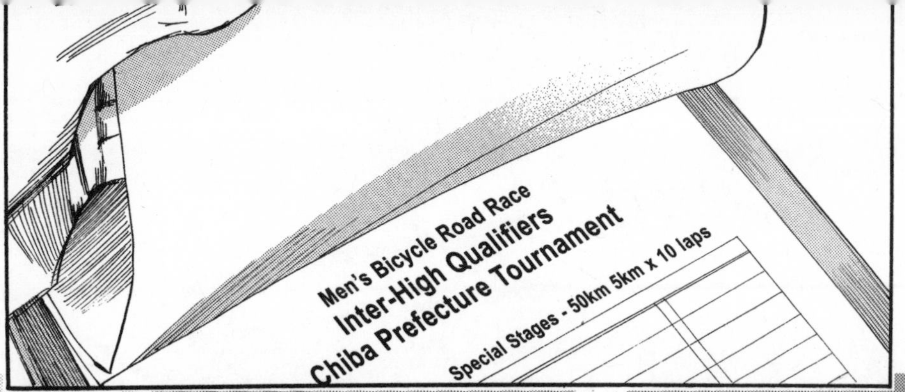
Men's Bicycle Road Race
Inter-High Qualifiers
Chiba Prefecture Tournament
Special Stages - 50km 5km x 10 laps

RIDE.38
THE INTER-HIGH QUALIFIERS

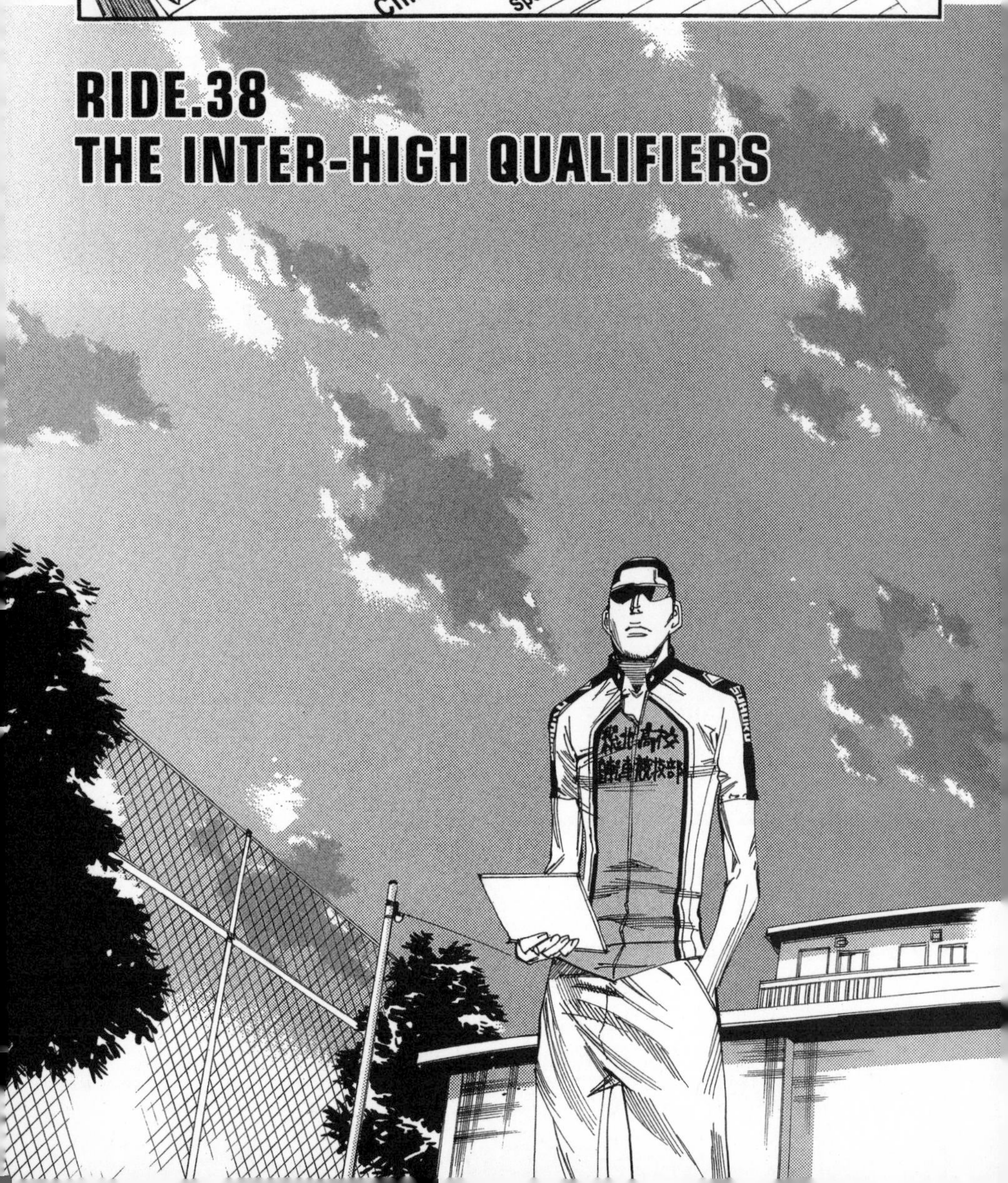

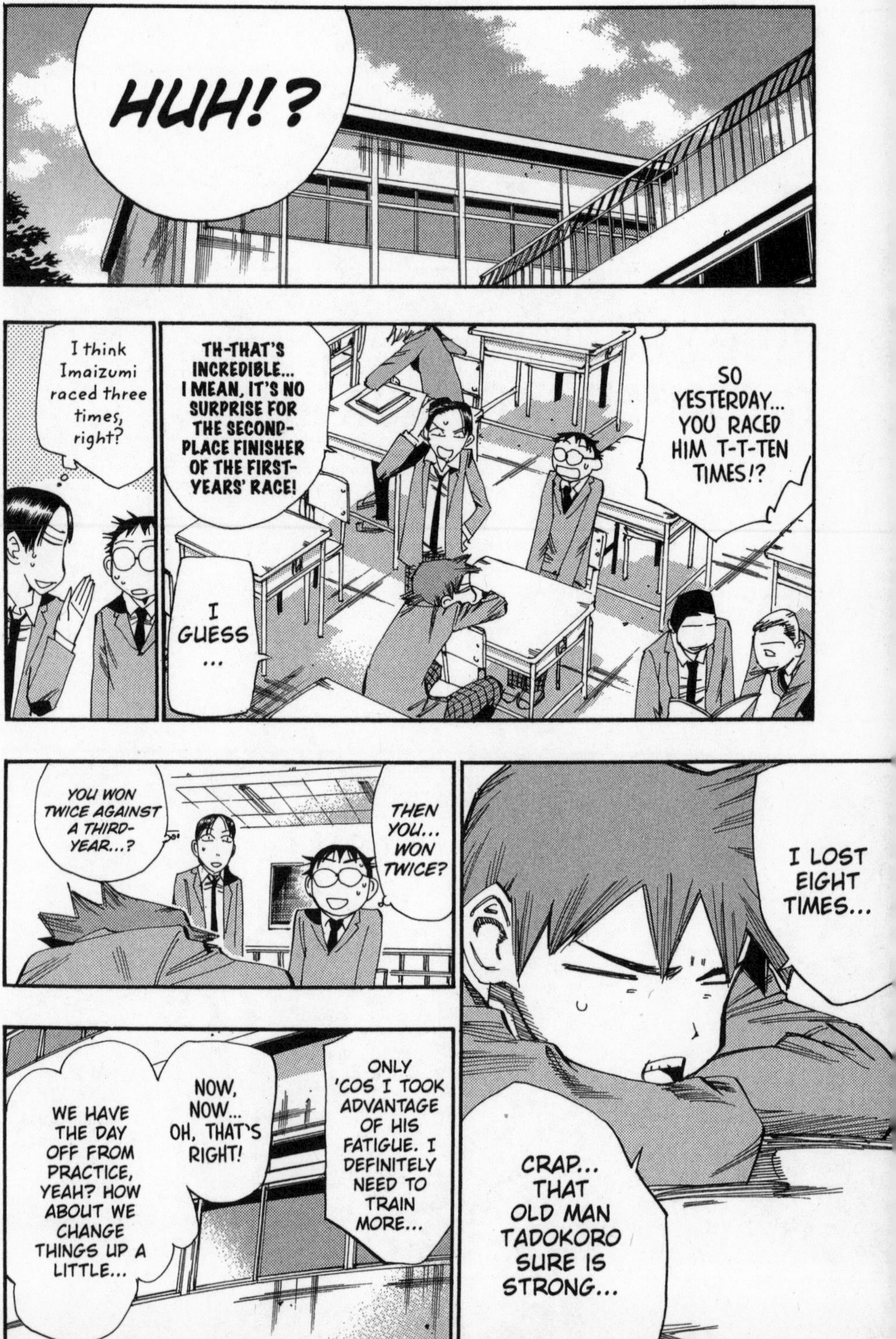
HUH!?
SO YESTERDAY... YOU RACED HIM T-T-TEN TIMES!?
TH-THAT'S INCREDIBLE... I MEAN, IT'S NO SURPRISE FOR THE SECOND-PLACE FINISHER OF THE FIRST-YEARS' RACE!
I GUESS ...
I think Imaizumi raced three times, right?
I LOST EIGHT TIMES...
CRAP... THAT OLD MAN TADOKORO SURE IS STRONG...
THEN YOU... WON TWICE?
YOU WON TWICE AGAINST A THIRD-YEAR...?
ONLY 'COS I TOOK ADVANTAGE OF HIS FATIGUE. I DEFINITELY NEED TO TRAIN MORE...
NOW, NOW... OH, THAT'S RIGHT!
WE HAVE THE DAY OFF FROM PRACTICE, YEAH? HOW ABOUT WE CHANGE THINGS UP A LITTLE...

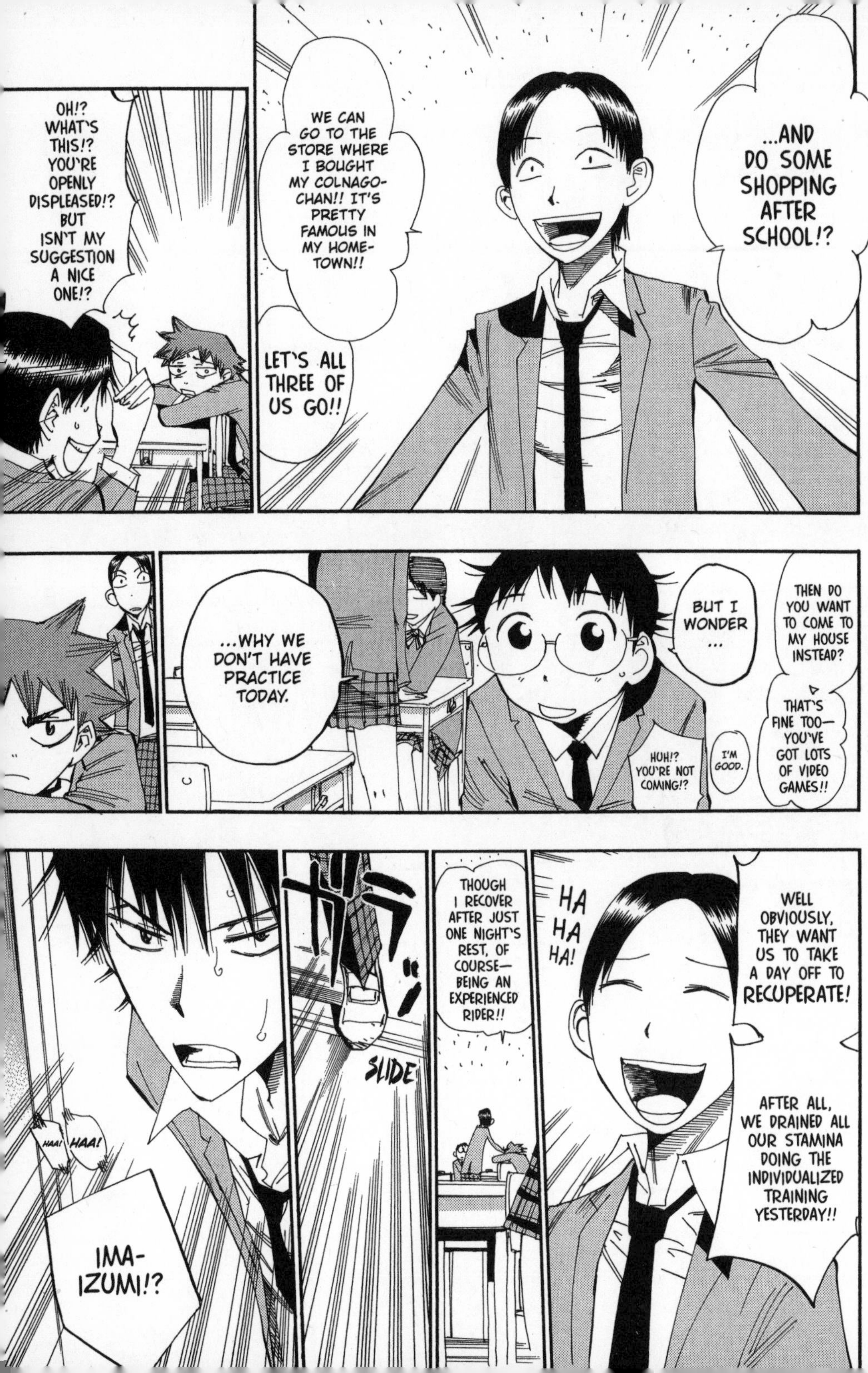

...AND DO SOME SHOPPING AFTER SCHOOL!?
WE CAN GO TO THE STORE WHERE I BOUGHT MY COLNAGO-CHAN!! IT'S PRETTY FAMOUS IN MY HOME-TOWN!!
LET'S ALL THREE OF US GO!!
OH!? WHAT'S THIS!? YOU'RE OPENLY DISPLEASED!? BUT ISN'T MY SUGGESTION A NICE ONE!?
THEN DO YOU WANT TO COME TO MY HOUSE INSTEAD?
THAT'S FINE TOO—YOU'VE GOT LOTS OF VIDEO GAMES!!
I'M GOOD.
HUH!? YOU'RE NOT COMING!?
BUT I WONDER ...
...WHY WE DON'T HAVE PRACTICE TODAY.
WELL OBVIOUSLY, THEY WANT US TO TAKE A DAY OFF TO RECUPERATE!
HA HA HA!
AFTER ALL, WE DRAINED ALL OUR STAMINA DOING THE INDIVIDUALIZED TRAINING YESTERDAY!!
THOUGH I RECOVER AFTER JUST ONE NIGHT'S REST, OF COURSE—BEING AN EXPERIENCED RIDER!!
SLIDE
HAA! HAA!
IMA-IZUMI!?

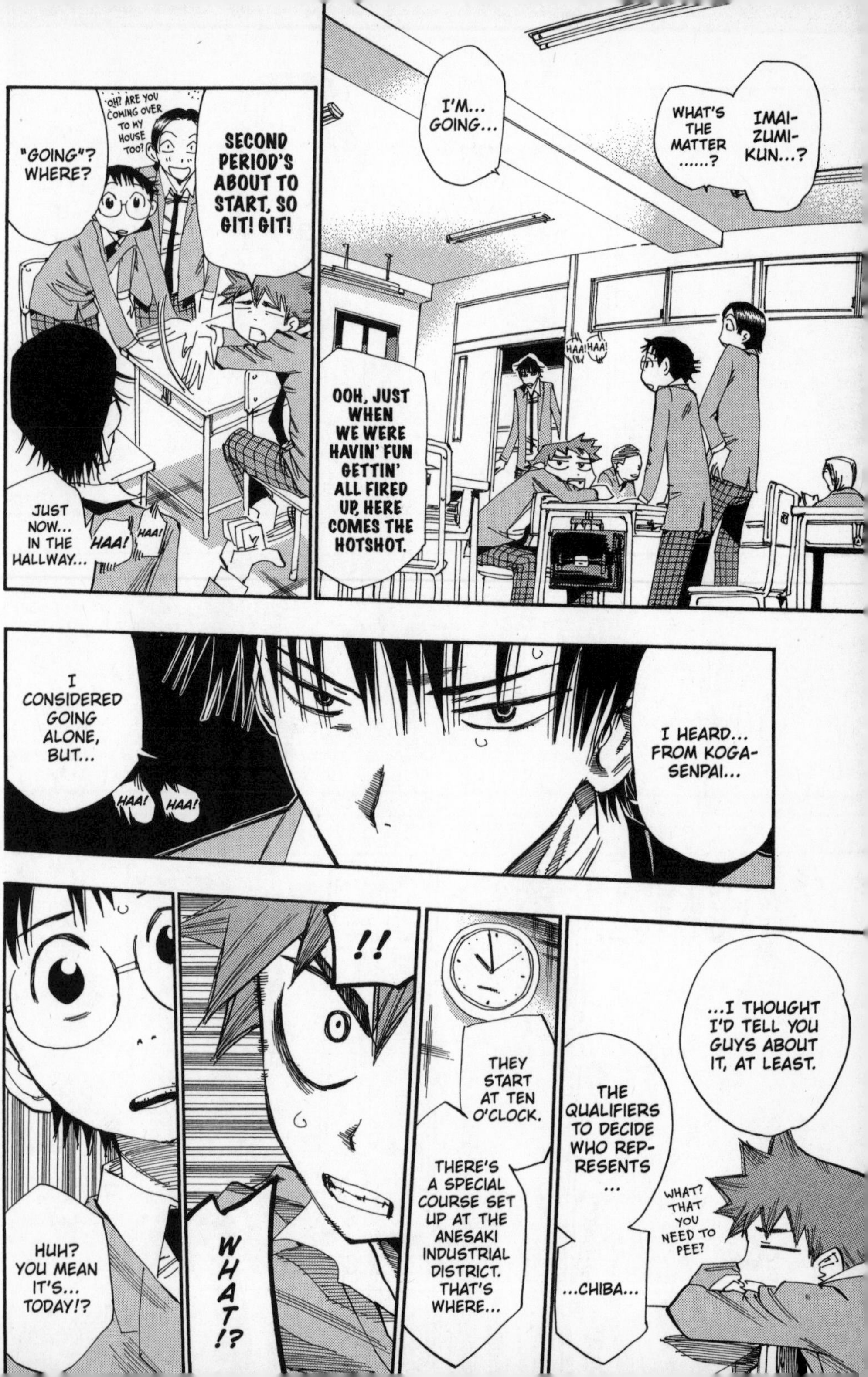
IMAI-ZUMI-KUN...?
WHAT'S THE MATTER ......?
I'M... GOING...
HAA! HAA!
OOH, JUST WHEN WE WERE HAVIN' FUN GETTIN' ALL FIRED UP, HERE COMES THE HOTSHOT.
SECOND PERIOD'S ABOUT TO START, SO GIT! GIT!
OH? ARE YOU COMING OVER TO MY HOUSE TOO?
"GOING"? WHERE?
JUST NOW... IN THE HALLWAY...
HAA! HAA!
I HEARD... FROM KOGA-SENPAI...
I CONSIDERED GOING ALONE, BUT...
HAA! HAA!
...I THOUGHT I'D TELL YOU GUYS ABOUT IT, AT LEAST.
WHAT? THAT YOU NEED TO PEE?
THE QUALIFIERS TO DECIDE WHO REPRESENTS ...
...CHIBA...
THEY START AT TEN O'CLOCK.
THERE'S A SPECIAL COURSE SET UP AT THE ANESAKI INDUSTRIAL DISTRICT. THAT'S WHERE...
!!
WHAT!?
HUH? YOU MEAN IT'S... TODAY!?

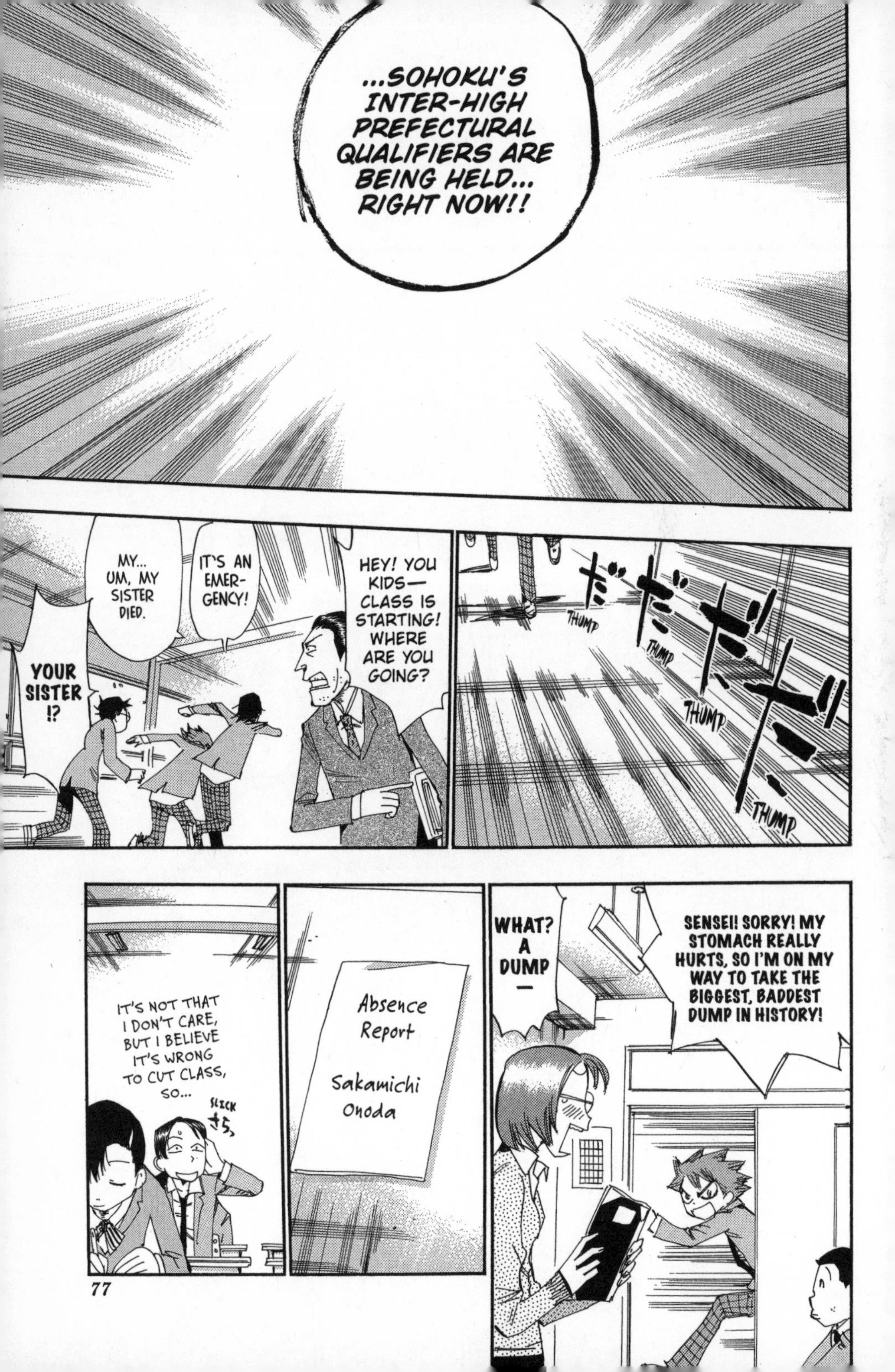
...SOHOKU'S INTER-HIGH PREFECTURAL QUALIFIERS ARE BEING HELD... RIGHT NOW!!
THUMP
THUMP
THUMP
THUMP
HEY! YOU KIDS—CLASS IS STARTING! WHERE ARE YOU GOING?
IT'S AN EMERGENCY!
MY... UM, MY SISTER DIED.
YOUR SISTER!?
SENSEI! SORRY! MY STOMACH REALLY HURTS, SO I'M ON MY WAY TO TAKE THE BIGGEST, BADDEST DUMP IN HISTORY!
WHAT? A DUMP—
Absence Report
Sakamichi Onoda
IT'S NOT THAT I DON'T CARE, BUT I BELIEVE IT'S WRONG TO CUT CLASS, SO...
SLICK

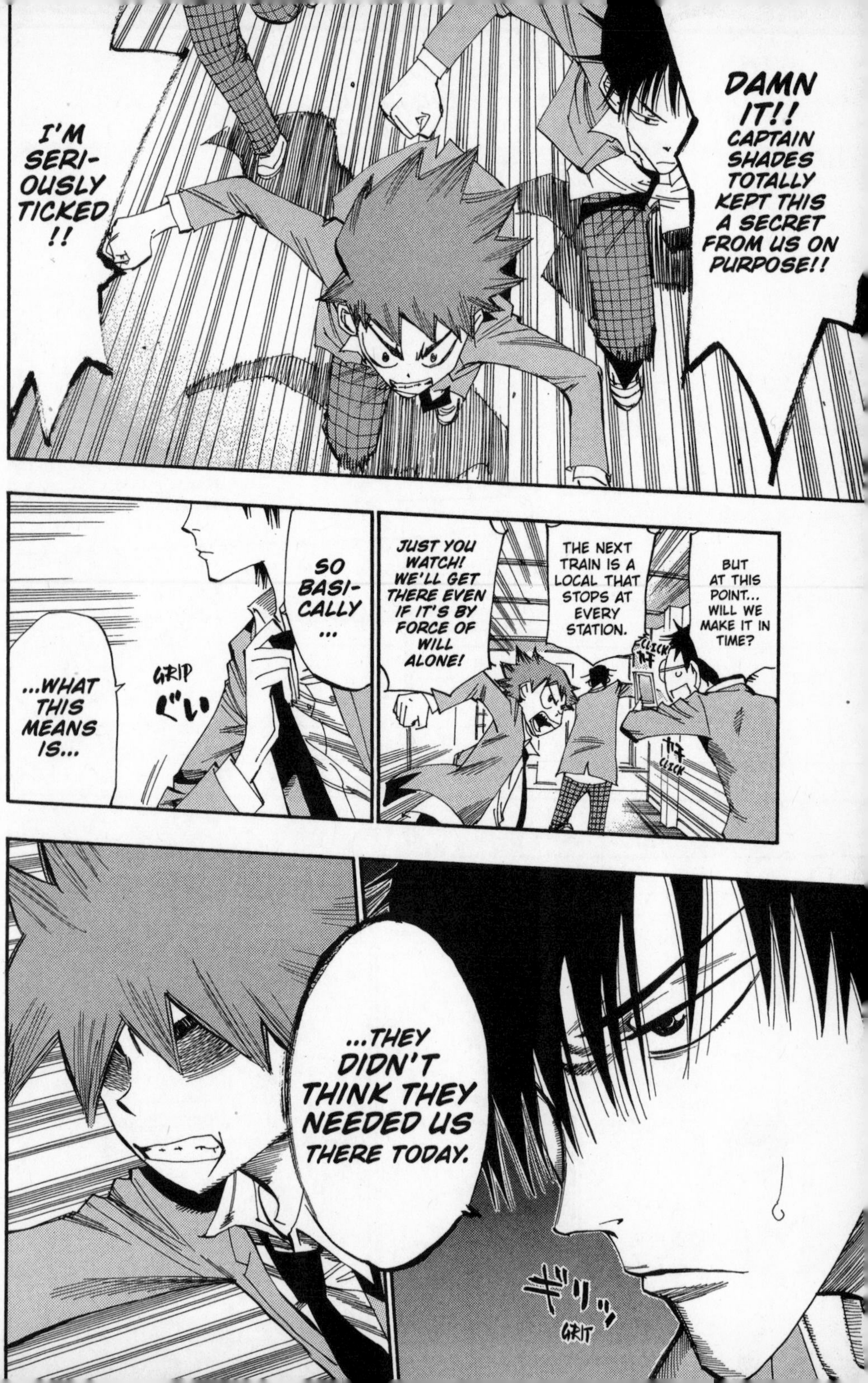
DAMN IT!! CAPTAIN SHADES TOTALLY KEPT THIS A SECRET FROM US ON PURPOSE!!
I'M SERI-OUSLY TICKED!!
BUT AT THIS POINT... WILL WE MAKE IT IN TIME?
THE NEXT TRAIN IS A LOCAL THAT STOPS AT EVERY STATION.
CLICK カチ
JUST YOU WATCH! WE'LL GET THERE EVEN IF IT'S BY FORCE OF WILL ALONE!
カチ CLICK
SO BASI-CALLY...
GRIP ぐい
...WHAT THIS MEANS IS...
...THEY DIDN'T THINK THEY NEEDED US THERE TODAY.
ギリッ GRIT

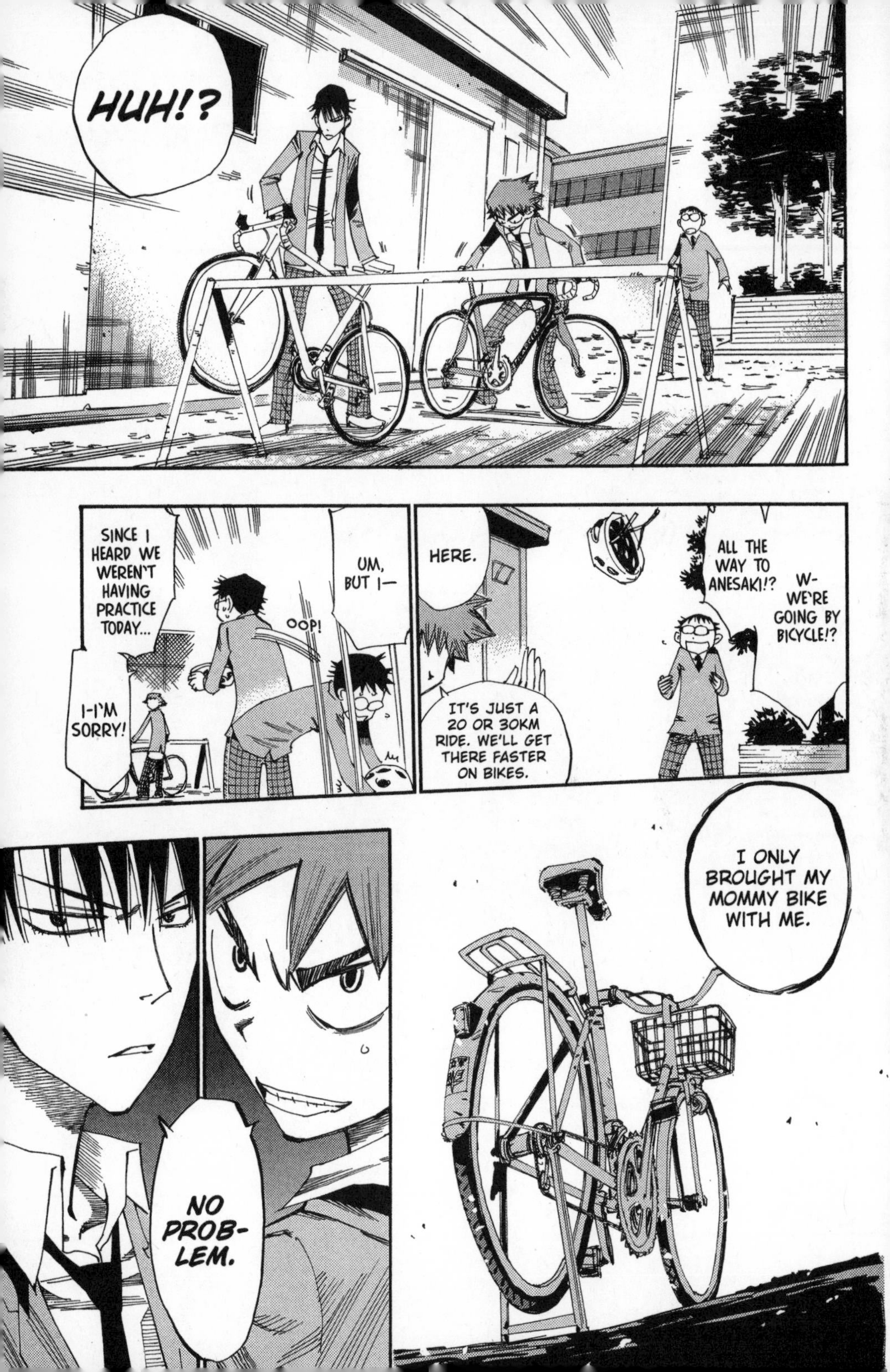
HUH!?
ALL THE WAY TO ANESAKI!?
W- WE'RE GOING BY BICYCLE!?
HERE.
IT'S JUST A 20 OR 30KM RIDE. WE'LL GET THERE FASTER ON BIKES.
UM, BUT I—
OOP!
SINCE I HEARD WE WEREN'T HAVING PRACTICE TODAY...
I-I'M SORRY!
I ONLY BROUGHT MY MOMMY BIKE WITH ME.
NO PROB-LEM.

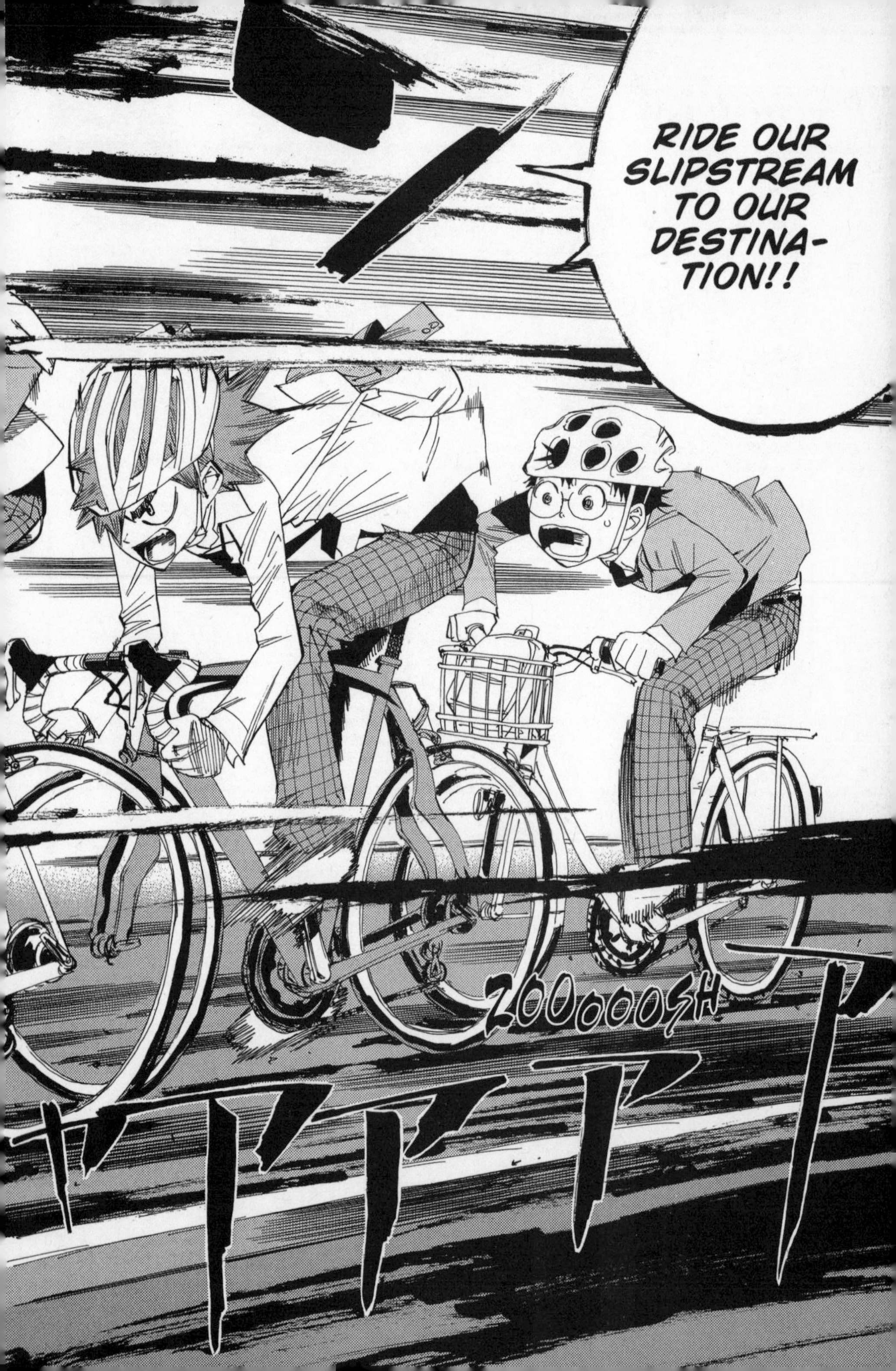
RIDE OUR SLIPSTREAM TO OUR DESTINATION!!
ZOOOOOOSH

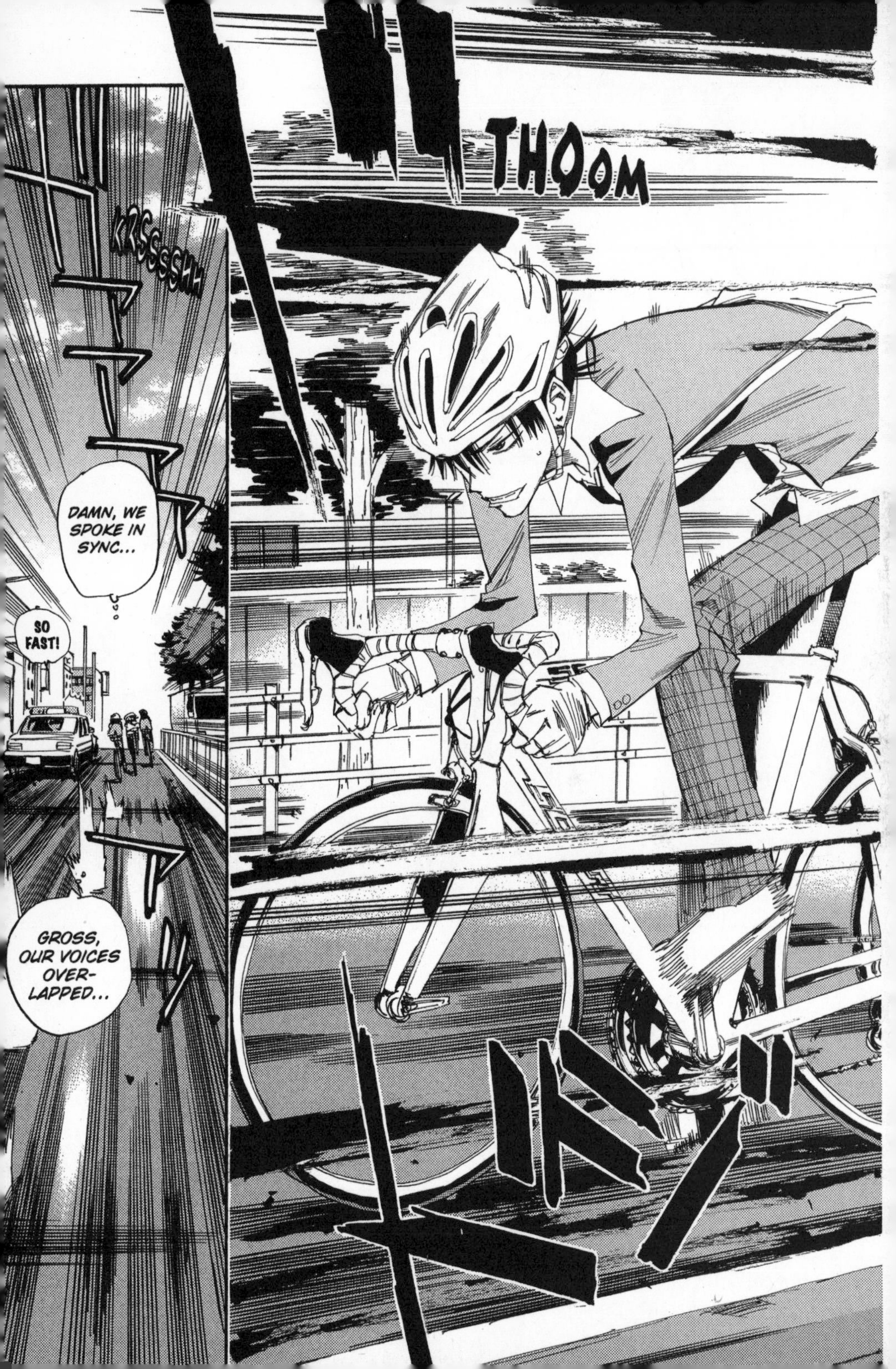
THOOM
KRSSSSHH
DAMN, WE SPOKE IN SYNC...
SO FAST!
GROSS, OUR VOICES OVER-LAPPED...

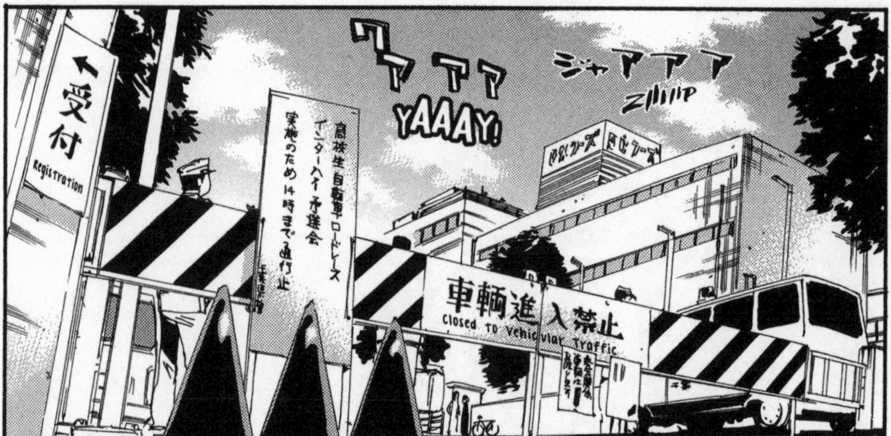
ワァアア
YAAAY!
ジャアアア
ZHIIIP
受付
Registration
高校生自転車ロードレース インターハイ予選会 実施のため14時まで通行止
車輌進入禁止
Closed to Vehicular Traffic
SIGN: ROAD CLOSED UNTIL 2 P.M. FOR THE HIGH SCHOOL BICYCLE ROAD RACE INTER-HIGH QUALIFIERS

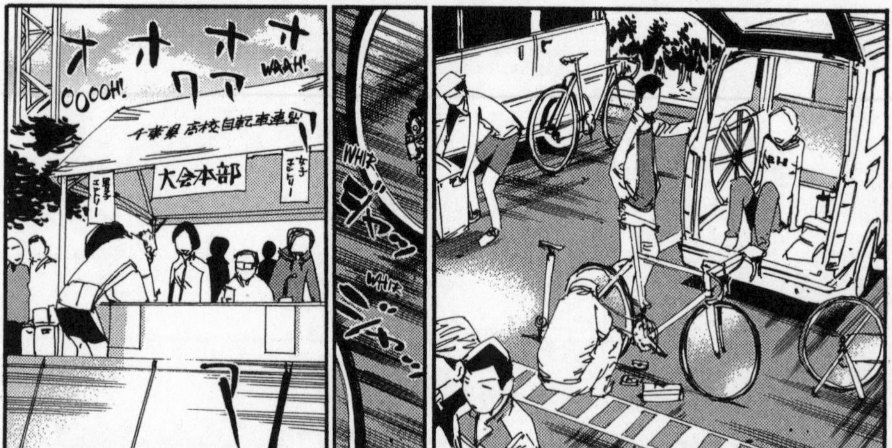
WHIR
ジャ~
WHIR
ジ~
オオオオ
OOOOH!
ワァ
WAAH!
千葉県 高校自転車連盟
大会本部
男子エントリー
女子エントリー
SIGNS: TOURNAMENT HQ, (LEFT) MALE ENTRANTS, (RIGHT) FEMALE ENTRANTS

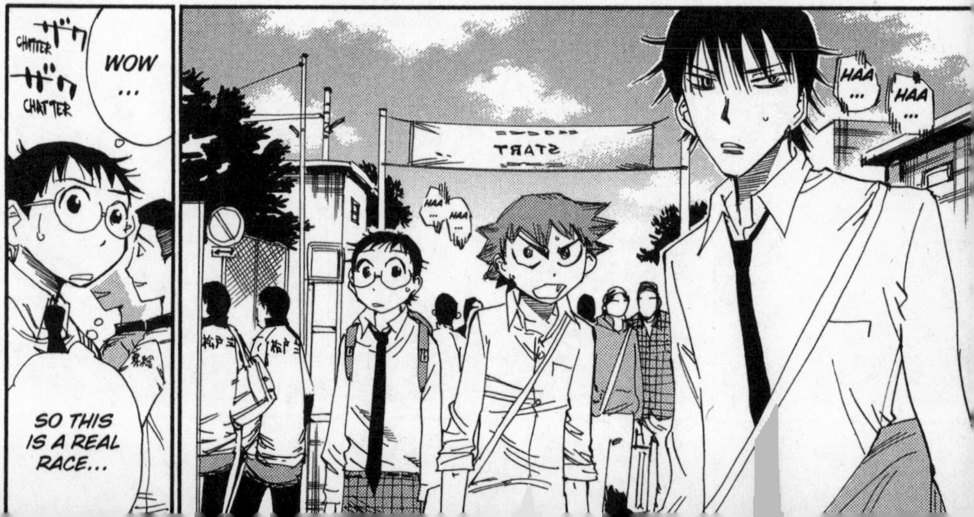
HAA...
HAA...
START
HAA...
HAA...
ザワ
CHATTER
ザワ
CHATTER
WOW...
SO THIS IS A REAL RACE...

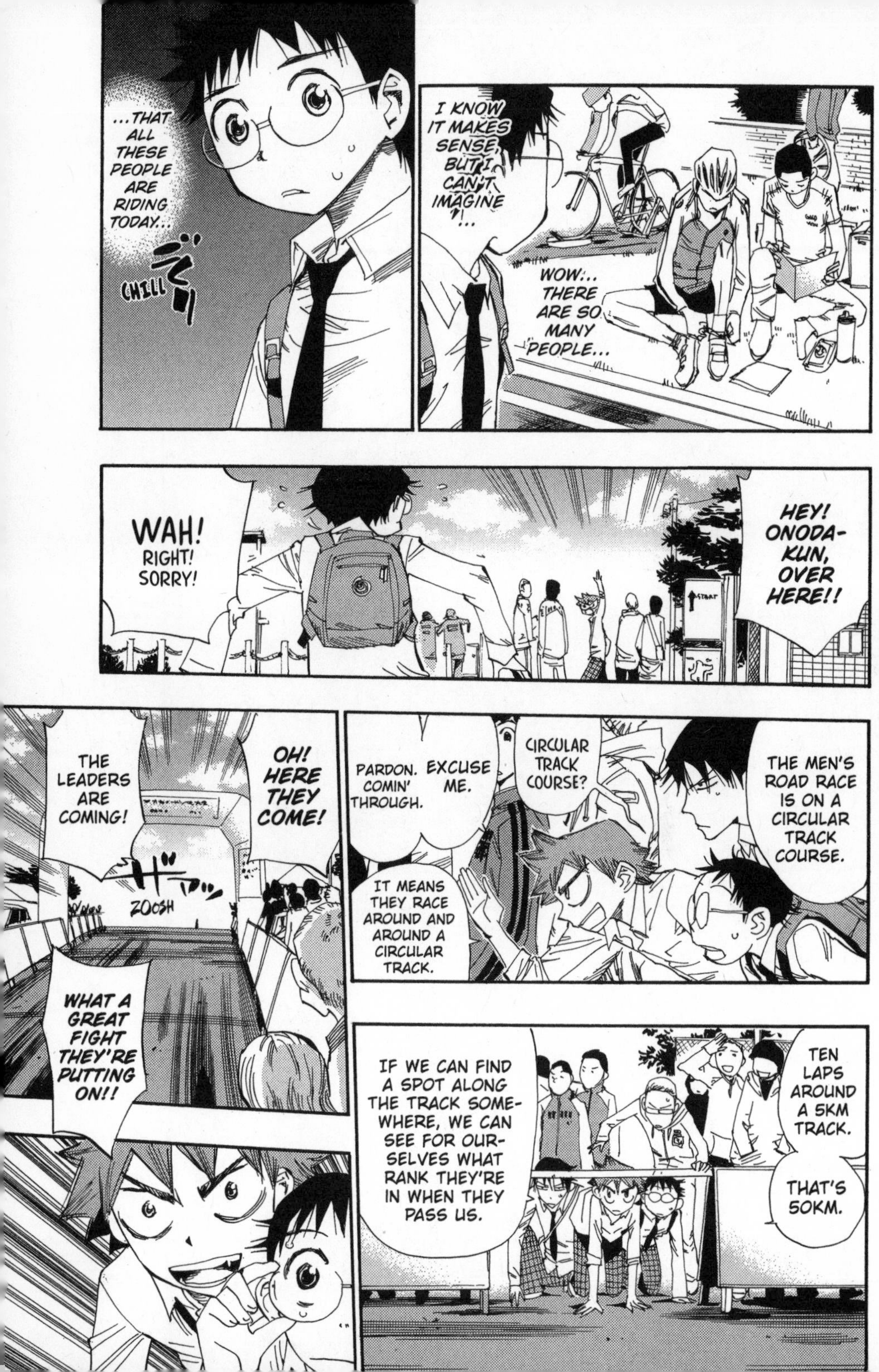
I KNOW IT MAKES SENSE, BUT I CAN'T IMAGINE...
WOW... THERE ARE SO MANY PEOPLE...
...THAT ALL THESE PEOPLE ARE RIDING TODAY...
CHILL
HEY! ONODA-KUN, OVER HERE!!
WAH! RIGHT! SORRY!
THE MEN'S ROAD RACE IS ON A CIRCULAR TRACK COURSE.
CIRCULAR TRACK COURSE?
EXCUSE ME.
PARDON. COMIN' THROUGH.
IT MEANS THEY RACE AROUND AND AROUND A CIRCULAR TRACK.
TEN LAPS AROUND A 5KM TRACK.
THAT'S 50KM.
IF WE CAN FIND A SPOT ALONG THE TRACK SOMEWHERE, WE CAN SEE FOR OURSELVES WHAT RANK THEY'RE IN WHEN THEY PASS US.
OH! HERE THEY COME!
THE LEADERS ARE COMING!
ZOOSH
WHAT A GREAT FIGHT THEY'RE PUTTING ON!!

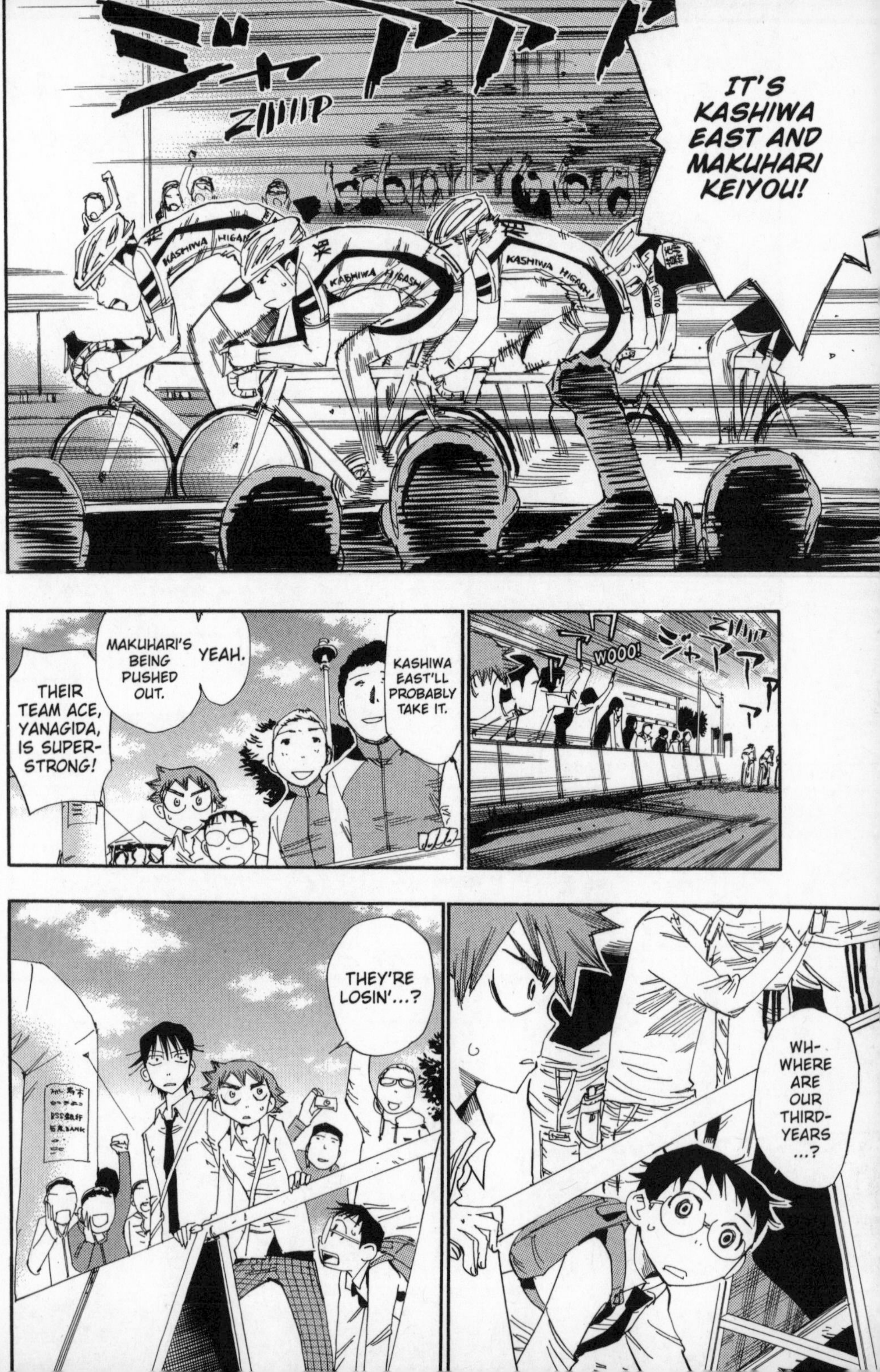
ジャアアー
ZIIIIP
IT'S KASHIWA EAST AND MAKUHARI KEIYOU!
ジャアアア
ZIIIIP
WOOO!
KASHIWA EAST'LL PROBABLY TAKE IT.
YEAH.
MAKUHARI'S BEING PUSHED OUT.
THEIR TEAM ACE, YANAGIDA, IS SUPER-STRONG!
WH-WHERE ARE OUR THIRD-YEARS ...?
THEY'RE LOSIN'...?

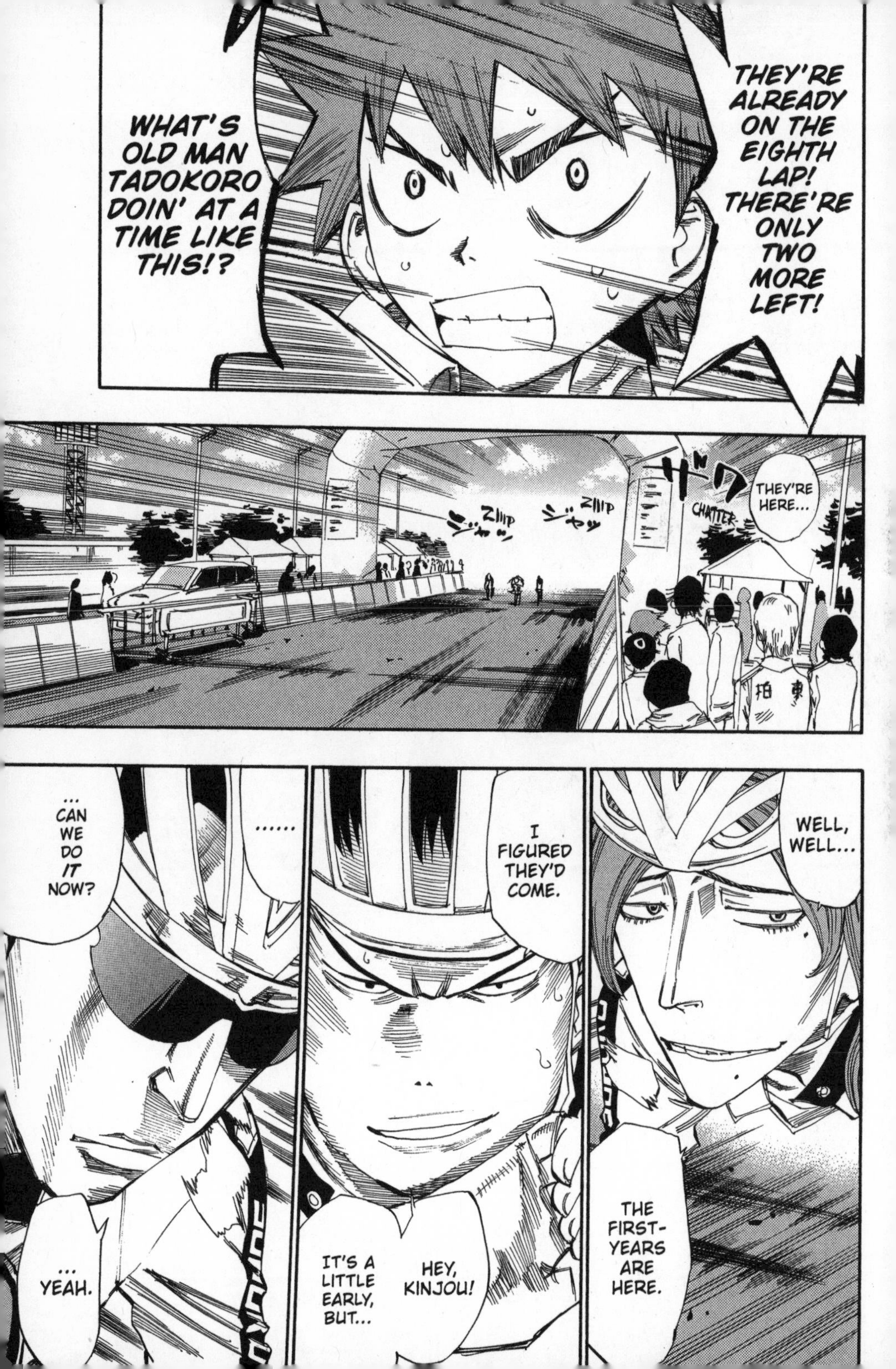
THEY'RE ALREADY ON THE EIGHTH LAP! THERE'RE ONLY TWO MORE LEFT!
WHAT'S OLD MAN TADOKORO DOIN' AT A TIME LIKE THIS!?
THEY'RE HERE...
CHATTER-
ZIIIP
ZIIIP
WELL, WELL...
THE FIRST-YEARS ARE HERE.
I FIGURED THEY'D COME.
......
HEY, KINJOU!
IT'S A LITTLE EARLY, BUT...
...CAN WE DO *IT* NOW?
...YEAH.

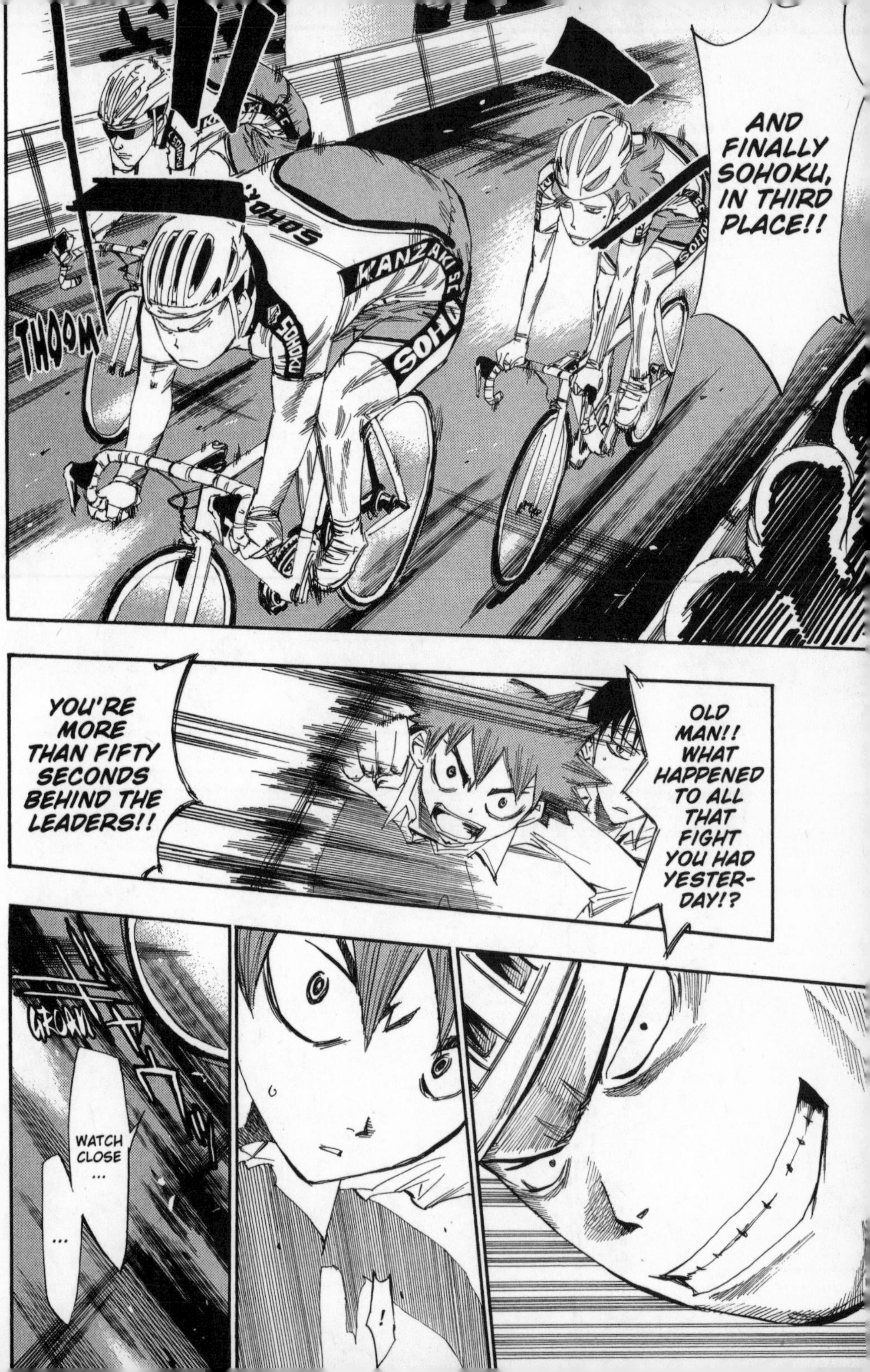
AND FINALLY SOHOKU, IN THIRD PLACE!!
THOOM
OLD MAN!! WHAT HAPPENED TO ALL THAT FIGHT YOU HAD YESTER-DAY!?
YOU'RE MORE THAN FIFTY SECONDS BEHIND THE LEADERS!!
!
WATCH CLOSE ...
...
GROAN

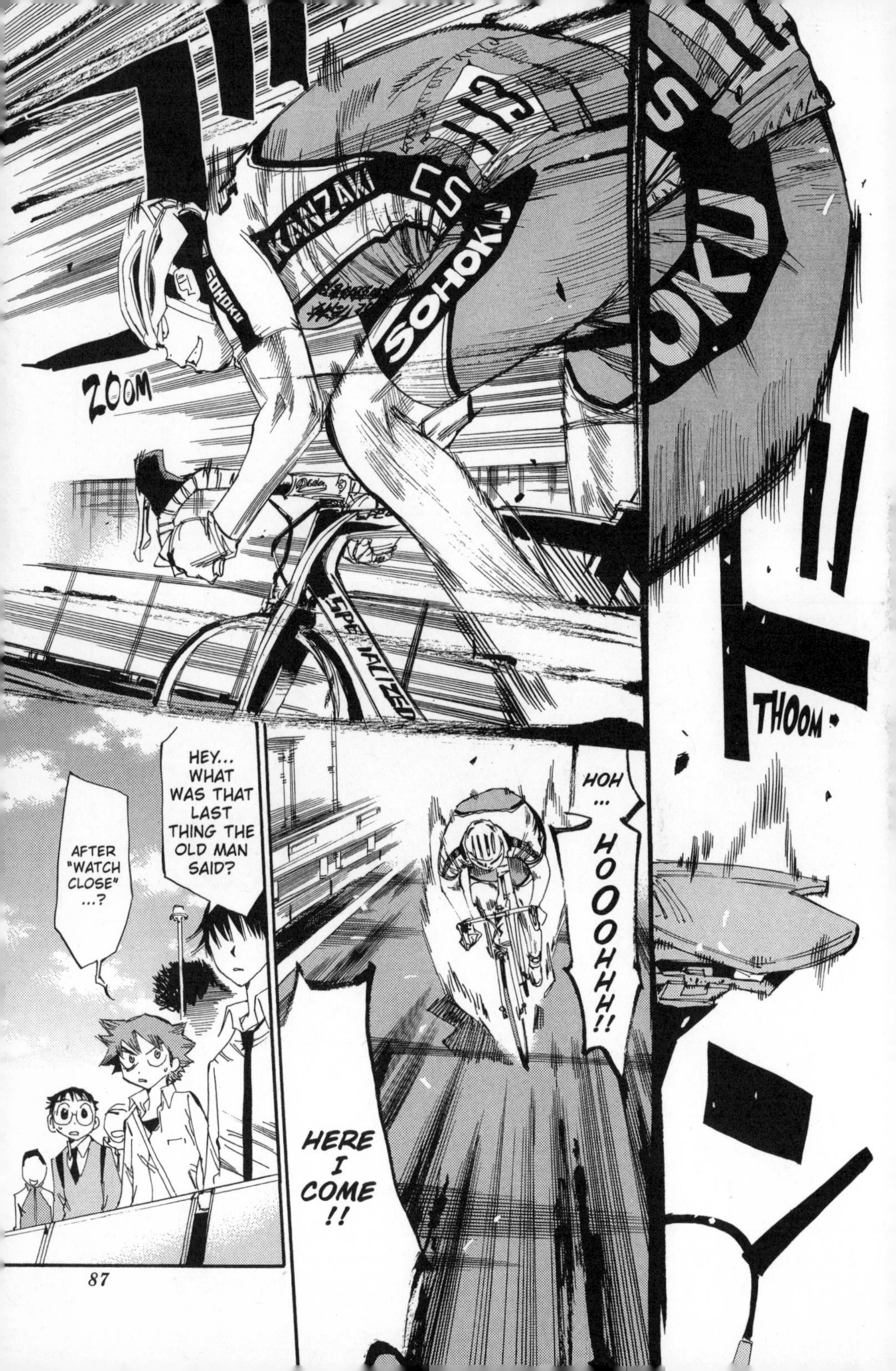
THOOM
ZOOM
HOH...
HOOOOHHHH!!
HERE I COME!!
HEY... WHAT WAS THAT LAST THING THE OLD MAN SAID?
AFTER "WATCH CLOSE"...?

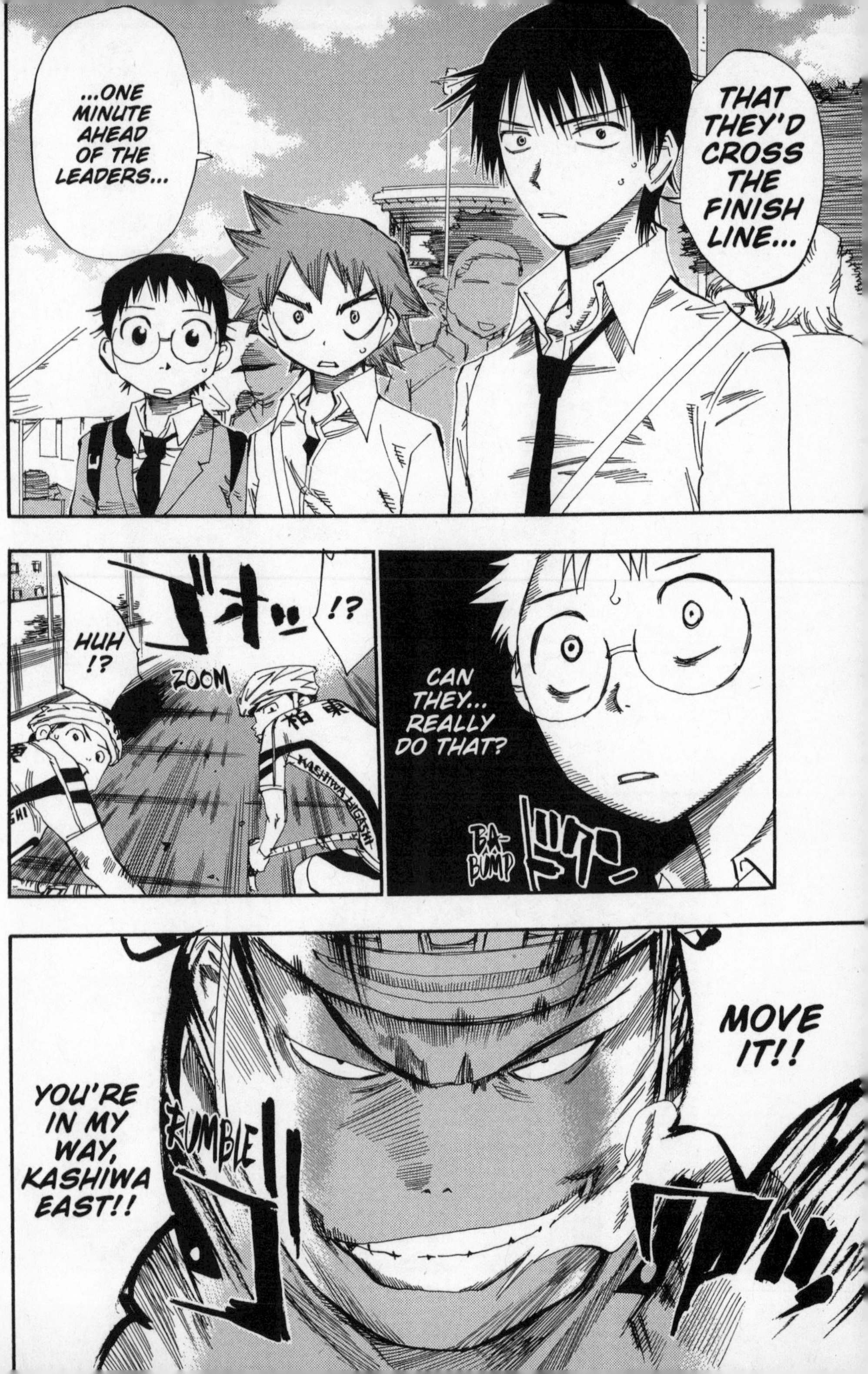
THAT THEY'D CROSS THE FINISH LINE...
...ONE MINUTE AHEAD OF THE LEADERS...
CAN THEY... REALLY DO THAT?
BA-BUMP
!?
HUH !?
ZOOM
KASHIWA HIGASHI
MOVE IT!!
RUMBLE
YOU'RE IN MY WAY, KASHIWA EAST!!

RIDE.39 SOHOKU

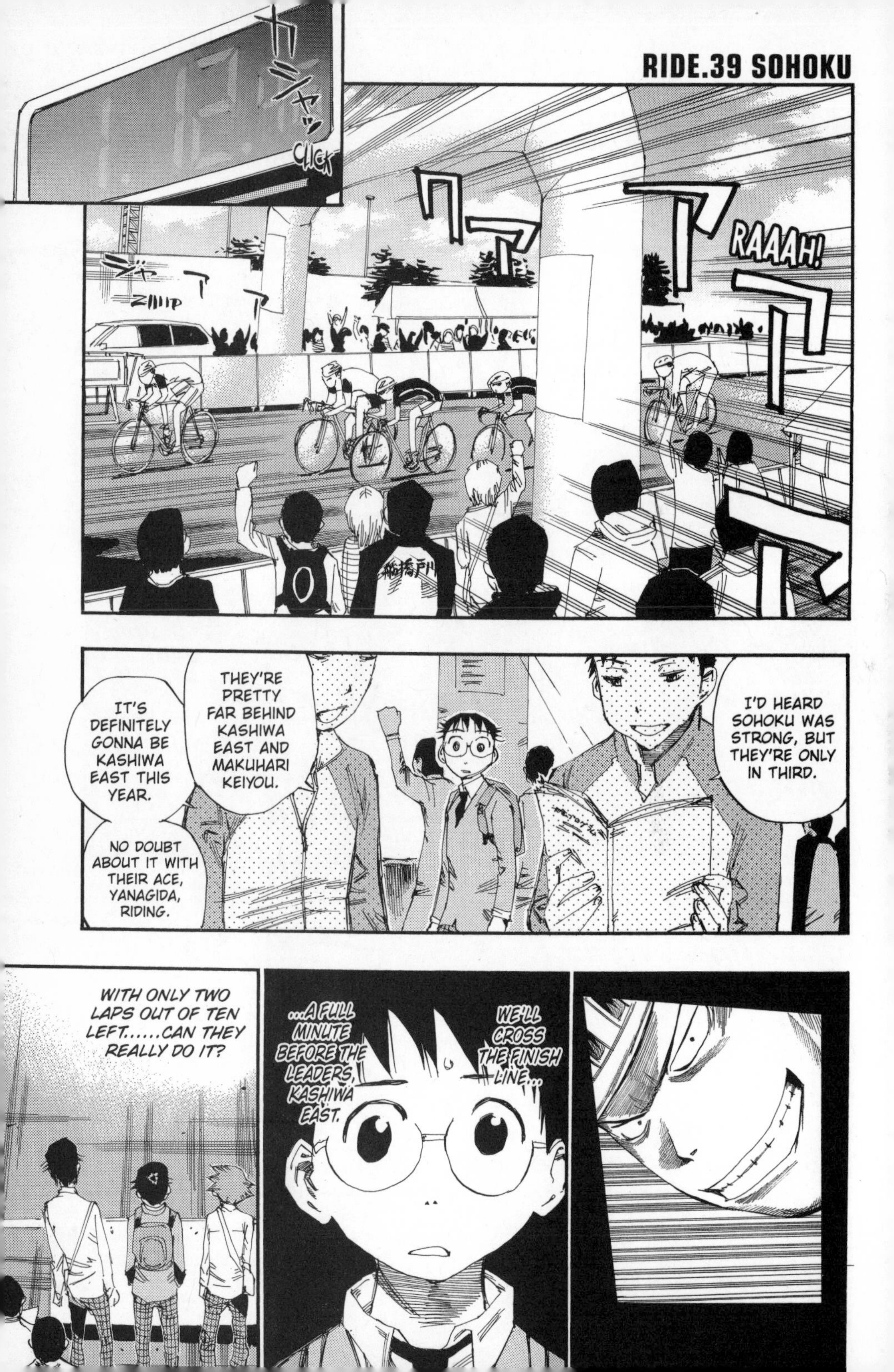
RAAAH!
ZIIIIP
カシャッ
CLICK
I'D HEARD SOHOKU WAS STRONG, BUT THEY'RE ONLY IN THIRD.
THEY'RE PRETTY FAR BEHIND KASHIWA EAST AND MAKUHARI KEIYOU.
IT'S DEFINITELY GONNA BE KASHIWA EAST THIS YEAR.
NO DOUBT ABOUT IT WITH THEIR ACE, YANAGIDA, RIDING.
WE'LL CROSS THE FINISH LINE...
...A FULL MINUTE BEFORE THE LEADERS, KASHIWA EAST.
WITH ONLY TWO LAPS OUT OF TEN LEFT......CAN THEY REALLY DO IT?

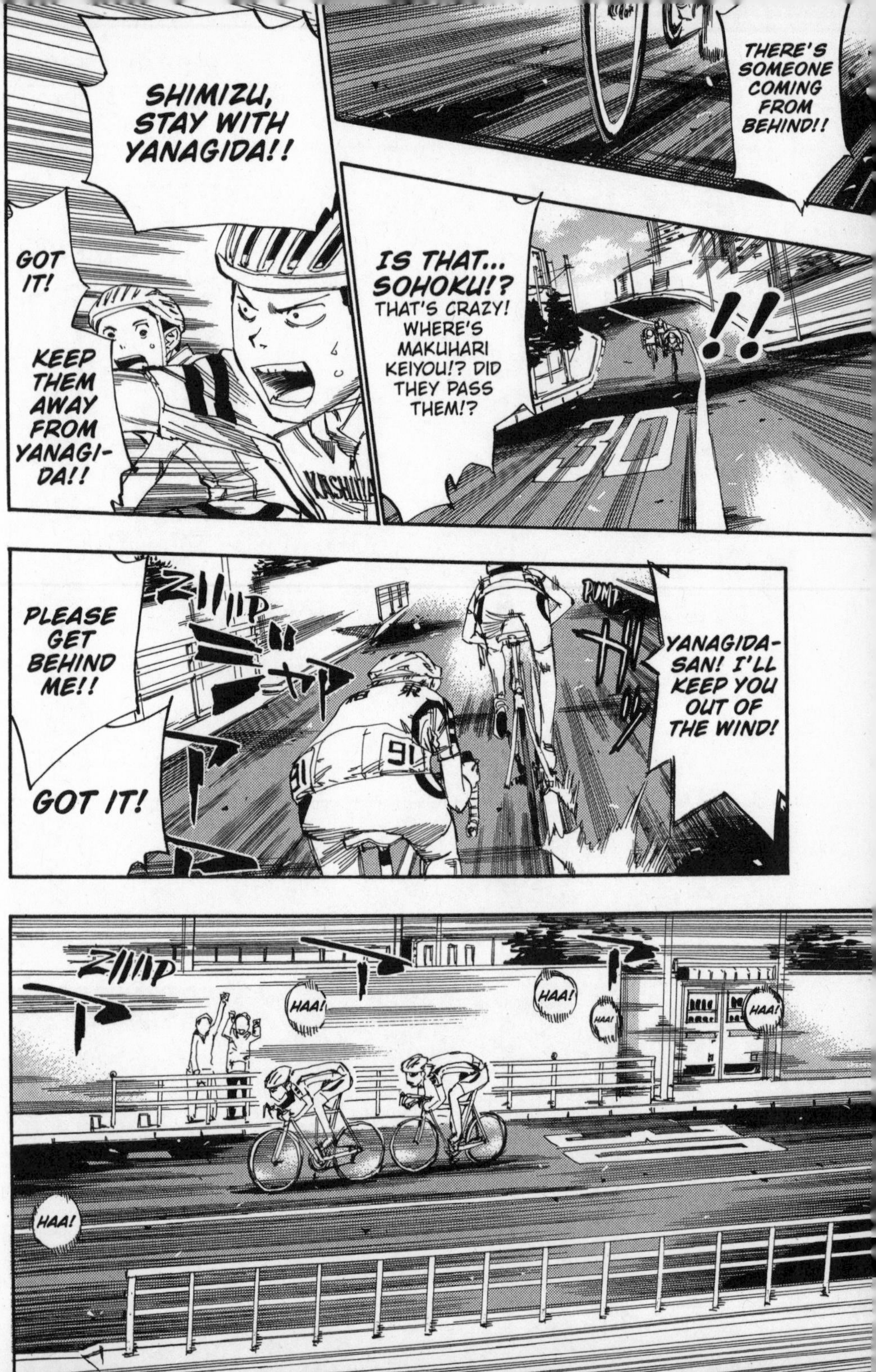
THERE'S SOMEONE COMING FROM BEHIND!!
IS THAT... SOHOKU!? THAT'S CRAZY! WHERE'S MAKUHARI KEIYOU!? DID THEY PASS THEM!?
!!
SHIMIZU, STAY WITH YANAGIDA!!
GOT IT!
KEEP THEM AWAY FROM YANAGIDA!!
YANAGIDA-SAN! I'LL KEEP YOU OUT OF THE WIND!
PUMP
PLEASE GET BEHIND ME!!
GOT IT!
ZIIIP
HAA!
HAA!
HAA!
HAA!
ZIIIP
HAA!

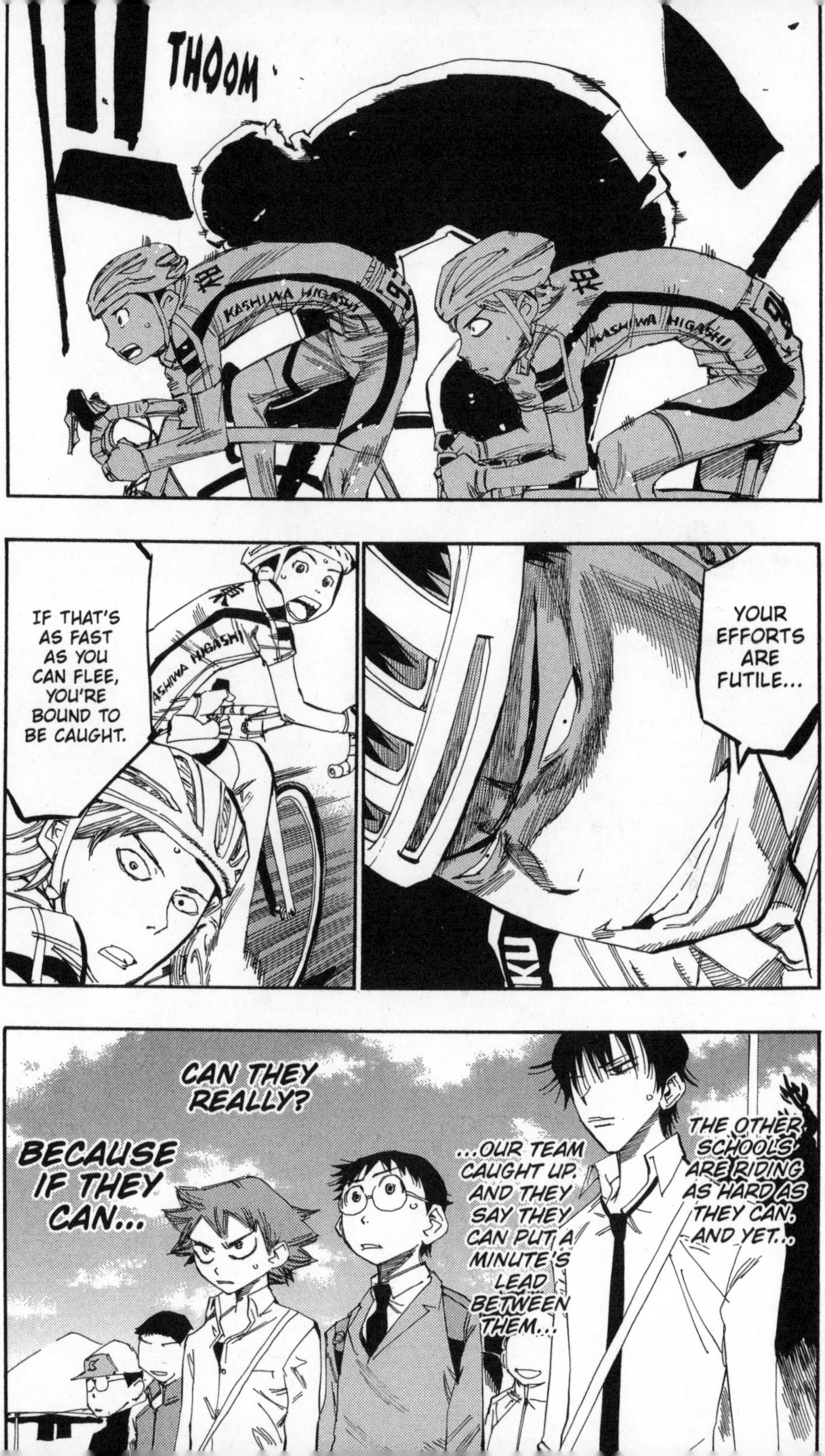
THOOM
YOUR EFFORTS ARE FUTILE...
IF THAT'S AS FAST AS YOU CAN FLEE, YOU'RE BOUND TO BE CAUGHT.
THE OTHER SCHOOLS ARE RIDING AS HARD AS THEY CAN, AND YET...
...OUR TEAM CAUGHT UP. AND THEY SAY THEY CAN PUT A MINUTE'S LEAD BETWEEN THEM...
CAN THEY REALLY?
BECAUSE IF THEY CAN...

RIDE.39 SOHOKU

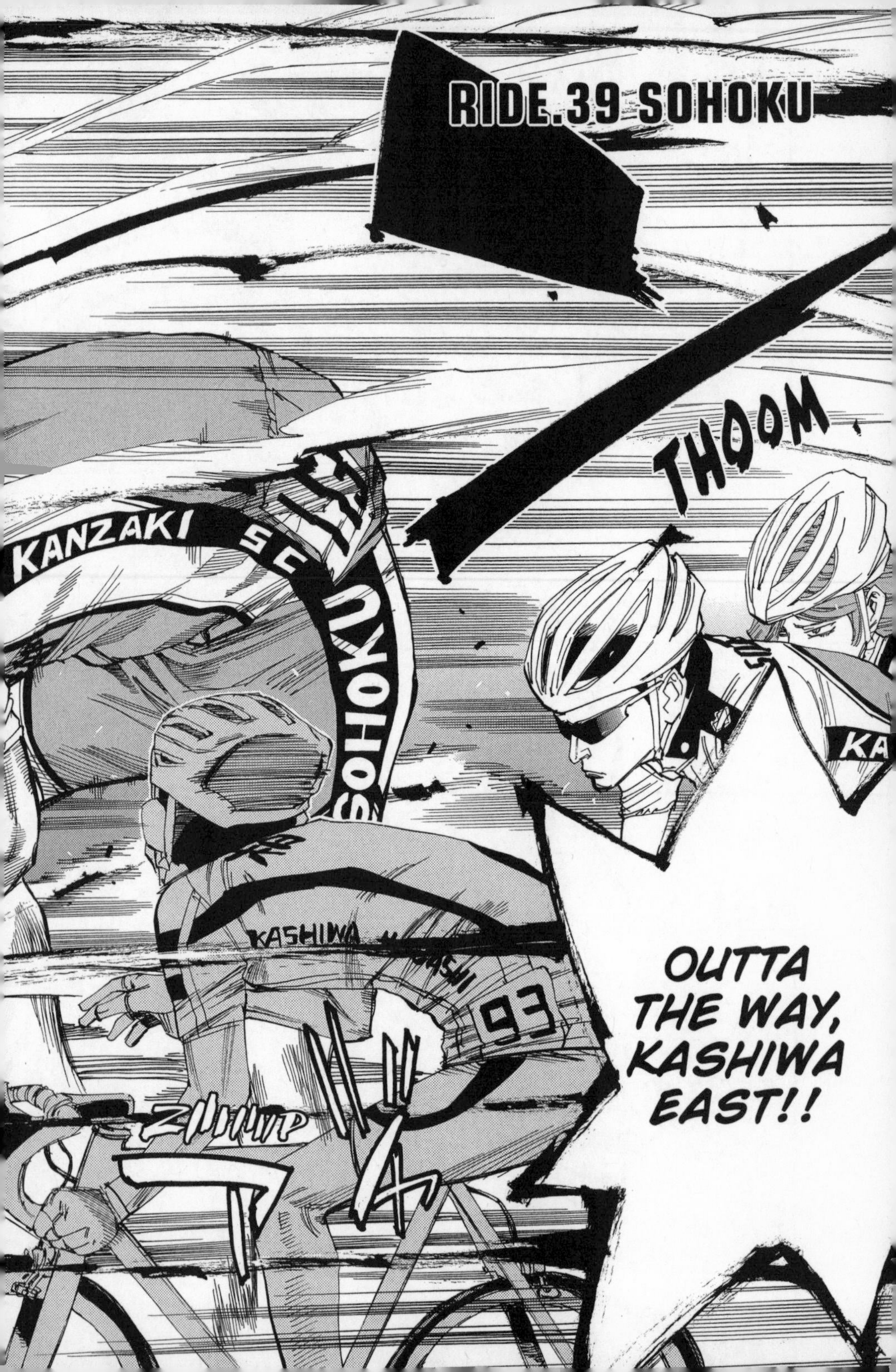
THOOM
OUTTA THE WAY, KASHIWA EAST!!
KANZAKI SC
SOHOKU
KASHIWA
93

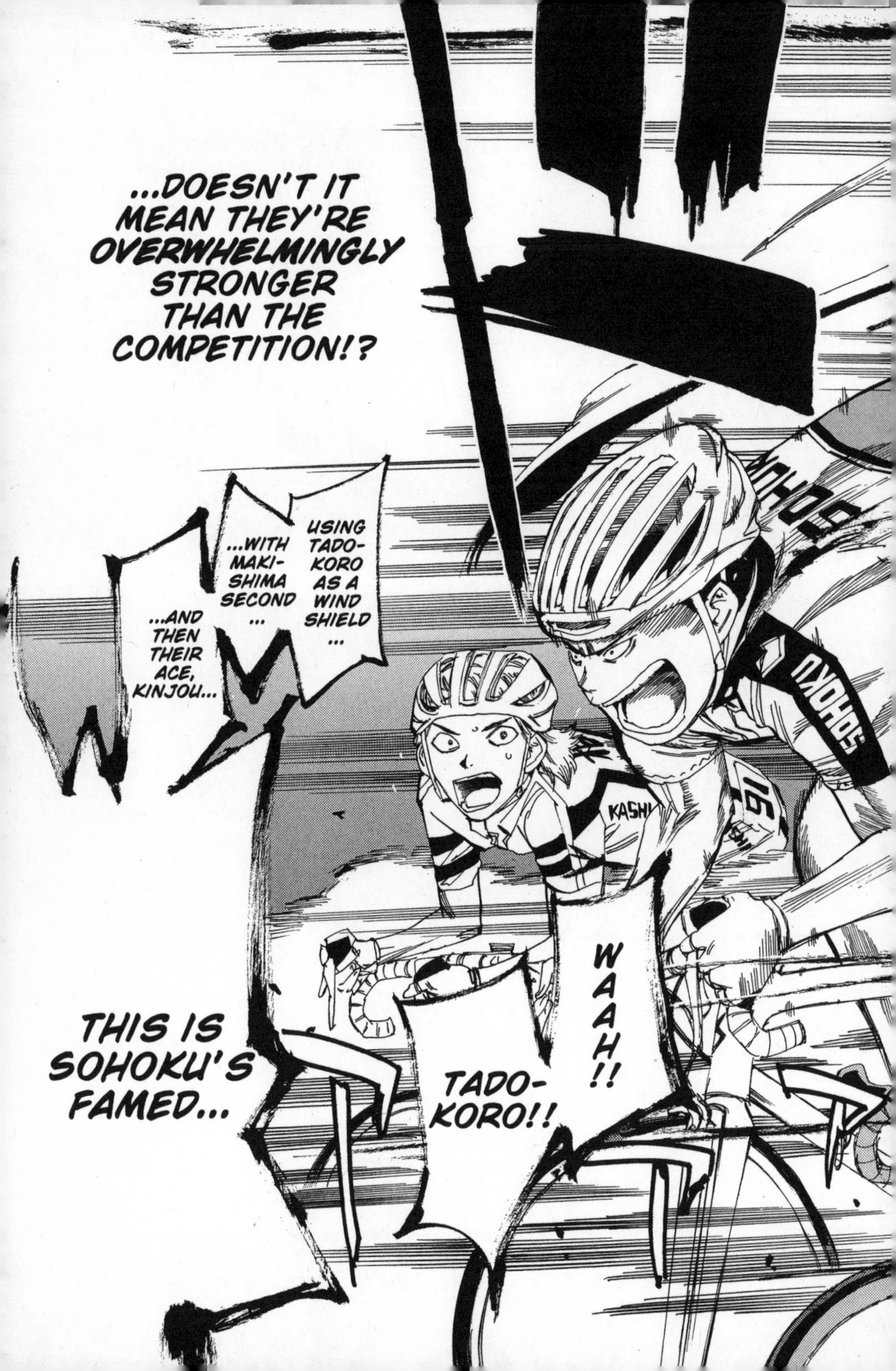
...DOESN'T IT MEAN THEY'RE OVERWHELMINGLY STRONGER THAN THE COMPETITION!?
USING TADO-KORO AS A WIND SHIELD...
...WITH MAKI-SHIMA SECOND...
...AND THEN THEIR ACE, KINJOU...
WAAH!!
TADO-KORO!!
THIS IS SOHOKU'S FAMED...

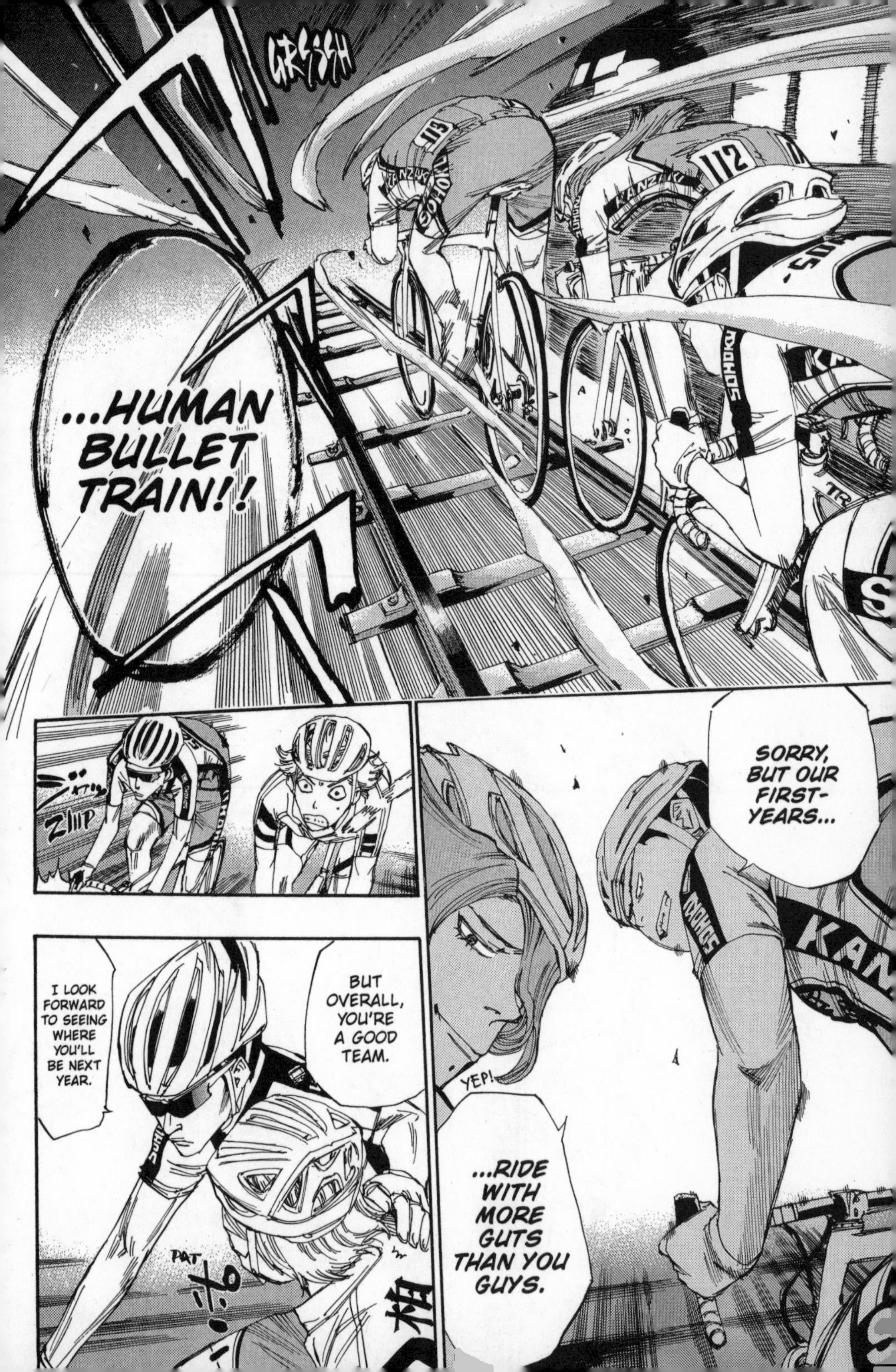
GRSSSH
...HUMAN BULLET TRAIN!!
SORRY, BUT OUR FIRST-YEARS...
YEP!
...RIDE WITH MORE GUTS THAN YOU GUYS.
ZIIIP
BUT OVERALL, YOU'RE A GOOD TEAM.
I LOOK FORWARD TO SEEING WHERE YOU'LL BE NEXT YEAR.
PAT

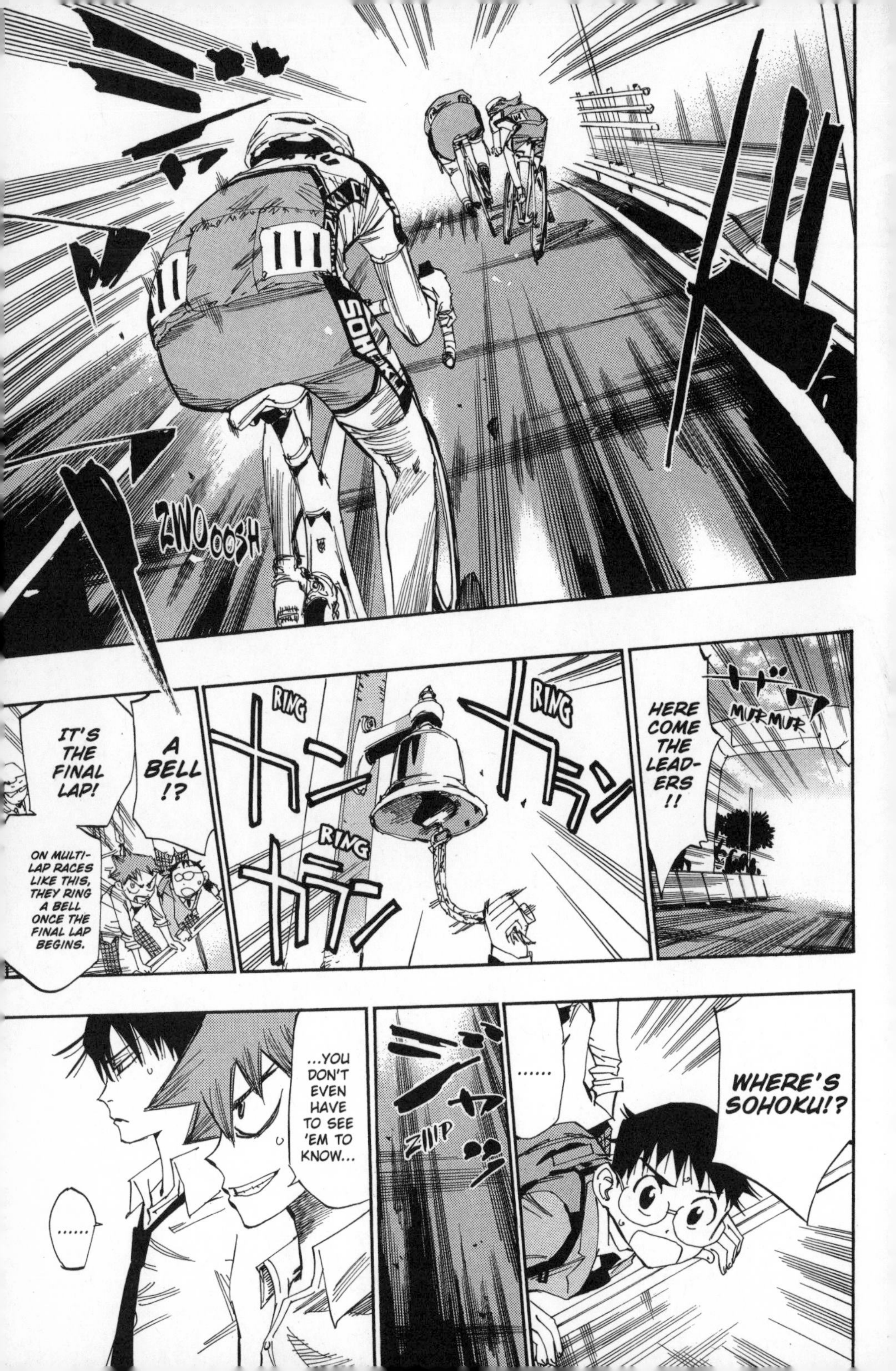
ZWOOOSH
MURMUR
HERE COME THE LEADERS!!
RING
RING
RING
A BELL!?
IT'S THE FINAL LAP!
ON MULTI-LAP RACES LIKE THIS, THEY RING A BELL ONCE THE FINAL LAP BEGINS.
WHERE'S SOHOKU!?
......
ZIIIP
...YOU DON'T EVEN HAVE TO SEE 'EM TO KNOW...
......

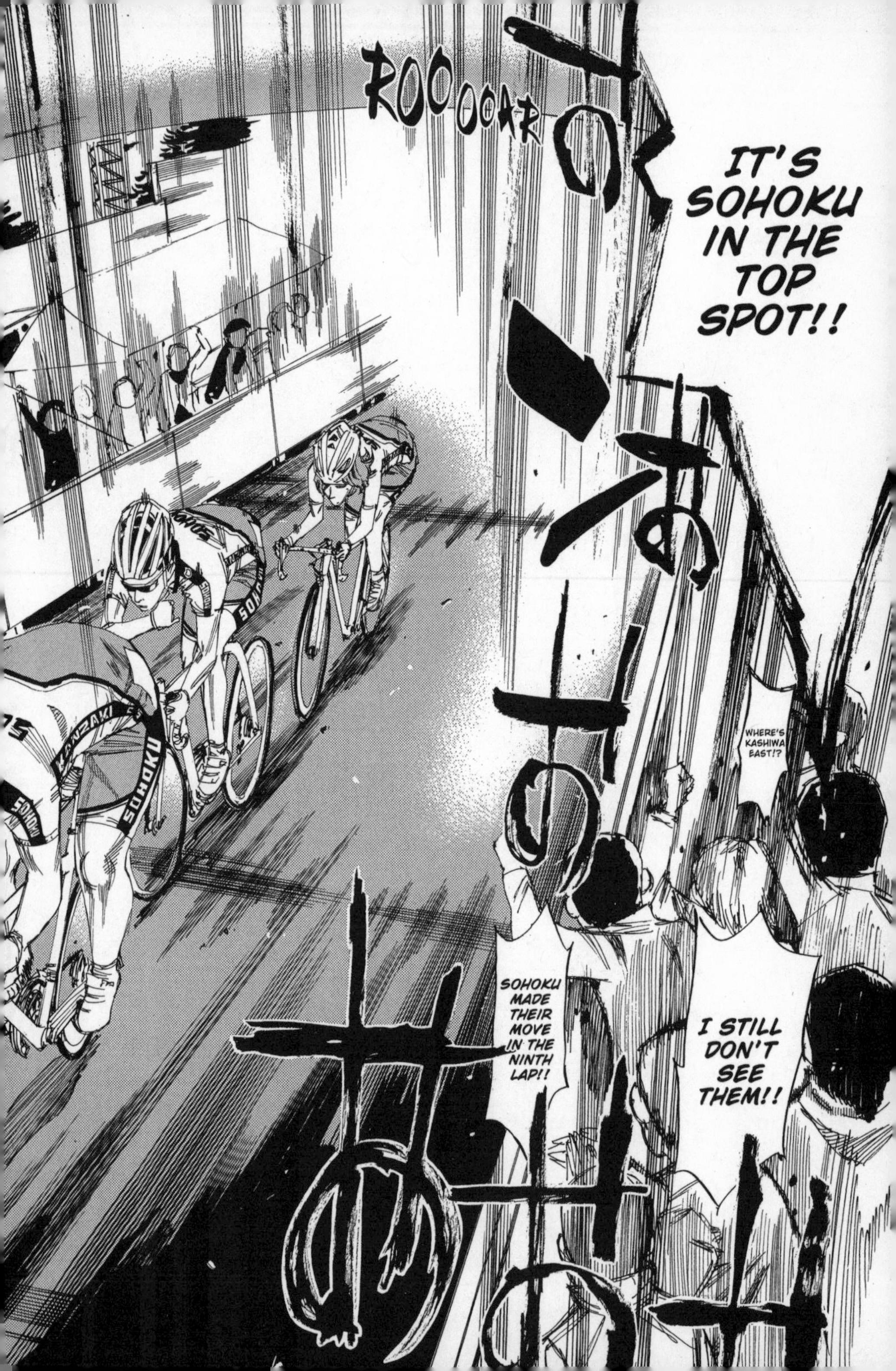
ROOOOAR
IT'S SOHOKU IN THE TOP SPOT!!
WHERE'S KASHIWA EAST!?
I STILL DON'T SEE THEM!!
SOHOKU MADE THEIR MOVE IN THE NINTH LAP!!

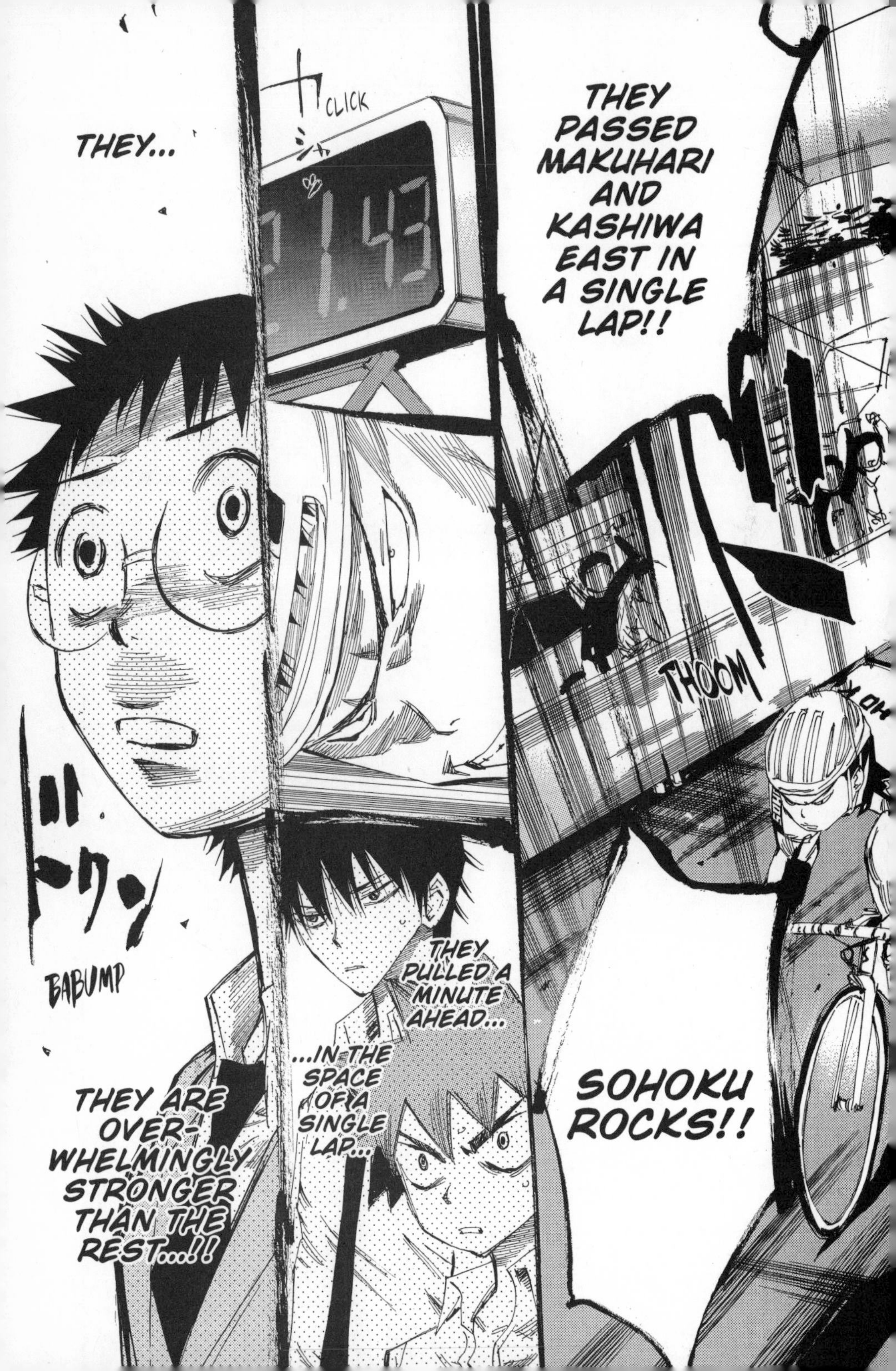
THEY PASSED MAKUHARI AND KASHIWA EAST IN A SINGLE LAP!!
THOOM
SOHOKU ROCKS!!
CLICK
THEY PULLED A MINUTE AHEAD...
...IN THE SPACE OF A SINGLE LAP...
THEY...
BABUMP
THEY ARE OVER-WHELMINGLY STRONGER THAN THE REST...!!

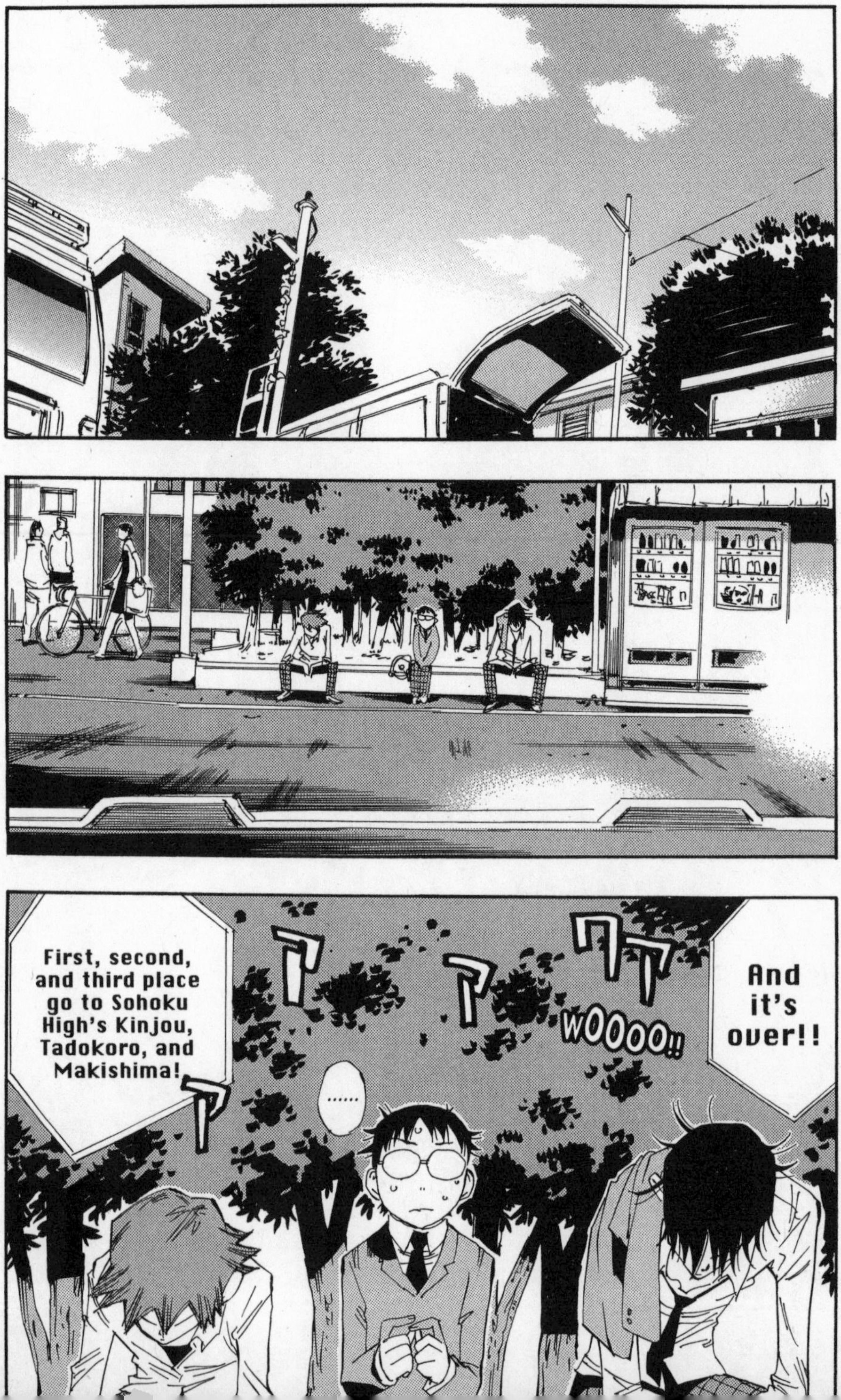

And it's over!!
WOOOO!!
First, second, and third place go to Sohoku High's Kinjou, Tadokoro, and Makishima!
......

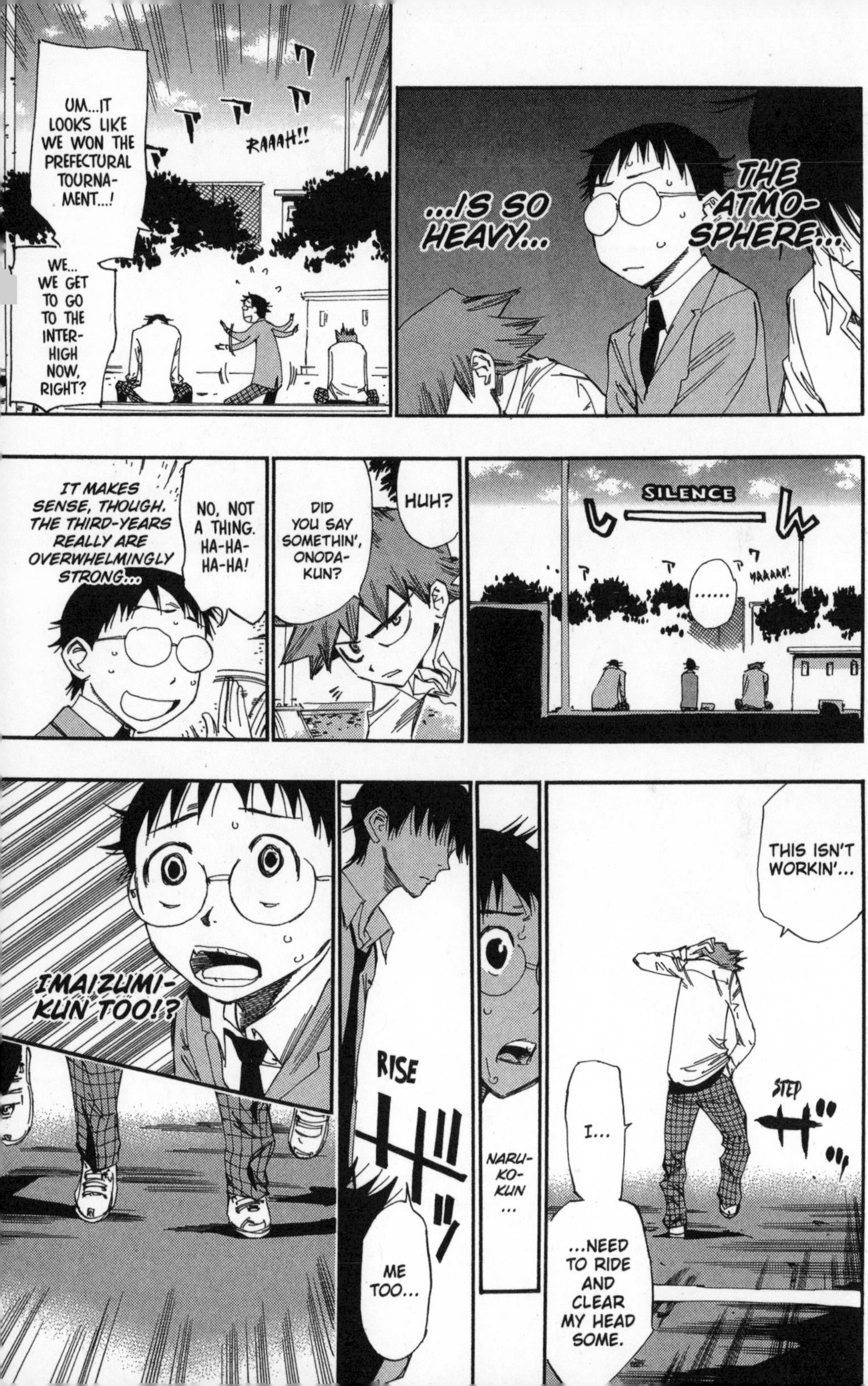

THE ATMO-SPHERE...
...IS SO HEAVY...
RAAAH!!
UM...IT LOOKS LIKE WE WON THE PREFECTURAL TOURNA-MENT...!
WE... WE GET TO GO TO THE INTER-HIGH NOW, RIGHT?
SILENCE
YAAAAY!
......
HUH?
DID YOU SAY SOMETHIN', ONODA-KUN?
NO, NOT A THING. HA-HA-HA-HA!
IT MAKES SENSE, THOUGH. THE THIRD-YEARS REALLY ARE OVERWHELMINGLY STRONG...
THIS ISN'T WORKIN'...
STEP
I...
...NEED TO RIDE AND CLEAR MY HEAD SOME.
NARU-KO-KUN...
RISE
ME TOO...
IMAIZUMI-KUN TOO!?

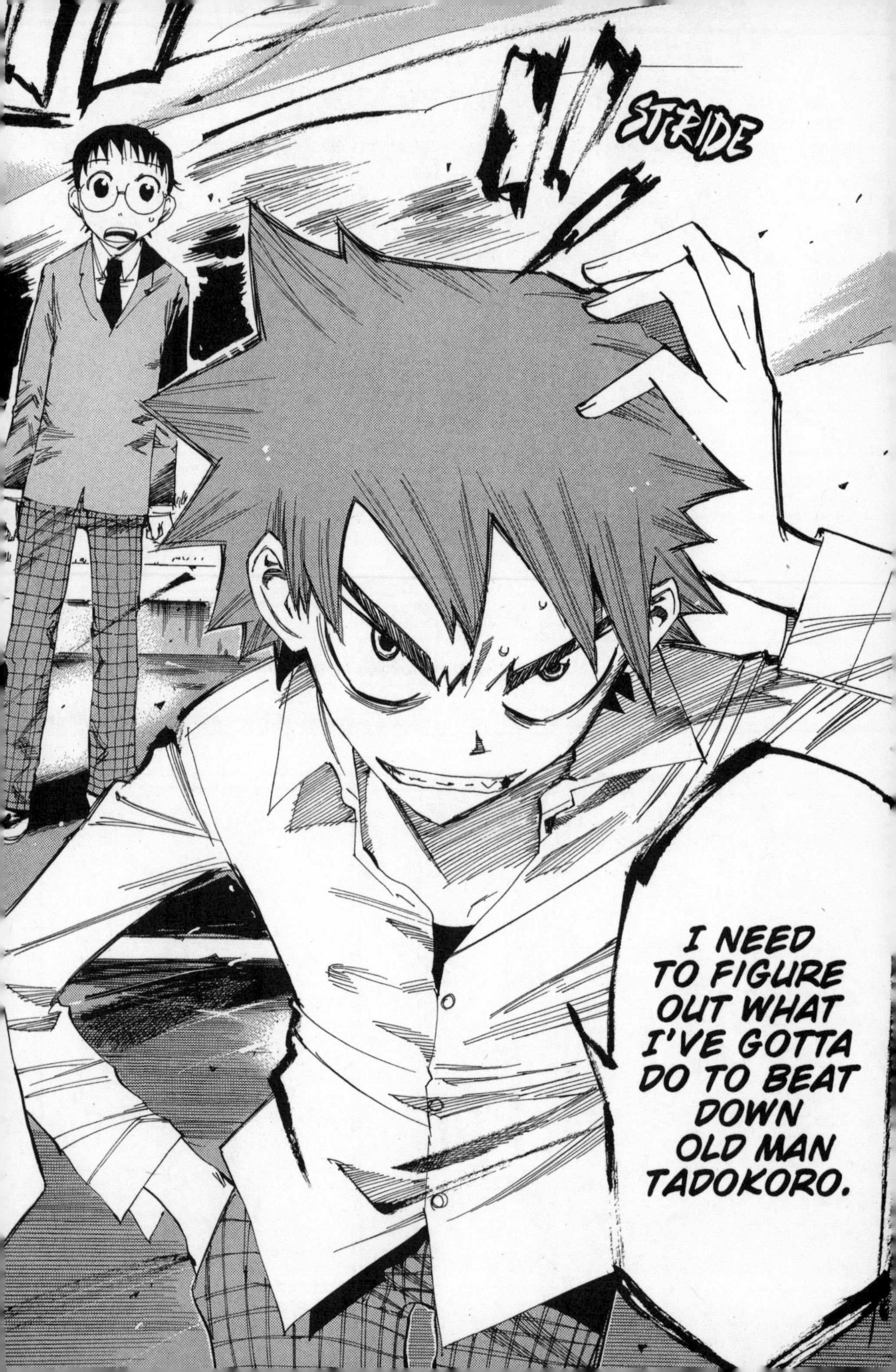
STRIDE
I NEED TO FIGURE OUT WHAT I'VE GOTTA DO TO BEAT DOWN OLD MAN TADOKORO.

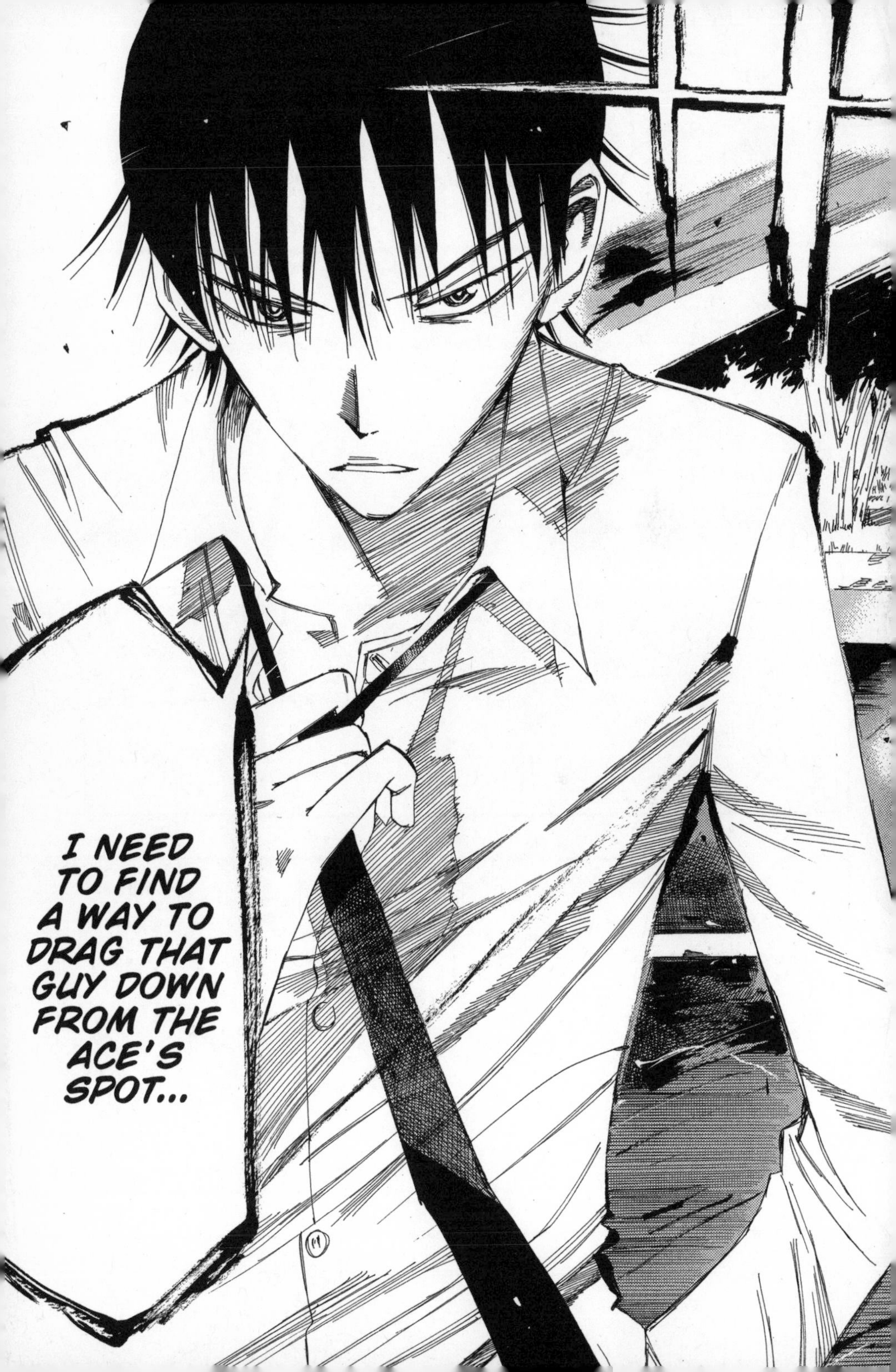
I NEED TO FIND A WAY TO DRAG THAT GUY DOWN FROM THE ACE'S SPOT...

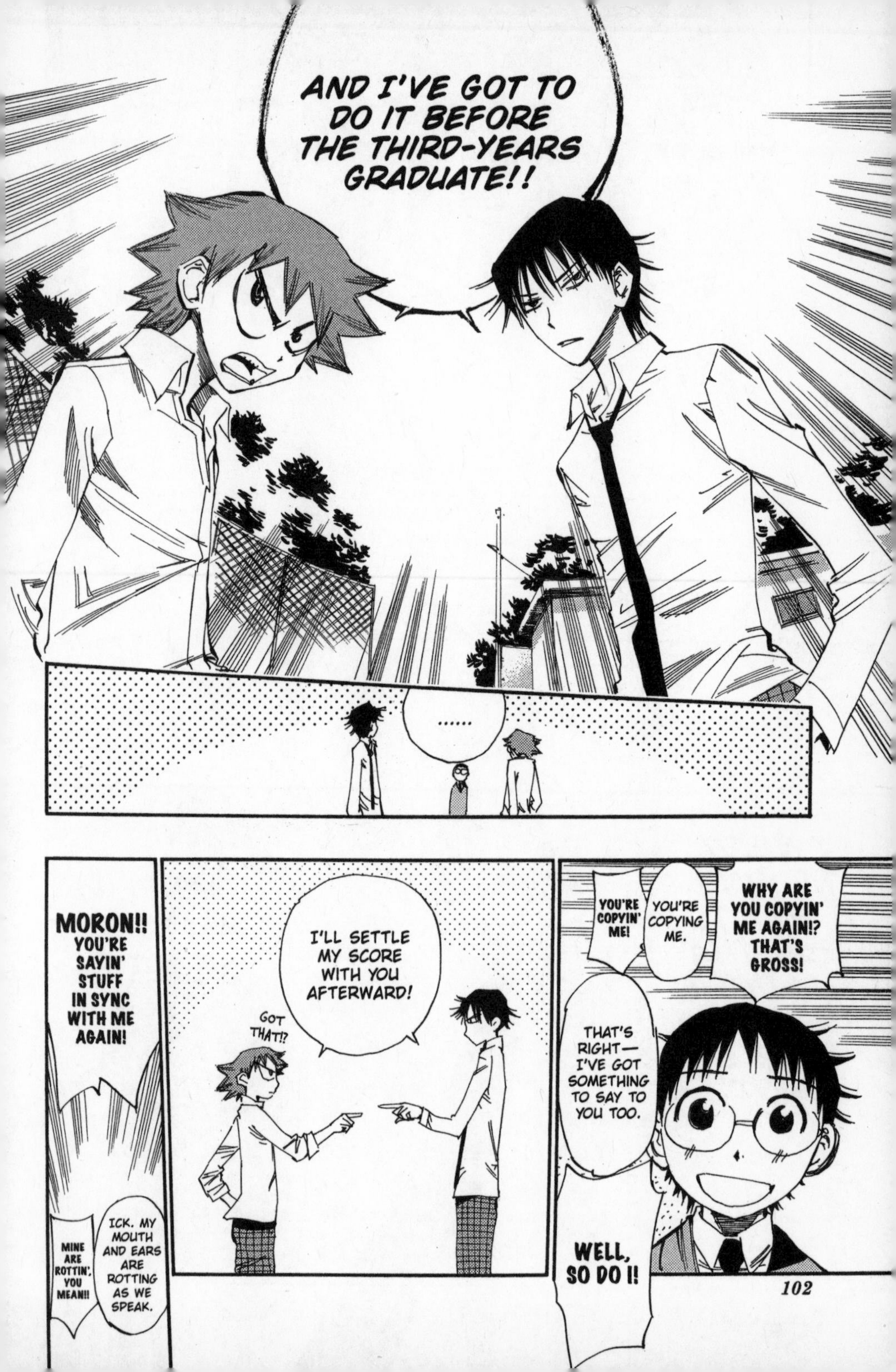
AND I'VE GOT TO DO IT BEFORE THE THIRD-YEARS GRADUATE!!
......
WHY ARE YOU COPYIN' ME AGAIN!? THAT'S GROSS!
YOU'RE COPYING ME.
YOU'RE COPYIN' ME!
THAT'S RIGHT— I'VE GOT SOMETHING TO SAY TO YOU TOO.
WELL, SO DO I!
I'LL SETTLE MY SCORE WITH YOU AFTERWARD!
GOT THAT!?
MORON!! YOU'RE SAYIN' STUFF IN SYNC WITH ME AGAIN!
ICK. MY MOUTH AND EARS ARE ROTTING AS WE SPEAK.
MINE ARE ROTTIN', YOU MEAN!!

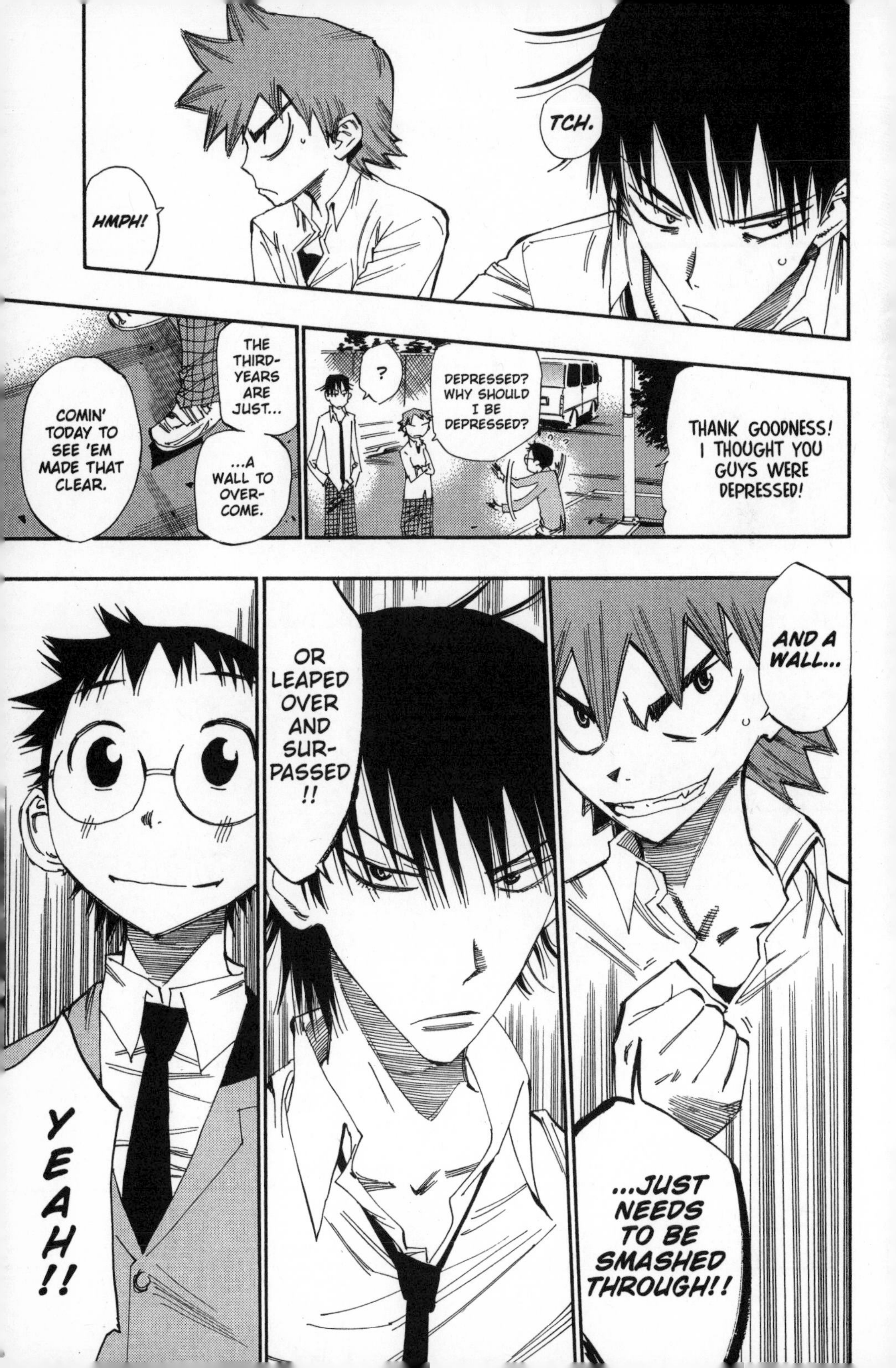
TCH.
HMPH!
THANK GOODNESS! I THOUGHT YOU GUYS WERE DEPRESSED!
DEPRESSED? WHY SHOULD I BE DEPRESSED?
?
THE THIRD-YEARS ARE JUST...
...A WALL TO OVER-COME.
COMIN' TODAY TO SEE 'EM MADE THAT CLEAR.
AND A WALL...
...JUST NEEDS TO BE SMASHED THROUGH!!
OR LEAPED OVER AND SUR-PASSED!!
YEAH!!

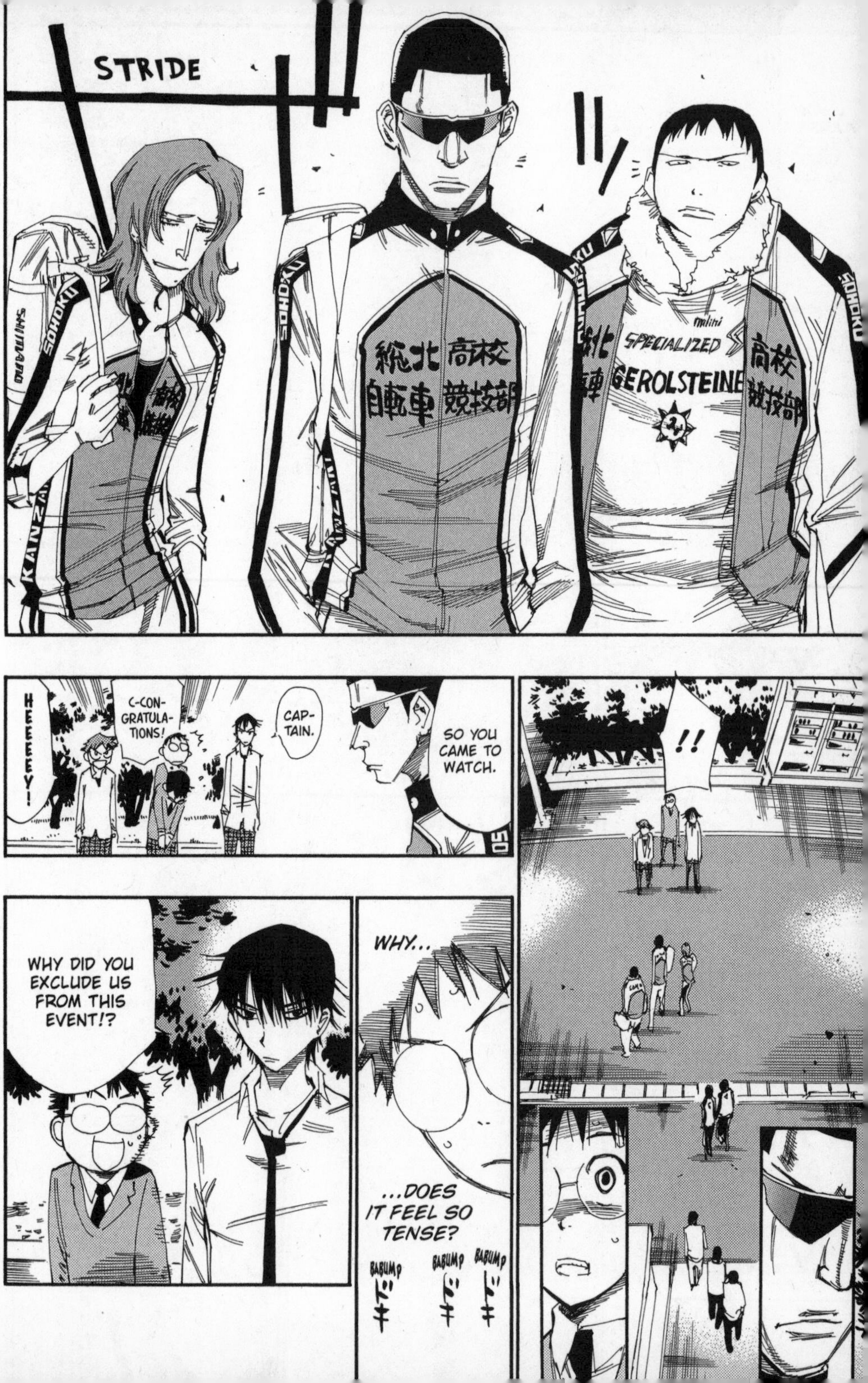
STRIDE
!!
SO YOU CAME TO WATCH.
CAP-TAIN.
C-CON-GRATULA-TIONS!
HEEEEEY!
WHY...
...DOES IT FEEL SO TENSE?
BABUMP ドキ
BABUMP ドキ
BABUMP ドキ
WHY DID YOU EXCLUDE US FROM THIS EVENT!?

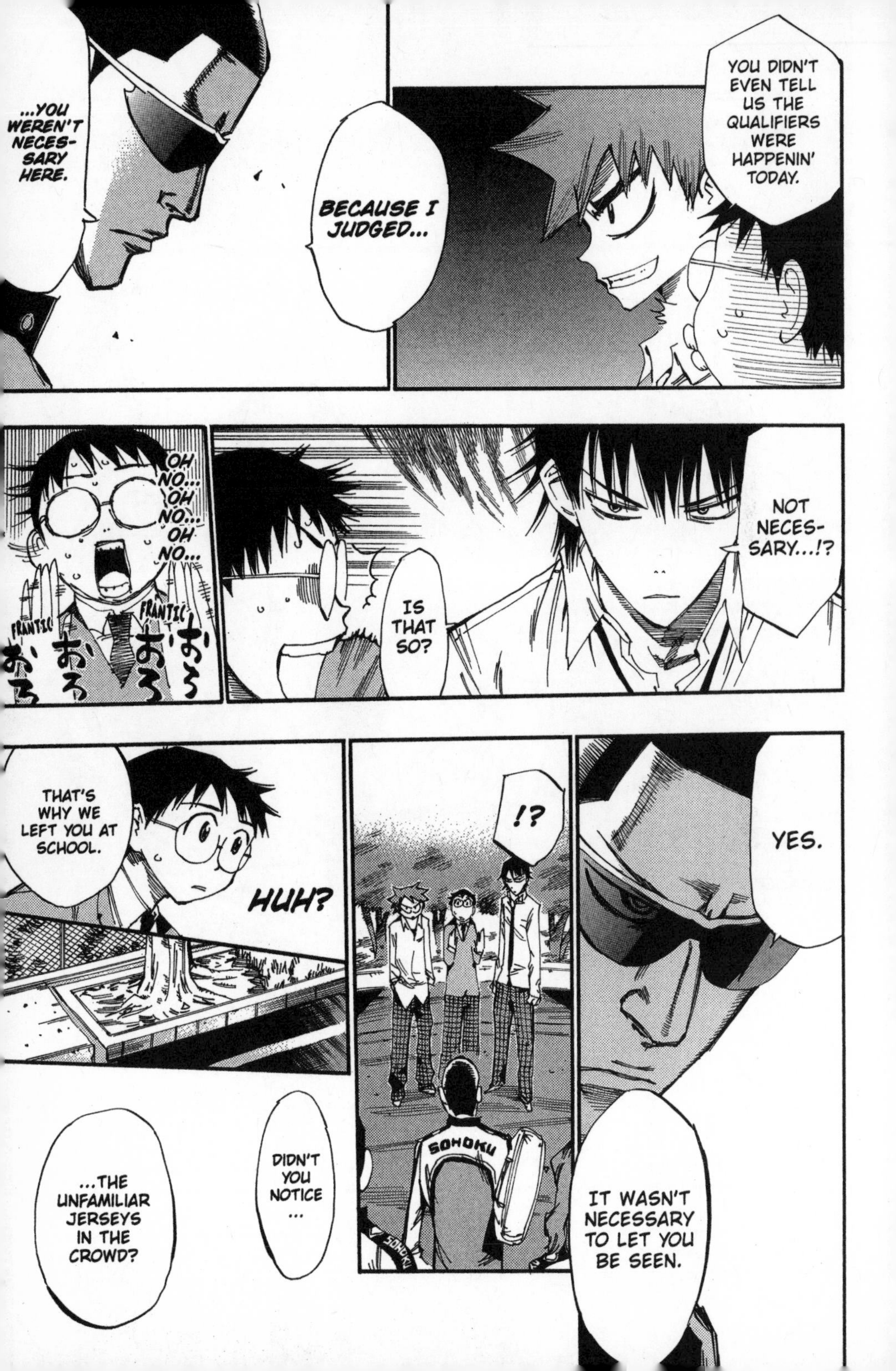
YOU DIDN'T EVEN TELL US THE QUALIFIERS WERE HAPPENIN' TODAY.
BECAUSE I JUDGED...
...YOU WEREN'T NECES-SARY HERE.
NOT NECES-SARY...!?
IS THAT SO?
OH NO... OH NO... OH NO...
FRANTIC
FRANTIC
おろ
おろ
おろ
YES.
IT WASN'T NECESSARY TO LET YOU BE SEEN.
!?
SOHOKU
THAT'S WHY WE LEFT YOU AT SCHOOL.
HUH?
DIDN'T YOU NOTICE...
...THE UNFAMILIAR JERSEYS IN THE CROWD?

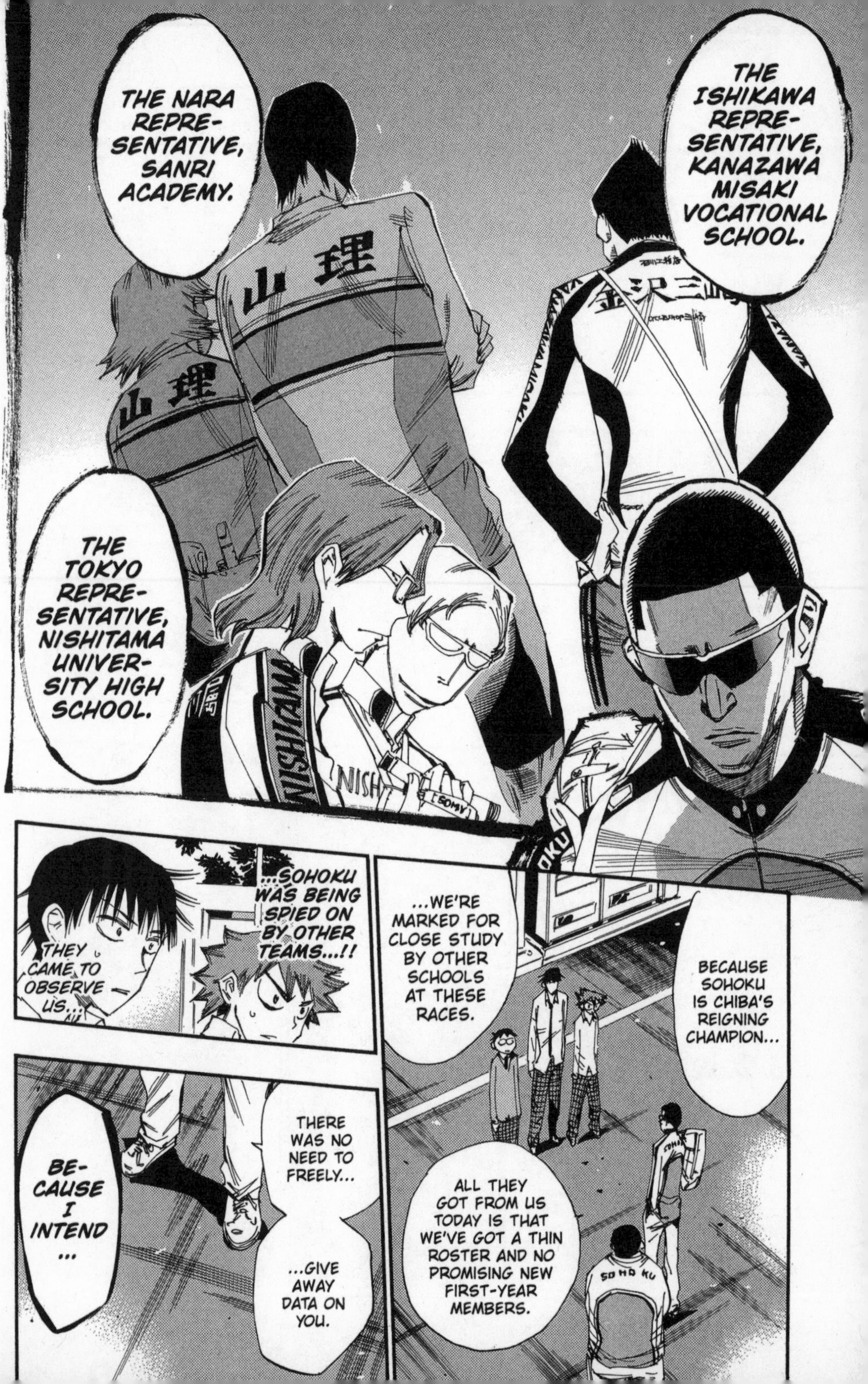
THE ISHIKAWA REPRESENTATIVE, KANAZAWA MISAKI VOCATIONAL SCHOOL.
THE NARA REPRESENTATIVE, SANRI ACADEMY.
THE TOKYO REPRESENTATIVE, NISHITAMA UNIVERSITY HIGH SCHOOL.
BECAUSE SOHOKU IS CHIBA'S REIGNING CHAMPION...
...WE'RE MARKED FOR CLOSE STUDY BY OTHER SCHOOLS AT THESE RACES.
ALL THEY GOT FROM US TODAY IS THAT WE'VE GOT A THIN ROSTER AND NO PROMISING NEW FIRST-YEAR MEMBERS.
...SOHOKU WAS BEING SPIED ON BY OTHER TEAMS...!!
THEY CAME TO OBSERVE US...
THERE WAS NO NEED TO FREELY...
...GIVE AWAY DATA ON YOU.
BECAUSE I INTEND ...

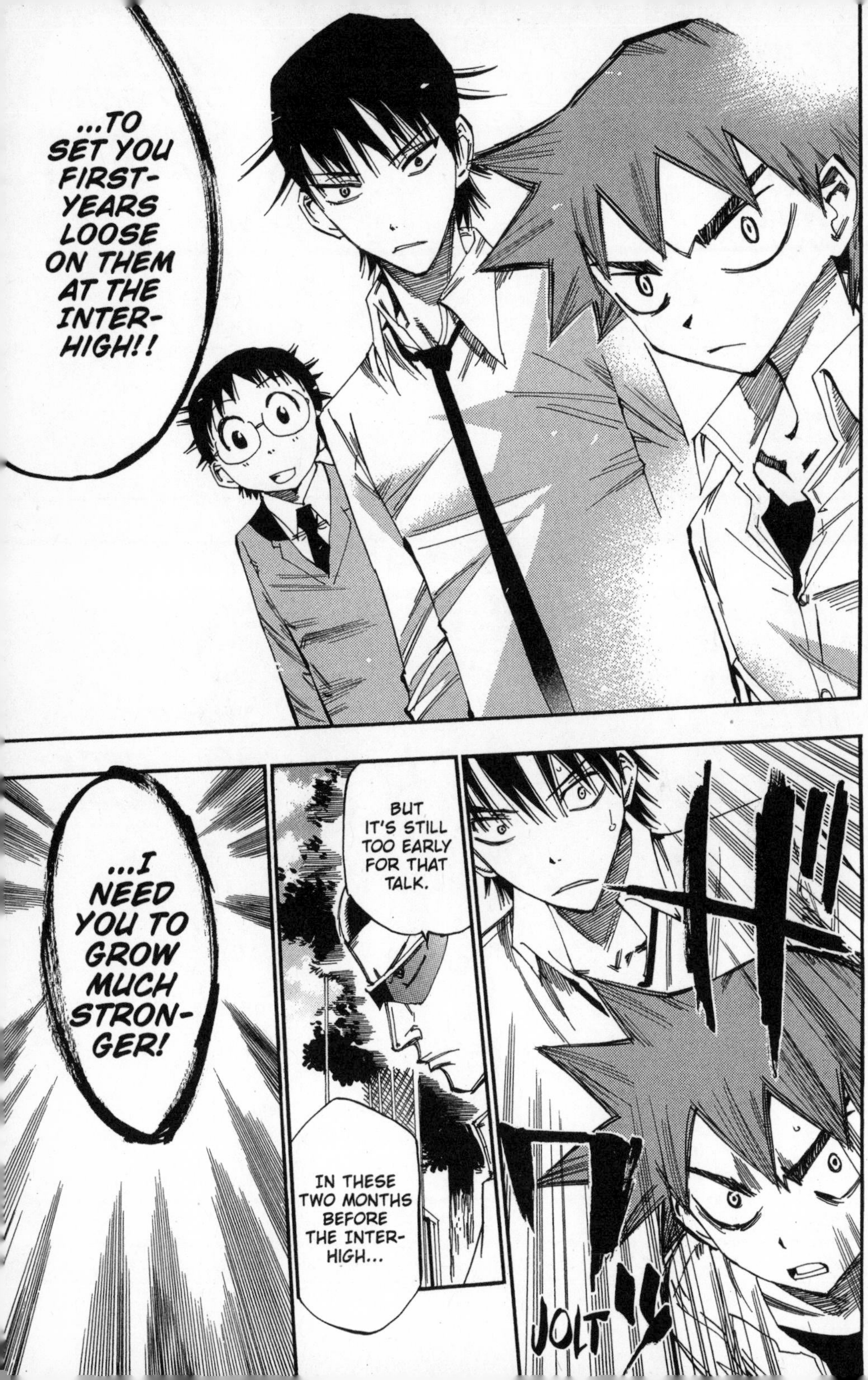
...TO SET YOU FIRST-YEARS LOOSE ON THEM AT THE INTER-HIGH!!
JOLT
BUT IT'S STILL TOO EARLY FOR THAT TALK.
IN THESE TWO MONTHS BEFORE THE INTER-HIGH...
...I NEED YOU TO GROW MUCH STRONGER!

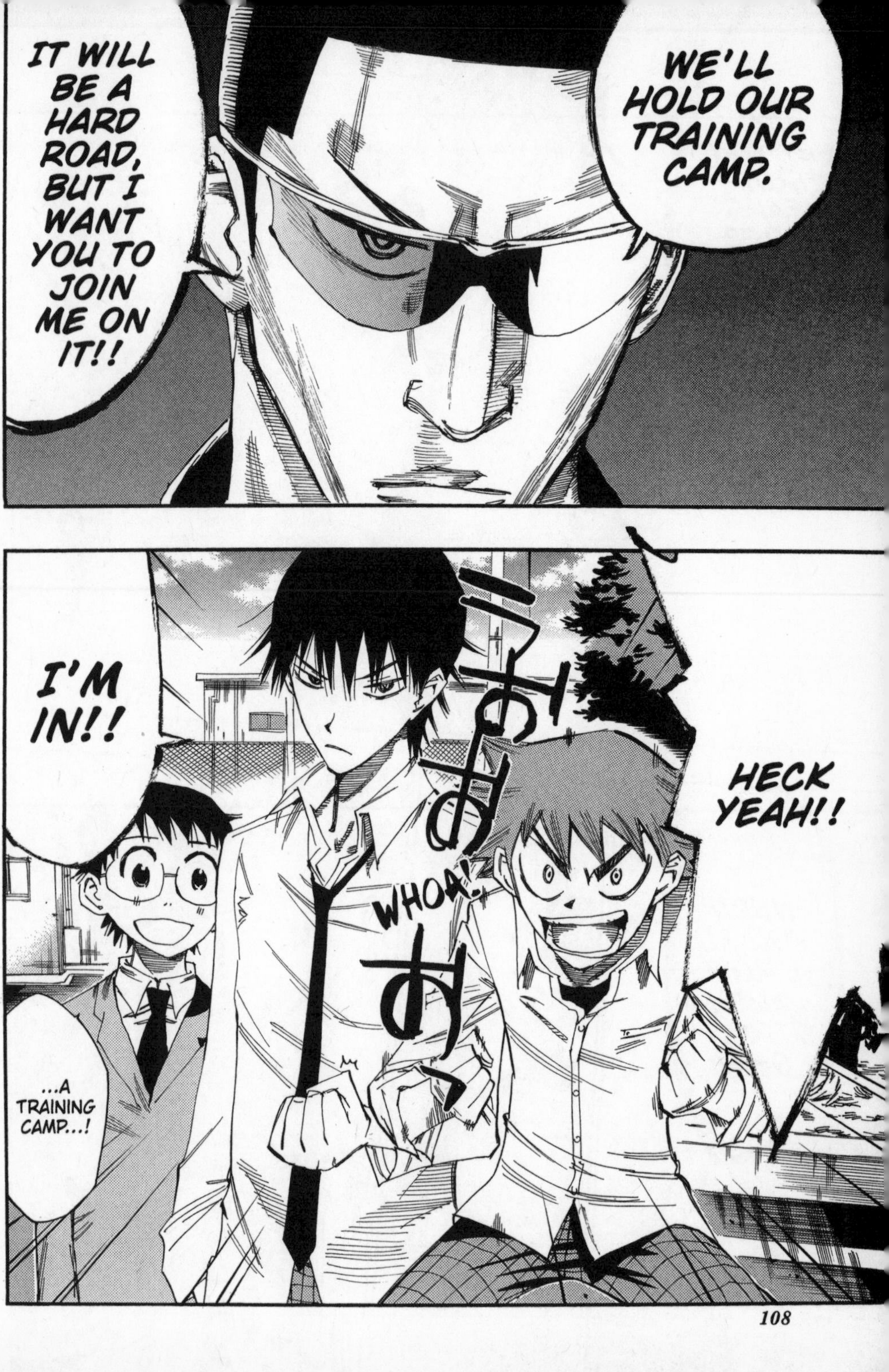
WE'LL HOLD OUR TRAINING CAMP.
IT WILL BE A HARD ROAD, BUT I WANT YOU TO JOIN ME ON IT!!
HECK YEAH!!
WHOA!
I'M IN!!
...A TRAINING CAMP...!

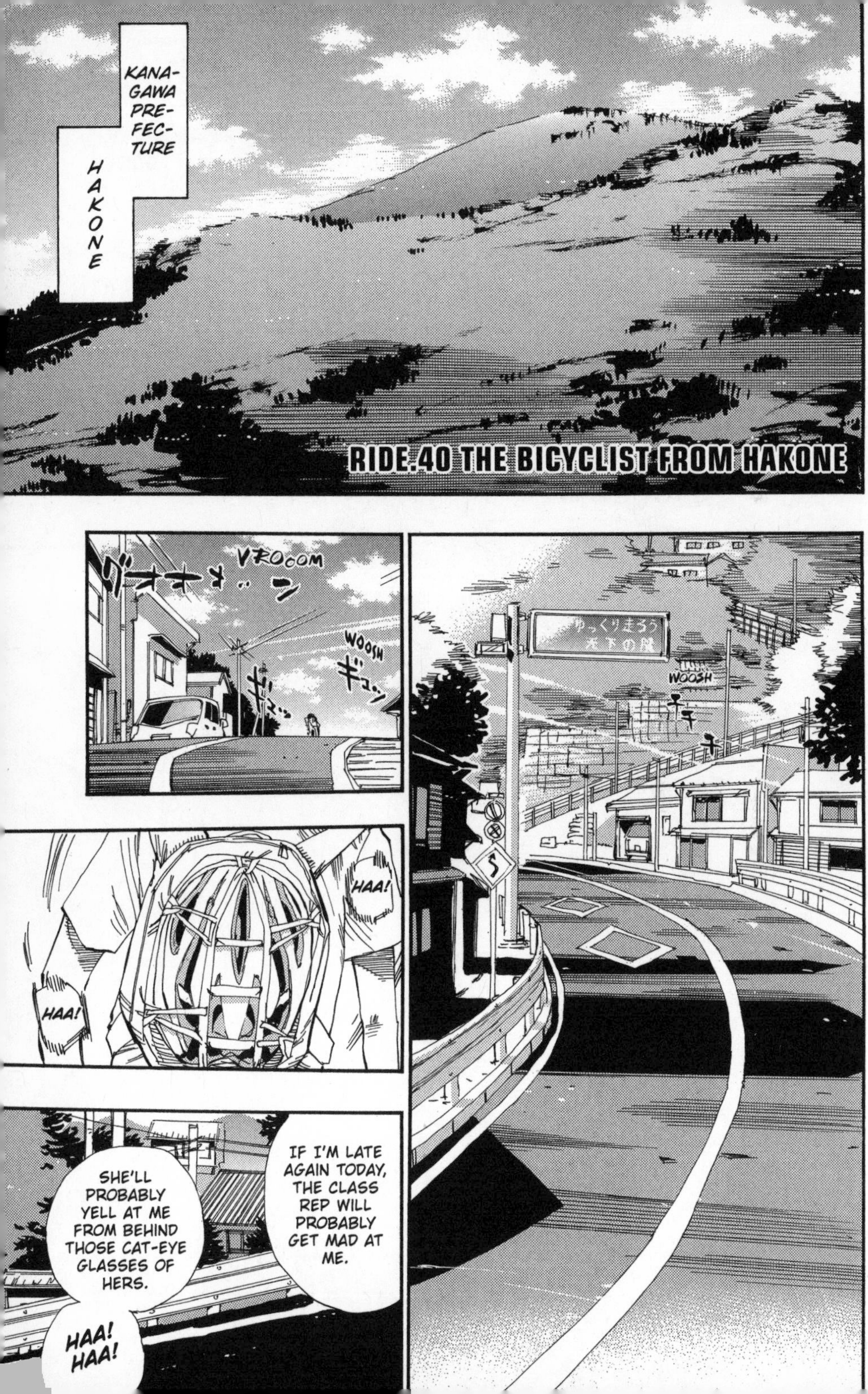
KANAGAWA PREFECTURE
HAKONE
RIDE.40 THE BICYCLIST FROM HAKONE
WOOSH
VROOOM
WOOSH
HAA!
HAA!
IF I'M LATE AGAIN TODAY, THE CLASS REP WILL PROBABLY GET MAD AT ME.
SHE'LL PROBABLY YELL AT ME FROM BEHIND THOSE CAT-EYE GLASSES OF HERS.
HAA! HAA!

RIDE.40
THE BICYCLIST FROM HAKONE

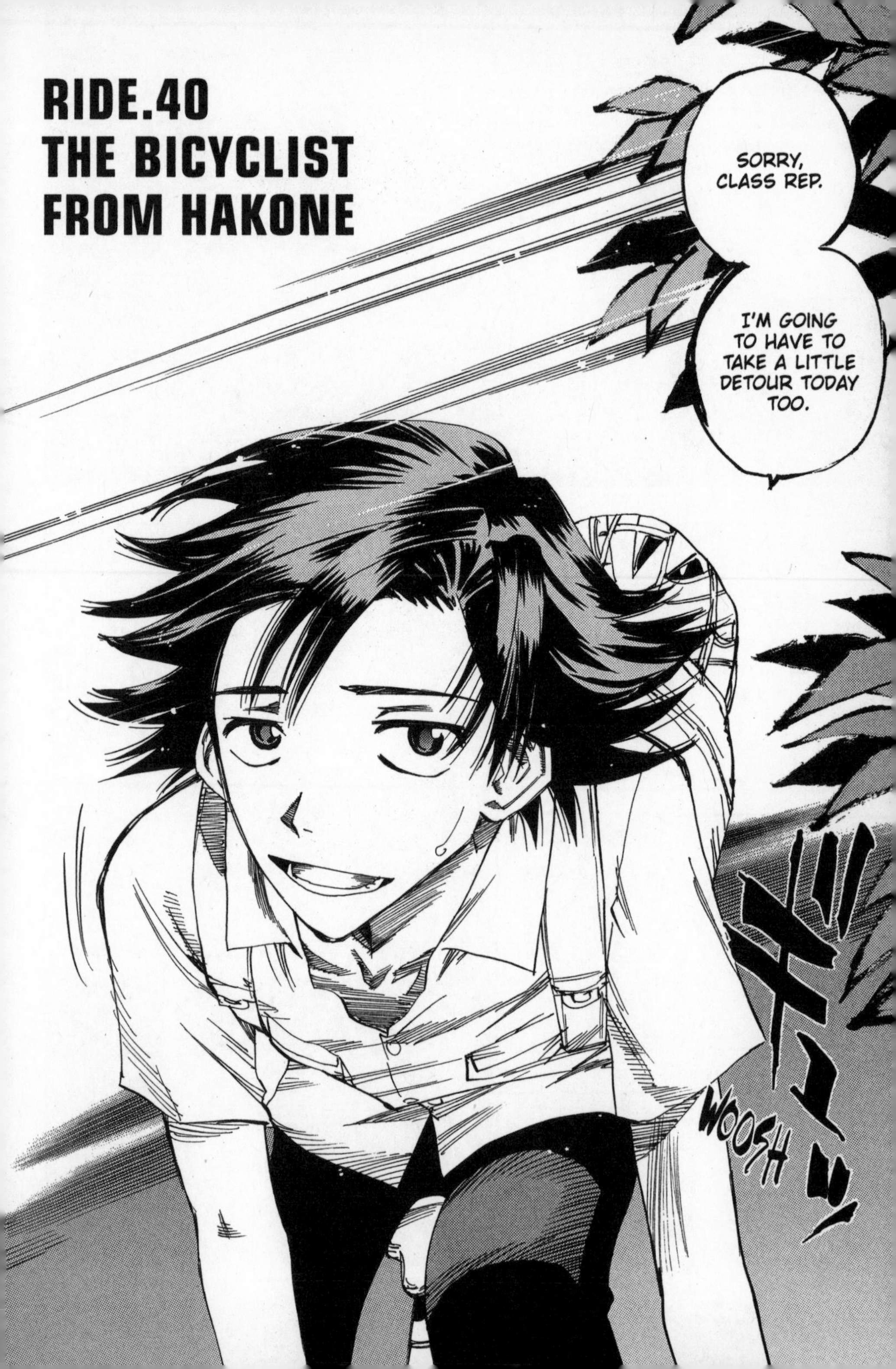
SORRY, CLASS REP.
I'M GOING TO HAVE TO TAKE A LITTLE DETOUR TODAY TOO.
WOOSH

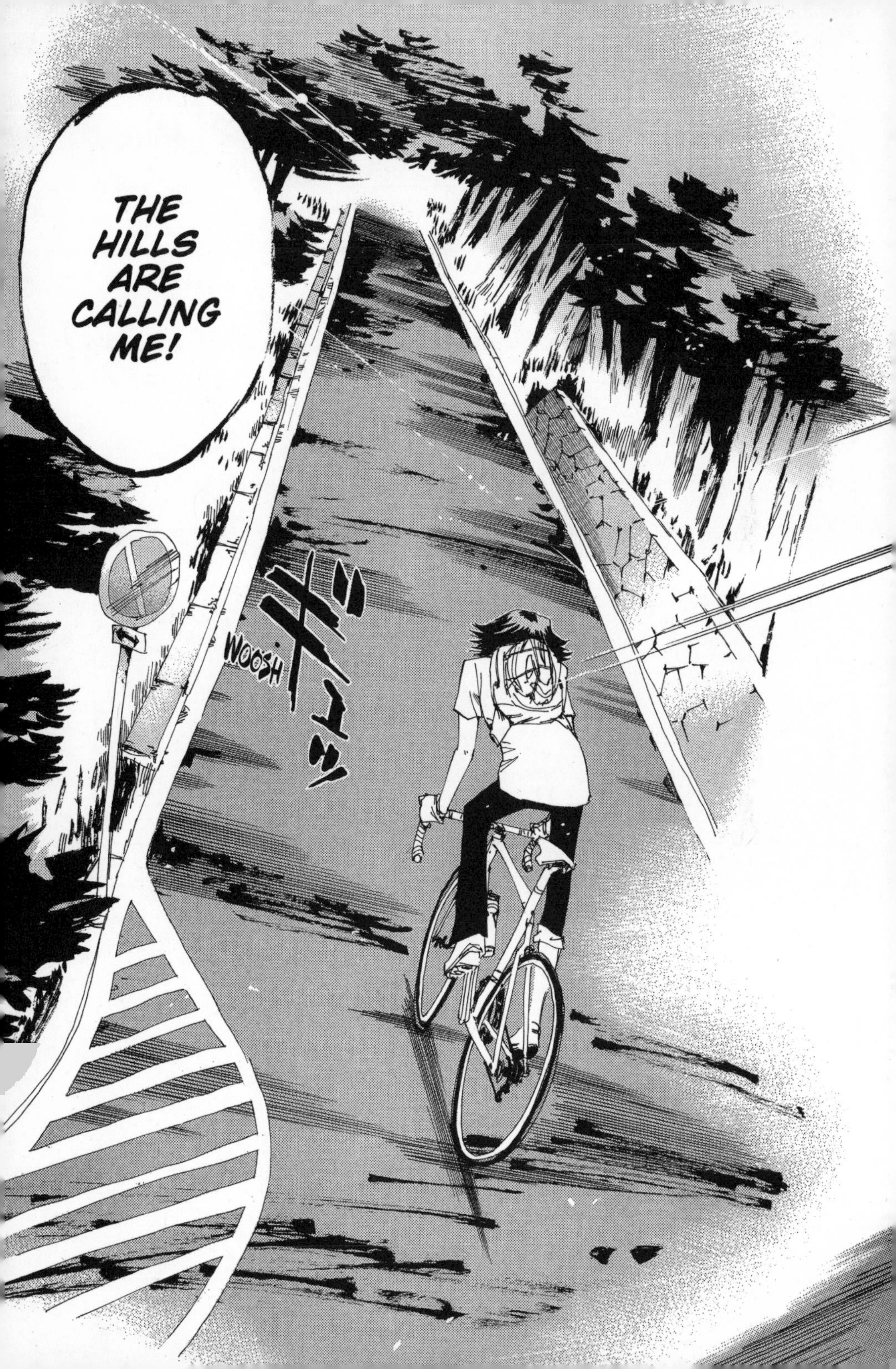
THE HILLS ARE CALLING ME!
WOOSH

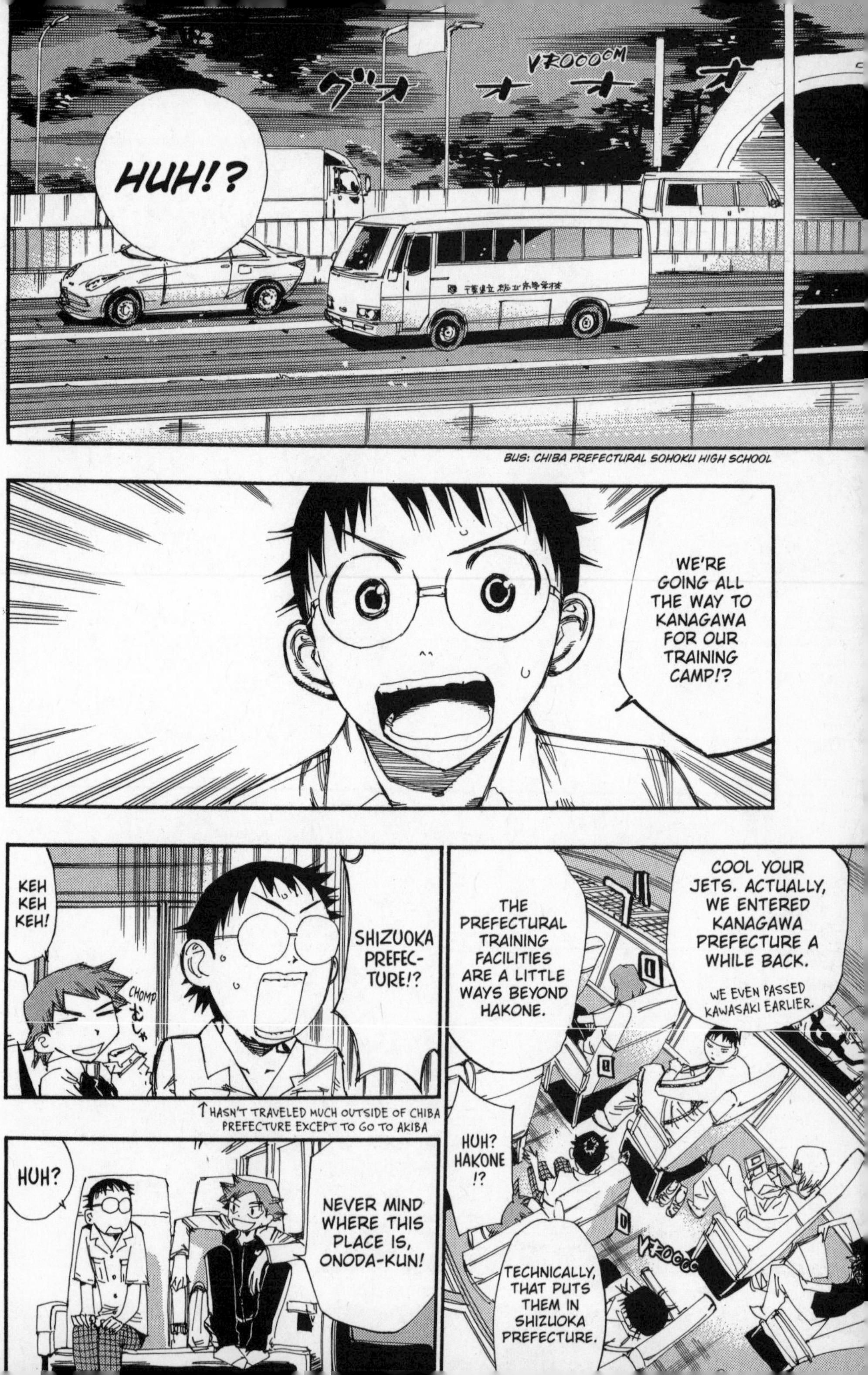
VROOOOM
グオォォォ
HUH!?
BUS: CHIBA PREFECTURAL SOHOKU HIGH SCHOOL
WE'RE GOING ALL THE WAY TO KANAGAWA FOR OUR TRAINING CAMP!?
COOL YOUR JETS. ACTUALLY, WE ENTERED KANAGAWA PREFECTURE A WHILE BACK.
WE EVEN PASSED KAWASAKI EARLIER.
THE PREFECTURAL TRAINING FACILITIES ARE A LITTLE WAYS BEYOND HAKONE.
HUH? HAKONE!?
TECHNICALLY, THAT PUTS THEM IN SHIZUOKA PREFECTURE.
VROOOO
SHIZUOKA PREFECTURE!?
KEH KEH KEH!
CHOMP
↑HASN'T TRAVELED MUCH OUTSIDE OF CHIBA PREFECTURE EXCEPT TO GO TO AKIBA
NEVER MIND WHERE THIS PLACE IS, ONODA-KUN!
HUH?

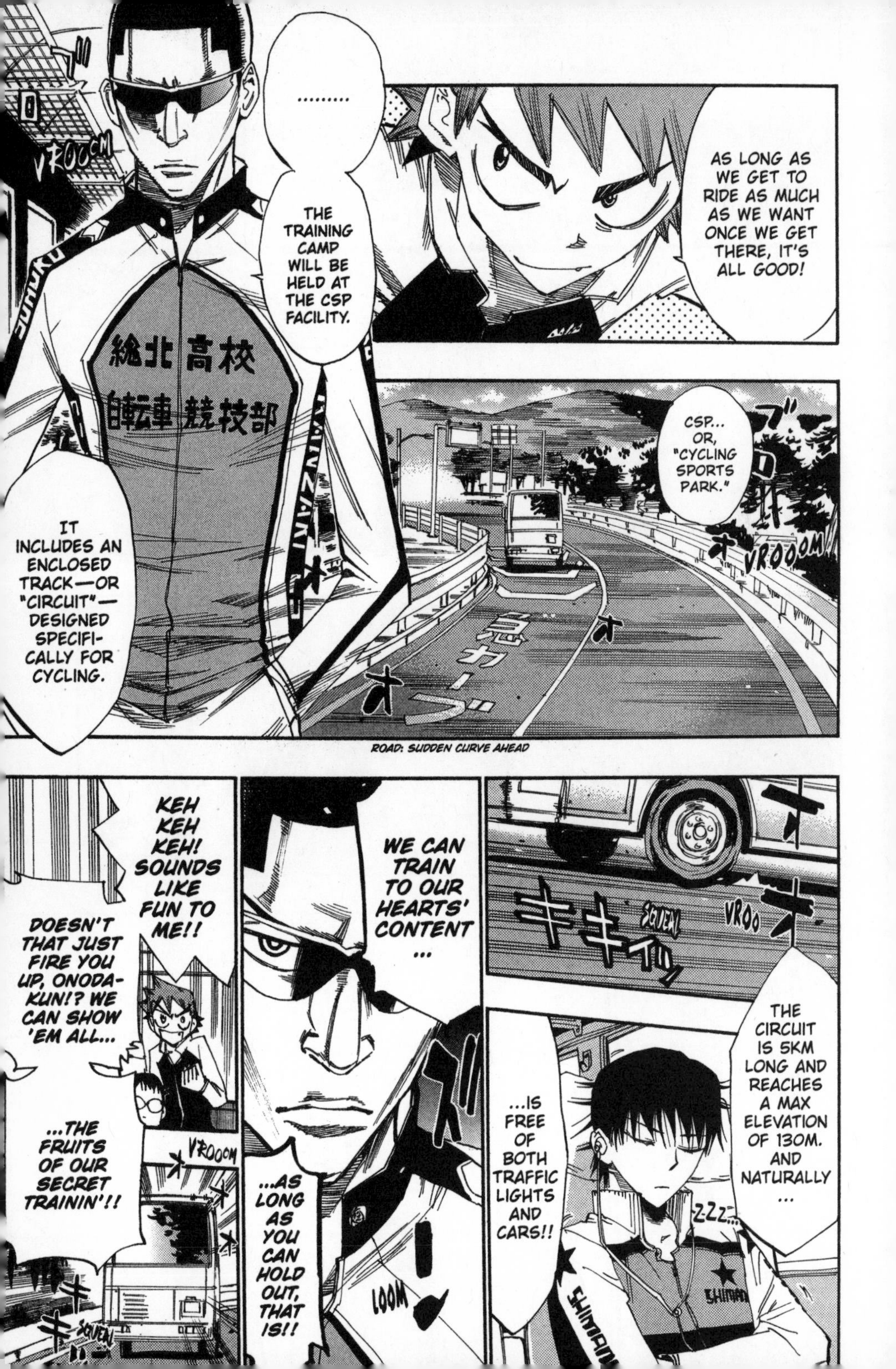
AS LONG AS WE GET TO RIDE AS MUCH AS WE WANT ONCE WE GET THERE, IT'S ALL GOOD!
....
THE TRAINING CAMP WILL BE HELD AT THE CSP FACILITY.
VROOOM
総北高校
自転車競技部
CSP... OR, "CYCLING SPORTS PARK."
VROOOM
IT INCLUDES AN ENCLOSED TRACK—OR "CIRCUIT"—DESIGNED SPECIFI-CALLY FOR CYCLING.
ROAD: SUDDEN CURVE AHEAD
SQUEAL
VROO
THE CIRCUIT IS 5KM LONG AND REACHES A MAX ELEVATION OF 130M. AND NATURALLY...
...IS FREE OF BOTH TRAFFIC LIGHTS AND CARS!!
Z-ZZ...
WE CAN TRAIN TO OUR HEARTS' CONTENT...
...AS LONG AS YOU CAN HOLD OUT, THAT IS!!
LOOM
KEH KEH KEH! SOUNDS LIKE FUN TO ME!!
DOESN'T THAT JUST FIRE YOU UP, ONODA-KUN!? WE CAN SHOW 'EM ALL...
...THE FRUITS OF OUR SECRET TRAININ'!!
VROOOM
SQUEAL

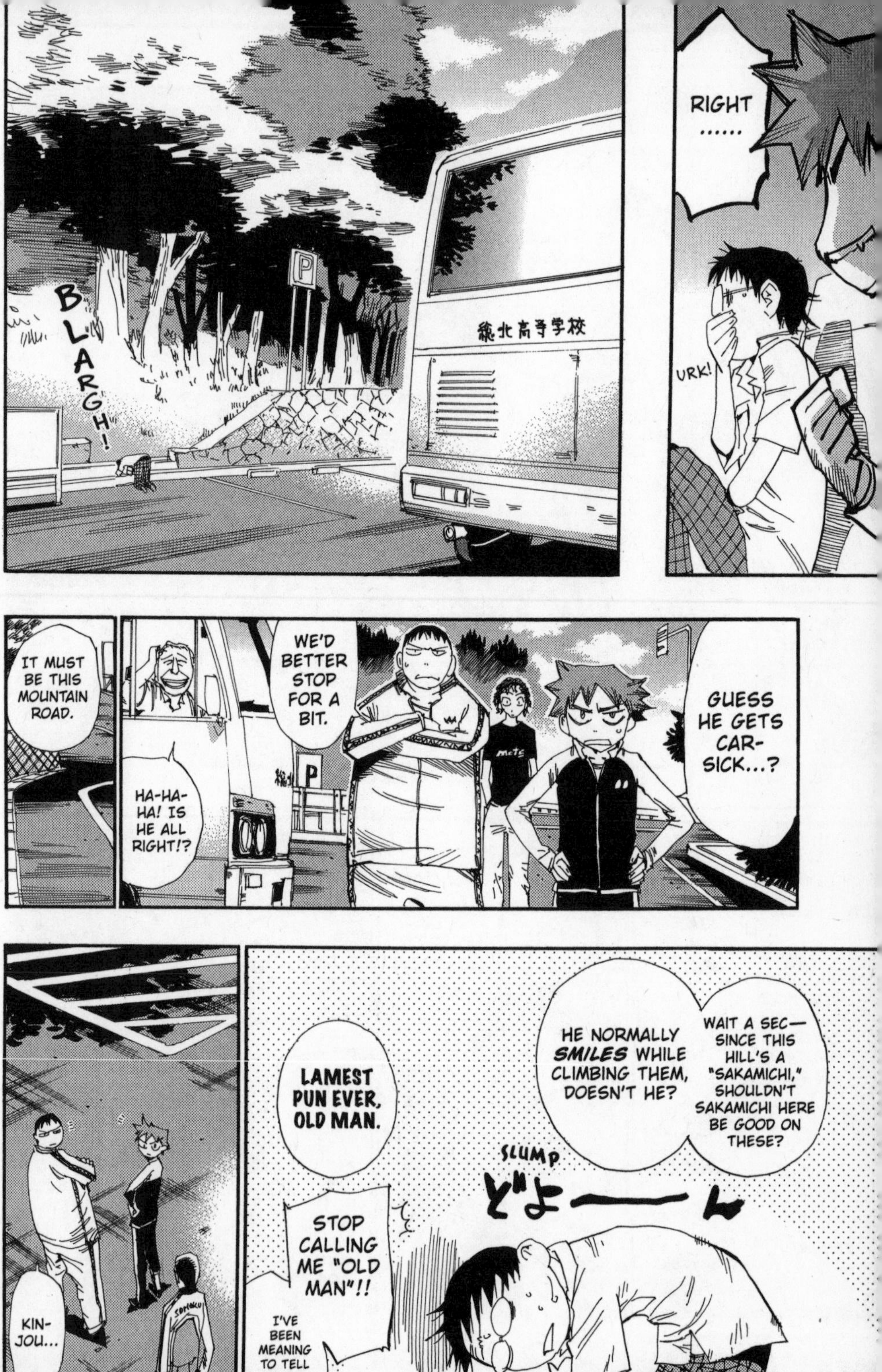
RIGHT ......
URK!
BLARGH!
GUESS HE GETS CAR-SICK...?
WE'D BETTER STOP FOR A BIT.
IT MUST BE THIS MOUNTAIN ROAD.
HA-HA-HA! IS HE ALL RIGHT!?
WAIT A SEC—SINCE THIS HILL'S A "SAKAMICHI," SHOULDN'T SAKAMICHI HERE BE GOOD ON THESE?
HE NORMALLY SMILES WHILE CLIMBING THEM, DOESN'T HE?
LAMEST PUN EVER, OLD MAN.
SLUMP
どよーーん
STOP CALLING ME "OLD MAN"!!
I'VE BEEN MEANING TO TELL YOU—
KIN-JOU...

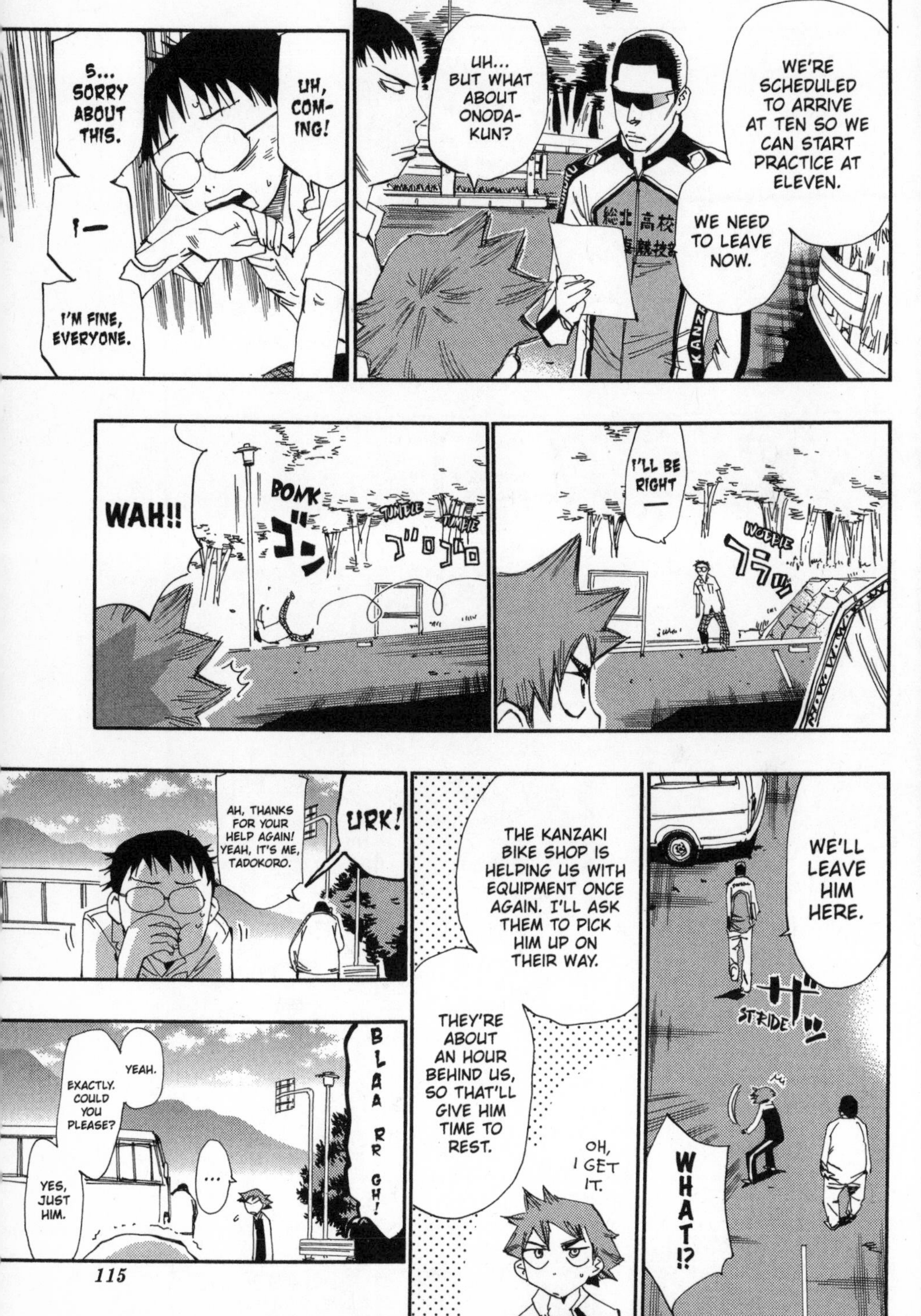
WE'RE SCHEDULED TO ARRIVE AT TEN SO WE CAN START PRACTICE AT ELEVEN.
WE NEED TO LEAVE NOW.
UH... BUT WHAT ABOUT ONODA-KUN?
UH, COMING!
S... SORRY ABOUT THIS.
I—
I'M FINE, EVERYONE.
I'LL BE RIGHT—
WOBBLE
フラッ
BONK
ゴン
TUMBLE TUMBLE
ゴロゴロ
WAH!!
WE'LL LEAVE HIM HERE.
STRIDE
ザッ
WHAT!?
THE KANZAKI BIKE SHOP IS HELPING US WITH EQUIPMENT ONCE AGAIN. I'LL ASK THEM TO PICK HIM UP ON THEIR WAY.
THEY'RE ABOUT AN HOUR BEHIND US, SO THAT'LL GIVE HIM TIME TO REST.
OH, I GET IT.
URK!
AH, THANKS FOR YOUR HELP AGAIN! YEAH, IT'S ME, TADOKORO.
BLAARRGH!
YEAH.
EXACTLY. COULD YOU PLEASE?
...
YES, JUST HIM.

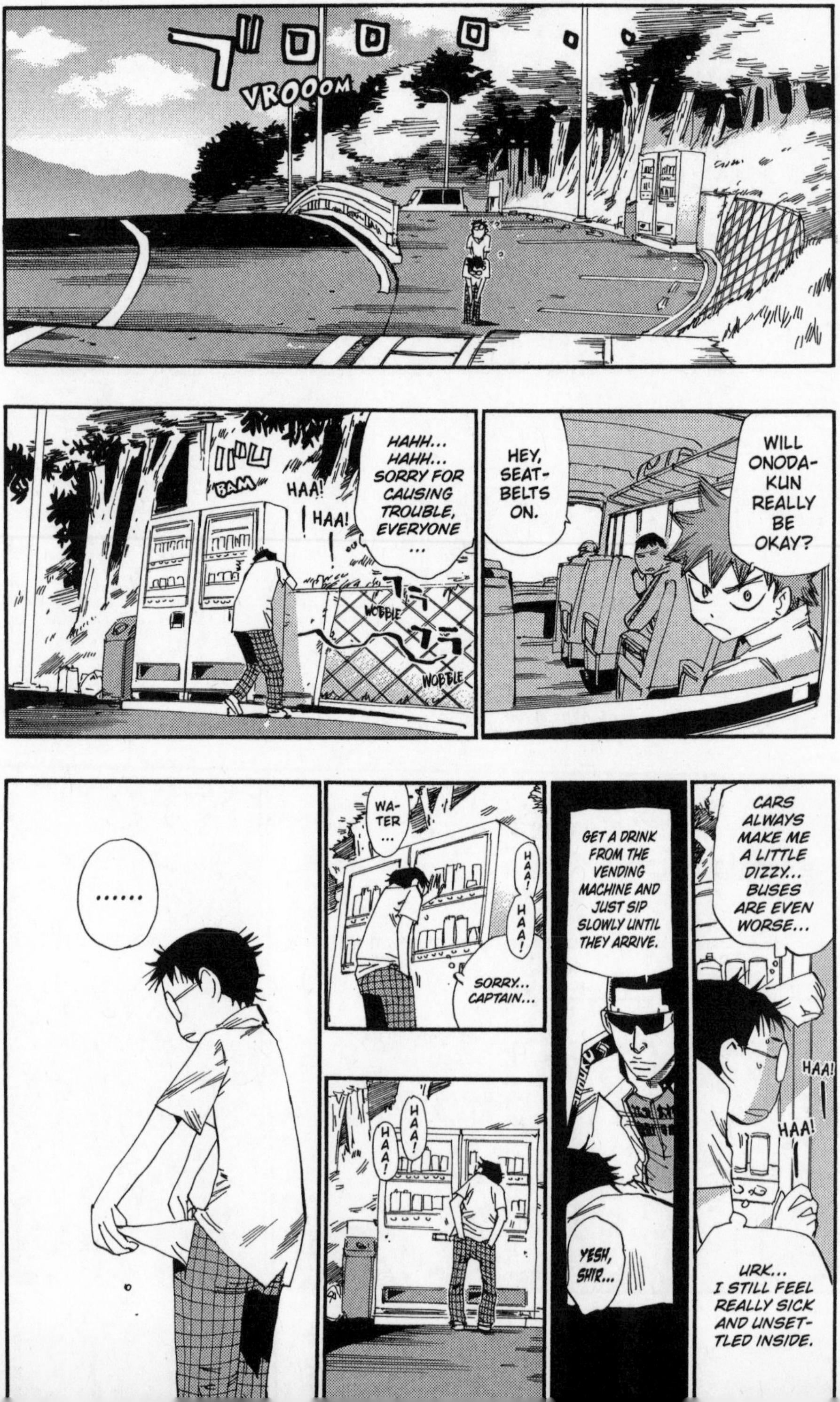
VROOOM
WILL ONODA-KUN REALLY BE OKAY?
HEY, SEAT-BELTS ON.
HAHH... HAHH... SORRY FOR CAUSING TROUBLE, EVERYONE...
BAM
HAA!
HAA!
WOBBLE
WOBBLE
CARS ALWAYS MAKE ME A LITTLE DIZZY... BUSES ARE EVEN WORSE...
HAA!
HAA!
URK... I STILL FEEL REALLY SICK AND UNSET-TLED INSIDE.
GET A DRINK FROM THE VENDING MACHINE AND JUST SIP SLOWLY UNTIL THEY ARRIVE.
YESH, SHIR...
WA-TER...
HAA!
HAA!
SORRY... CAPTAIN...
HAA!
HAA!
......

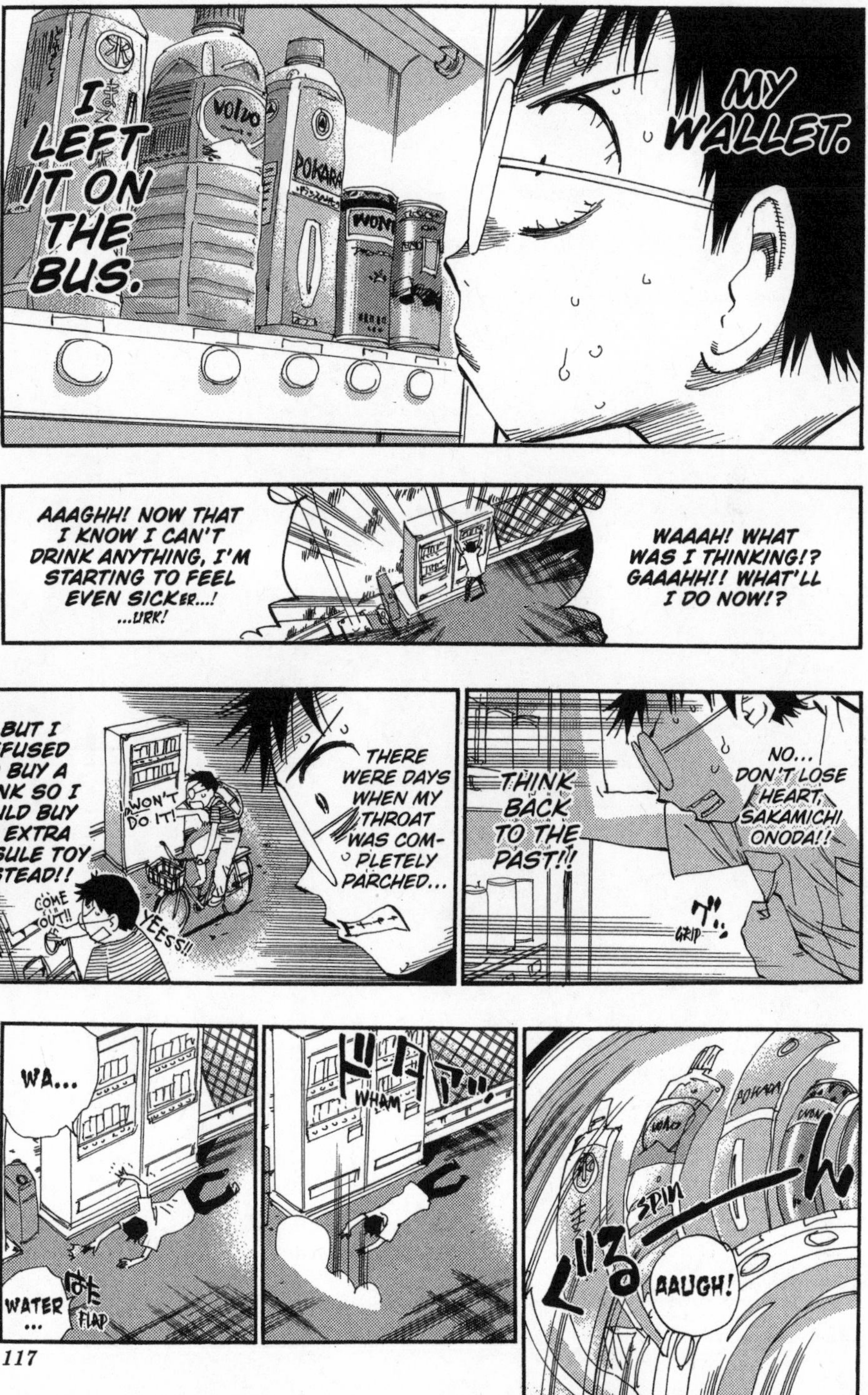
MY WALLET.
I LEFT IT ON THE BUS.
WAAAH! WHAT WAS I THINKING!? GAAAHH!! WHAT'LL I DO NOW!?
AAAGHH! NOW THAT I KNOW I CAN'T DRINK ANYTHING, I'M STARTING TO FEEL EVEN SICKer...! ...URK!
NO... DON'T LOSE HEART, SAKAMICHI ONODA!!
THINK BACK TO THE PAST!!
GRIP
THERE WERE DAYS WHEN MY THROAT WAS COMPLETELY PARCHED...
...BUT I REFUSED TO BUY A DRINK SO I COULD BUY AN EXTRA CAPSULE TOY INSTEAD!!
I WON'T DO IT!
YEESS!!
COME OUT!!
SPIN
AAUGH!
WHAM
WA...
WATER ...
FLAP

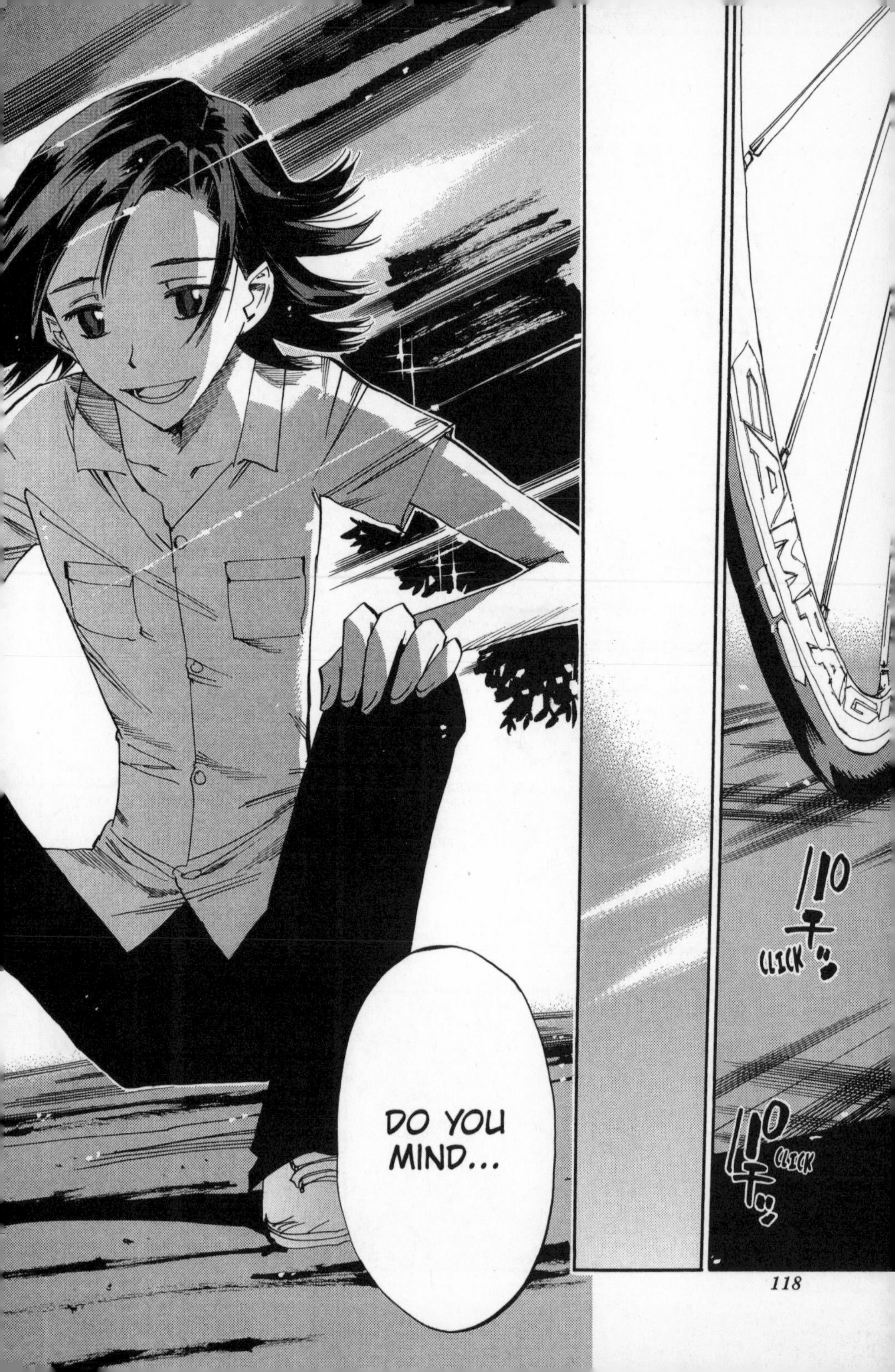
CLICK
CLICK
DO YOU MIND...

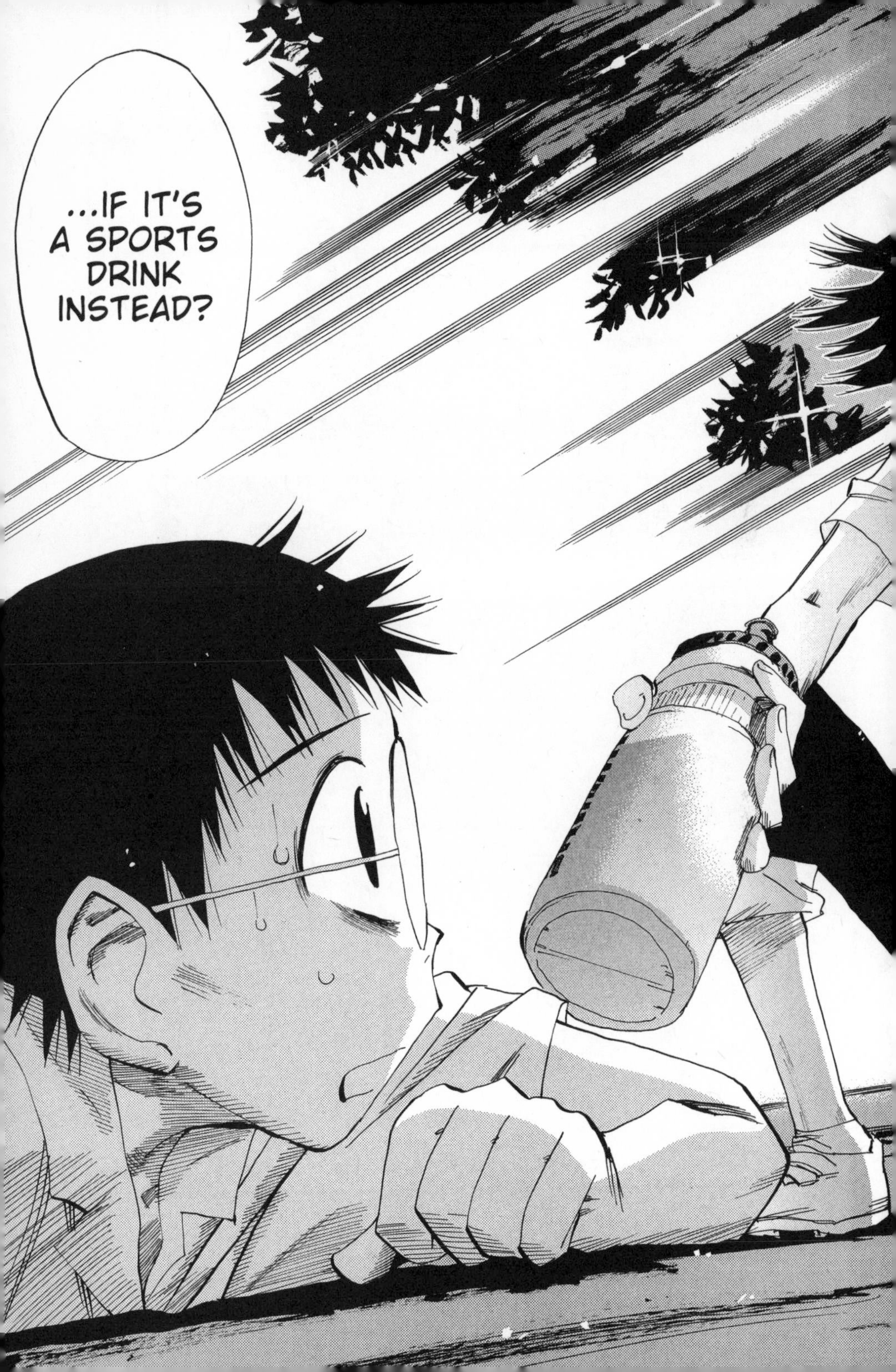
...IF IT'S A SPORTS DRINK INSTEAD?

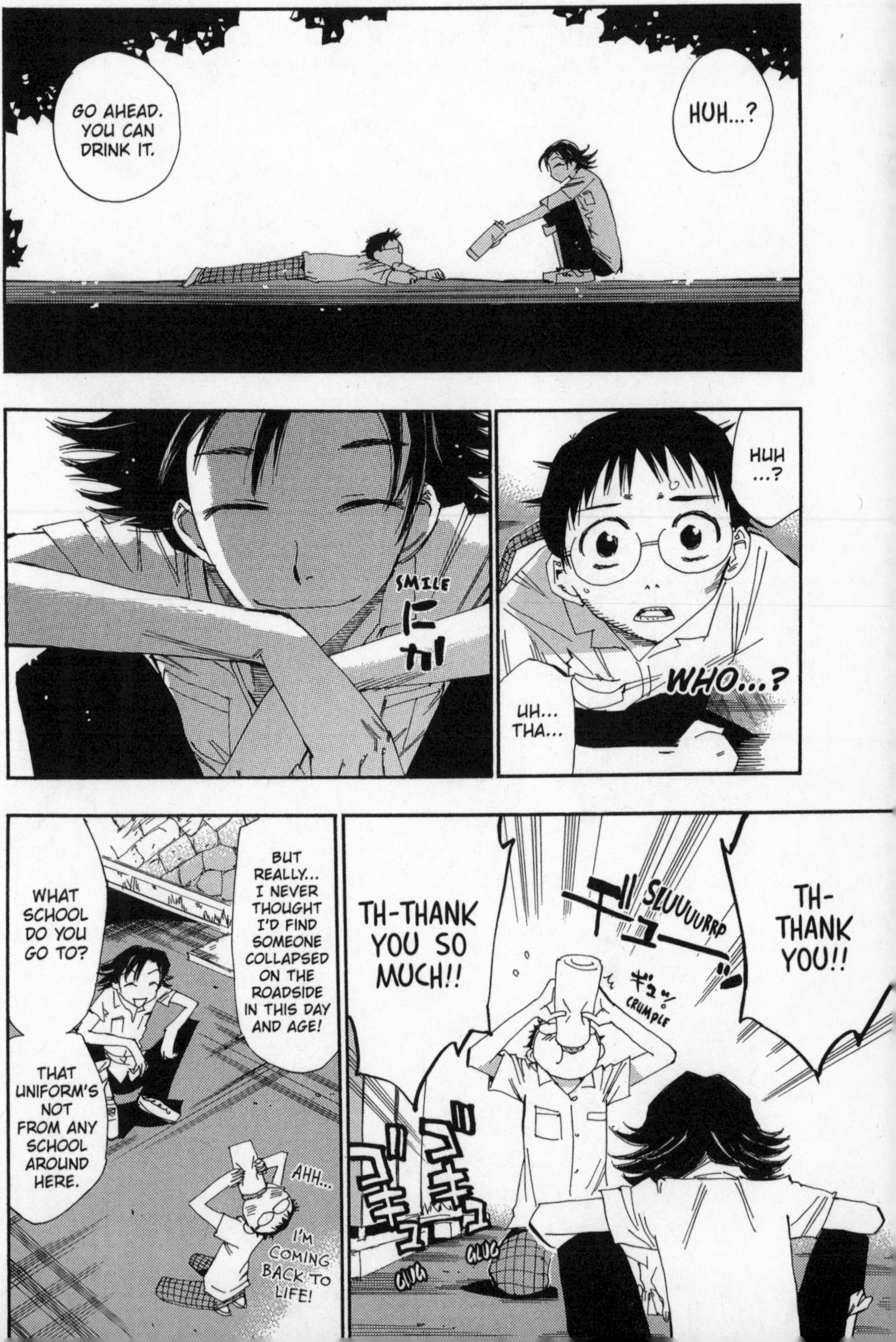
HUH...?
GO AHEAD. YOU CAN DRINK IT.
HUH ...?
WHO...?
UH... THA...
SMILE
ニカ
TH-THANK YOU!!
SLUUUURRP
ギュッ
CRUMPLE
TH-THANK YOU SO MUCH!!
GLUG
GLUG
BUT REALLY... I NEVER THOUGHT I'D FIND SOMEONE COLLAPSED ON THE ROADSIDE IN THIS DAY AND AGE!
WHAT SCHOOL DO YOU GO TO?
THAT UNIFORM'S NOT FROM ANY SCHOOL AROUND HERE.
AHH...
I'M COMING BACK TO LIFE!

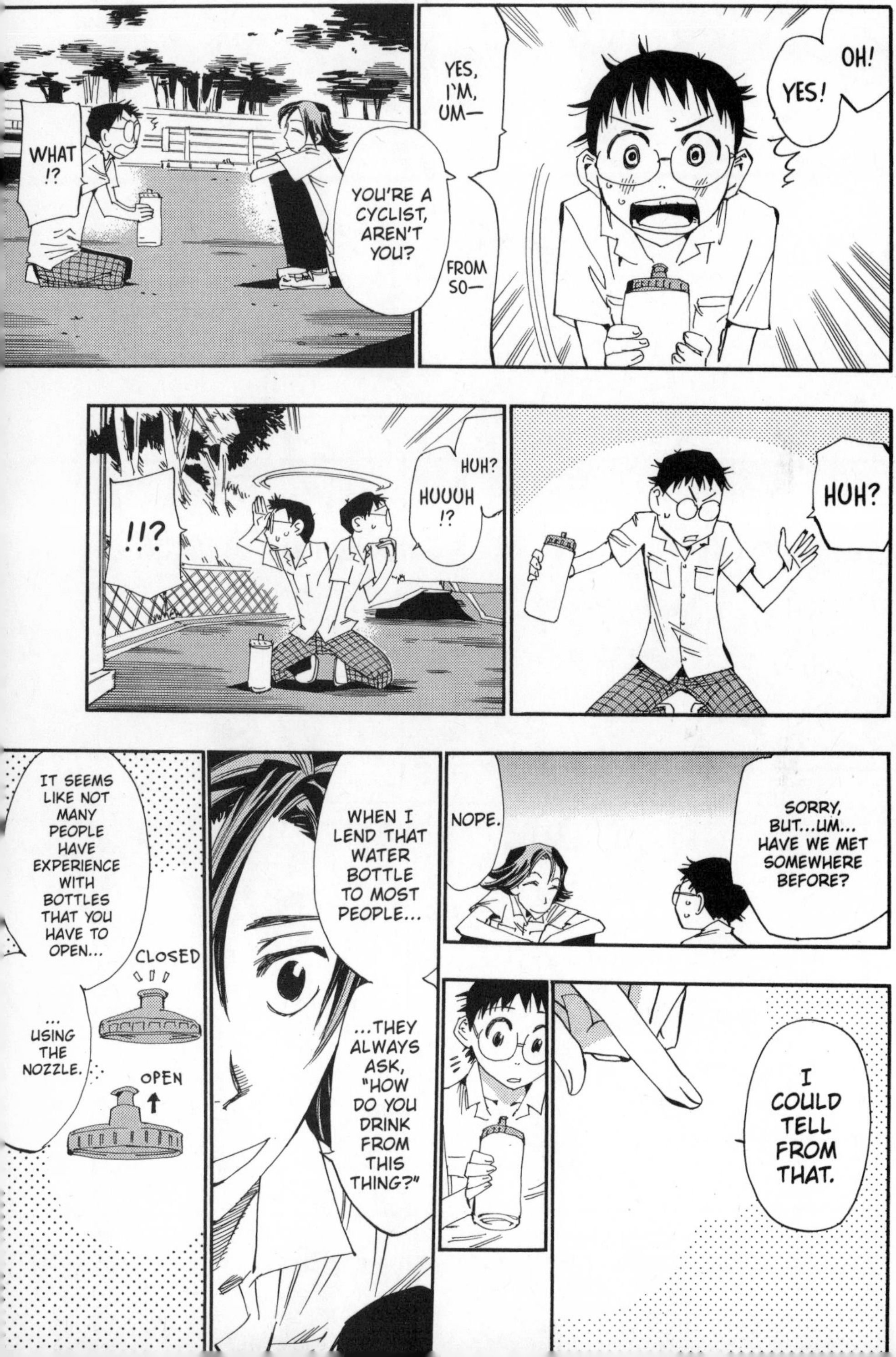
OH! YES!
YES, I'M, UM—
FROM SO—
YOU'RE A CYCLIST, AREN'T YOU?
WHAT !?
HUH?
HUH? HUUUH !?
!!?
SORRY, BUT...UM... HAVE WE MET SOMEWHERE BEFORE?
NOPE.
I COULD TELL FROM THAT.
WHEN I LEND THAT WATER BOTTLE TO MOST PEOPLE...
...THEY ALWAYS ASK, "HOW DO YOU DRINK FROM THIS THING?"
IT SEEMS LIKE NOT MANY PEOPLE HAVE EXPERIENCE WITH BOTTLES THAT YOU HAVE TO OPEN...
...USING THE NOZZLE.
CLOSED
OPEN

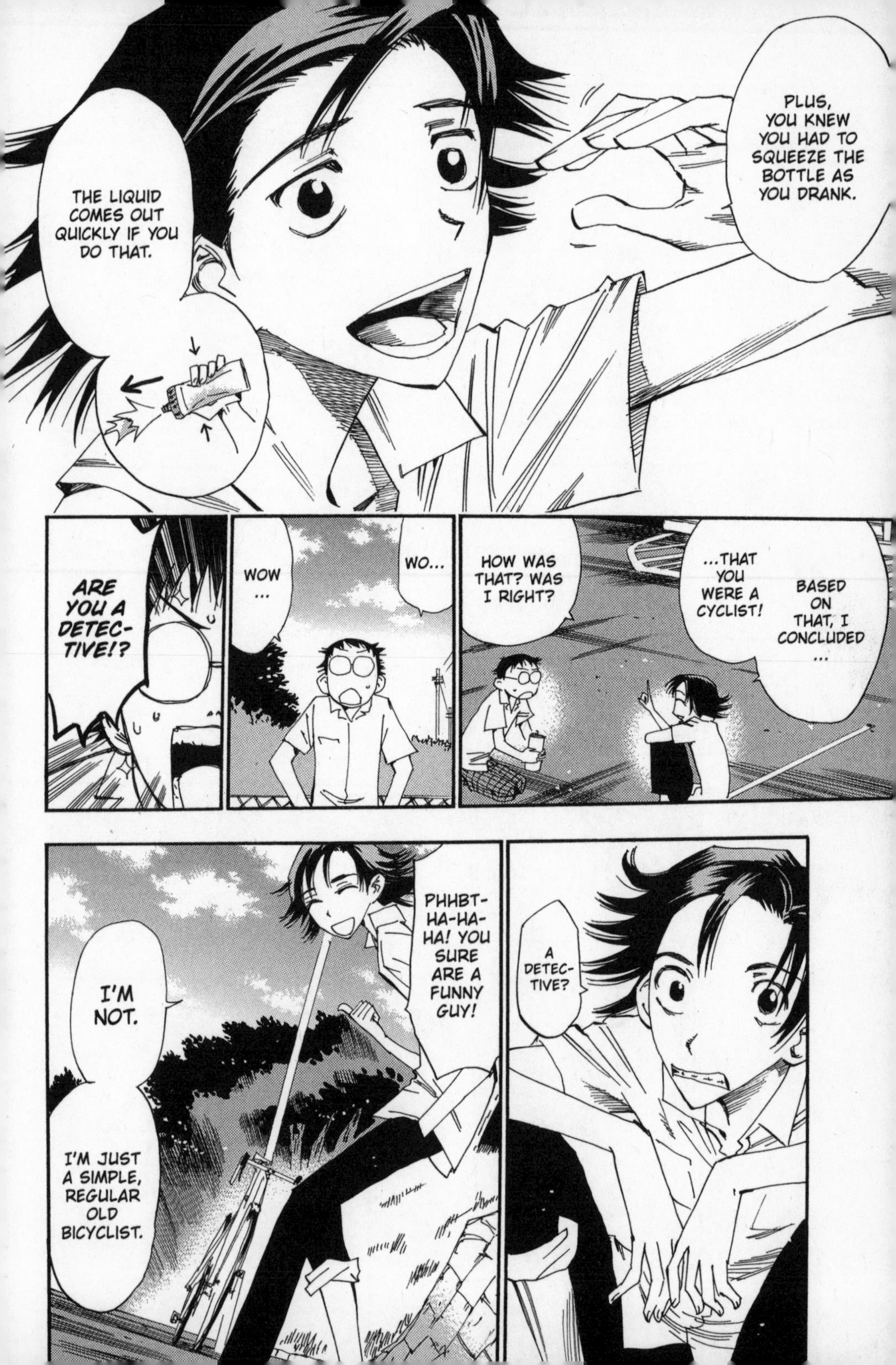
PLUS, YOU KNEW YOU HAD TO SQUEEZE THE BOTTLE AS YOU DRANK.
THE LIQUID COMES OUT QUICKLY IF YOU DO THAT.
BASED ON THAT, I CONCLUDED ...
...THAT YOU WERE A CYCLIST!
HOW WAS THAT? WAS I RIGHT?
WO...
WOW ...
ARE YOU A DETECTIVE!?
A DETECTIVE?
PHHBT-HA-HA-HA! YOU SURE ARE A FUNNY GUY!
I'M NOT.
I'M JUST A SIMPLE, REGULAR OLD BICYCLIST.

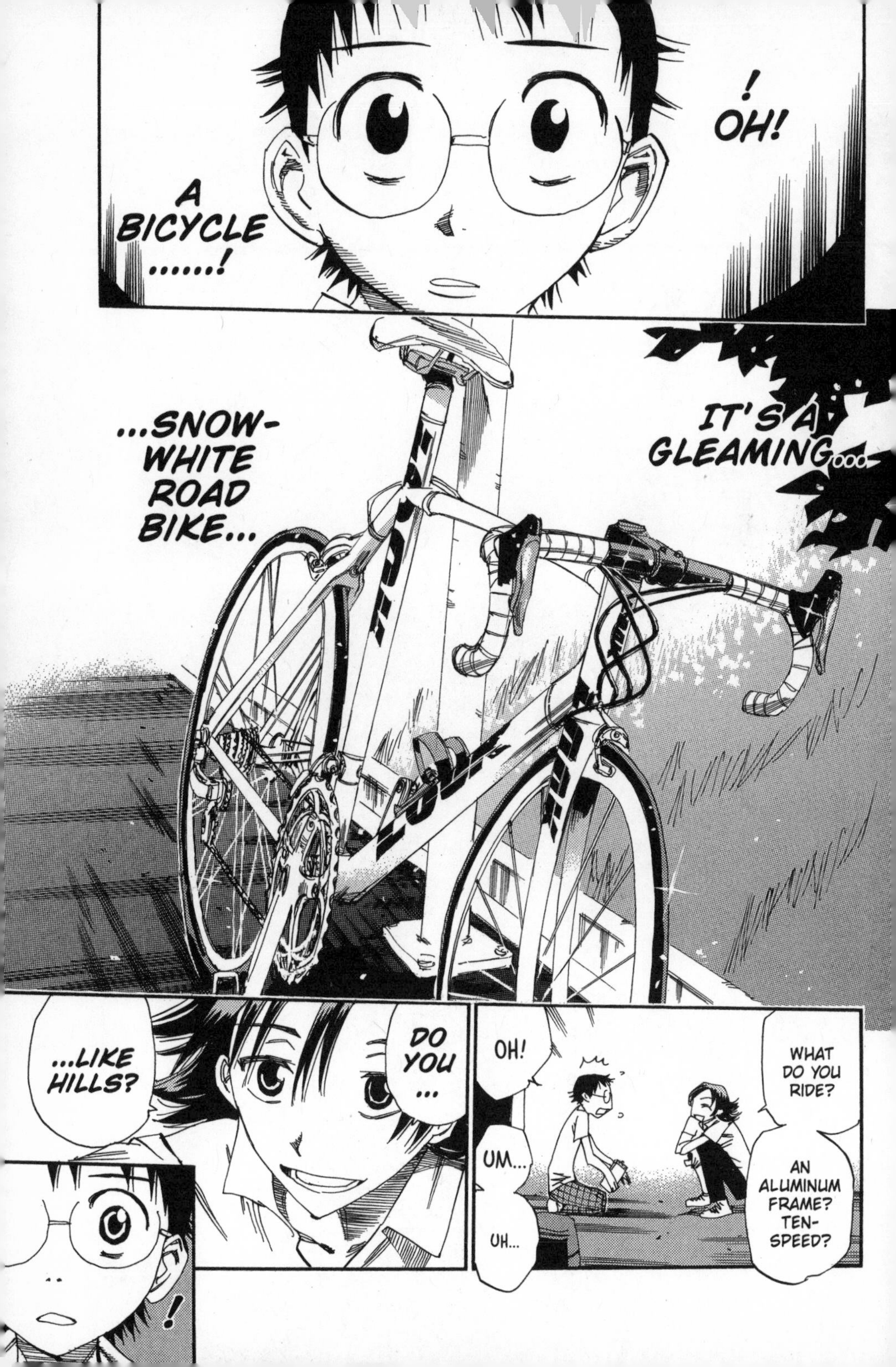
! OH!
A BICYCLE ......!
IT'S A GLEAMING...
...SNOW-WHITE ROAD BIKE...
WHAT DO YOU RIDE?
AN ALUMINUM FRAME? TEN-SPEED?
OH!
UM...
UH...
DO YOU ...
...LIKE HILLS?
!

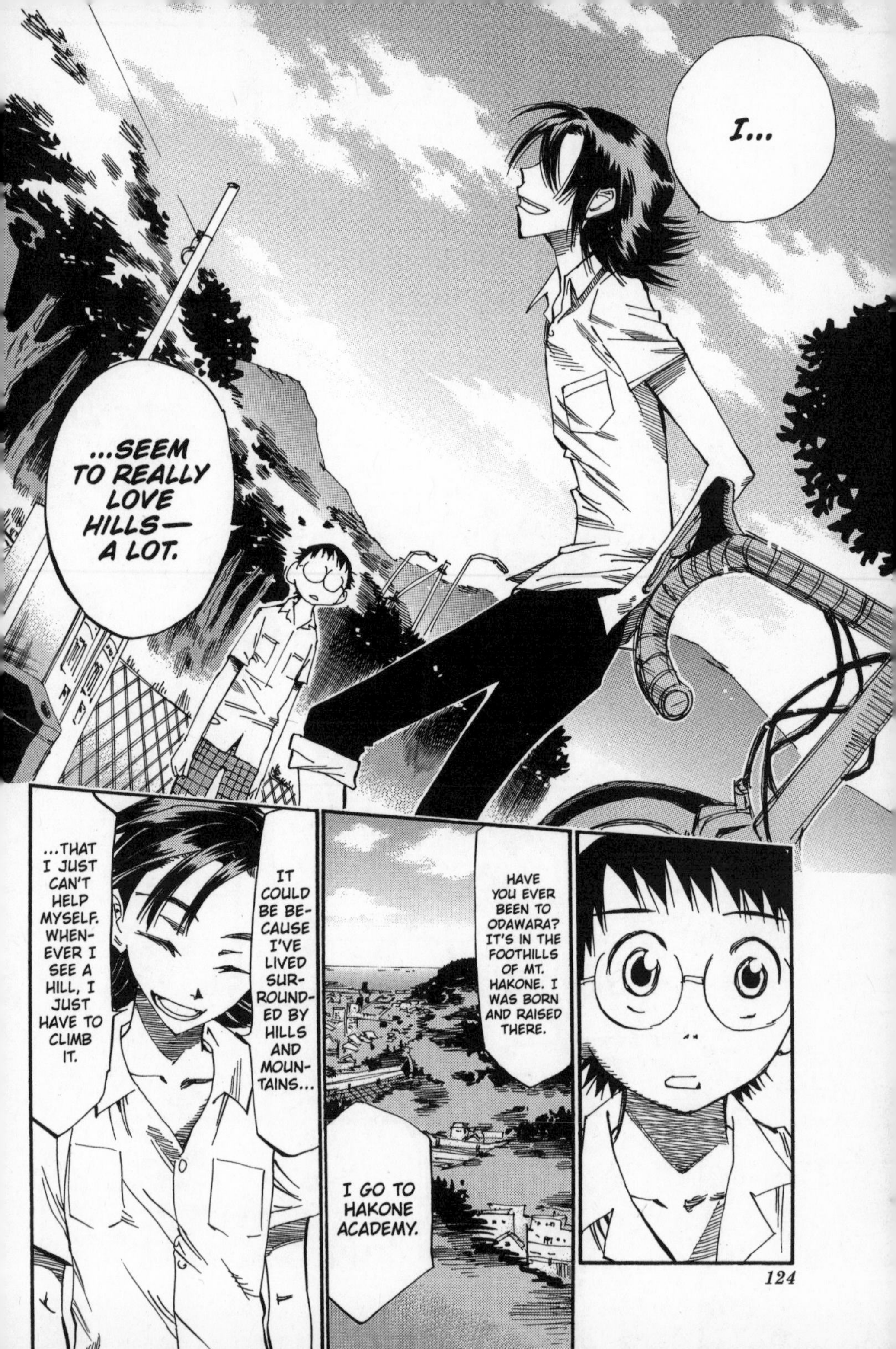
I...
...SEEM TO REALLY LOVE HILLS— A LOT.
HAVE YOU EVER BEEN TO ODAWARA? IT'S IN THE FOOTHILLS OF MT. HAKONE. I WAS BORN AND RAISED THERE.
I GO TO HAKONE ACADEMY.
IT COULD BE BE-CAUSE I'VE LIVED SUR-ROUND-ED BY HILLS AND MOUN-TAINS...
...THAT I JUST CAN'T HELP MYSELF. WHEN-EVER I SEE A HILL, I JUST HAVE TO CLIMB IT.

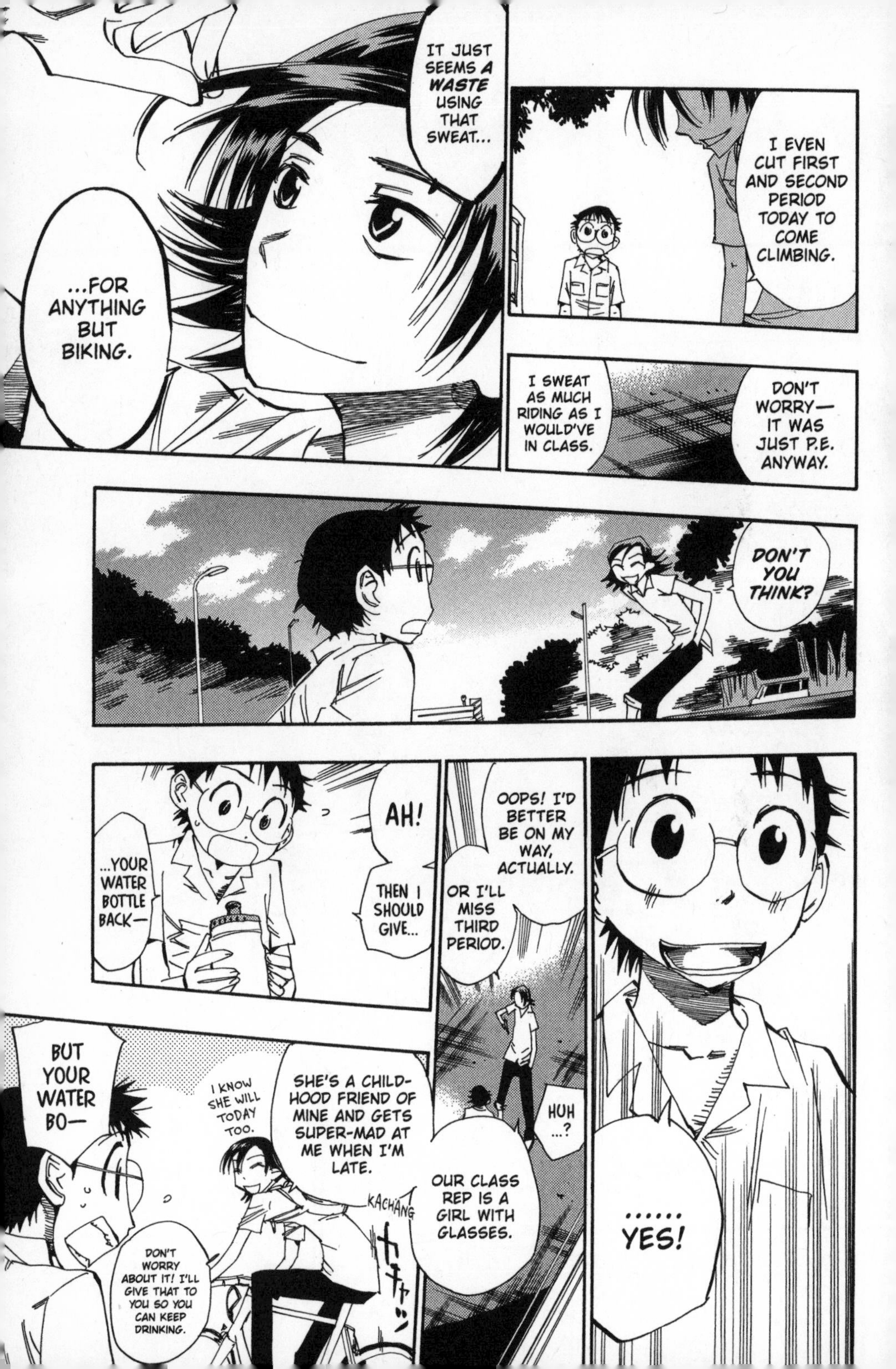
I EVEN CUT FIRST AND SECOND PERIOD TODAY TO COME CLIMBING.
DON'T WORRY— IT WAS JUST P.E. ANYWAY.
I SWEAT AS MUCH RIDING AS I WOULD'VE IN CLASS.
IT JUST SEEMS A WASTE USING THAT SWEAT...
...FOR ANYTHING BUT BIKING.
DON'T YOU THINK?
......YES!
OOPS! I'D BETTER BE ON MY WAY, ACTUALLY.
OR I'LL MISS THIRD PERIOD.
HUH ...?
OUR CLASS REP IS A GIRL WITH GLASSES.
AH!
THEN I SHOULD GIVE...
...YOUR WATER BOTTLE BACK—
SHE'S A CHILDHOOD FRIEND OF MINE AND GETS SUPER-MAD AT ME WHEN I'M LATE.
I KNOW SHE WILL TODAY TOO.
KACHANG
BUT YOUR WATER BO—
DON'T WORRY ABOUT IT! I'LL GIVE THAT TO YOU SO YOU CAN KEEP DRINKING.

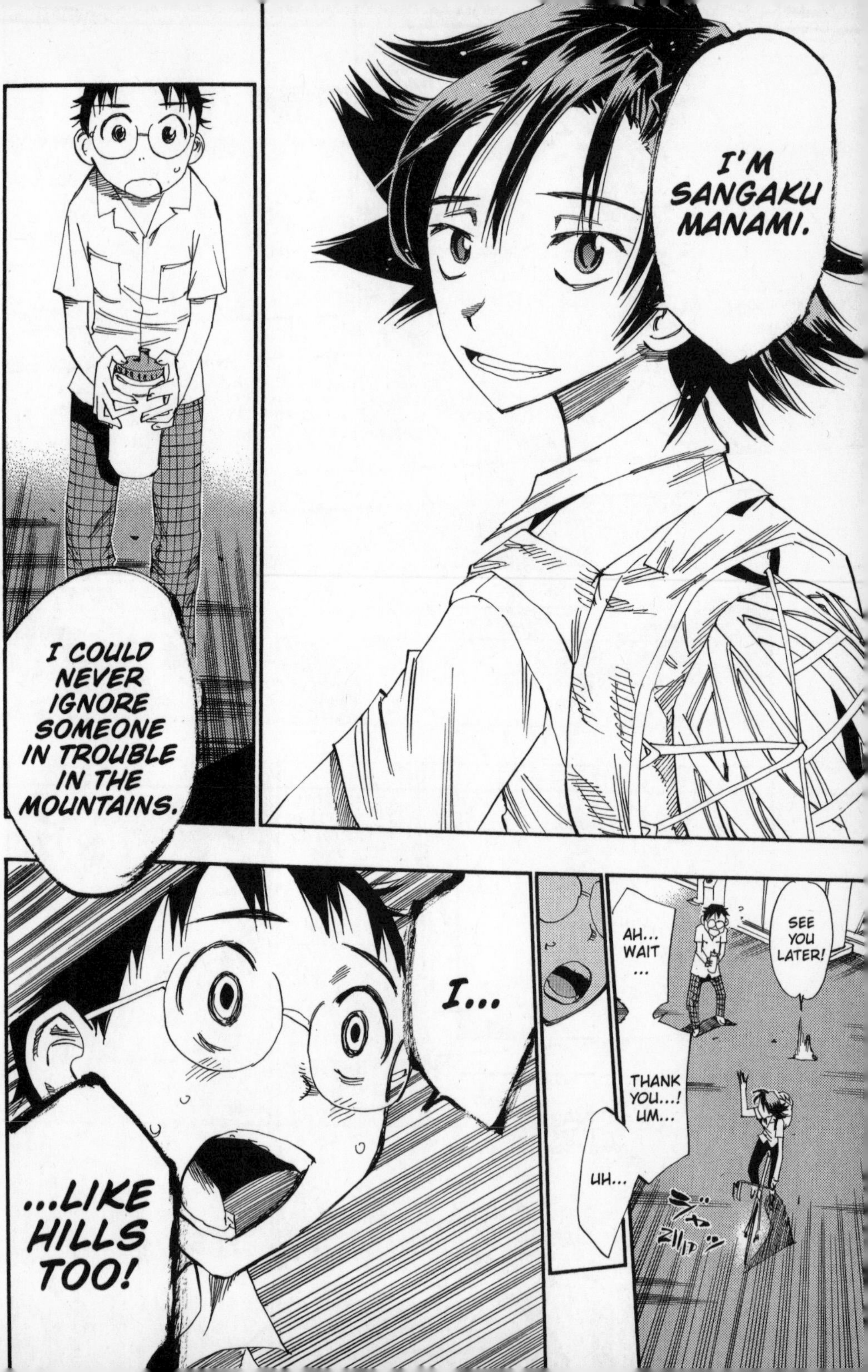
I'M SANGAKU MANAMI.
I COULD NEVER IGNORE SOMEONE IN TROUBLE IN THE MOUNTAINS.
SEE YOU LATER!
AH... WAIT ...
THANK YOU...! UM...
UH...
ZIIIP
I...
...LIKE HILLS TOO!

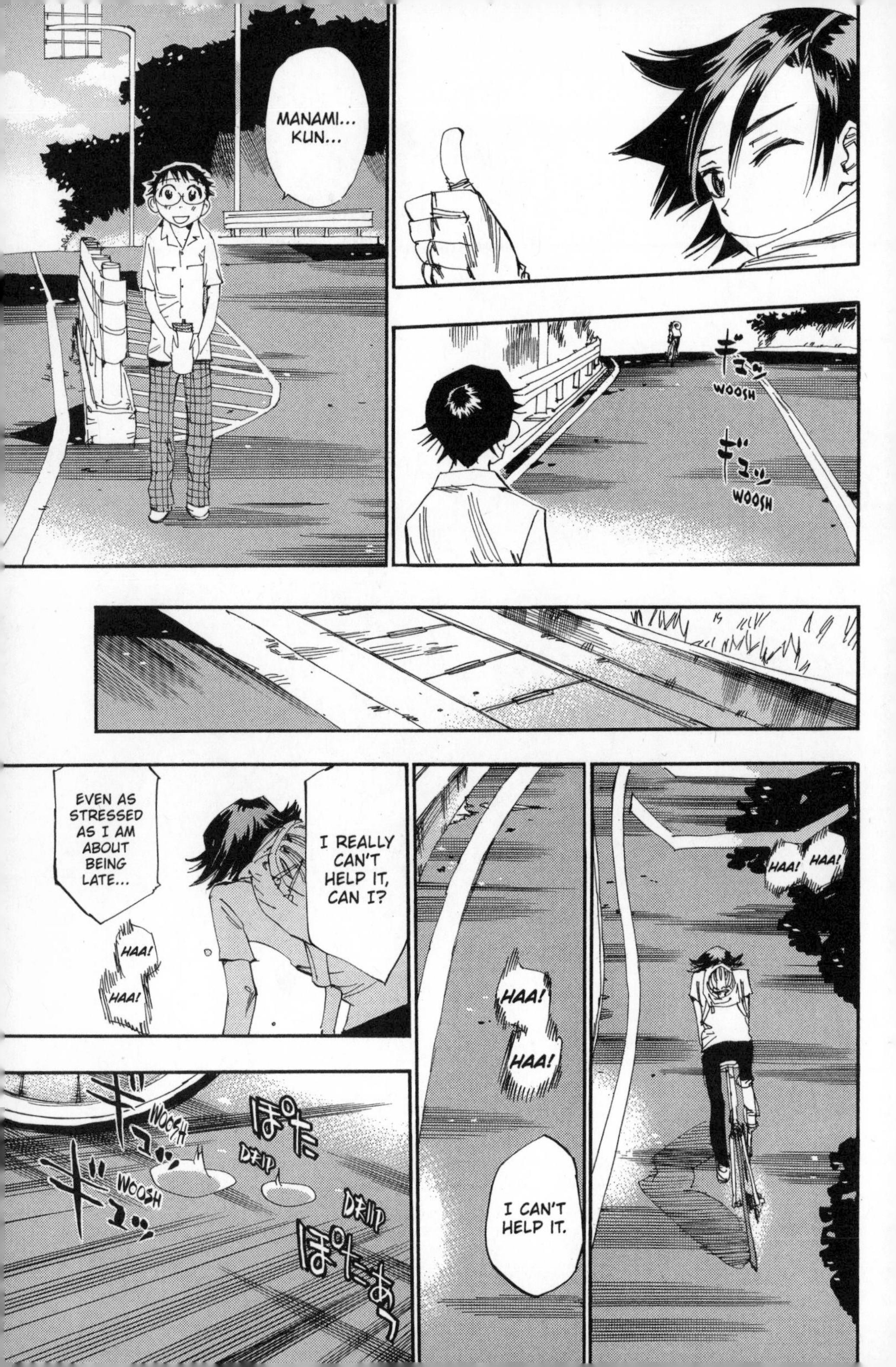

ギコッ
WOOSH
ギコッ
WOOSH
MANAMI... KUN...
HAA! HAA!
HAA!
HAA!
I CAN'T HELP IT.
I REALLY CAN'T HELP IT, CAN I?
EVEN AS STRESSED AS I AM ABOUT BEING LATE...
HAA!
HAA!
ぽた
DRIP
ぽたぁっ
DRIP
ギコッ
WOOSH
ギコッ
WOOSH

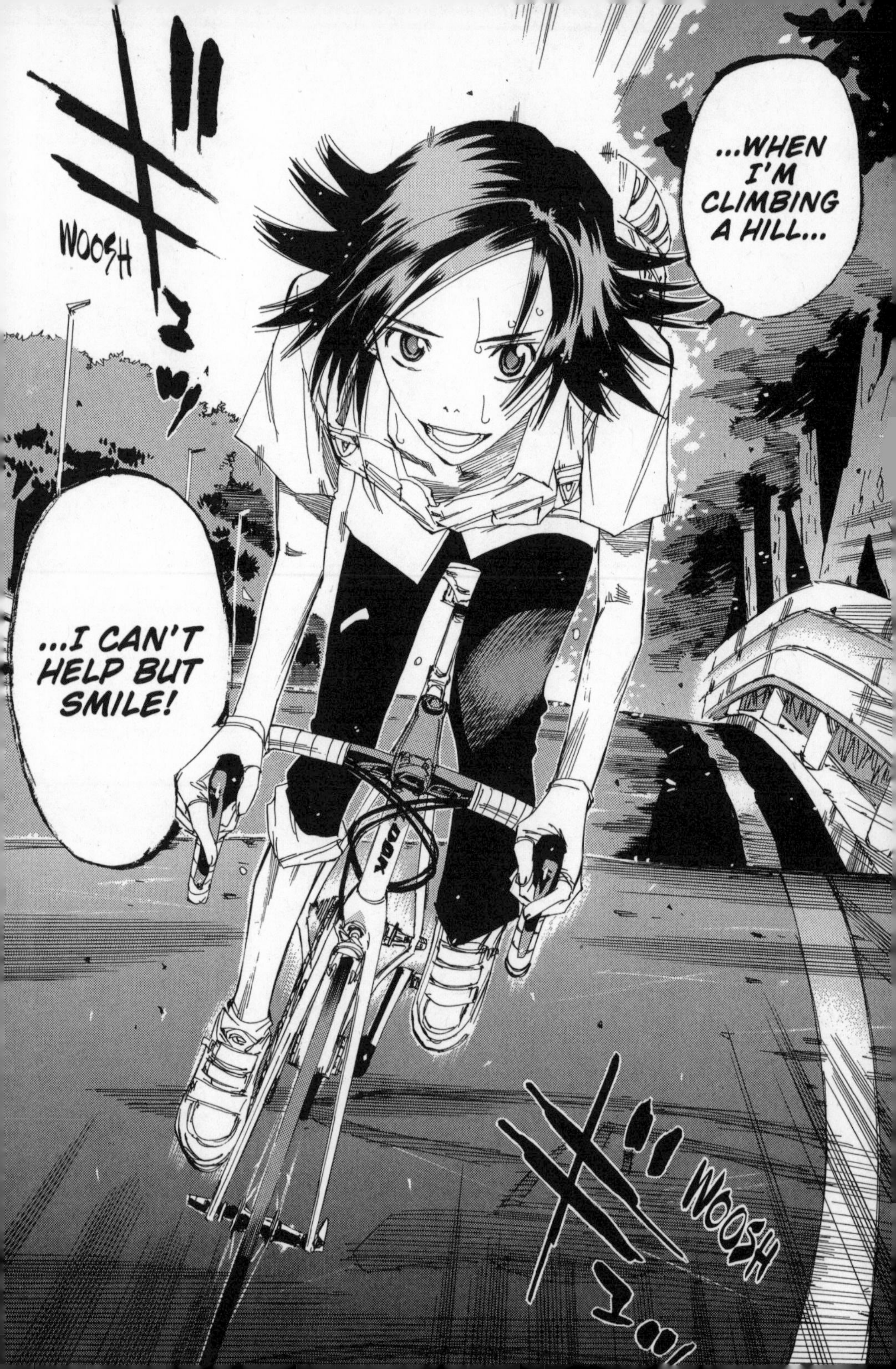
...WHEN I'M CLIMBING A HILL...
WOOSH
...I CAN'T HELP BUT SMILE!
WOOSH

RIDE.41 THE FIRST DAY OF TRAINING CAMP!

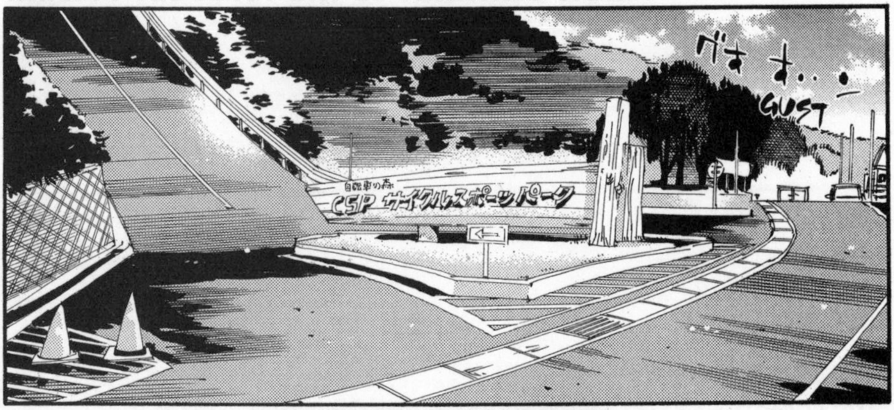
GUST

SIGN: BICYCLE FOREST, CSP CYCLING SPORTS PARK

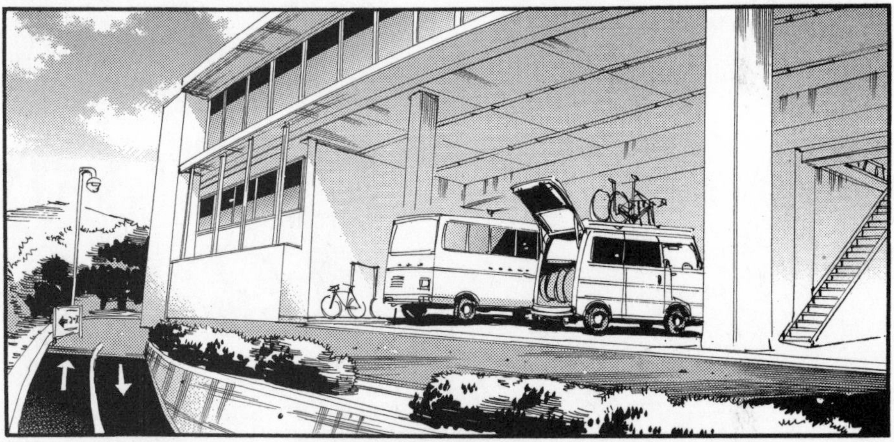

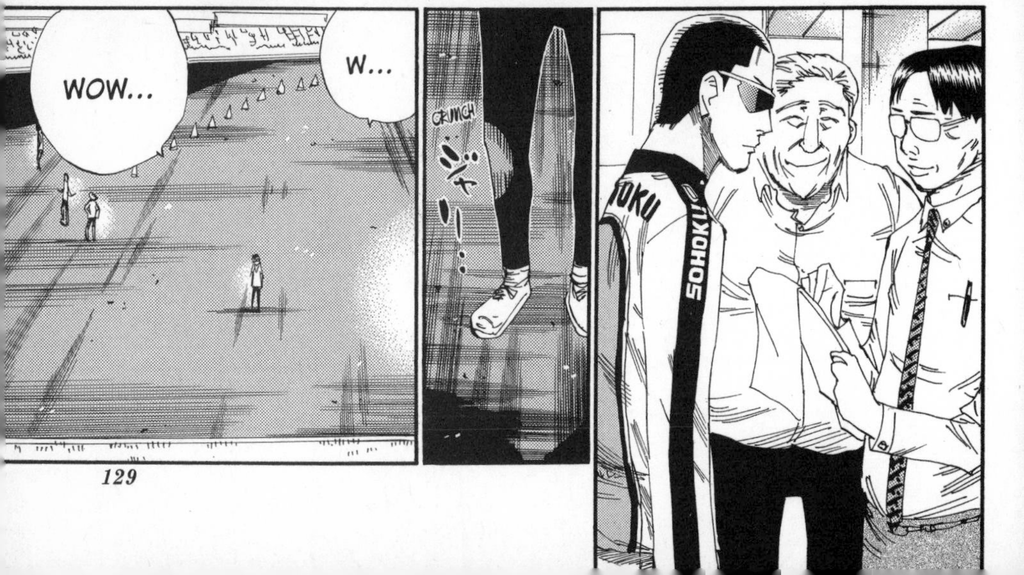
SOHOKU
CRUNCH
W...
WOW...

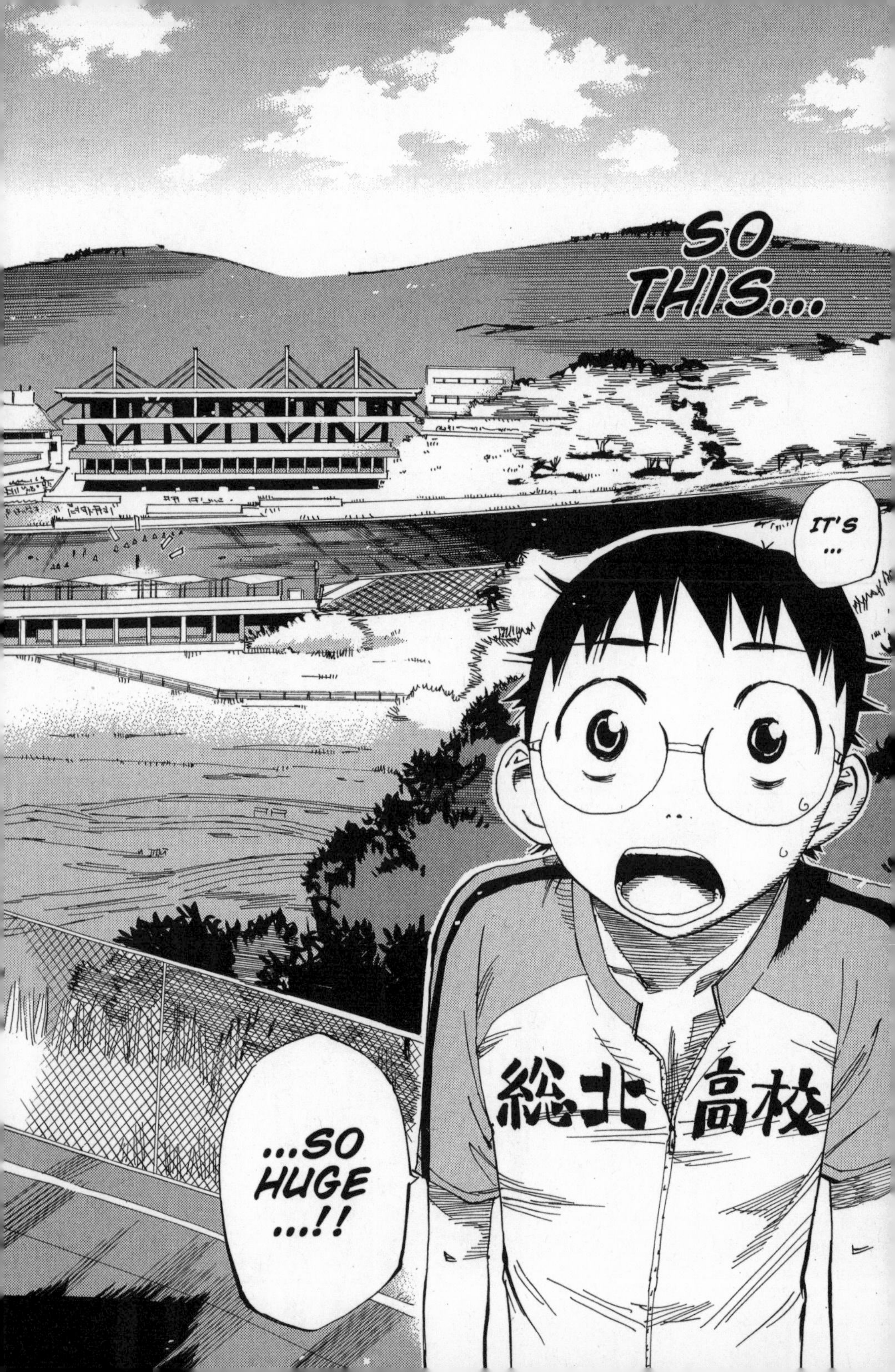
SO THIS...
IT'S ...
総北 高校
...SO HUGE ...!!

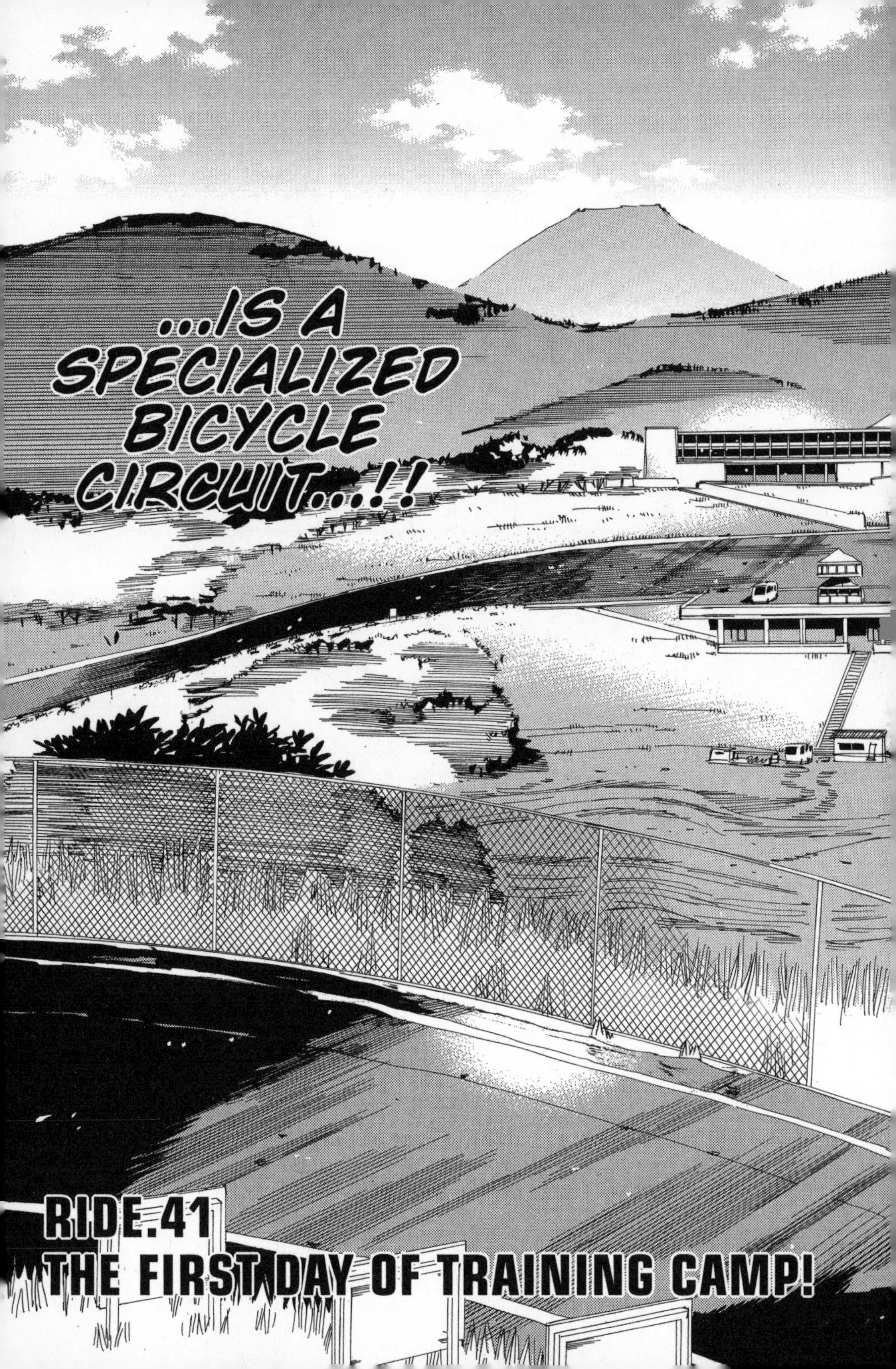
...IS A SPECIALIZED BICYCLE CIRCUIT...!!
RIDE.41
THE FIRST DAY OF TRAINING CAMP!

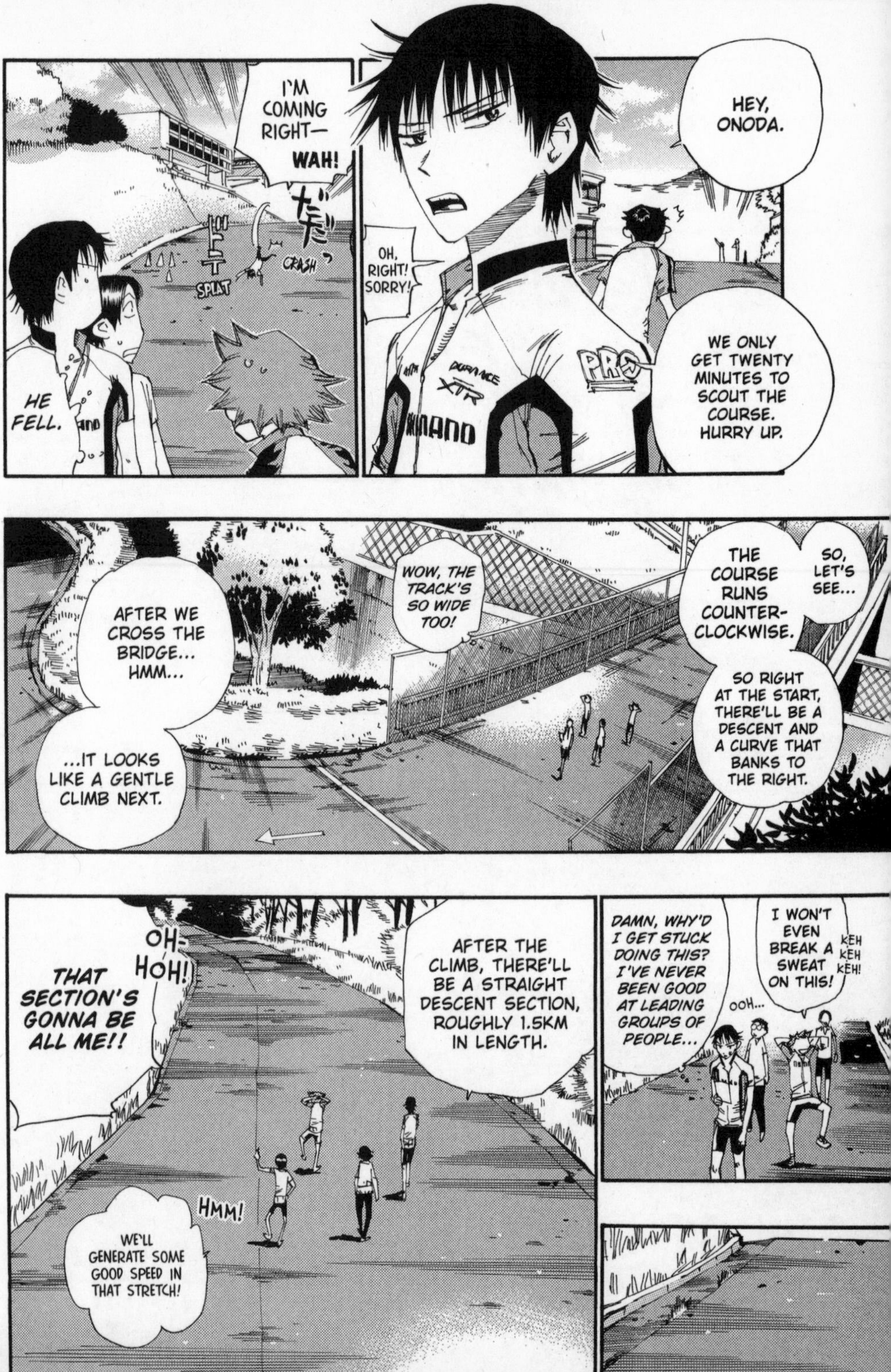
HEY, ONODA.
WE ONLY GET TWENTY MINUTES TO SCOUT THE COURSE. HURRY UP.
OH, RIGHT! SORRY!
I'M COMING RIGHT—
WAH!
CRASH
SPLAT
HE FELL.
SO, LET'S SEE...
THE COURSE RUNS COUNTER-CLOCKWISE.
SO RIGHT AT THE START, THERE'LL BE A DESCENT AND A CURVE THAT BANKS TO THE RIGHT.
WOW, THE TRACK'S SO WIDE TOO!
AFTER WE CROSS THE BRIDGE... HMM...
...IT LOOKS LIKE A GENTLE CLIMB NEXT.
I WON'T EVEN BREAK A SWEAT ON THIS!
KEH KEH KEH!
DAMN, WHY'D I GET STUCK DOING THIS? I'VE NEVER BEEN GOOD AT LEADING GROUPS OF PEOPLE...
OOH...
AFTER THE CLIMB, THERE'LL BE A STRAIGHT DESCENT SECTION, ROUGHLY 1.5KM IN LENGTH.
OH-HOH!
THAT SECTION'S GONNA BE ALL ME!!
HMM!
WE'LL GENERATE SOME GOOD SPEED IN THAT STRETCH!

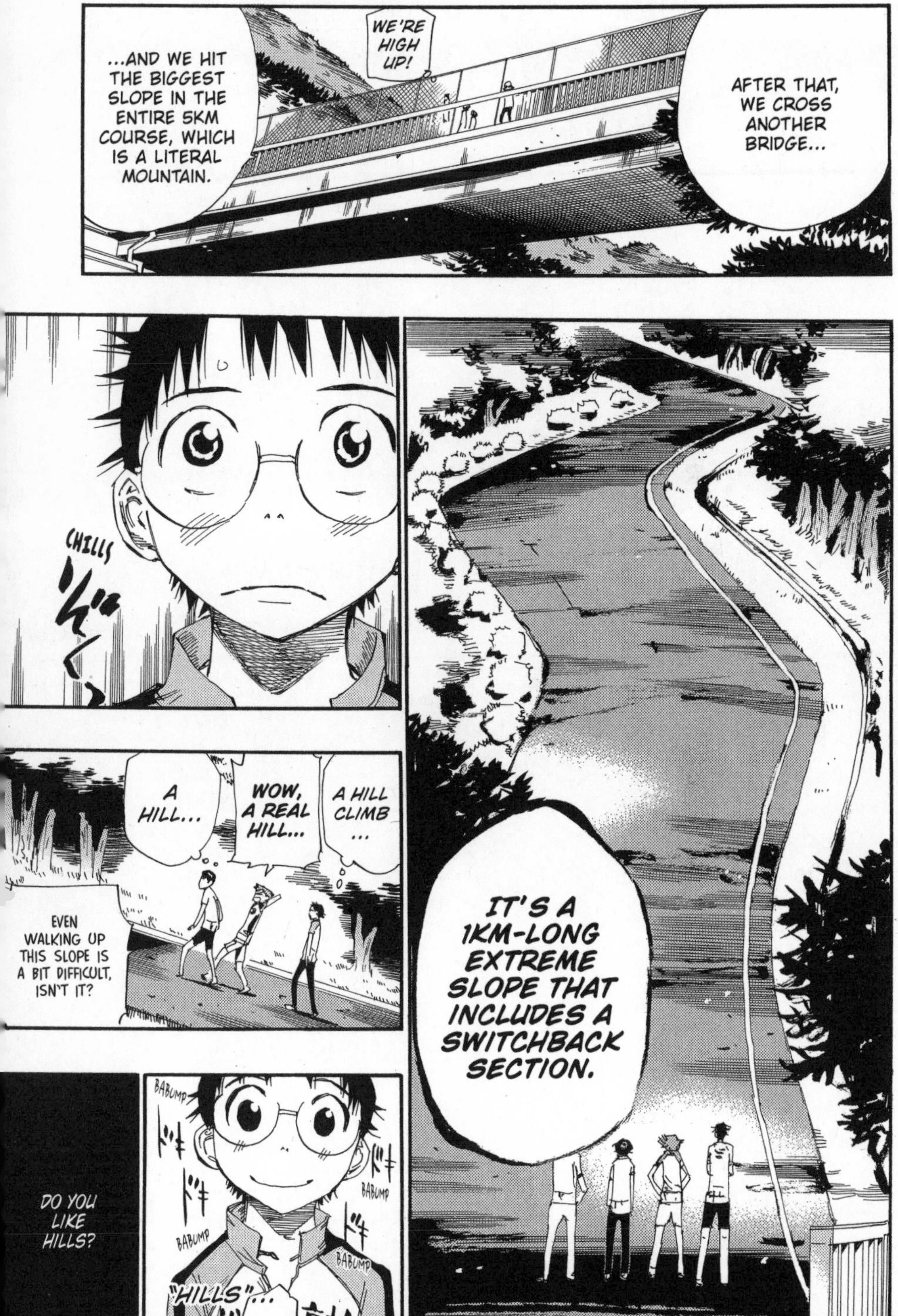
AFTER THAT, WE CROSS ANOTHER BRIDGE...
WE'RE HIGH UP!
...AND WE HIT THE BIGGEST SLOPE IN THE ENTIRE 5KM COURSE, WHICH IS A LITERAL MOUNTAIN.
IT'S A 1KM-LONG EXTREME SLOPE THAT INCLUDES A SWITCHBACK SECTION.
CHILLS
A HILL CLIMB...
WOW, A REAL HILL...
A HILL...
EVEN WALKING UP THIS SLOPE IS A BIT DIFFICULT, ISN'T IT?
BABUMP
BABUMP
BABUMP
BABUMP
"HILLS"...
高校
DO YOU LIKE HILLS?

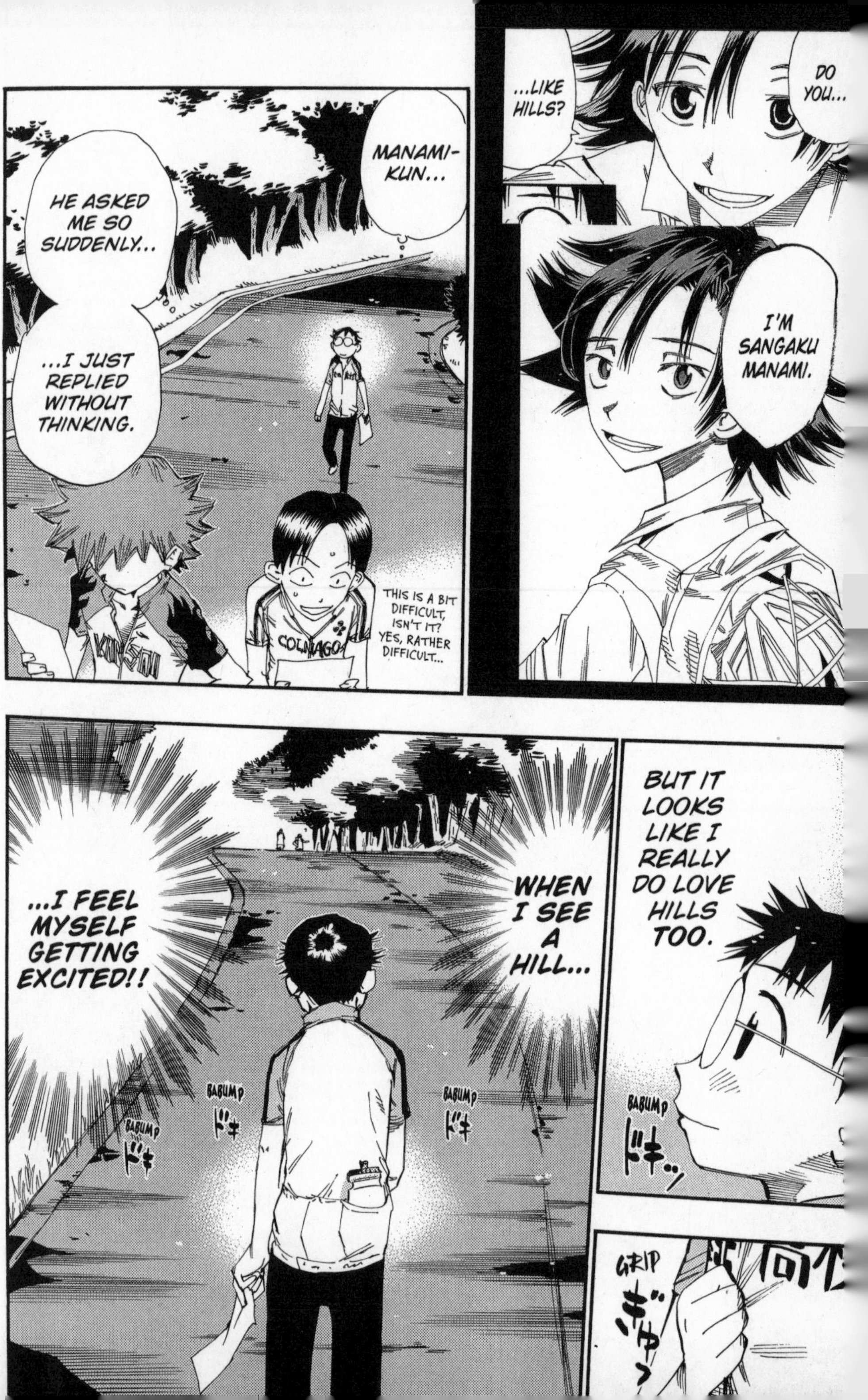
DO YOU...
...LIKE HILLS?
I'M SANGAKU MANAMI.
MANAMI-KUN...
HE ASKED ME SO SUDDENLY...
...I JUST REPLIED WITHOUT THINKING.
THIS IS A BIT DIFFICULT, ISN'T IT? YES, RATHER DIFFICULT...
BUT IT LOOKS LIKE I REALLY DO LOVE HILLS TOO.
BABUMP
ドキッ
GRIP
WHEN I SEE A HILL...
...I FEEL MYSELF GETTING EXCITED!!
BABUMP
ドキ
BABUMP
ドキ
BABUMP
ドキ

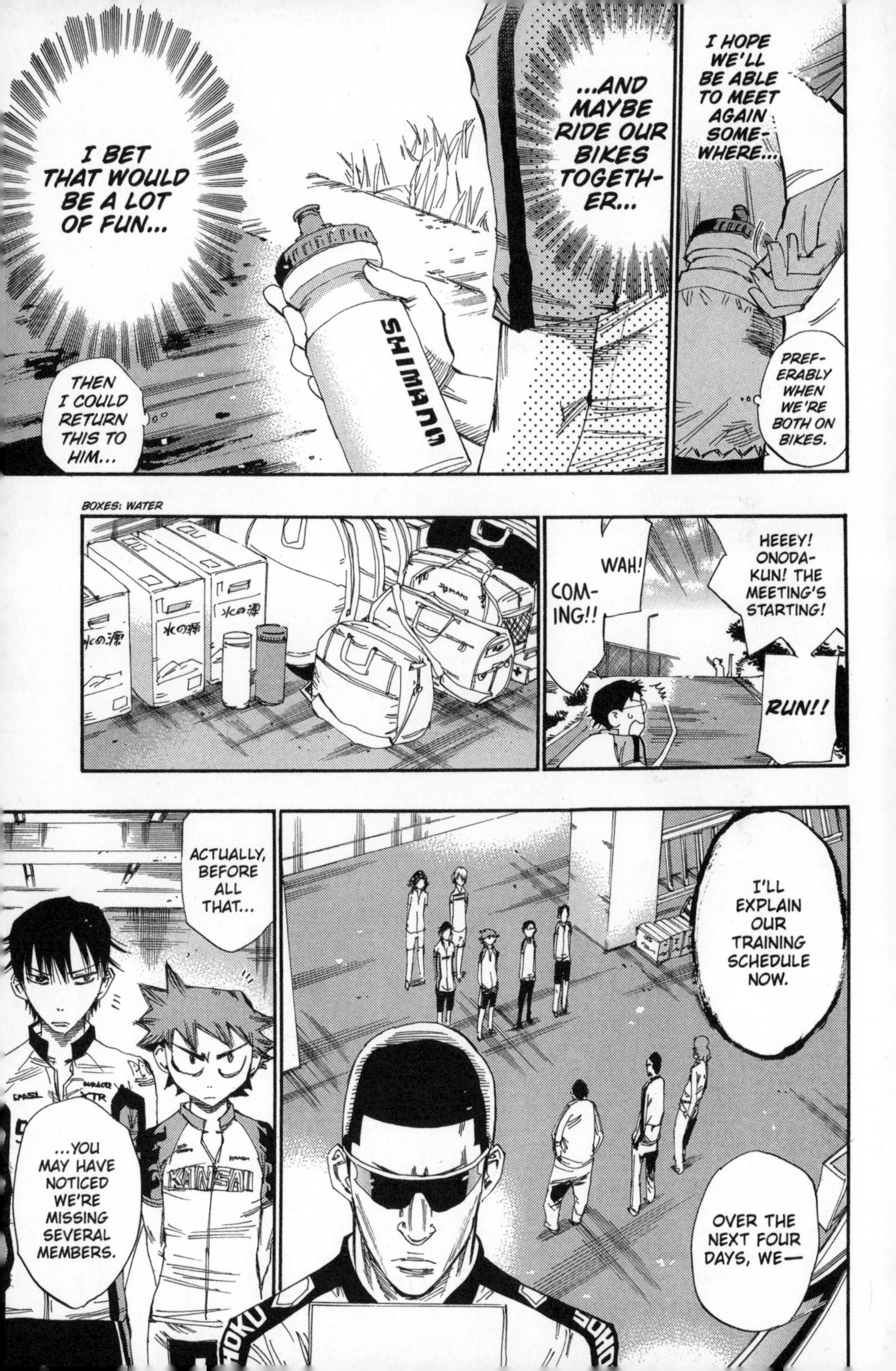
I HOPE WE'LL BE ABLE TO MEET AGAIN SOME-WHERE...
PREF-ERABLY WHEN WE'RE BOTH ON BIKES.
...AND MAYBE RIDE OUR BIKES TOGETH-ER...
I BET THAT WOULD BE A LOT OF FUN...
SHIMANO
THEN I COULD RETURN THIS TO HIM...
HEEEY! ONODA-KUN! THE MEETING'S STARTING!
WAH!
COM-ING!!
RUN!!
BOXES: WATER
水の源
I'LL EXPLAIN OUR TRAINING SCHEDULE NOW.
OVER THE NEXT FOUR DAYS, WE—
ACTUALLY, BEFORE ALL THAT...
...YOU MAY HAVE NOTICED WE'RE MISSING SEVERAL MEMBERS.
KANSAI

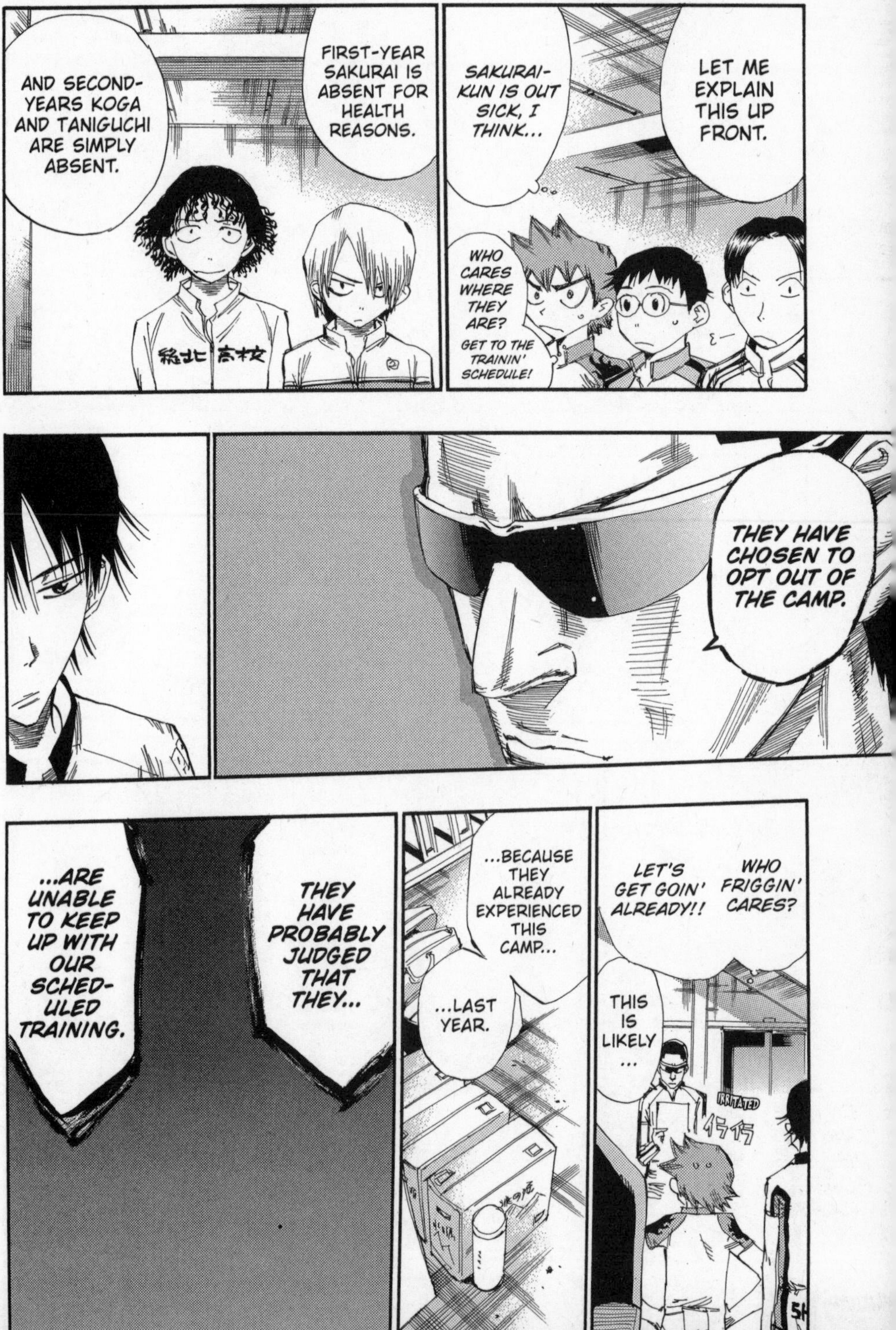
LET ME EXPLAIN THIS UP FRONT.
SAKURAI-KUN IS OUT SICK, I THINK...
WHO CARES WHERE THEY ARE? GET TO THE TRAININ' SCHEDULE!
FIRST-YEAR SAKURAI IS ABSENT FOR HEALTH REASONS.
AND SECOND-YEARS KOGA AND TANIGUCHI ARE SIMPLY ABSENT.
THEY HAVE CHOSEN TO OPT OUT OF THE CAMP.
WHO FRIGGIN' CARES?
LET'S GET GOIN' ALREADY!!
THIS IS LIKELY...
IRRITATED
...BECAUSE THEY ALREADY EXPERIENCED THIS CAMP...
...LAST YEAR.
THEY HAVE PROBABLY JUDGED THAT THEY...
...ARE UNABLE TO KEEP UP WITH OUR SCHED-ULED TRAINING.

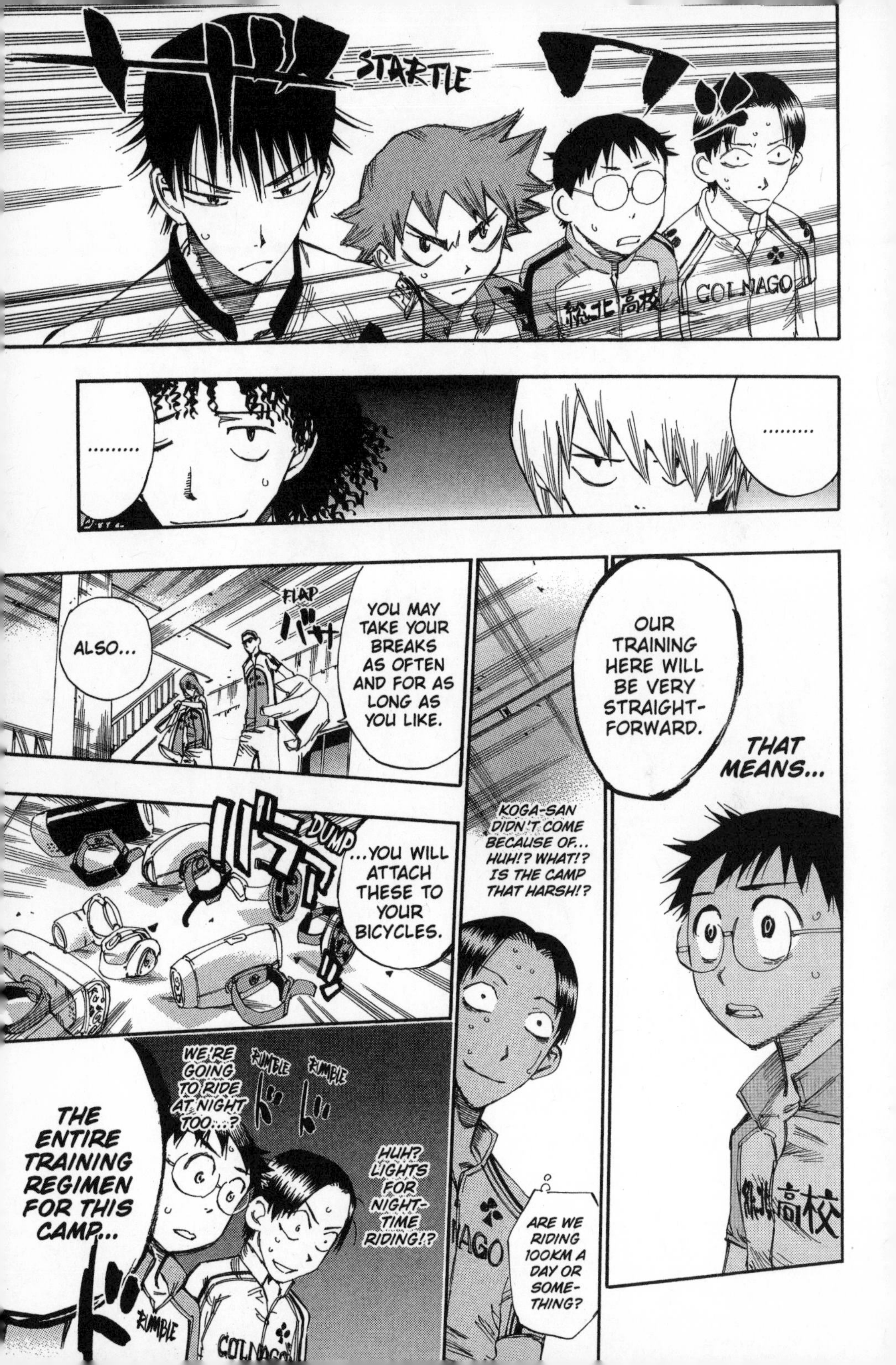
STARTLE
....
....
OUR TRAINING HERE WILL BE VERY STRAIGHT-FORWARD.
THAT MEANS...
FLAP
YOU MAY TAKE YOUR BREAKS AS OFTEN AND FOR AS LONG AS YOU LIKE.
ALSO...
KOGA-SAN DIDN'T COME BECAUSE OF... HUH!? WHAT!? IS THE CAMP THAT HARSH!?
ARE WE RIDING 100KM A DAY OR SOME-THING?
DUMP
...YOU WILL ATTACH THESE TO YOUR BICYCLES.
HUH? LIGHTS FOR NIGHT-TIME RIDING!?
RUMBLE RUMBLE
WE'RE GOING TO RIDE AT NIGHT TOO...?
THE ENTIRE TRAINING REGIMEN FOR THIS CAMP...
RUMBLE

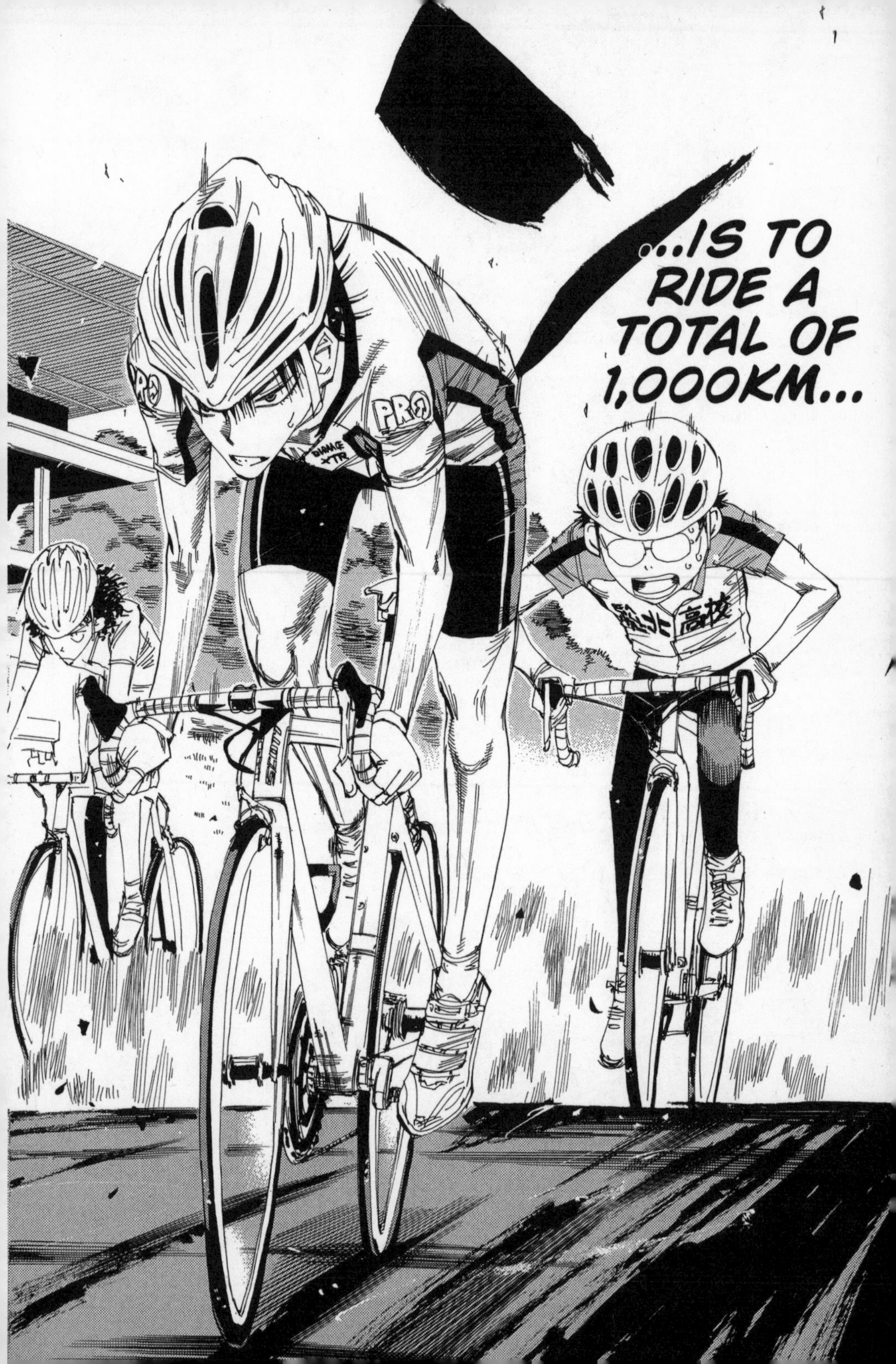
...IS TO RIDE A TOTAL OF 1,000KM...

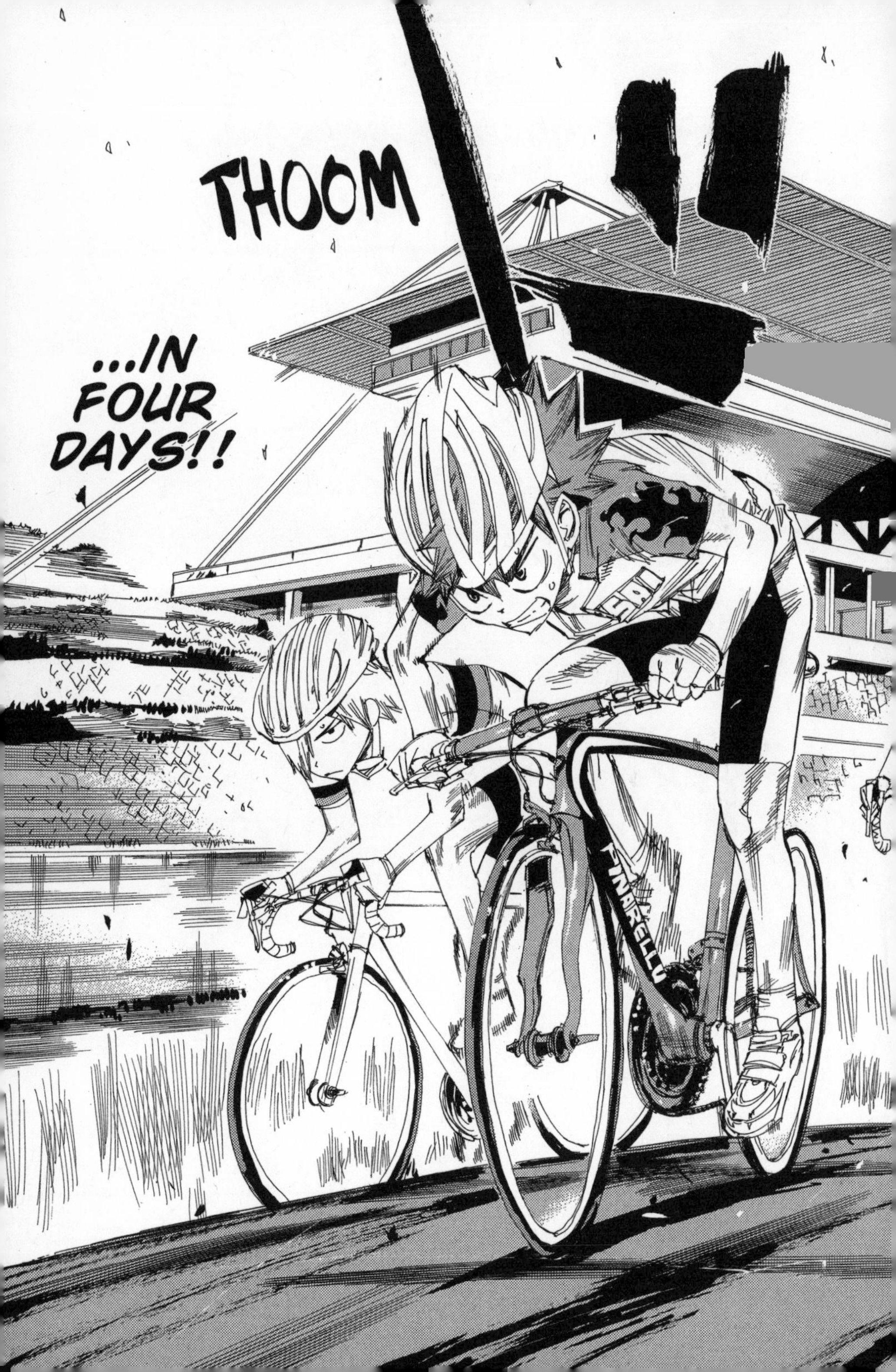
THOOM
...IN FOUR DAYS!!

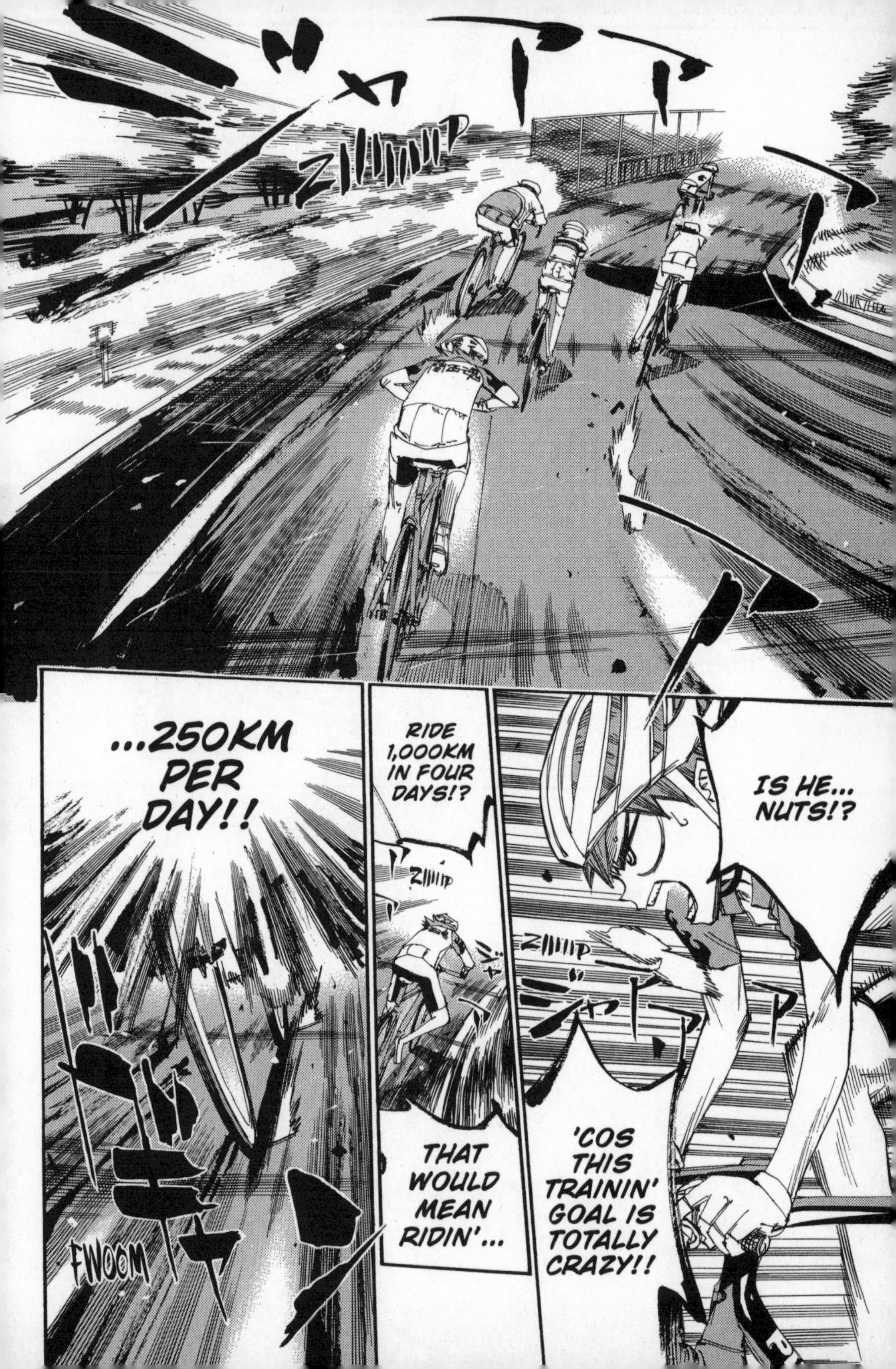
ZIIIIIIIIP
IS HE... NUTS!?
ZIIIIP
'COS THIS TRAININ' GOAL IS TOTALLY CRAZY!!
RIDE 1,000KM IN FOUR DAYS!?
ZIIIIP
THAT WOULD MEAN RIDIN'...
...250KM PER DAY!!
FWOOM

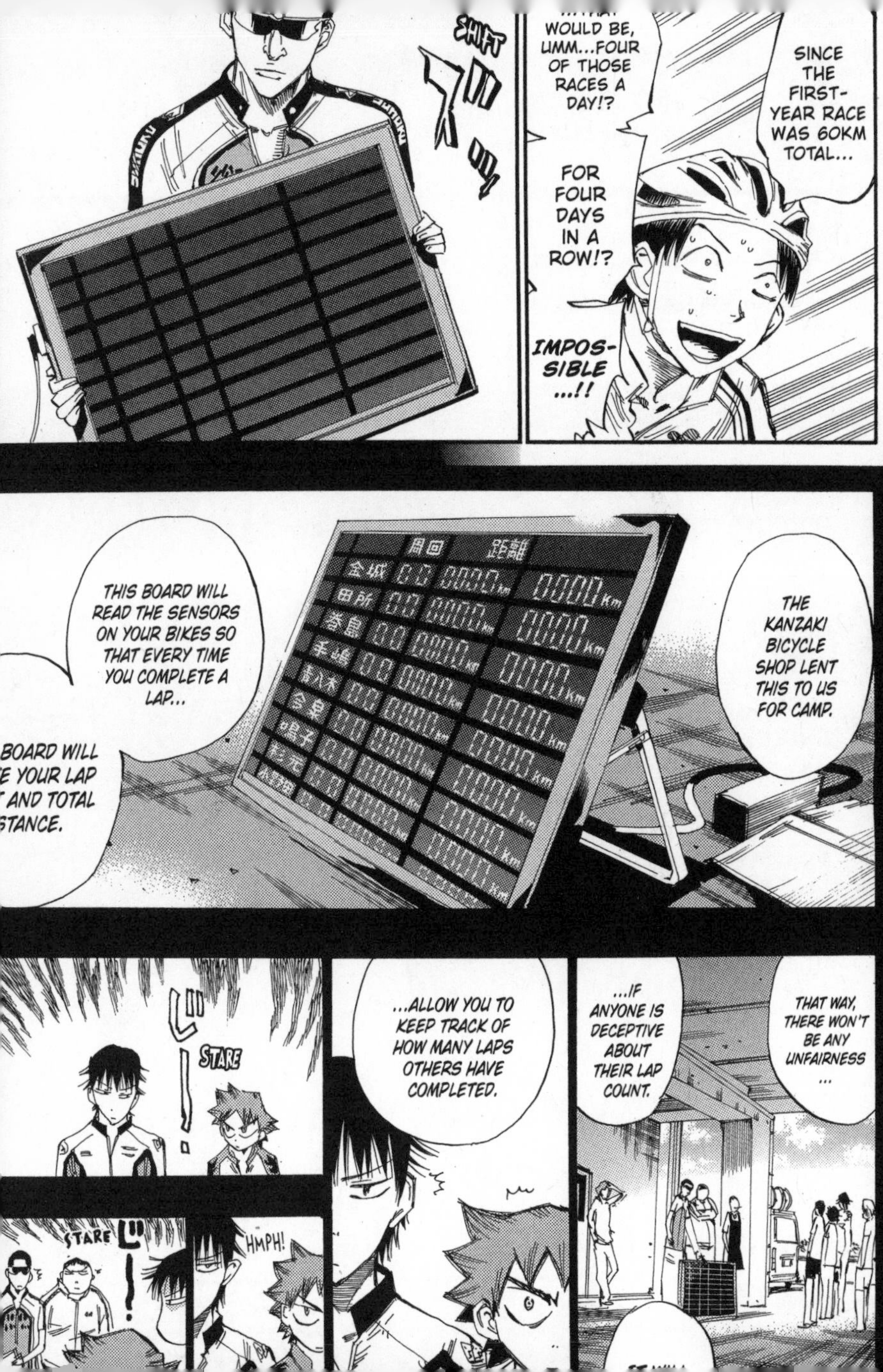
SINCE THE FIRST-YEAR RACE WAS 60KM TOTAL...
WOULD BE, UMM...FOUR OF THOSE RACES A DAY!?
FOR FOUR DAYS IN A ROW!?
IMPOSSIBLE...!!
SHIFT
THE KANZAKI BICYCLE SHOP LENT THIS TO US FOR CAMP.
周回 距離
THIS BOARD WILL READ THE SENSORS ON YOUR BIKES SO THAT EVERY TIME YOU COMPLETE A LAP...
BOARD WILL
YOUR LAP
AND TOTAL
STANCE.
THAT WAY, THERE WON'T BE ANY UNFAIRNESS...
...IF ANYONE IS DECEPTIVE ABOUT THEIR LAP COUNT.
...ALLOW YOU TO KEEP TRACK OF HOW MANY LAPS OTHERS HAVE COMPLETED.
STARE
HMPH!
STARE

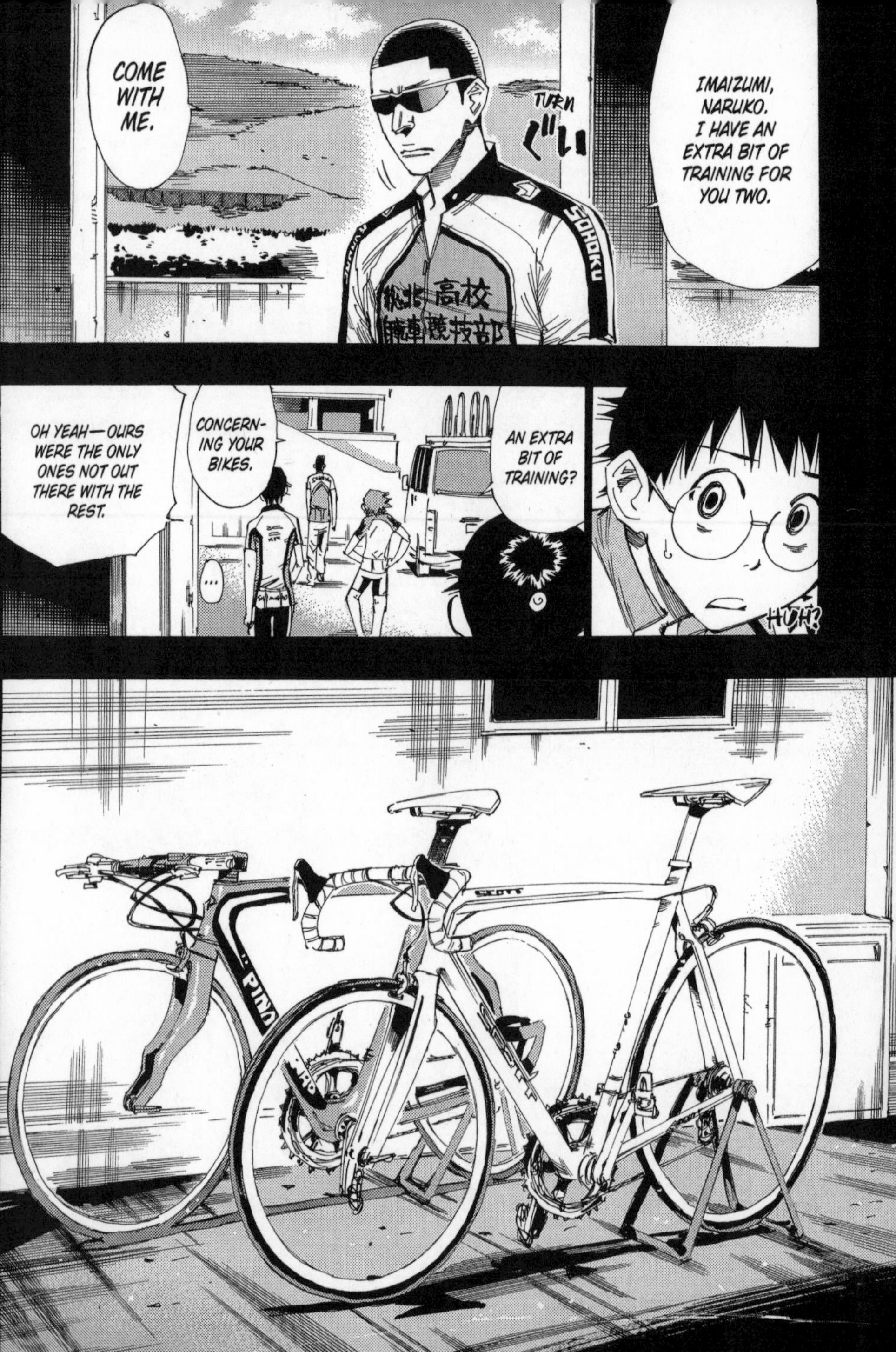
IMAIZUMI, NARUKO. I HAVE AN EXTRA BIT OF TRAINING FOR YOU TWO.
TURN
ぐい
COME WITH ME.
AN EXTRA BIT OF TRAINING?
HUH?
CONCERNING YOUR BIKES.
OH YEAH—OURS WERE THE ONLY ONES NOT OUT THERE WITH THE REST.
...

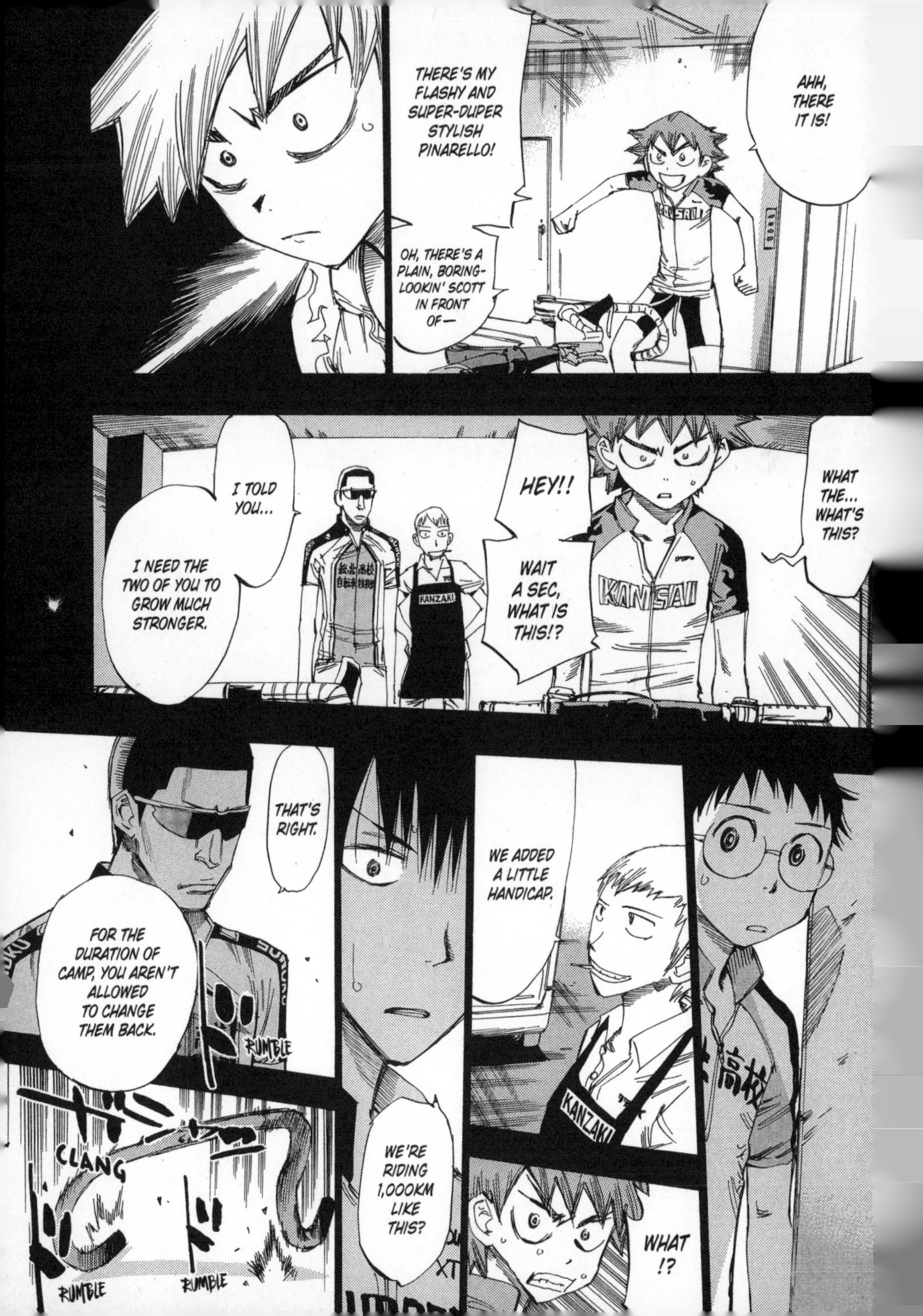
AHH, THERE IT IS!
THERE'S MY FLASHY AND SUPER-DUPER STYLISH PINARELLO!
OH, THERE'S A PLAIN, BORING-LOOKIN' SCOTT IN FRONT OF—
WHAT THE... WHAT'S THIS?
HEY!!
WAIT A SEC, WHAT IS THIS!?
I TOLD YOU...
I NEED THE TWO OF YOU TO GROW MUCH STRONGER.
WE ADDED A LITTLE HANDICAP.
WHAT !?
WE'RE RIDING 1,000KM LIKE THIS?
THAT'S RIGHT.
FOR THE DURATION OF CAMP, YOU AREN'T ALLOWED TO CHANGE THEM BACK.
RUMBLE
CLANG
RUMBLE
RUMBLE

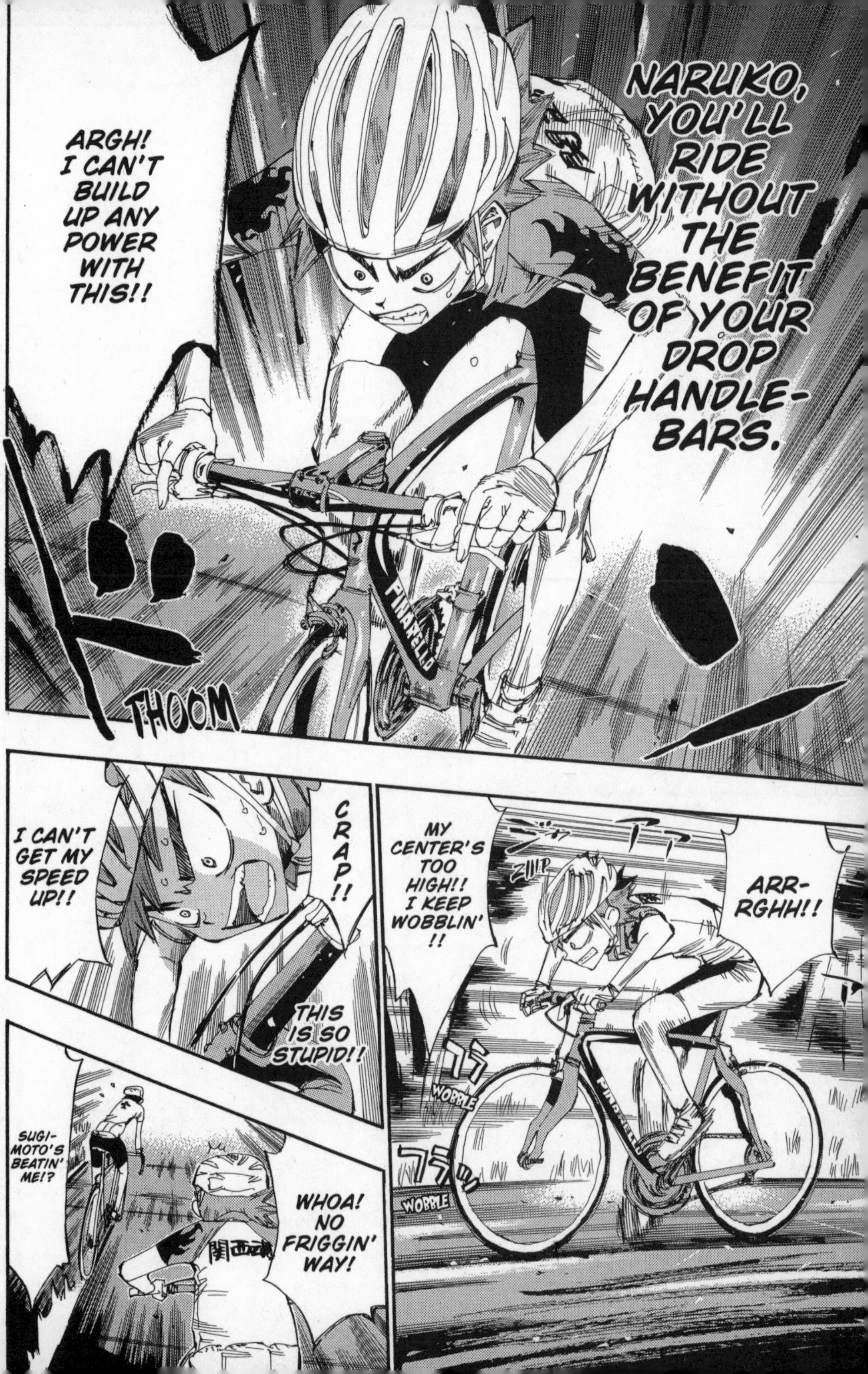

NARUKO, YOU'LL RIDE WITHOUT THE BENEFIT OF YOUR DROP HANDLE-BARS.
ARGH! I CAN'T BUILD UP ANY POWER WITH THIS!!
THOOM
ARR-RGHH!!
MY CENTER'S TOO HIGH!! I KEEP WOBBLIN' !!
WOBBLE
WOBBLE
CRAP!!
I CAN'T GET MY SPEED UP!!
THIS IS SO STUPID!!
WHOA! NO FRIGGIN' WAY!
SUGI-MOTO'S BEATIN' ME!?

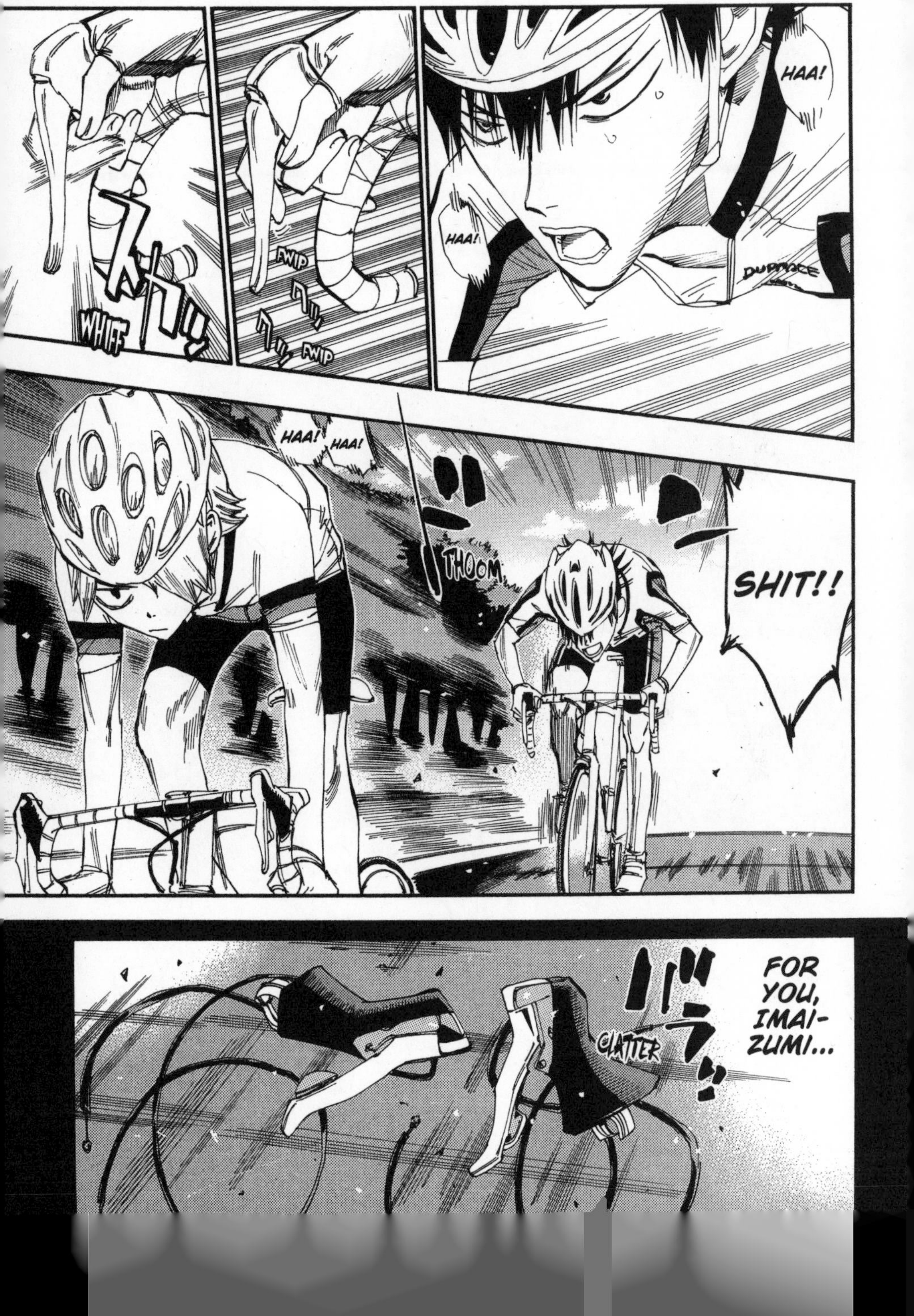
HAA!
HAA!
FWIP
FWIP
WHIFF
SHIT!!
HAA! HAA!
THOOM
FOR YOU, IMAI-ZUMI...
CLATTER

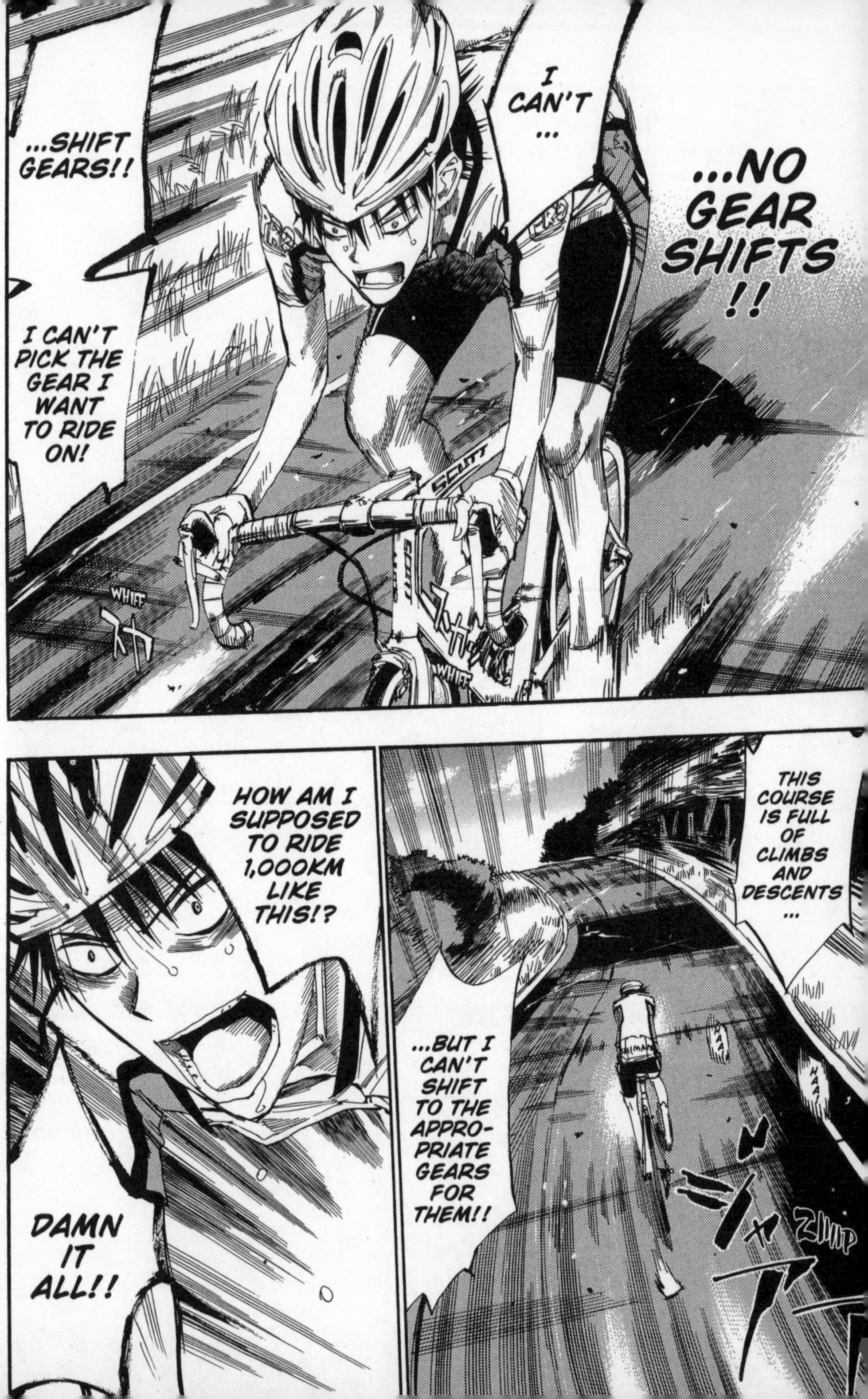
I CAN'T ...
...NO GEAR SHIFTS!!
...SHIFT GEARS!!
I CAN'T PICK THE GEAR I WANT TO RIDE ON!
WHIFF
WHIFF
THIS COURSE IS FULL OF CLIMBS AND DESCENTS ...
...BUT I CAN'T SHIFT TO THE APPRO-PRIATE GEARS FOR THEM!!
HAA
HAA
ZIIIIP
HOW AM I SUPPOSED TO RIDE 1,000KM LIKE THIS!?
DAMN IT ALL!!

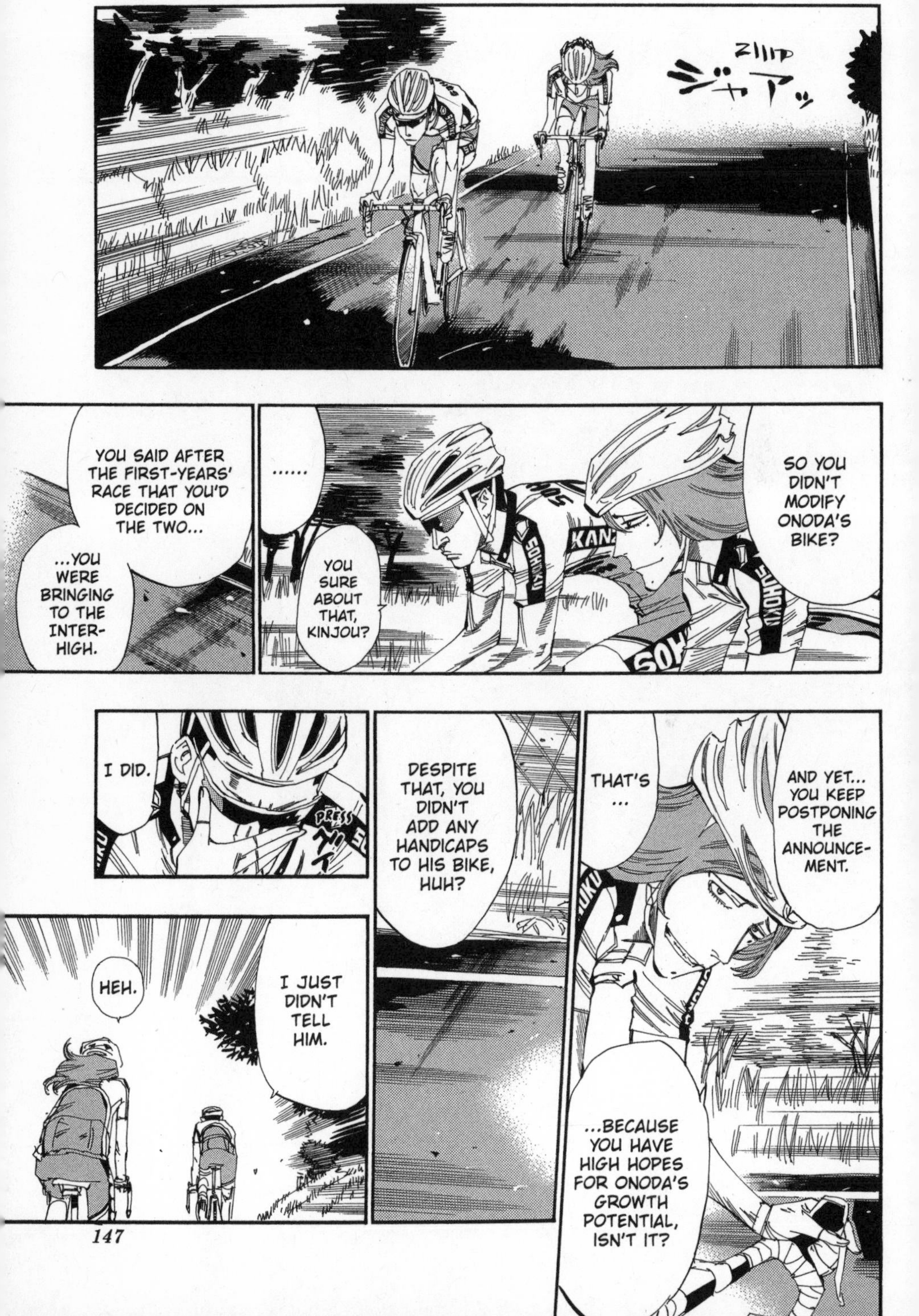
ZIIIP
ジャアッ
SO YOU DIDN'T MODIFY ONODA'S BIKE?
YOU SURE ABOUT THAT, KINJOU?
......
YOU SAID AFTER THE FIRST-YEARS' RACE THAT YOU'D DECIDED ON THE TWO...
...YOU WERE BRINGING TO THE INTER-HIGH.
AND YET... YOU KEEP POSTPONING THE ANNOUNCEMENT.
THAT'S ...
...BECAUSE YOU HAVE HIGH HOPES FOR ONODA'S GROWTH POTENTIAL, ISN'T IT?
DESPITE THAT, YOU DIDN'T ADD ANY HANDICAPS TO HIS BIKE, HUH?
I DID.
PRESS
I JUST DIDN'T TELL HIM.
HEH.

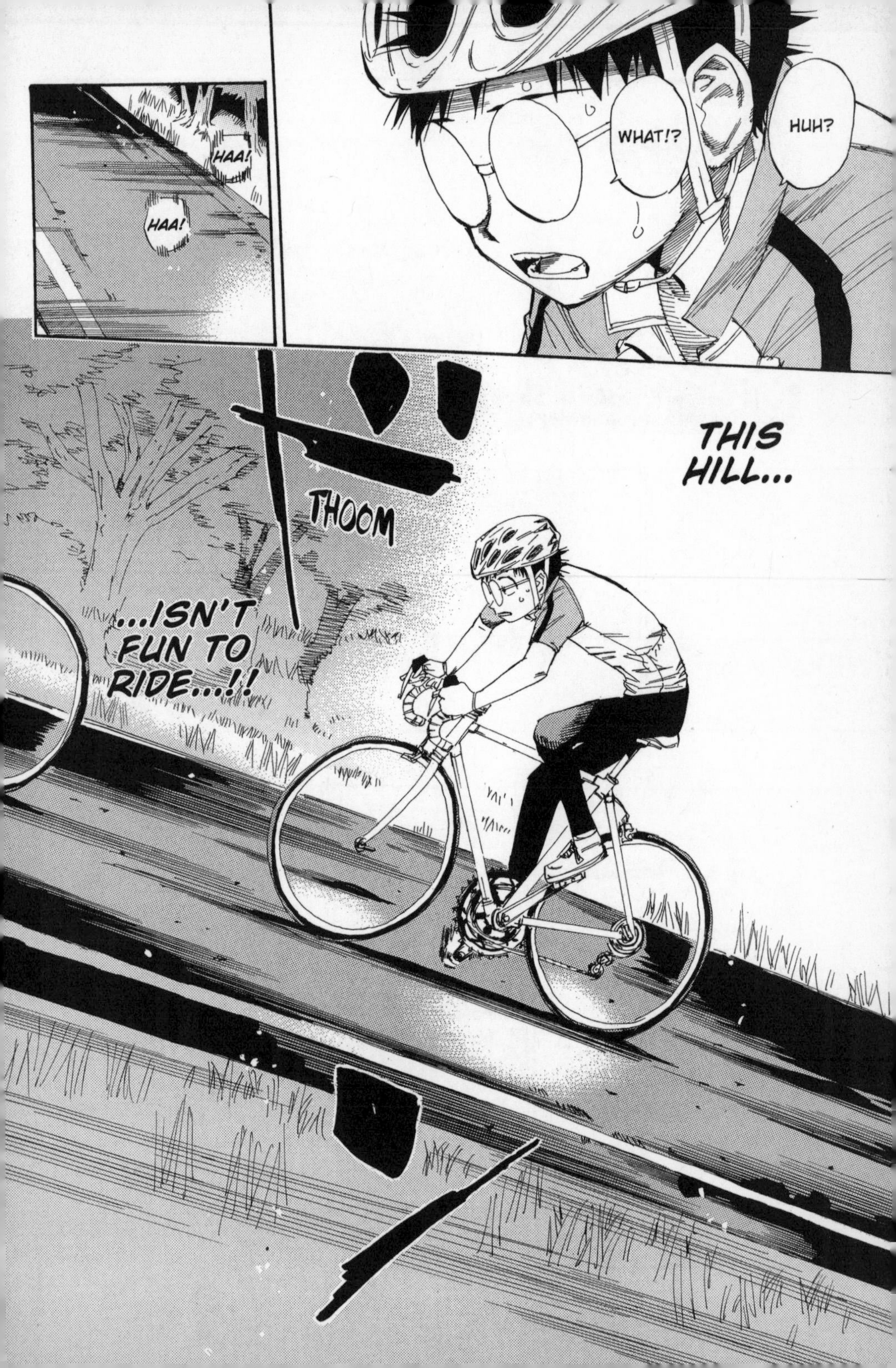
HUH?
WHAT!?
HAA!
HAA!
THIS HILL...
THOOM
...ISN'T FUN TO RIDE...!!

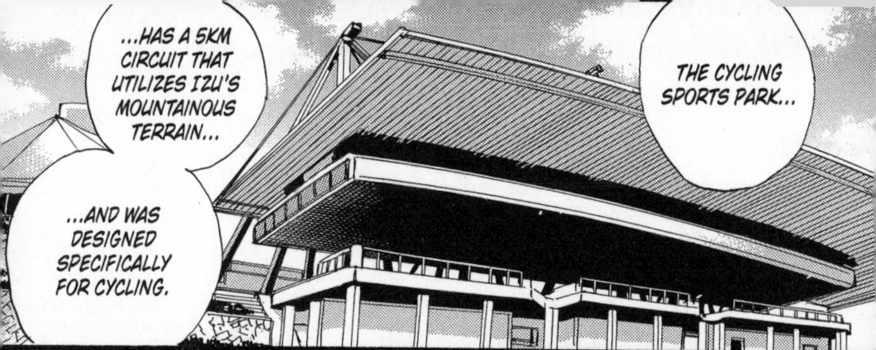
THE CYCLING SPORTS PARK...
...HAS A 5KM CIRCUIT THAT UTILIZES IZU'S MOUNTAINOUS TERRAIN...
...AND WAS DESIGNED SPECIFICALLY FOR CYCLING.

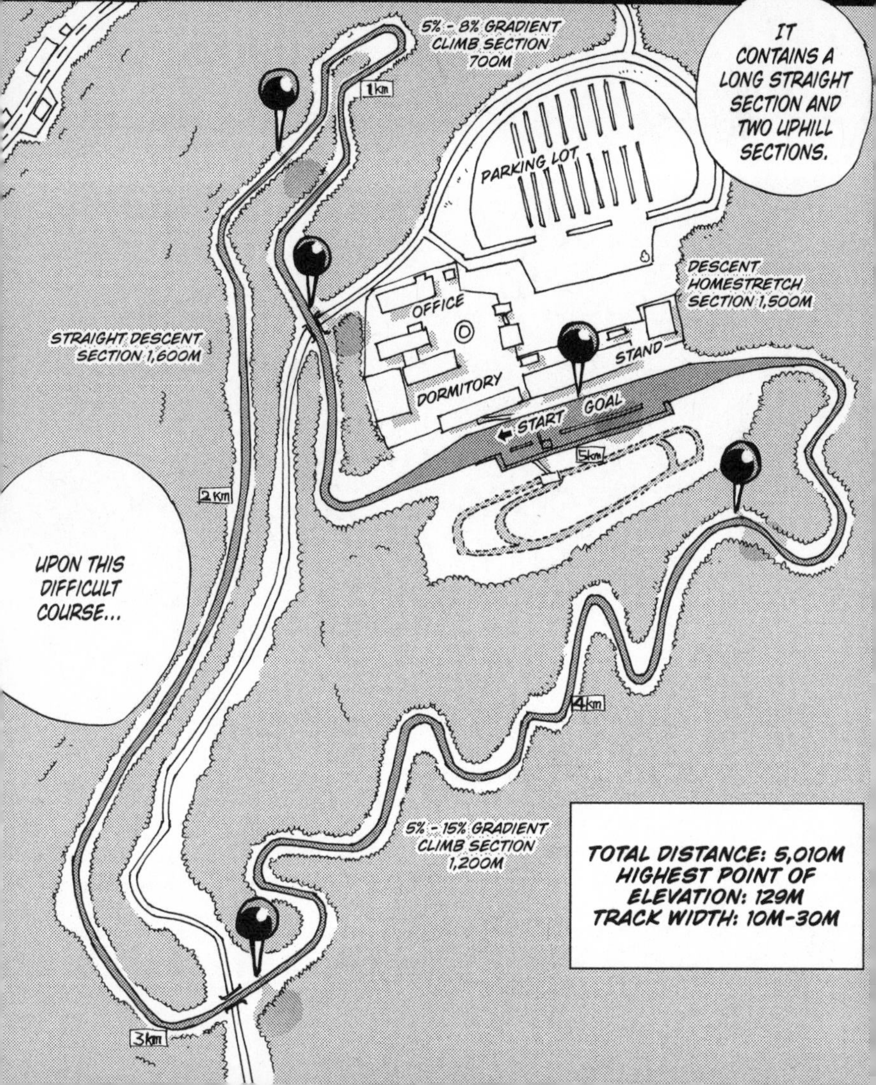
IT CONTAINS A LONG STRAIGHT SECTION AND TWO UPHILL SECTIONS.
5% - 8% GRADIENT CLIMB SECTION 700M
1km
PARKING LOT
DESCENT HOMESTRETCH SECTION 1,500M
OFFICE
STAND
DORMITORY
GOAL
START
5km
STRAIGHT DESCENT SECTION 1,600M
2km
UPON THIS DIFFICULT COURSE...
4km
5% - 15% GRADIENT CLIMB SECTION 1,200M
3km
TOTAL DISTANCE: 5,010M
HIGHEST POINT OF ELEVATION: 129M
TRACK WIDTH: 10M-30M

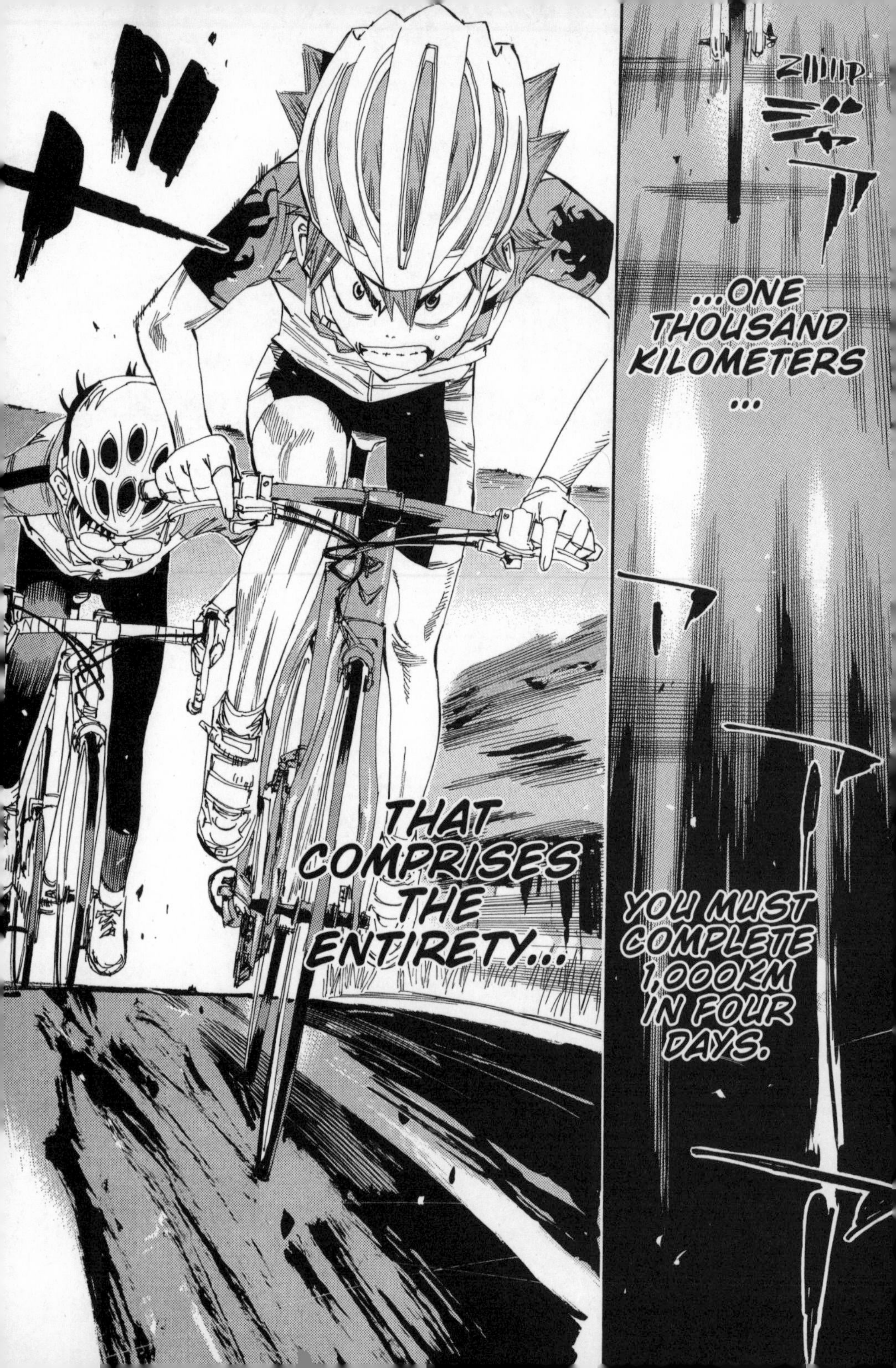
ZIIIIP
...ONE THOUSAND KILOMETERS...
YOU MUST COMPLETE 1,000KM IN FOUR DAYS.
THAT COMPRISES THE ENTIRETY...

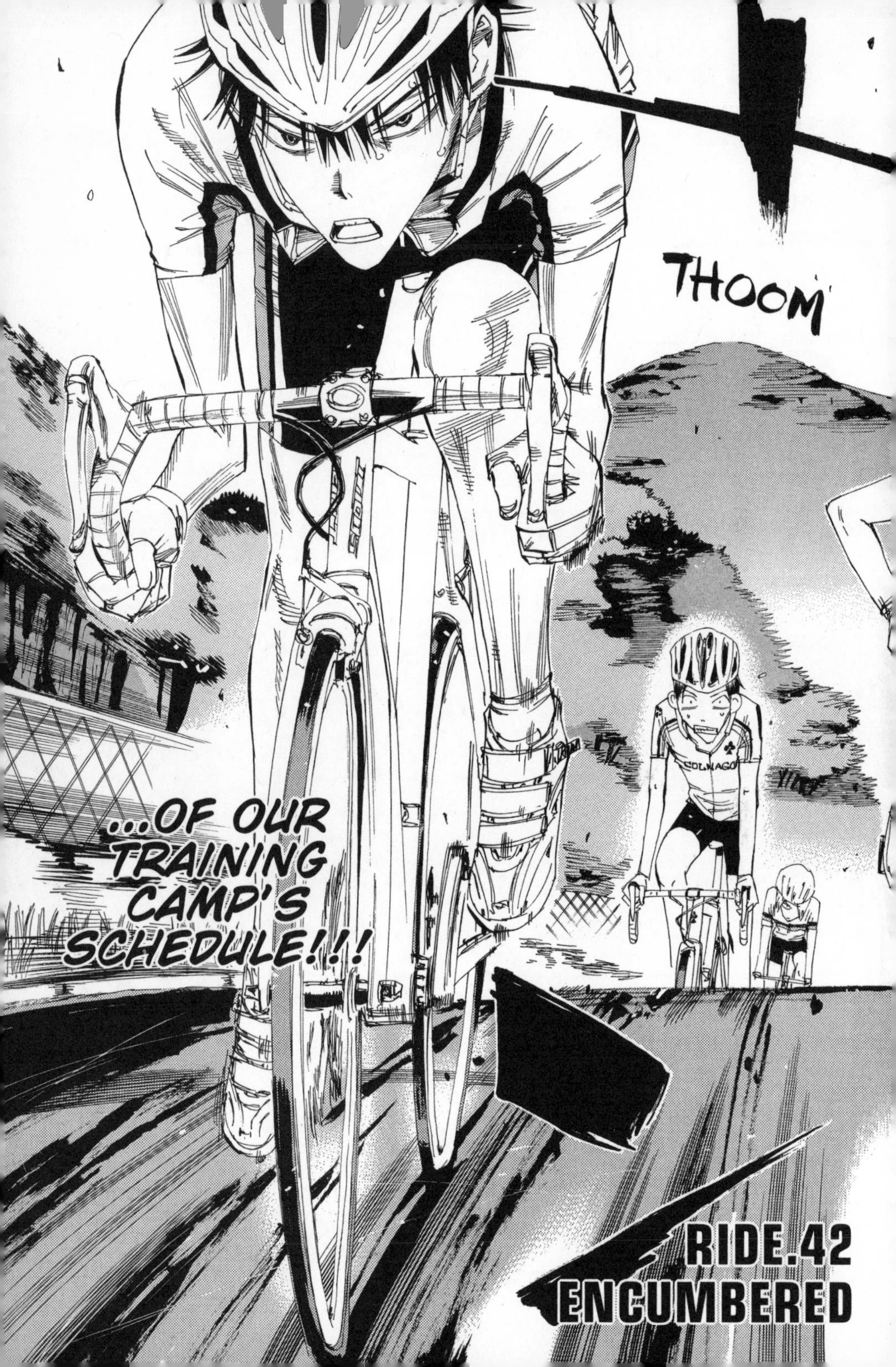
THOOM
...OF OUR TRAINING CAMP'S SCHEDULE!!!
RIDE.42
ENCUMBERED

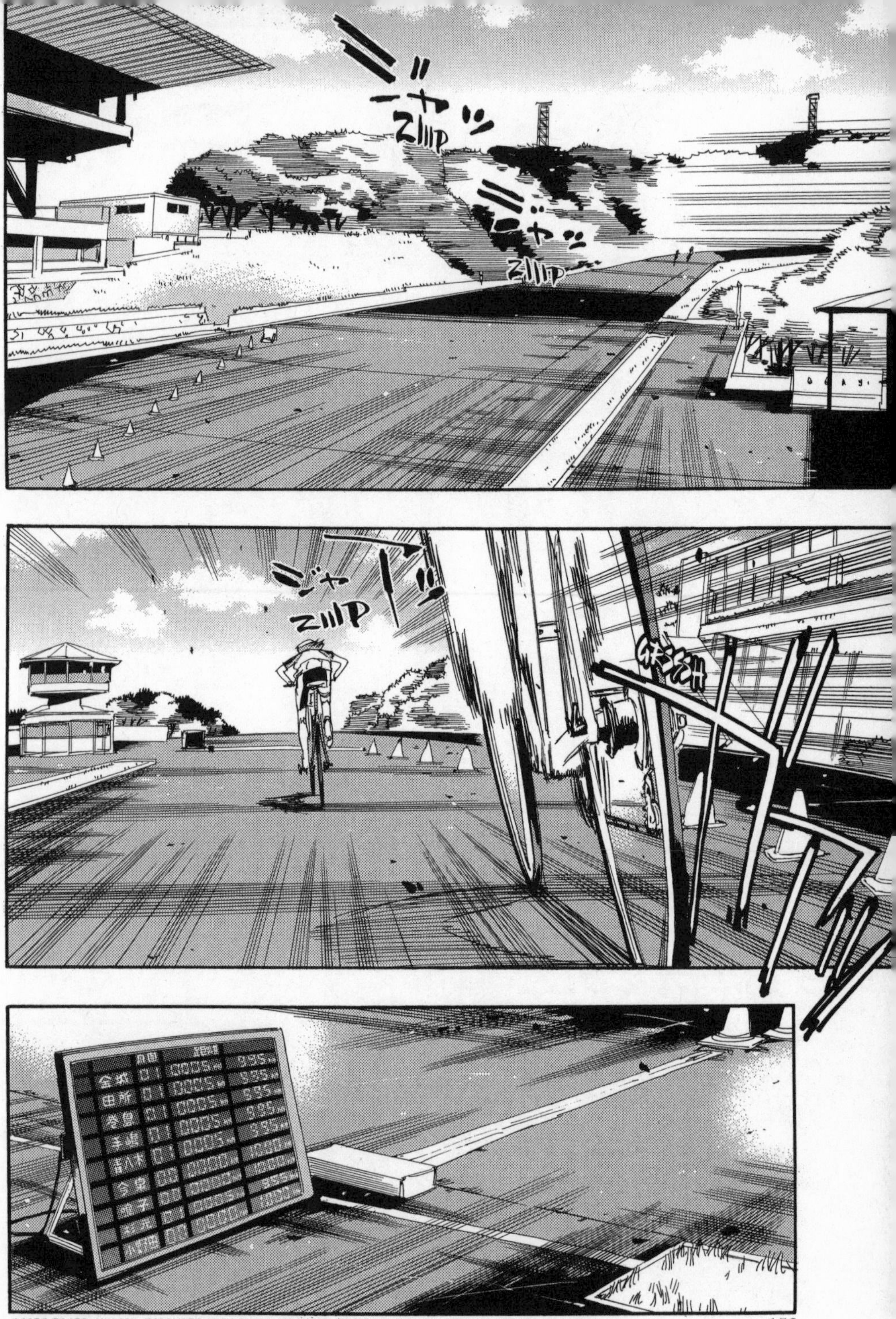
ジャーッ
ZIIIP
ジャッ
ZIIIP
ジャーッ
ZIIIP
GRSCH

SCORE BOARD: KINJOU, TADOKORO, MAKISHIMA, TESHIMA, AOYAGI, IMAIZUMI, NARUKO, SUGIMOTO, ONODA

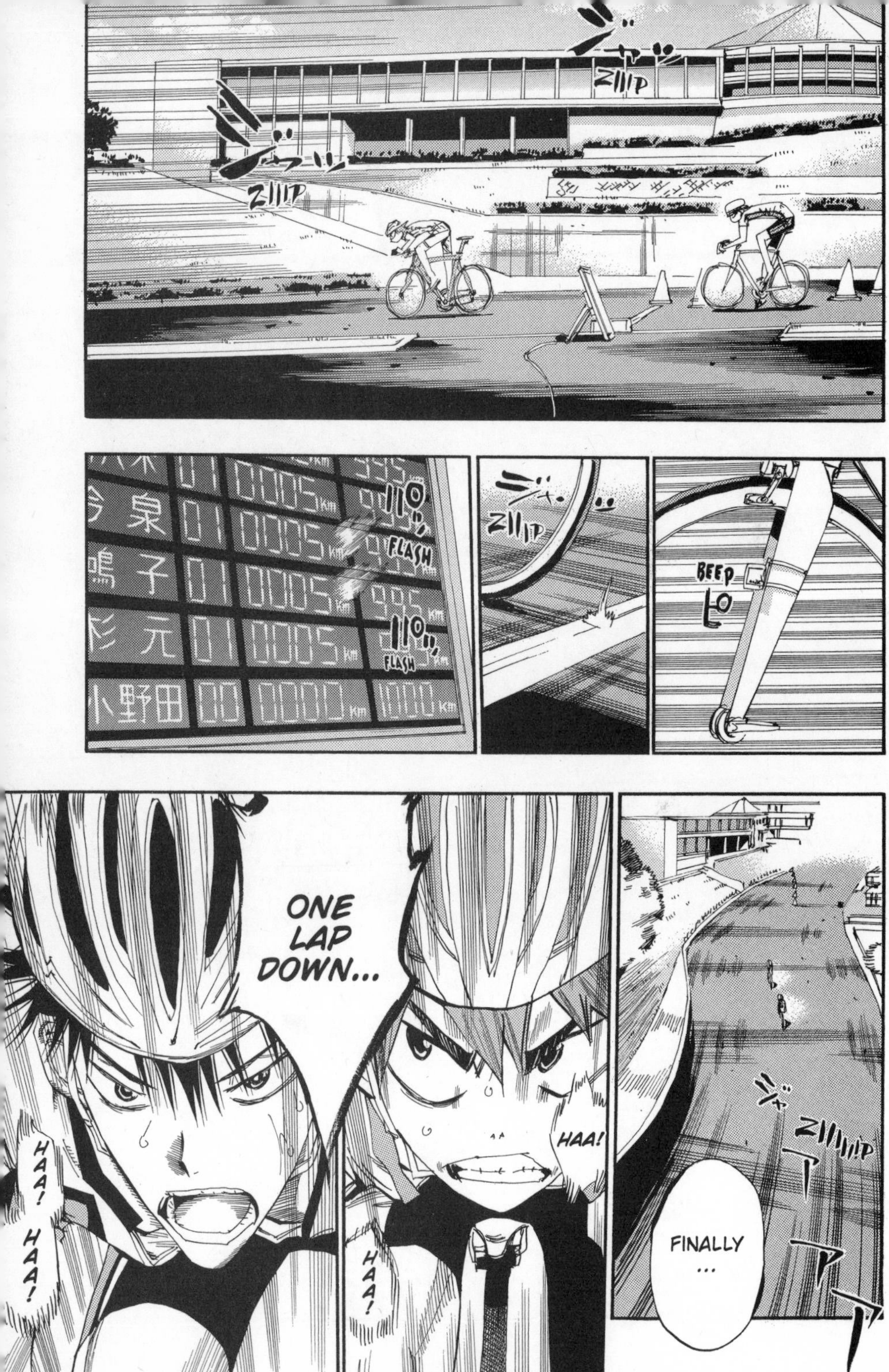

ZIIIP
ZIIIP
BEEP
ZIIIP
FLASH
FLASH
今泉
鳴子
杉元
小野田
ZIIIIIP
FINALLY ...
ONE LAP DOWN...
HAA!
HAA!
HAA! HAA!

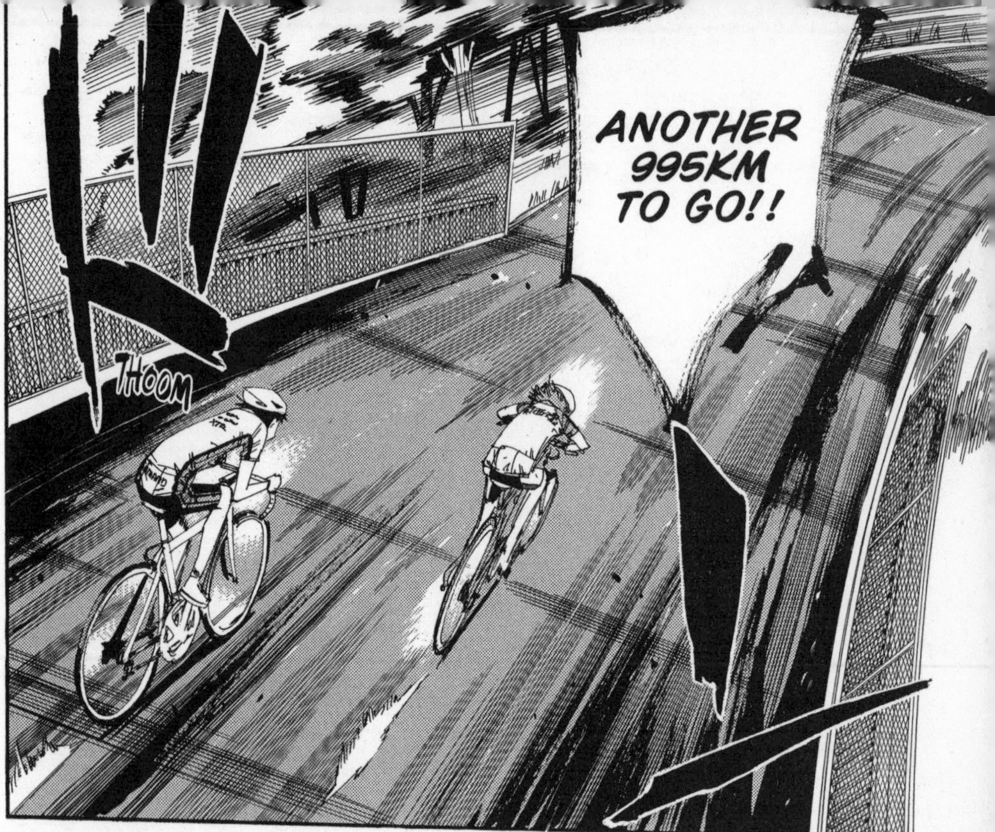
ANOTHER 995KM TO GO!!
THOOM
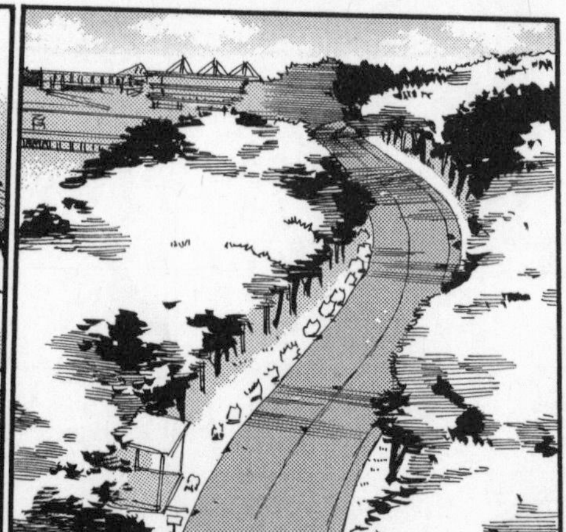
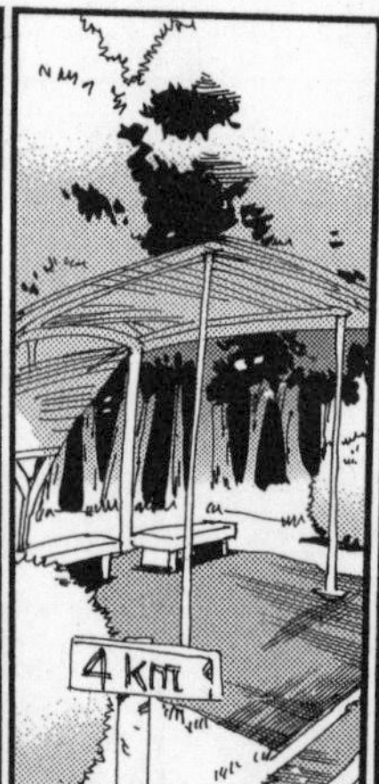
4 km
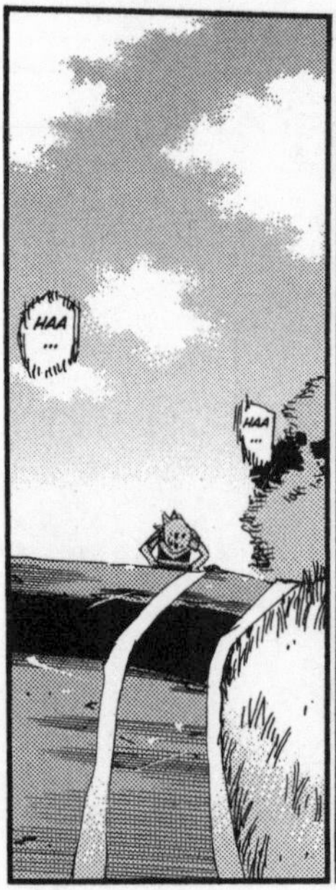
HAA ...
HAA ...

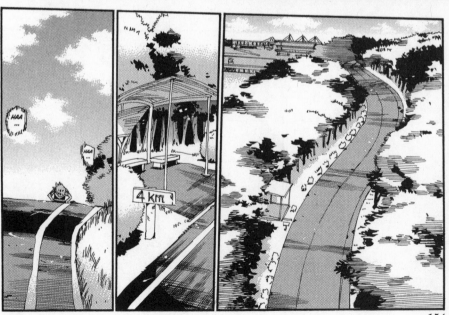

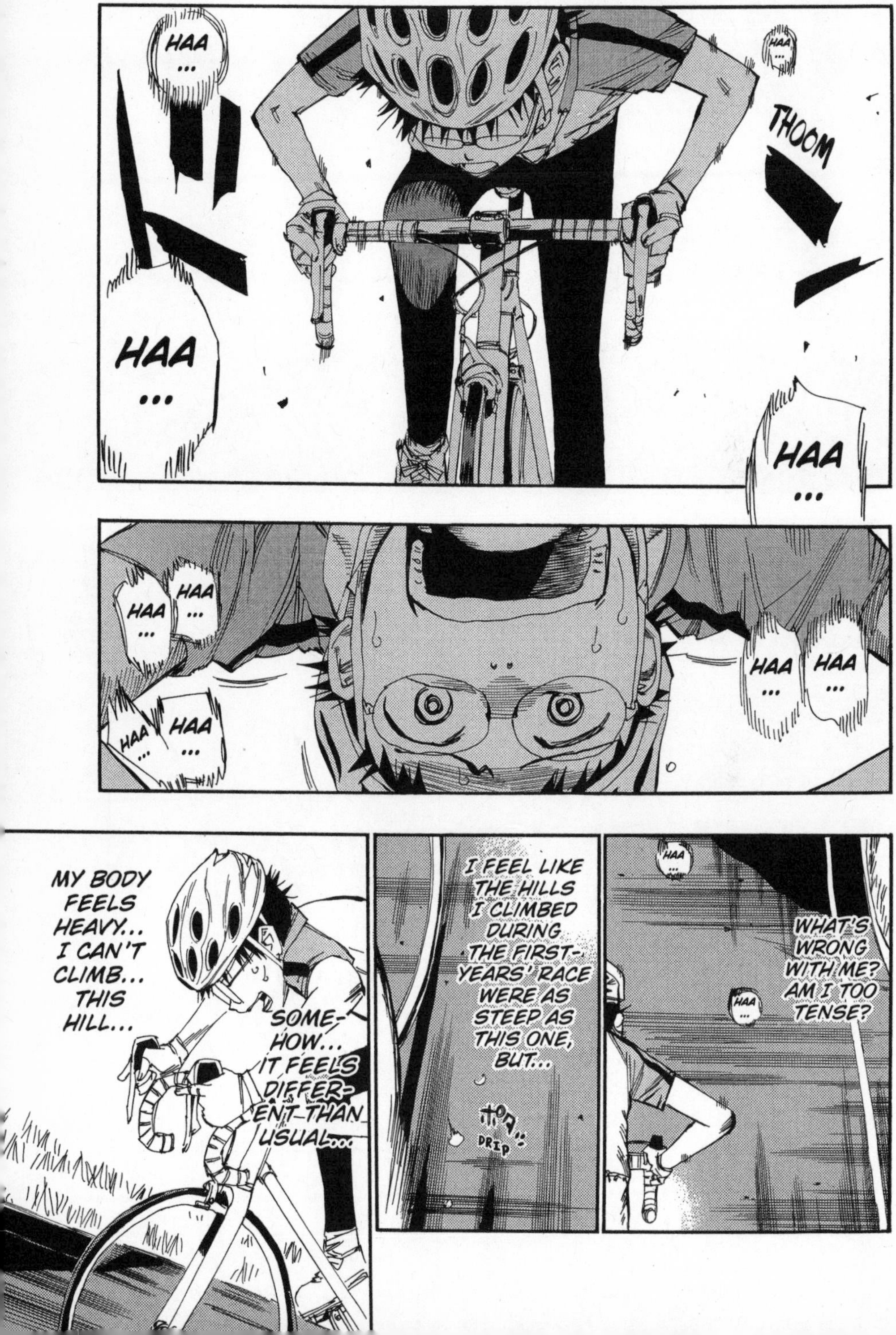
HAA...
THOOM
HAA...
HAA...
HAA...
HAA...
HAA...
HAA...
HAA...
HAA...
HAA...
HAA...
WHAT'S WRONG WITH ME? AM I TOO TENSE?
HAA...
I FEEL LIKE THE HILLS I CLIMBED DURING THE FIRST-YEARS' RACE WERE AS STEEP AS THIS ONE, BUT...
DRIP
MY BODY FEELS HEAVY... I CAN'T CLIMB... THIS HILL...
SOME-HOW... IT FEELS DIFFER-ENT THAN USUAL...

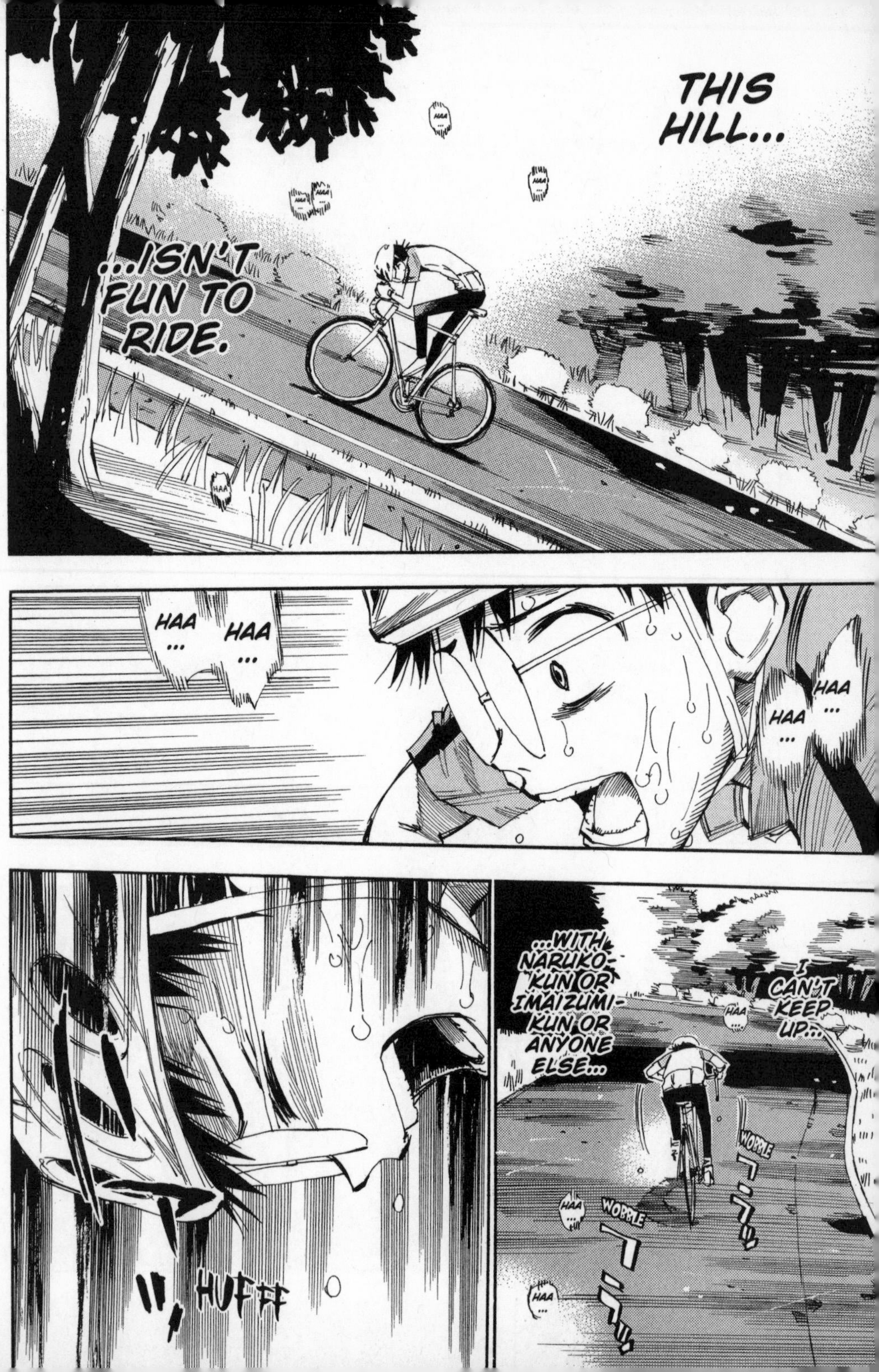
THIS HILL...
HAA...
HAA...
HAA...
HAA...
...ISN'T FUN TO RIDE.
HAA
HAA...
HAA...
HAA...
HAA...
I CAN'T KEEP UP...
...WITH NARUKO-KUN OR IMAIZUMI-KUN OR ANYONE ELSE...
HAA...
WOBBLE
HAA...
WOBBLE
HAA...
HUFF

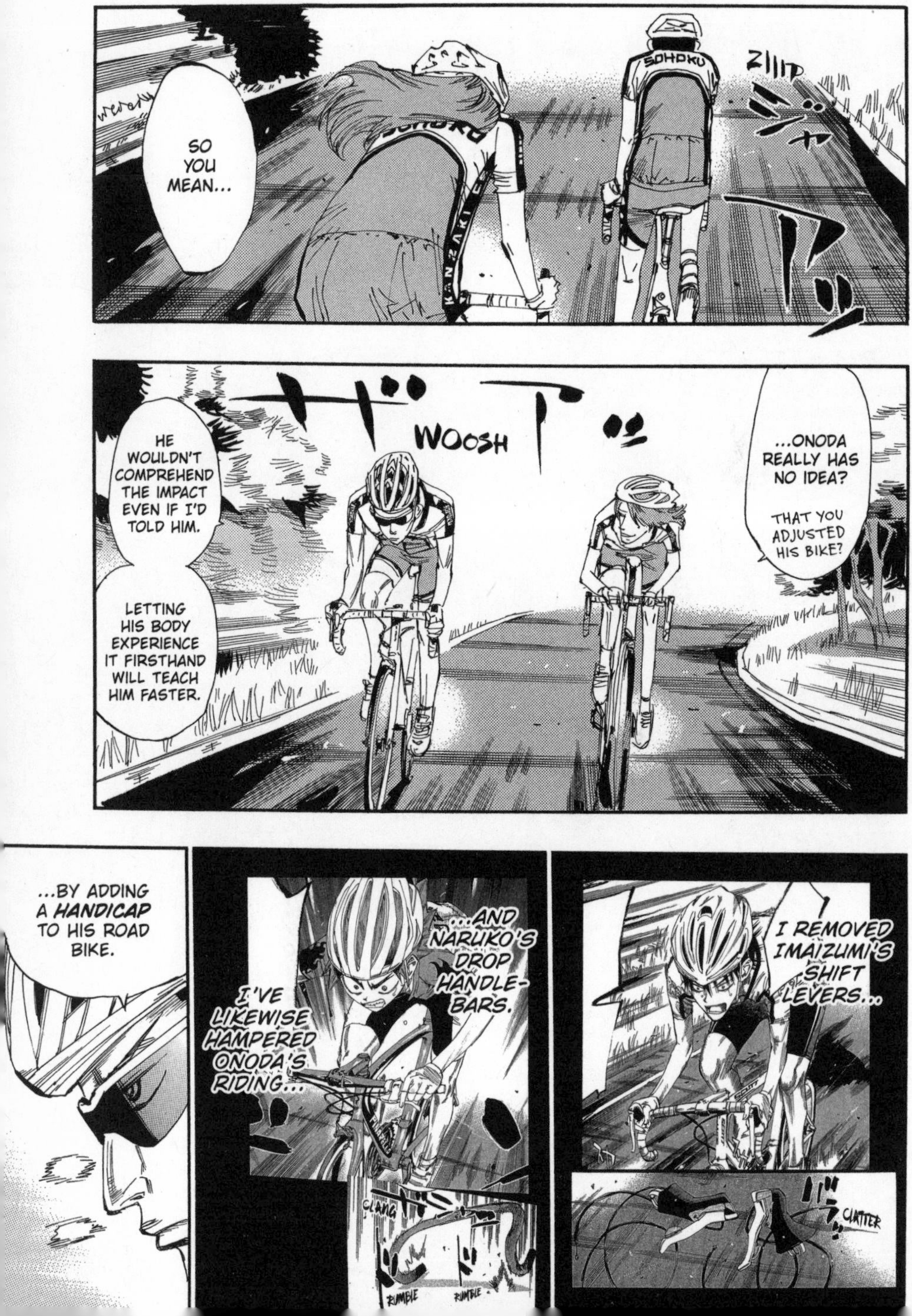
SO YOU MEAN...
ZIIIP
...ONODA REALLY HAS NO IDEA?
THAT YOU ADJUSTED HIS BIKE?
WOOSH
HE WOULDN'T COMPREHEND THE IMPACT EVEN IF I'D TOLD HIM.
LETTING HIS BODY EXPERIENCE IT FIRSTHAND WILL TEACH HIM FASTER.
I REMOVED IMAIZUMI'S SHIFT LEVERS...
CLATTER
...AND NARUKO'S DROP HANDLEBARS.
I'VE LIKEWISE HAMPERED ONODA'S RIDING...
CLANG
RUMBLE
RUMBLE
...BY ADDING A *HANDICAP* TO HIS ROAD BIKE.

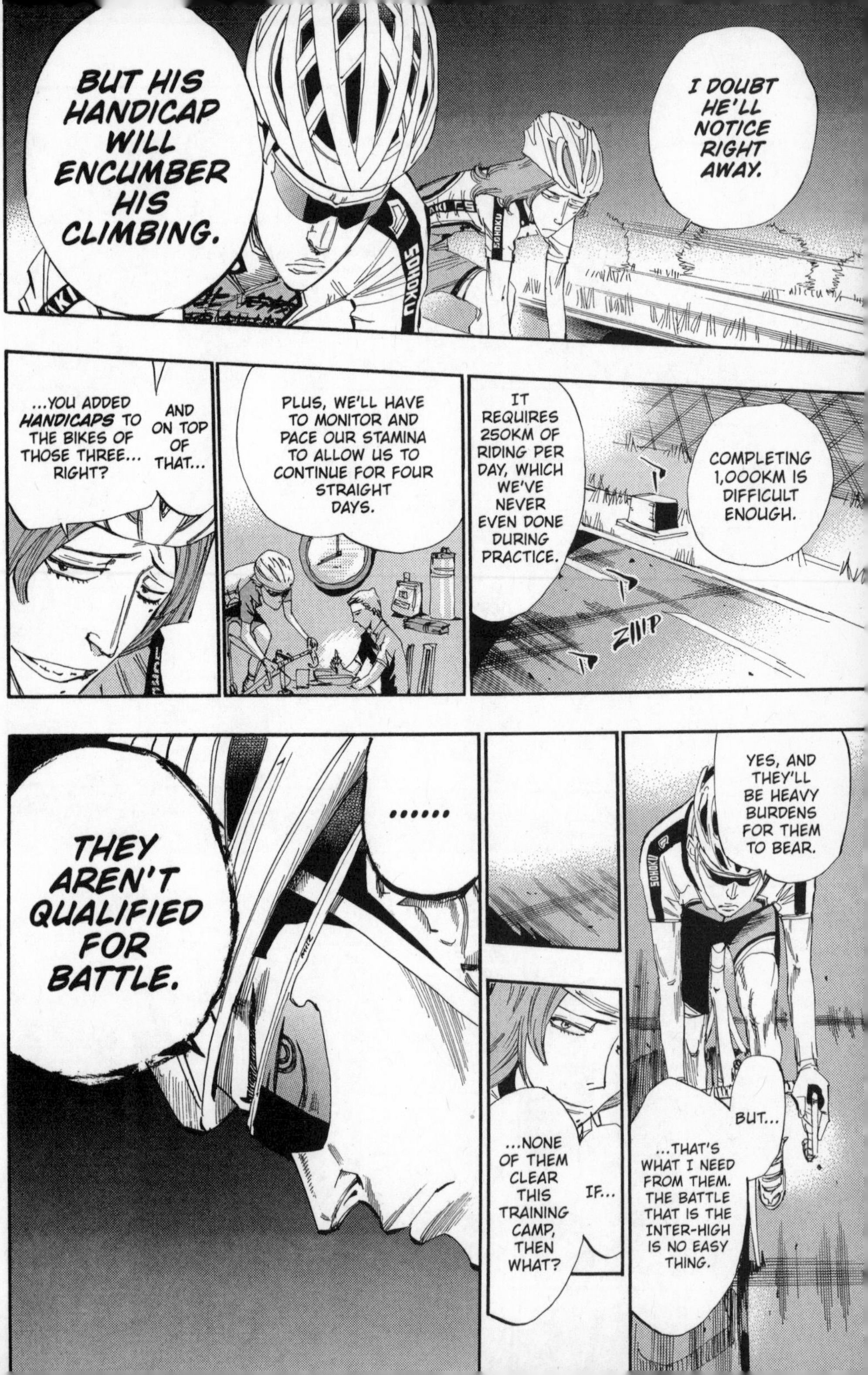
I DOUBT HE'LL NOTICE RIGHT AWAY.
BUT HIS HANDICAP WILL ENCUMBER HIS CLIMBING.
COMPLETING 1,000KM IS DIFFICULT ENOUGH.
IT REQUIRES 250KM OF RIDING PER DAY, WHICH WE'VE NEVER EVEN DONE DURING PRACTICE.
ZIIIP
PLUS, WE'LL HAVE TO MONITOR AND PACE OUR STAMINA TO ALLOW US TO CONTINUE FOR FOUR STRAIGHT DAYS.
AND ON TOP OF THAT...
...YOU ADDED *HANDICAPS* TO THE BIKES OF THOSE THREE... RIGHT?
YES, AND THEY'LL BE HEAVY BURDENS FOR THEM TO BEAR.
BUT...
...THAT'S WHAT I NEED FROM THEM. THE BATTLE THAT IS THE INTER-HIGH IS NO EASY THING.
IF...
...NONE OF THEM CLEAR THIS TRAINING CAMP, THEN WHAT?
......
THEY AREN'T QUALIFIED FOR BATTLE.

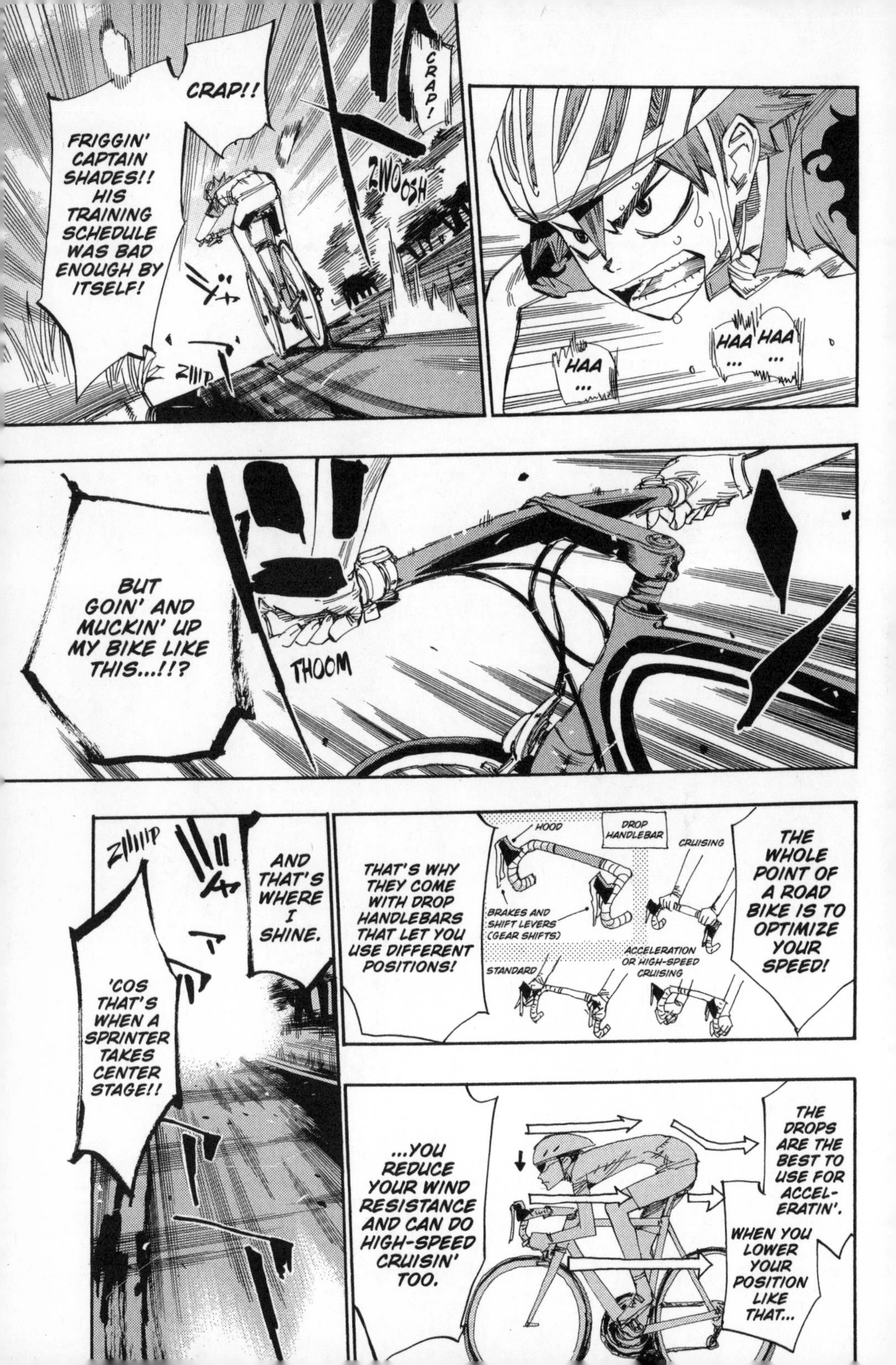
HAA ...
HAA ...
HAA ...
CRAP!
ZWOOSH
CRAP!!
FRIGGIN' CAPTAIN SHADES!! HIS TRAINING SCHEDULE WAS BAD ENOUGH BY ITSELF!
ZIIIP
BUT GOIN' AND MUCKIN' UP MY BIKE LIKE THIS...!!?
THOOM
THE WHOLE POINT OF A ROAD BIKE IS TO OPTIMIZE YOUR SPEED!
DROP HANDLEBAR
HOOD
CRUISING
BRAKES AND SHIFT LEVERS (GEAR SHIFTS)
ACCELERATION OR HIGH-SPEED CRUISING
STANDARD
THAT'S WHY THEY COME WITH DROP HANDLEBARS THAT LET YOU USE DIFFERENT POSITIONS!
THE DROPS ARE THE BEST TO USE FOR ACCEL-ERATIN'.
WHEN YOU LOWER YOUR POSITION LIKE THAT...
...YOU REDUCE YOUR WIND RESISTANCE AND CAN DO HIGH-SPEED CRUISIN' TOO.
AND THAT'S WHERE I SHINE.
'COS THAT'S WHEN A SPRINTER TAKES CENTER STAGE!!
ZIIIP

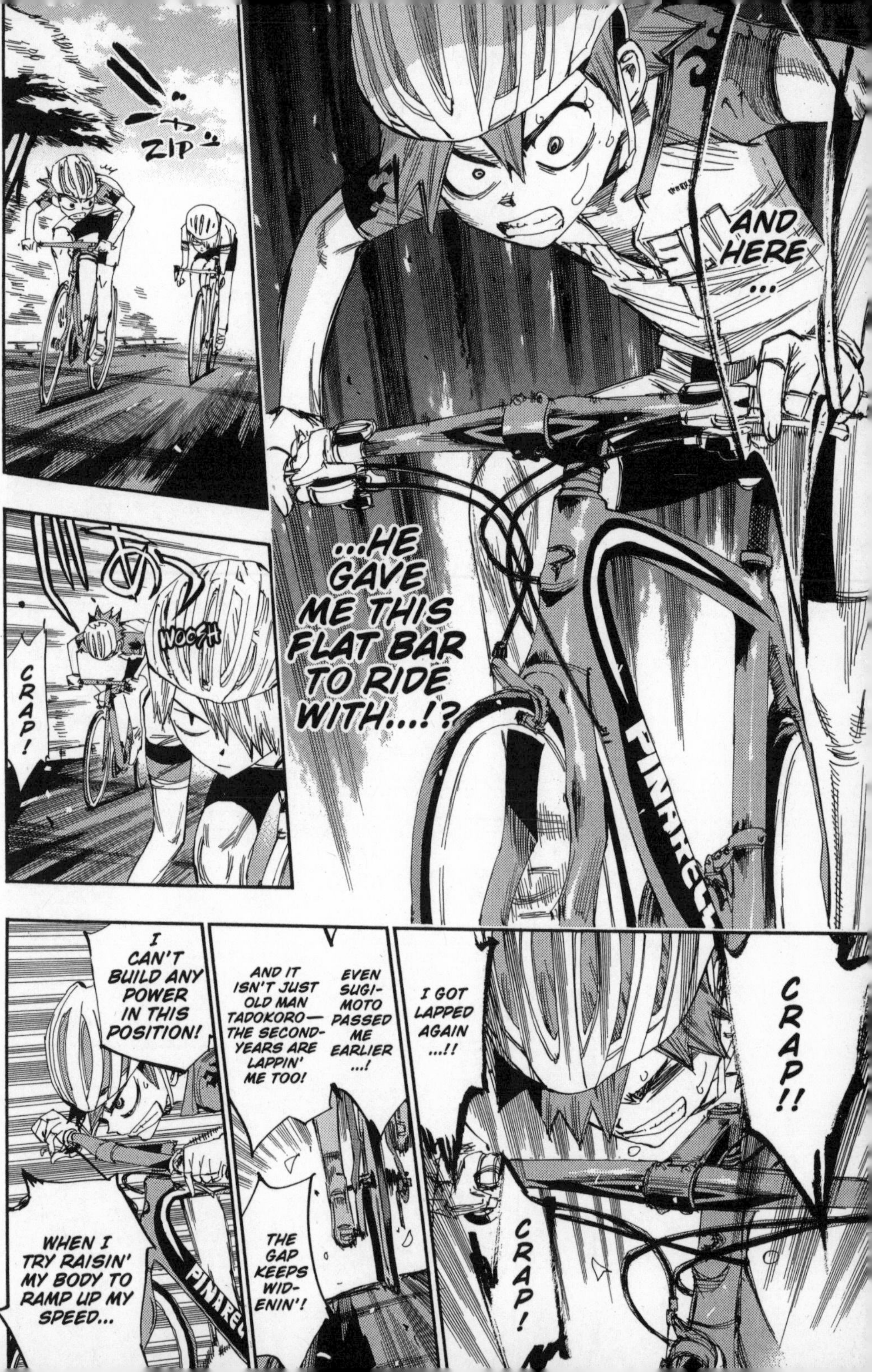
AND HERE...
...HE GAVE ME THIS FLAT BAR TO RIDE WITH...!?
ZIP
WOOSH
CRAP!
CRAP!!
I GOT LAPPED AGAIN...!!
CRAP!
EVEN SUGIMOTO PASSED ME EARLIER...!
AND IT ISN'T JUST OLD MAN TADOKORO—THE SECOND-YEARS ARE LAPPIN' ME TOO!
THE GAP KEEPS WIDENIN'!
I CAN'T BUILD ANY POWER IN THIS POSITION!
WHEN I TRY RAISIN' MY BODY TO RAMP UP MY SPEED...

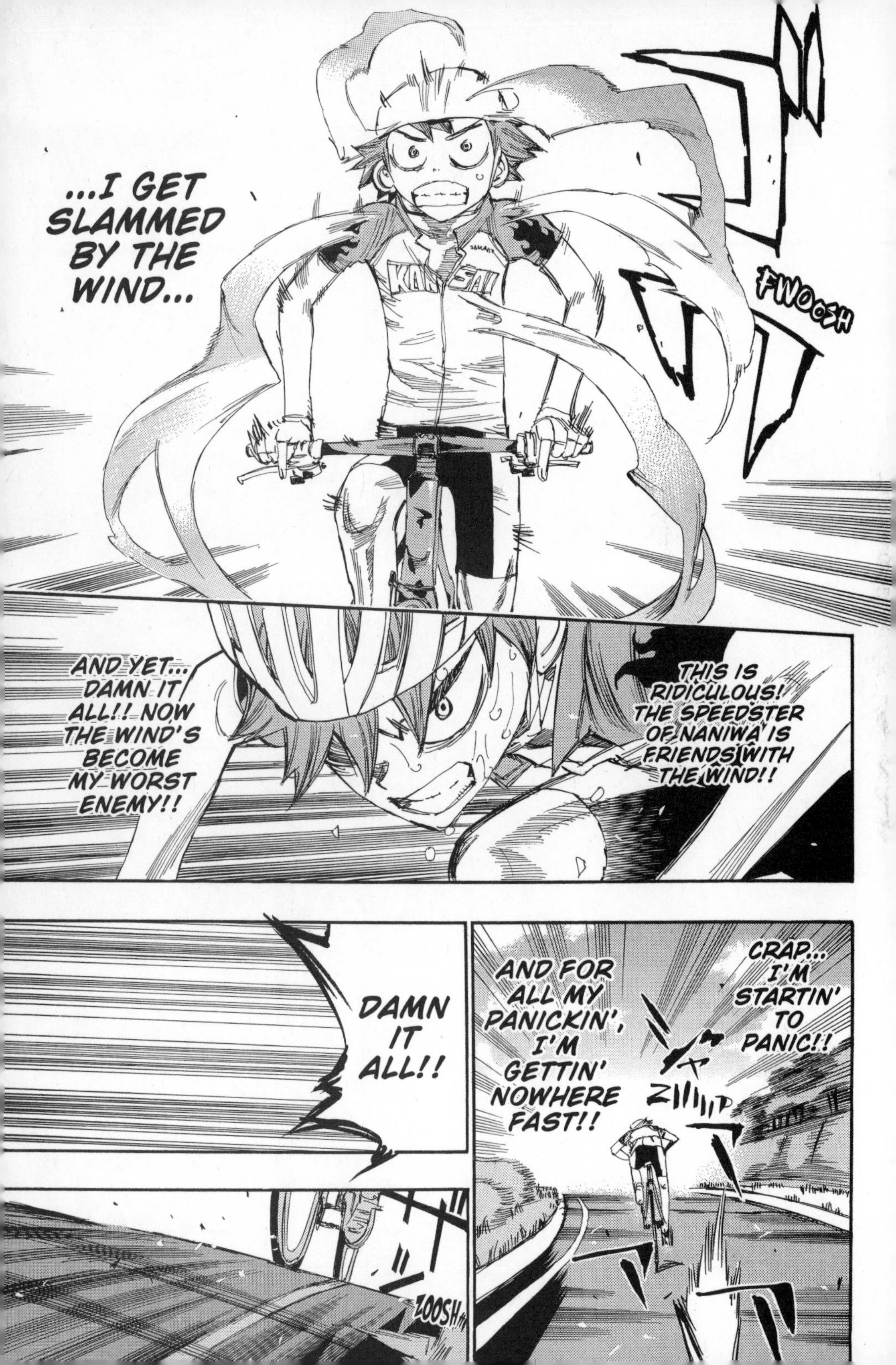
FWOOSH
...I GET SLAMMED BY THE WIND...
THIS IS RIDICULOUS! THE SPEEDSTER OF NANIWA IS FRIENDS WITH THE WIND!!
AND YET... DAMN IT ALL!! NOW THE WIND'S BECOME MY WORST ENEMY!!
CRAP... I'M STARTIN' TO PANIC!!
AND FOR ALL MY PANICKIN', I'M GETTIN' NOWHERE FAST!!
ZIIIIIP
DAMN IT ALL!!
ZOOSH

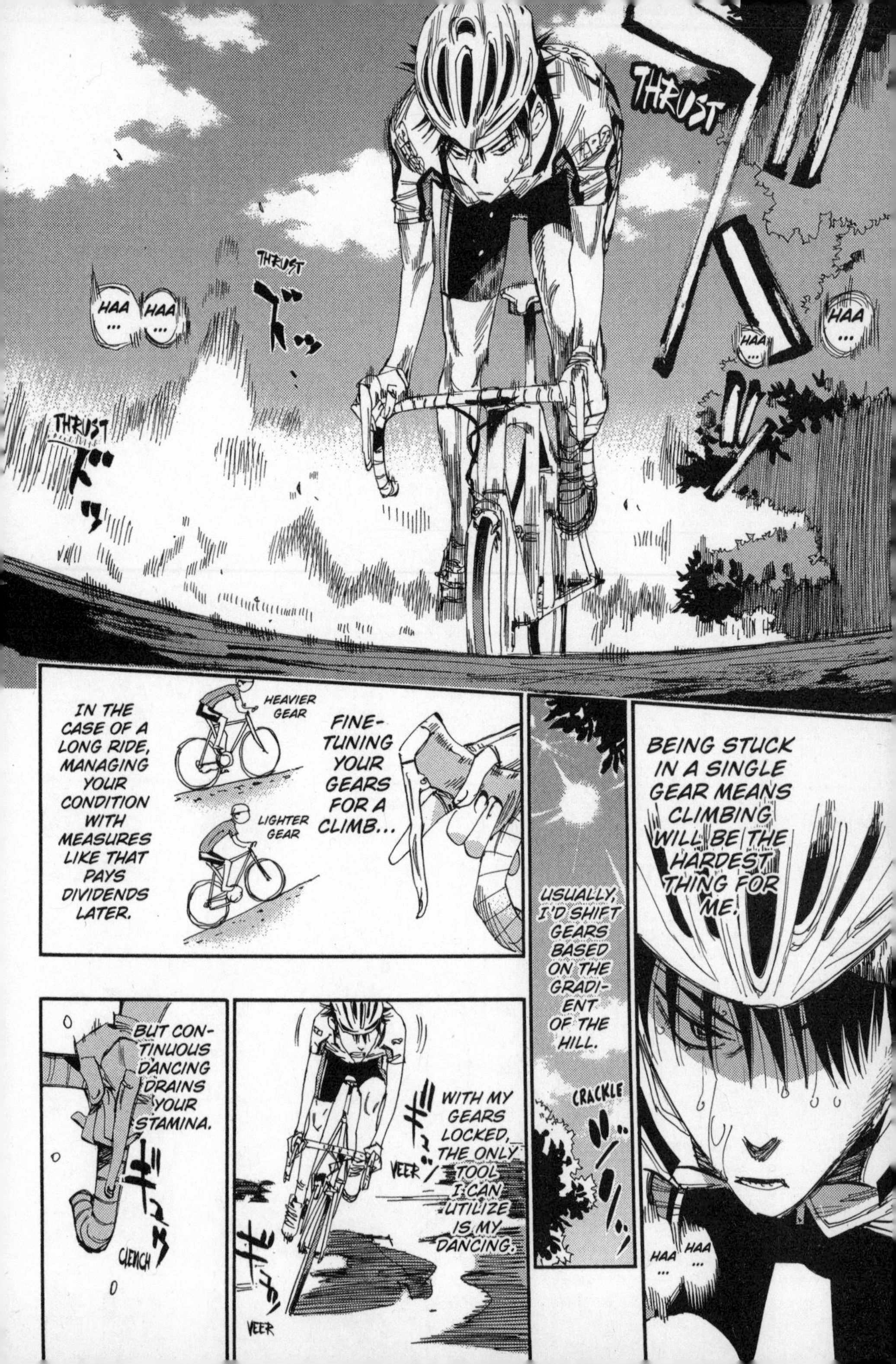

THRUST
HAA...
HAA...
THRUST
HAA...
HAA...
THRUST
BEING STUCK IN A SINGLE GEAR MEANS CLIMBING WILL BE THE HARDEST THING FOR ME.
HAA...
HAA...
USUALLY, I'D SHIFT GEARS BASED ON THE GRADIENT OF THE HILL.
CRACKLE
FINE-TUNING YOUR GEARS FOR A CLIMB...
HEAVIER GEAR
LIGHTER GEAR
IN THE CASE OF A LONG RIDE, MANAGING YOUR CONDITION WITH MEASURES LIKE THAT PAYS DIVIDENDS LATER.
WITH MY GEARS LOCKED, THE ONLY TOOL I CAN UTILIZE IS MY DANCING.
VEER
VEER
BUT CONTINUOUS DANCING DRAINS YOUR STAMINA.
CLENCH

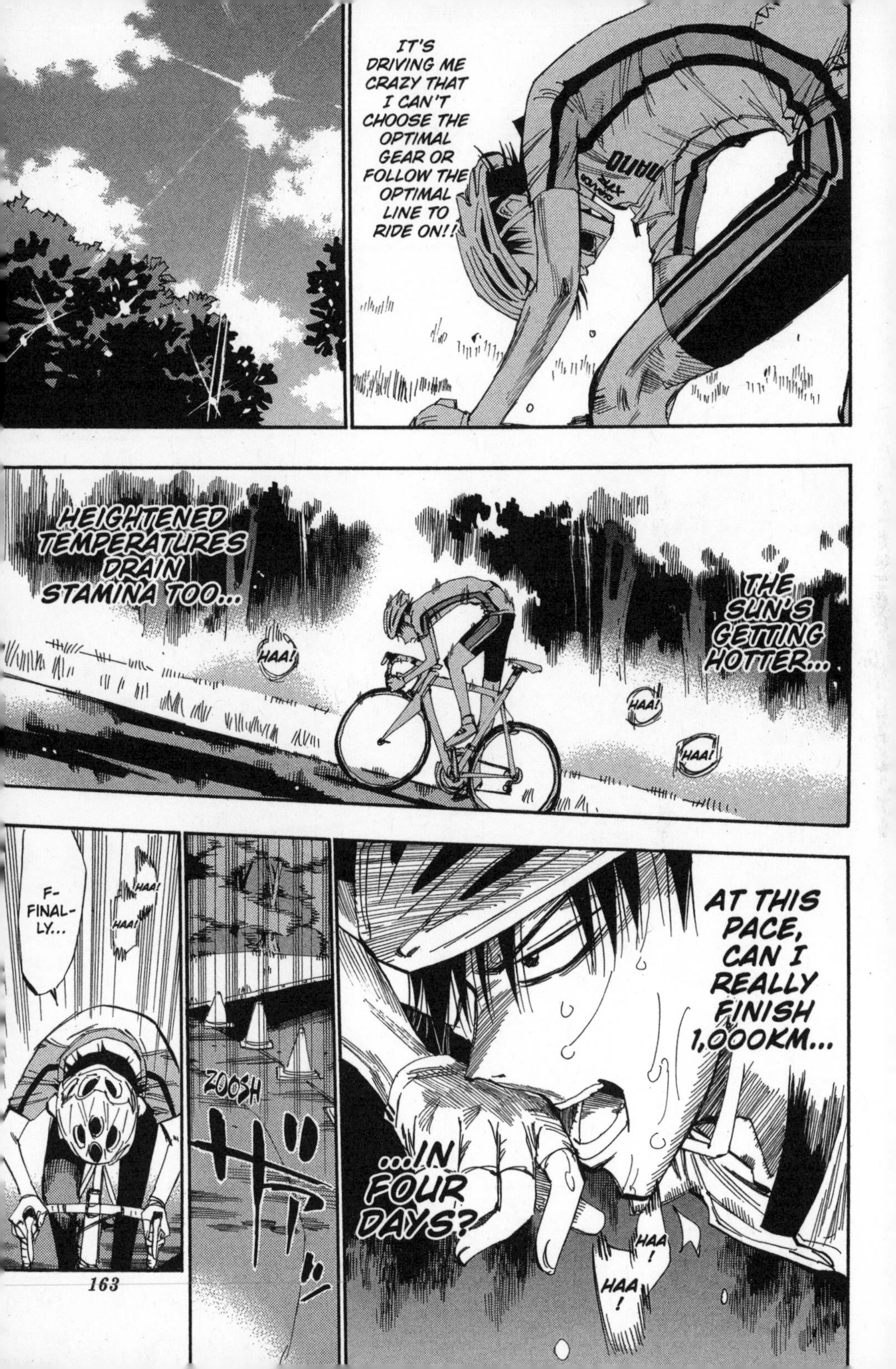
IT'S DRIVING ME CRAZY THAT I CAN'T CHOOSE THE OPTIMAL GEAR OR FOLLOW THE OPTIMAL LINE TO RIDE ON!!
THE SUN'S GETTING HOTTER...
HAA!
HAA!
HAA!
HEIGHTENED TEMPERATURES DRAIN STAMINA TOO...
AT THIS PACE, CAN I REALLY FINISH 1,000KM...
...IN FOUR DAYS?
HAA!
HAA!
ZOOSH
HAA!
HAA!
F-FINAL-LY...

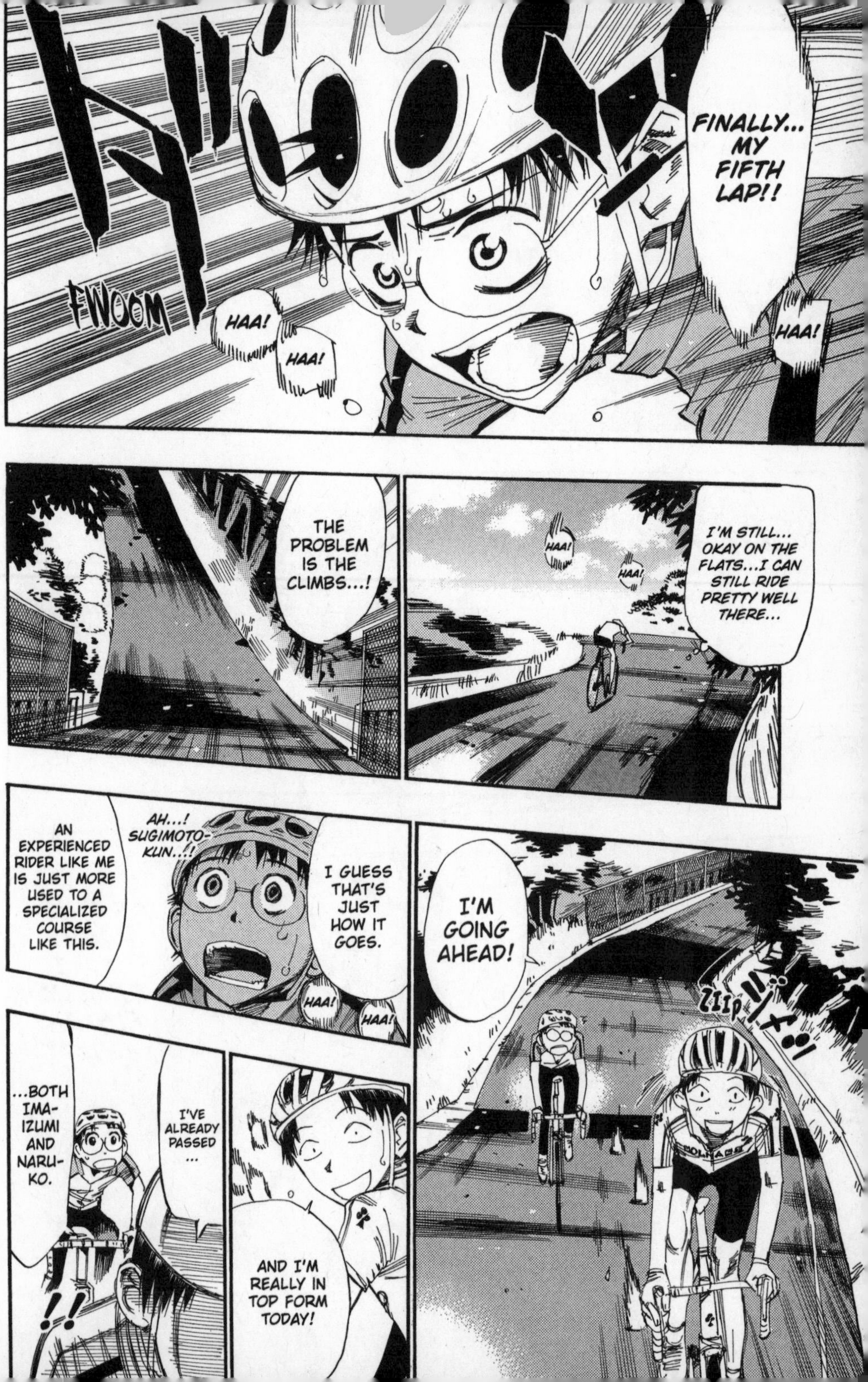
FINALLY... MY FIFTH LAP!!
HAA!
HAA!
HAA!
FWOOM
I'M STILL... OKAY ON THE FLATS...I CAN STILL RIDE PRETTY WELL THERE...
HAA!
HAA!
THE PROBLEM IS THE CLIMBS...!
I'M GOING AHEAD!
ZIIP
I GUESS THAT'S JUST HOW IT GOES.
AH...! SUGIMOTO-KUN...!
AN EXPERIENCED RIDER LIKE ME IS JUST MORE USED TO A SPECIALIZED COURSE LIKE THIS.
HAA!
HAA!
I'VE ALREADY PASSED ...
...BOTH IMAIZUMI AND NARUKO.
AND I'M REALLY IN TOP FORM TODAY!
!!

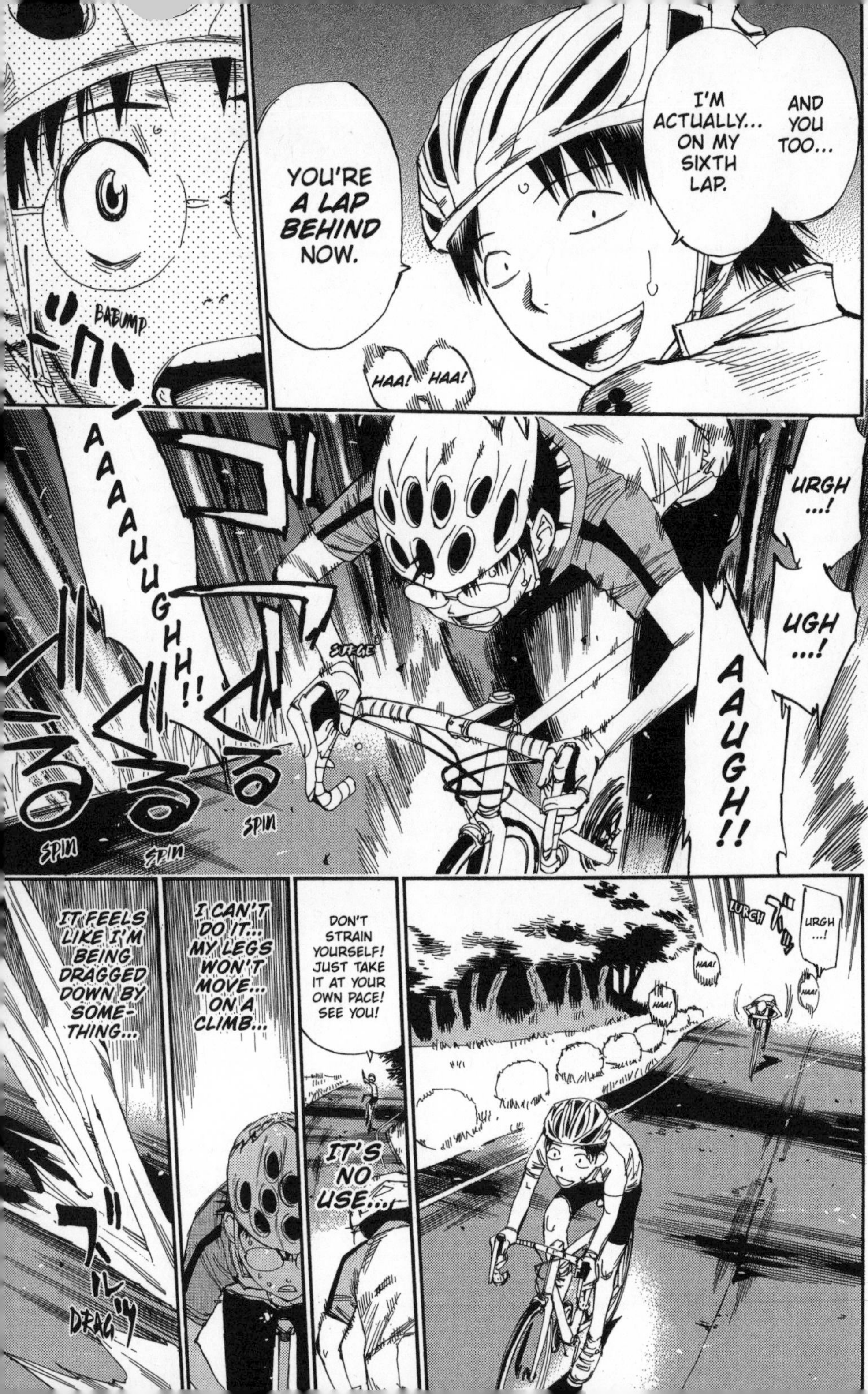
AND YOU TOO...
I'M ACTUALLY... ON MY SIXTH LAP.
YOU'RE A LAP BEHIND NOW.
HAA! HAA!
BABUMP
URGH ...!
UGH ...!
AAUGH!!
AAAAAUUGHH!!
SURGE
SPIN
SPIN
SPIN
ZURCH
URGH ...!
HAA!
HAA!
HAA!
DON'T STRAIN YOURSELF! JUST TAKE IT AT YOUR OWN PACE! SEE YOU!
IT'S NO USE...
I CAN'T DO IT... MY LEGS WON'T MOVE... ON A CLIMB...
IT FEELS LIKE I'M BEING DRAGGED DOWN BY SOME-THING...
DRAG

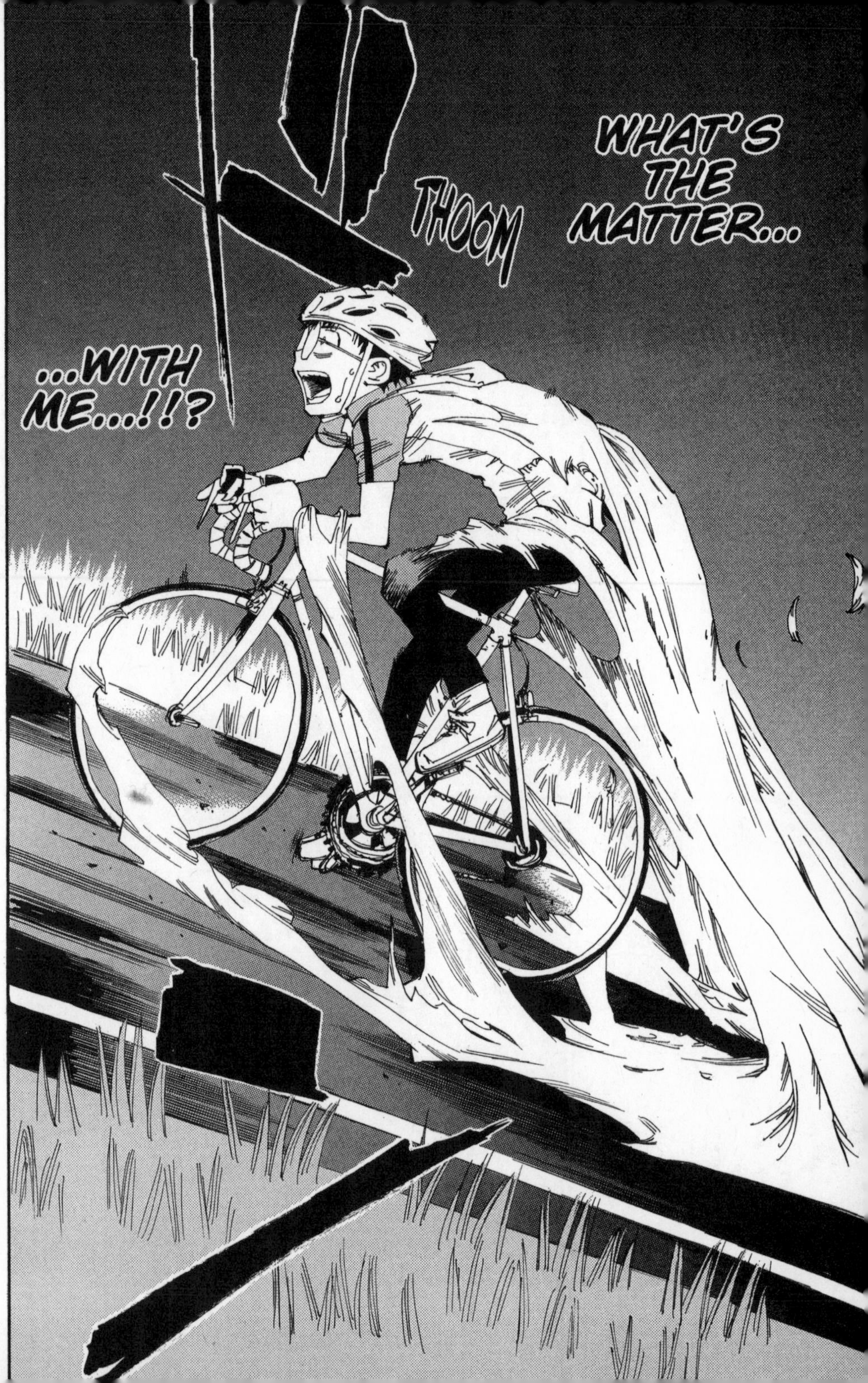
WHAT'S THE MATTER...
THOOM
...WITH ME...!!?

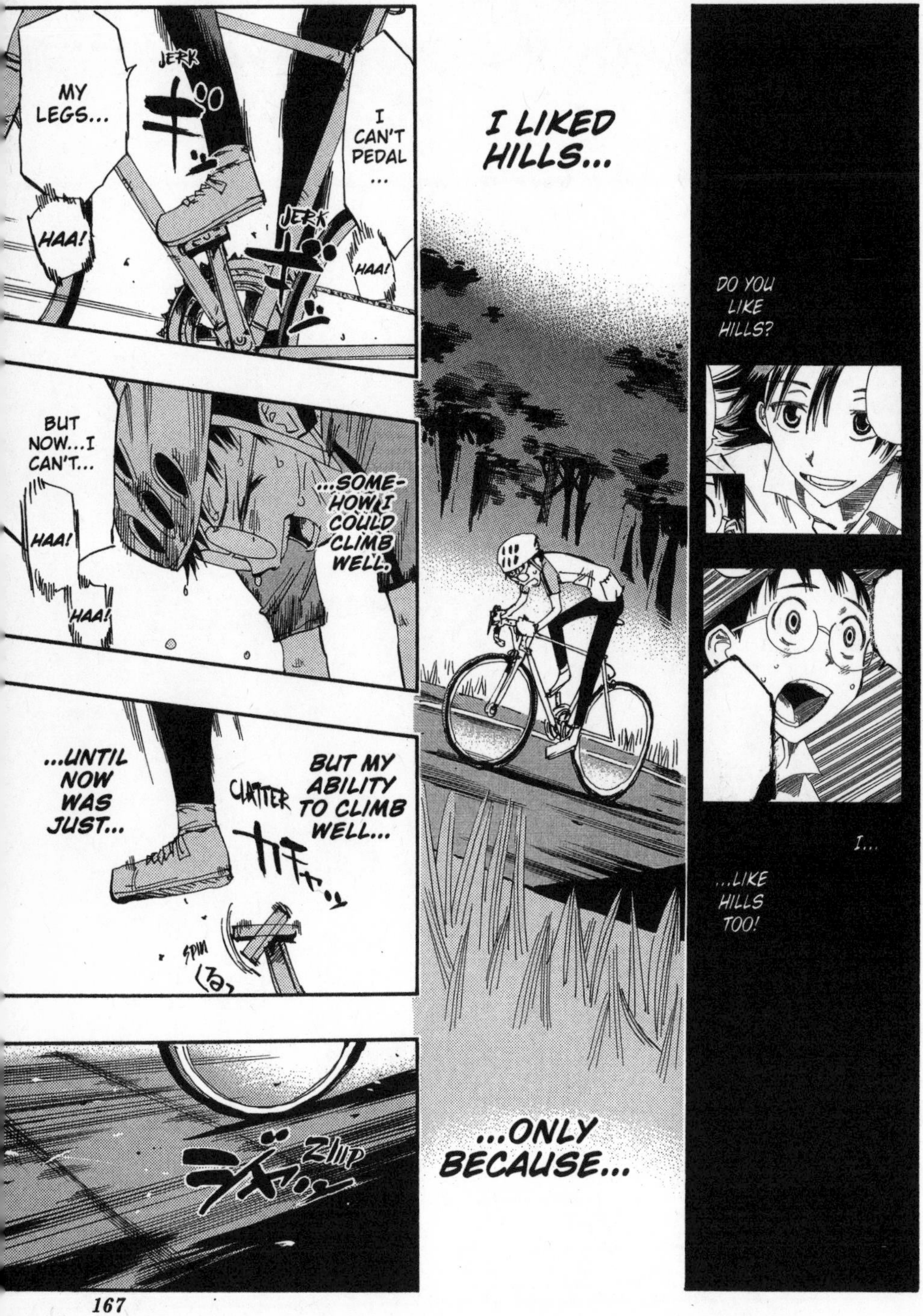
DO YOU LIKE HILLS?
I...
...LIKE HILLS TOO!
I LIKED HILLS...
...ONLY BECAUSE...
JERK
MY LEGS...
I CAN'T PEDAL ...
JERK
HAA!
HAA!
...SOME-HOW, I COULD CLIMB WELL.
BUT NOW...I CAN'T...
HAA!
HAA!
BUT MY ABILITY TO CLIMB WELL...
...UNTIL NOW WAS JUST...
CLATTER
SPIN
ZIIIP

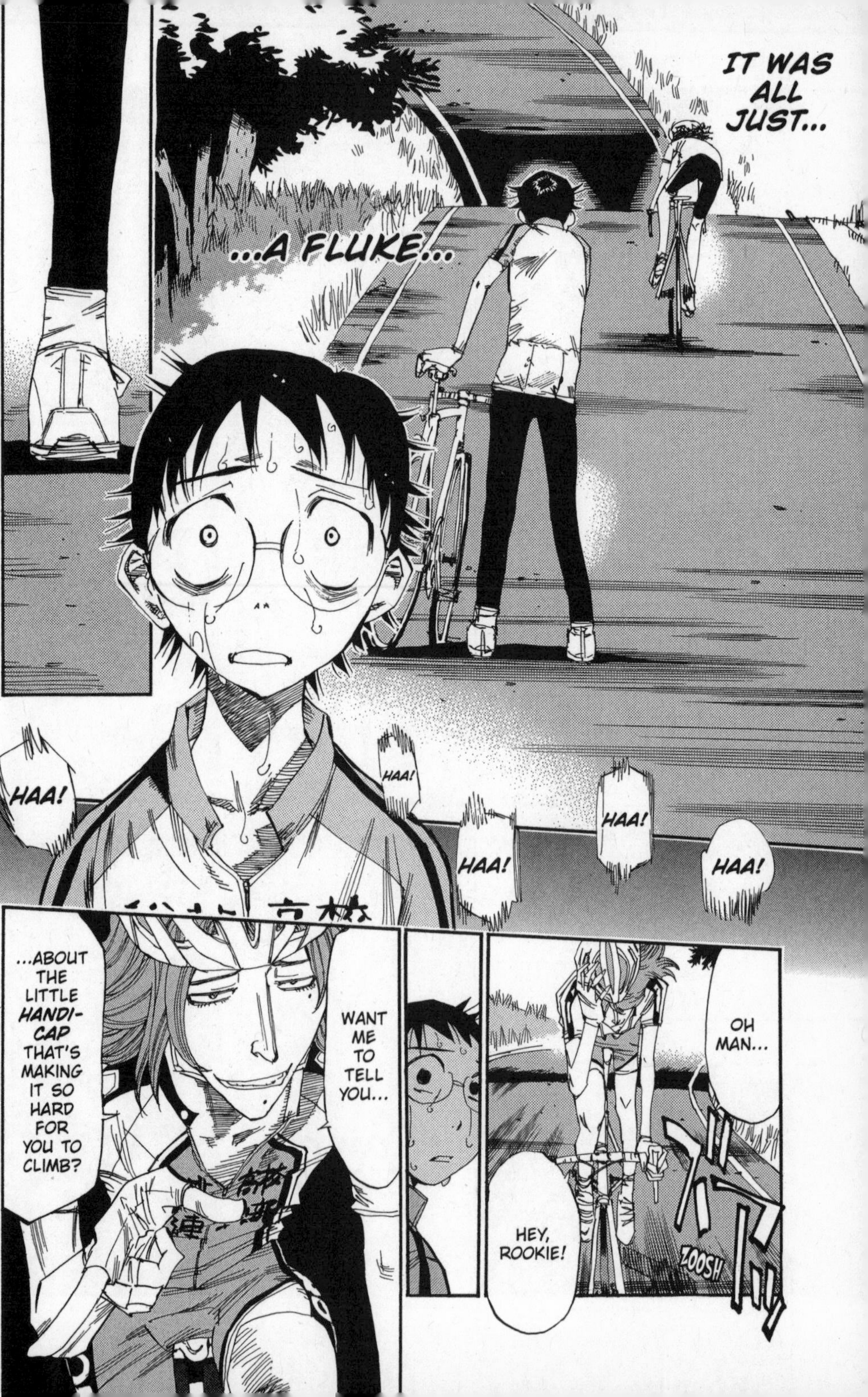
IT WAS ALL JUST...
...A FLUKE...
HAA!
HAA!
HAA!
HAA!
HAA!
OH MAN...
HEY, ROOKIE!
ZOOSH
WANT ME TO TELL YOU...
...ABOUT THE LITTLE HANDI-CAP THAT'S MAKING IT SO HARD FOR YOU TO CLIMB?

RIDE.43 THE HANDICAP HURDLE

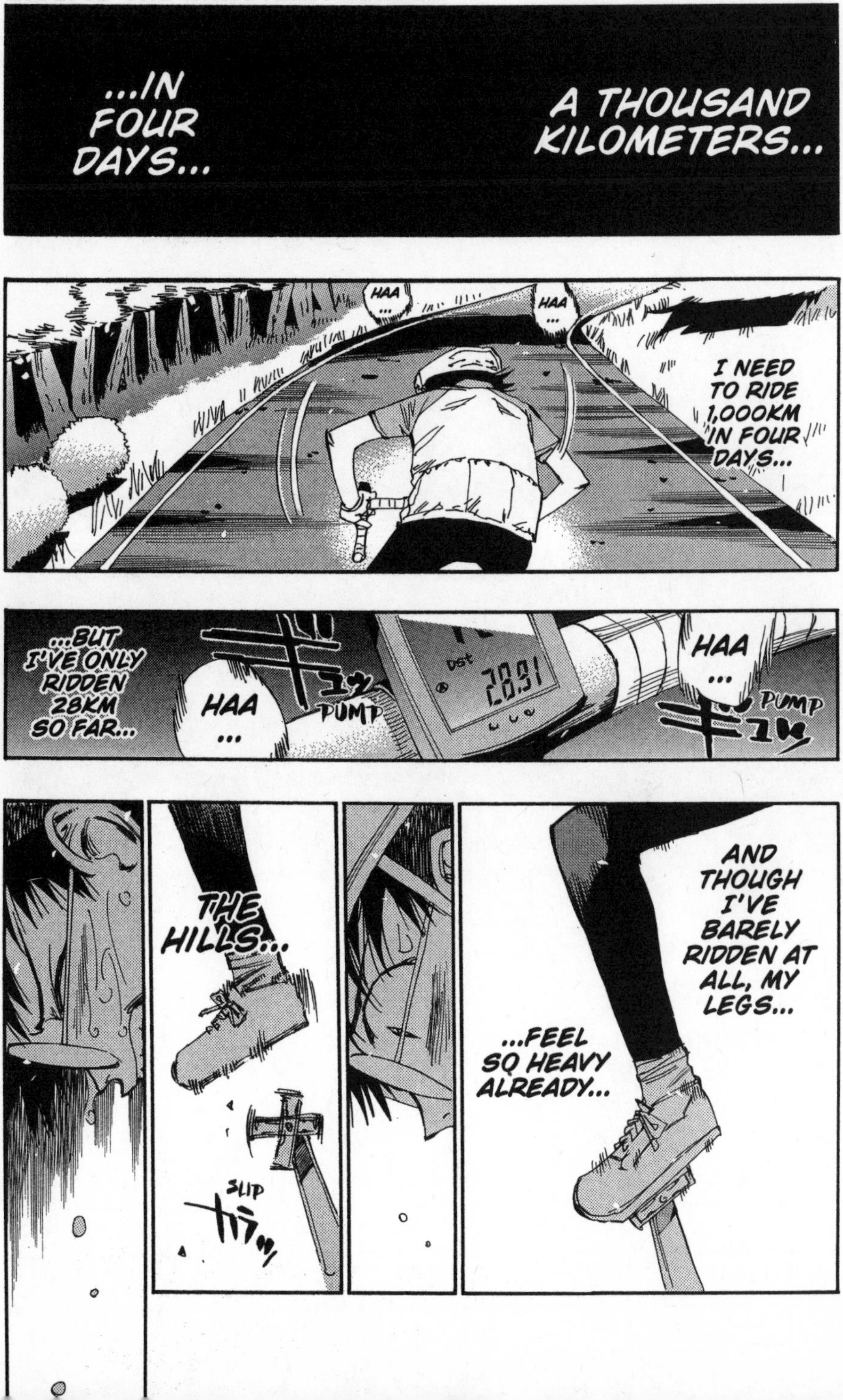
A THOUSAND KILOMETERS...
...IN FOUR DAYS...
HAA...
HAA...
I NEED TO RIDE 1,000KM IN FOUR DAYS...
HAA...
PUMP
DST
28.91
PUMP
HAA...
...BUT I'VE ONLY RIDDEN 28KM SO FAR...
AND THOUGH I'VE BARELY RIDDEN AT ALL, MY LEGS...
...FEEL SO HEAVY ALREADY...
THE HILLS...
SLIP

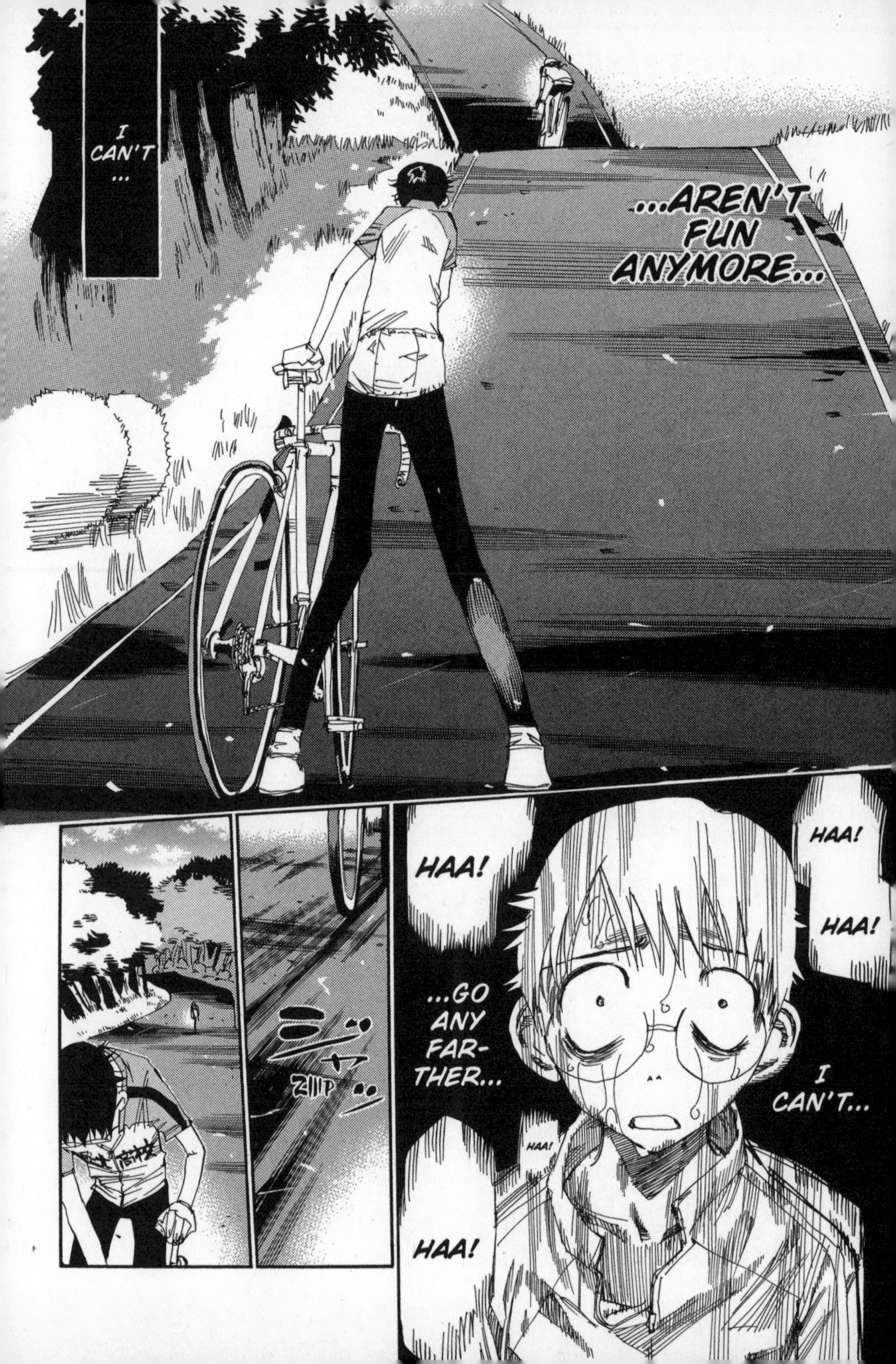
...AREN'T FUN ANYMORE...
I CAN'T ...
HAA!
HAA!
I CAN'T...
HAA!
...GO ANY FAR-THER...
HAA!
HAA!
ZIIP

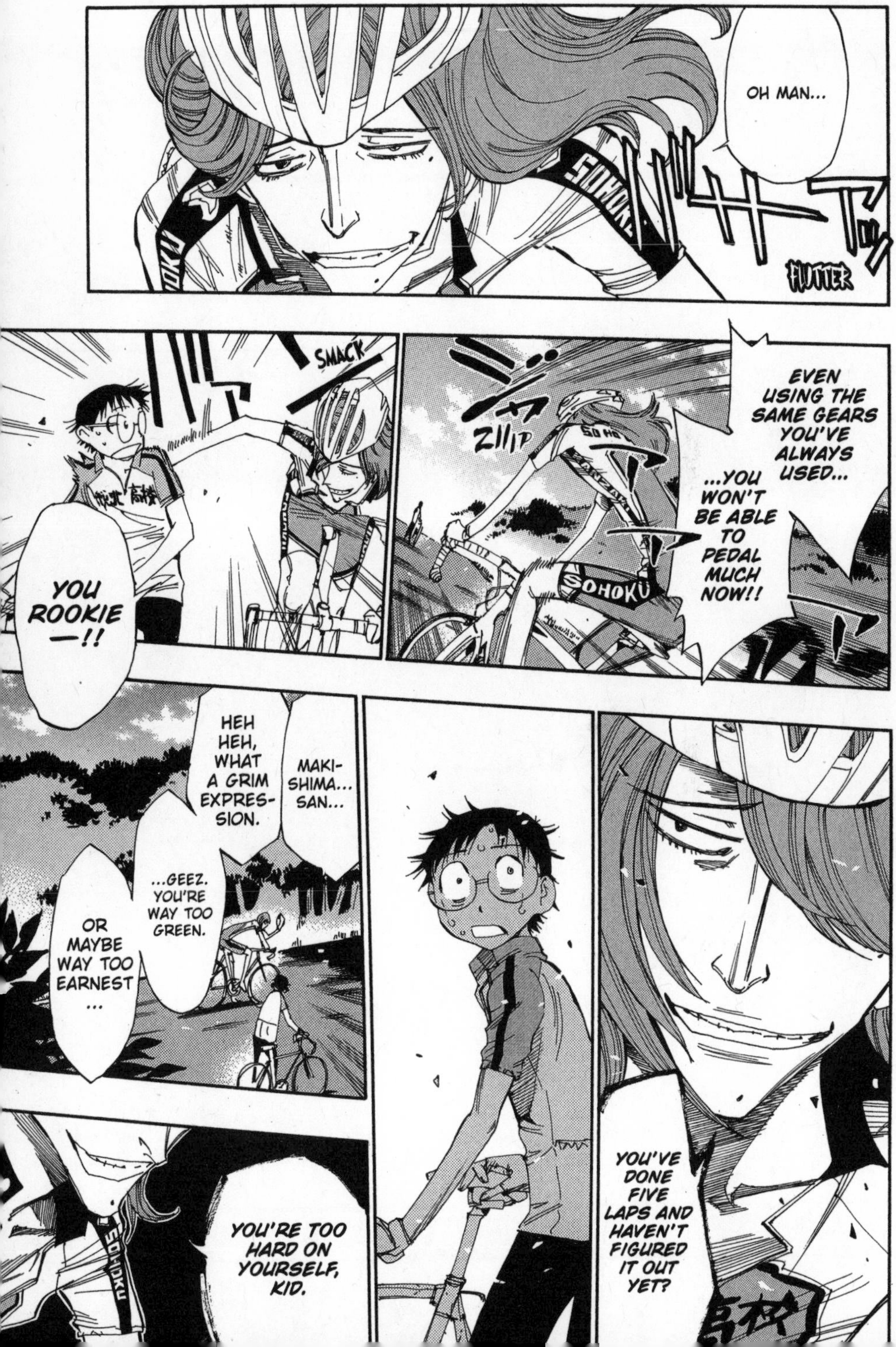
OH MAN...
FLUTTER
EVEN USING THE SAME GEARS YOU'VE ALWAYS USED...
...YOU WON'T BE ABLE TO PEDAL MUCH NOW!!
ZIIIP
SMACK
YOU ROOKIE—!!
YOU'VE DONE FIVE LAPS AND HAVEN'T FIGURED IT OUT YET?
MAKI-SHIMA... SAN...
HEH HEH, WHAT A GRIM EXPRES-SION.
...GEEZ. YOU'RE WAY TOO GREEN.
OR MAYBE WAY TOO EARNEST ...
YOU'RE TOO HARD ON YOURSELF, KID.

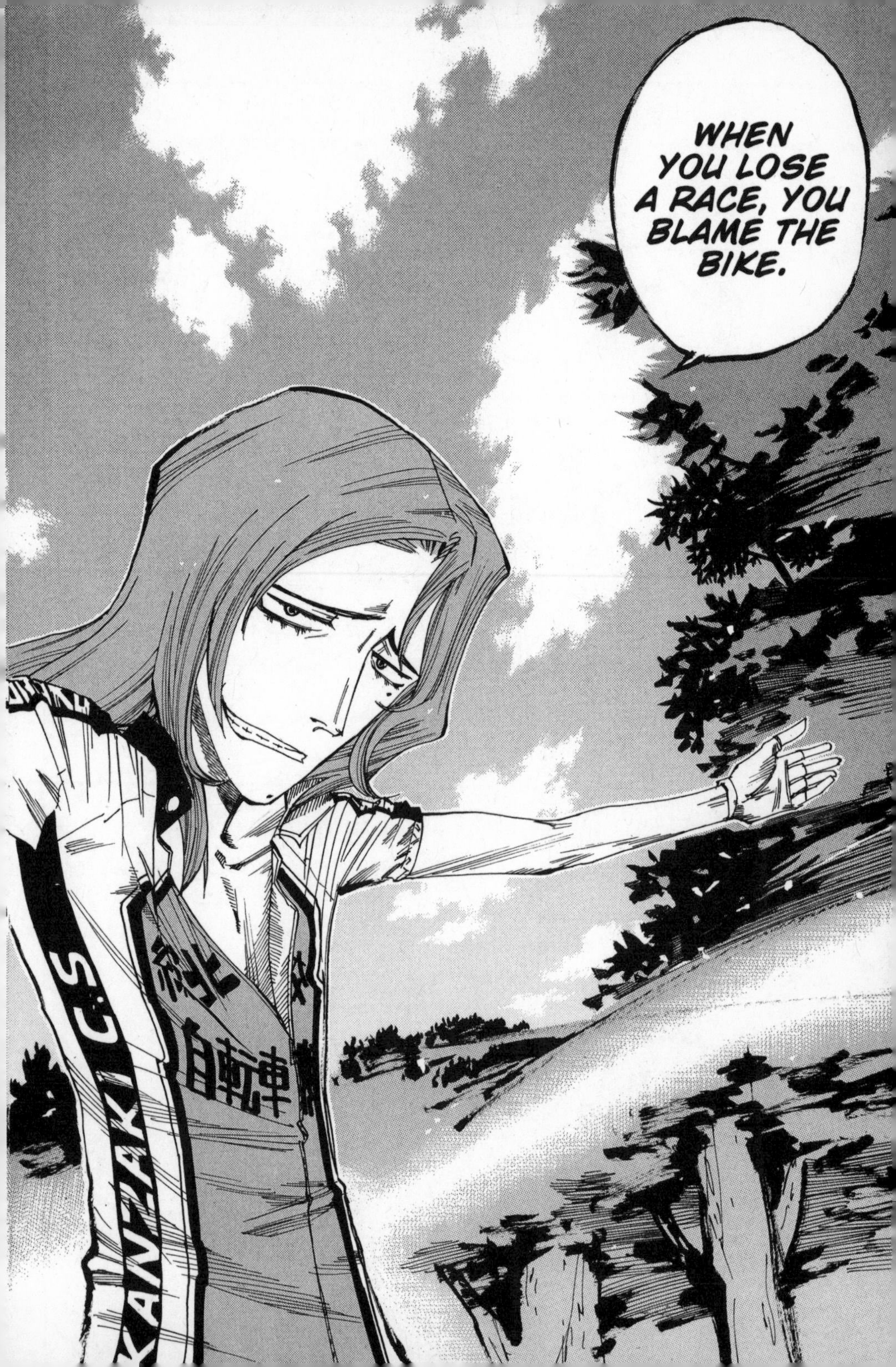
WHEN YOU LOSE A RACE, YOU BLAME THE BIKE.
KANZAKI C.S
自転車

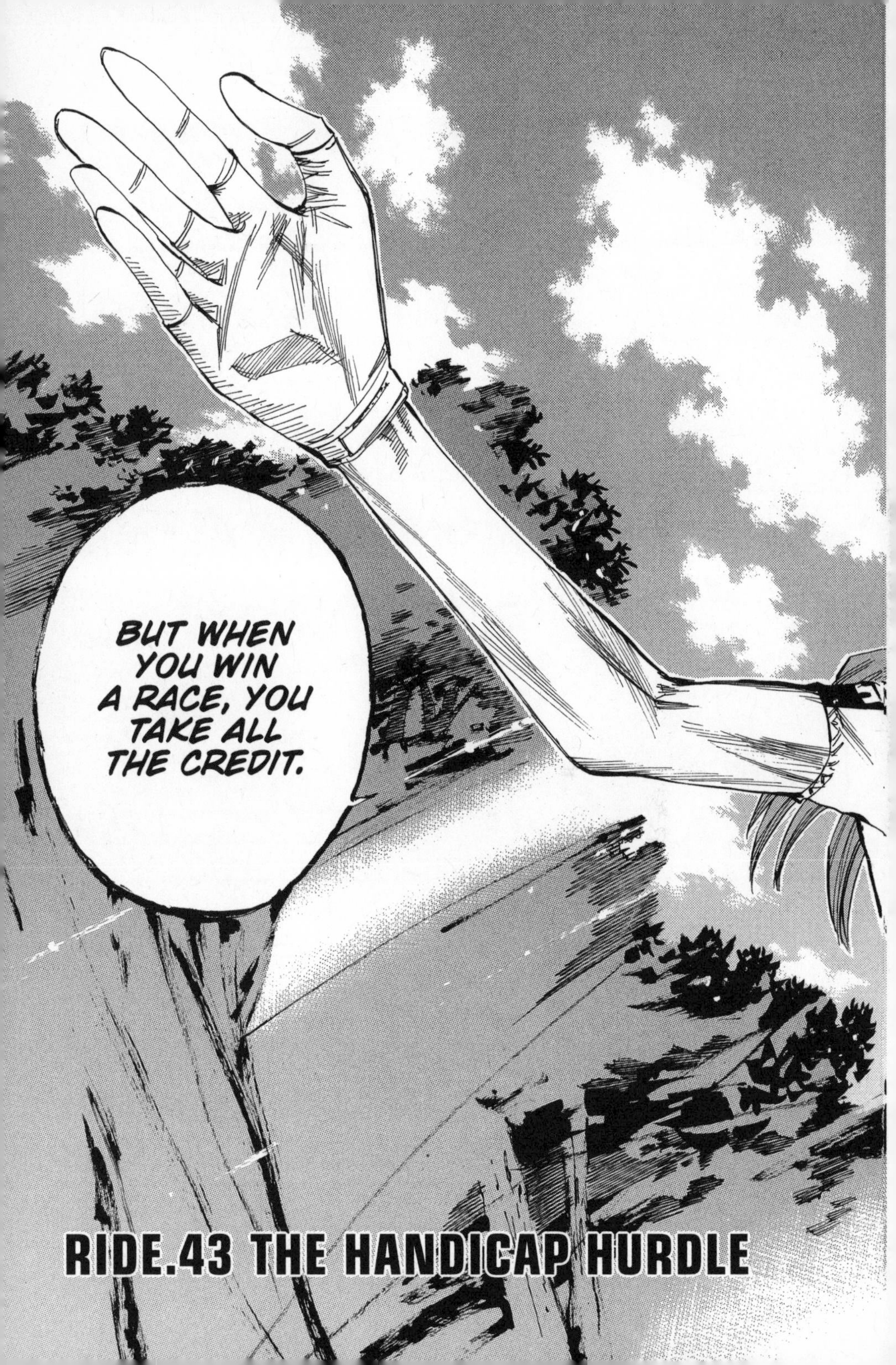
BUT WHEN YOU WIN A RACE, YOU TAKE ALL THE CREDIT.
RIDE.43 THE HANDICAP HURDLE

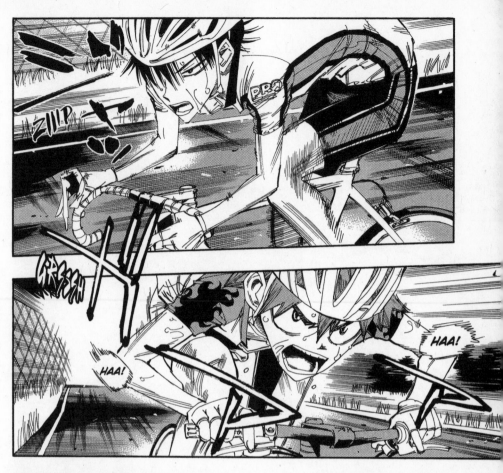

ZIIIP

GREEEN

HAA!

HAA!

WHA...
WHAT
DO YOU
MEAN?

HUH
...?

ゴ!!
ZOOM

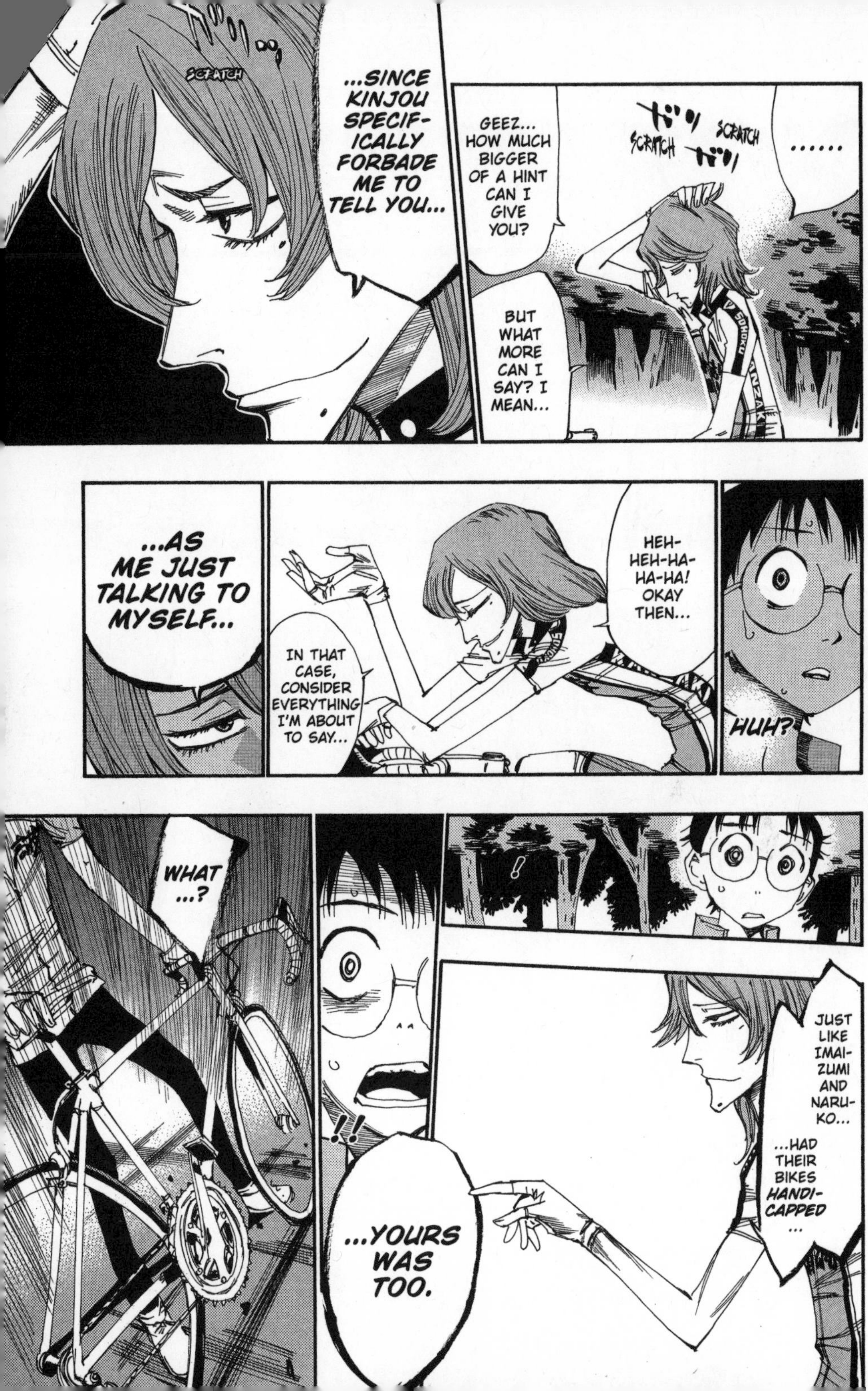
......
SCRATCH
SCRATCH
GEEZ... HOW MUCH BIGGER OF A HINT CAN I GIVE YOU?
BUT WHAT MORE CAN I SAY? I MEAN...
SCRATCH
...SINCE KINJOU SPECIFICALLY FORBADE ME TO TELL YOU...
HUH?
HEH-HEH-HA-HA-HA! OKAY THEN...
IN THAT CASE, CONSIDER EVERYTHING I'M ABOUT TO SAY...
...AS ME JUST TALKING TO MYSELF...
!
JUST LIKE IMAIZUMI AND NARUKO...
...HAD THEIR BIKES HANDICAPPED...
...YOURS WAS TOO.
!!
WHAT ...?

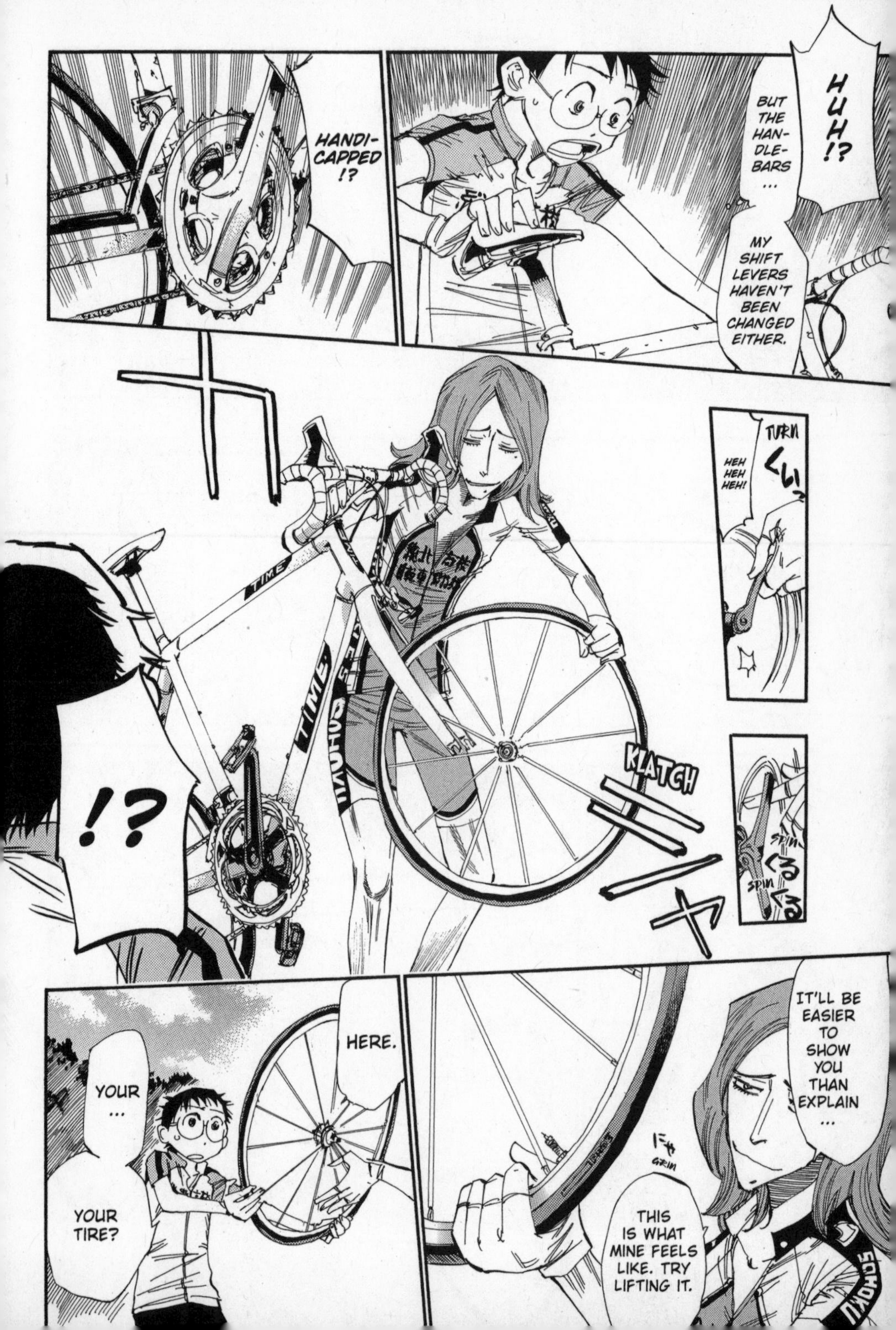
HUH!?
BUT THE HANDLEBARS...
MY SHIFT LEVERS HAVEN'T BEEN CHANGED EITHER.
HANDICAPPED!?
TURN
HEH HEH HEH!
SPIN
SPIN
KLATCH
!?
IT'LL BE EASIER TO SHOW YOU THAN EXPLAIN...
GRIN
THIS IS WHAT MINE FEELS LIKE. TRY LIFTING IT.
HERE.
YOUR...
YOUR TIRE?

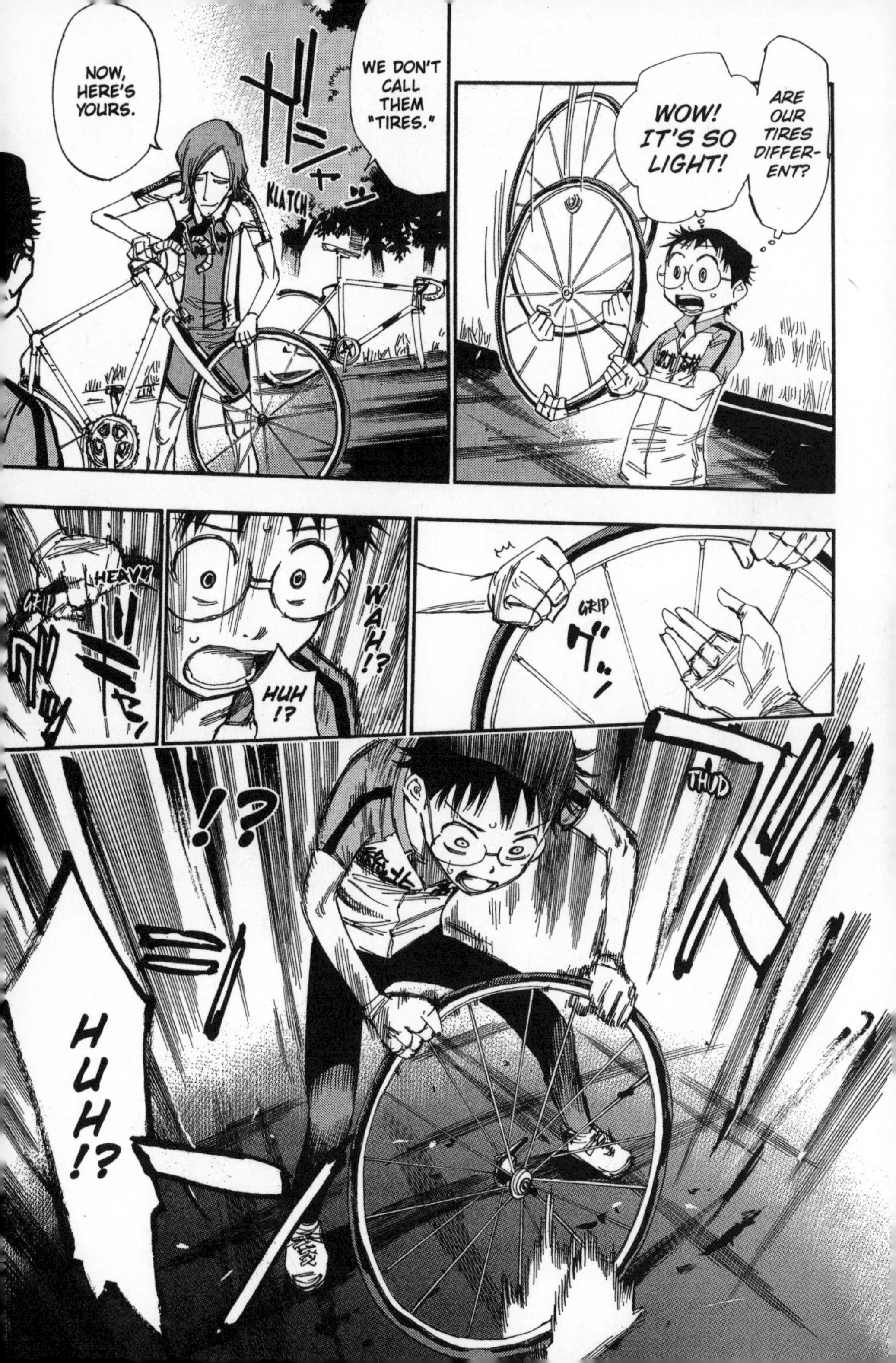
ARE OUR TIRES DIFFERENT?
WOW! IT'S SO LIGHT!
WE DON'T CALL THEM "TIRES."
KLATCH
NOW, HERE'S YOURS.
GRIP
WAH!?
HUH!?
HEAVY
GRIP
THUD
!?
HUH!?

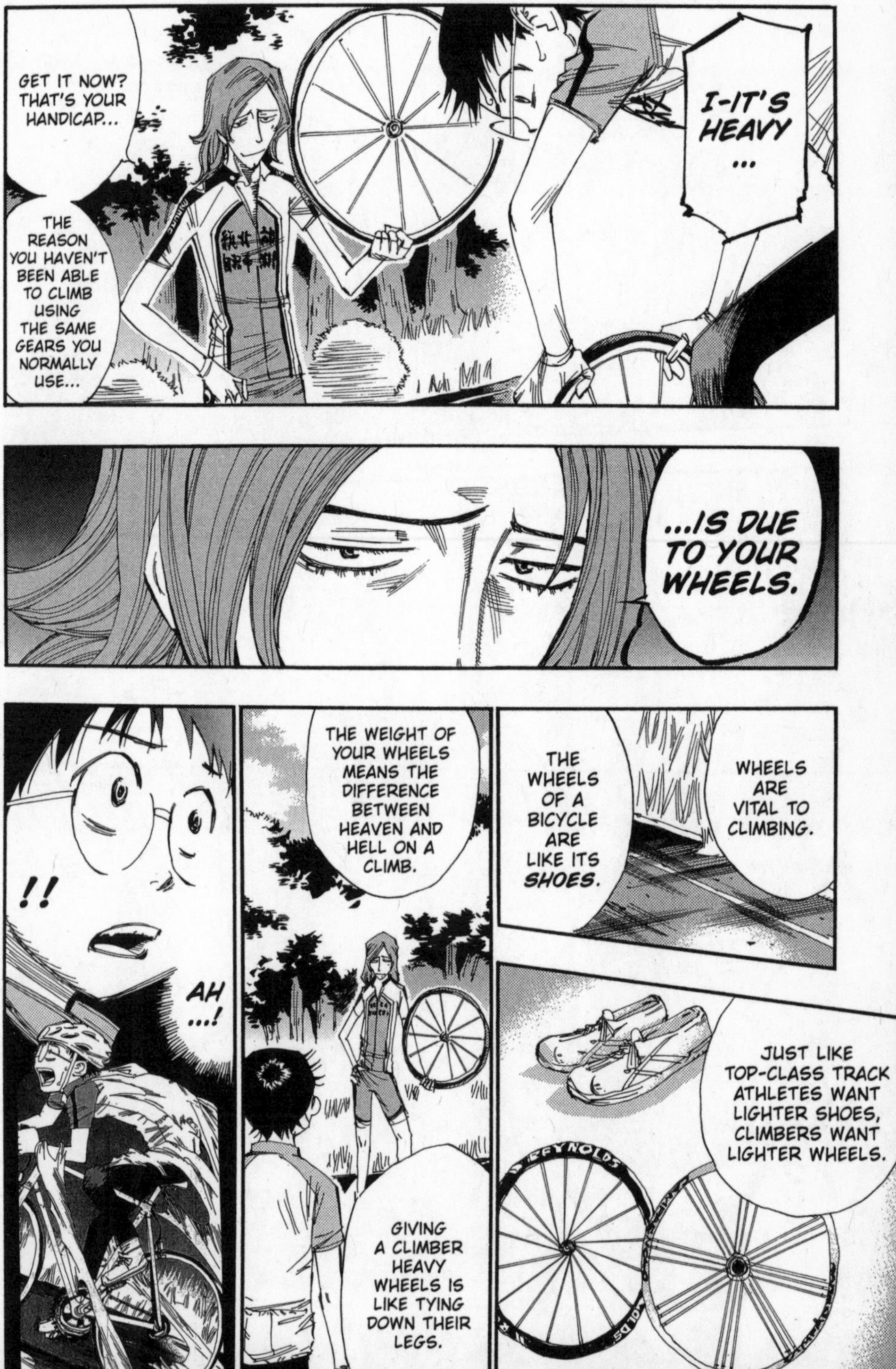
I-IT'S HEAVY ...
GET IT NOW? THAT'S YOUR HANDICAP...
THE REASON YOU HAVEN'T BEEN ABLE TO CLIMB USING THE SAME GEARS YOU NORMALLY USE...
...IS DUE TO YOUR WHEELS.
WHEELS ARE VITAL TO CLIMBING.
THE WHEELS OF A BICYCLE ARE LIKE ITS SHOES.
JUST LIKE TOP-CLASS TRACK ATHLETES WANT LIGHTER SHOES, CLIMBERS WANT LIGHTER WHEELS.
THE WEIGHT OF YOUR WHEELS MEANS THE DIFFERENCE BETWEEN HEAVEN AND HELL ON A CLIMB.
GIVING A CLIMBER HEAVY WHEELS IS LIKE TYING DOWN THEIR LEGS.
!!
AH ...!

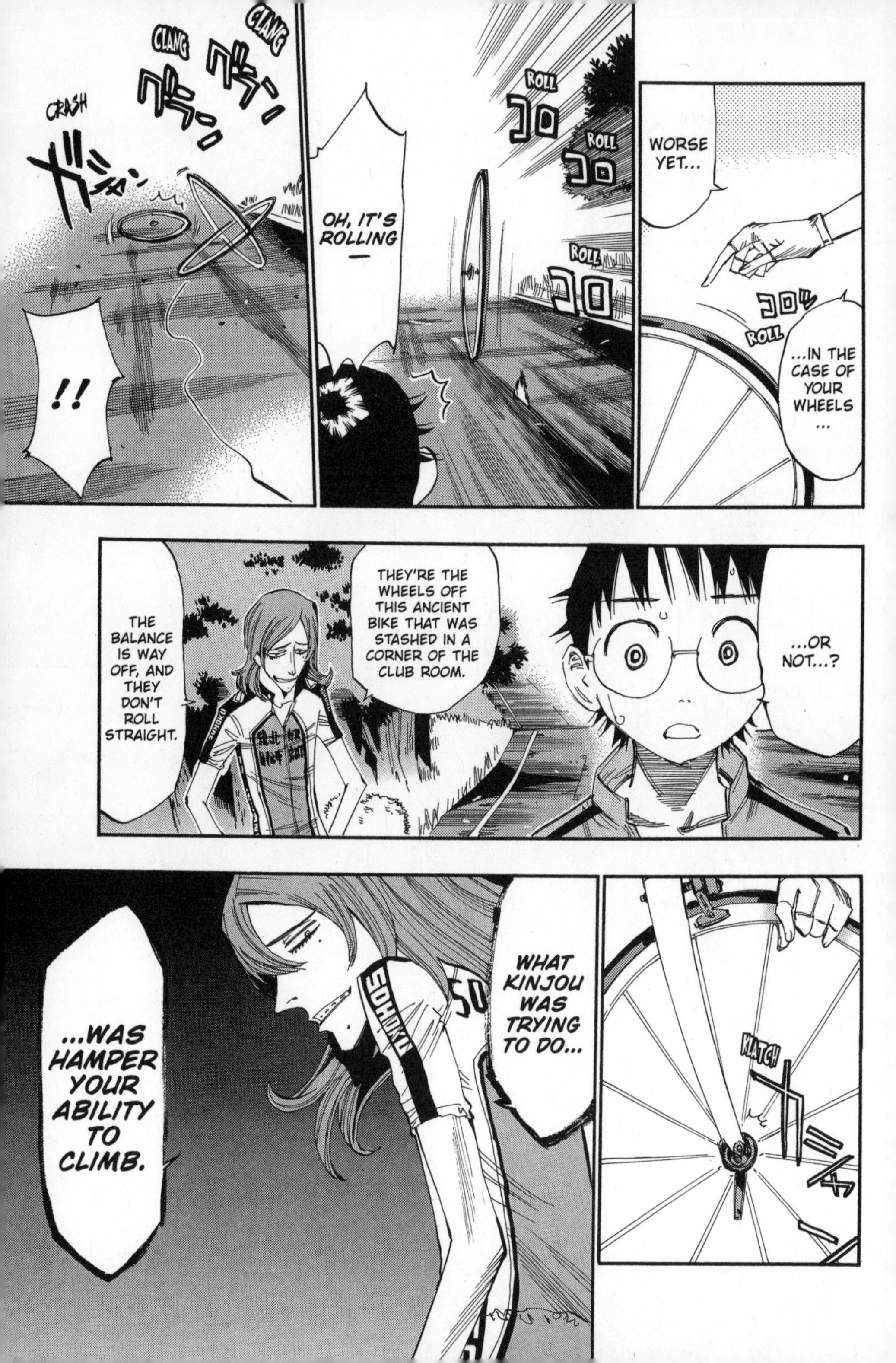
WORSE YET...
ROLL
...IN THE CASE OF YOUR WHEELS ...
ROLL
ROLL
ROLL
OH, IT'S ROLLING —
CLANG
CLANG
CRASH
!!
...OR NOT...?
THEY'RE THE WHEELS OFF THIS ANCIENT BIKE THAT WAS STASHED IN A CORNER OF THE CLUB ROOM.
THE BALANCE IS WAY OFF, AND THEY DON'T ROLL STRAIGHT.
KLATCH
WHAT KINJOU WAS TRYING TO DO...
...WAS HAMPER YOUR ABILITY TO CLIMB.

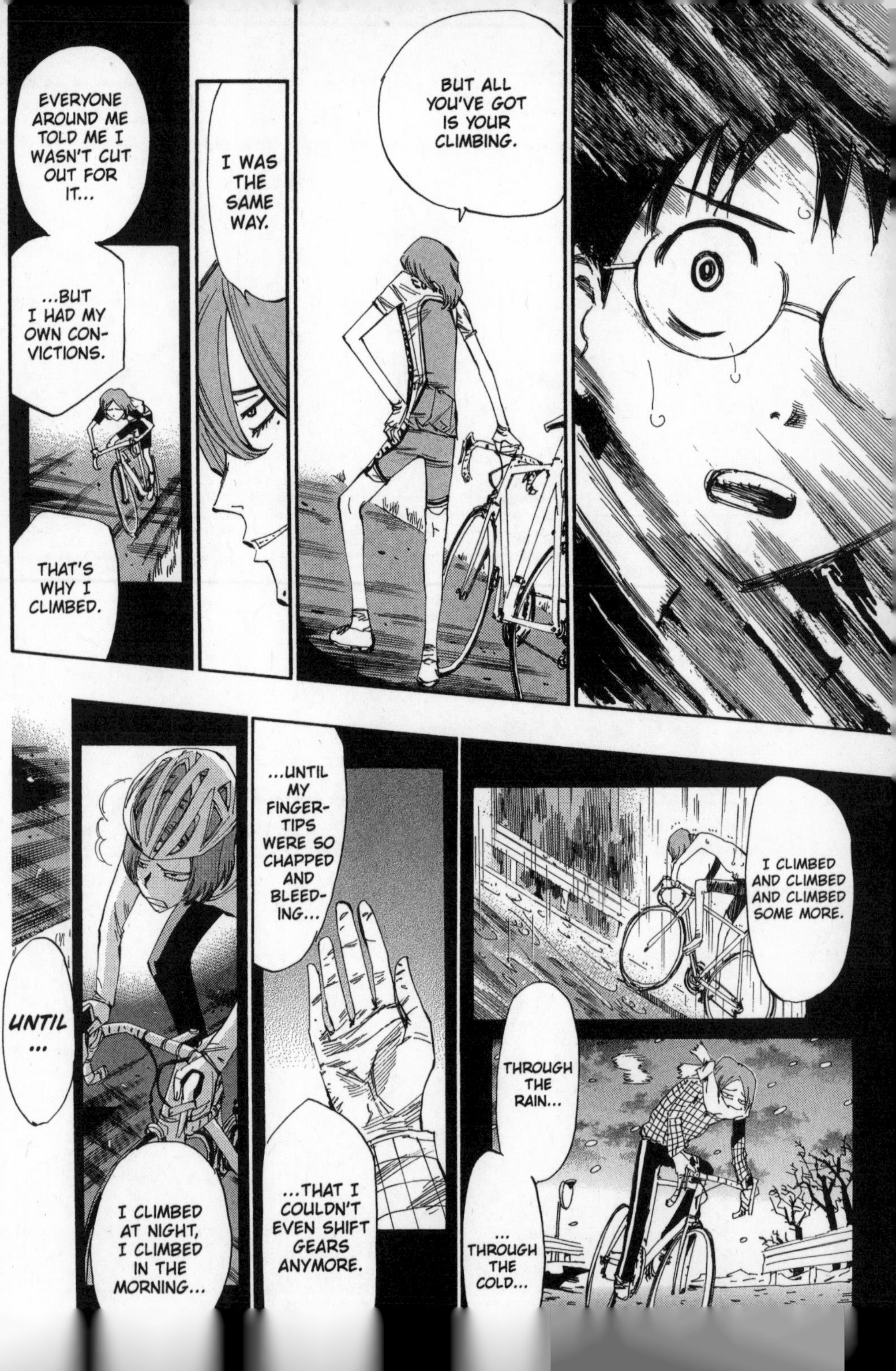
BUT ALL YOU'VE GOT IS YOUR CLIMBING.
I WAS THE SAME WAY.
EVERYONE AROUND ME TOLD ME I WASN'T CUT OUT FOR IT...
...BUT I HAD MY OWN CONVICTIONS.
THAT'S WHY I CLIMBED.
I CLIMBED AND CLIMBED AND CLIMBED SOME MORE.
THROUGH THE RAIN...
...THROUGH THE COLD...
...UNTIL MY FINGERTIPS WERE SO CHAPPED AND BLEEDING...
...THAT I COULDN'T EVEN SHIFT GEARS ANYMORE.
UNTIL...
I CLIMBED AT NIGHT, I CLIMBED IN THE MORNING...

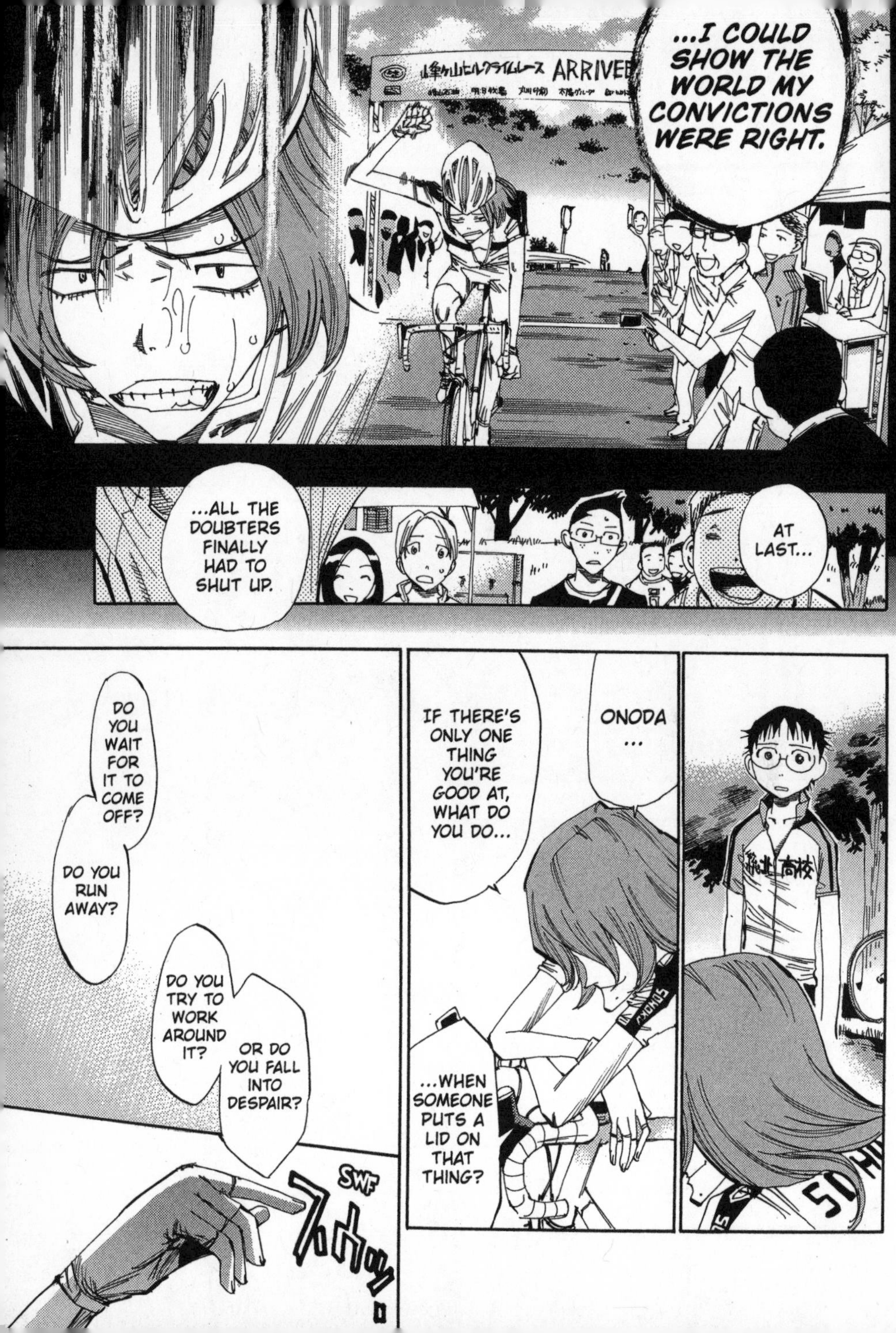
ARRIVEE
...I COULD SHOW THE WORLD MY CONVICTIONS WERE RIGHT.
AT LAST...
...ALL THE DOUBTERS FINALLY HAD TO SHUT UP.
ONODA ...
IF THERE'S ONLY ONE THING YOU'RE GOOD AT, WHAT DO YOU DO...
...WHEN SOMEONE PUTS A LID ON THAT THING?
DO YOU WAIT FOR IT TO COME OFF?
DO YOU RUN AWAY?
DO YOU TRY TO WORK AROUND IT?
OR DO YOU FALL INTO DESPAIR?
SWF

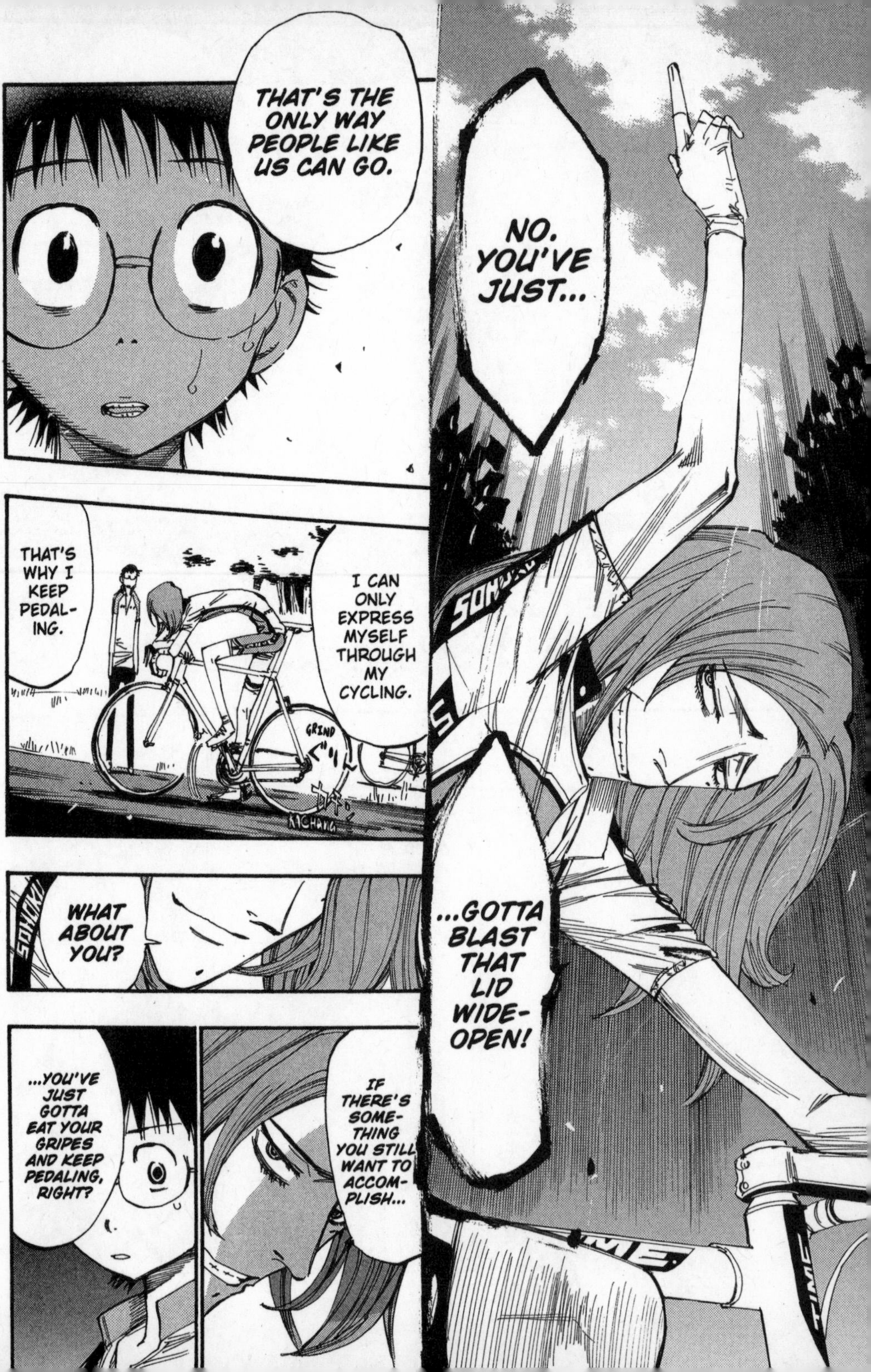
THAT'S THE ONLY WAY PEOPLE LIKE US CAN GO.
I CAN ONLY EXPRESS MYSELF THROUGH MY CYCLING.
THAT'S WHY I KEEP PEDAL-ING.
GRIND
KACHANG
WHAT ABOUT YOU?
IF THERE'S SOME-THING YOU STILL WANT TO ACCOM-PLISH...
...YOU'VE JUST GOTTA EAT YOUR GRIPES AND KEEP PEDALING, RIGHT?
NO. YOU'VE JUST...
...GOTTA BLAST THAT LID WIDE-OPEN!

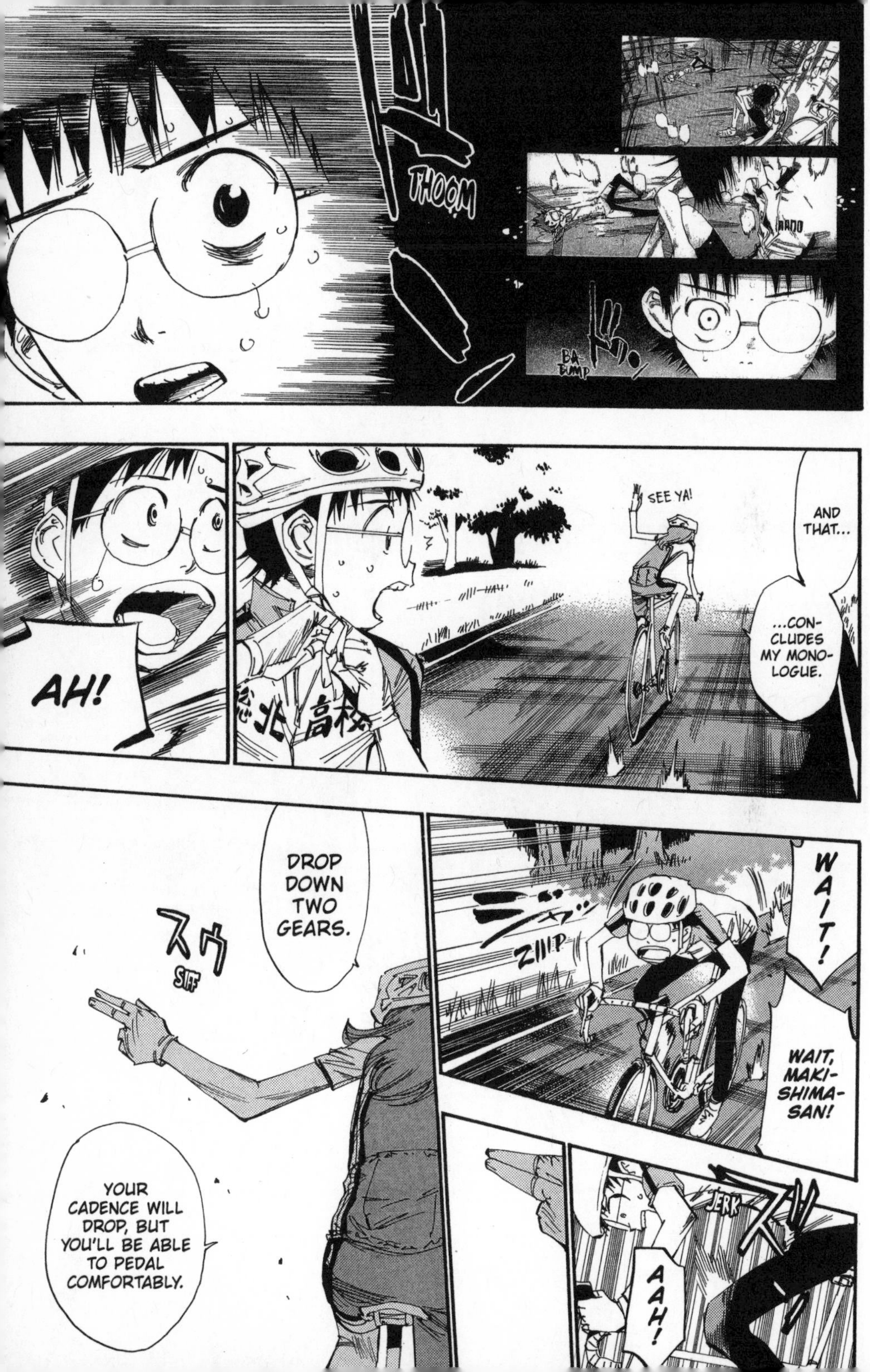
BA-BUMP
THOOM
SEE YA!
AND THAT...
...CON-CLUDES MY MONO-LOGUE.
AH!
WAIT!
ZIP
WAIT, MAKI-SHIMA-SAN!
JERK
AAH!
DROP DOWN TWO GEARS.
スウ
SIFF
YOUR CADENCE WILL DROP, BUT YOU'LL BE ABLE TO PEDAL COMFORTABLY.

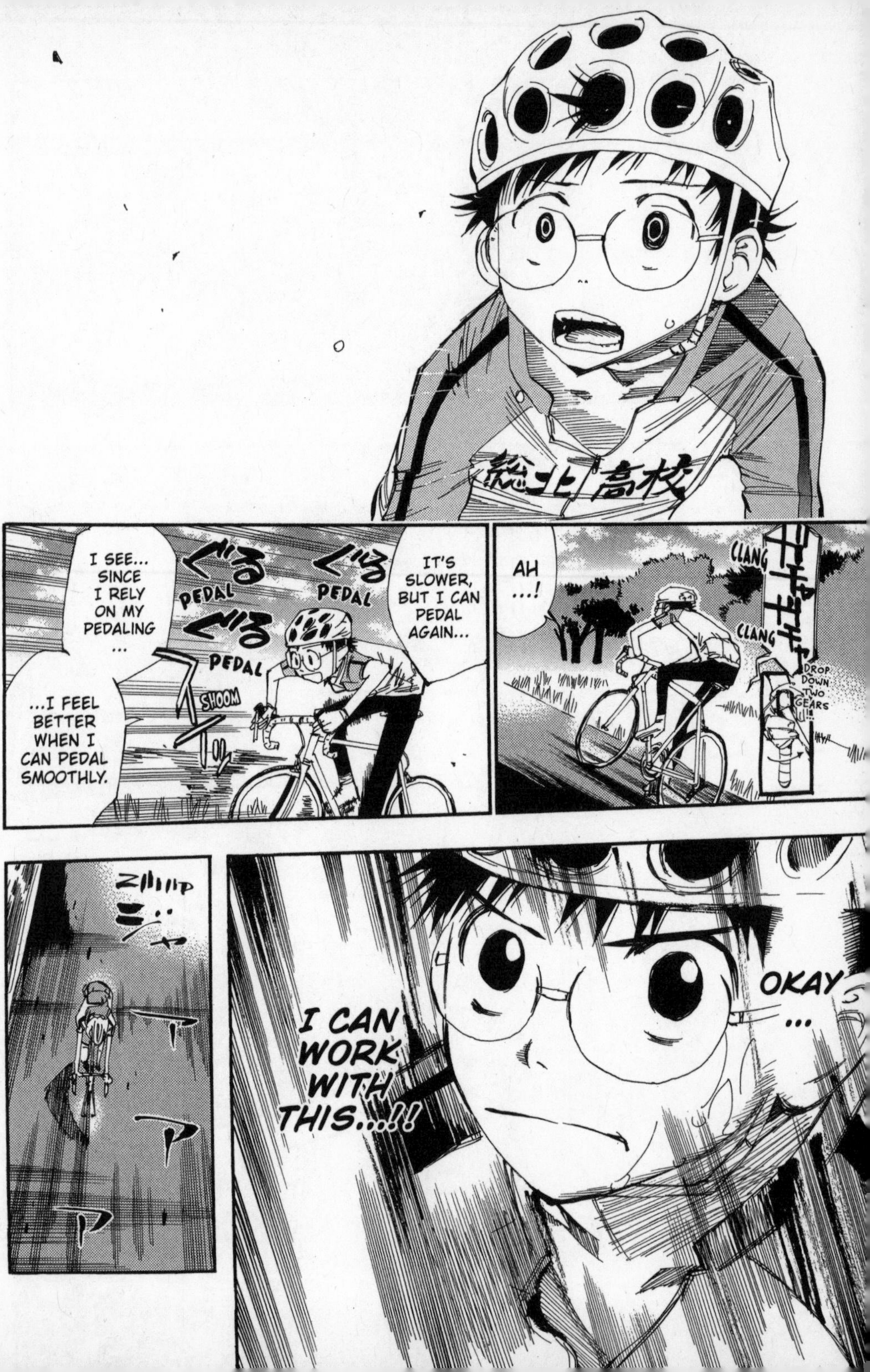
総北高校
CLANG
AH ...!
CLANG
DROP DOWN TWO GEARS!!
IT'S SLOWER, BUT I CAN PEDAL AGAIN...
PEDAL
PEDAL
PEDAL
I SEE... SINCE I RELY ON MY PEDALING ...
...I FEEL BETTER WHEN I CAN PEDAL SMOOTHLY.
SHOOM
OKAY ...
I CAN WORK WITH THIS...!!

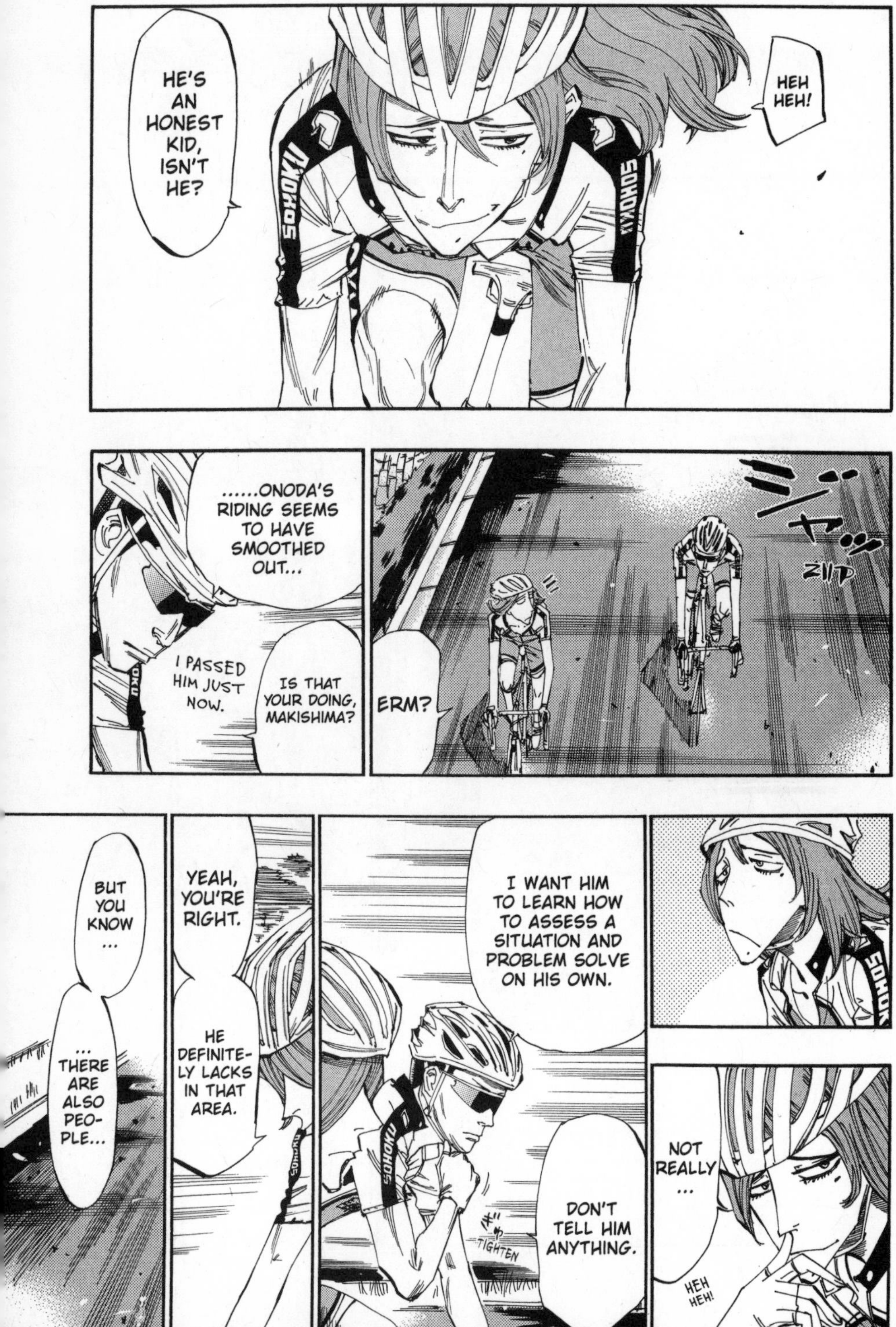
HEH HEH!
HE'S AN HONEST KID, ISN'T HE?
ZIIP
ERM?
......ONODA'S RIDING SEEMS TO HAVE SMOOTHED OUT...
IS THAT YOUR DOING, MAKISHIMA?
I PASSED HIM JUST NOW.
NOT REALLY ...
HEH HEH!
DON'T TELL HIM ANYTHING.
I WANT HIM TO LEARN HOW TO ASSESS A SITUATION AND PROBLEM SOLVE ON HIS OWN.
TIGHTEN
YEAH, YOU'RE RIGHT.
HE DEFINITE-LY LACKS IN THAT AREA.
BUT YOU KNOW ...
... THERE ARE ALSO PEO-PLE...

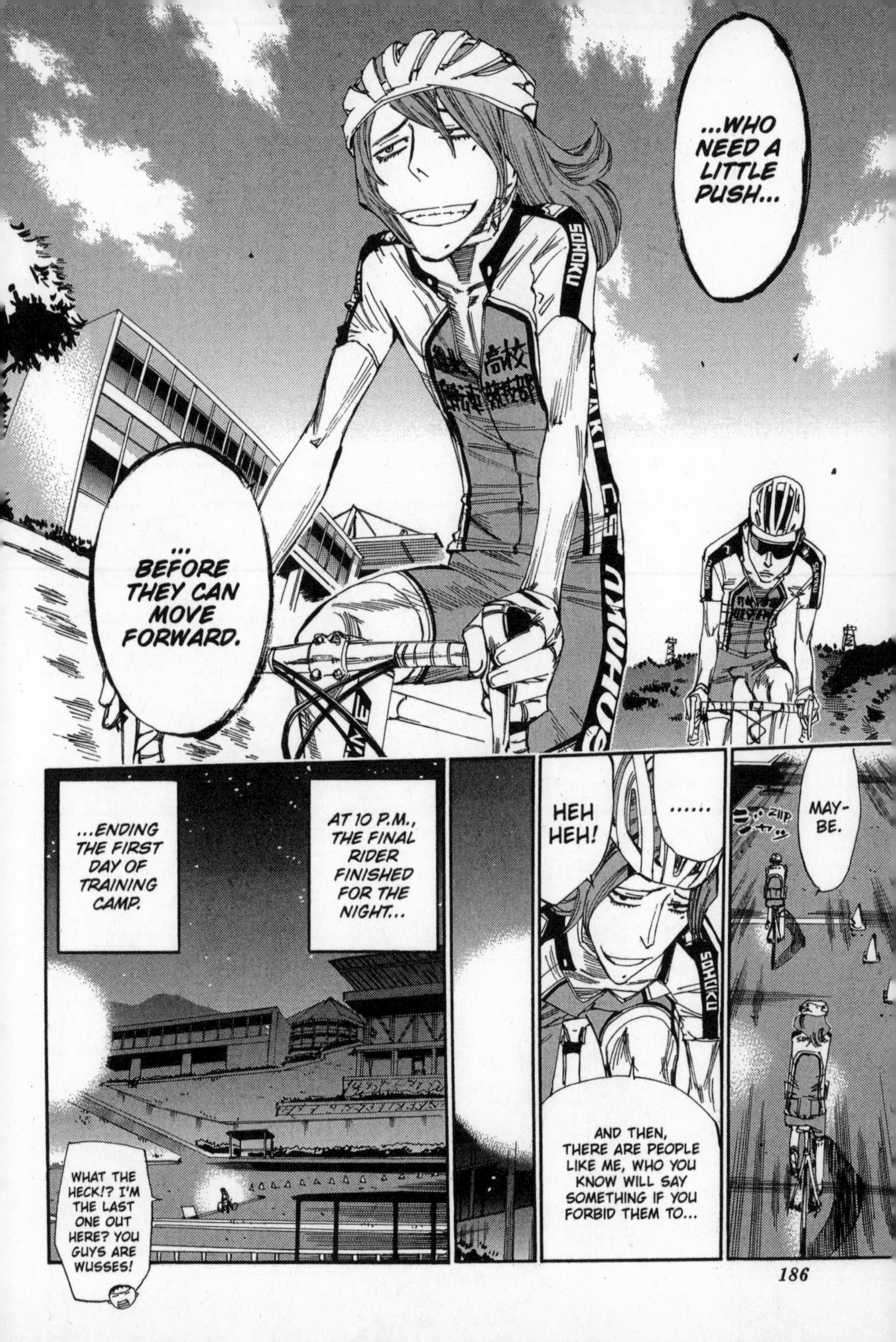
...WHO NEED A LITTLE PUSH...
...BEFORE THEY CAN MOVE FORWARD.
MAY-BE.
......
HEH HEH!
AND THEN, THERE ARE PEOPLE LIKE ME, WHO YOU KNOW WILL SAY SOMETHING IF YOU FORBID THEM TO...
AT 10 P.M., THE FINAL RIDER FINISHED FOR THE NIGHT...
...ENDING THE FIRST DAY OF TRAINING CAMP.
WHAT THE HECK!? I'M THE LAST ONE OUT HERE? YOU GUYS ARE WUSSES!

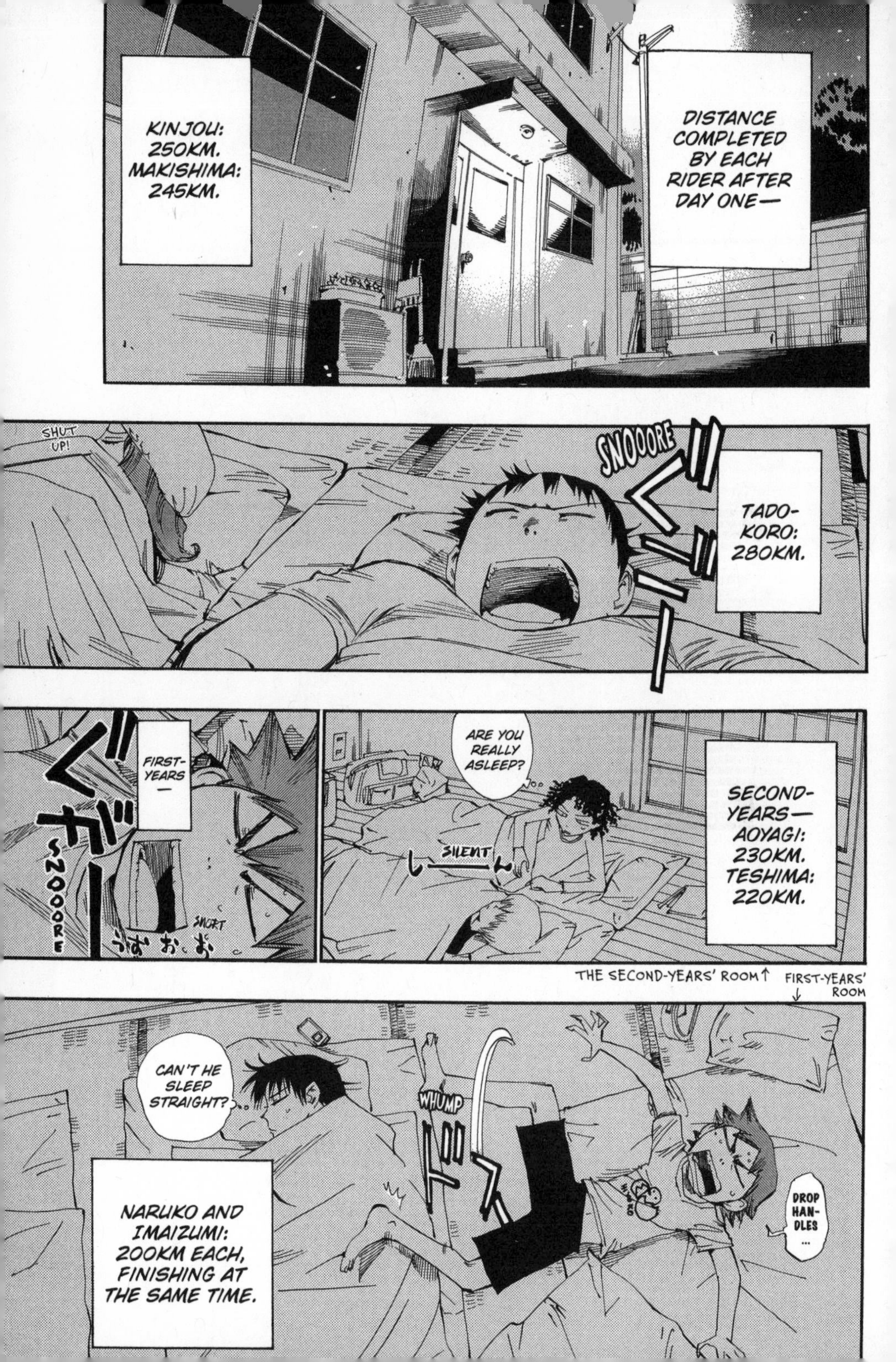
DISTANCE COMPLETED BY EACH RIDER AFTER DAY ONE—
KINJOU: 250KM. MAKISHIMA: 245KM.
SNOOORE
TADO-KORO: 280KM.
SHUT UP!
SECOND-YEARS— AOYAGI: 230KM. TESHIMA: 220KM.
ARE YOU REALLY ASLEEP?
SILENT
FIRST-YEARS —
SNOOORE
SNORT
THE SECOND-YEARS' ROOM↑
FIRST-YEARS' ROOM ↓
DROP HANDLES ...
WHUMP
CAN'T HE SLEEP STRAIGHT?...
NARUKO AND IMAIZUMI: 200KM EACH, FINISHING AT THE SAME TIME.

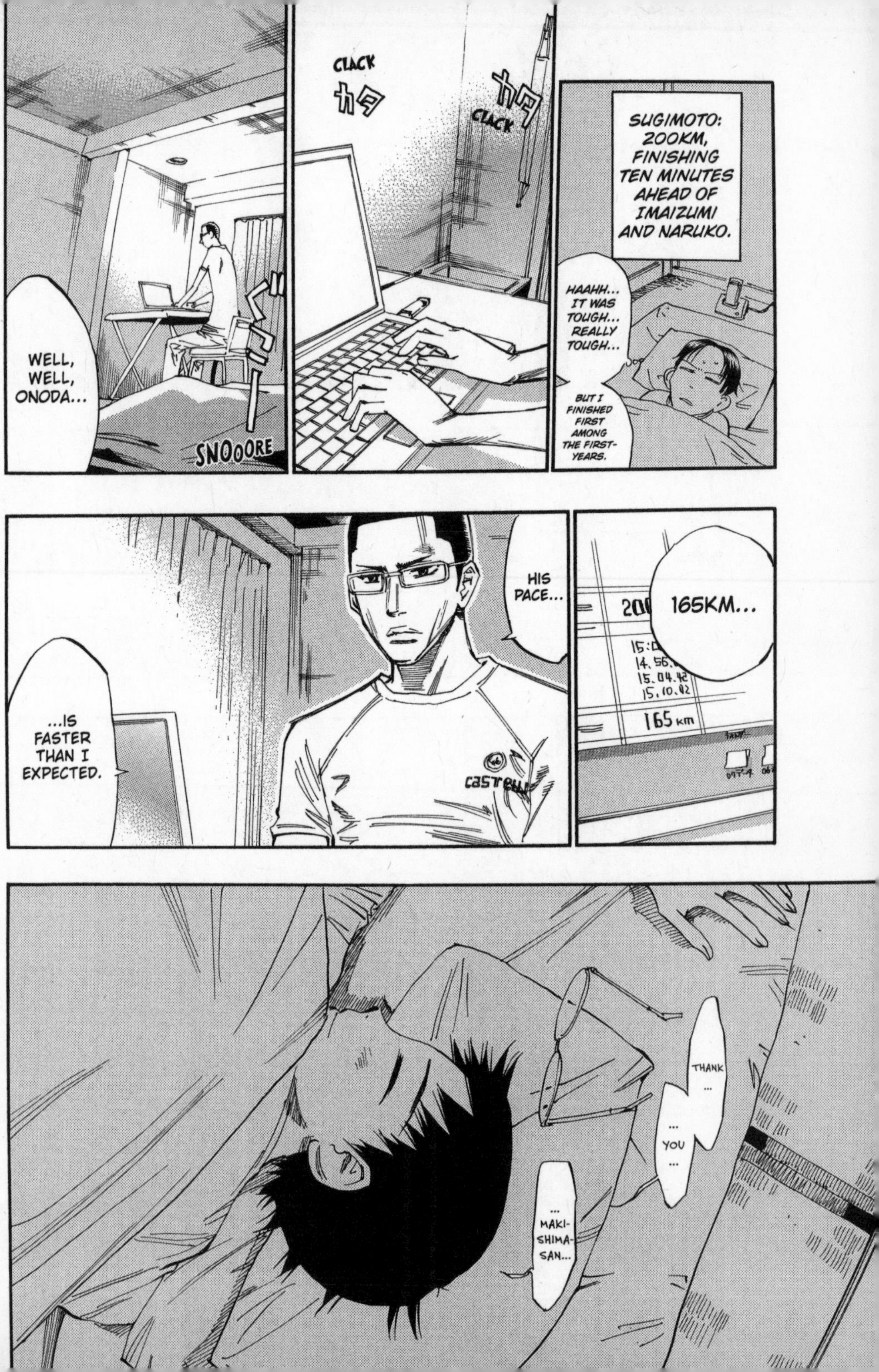
SUGIMOTO: 200KM, FINISHING TEN MINUTES AHEAD OF IMAIZUMI AND NARUKO.
HAAHH... IT WAS TOUGH... REALLY TOUGH...
BUT I FINISHED FIRST AMONG THE FIRST-YEARS.
CLACK
カタ
カタ
CLACK
WELL, WELL, ONODA...
SNOooRE
165KM...
HIS PACE...
...IS FASTER THAN I EXPECTED.
THANK... ...YOU...
...MAKISHIMA-SAN...

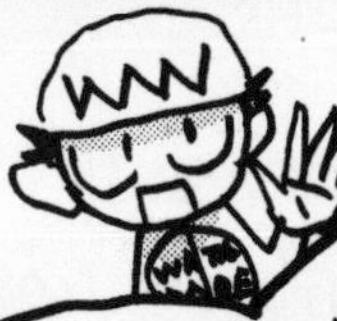

LET'S EXPLAIN SOME STUFF

YOWAMUSHI PEDAL BICYCLES ARE FUN CORNER

THE POLKA DOT JERSEY AND THE YELLOW JERSEY

THE RACING JERSEYS THAT SAKAMICHI AND IMAIZUMI ARE WEARING ON THE BACK COVER OF THIS VOLUME ACTUALLY HAVE SPECIAL SIGNIFICANCE. I MENTIONED IT ONCE BEFORE DURING THE STORY, BUT IN BIG ROAD RACES, SPECIAL JERSEYS ARE AWARDED TO OUTSTANDING CYCLISTS.

IN VOLUME 2, RIDE.28

AMONG THESE RACES, THE ONE WITH THE HIGHEST MOUNTAIN PEAK IS THE **TOUR DE FRANCE**. EVEN WITHOUT THAT, JUST RIDING IN THE TOUR IS BRUTAL—IT'S A 23-DAY RACE THAT TAKES YOU ON A CIRCUIT ALL OVER FRANCE. DESPITE THAT, ABOUT TWO HUNDRED CYCLISTS FROM AROUND THE WORLD GATHER EVERY SUMMER TO COMPETE TO BE THE WORLD'S FASTEST. HERE SPECIAL JERSEYS ARE GIVEN TO "THE FASTEST CYCLIST" AND "THE CYCLIST WHO CLIMBS THE MOUNTAIN FASTEST."

OVER THE COURSE OF 23 DAYS, SEVERAL DIFFERENT PEOPLE TAKE THESE TOP HONORS.

THE HELMET DESIGN FOR THE MAILLOT BLANC.

FASTEST RIDER GETS THE TOP-SPEED JERSEY

MAILLOT JAUNE

FRENCH FOR "YELLOW JERSEY"

AHH, THE COLOR EVERYONE DESIRES. THE RIGHT TO WEAR THIS JERSEY FOR EVEN A SINGLE DAY WOULD GUARANTEE YOUR NAME WOULD GO DOWN IN HISTORY. IT'S AN INCREDIBLY HUGE HONOR!!

THE ORIGIN OF THE YELLOW COLOR WAS SO THAT THE RIDER WOULD STAND OUT ON A TV BROADCAST.

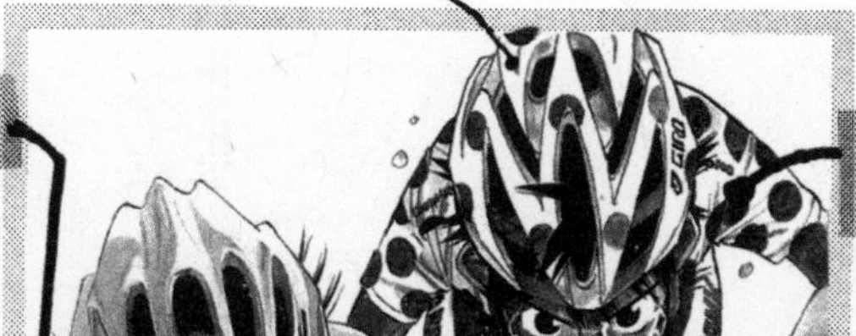

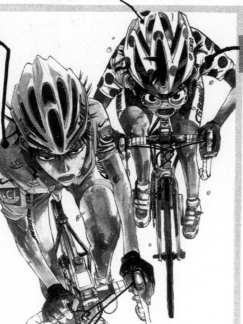

KING OF THE MOUNTAINS JERSEY

MAILLOT BLANC À POIS ROUGE

FRENCH FOR "RED DOTS ON WHITE"

THOUGH THEY ACTUALLY LOOK MORE REDDISH-BROWN

THE CURRENT SPONSOR OF THIS JERSEY IS THE FRENCH SUPERMARKET CHAIN "CHAMPION."

※ INCIDENTALLY, EACH TEAM BRINGS THEIR OWN YELLOW AND POLKA-DOT JERSEYS TO THE RACE, SO IF YOU WERE THINKING, "EWW, WOULDN'T IT BE SMELLY IF IT WERE WORN BY SOMEONE ELSE THE PREVIOUS DAY?" THE ANSWER IS NO. DON'T WORRY. (LOL)

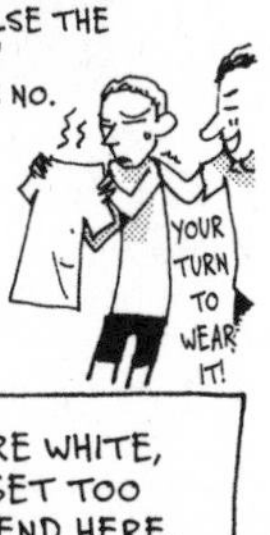
YOUR TURN TO WEAR IT!

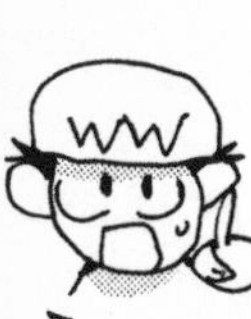

THE MAILLOT JAUNE AND MAILLOT BLANC ARE JERSEYS ANY PRO CYCLIST DREAMS OF WEARING. I BASICALLY DREW THIS ILLUSTRATION TO EXPRESS THAT DREAM!!

※ THERE ARE OTHER JERSEYS THAT ARE WHITE, GREEN, ETC. AS WELL, BUT IT WOULD GET TOO LONG IF I LISTED THEM ALL. SO LET'S END HERE.

LET'S EXPLAIN SOME STUFF PART 2

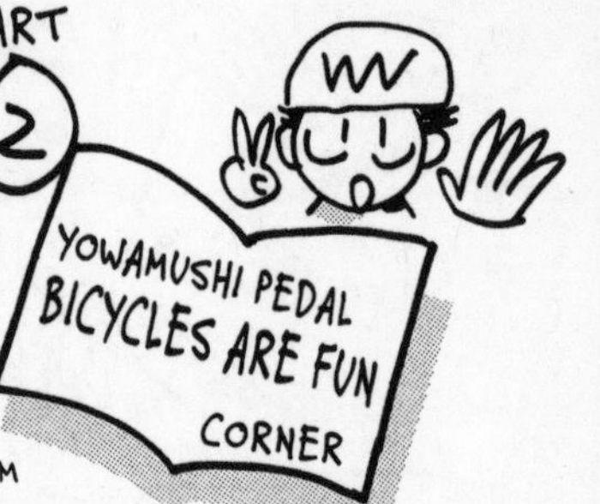
YOWAMUSHI PEDAL
BICYCLES ARE FUN
CORNER

SPEAKING OF JERSEYS, LET'S TALK ABOUT

JERSEYS FOR CYCLING

IN GENERAL, THE JERSEYS AVAILABLE ON THE MARKET RANGE FROM VERY FLASHY-LOOKING TO VERY PLAIN. ONE NEAT FEATURE THEY HAVE IS THESE **POCKETS ON THE BACKSIDE.** ← THEY'RE INCREDIBLY USEFUL!!

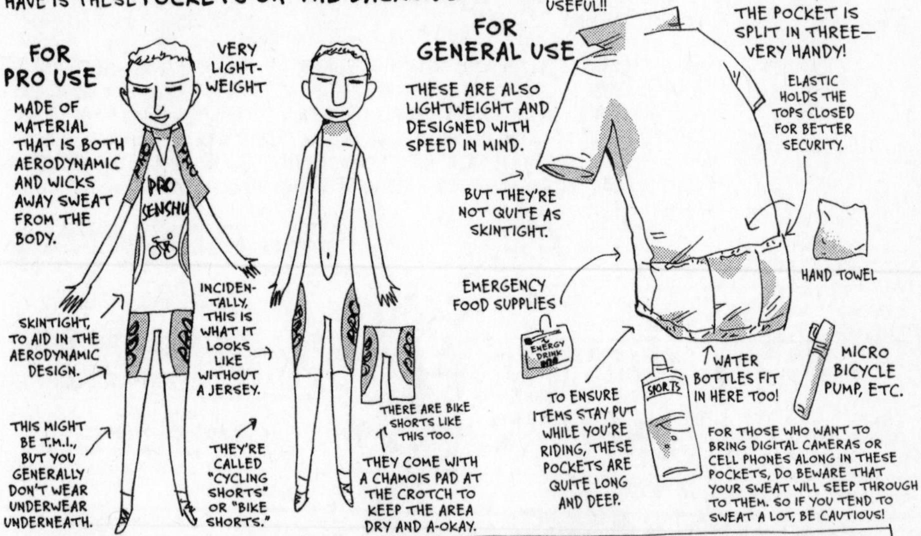
FOR PRO USE
MADE OF MATERIAL THAT IS BOTH AERODYNAMIC AND WICKS AWAY SWEAT FROM THE BODY.
VERY LIGHT-WEIGHT
PRO
PRO
PRO SENSHU
SKINTIGHT, TO AID IN THE AERODYNAMIC DESIGN.
INCIDENTALLY, THIS IS WHAT IT LOOKS LIKE WITHOUT A JERSEY.
THIS MIGHT BE T.M.I., BUT YOU GENERALLY DON'T WEAR UNDERWEAR UNDERNEATH.
THEY'RE CALLED "CYCLING SHORTS" OR "BIKE SHORTS."
THERE ARE BIKE SHORTS LIKE THIS TOO.
THEY COME WITH A CHAMOIS PAD AT THE CROTCH TO KEEP THE AREA DRY AND A-OKAY.
FOR GENERAL USE
THESE ARE ALSO LIGHTWEIGHT AND DESIGNED WITH SPEED IN MIND.
BUT THEY'RE NOT QUITE AS SKINTIGHT.
THE POCKET IS SPLIT IN THREE—VERY HANDY!
ELASTIC HOLDS THE TOPS CLOSED FOR BETTER SECURITY.
HAND TOWEL
EMERGENCY FOOD SUPPLIES
ENERGY DRINK
WATER BOTTLES FIT IN HERE TOO!
SPORTS
MICRO BICYCLE PUMP, ETC.
TO ENSURE ITEMS STAY PUT WHILE YOU'RE RIDING, THESE POCKETS ARE QUITE LONG AND DEEP.
FOR THOSE WHO WANT TO BRING DIGITAL CAMERAS OR CELL PHONES ALONG IN THESE POCKETS, DO BEWARE THAT YOUR SWEAT WILL SEEP THROUGH TO THEM. SO IF YOU TEND TO SWEAT A LOT, BE CAUTIOUS!

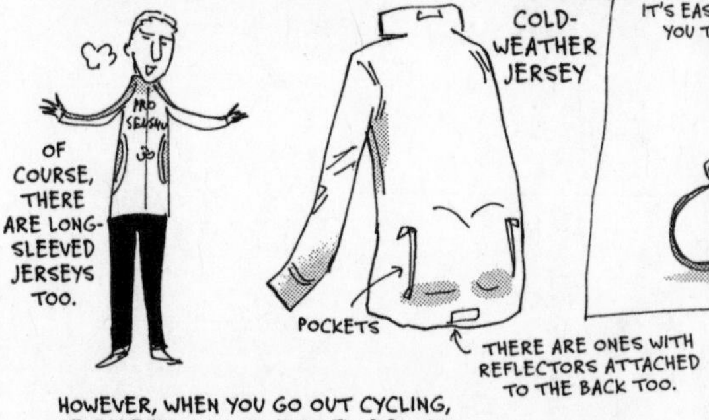
PRO SENSHU
OF COURSE, THERE ARE LONG-SLEEVED JERSEYS TOO.
COLD-WEATHER JERSEY
POCKETS
THERE ARE ONES WITH REFLECTORS ATTACHED TO THE BACK TOO.

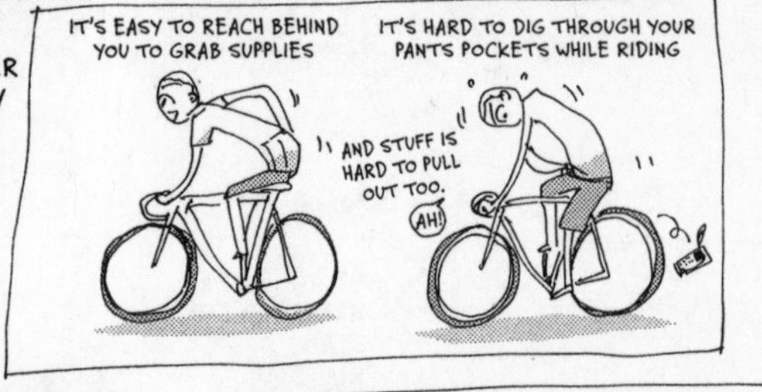
IT'S EASY TO REACH BEHIND YOU TO GRAB SUPPLIES
IT'S HARD TO DIG THROUGH YOUR PANTS POCKETS WHILE RIDING
AND STUFF IS HARD TO PULL OUT TOO.
AH!

HOWEVER, WHEN YOU GO OUT CYCLING, BE CAREFUL NOT TO JUST FLOP DOWN ON THE GRASS, ETC, OR YOU'LL SQUISH YOUR STUFF.

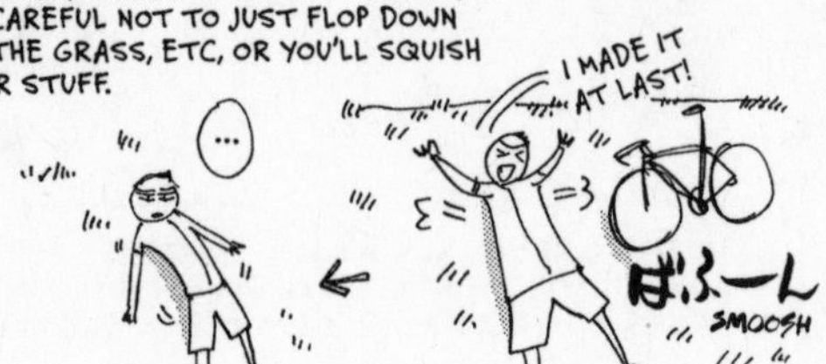
...
I MADE IT AT LAST!
ぼふーん
SMOOSH

THERE ARE MANY DIFFERENT KINDS OF JERSEYS AT STORES (BIG CYCLING SHOPS) SO IT'S VERY FUN TO GO CHECK THEM OUT. PICK ONE YOU LIKE AND COLOR THE MOUNTAINS AND FIELDS!

THE FLASHY COLORS MAKE IT EASIER FOR DRIVERS TO SPOT YOU, MAKING IT THAT MUCH SAFER.

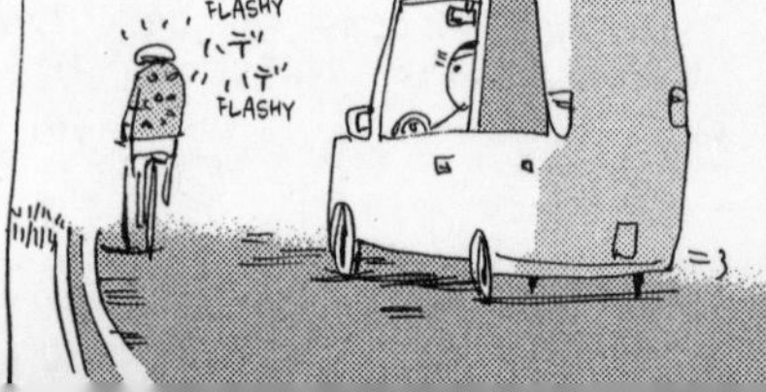
FLASHY
ハデ
ハデ
FLASHY

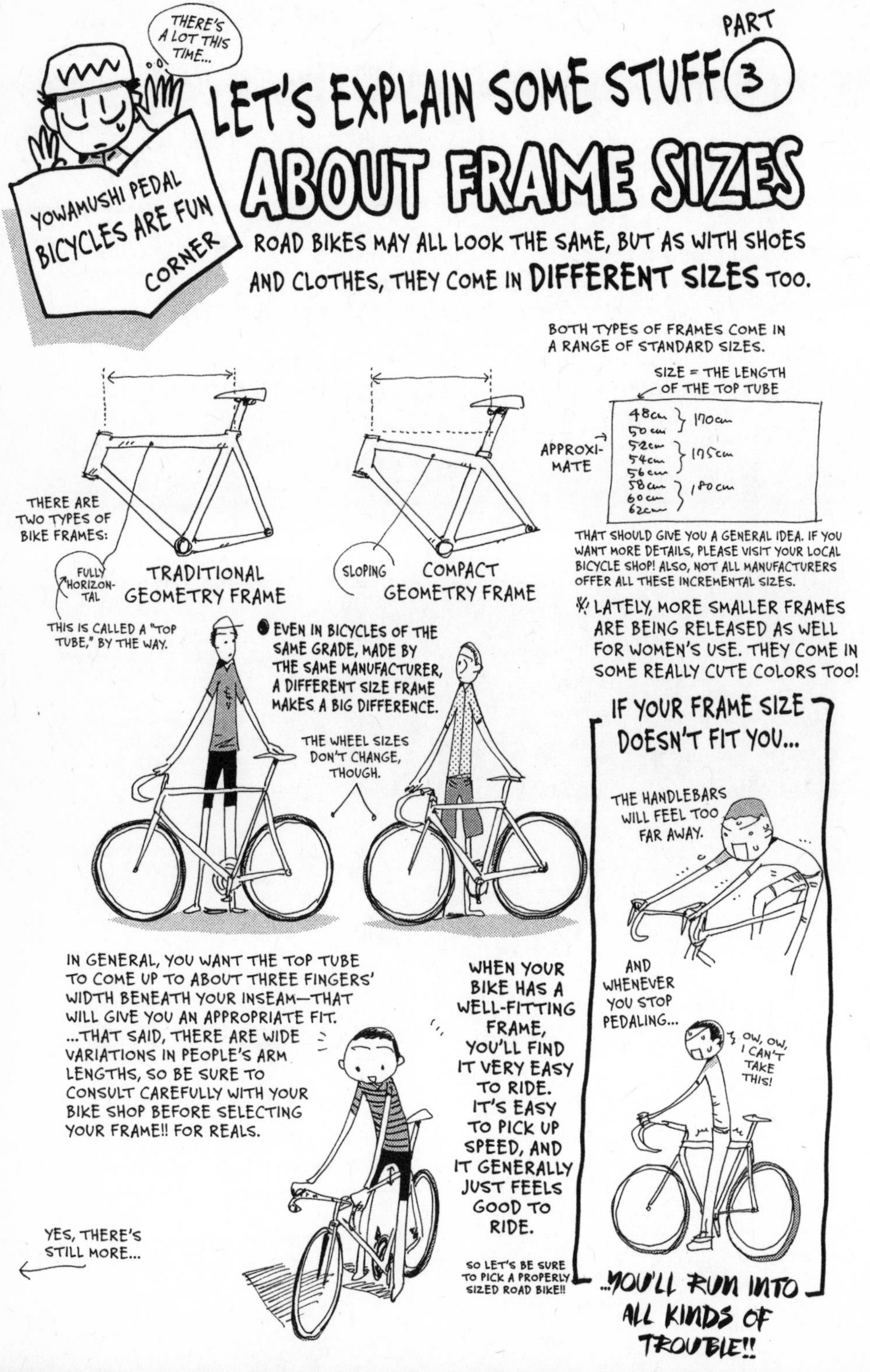

THERE'S A LOT THIS TIME...
LET'S EXPLAIN SOME STUFF PART 3
ABOUT FRAME SIZES
YOWAMUSHI PEDAL BICYCLES ARE FUN CORNER
ROAD BIKES MAY ALL LOOK THE SAME, BUT AS WITH SHOES AND CLOTHES, THEY COME IN DIFFERENT SIZES TOO.
BOTH TYPES OF FRAMES COME IN A RANGE OF STANDARD SIZES.
SIZE = THE LENGTH OF THE TOP TUBE
APPROXIMATE
48cm
50cm
170cm
52cm
54cm
56cm
175cm
58cm
60cm
62cm
180cm
THAT SHOULD GIVE YOU A GENERAL IDEA. IF YOU WANT MORE DETAILS, PLEASE VISIT YOUR LOCAL BICYCLE SHOP! ALSO, NOT ALL MANUFACTURERS OFFER ALL THESE INCREMENTAL SIZES.
※ LATELY, MORE SMALLER FRAMES ARE BEING RELEASED AS WELL FOR WOMEN'S USE. THEY COME IN SOME REALLY CUTE COLORS TOO!
THERE ARE TWO TYPES OF BIKE FRAMES:
FULLY HORIZONTAL
TRADITIONAL GEOMETRY FRAME
SLOPING
COMPACT GEOMETRY FRAME
THIS IS CALLED A "TOP TUBE," BY THE WAY.
EVEN IN BICYCLES OF THE SAME GRADE, MADE BY THE SAME MANUFACTURER, A DIFFERENT SIZE FRAME MAKES A BIG DIFFERENCE.
THE WHEEL SIZES DON'T CHANGE, THOUGH.
IF YOUR FRAME SIZE DOESN'T FIT YOU...
THE HANDLEBARS WILL FEEL TOO FAR AWAY.
AND WHENEVER YOU STOP PEDALING...
OW, OW, I CAN'T TAKE THIS!
...YOU'LL RUN INTO ALL KINDS OF TROUBLE!!
IN GENERAL, YOU WANT THE TOP TUBE TO COME UP TO ABOUT THREE FINGERS' WIDTH BENEATH YOUR INSEAM—THAT WILL GIVE YOU AN APPROPRIATE FIT. ...THAT SAID, THERE ARE WIDE VARIATIONS IN PEOPLE'S ARM LENGTHS, SO BE SURE TO CONSULT CAREFULLY WITH YOUR BIKE SHOP BEFORE SELECTING YOUR FRAME!! FOR REALS.
WHEN YOUR BIKE HAS A WELL-FITTING FRAME, YOU'LL FIND IT VERY EASY TO RIDE. IT'S EASY TO PICK UP SPEED, AND IT GENERALLY JUST FEELS GOOD TO RIDE.
SO LET'S BE SURE TO PICK A PROPERLY SIZED ROAD BIKE!!
YES, THERE'S STILL MORE...

THE SPECIALIZED CYCLING CIRCUIT ACTUALLY EXISTS!

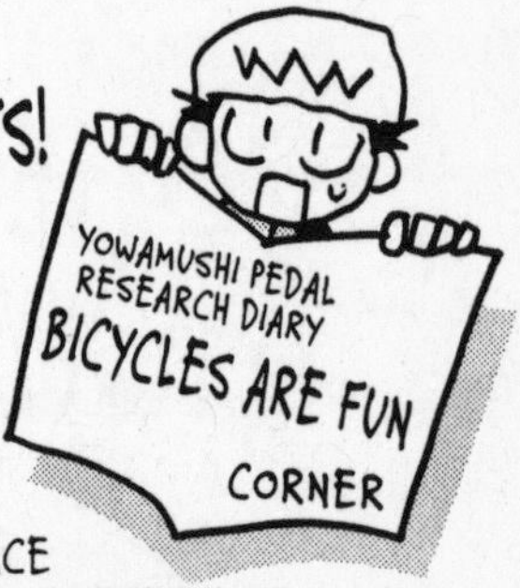
YOWAMUSHI PEDAL RESEARCH DIARY
BICYCLES ARE FUN
CORNER

IN THE MANGA, OUR HEROES GO TO A TRAINING FACILITY CALLED "CSP / CYCLING SPORTS PARK" THAT HAS A TRACK SPECIFICALLY DESIGNED FOR BICYCLES. I BET YOU WERE THINKING SOMETHING THAT COOL COULDN'T POSSIBLY EXIST, RIGHT!?

BUT IT DOES!! *THOOM*

IN FACT, WHAT I USED AS A MODEL FOR THE CSP IS AN ACTUAL PLACE CALLED THE CYCLING SPORTS CENTER (CSC) IN IZU CITY, SHIZUOKA PREFECTURE. IT HAS A 5KM CIRCUIT DESIGNED JUST FOR CYCLING, AS WELL AS A HILLY COURSE FOR MTBS! THEY PROVIDE BICYCLES YOU CAN RENT THERE TOO, OF COURSE. IN SHORT, IT'S BICYCLE HEAVEN!! A FACILITY MADE SOLELY FOR BICYCLE-RELATED ACTIVITIES!!

ENTERTAINMENT

"THE LAND OF BICYCLES: CYCLING SPORTS CENTER"

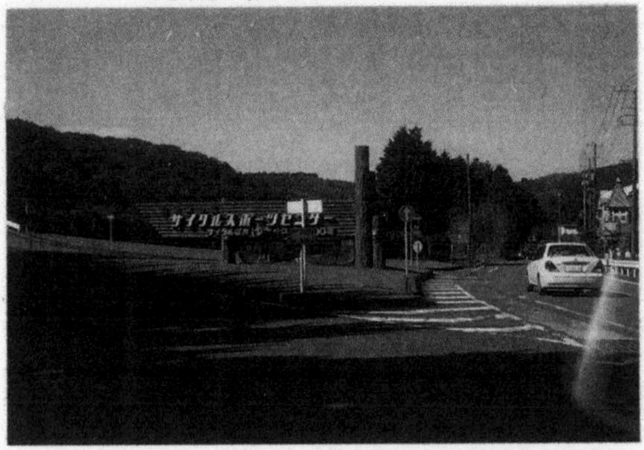

← THERE'S A SMALL AMUSEMENT PARK AREA INTEGRATED WITH IT TOO, SO THE WHOLE FAMILY CAN HAVE FUN!!

← THEY ALSO HAVE A HOT SPRINGS ONSITE, SO YOU CAN WASH AWAY ALL YOUR FATIGUE AFTER RIDING.

← THERE'S NO MINIMUM QUALIFICATION TO RIDE HERE. EVEN GRADE SCHOOLERS CAN RIDE.

THE ENTRANCE

THE HOMESTRETCH SECTION. IT'S SO WIDE!!

YOU FEEL LIKE A PRO CYCLIST RIDING HERE! LOL

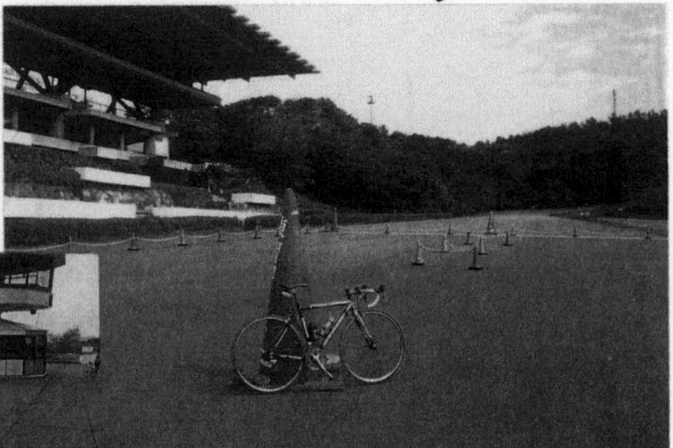

BIG CONES TOO...

THERE'S A QUITE ODDLY SHAPED OBSERVATION TOWER TOO!!

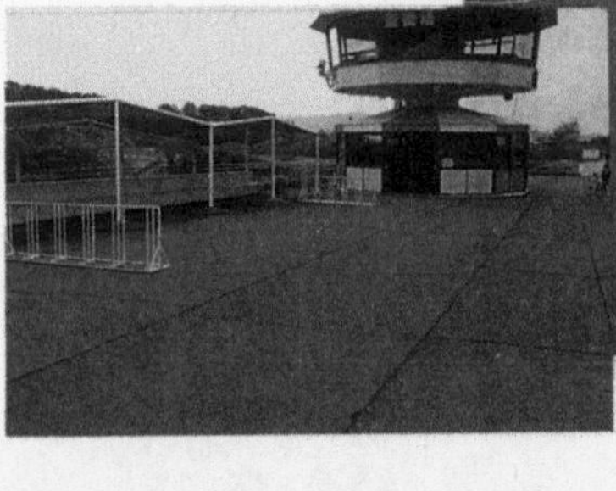

175~
165~

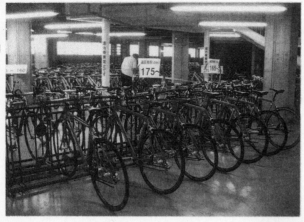

YOU CAN RENT VARIOUS KINDS OF BICYCLES, INCLUDING ROAD BIKES, CITY BIKES, MTBS, ETC. SO YOU CAN GO THERE AND EXPERIENCE WHAT IT'S LIKE RIDING A ROAD BIKE WITHOUT BUYING ONE! (BUT THEY HAVE REGULAR PEDALS, SO YOU CAN JUST WEAR YOUR SNEAKERS, ETC.) THEY RENT OUT HELMETS TOO.

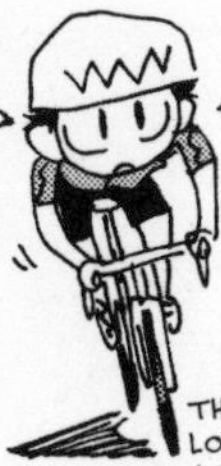

YOU REALLY GO FAST ON THE DESCENTS, SO BE CAREFUL!

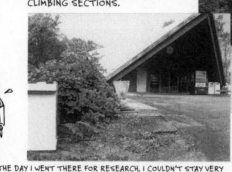

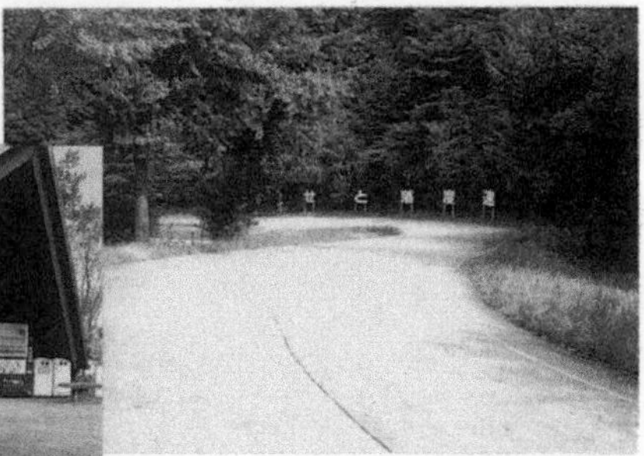

BECAUSE THE UPHILL SECTIONS MIGHT BE A BIT DIFFICULT FOR PEOPLE AT FIRST, THERE ARE BENCHES PLACED ALONG THE TRACK SO YOU CAN STOP AND REST ALONG THE WAY.

THE COURSE USUALLY HAS REST AREAS AT THE TOPS OF THE CLIMBING SECTIONS.

THE DAY I WENT THERE FOR RESEARCH, I COULDN'T STAY VERY LONG. SO I ONLY GOT TO DO ABOUT SIX LAPS ON THE CIRCUIT... A BIG THANK YOU TO EVERYONE AT THE CSC!.

IF YOU'RE INTERESTED, PLEASE GO CHECK IT OUT!

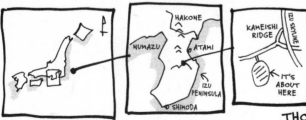

HAKONE
NUMAZU
ATAMI
IZU PENINSULA
SHIMODA
KAMEISHI RIDGE
IZU SKYLINE
IT'S ABOUT HERE

ACTUALLY, A PART OF THE JAPAN KEIRIN SCHOOL'S COURSE IS CONNECTED TO THE CSC. (THOUGH OF COURSE, THE GENERAL PUBLIC CAN'T GO ON THERE.)

THOUGH ACTUALLY, STUDENTS FROM THE KEIRIN SCHOOL WILL SOMETIMES COME OVER TO THE CSC TO PRACTICE.

THERE ARE DAYS WHEN THE CSC IS CLOSED FOR CYCLING RACES AND OTHER EVENTS, SO IF YOU'RE INTERESTED IN GOING, DO GIVE THEM A CALL TO MAKE SURE THEY'RE OPEN WHEN YOU WANT TO GO.

THE CYCLING SPORTS CENTER - 0558-79-0001 HTTP://WWW.CSC.OR.JP

YOWAMUSHI PEDAL

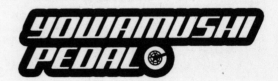

RIDE.44 IMAIZUMI'S AND NARUKO'S 1,000 KILOMETERS

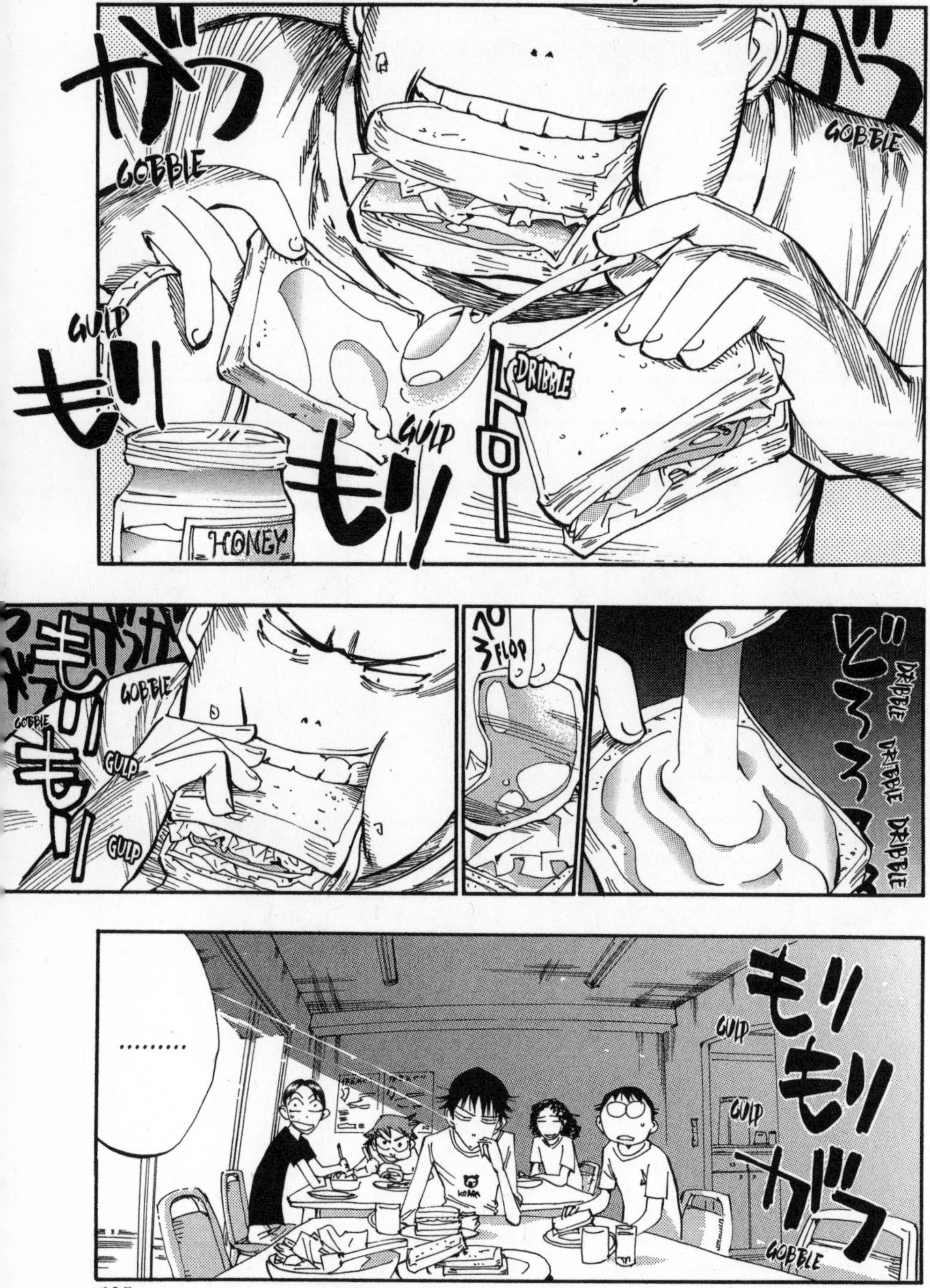

がつ
GOBBLE
がつ
GOBBLE
GULP
もり
DRIBBLE
GULP
もり
HONEY
DRIBBLE
DRIBBLE
DRIBBLE
FLOP
GOBBLE
GOBBLE
GULP
GULP
....
GULP
GULP
GOBBLE
KOARA

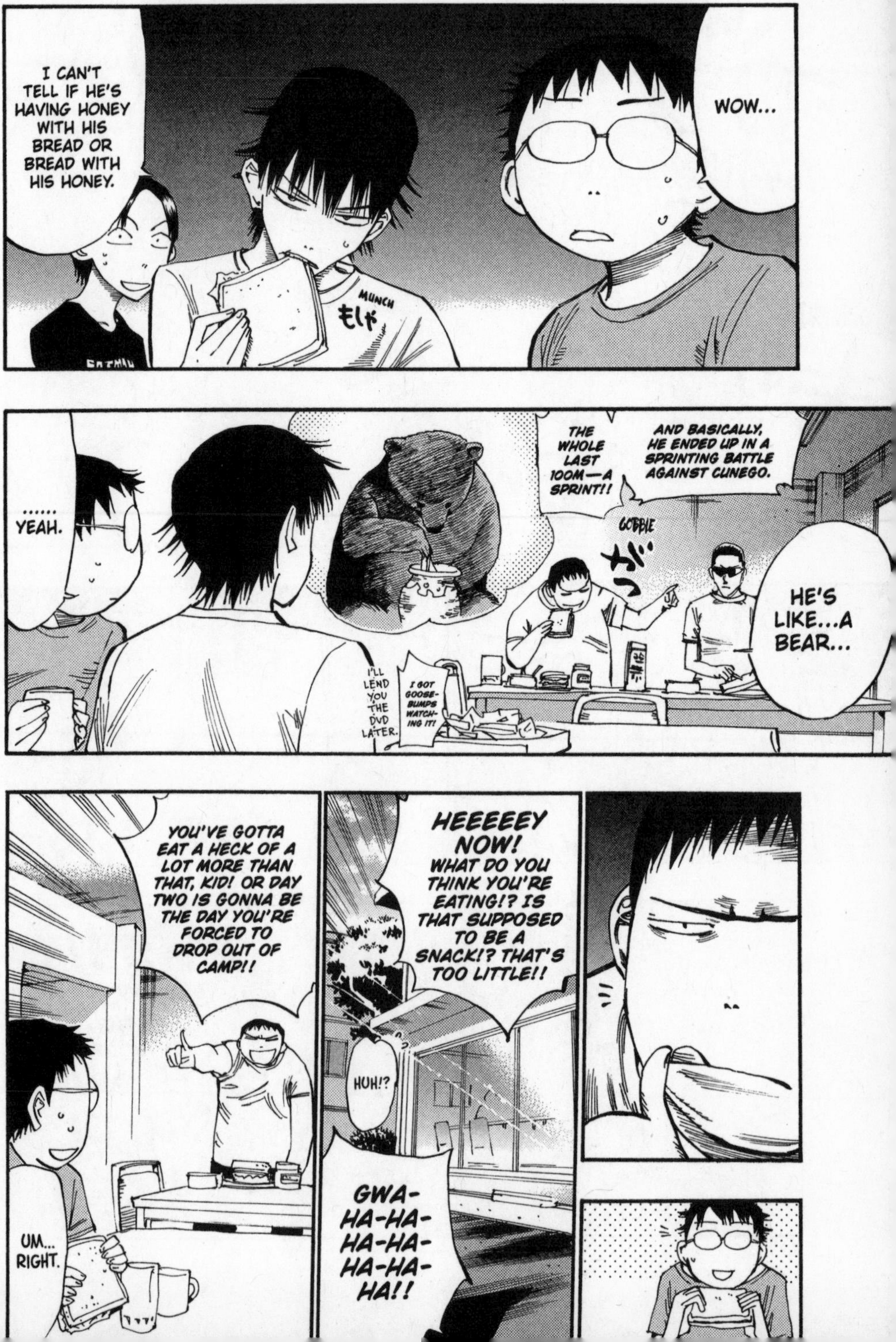
WOW...
I CAN'T TELL IF HE'S HAVING HONEY WITH HIS BREAD OR BREAD WITH HIS HONEY.
MUNCH
もしゃ
HE'S LIKE...A BEAR...
AND BASICALLY, HE ENDED UP IN A SPRINTING BATTLE AGAINST CUNEGO.
THE WHOLE LAST 100M—A SPRINT!!
GOBBIE
がつ
I GOT GOOSE-BUMPS WATCHING IT!
I'LL LEND YOU THE DVD LATER.
......YEAH.
HEEEEEY NOW! WHAT DO YOU THINK YOU'RE EATING!? IS THAT SUPPOSED TO BE A SNACK!? THAT'S TOO LITTLE!!
HUH!?
GWA-HA-HA-HA-HA-HA-HA-HA!!
YOU'VE GOTTA EAT A HECK OF A LOT MORE THAN THAT, KID! OR DAY TWO IS GONNA BE THE DAY YOU'RE FORCED TO DROP OUT OF CAMP!!
UM... RIGHT.

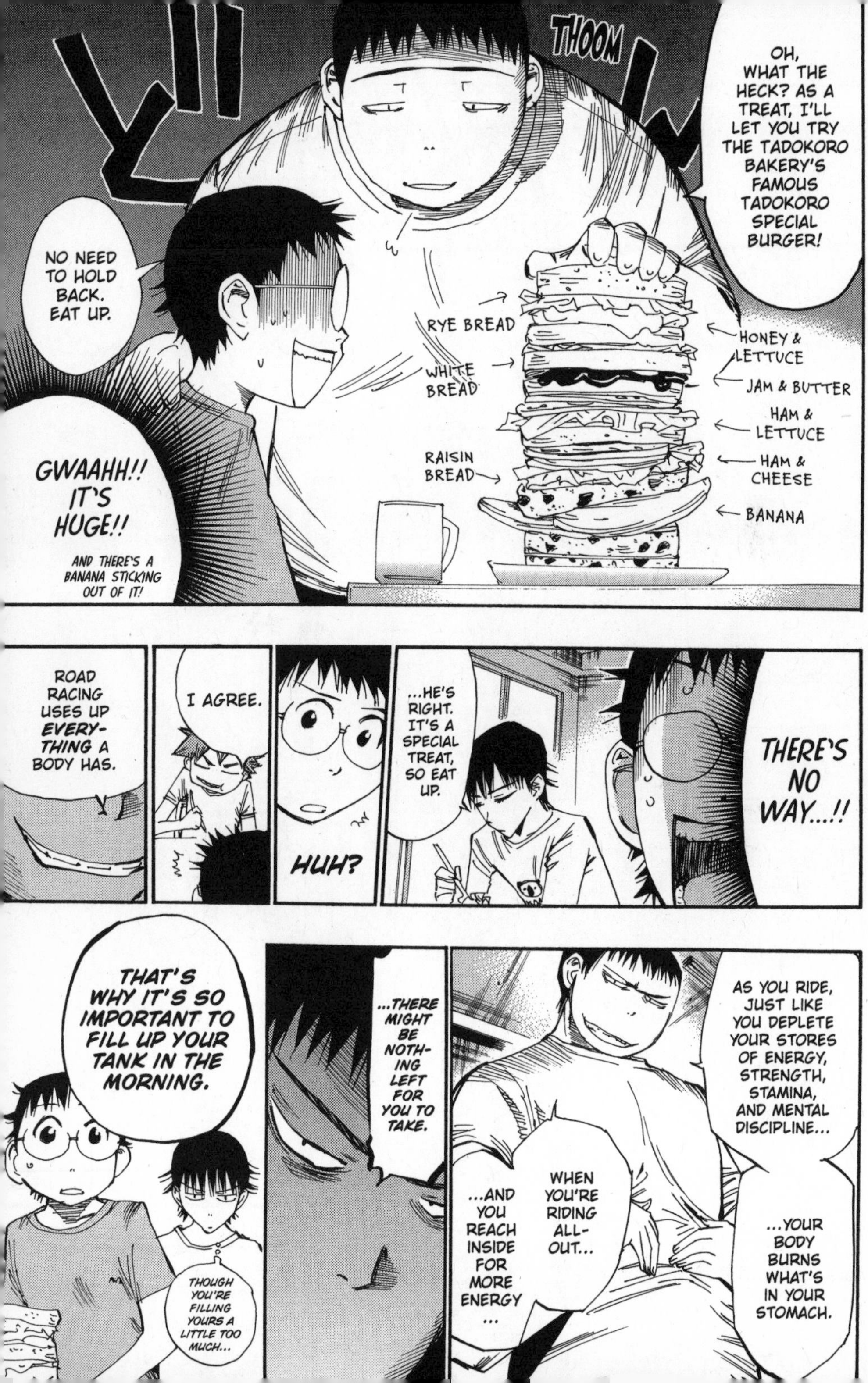
THOOM
OH, WHAT THE HECK? AS A TREAT, I'LL LET YOU TRY THE TADOKORO BAKERY'S FAMOUS TADOKORO SPECIAL BURGER!
NO NEED TO HOLD BACK. EAT UP.
HONEY & LETTUCE
JAM & BUTTER
HAM & LETTUCE
HAM & CHEESE
BANANA
RYE BREAD
WHITE BREAD
RAISIN BREAD
GWAAHH!! IT'S HUGE!!
AND THERE'S A BANANA STICKING OUT OF IT!
THERE'S NO WAY...!!
...HE'S RIGHT. IT'S A SPECIAL TREAT, SO EAT UP.
HUH?
I AGREE.
ROAD RACING USES UP EVERYTHING A BODY HAS.
AS YOU RIDE, JUST LIKE YOU DEPLETE YOUR STORES OF ENERGY, STRENGTH, STAMINA, AND MENTAL DISCIPLINE...
...YOUR BODY BURNS WHAT'S IN YOUR STOMACH.
WHEN YOU'RE RIDING ALL-OUT...
...AND YOU REACH INSIDE FOR MORE ENERGY...
...THERE MIGHT BE NOTHING LEFT FOR YOU TO TAKE.
THAT'S WHY IT'S SO IMPORTANT TO FILL UP YOUR TANK IN THE MORNING.
THOUGH YOU'RE FILLING YOURS A LITTLE TOO MUCH...

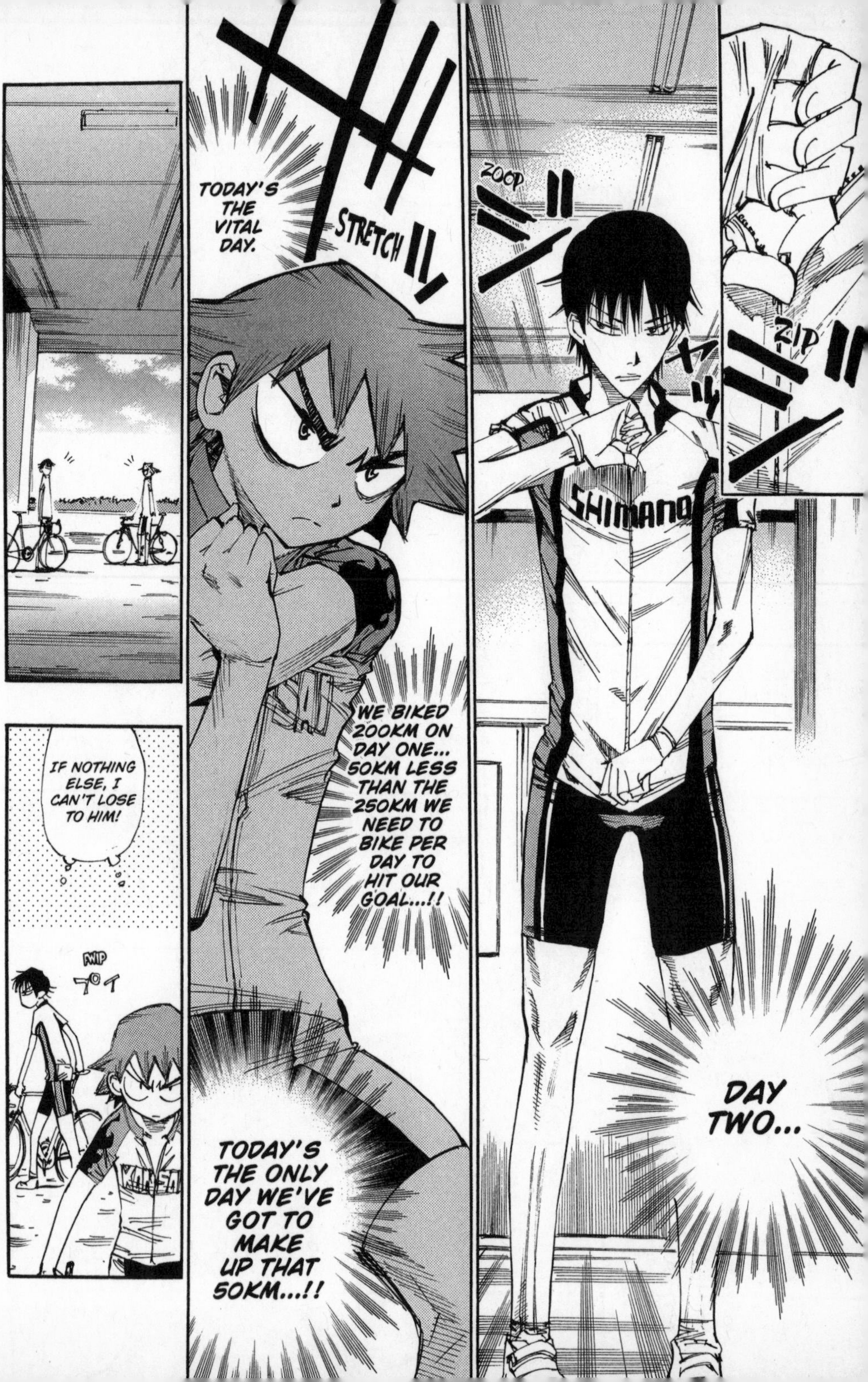

ZIP
ZOOP
DAY TWO...
STRETCH
TODAY'S THE VITAL DAY.
WE BIKED 200KM ON DAY ONE... 50KM LESS THAN THE 250KM WE NEED TO BIKE PER DAY TO HIT OUR GOAL...!!
TODAY'S THE ONLY DAY WE'VE GOT TO MAKE UP THAT 50KM...!!
IF NOTHING ELSE, I CAN'T LOSE TO HIM!
FWIP

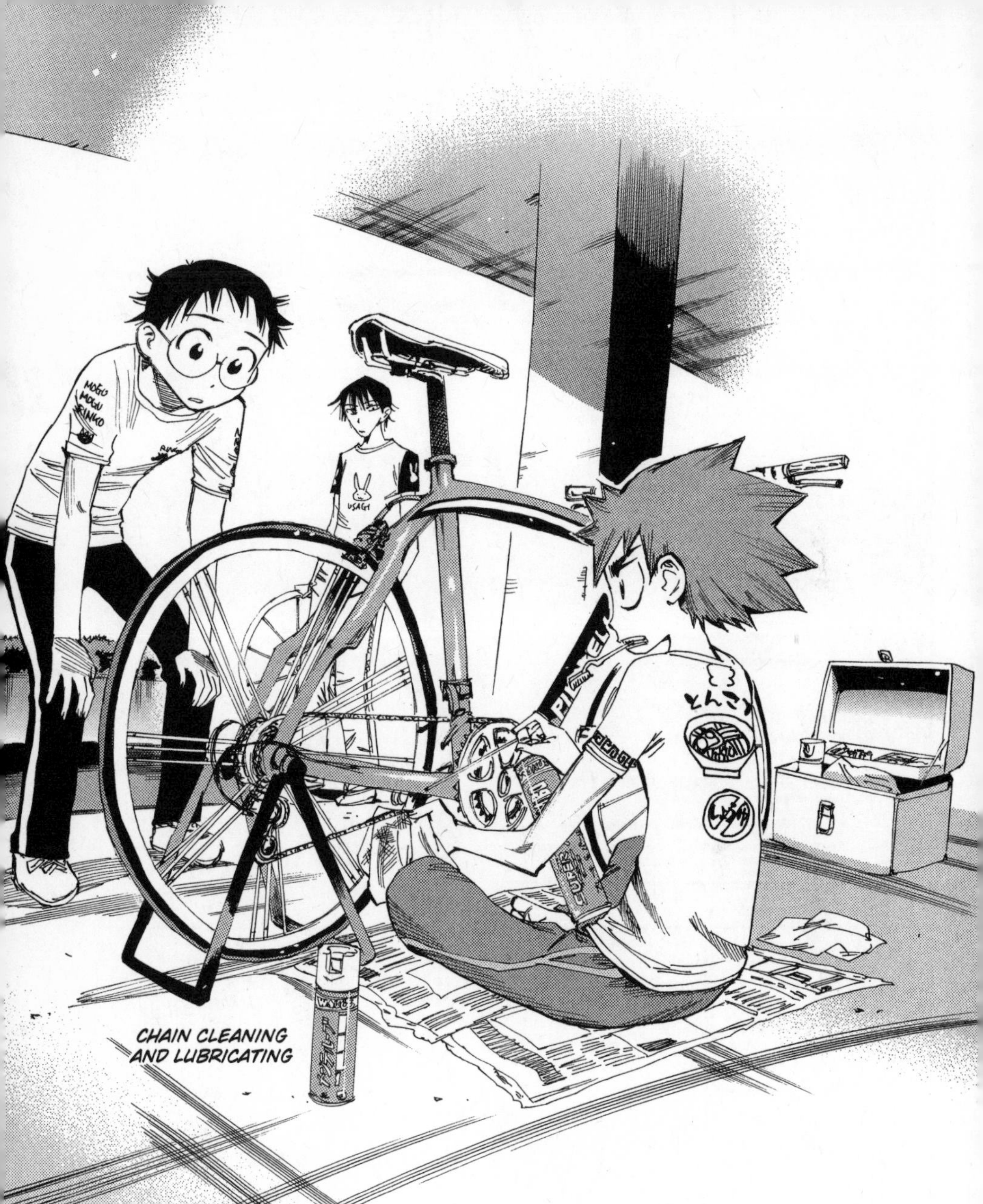
CHAIN CLEANING AND LUBRICATING

RIDE.44 IMAIZUMI'S AND NARUKO'S 1,000 KILOMETERS

BE SURE TO LUBRICATE YOUR BIKE CHAIN FREQUENTLY!

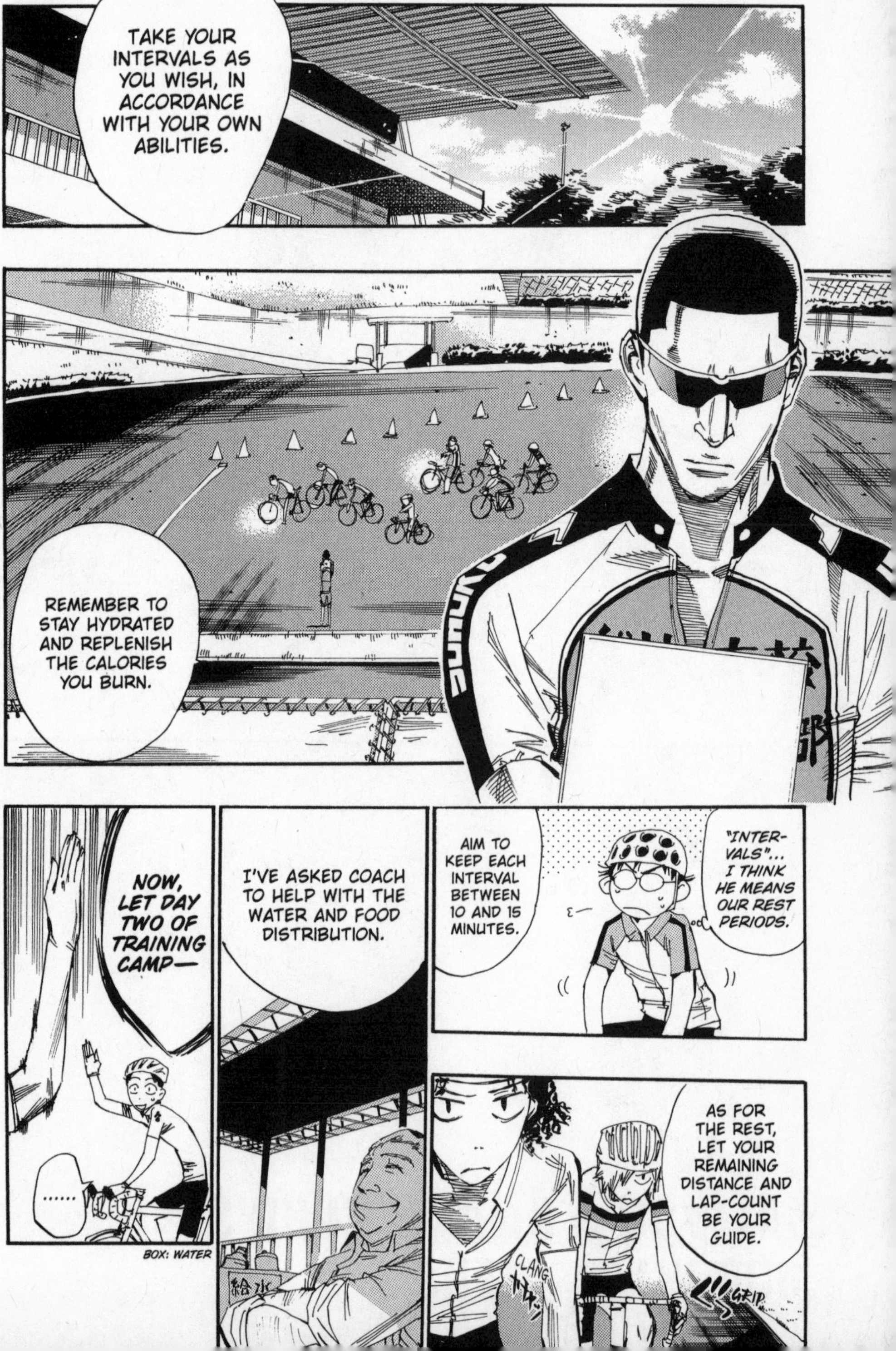
TAKE YOUR INTERVALS AS YOU WISH, IN ACCORDANCE WITH YOUR OWN ABILITIES.
REMEMBER TO STAY HYDRATED AND REPLENISH THE CALORIES YOU BURN.
"INTER-VALS"... I THINK HE MEANS OUR REST PERIODS.
AIM TO KEEP EACH INTERVAL BETWEEN 10 AND 15 MINUTES.
AS FOR THE REST, LET YOUR REMAINING DISTANCE AND LAP-COUNT BE YOUR GUIDE.
CLANG
GRIP
I'VE ASKED COACH TO HELP WITH THE WATER AND FOOD DISTRIBUTION.
給水
NOW, LET DAY TWO OF TRAINING CAMP—
......
BOX: WATER

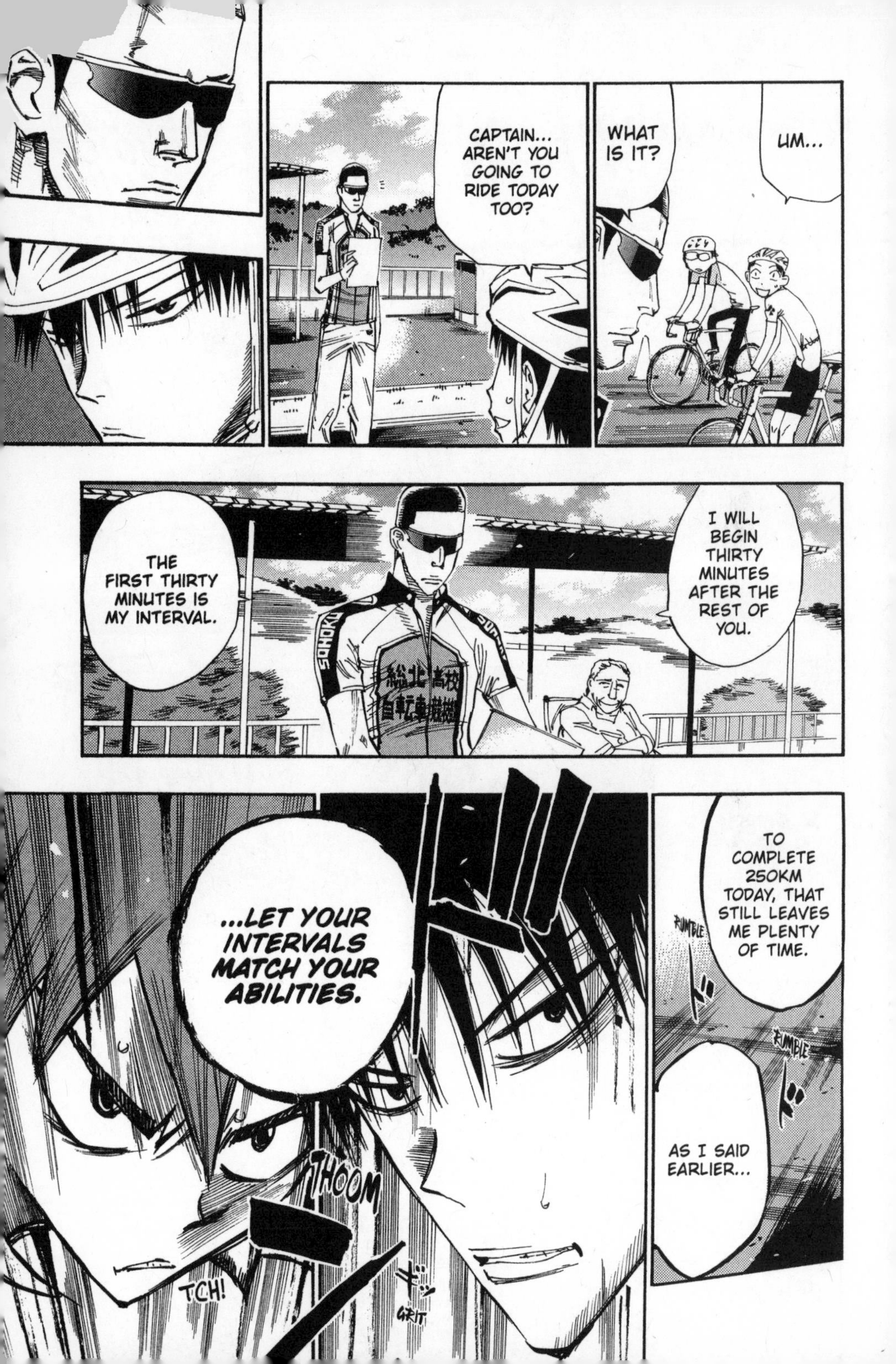
UM...
WHAT IS IT?
CAPTAIN... AREN'T YOU GOING TO RIDE TODAY TOO?
I WILL BEGIN THIRTY MINUTES AFTER THE REST OF YOU.
THE FIRST THIRTY MINUTES IS MY INTERVAL.
TO COMPLETE 250KM TODAY, THAT STILL LEAVES ME PLENTY OF TIME.
RUMBLE
RUMBLE
AS I SAID EARLIER...
...LET YOUR INTERVALS MATCH YOUR ABILITIES.
THOOM
TCH!
GRIT

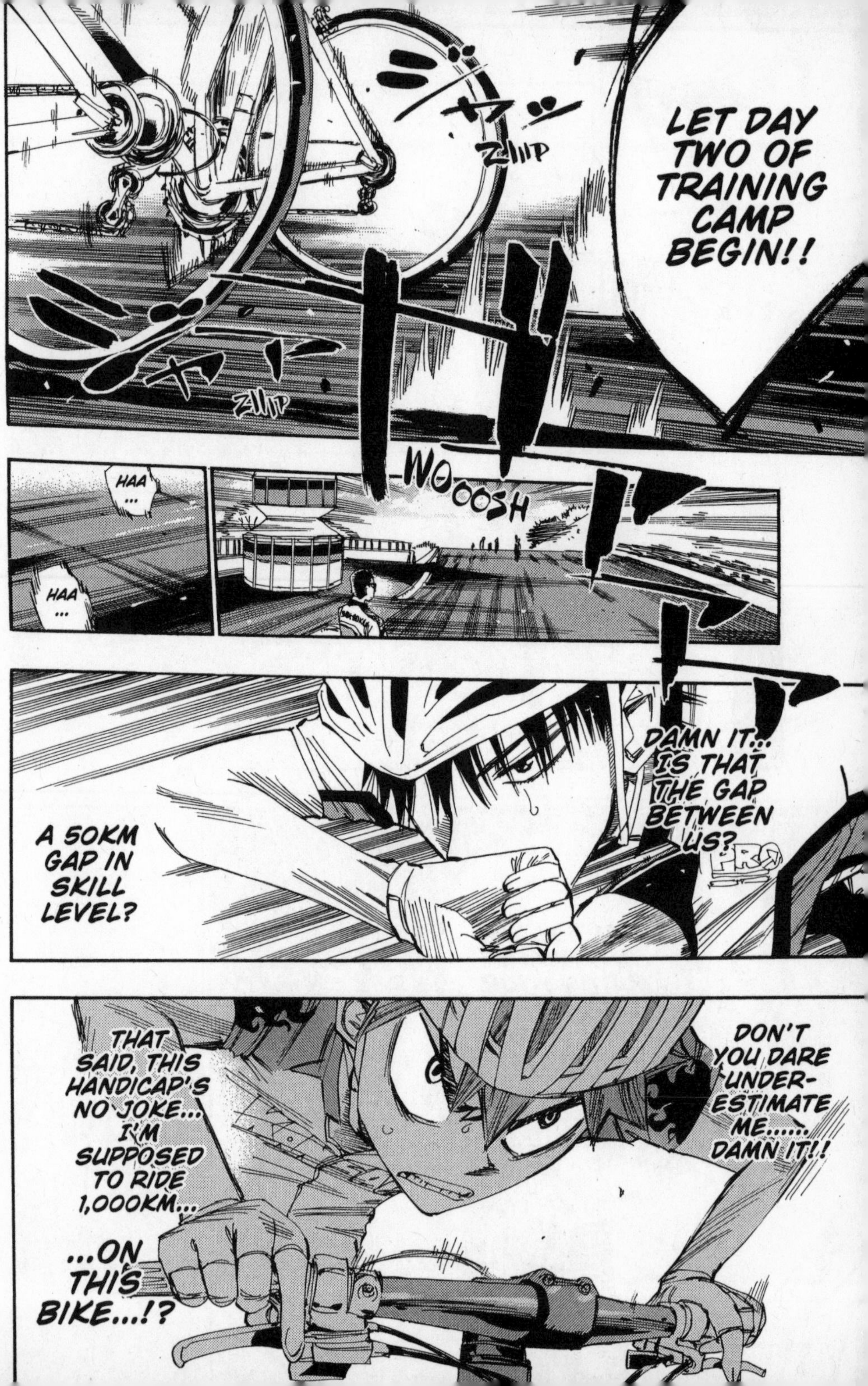
LET DAY TWO OF TRAINING CAMP BEGIN!!
ZIIIP
ZIIIP
WOOOSH
HAA ...
HAA ...
DAMN IT... IS THAT THE GAP BETWEEN US?
A 50KM GAP IN SKILL LEVEL?
DON'T YOU DARE UNDER-ESTIMATE ME...... DAMN IT!!
THAT SAID, THIS HANDICAP'S NO JOKE... I'M SUPPOSED TO RIDE 1,000KM...
...ON THIS BIKE...!?

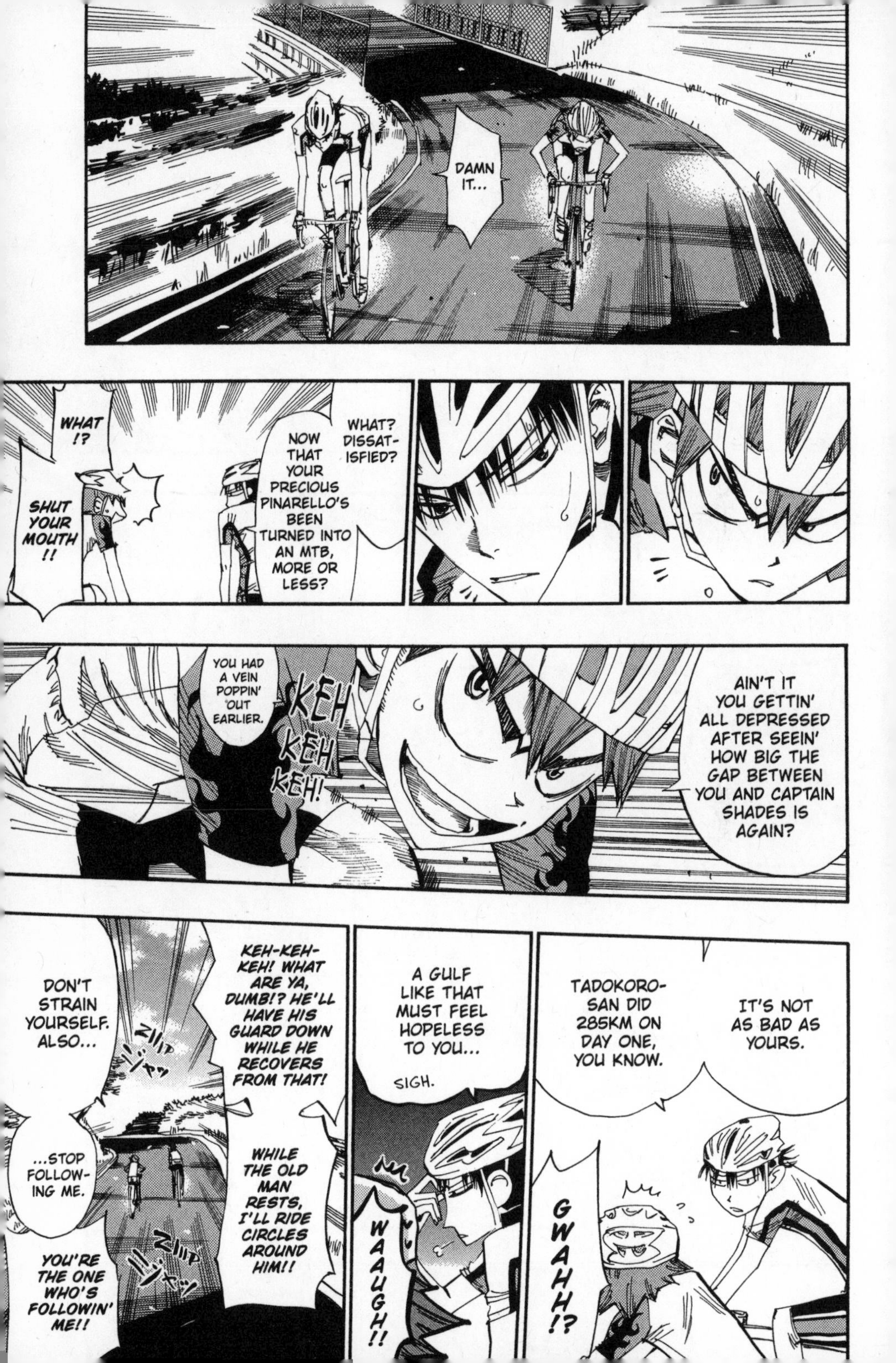
DAMN IT...
WHAT? DISSATISFIED?
NOW THAT YOUR PRECIOUS PINARELLO'S BEEN TURNED INTO AN MTB, MORE OR LESS?
WHAT!?
SHUT YOUR MOUTH!!
AIN'T IT YOU GETTIN' ALL DEPRESSED AFTER SEEIN' HOW BIG THE GAP BETWEEN YOU AND CAPTAIN SHADES IS AGAIN?
KEH KEH KEH!
YOU HAD A VEIN POPPIN' OUT EARLIER.
IT'S NOT AS BAD AS YOURS.
TADOKORO-SAN DID 285KM ON DAY ONE, YOU KNOW.
GWAHH!?
A GULF LIKE THAT MUST FEEL HOPELESS TO YOU...
SIGH.
WAAUGH!!
KEH-KEH-KEH! WHAT ARE YA, DUMB!? HE'LL HAVE HIS GUARD DOWN WHILE HE RECOVERS FROM THAT!
DON'T STRAIN YOURSELF. ALSO...
ZIIP
WHILE THE OLD MAN RESTS, I'LL RIDE CIRCLES AROUND HIM!!
...STOP FOLLOWING ME.
ZIIP
YOU'RE THE ONE WHO'S FOLLOWIN' ME!!

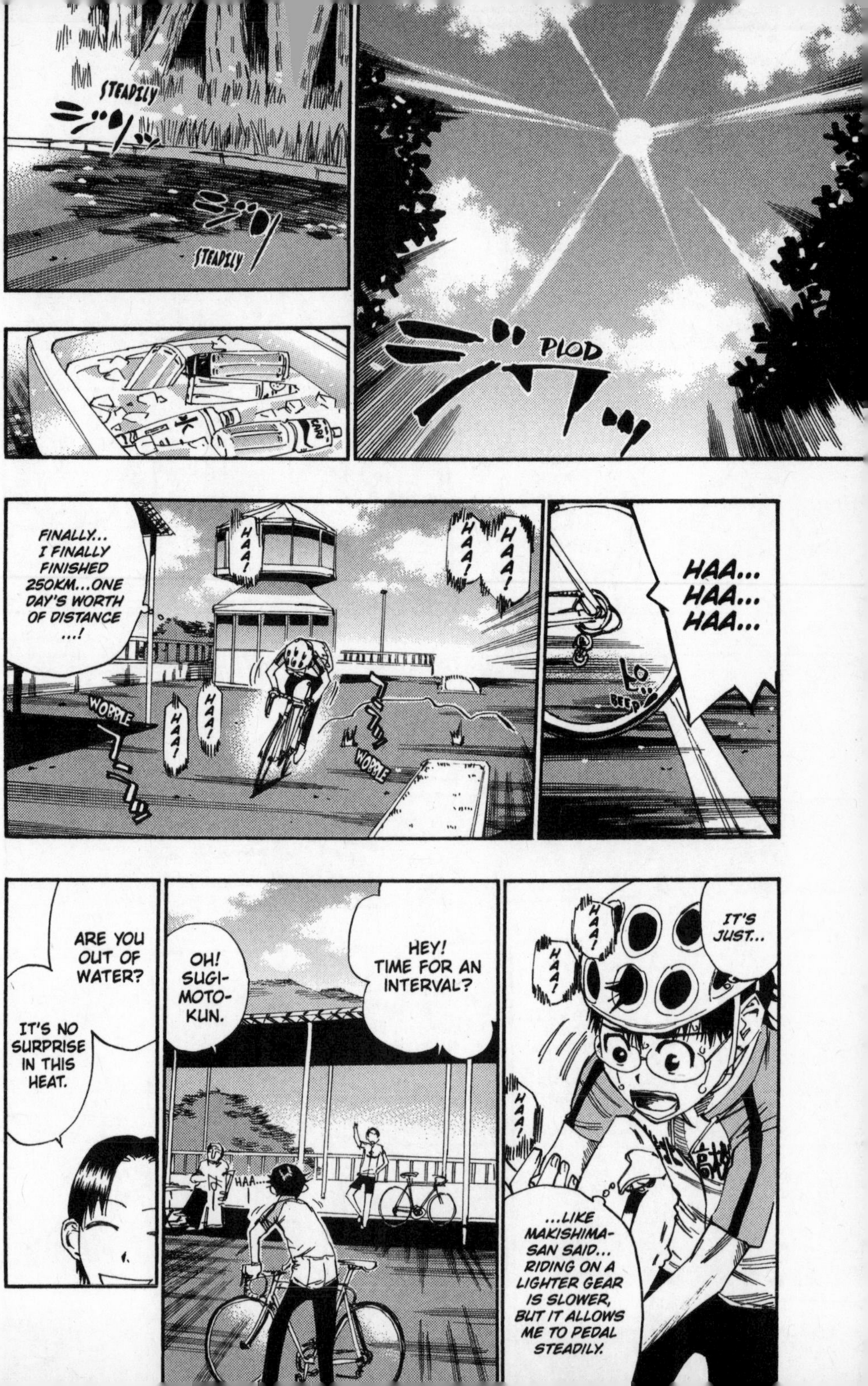
PLOD
STEADILY
STEADILY
HAA... HAA... HAA...
BEEP
HAA! HAA!
FINALLY... I FINALLY FINISHED 250KM...ONE DAY'S WORTH OF DISTANCE ...!
HAA! HAA!
WOBBLE
WOBBLE
IT'S JUST...
HAA! HAA!
HAA!
...LIKE MAKISHIMA-SAN SAID... RIDING ON A LIGHTER GEAR IS SLOWER, BUT IT ALLOWS ME TO PEDAL STEADILY.
HEY! TIME FOR AN INTERVAL?
OH! SUGI-MOTO-KUN.
HAA...
ARE YOU OUT OF WATER?
IT'S NO SURPRISE IN THIS HEAT.

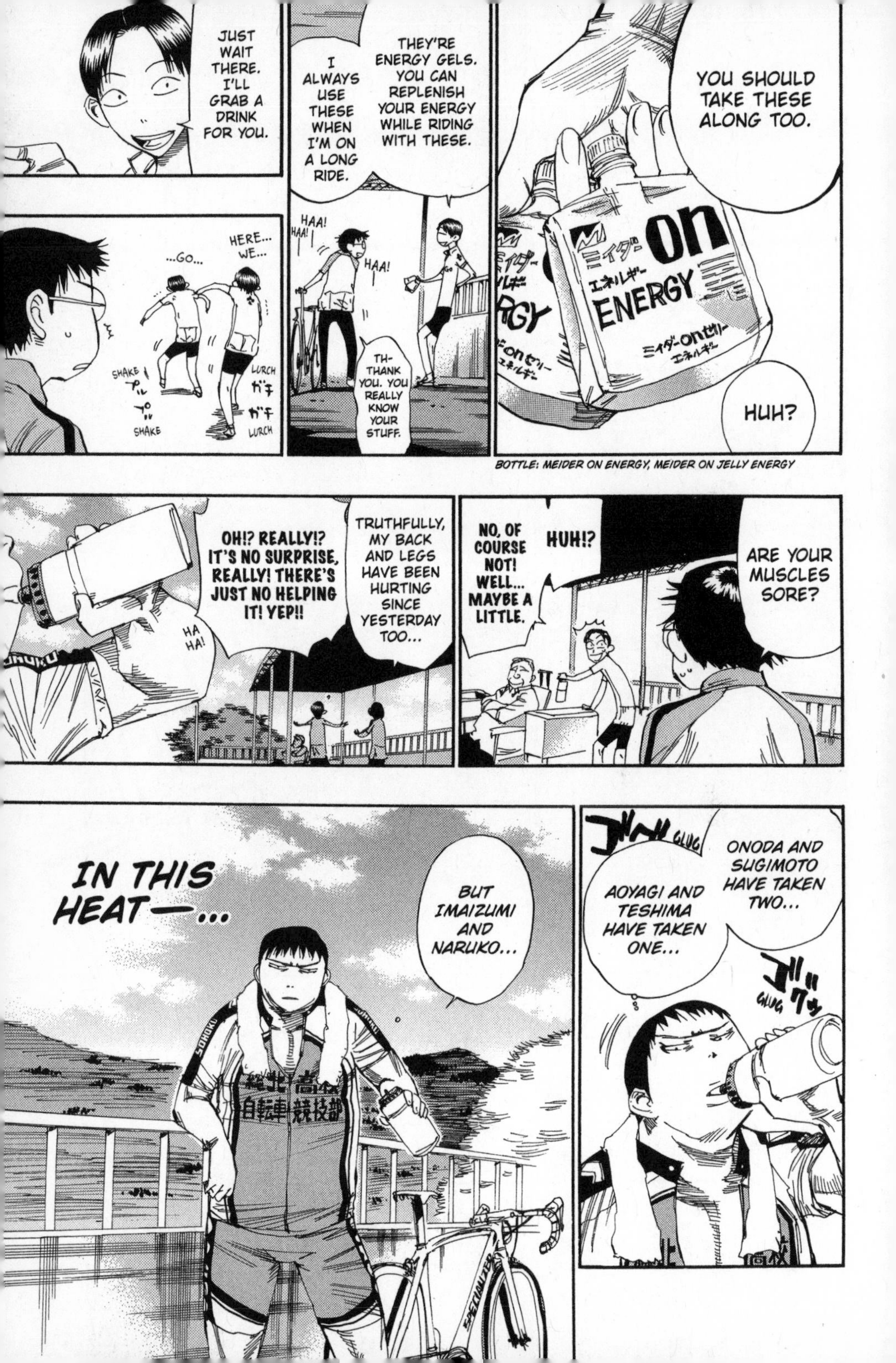
YOU SHOULD TAKE THESE ALONG TOO.
ON
ENERGY
HUH?
THEY'RE ENERGY GELS. YOU CAN REPLENISH YOUR ENERGY WHILE RIDING WITH THESE.
I ALWAYS USE THESE WHEN I'M ON A LONG RIDE.
HAA! HAA!
HAA!
TH-THANK YOU. YOU REALLY KNOW YOUR STUFF.
JUST WAIT THERE. I'LL GRAB A DRINK FOR YOU.
HERE... WE...
...GO...
LURCH LURCH
SHAKE SHAKE
BOTTLE: MEIDER ON ENERGY, MEIDER ON JELLY ENERGY
ARE YOUR MUSCLES SORE?
HUH!?
NO, OF COURSE NOT! WELL... MAYBE A LITTLE.
TRUTHFULLY, MY BACK AND LEGS HAVE BEEN HURTING SINCE YESTERDAY TOO...
OH!? REALLY!? IT'S NO SURPRISE, REALLY! THERE'S JUST NO HELPING IT! YEP!!
HA HA!
GLUG
ONODA AND SUGIMOTO HAVE TAKEN TWO...
AOYAGI AND TESHIMA HAVE TAKEN ONE...
GLUG
BUT IMAIZUMI AND NARUKO...
IN THIS HEAT—...

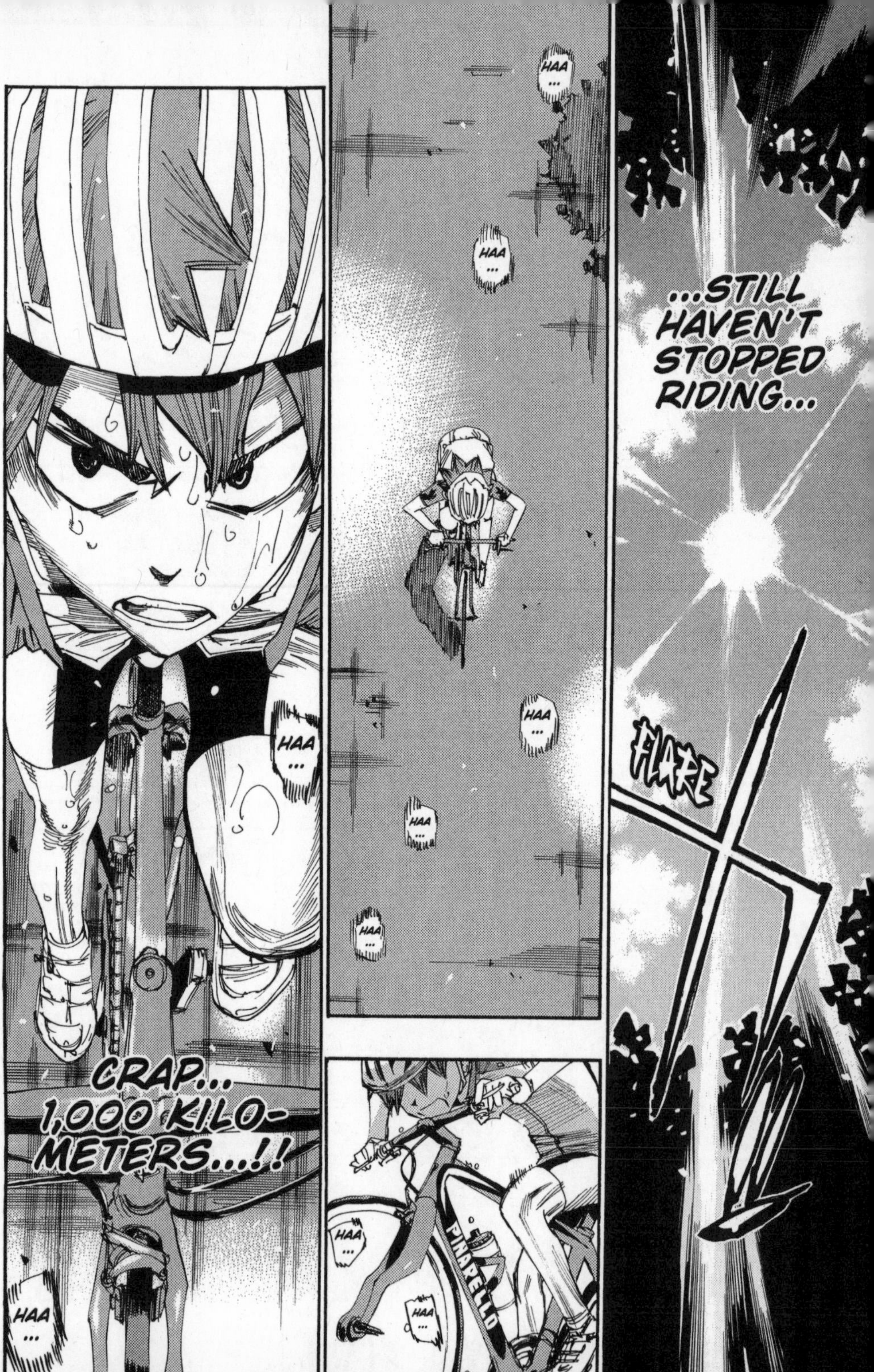
...STILL HAVEN'T STOPPED RIDING...
FLARE
HAA ...
HAA ...
HAA ...
HAA ...
HAA ...
HAA ...
HAA ...
HAA ...
CRAP... 1,000 KILO-METERS...!!
HAA ...

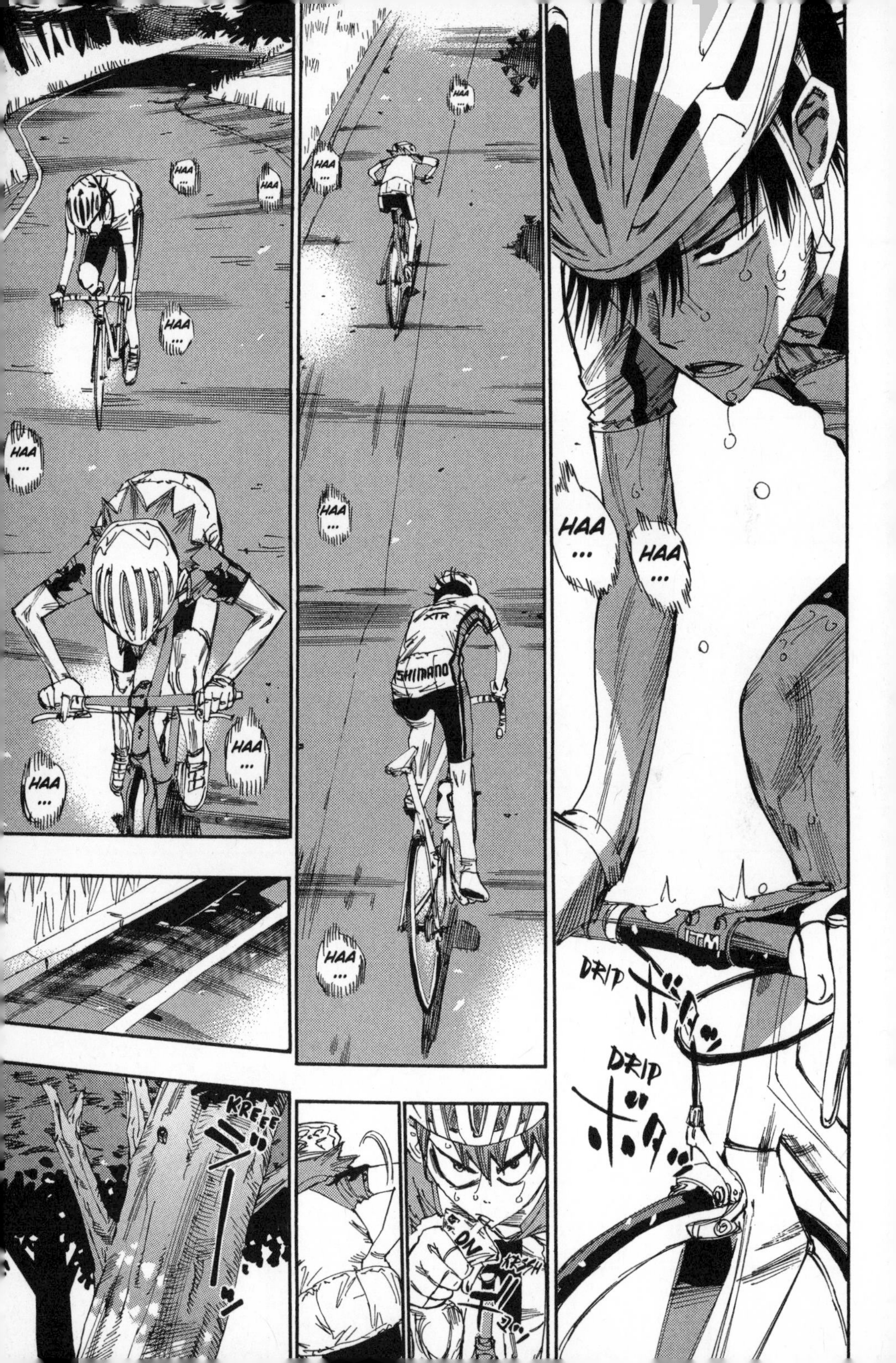
HAA ...
HAA ...
DRIP
DRIP
HAA ...
HAA ...
HAA ...
HAA ...
HAA ...
DN
KRSH
HAA ...
HAA ...
HAA ...
HAA ...
HAA ...
HAA ...
KREEE

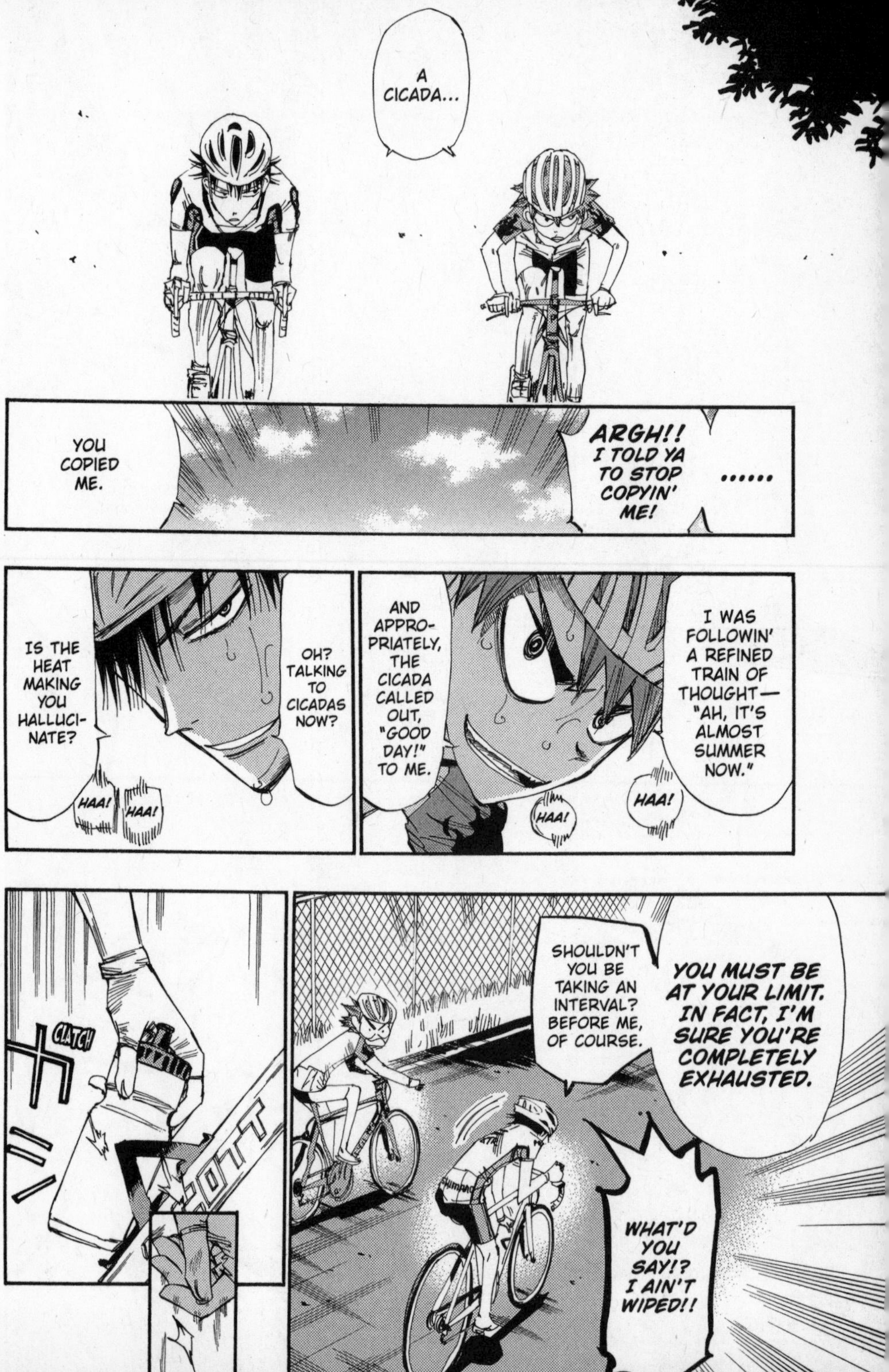
A CICADA...
......
ARGH!! I TOLD YA TO STOP COPYIN' ME!
YOU COPIED ME.
I WAS FOLLOWIN' A REFINED TRAIN OF THOUGHT—"AH, IT'S ALMOST SUMMER NOW."
HAA!
AND APPROPRIATELY, THE CICADA CALLED OUT, "GOOD DAY!" TO ME.
HAA!
OH? TALKING TO CICADAS NOW?
IS THE HEAT MAKING YOU HALLUCINATE?
HAA!
HAA!
YOU MUST BE AT YOUR LIMIT. IN FACT, I'M SURE YOU'RE COMPLETELY EXHAUSTED.
SHOULDN'T YOU BE TAKING AN INTERVAL? BEFORE ME, OF COURSE.
WHAT'D YOU SAY!? I AIN'T WIPED!!
CLATCH

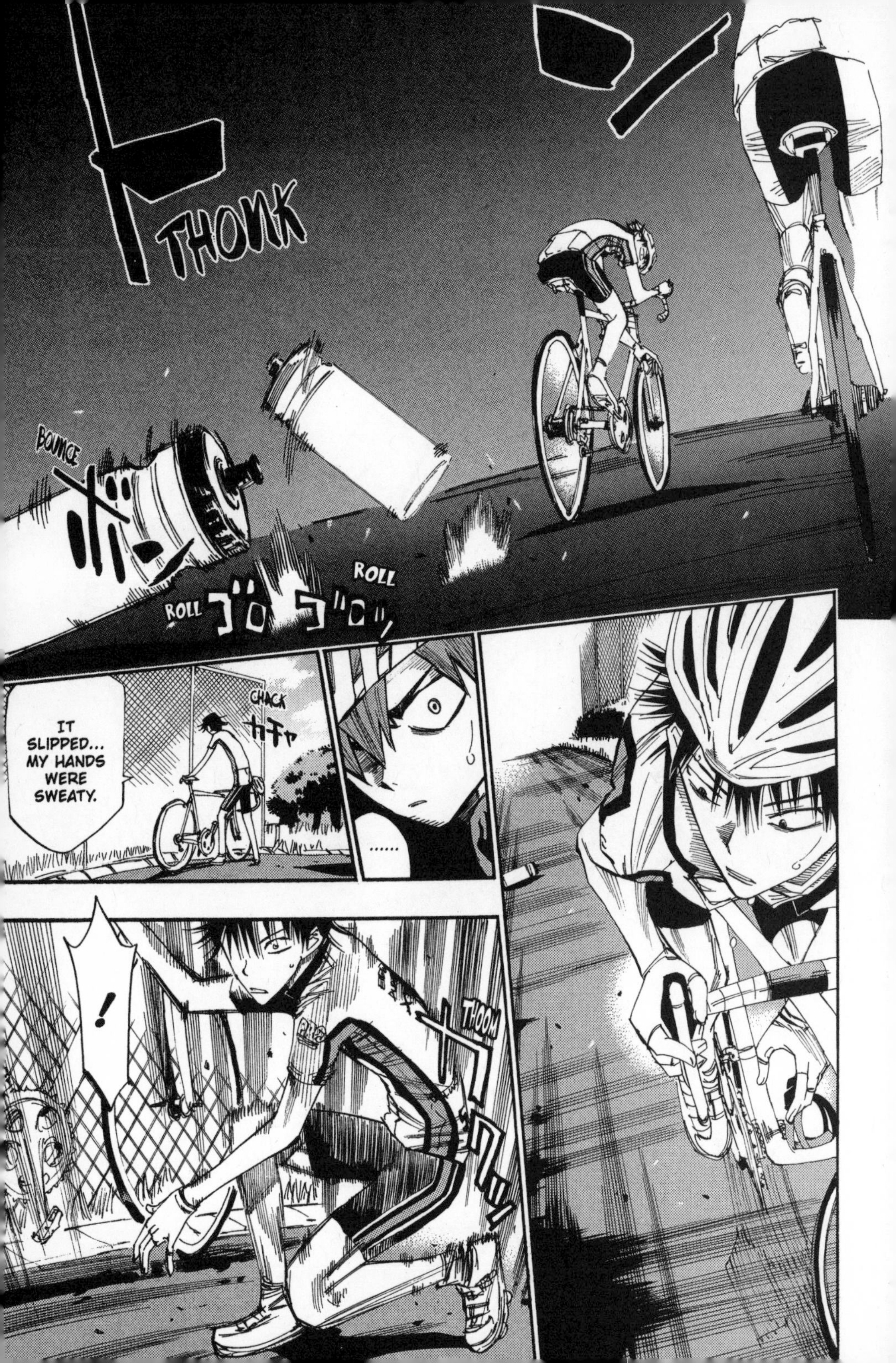
THONK
BOUNCE
ROLL
ROLL
……
CHACK
カチャ
IT SLIPPED… MY HANDS WERE SWEATY.
THOOM
!

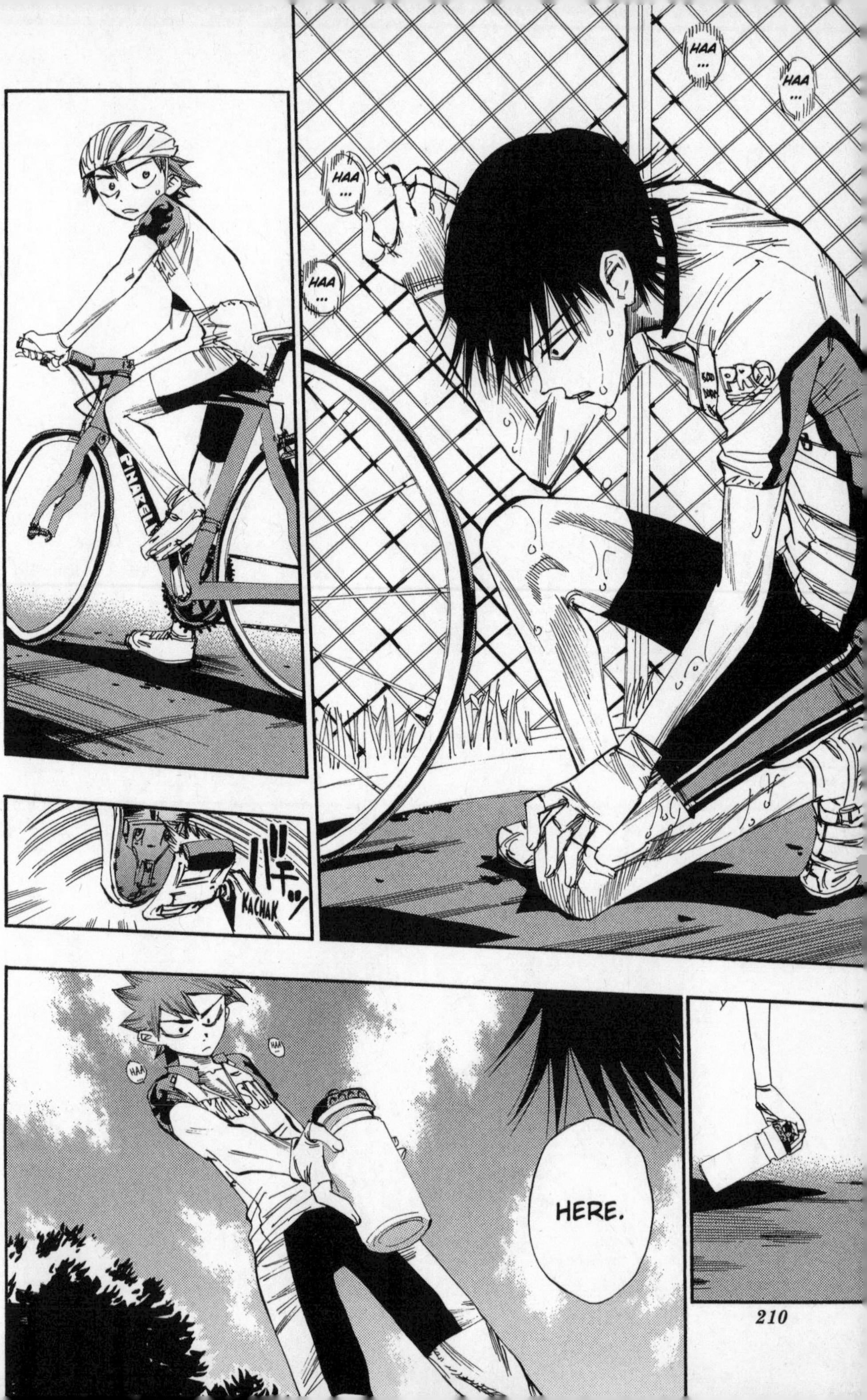
HAA...
HAA...
HAA...
HAA...
KACHAK
HERE.
HAA
HAA

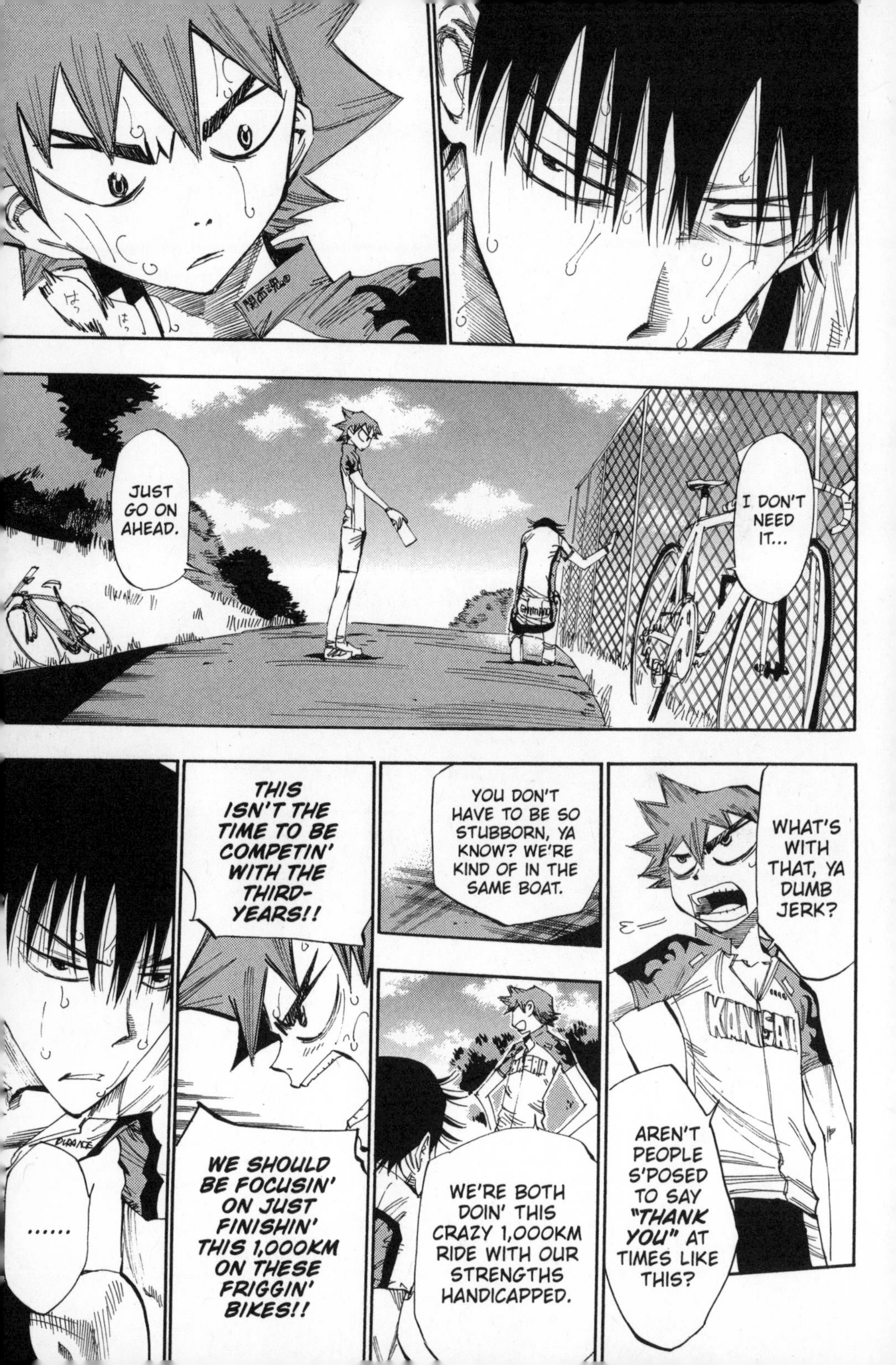

はっ
はっ
I DON'T NEED IT...
JUST GO ON AHEAD.
WHAT'S WITH THAT, YA DUMB JERK?
AREN'T PEOPLE S'POSED TO SAY "THANK YOU" AT TIMES LIKE THIS?
YOU DON'T HAVE TO BE SO STUBBORN, YA KNOW? WE'RE KIND OF IN THE SAME BOAT.
WE'RE BOTH DOIN' THIS CRAZY 1,000KM RIDE WITH OUR STRENGTHS HANDICAPPED.
THIS ISN'T THE TIME TO BE COMPETIN' WITH THE THIRD-YEARS!!
WE SHOULD BE FOCUSIN' ON JUST FINISHIN' THIS 1,000KM ON THESE FRIGGIN' BIKES!!
......

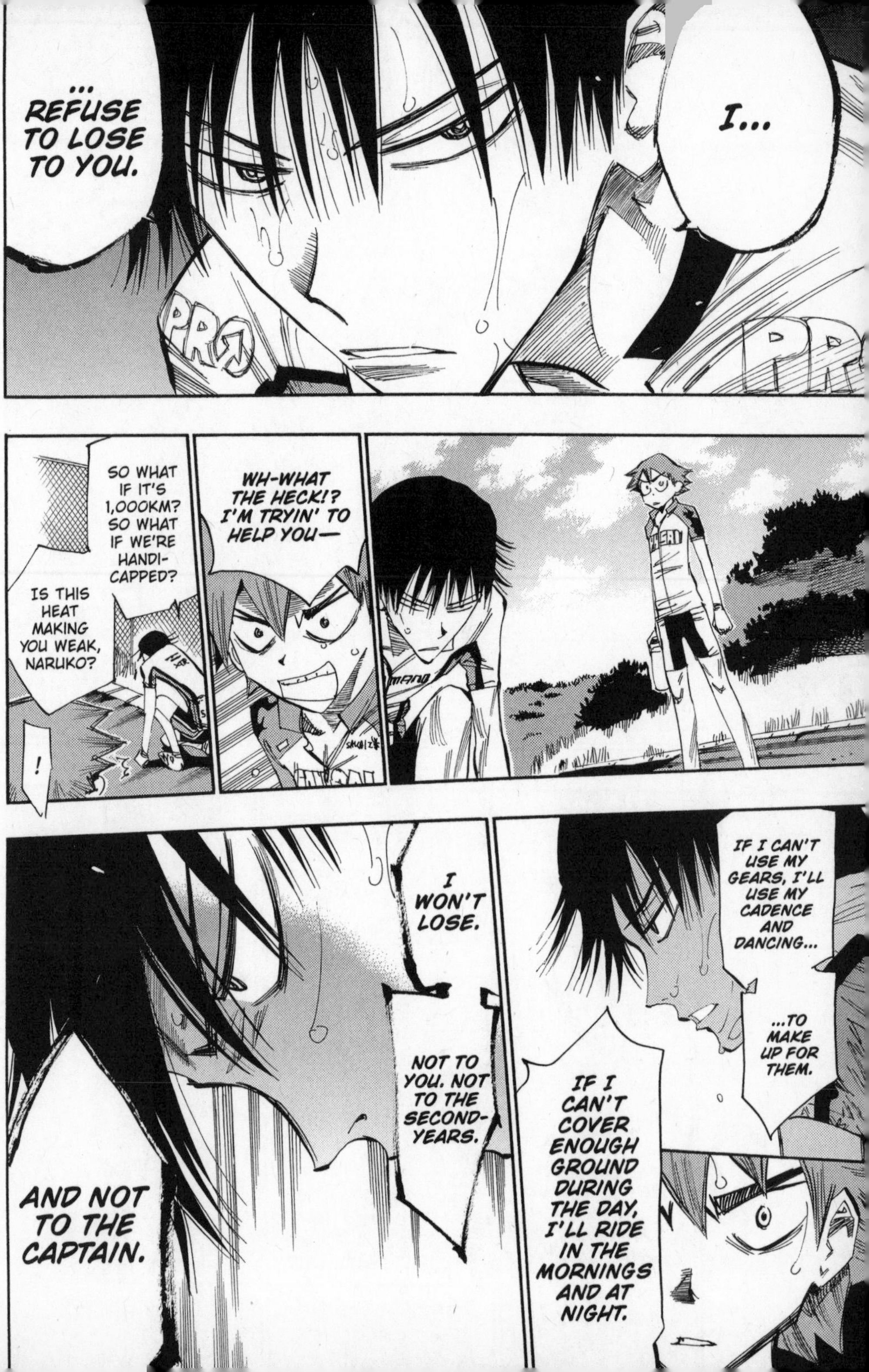
I...
...REFUSE TO LOSE TO YOU.
WH-WHAT THE HECK!? I'M TRYIN' TO HELP YOU—
SO WHAT IF IT'S 1,000KM? SO WHAT IF WE'RE HANDI-CAPPED?
IS THIS HEAT MAKING YOU WEAK, NARUKO?
!
IF I CAN'T USE MY GEARS, I'LL USE MY CADENCE AND DANCING...
...TO MAKE UP FOR THEM.
IF I CAN'T COVER ENOUGH GROUND DURING THE DAY, I'LL RIDE IN THE MORNINGS AND AT NIGHT.
I WON'T LOSE.
NOT TO YOU. NOT TO THE SECOND-YEARS.
AND NOT TO THE CAPTAIN.

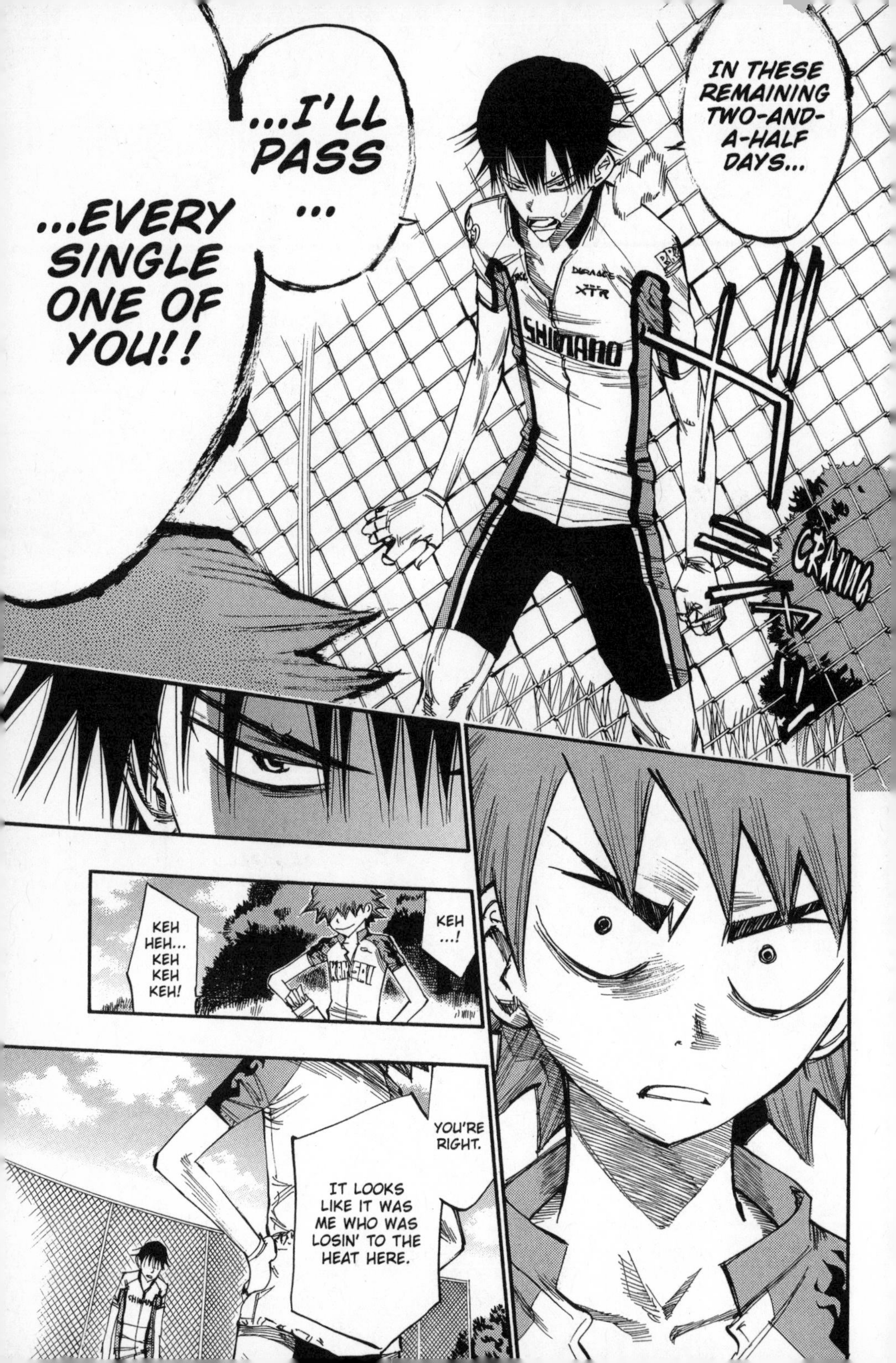
IN THESE REMAINING TWO-AND-A-HALF DAYS...
...I'LL PASS ...
...EVERY SINGLE ONE OF YOU!!
CRANNG
KEH ...!
KEH HEH... KEH KEH KEH!
YOU'RE RIGHT.
IT LOOKS LIKE IT WAS ME WHO WAS LOSIN' TO THE HEAT HERE.

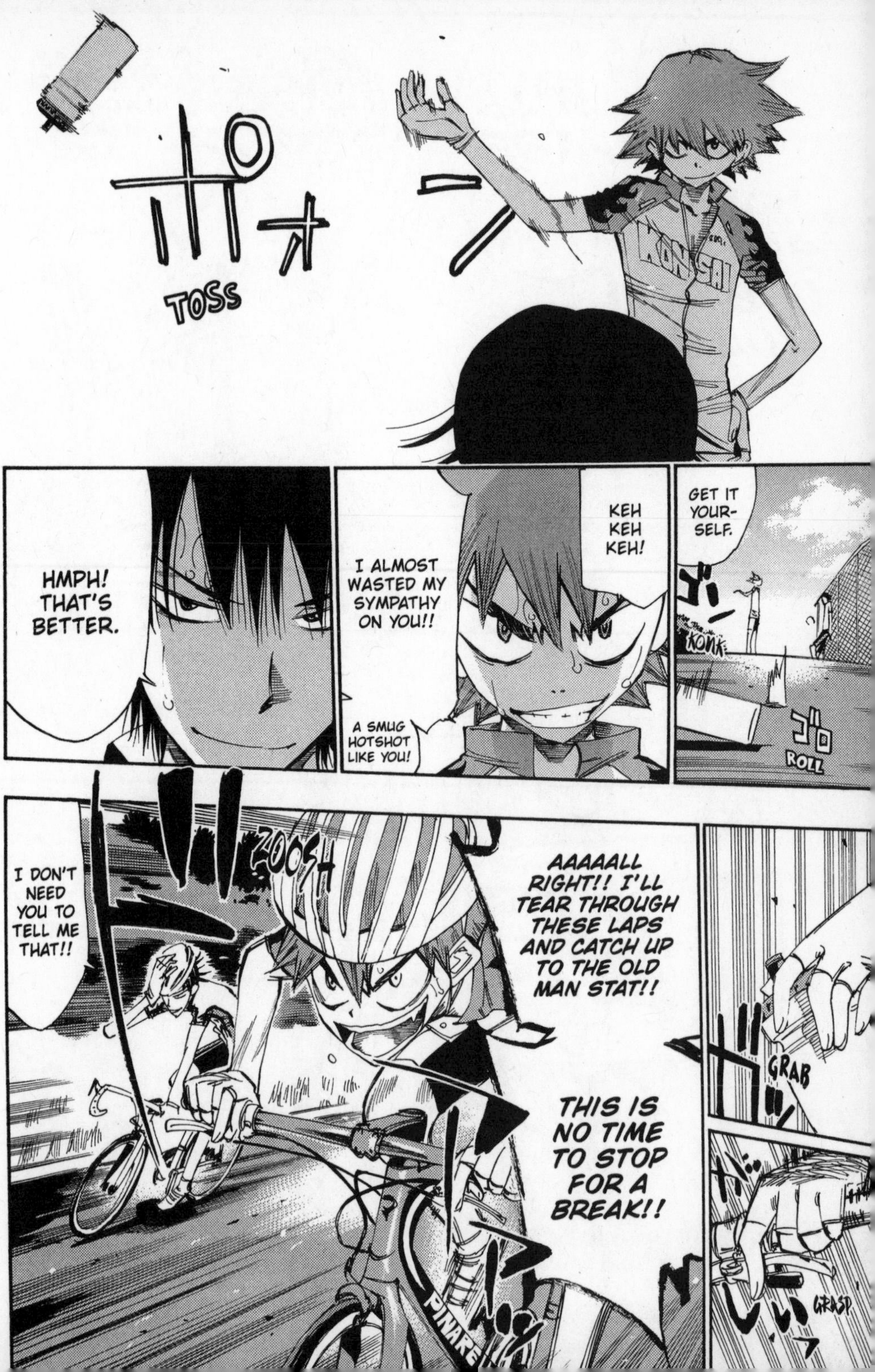
TOSS
GET IT YOURSELF.
KONK
ROLL
KEH KEH KEH!
I ALMOST WASTED MY SYMPATHY ON YOU!!
A SMUG HOTSHOT LIKE YOU!
HMPH! THAT'S BETTER.
GRAB
GRASP
AAAAALL RIGHT!! I'LL TEAR THROUGH THESE LAPS AND CATCH UP TO THE OLD MAN STAT!!
ZOOSH
I DON'T NEED YOU TO TELL ME THAT!!
THIS IS NO TIME TO STOP FOR A BREAK!!

RIDE.45 HAKONE ACADEMY

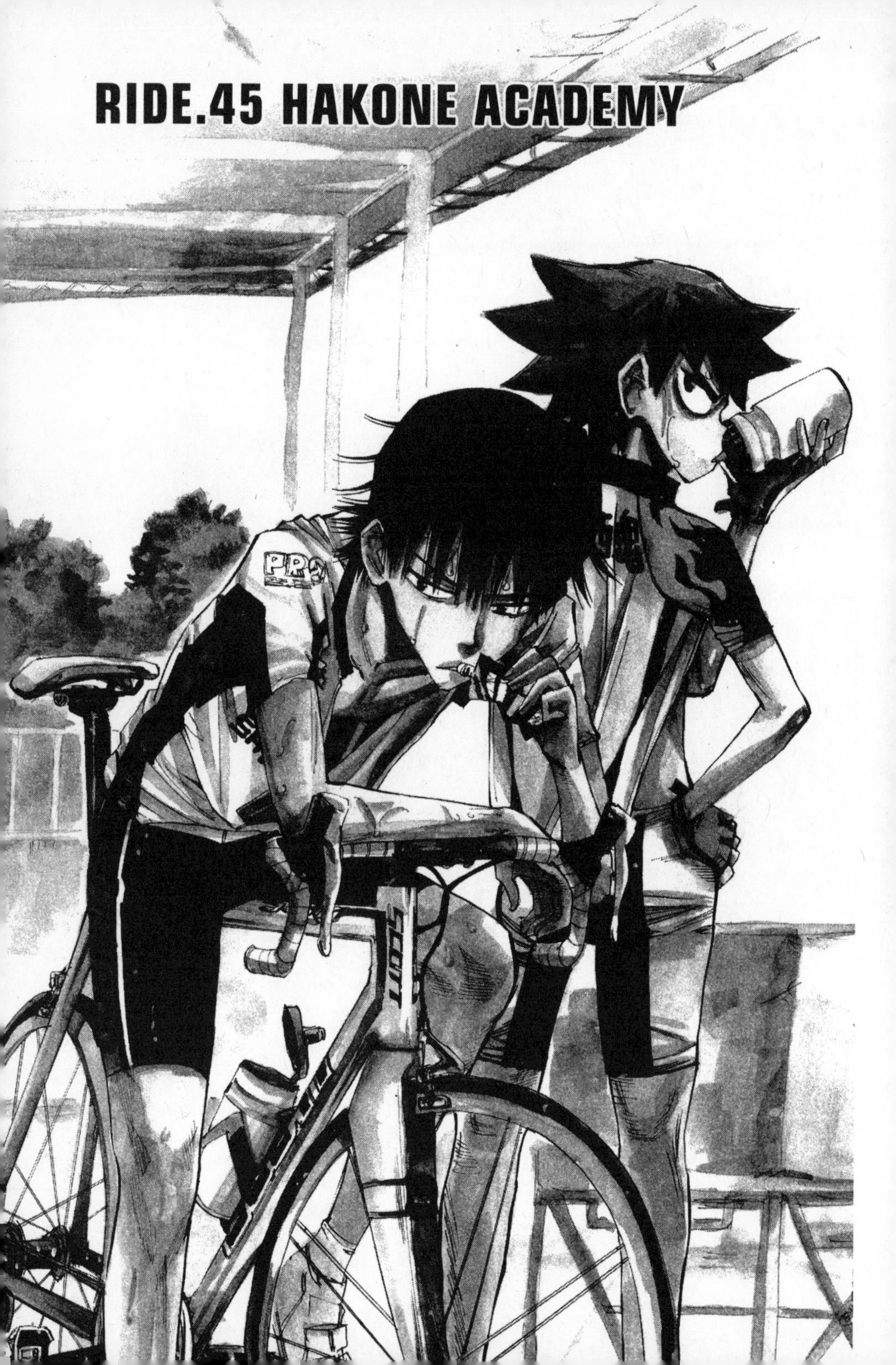

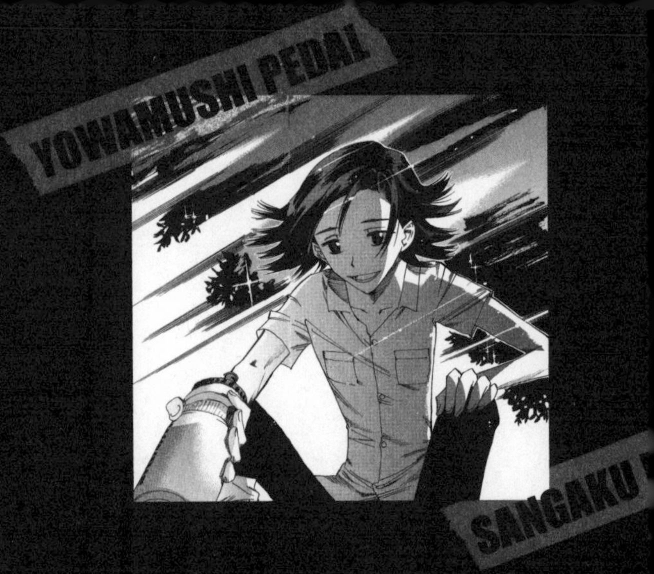
YOWAMUSHI PEDAL
SANGAKU

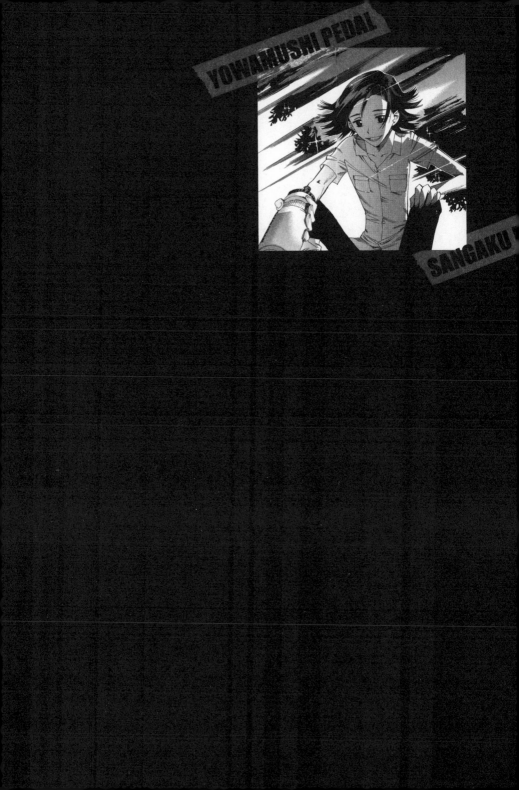

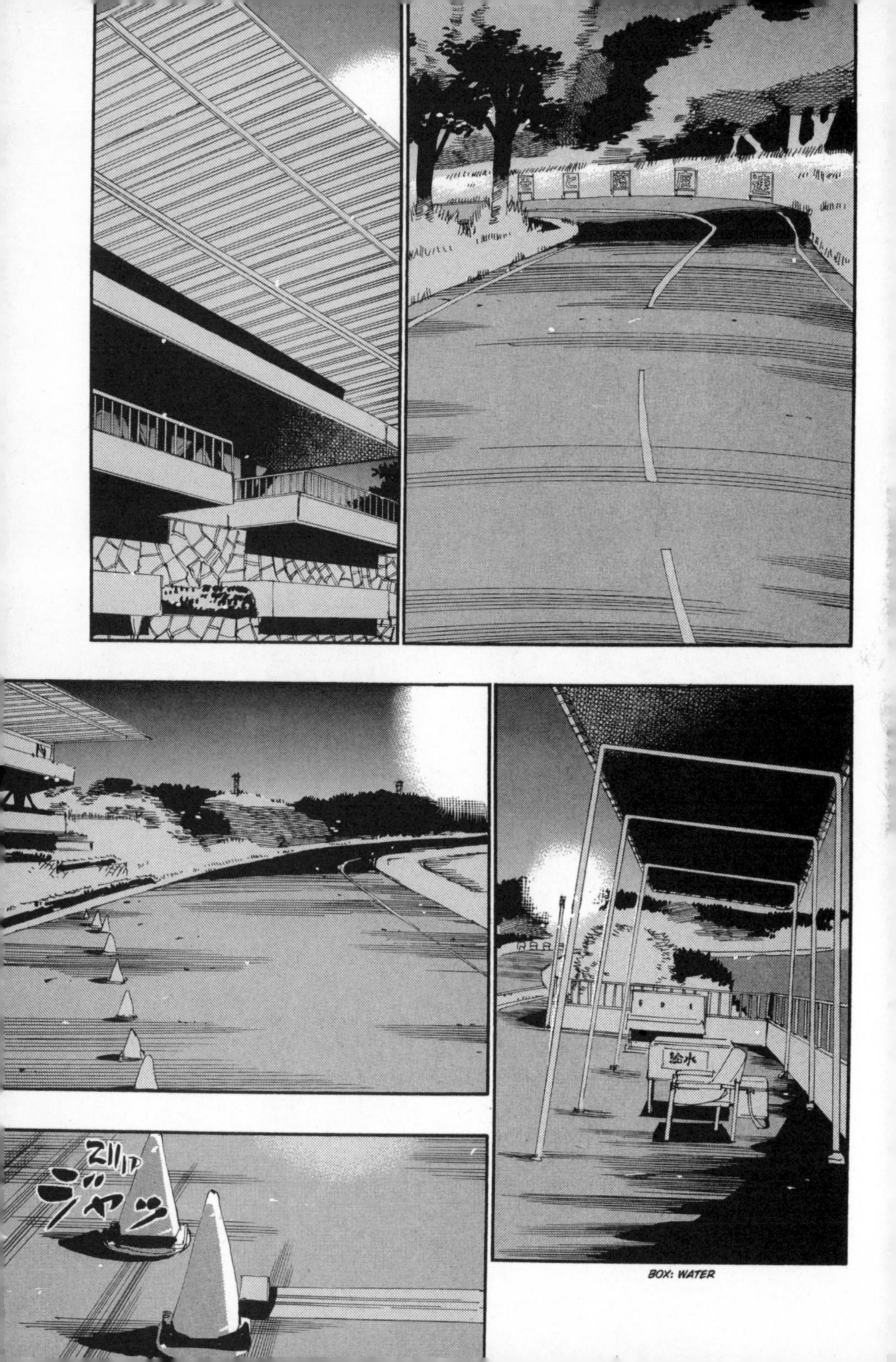
給水
ZIIP
ジャッ

BOX: WATER

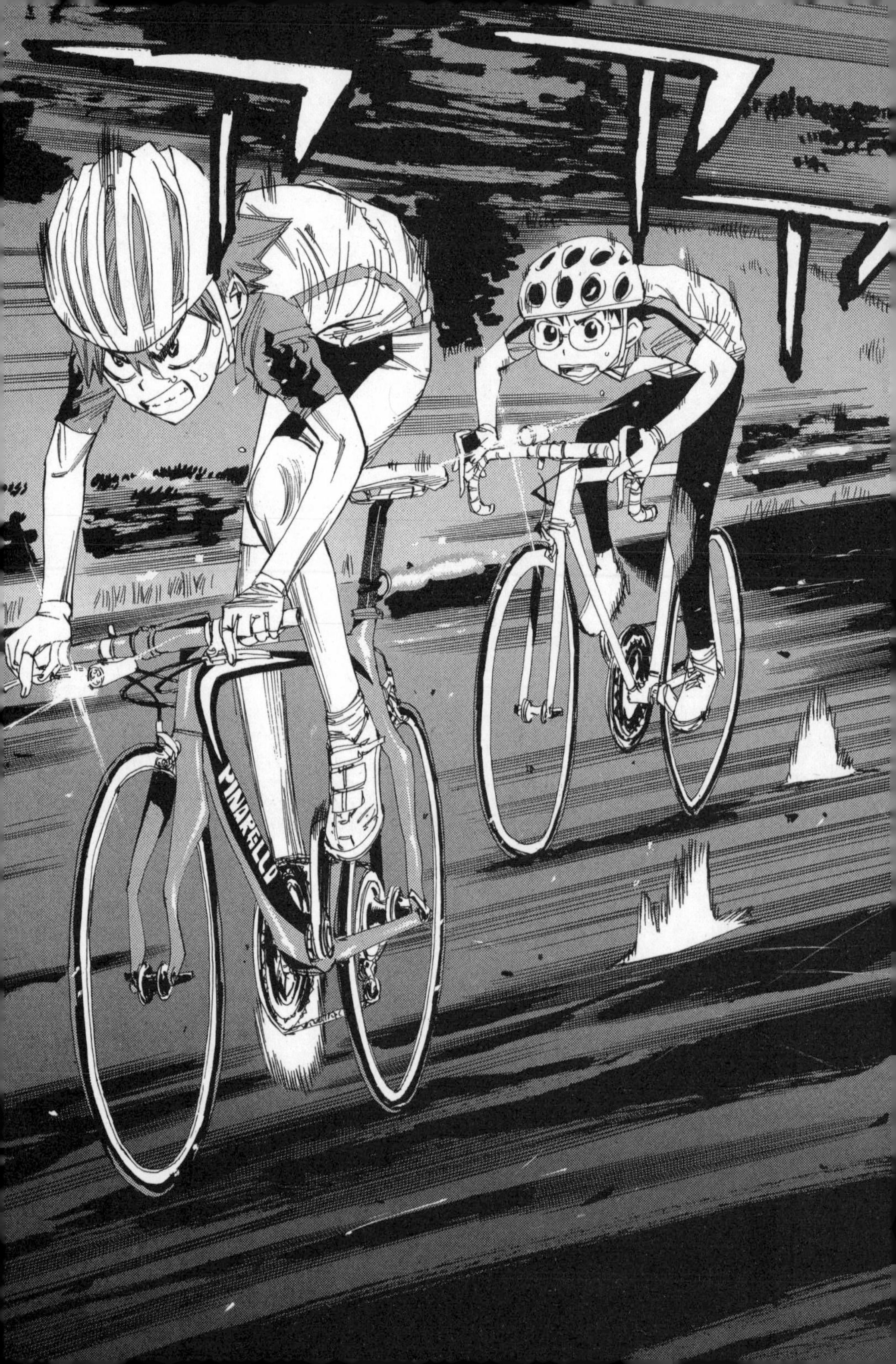
PINARELLO

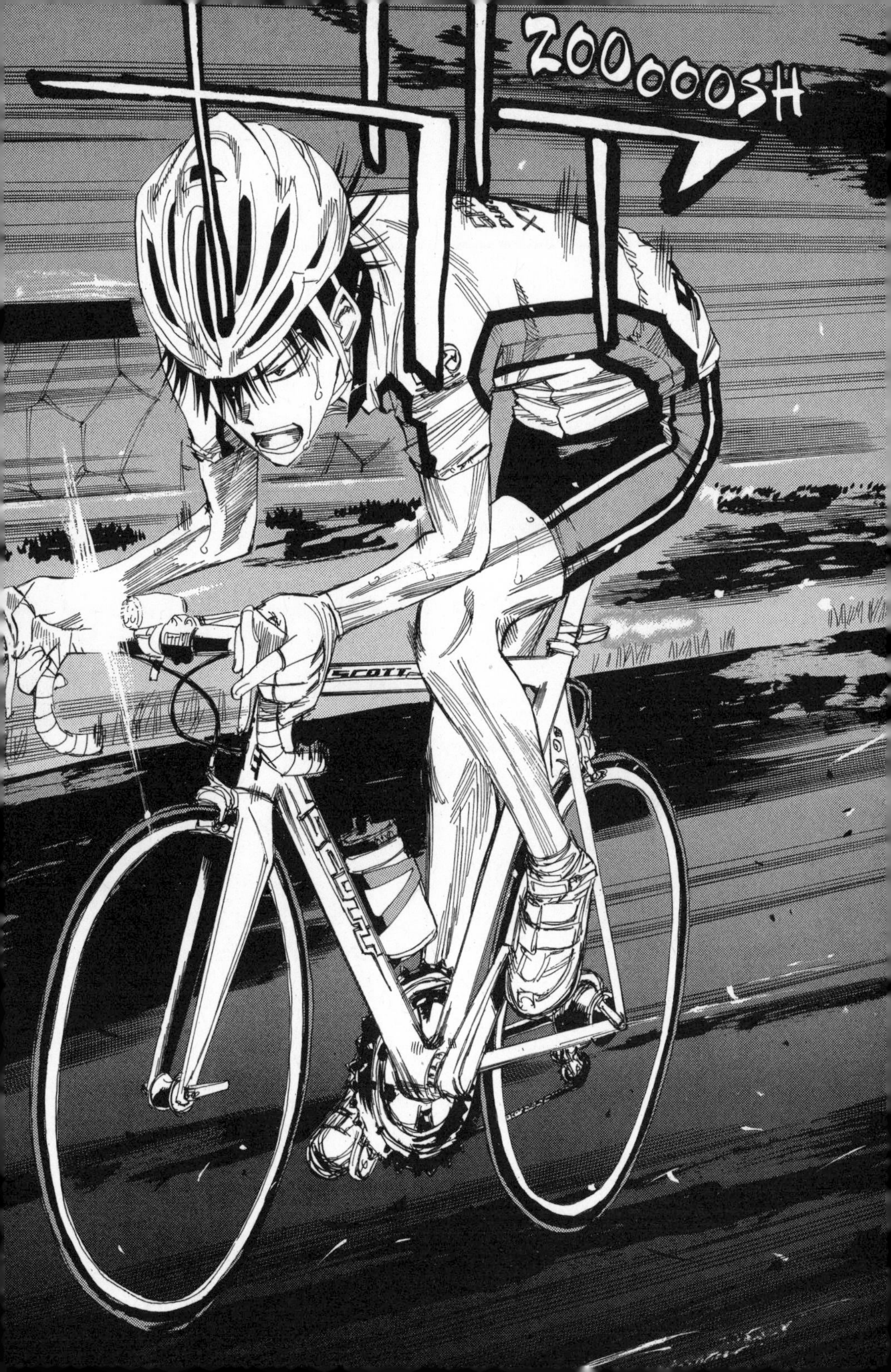
ZOOOOOOSH

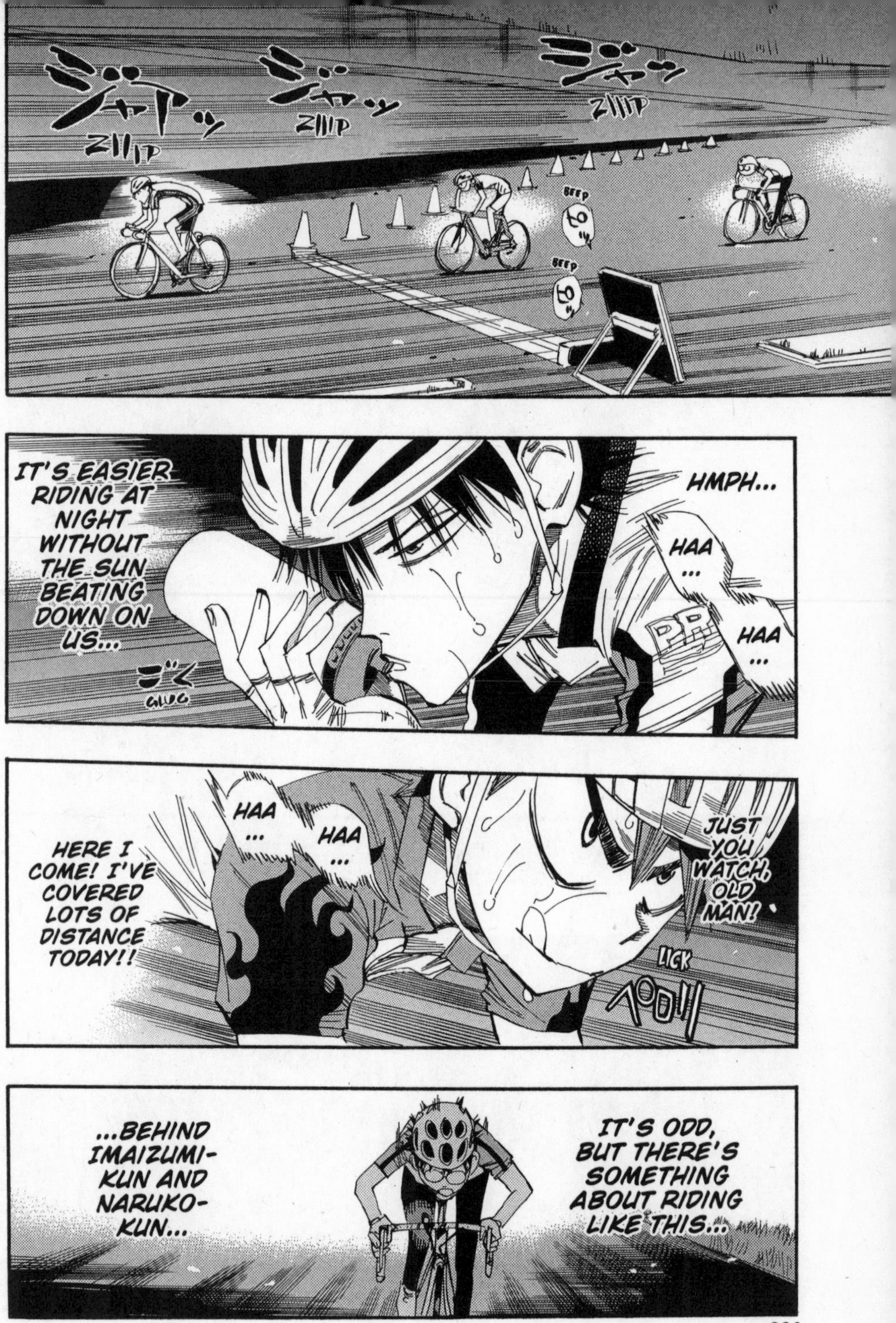
ZIIIP
ZIIIP
ZIIIP
BEEP
BEEP
HMPH...
HAA...
HAA...
IT'S EASIER RIDING AT NIGHT WITHOUT THE SUN BEATING DOWN ON US...
GULP
JUST YOU WATCH, OLD MAN!
LICK
HAA...
HAA...
HERE I COME! I'VE COVERED LOTS OF DISTANCE TODAY!!
IT'S ODD, BUT THERE'S SOMETHING ABOUT RIDING LIKE THIS...
...BEHIND IMAIZUMI-KUN AND NARUKO-KUN...

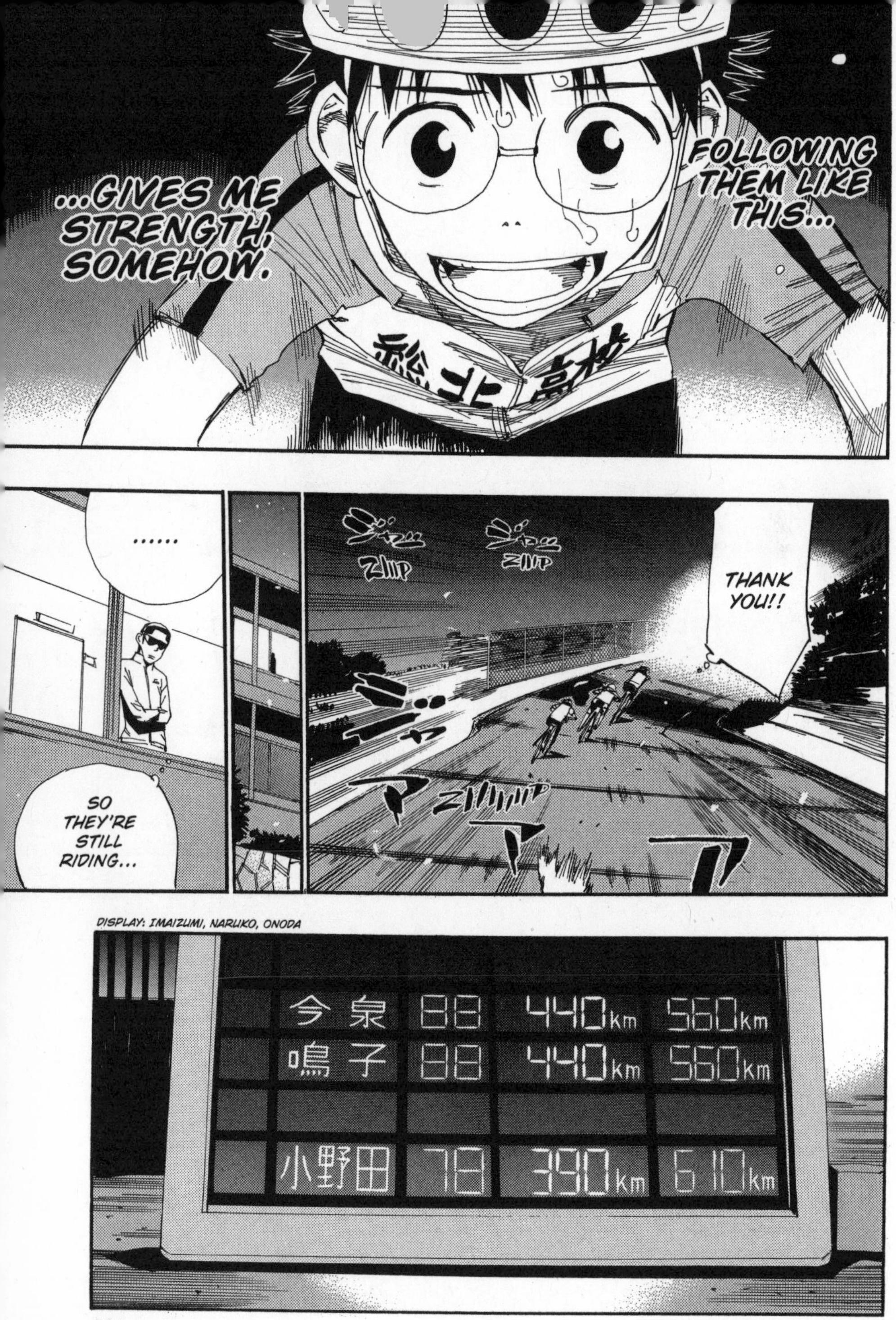
FOLLOWING THEM LIKE THIS...
...GIVES ME STRENGTH, SOMEHOW.
ZIIIP
ZIIIP
ZIIIIIP
THANK YOU!!
......
SO THEY'RE STILL RIDING...
DISPLAY: IMAIZUMI, NARUKO, ONODA
今泉 88 440km 560km
鳴子 88 440km 560km
小野田 78 390km 610km

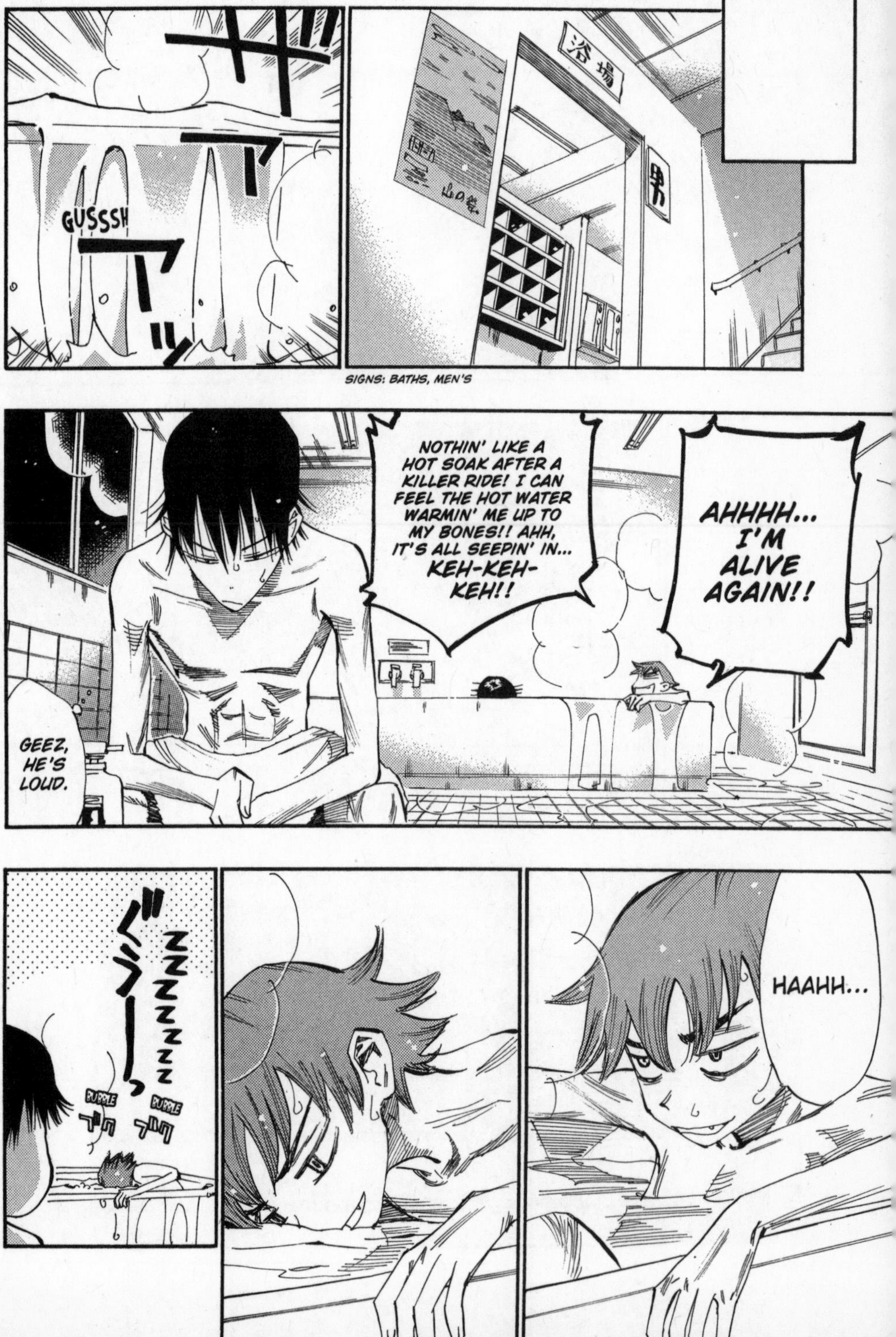
浴場
男
GUSSSH
AHHHH... I'M ALIVE AGAIN!!
NOTHIN' LIKE A HOT SOAK AFTER A KILLER RIDE! I CAN FEEL THE HOT WATER WARMIN' ME UP TO MY BONES!! AHH, IT'S ALL SEEPIN' IN... KEH-KEH-KEH!!
GEEZ, HE'S LOUD.
HAAHH...
BUBBLE
BUBBLE

SIGNS: BATHS, MEN'S

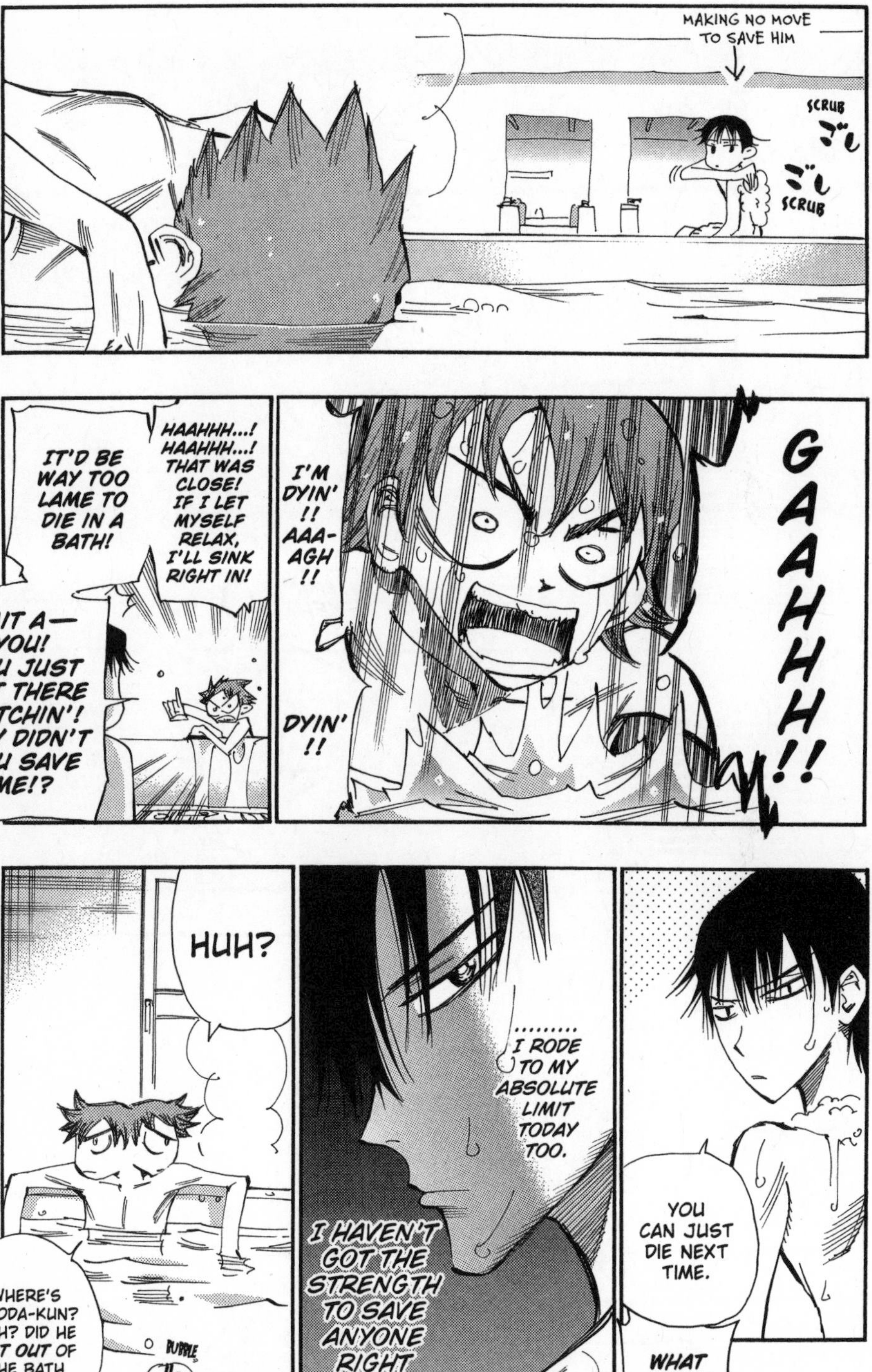
MAKING NO MOVE TO SAVE HIM
SCRUB
ごし
ごし
SCRUB
GAAHHH!!
I'M DYIN'!! AAA-AGH!!
DYIN'!!
HAAHHH...! HAAHHH...! THAT WAS CLOSE! IF I LET MYSELF RELAX, I'LL SINK RIGHT IN!
IT'D BE WAY TOO LAME TO DIE IN A BATH!
WAIT A— YOU! YOU JUST SAT THERE WATCHIN'! WHY DIDN'T YOU SAVE ME!?
YOU CAN JUST DIE NEXT TIME.
WHAT WAS THAT!?
.... I RODE TO MY ABSOLUTE LIMIT TODAY TOO.
I HAVEN'T GOT THE STRENGTH TO SAVE ANYONE RIGHT NOW.
HUH?
WHERE'S ONODA-KUN? HUH? DID HE GET OUT OF THE BATH ALREADY?
BUBBLE

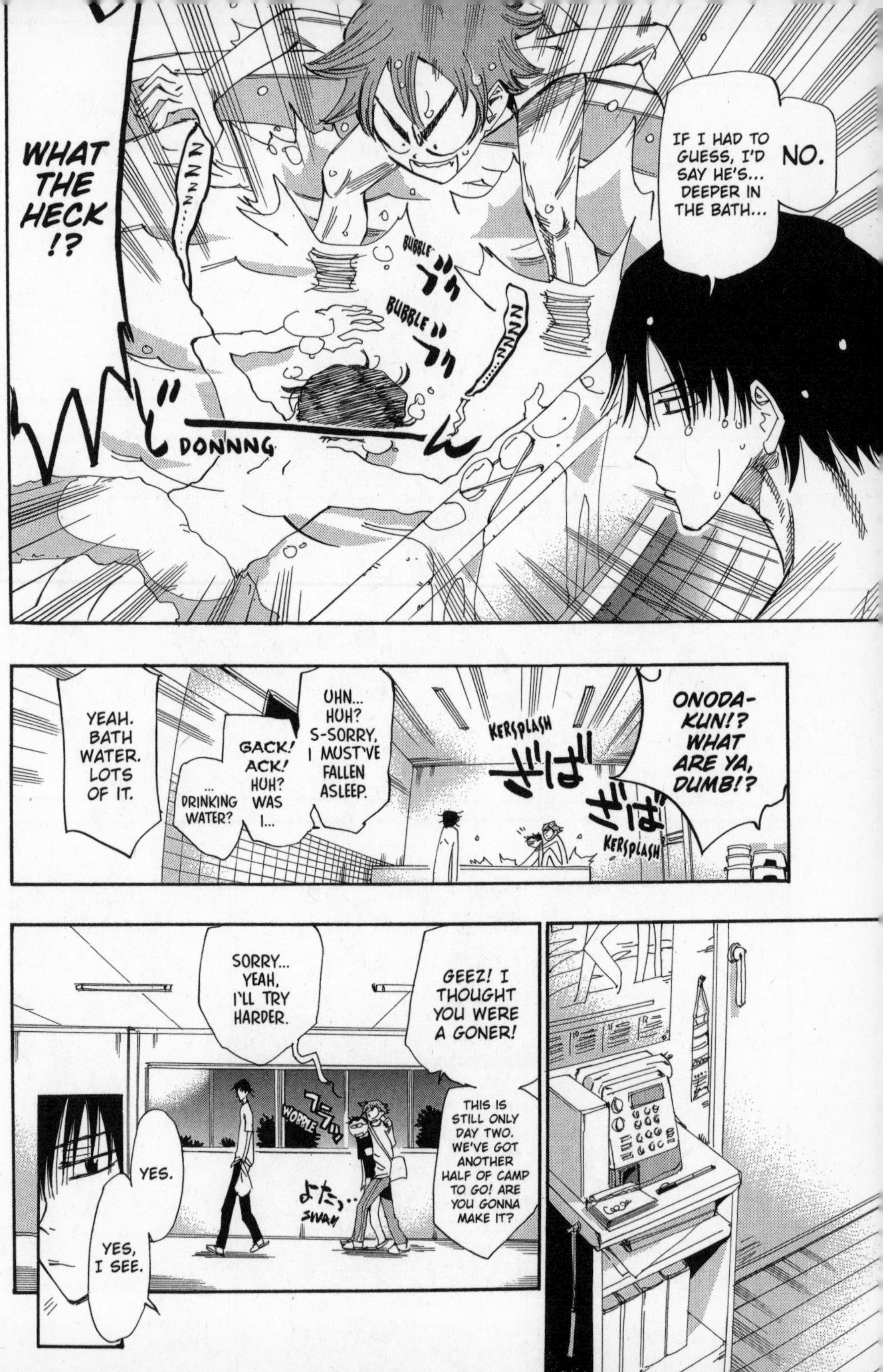
NO.
IF I HAD TO GUESS, I'D SAY HE'S... DEEPER IN THE BATH...
BUBBLE
BUBBLE
DONNNG
WHAT THE HECK!?
ONODA-KUN!? WHAT ARE YA, DUMB!?
KERSPLASH
KERSPLASH
UHN... HUH? S-SORRY, I MUST'VE FALLEN ASLEEP.
GACK! ACK! HUH? WAS I...
...DRINKING WATER?
YEAH. BATH WATER. LOTS OF IT.
GEEZ! I THOUGHT YOU WERE A GONER!
THIS IS STILL ONLY DAY TWO. WE'VE GOT ANOTHER HALF OF CAMP TO GO! ARE YOU GONNA MAKE IT?
SORRY... YEAH, I'LL TRY HARDER.
WOBBLE
SWAY
YES.
YES, I SEE.

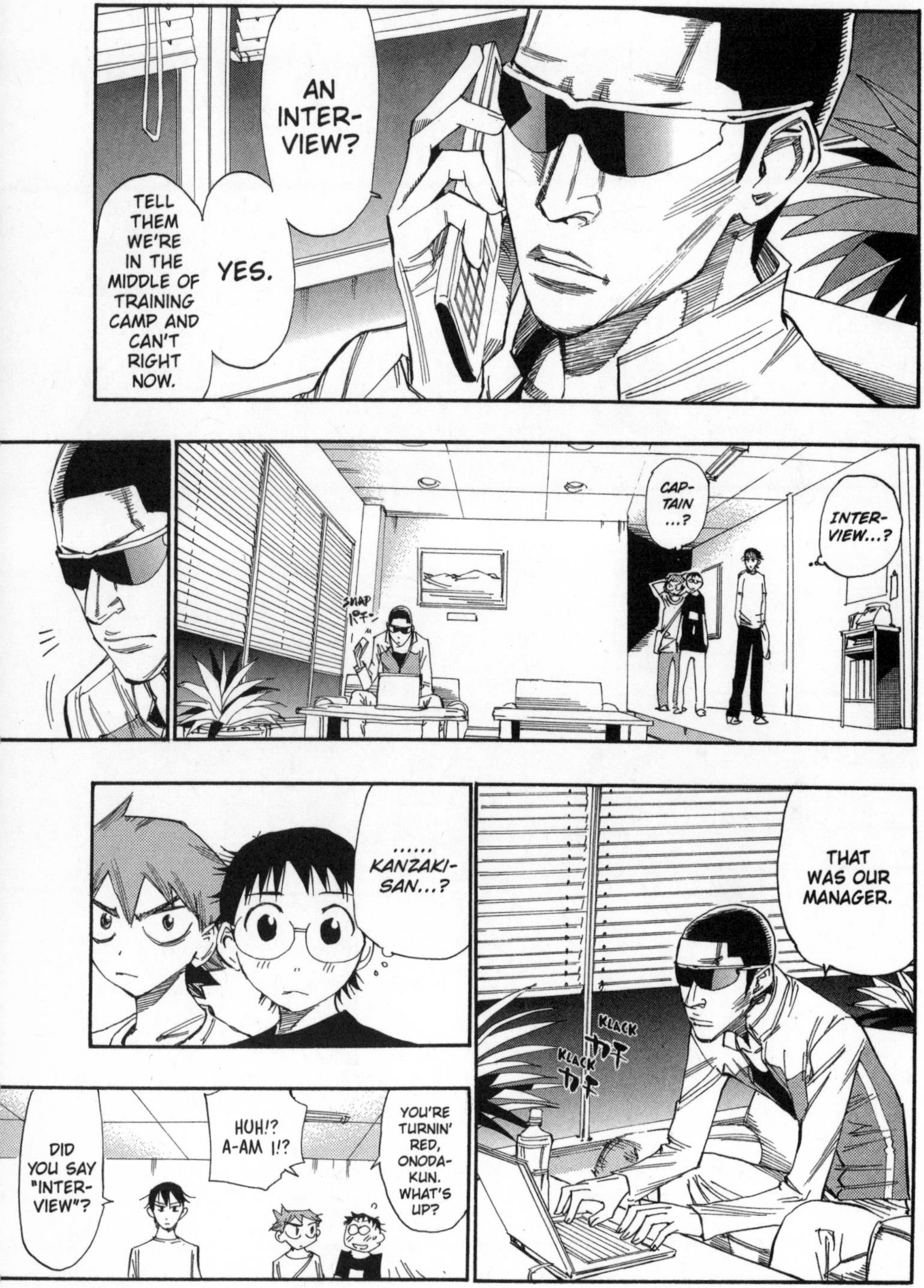
AN INTER-VIEW?
YES.
TELL THEM WE'RE IN THE MIDDLE OF TRAINING CAMP AND CAN'T RIGHT NOW.
INTER-VIEW...?
CAP-TAIN ...?
SNAP
THAT WAS OUR MANAGER.
KLACK
KLACK
...... KANZAKI-SAN...?
YOU'RE TURNIN' RED, ONODA-KUN. WHAT'S UP?
HUH!? A-AM I!?
DID YOU SAY "INTER-VIEW"?

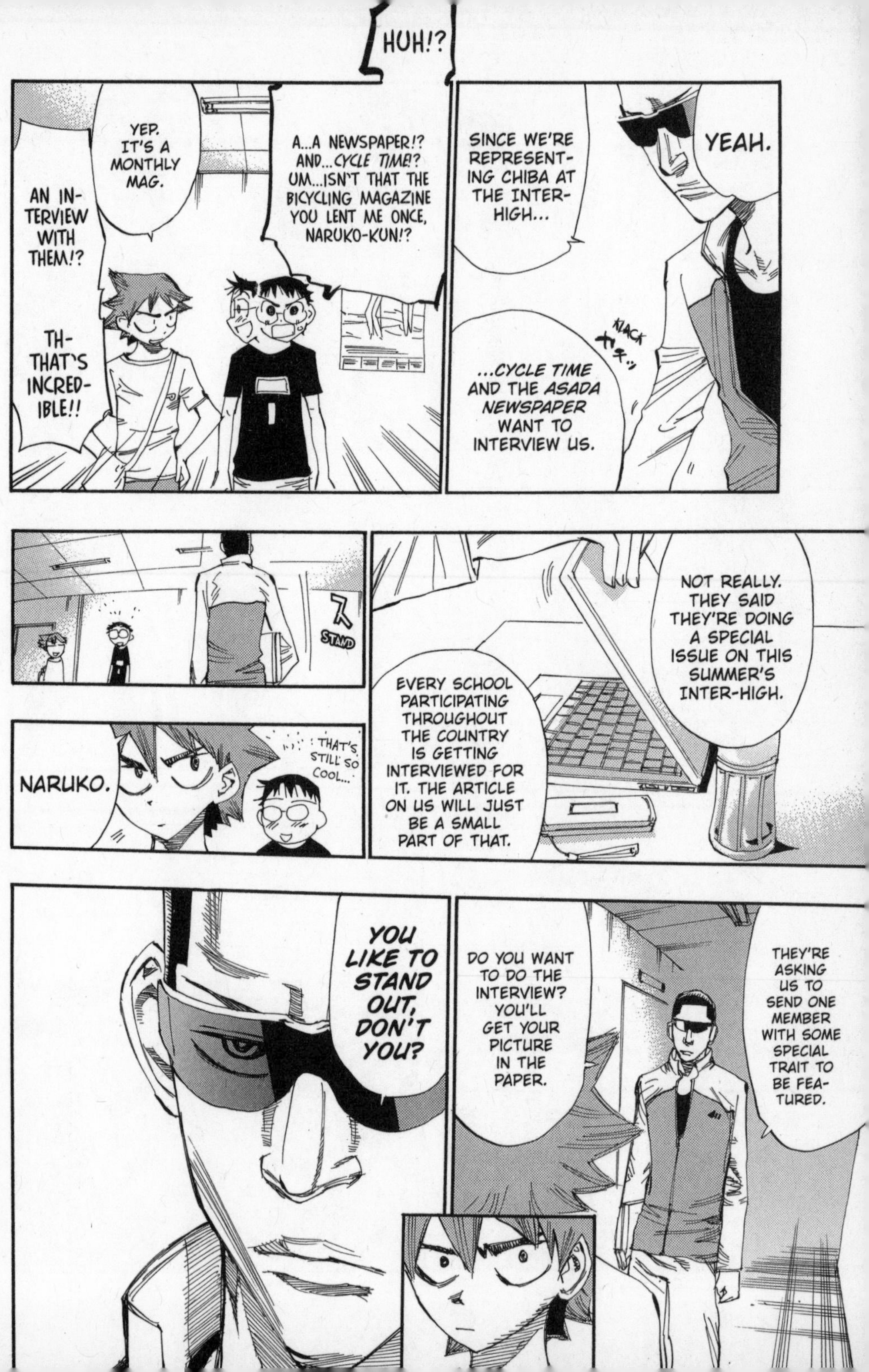
HUH!?
YEAH.
SINCE WE'RE REPRESENTING CHIBA AT THE INTER-HIGH...
KLACK
...CYCLE TIME AND THE ASADA NEWSPAPER WANT TO INTERVIEW US.
A...A NEWSPAPER!? AND...CYCLE TIME!? UM...ISN'T THAT THE BICYCLING MAGAZINE YOU LENT ME ONCE, NARUKO-KUN!?
YEP. IT'S A MONTHLY MAG.
AN INTERVIEW WITH THEM!?
TH-THAT'S INCREDIBLE!!
NOT REALLY. THEY SAID THEY'RE DOING A SPECIAL ISSUE ON THIS SUMMER'S INTER-HIGH.
EVERY SCHOOL PARTICIPATING THROUGHOUT THE COUNTRY IS GETTING INTERVIEWED FOR IT. THE ARTICLE ON US WILL JUST BE A SMALL PART OF THAT.
STAND
THAT'S STILL SO COOL...
NARUKO.
THEY'RE ASKING US TO SEND ONE MEMBER WITH SOME SPECIAL TRAIT TO BE FEATURED.
DO YOU WANT TO DO THE INTERVIEW? YOU'LL GET YOUR PICTURE IN THE PAPER.
YOU LIKE TO STAND OUT, DON'T YOU?

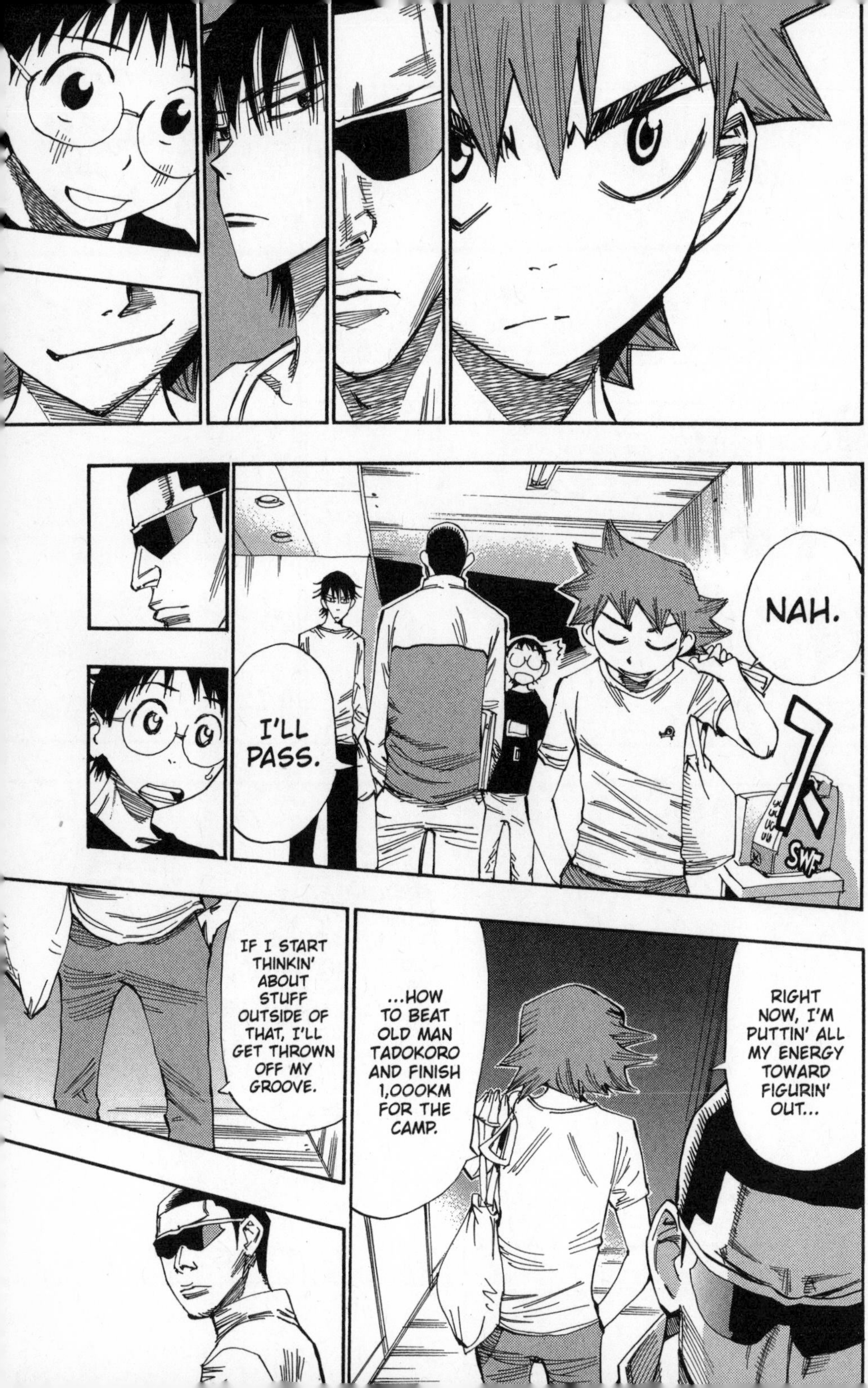
NAH.
I'LL PASS.
SWF
RIGHT NOW, I'M PUTTIN' ALL MY ENERGY TOWARD FIGURIN' OUT...
...HOW TO BEAT OLD MAN TADOKORO AND FINISH 1,000KM FOR THE CAMP.
IF I START THINKIN' ABOUT STUFF OUTSIDE OF THAT, I'LL GET THROWN OFF MY GROOVE.

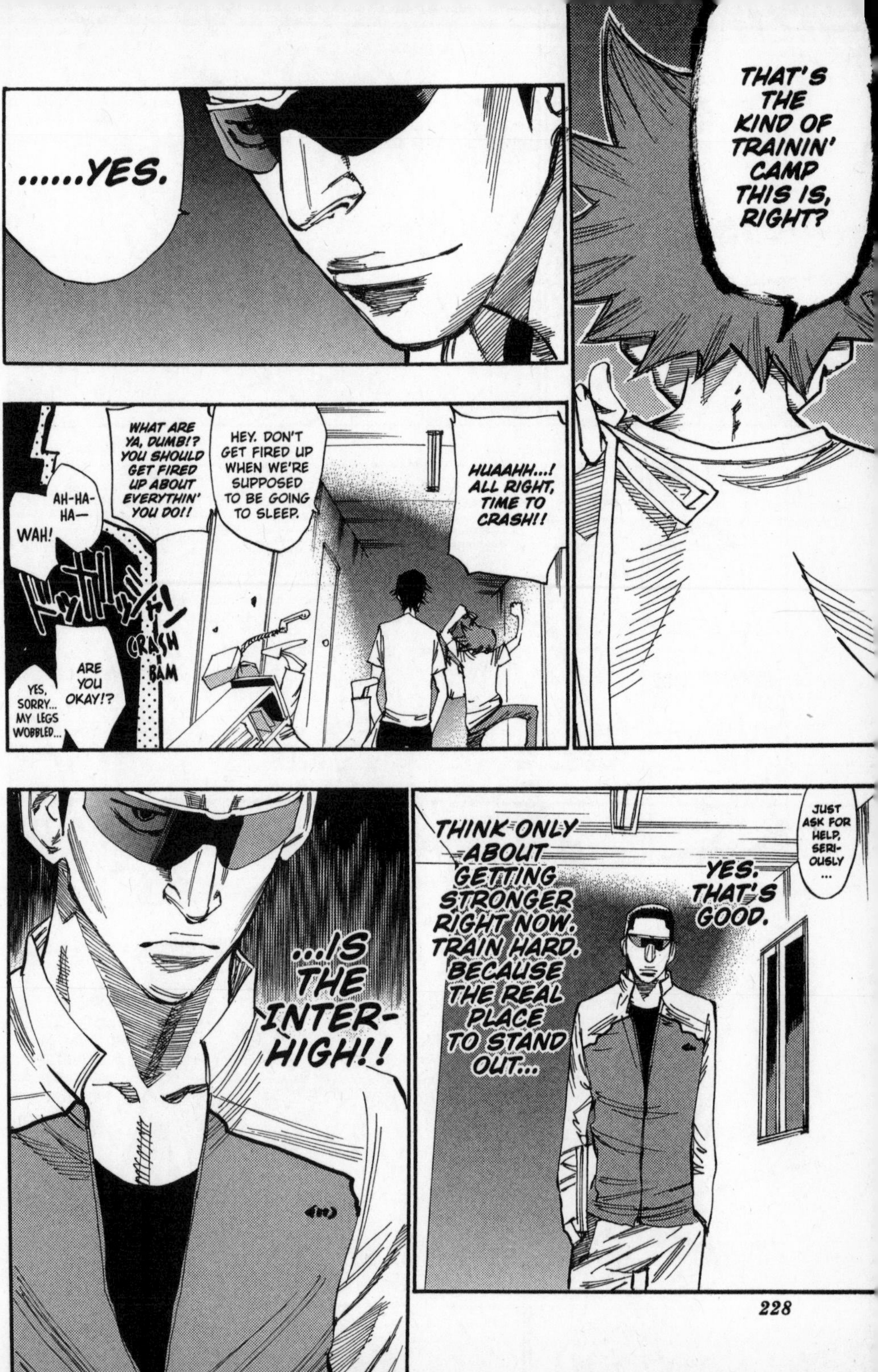
THAT'S THE KIND OF TRAININ' CAMP THIS IS, RIGHT?
......YES.
HUAAHH...! ALL RIGHT, TIME TO CRASH!!
HEY. DON'T GET FIRED UP WHEN WE'RE SUPPOSED TO BE GOING TO SLEEP.
WHAT ARE YA, DUMB!? YOU SHOULD GET FIRED UP ABOUT EVERYTHIN' YOU DO!!
AH-HA-HA—
WAH!
CRASH
BAM
ARE YOU OKAY!?
YES, SORRY... MY LEGS WOBBLED...
JUST ASK FOR HELP, SERIOUSLY...
YES. THAT'S GOOD.
THINK ONLY ABOUT GETTING STRONGER RIGHT NOW. TRAIN HARD. BECAUSE THE REAL PLACE TO STAND OUT...
...IS THE INTER-HIGH!!

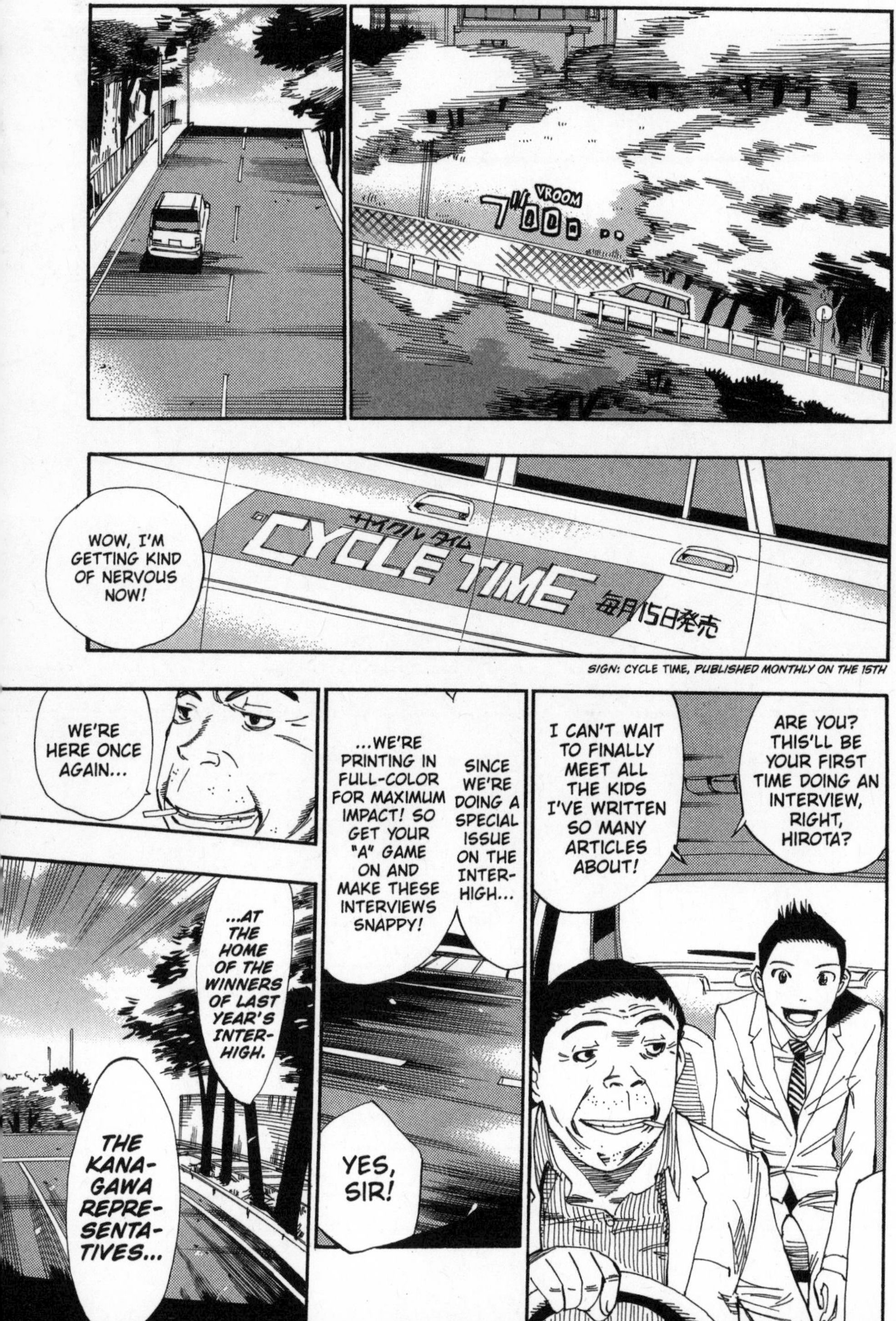
VROOM
ブォォォ
WOW, I'M GETTING KIND OF NERVOUS NOW!
サイクルタイム
CYCLE TIME
毎月15日発売
ARE YOU? THIS'LL BE YOUR FIRST TIME DOING AN INTERVIEW, RIGHT, HIROTA?
I CAN'T WAIT TO FINALLY MEET ALL THE KIDS I'VE WRITTEN SO MANY ARTICLES ABOUT!
SINCE WE'RE DOING A SPECIAL ISSUE ON THE INTER-HIGH...
...WE'RE PRINTING IN FULL-COLOR FOR MAXIMUM IMPACT! SO GET YOUR "A" GAME ON AND MAKE THESE INTERVIEWS SNAPPY!
YES, SIR!
WE'RE HERE ONCE AGAIN...
...AT THE HOME OF THE WINNERS OF LAST YEAR'S INTER-HIGH.
THE KANAGAWA REPRESENTATIVES...
SIGN: CYCLE TIME, PUBLISHED MONTHLY ON THE 15TH

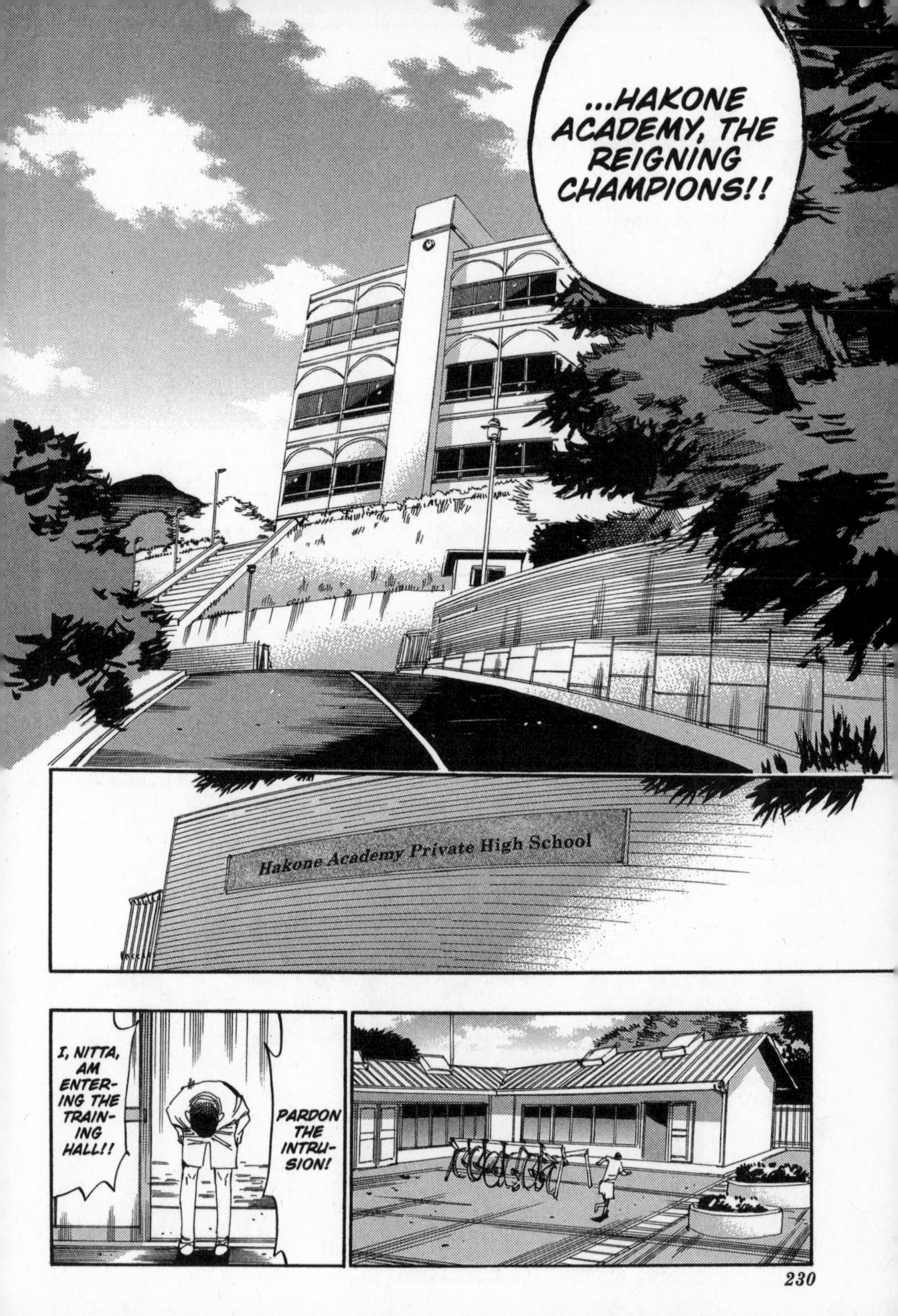
...HAKONE ACADEMY, THE REIGNING CHAMPIONS!!
Hakone Academy Private High School
PARDON THE INTRUSION!
I, NITTA, AM ENTERING THE TRAINING HALL!!

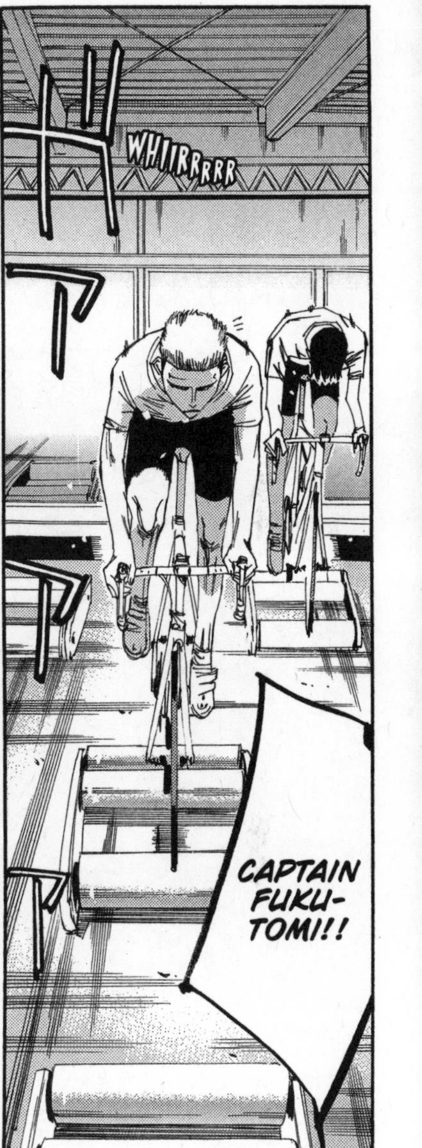
WHIIRRRRR
CAPTAIN FUKU-TOMI!!
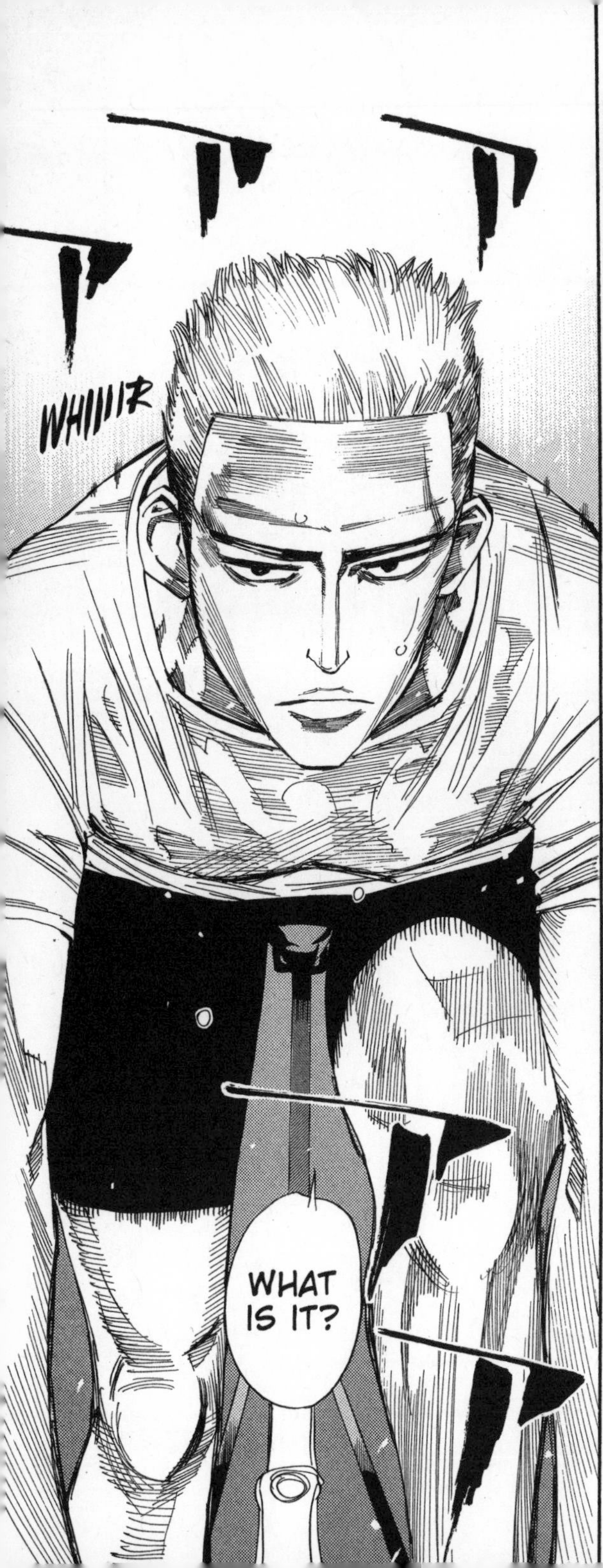
WHIIIIR
WHAT IS IT?

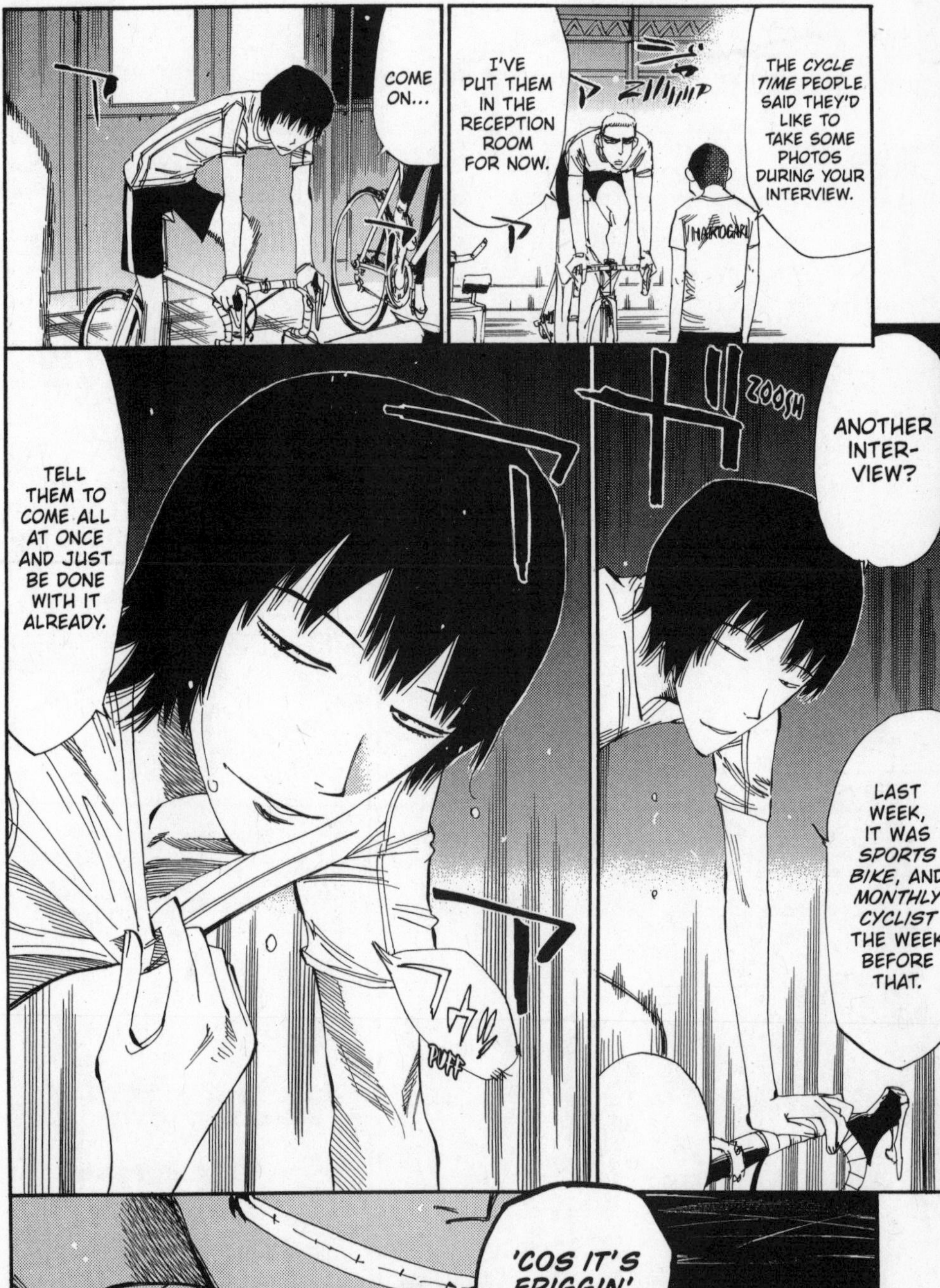
THE *CYCLE TIME* PEOPLE SAID THEY'D LIKE TO TAKE SOME PHOTOS DURING YOUR INTERVIEW.
ZIIIIIIP
I'VE PUT THEM IN THE RECEPTION ROOM FOR NOW.
COME ON...
ZOOSH
ANOTHER INTER-VIEW?
LAST WEEK, IT WAS *SPORTS BIKE*, AND *MONTHLY CYCLIST* THE WEEK BEFORE THAT.
TELL THEM TO COME ALL AT ONCE AND JUST BE DONE WITH IT ALREADY.
PUFF
'COS IT'S FRIGGIN' ANNOYING.

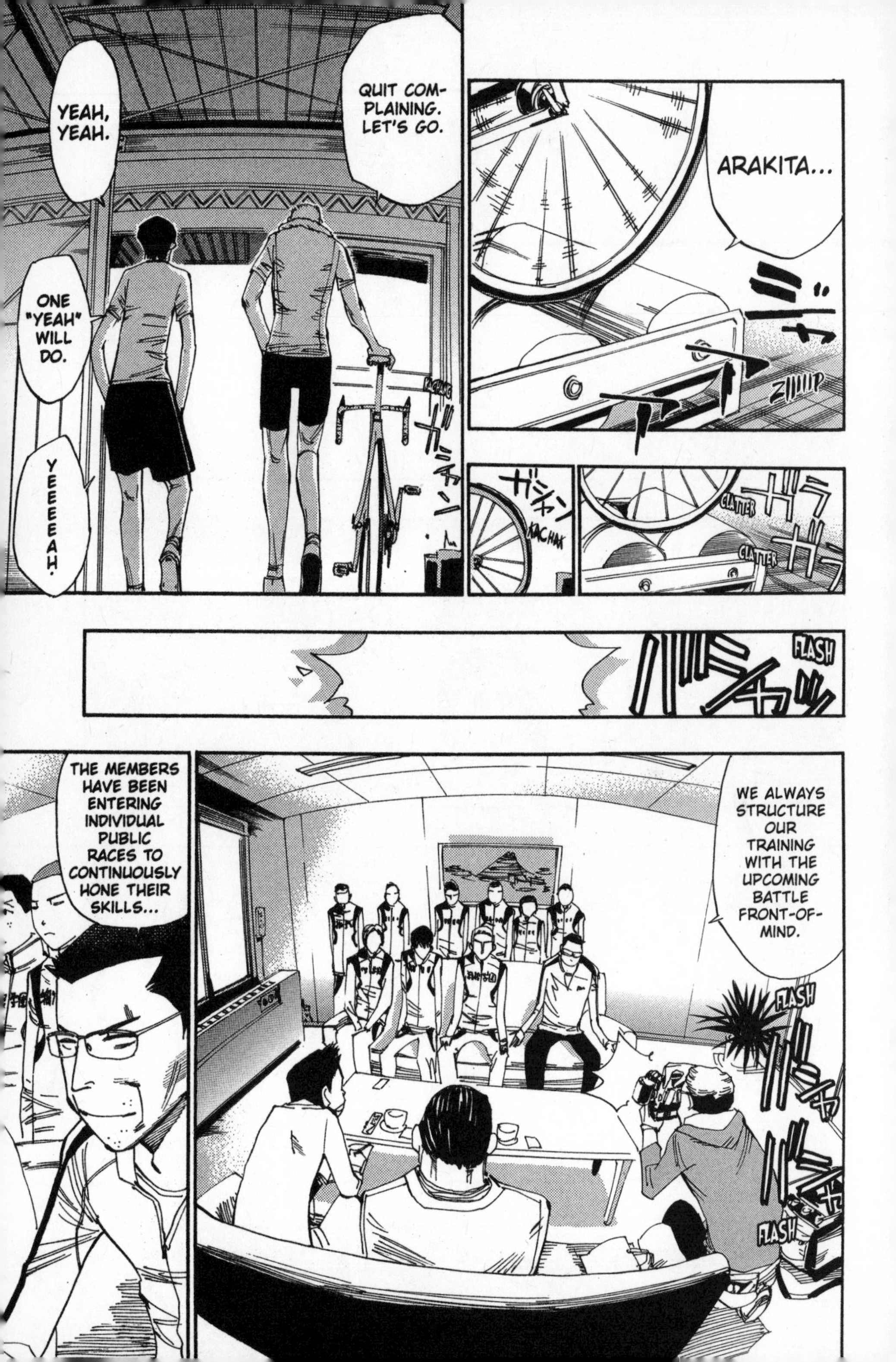
ARAKITA...
ZIIIIP
CLATTER
CLATTER
KACHAK
QUIT COM-PLAINING. LET'S GO.
YEAH, YEAH.
ONE "YEAH" WILL DO.
YEEEEAH.
KACHANG
FLASH
WE ALWAYS STRUCTURE OUR TRAINING WITH THE UPCOMING BATTLE FRONT-OF-MIND.
FLASH
FLASH
THE MEMBERS HAVE BEEN ENTERING INDIVIDUAL PUBLIC RACES TO CONTINUOUSLY HONE THEIR SKILLS...

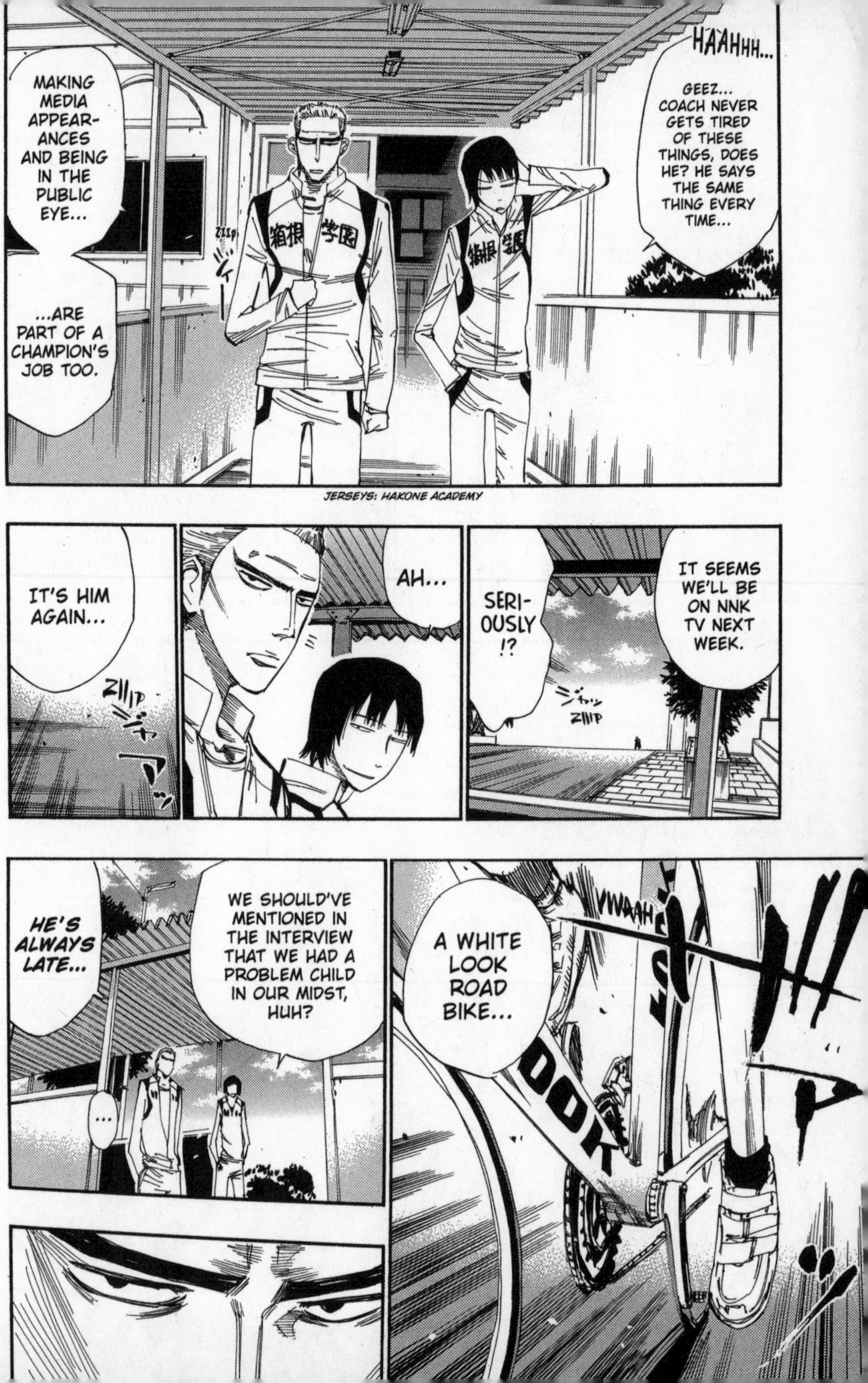
HAAHHH...
GEEZ... COACH NEVER GETS TIRED OF THESE THINGS, DOES HE? HE SAYS THE SAME THING EVERY TIME...
MAKING MEDIA APPEAR-ANCES AND BEING IN THE PUBLIC EYE...
...ARE PART OF A CHAMPION'S JOB TOO.
ZIIIP
IT SEEMS WE'LL BE ON NNK TV NEXT WEEK.
SERI-OUSLY!?
ZIIIP
AH...
IT'S HIM AGAIN...
ZIIIP
VWAAH
A WHITE LOOK ROAD BIKE...
WE SHOULD'VE MENTIONED IN THE INTERVIEW THAT WE HAD A PROBLEM CHILD IN OUR MIDST, HUH?
HE'S ALWAYS LATE...
...
JERSEYS: HAKONE ACADEMY

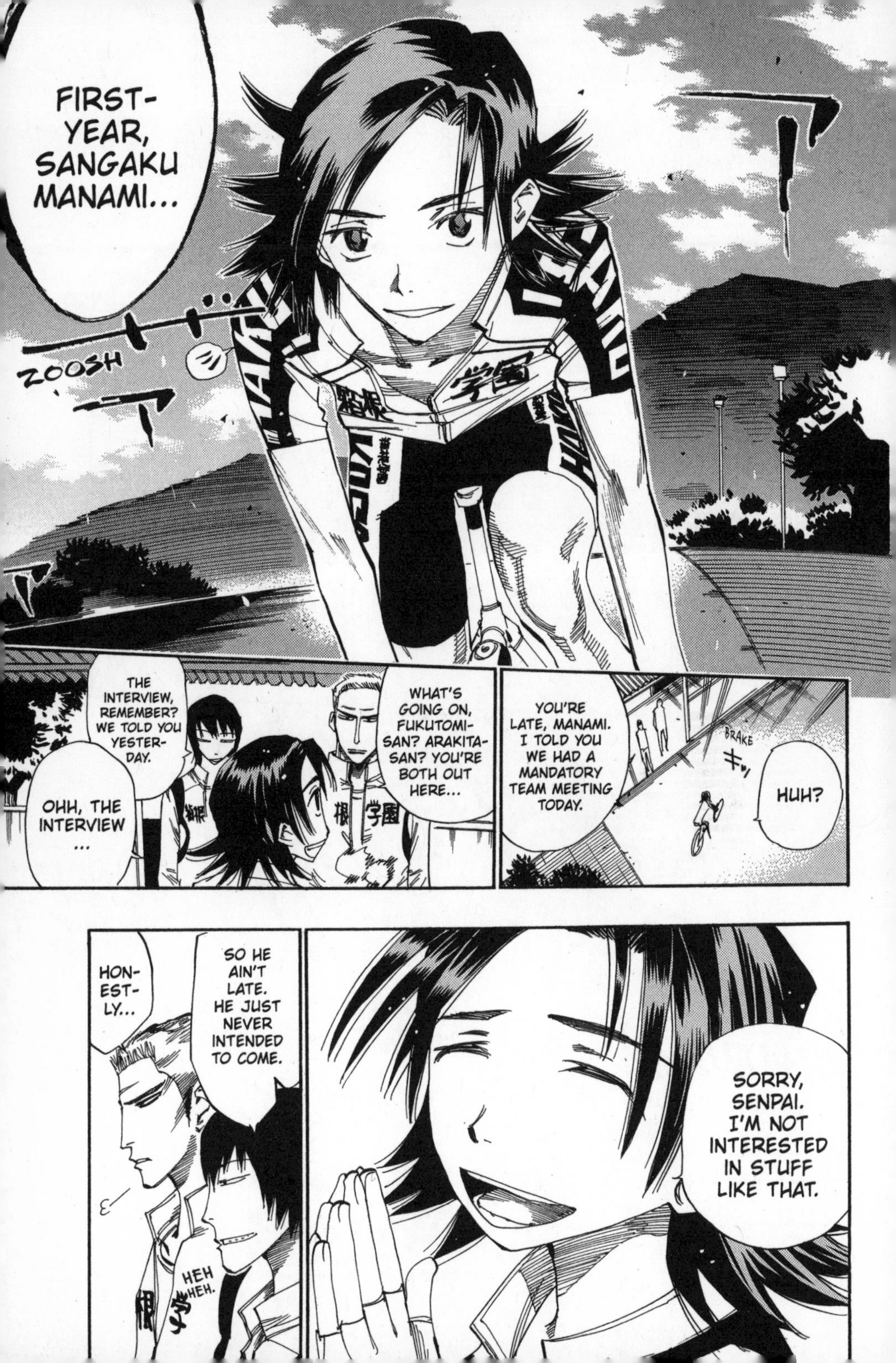
FIRST-YEAR, SANGAKU MANAMI...
ZOOSH
BRAKE
HUH?
YOU'RE LATE, MANAMI. I TOLD YOU WE HAD A MANDATORY TEAM MEETING TODAY.
WHAT'S GOING ON, FUKUTOMI-SAN? ARAKITA-SAN? YOU'RE BOTH OUT HERE...
THE INTERVIEW, REMEMBER? WE TOLD YOU YESTER-DAY.
OHH, THE INTERVIEW ...
SORRY, SENPAI. I'M NOT INTERESTED IN STUFF LIKE THAT.
SO HE AIN'T LATE. HE JUST NEVER INTENDED TO COME.
HON-EST-LY...
HEH HEH.

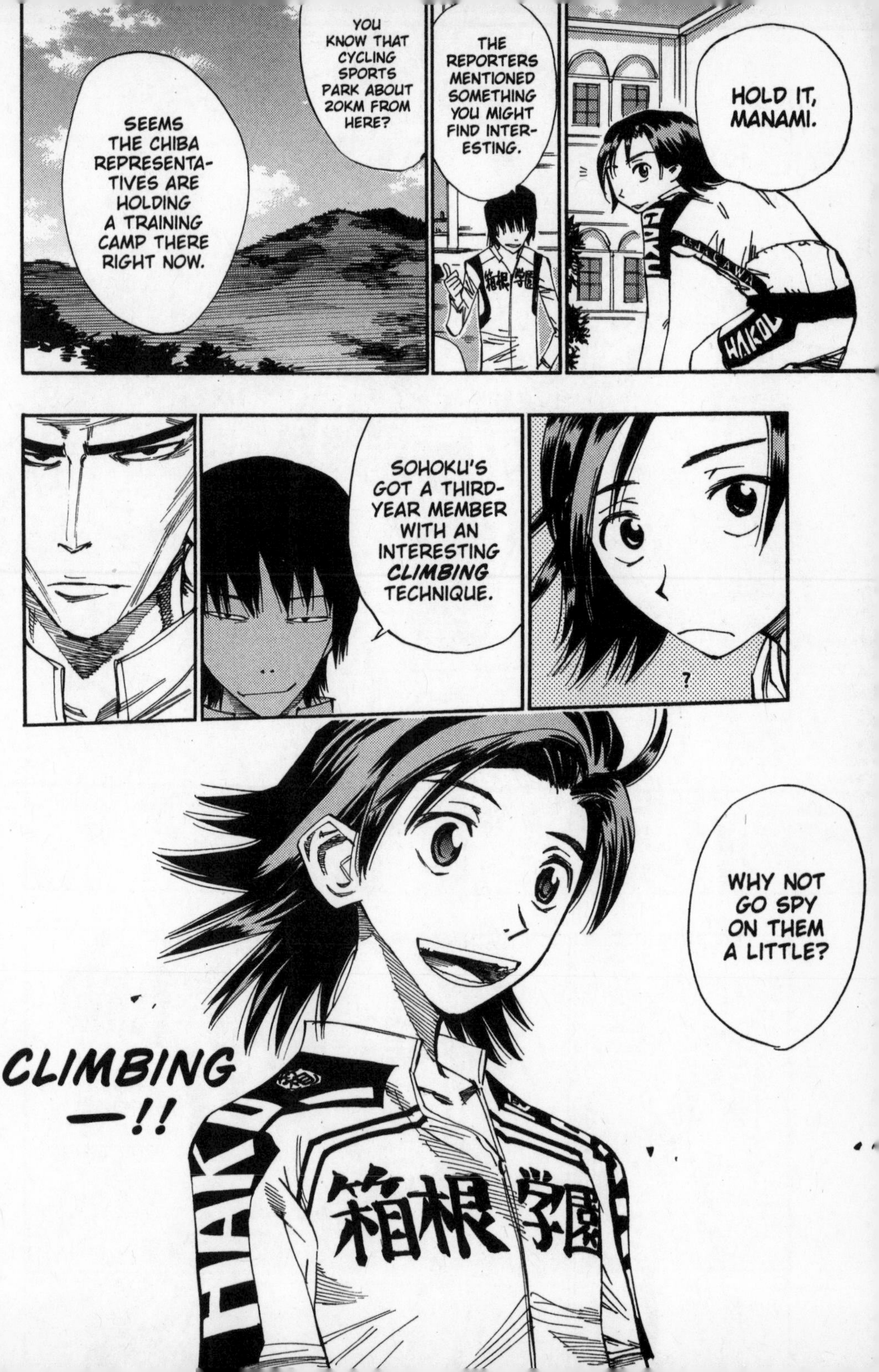
HOLD IT, MANAMI.
THE REPORTERS MENTIONED SOMETHING YOU MIGHT FIND INTER-ESTING.
YOU KNOW THAT CYCLING SPORTS PARK ABOUT 20KM FROM HERE?
SEEMS THE CHIBA REPRESENTA-TIVES ARE HOLDING A TRAINING CAMP THERE RIGHT NOW.
?
SOHOKU'S GOT A THIRD-YEAR MEMBER WITH AN INTERESTING *CLIMBING* TECHNIQUE.
WHY NOT GO SPY ON THEM A LITTLE?
CLIMBING —!!

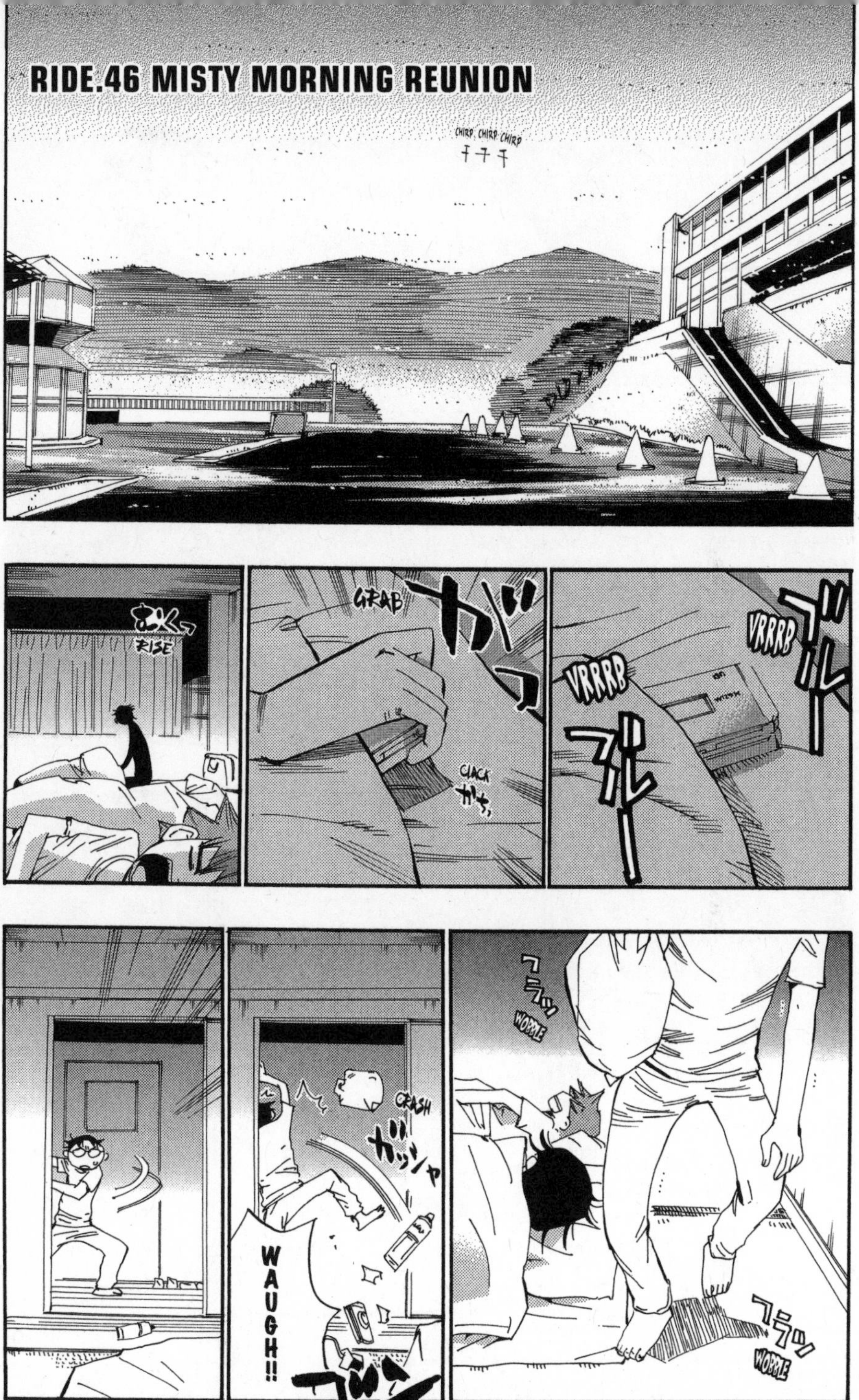
RIDE.46 MISTY MORNING REUNION
CHIRP, CHIRP, CHIRP
VRRRB
VRRRB
GRAB
CLACK
RISE
WOBBLE
WOBBLE
CRASH
WAUGH!!
BAM

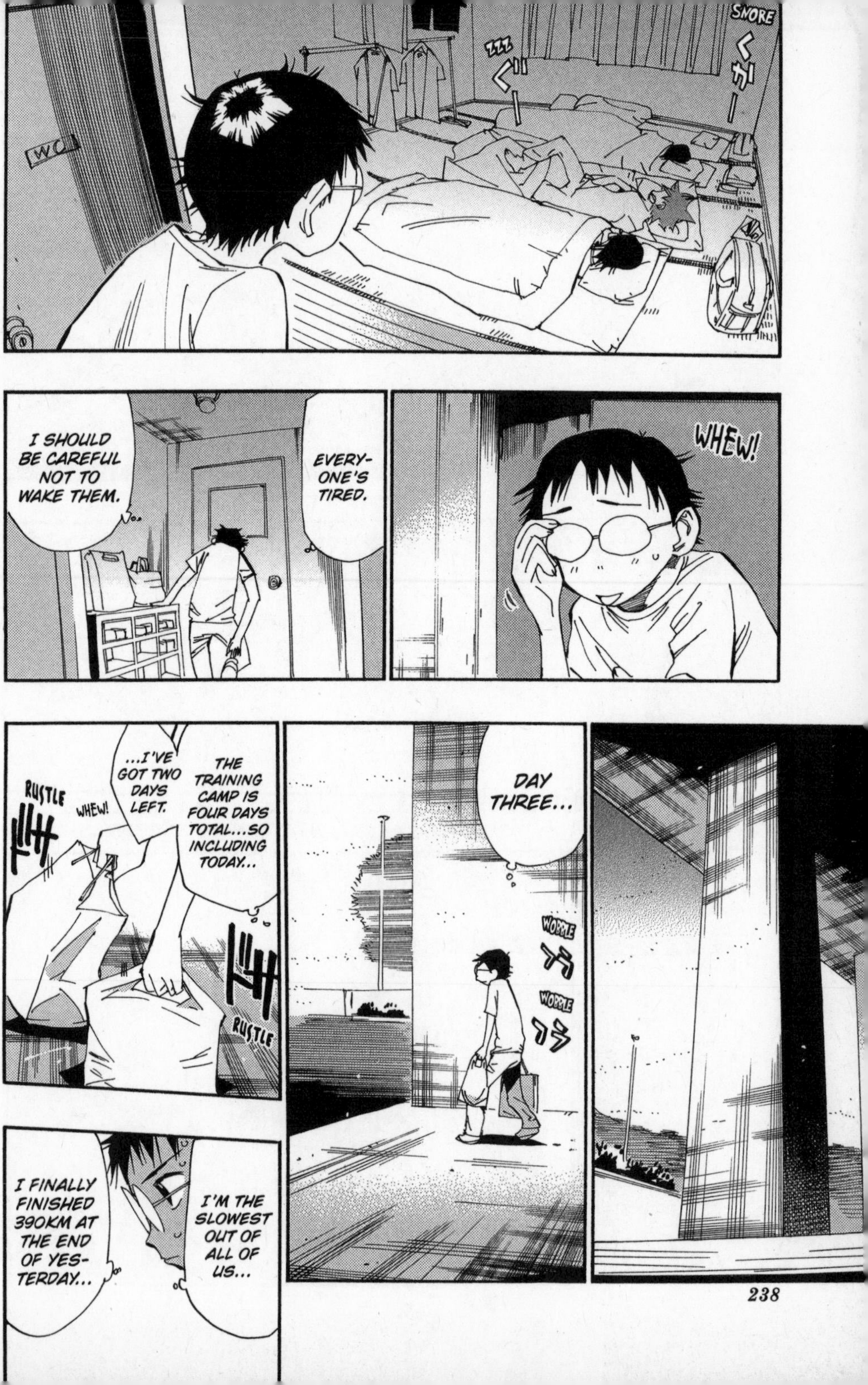
SNORE
ZZZ
WHEW!
EVERY-ONE'S TIRED.
I SHOULD BE CAREFUL NOT TO WAKE THEM.
DAY THREE...
WOBBLE
WOBBLE
THE TRAINING CAMP IS FOUR DAYS TOTAL...SO INCLUDING TODAY...
...I'VE GOT TWO DAYS LEFT.
WHEW!
RUSTLE
RUSTLE
I'M THE SLOWEST OUT OF ALL OF US...
I FINALLY FINISHED 390KM AT THE END OF YES-TERDAY...

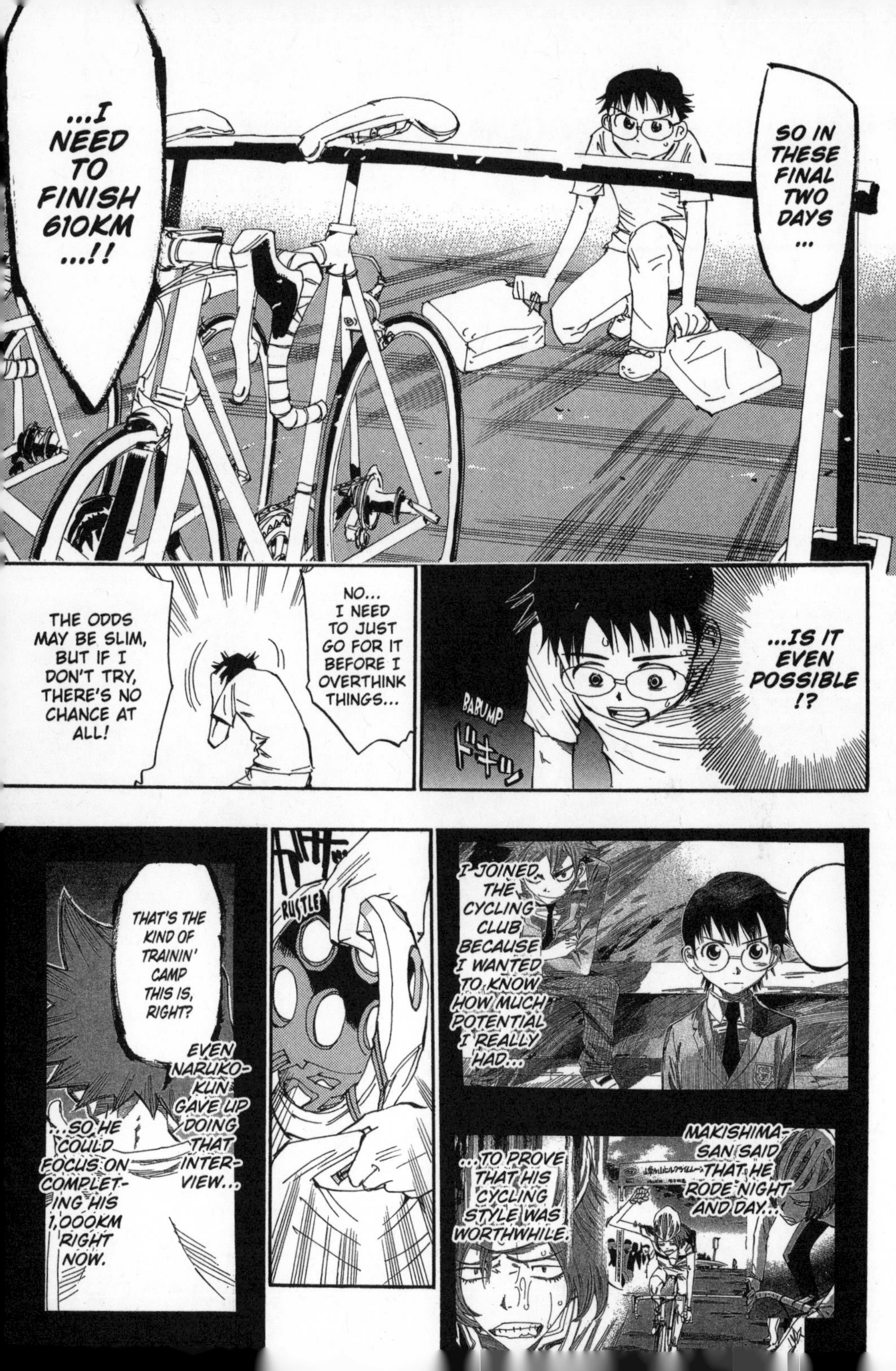
SO IN THESE FINAL TWO DAYS...
...I NEED TO FINISH 610KM ...!!
...IS IT EVEN POSSIBLE!?
BABUMP
ドキッ
NO... I NEED TO JUST GO FOR IT BEFORE I OVERTHINK THINGS...
THE ODDS MAY BE SLIM, BUT IF I DON'T TRY, THERE'S NO CHANCE AT ALL!
I JOINED THE CYCLING CLUB BECAUSE I WANTED TO KNOW HOW MUCH POTENTIAL I REALLY HAD...
MAKISHIMA-SAN SAID THAT HE RODE NIGHT AND DAY...
...TO PROVE THAT HIS CYCLING STYLE WAS WORTHWHILE.
RUSTLE
THAT'S THE KIND OF TRAININ' CAMP THIS IS, RIGHT?
EVEN NARUKO-KUN GAVE UP DOING THAT INTERVIEW...
...SO HE COULD FOCUS ON COMPLETING HIS 1,000KM RIGHT NOW.

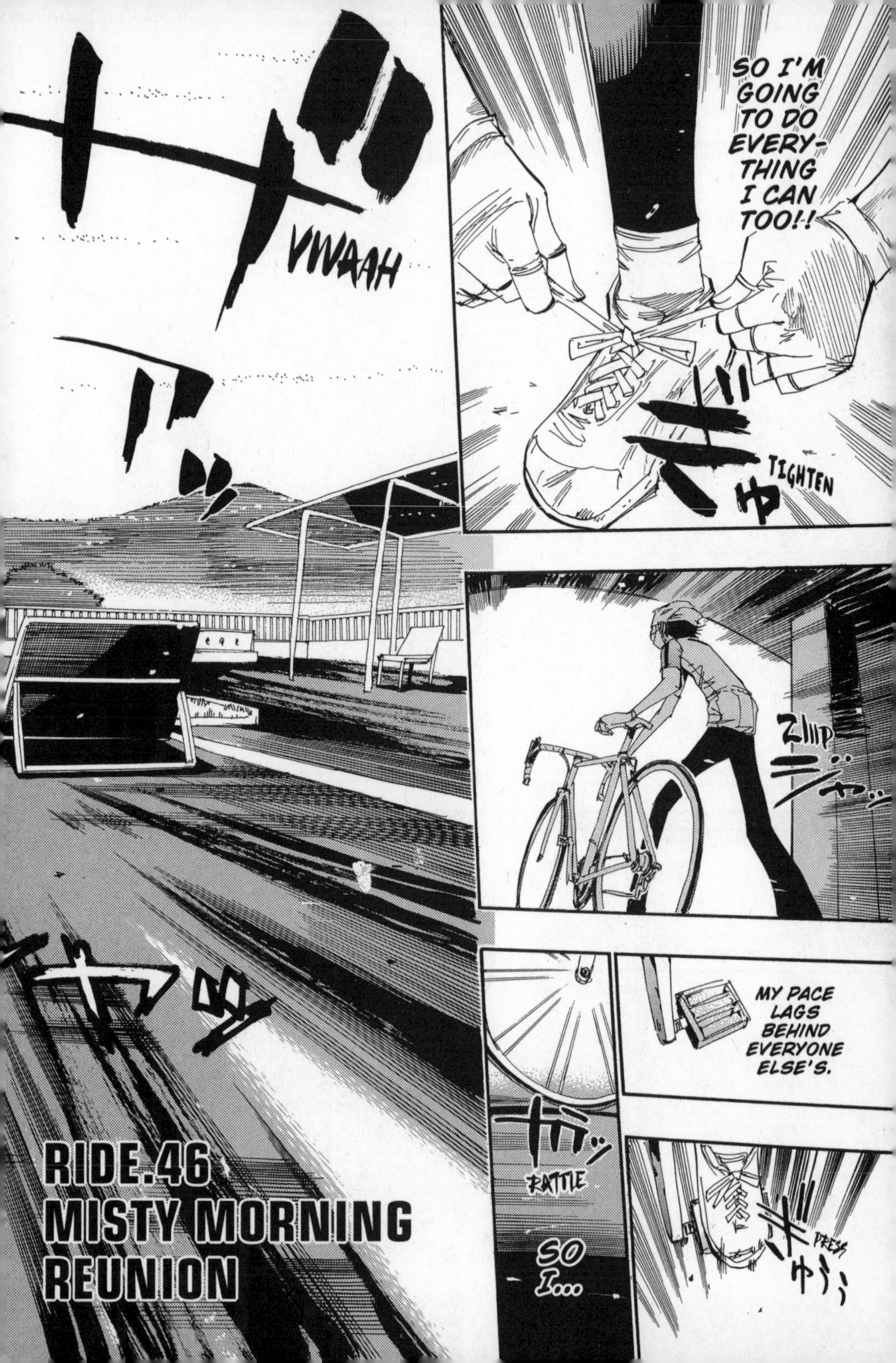
SO I'M GOING TO DO EVERYTHING I CAN TOO!!
TIGHTEN
ZIIIP
MY PACE LAGS BEHIND EVERYONE ELSE'S.
RATTLE
SO I...
PRESS
VWAAH
RIDE.46 MISTY MORNING REUNION

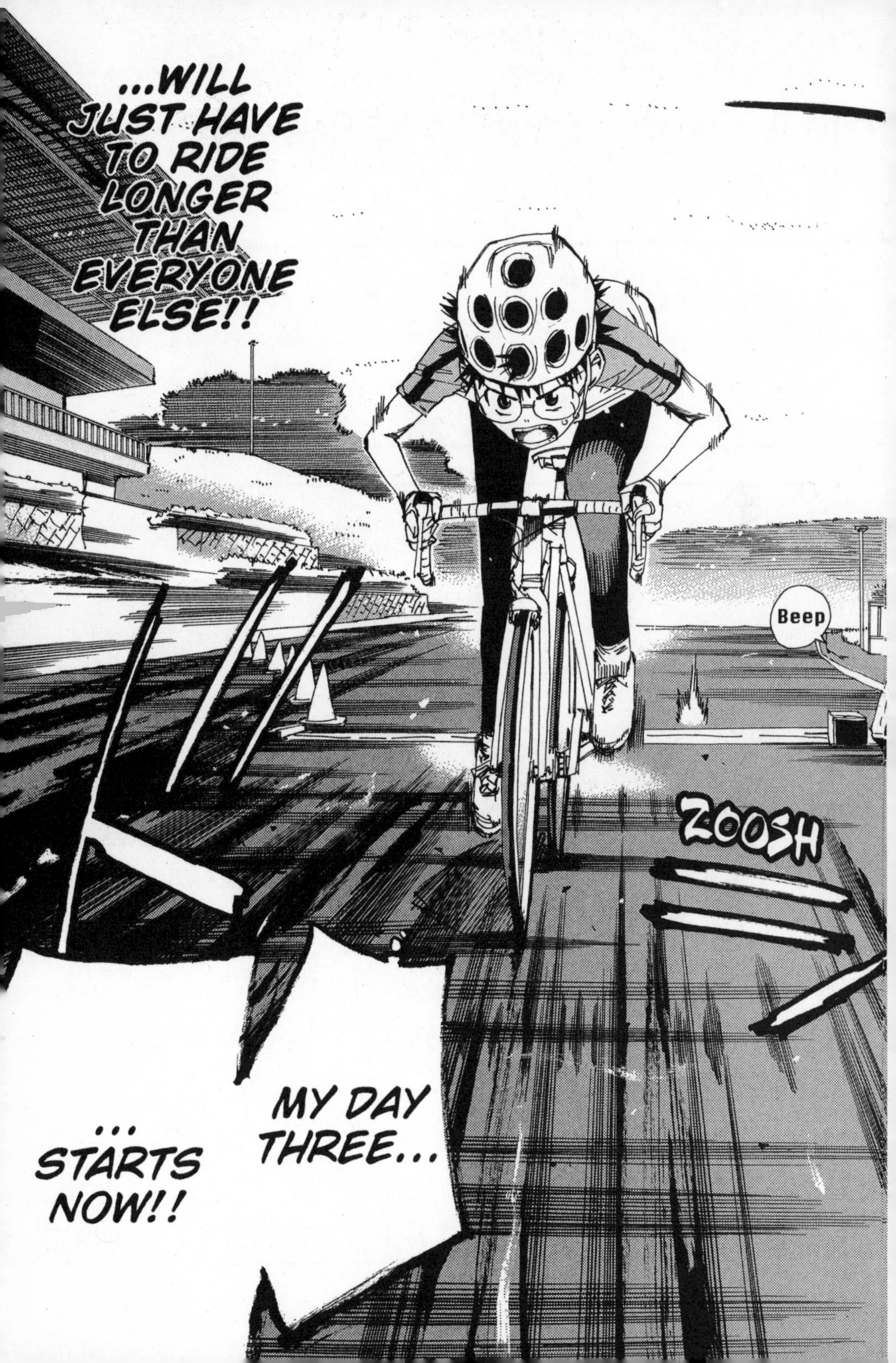
...WILL JUST HAVE TO RIDE LONGER THAN EVERYONE ELSE!!
Beep
ZOOSH
MY DAY THREE...
...STARTS NOW!!

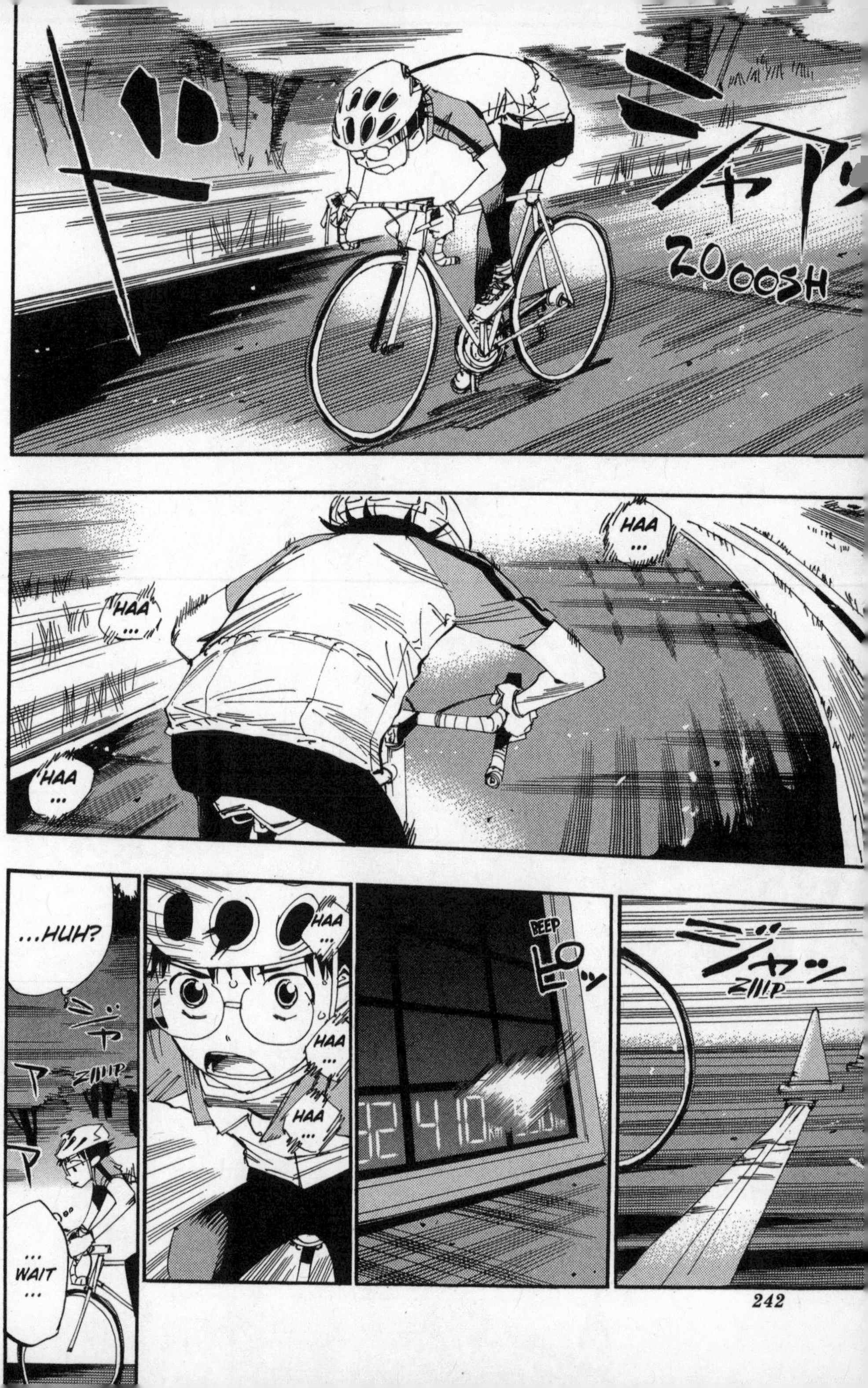
ZOOOSH
HAA ...
HAA ...
HAA ...
ZIIIP
BEEP
HAA ...
HAA ...
HAA ...
...HUH?
ZIIIP
... WAIT ...

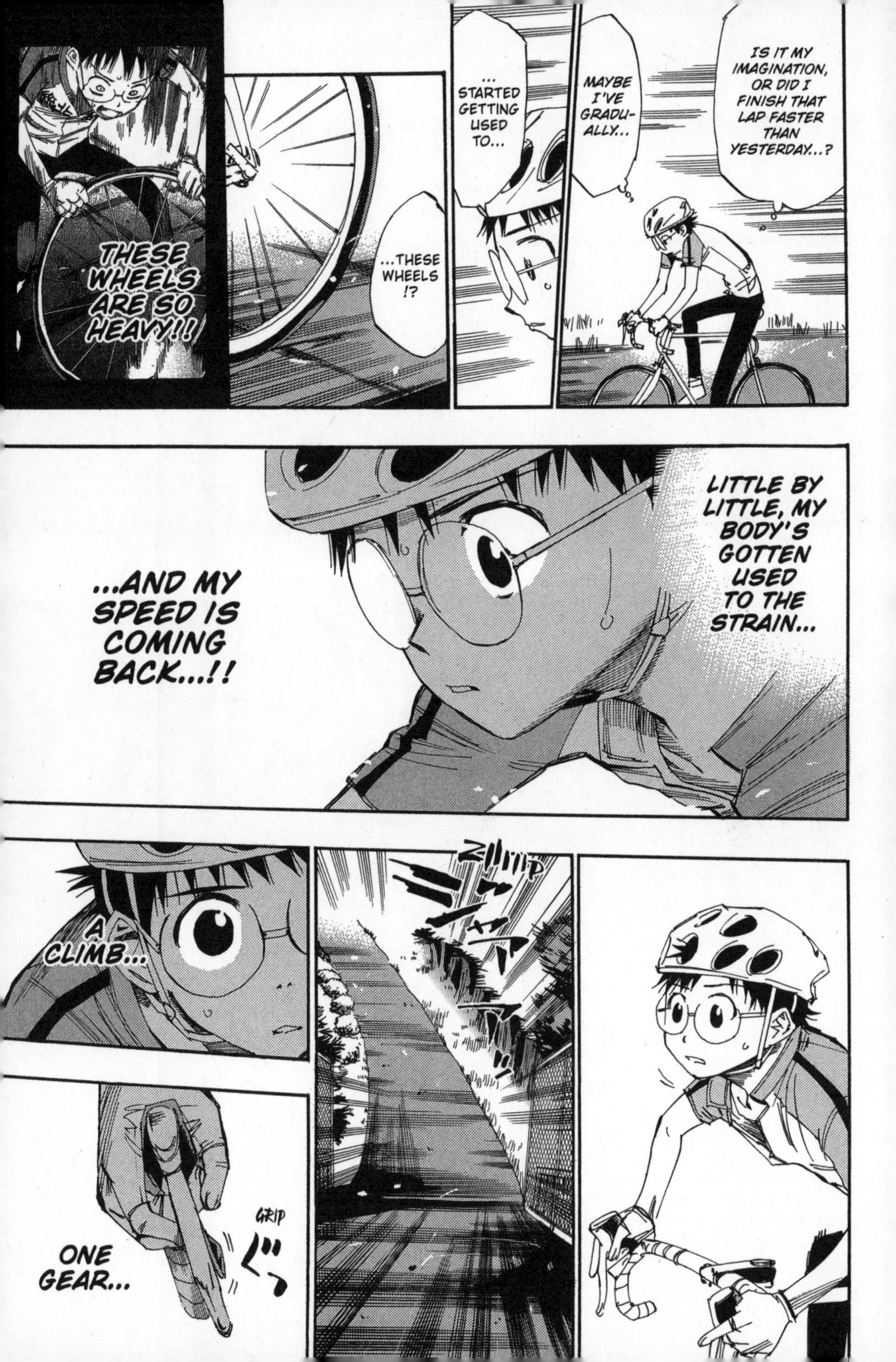
IS IT MY IMAGINATION, OR DID I FINISH THAT LAP FASTER THAN YESTERDAY...?
MAYBE I'VE GRADU-ALLY...
... STARTED GETTING USED TO...
...THESE WHEELS !?
THESE WHEELS ARE SO HEAVY!!
LITTLE BY LITTLE, MY BODY'S GOTTEN USED TO THE STRAIN...
...AND MY SPEED IS COMING BACK...!!
ZIIIIP
A CLIMB...
GRIP
ONE GEAR...

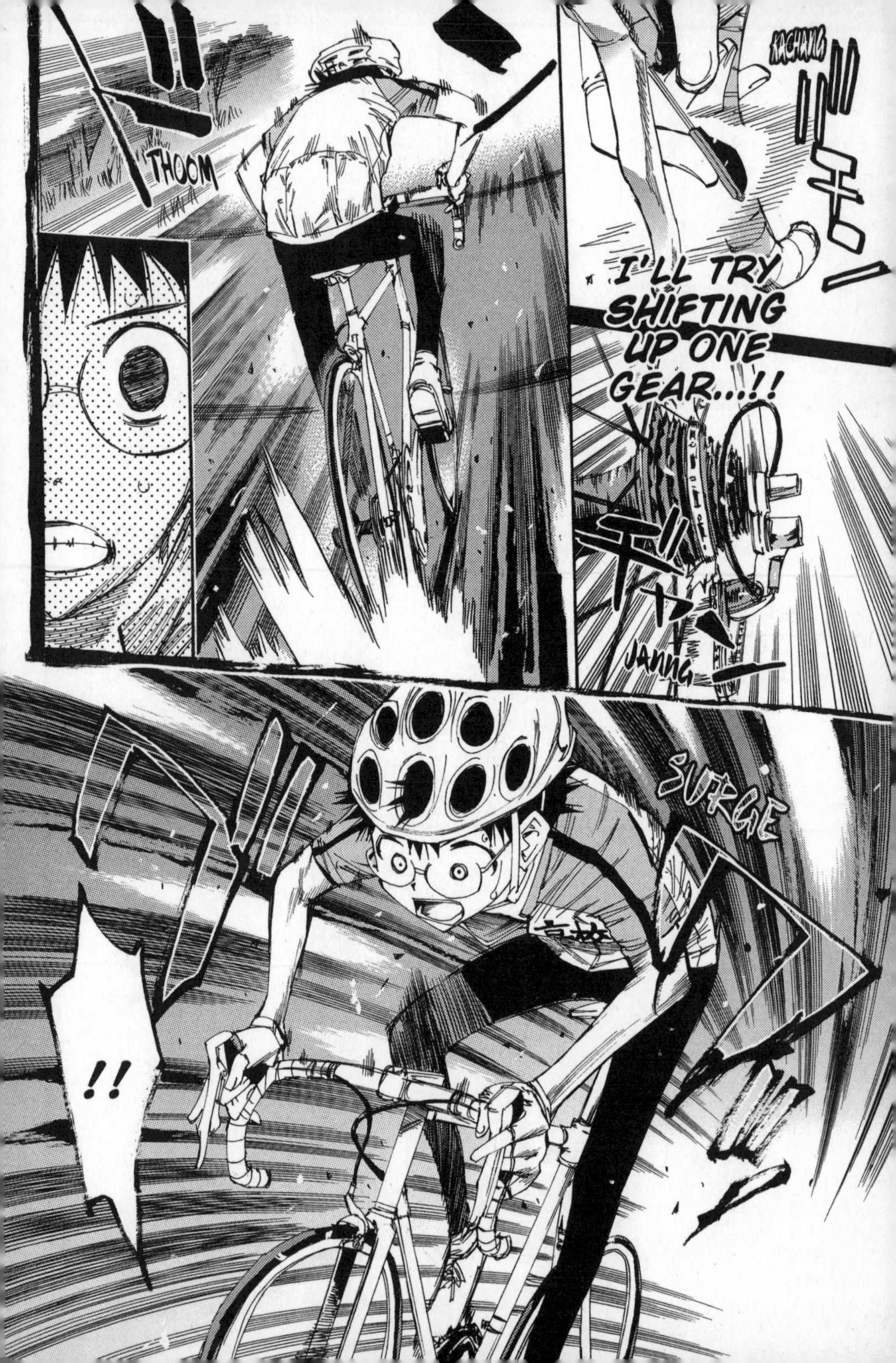
KACHANG
I'LL TRY SHIFTING UP ONE GEAR...!!
JANNG
THOOM
SURGE
!!

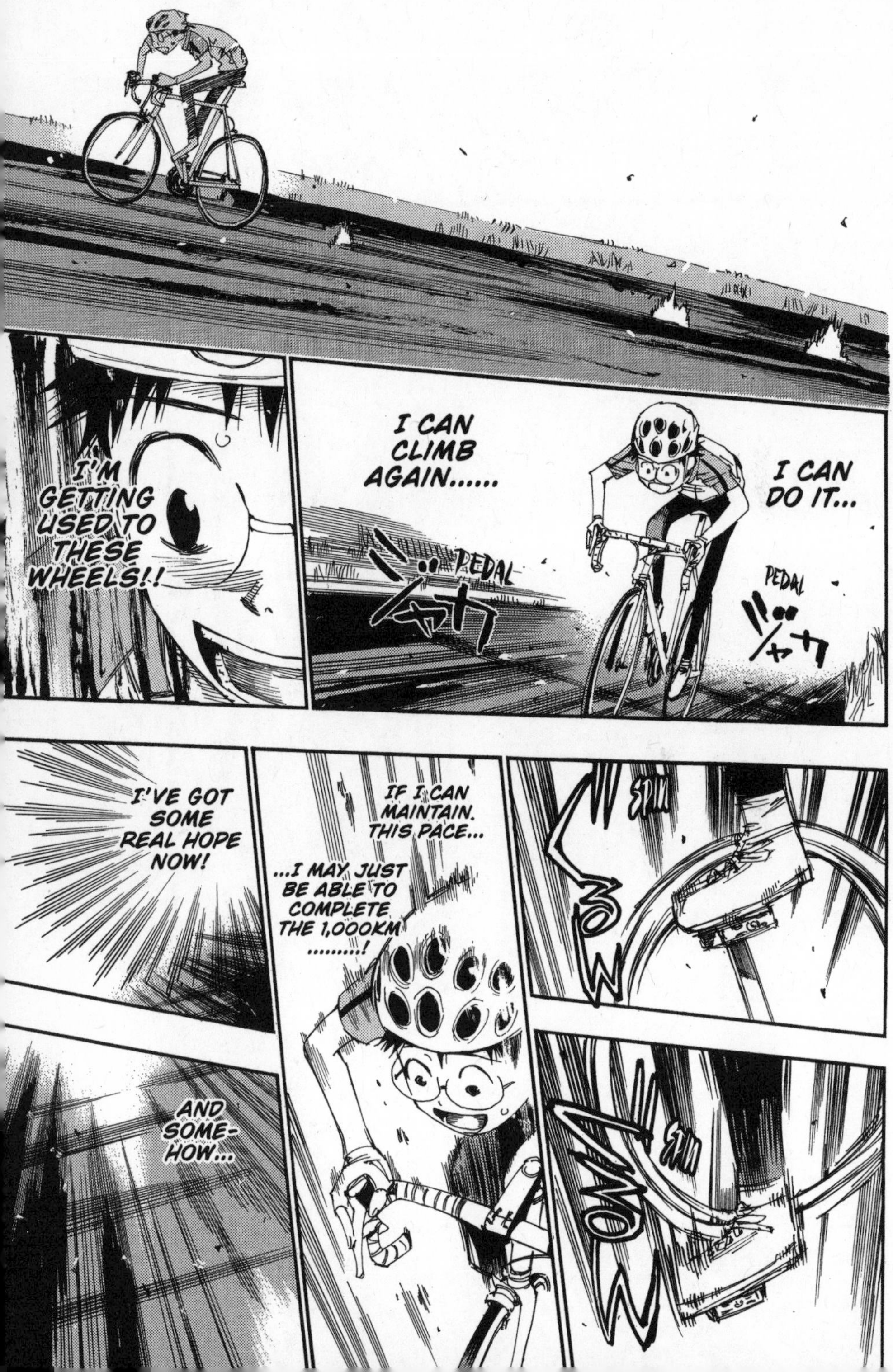
I CAN DO IT...
PEDAL
I CAN CLIMB AGAIN......
PEDAL
I'M GETTING USED TO THESE WHEELS!!
SPIN
IF I CAN MAINTAIN. THIS PACE...
...I MAY JUST BE ABLE TO COMPLETE THE 1,000KM ....!
I'VE GOT SOME REAL HOPE NOW!
SPIN
AND SOME-HOW...

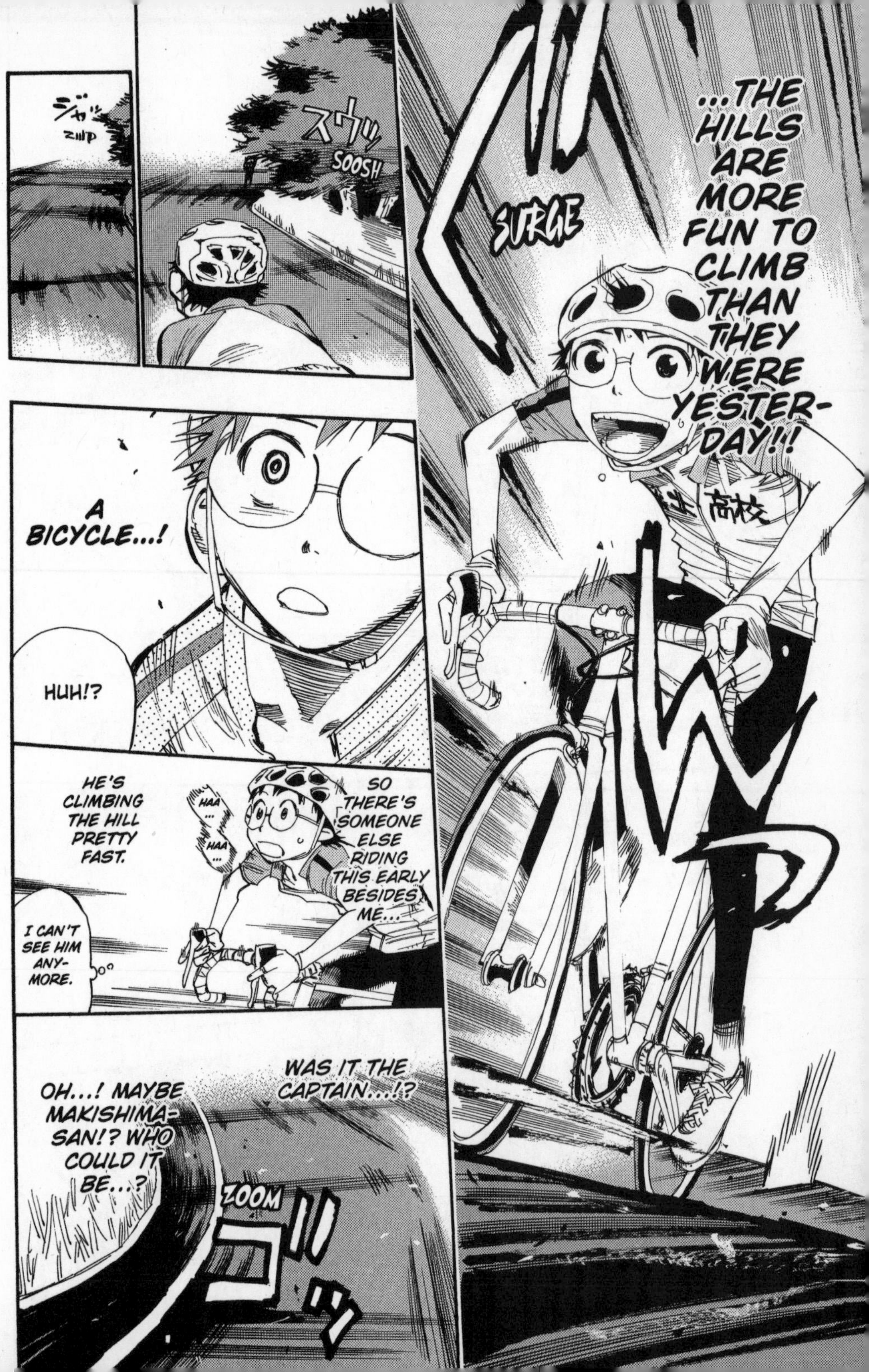
...THE HILLS ARE MORE FUN TO CLIMB THAN THEY WERE YESTER-DAY!!
SURGE
スウッ
SOOSH
ジャッ
ZIIP
A BICYCLE...!
HUH!?
SO THERE'S SOMEONE ELSE RIDING THIS EARLY BESIDES ME...
HAA...
HAA...
HE'S CLIMBING THE HILL PRETTY FAST.
I CAN'T SEE HIM ANY-MORE.
WAS IT THE CAPTAIN...!?
OH...! MAYBE MAKISHIMA-SAN!? WHO COULD IT BE...?
ZOOM
ゴーッ

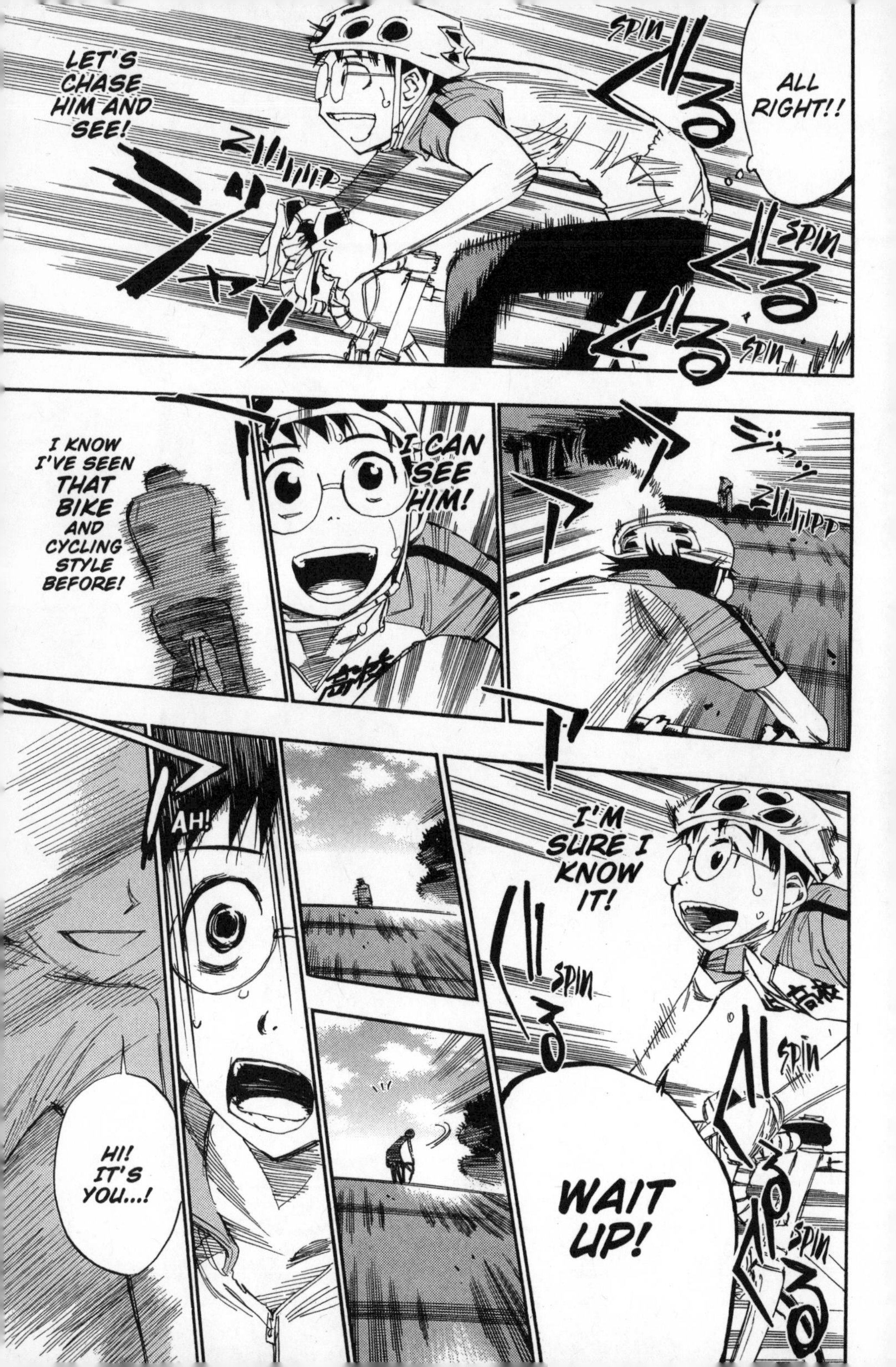
ALL RIGHT!!
SPIN
SPIN
SPIN
LET'S CHASE HIM AND SEE!
ZIIIIIIIP
ZIIIIIPP
I CAN SEE HIM!
I KNOW I'VE SEEN THAT BIKE AND CYCLING STYLE BEFORE!
I'M SURE I KNOW IT!
SPIN
SPIN
SPIN
WAIT UP!
AH!
HI! IT'S YOU...!

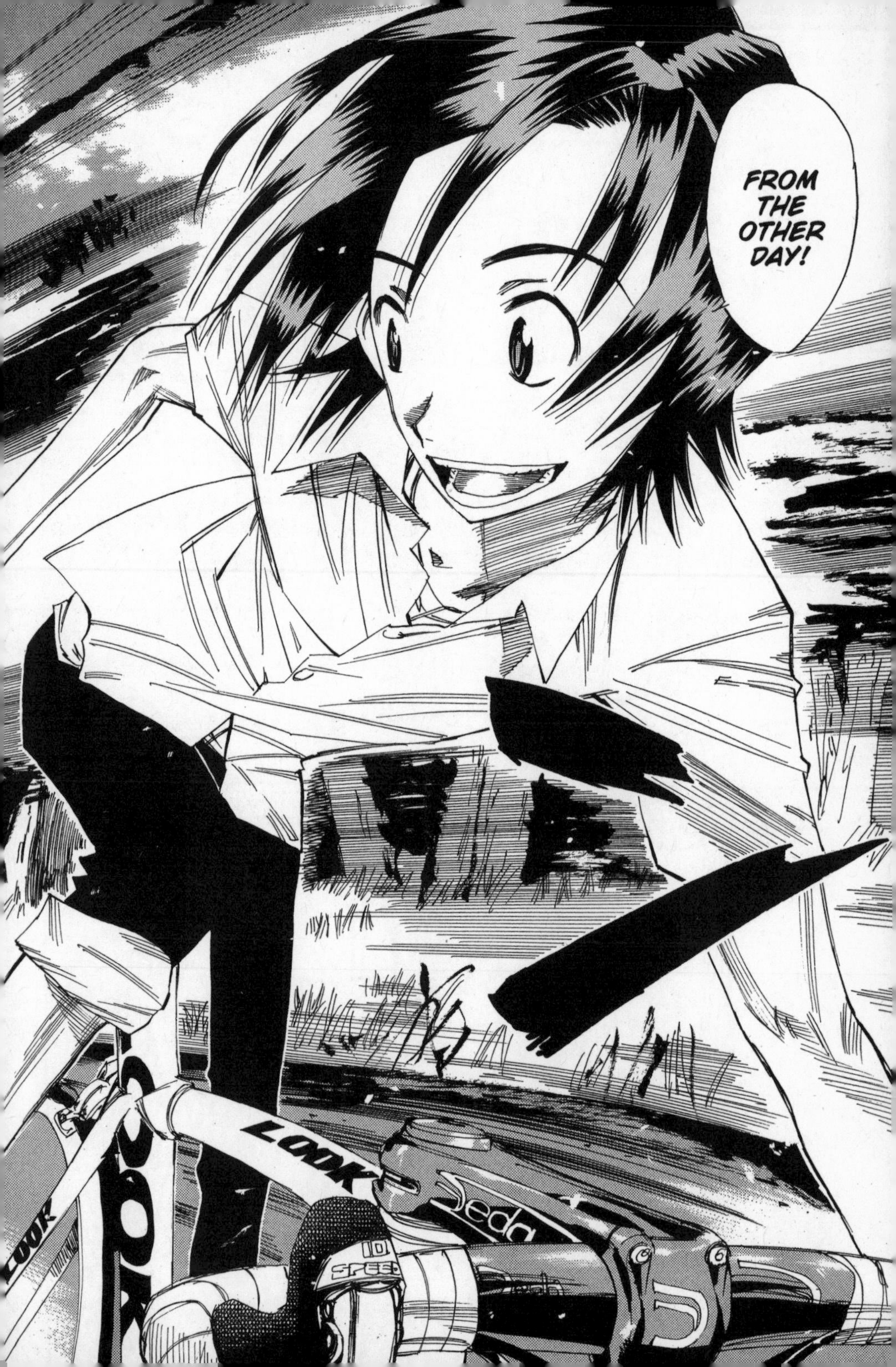
FROM THE OTHER DAY!
LOOK
LOOK
Deda
10 SPEED

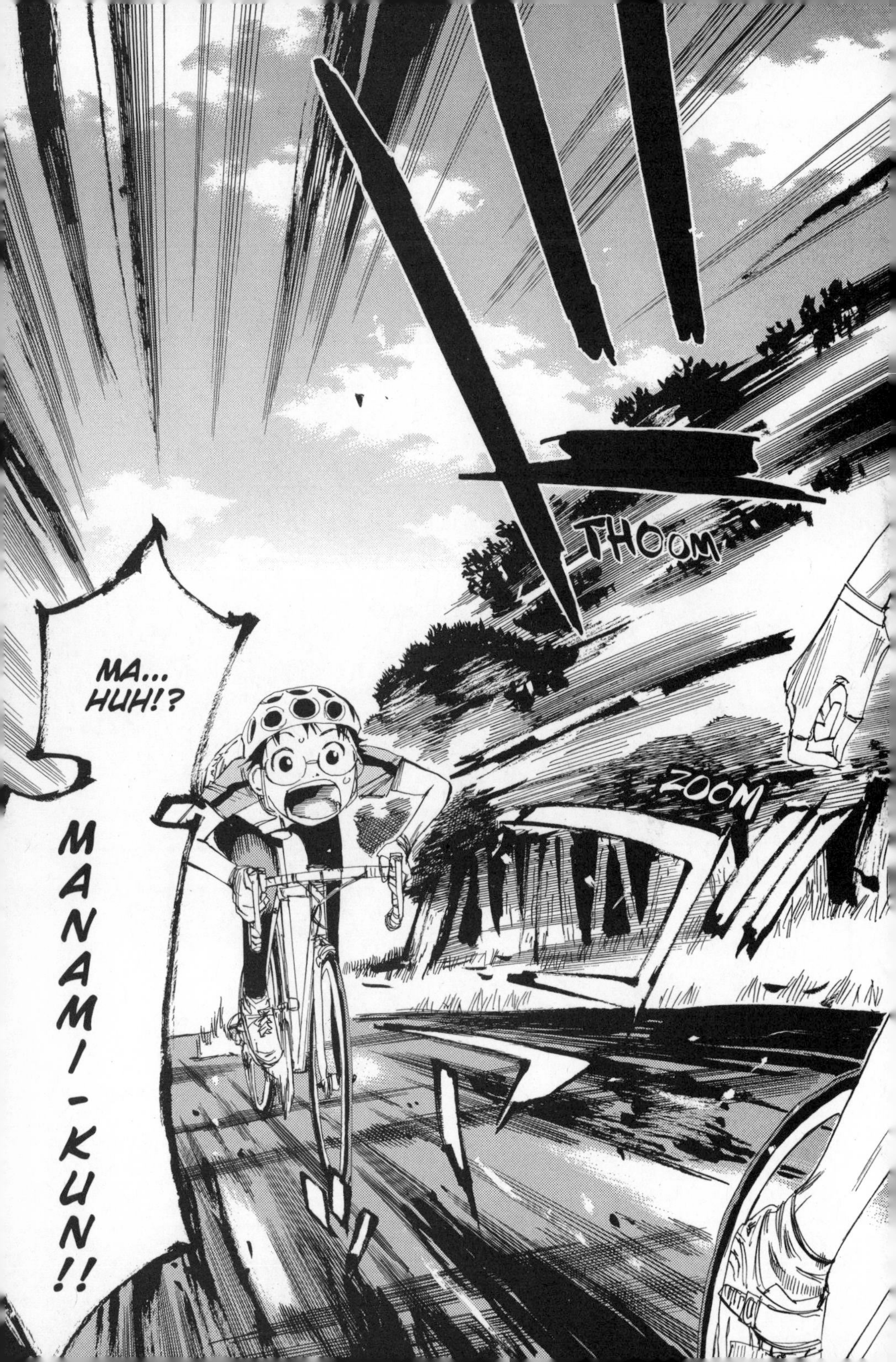
THOOM
ZOOM
MA... HUH!?
MANAMI-KUN!!

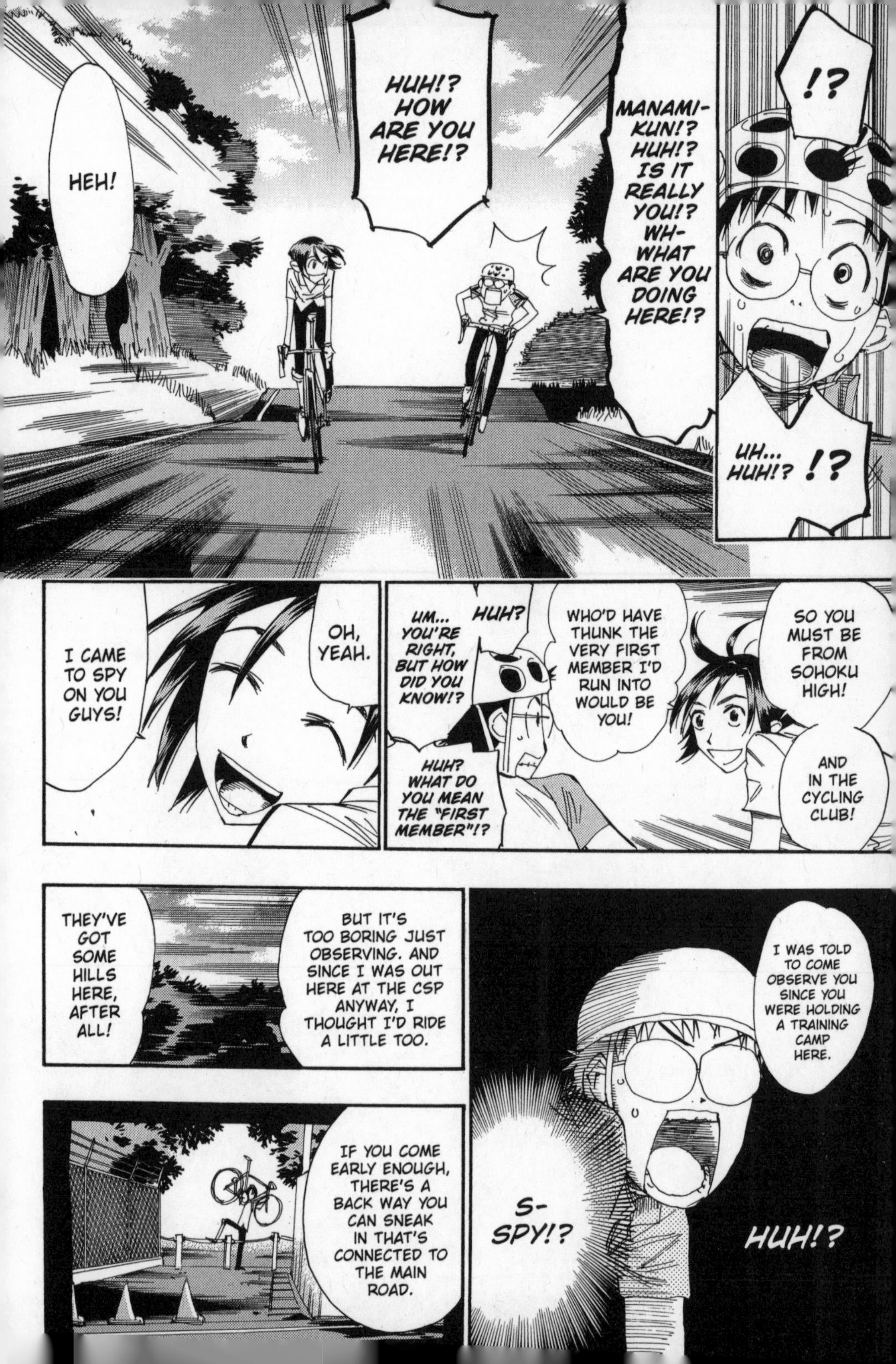
!?
UH... HUH!? !?
MANAMI-KUN!? HUH!? IS IT REALLY YOU!? WH-WHAT ARE YOU DOING HERE!?
HUH!? HOW ARE YOU HERE!?
HEH!
SO YOU MUST BE FROM SOHOKU HIGH!
AND IN THE CYCLING CLUB!
WHO'D HAVE THUNK THE VERY FIRST MEMBER I'D RUN INTO WOULD BE YOU!
HUH?
UM... YOU'RE RIGHT, BUT HOW DID YOU KNOW!?
HUH? WHAT DO YOU MEAN THE "FIRST MEMBER"!?
OH, YEAH.
I CAME TO SPY ON YOU GUYS!
I WAS TOLD TO COME OBSERVE YOU SINCE YOU WERE HOLDING A TRAINING CAMP HERE.
HUH!?
S-SPY!?
BUT IT'S TOO BORING JUST OBSERVING. AND SINCE I WAS OUT HERE AT THE CSP ANYWAY, I THOUGHT I'D RIDE A LITTLE TOO.
THEY'VE GOT SOME HILLS HERE, AFTER ALL!
IF YOU COME EARLY ENOUGH, THERE'S A BACK WAY YOU CAN SNEAK IN THAT'S CONNECTED TO THE MAIN ROAD.

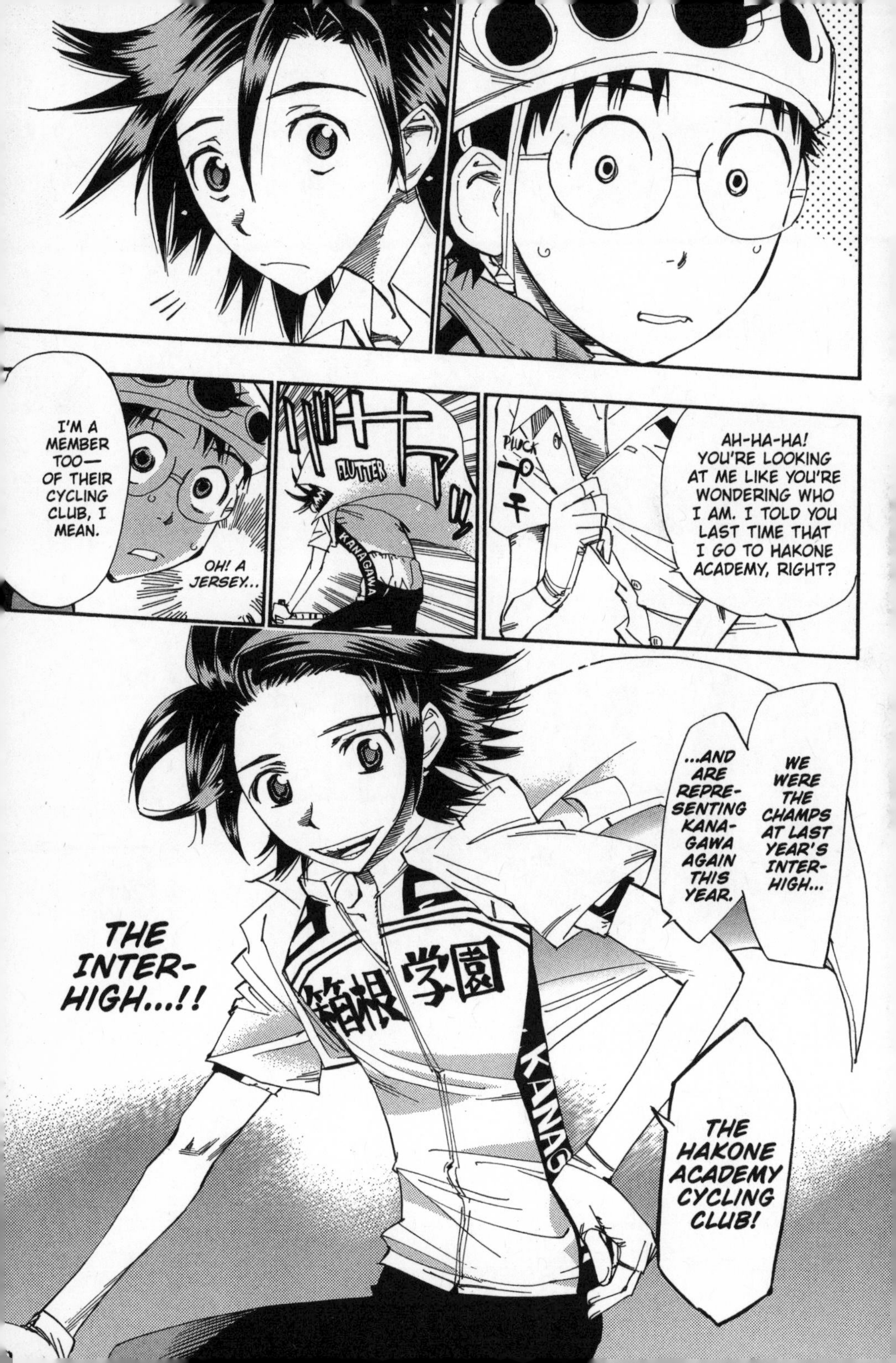
PLUCK
AH-HA-HA! YOU'RE LOOKING AT ME LIKE YOU'RE WONDERING WHO I AM. I TOLD YOU LAST TIME THAT I GO TO HAKONE ACADEMY, RIGHT?
FLUTTER
KANAGAWA
I'M A MEMBER TOO— OF THEIR CYCLING CLUB, I MEAN.
OH! A JERSEY...
WE WERE THE CHAMPS AT LAST YEAR'S INTER-HIGH...
...AND ARE REPRESENTING KANAGAWA AGAIN THIS YEAR.
箱根学園
KANAG
THE HAKONE ACADEMY CYCLING CLUB!
THE INTER-HIGH...!!

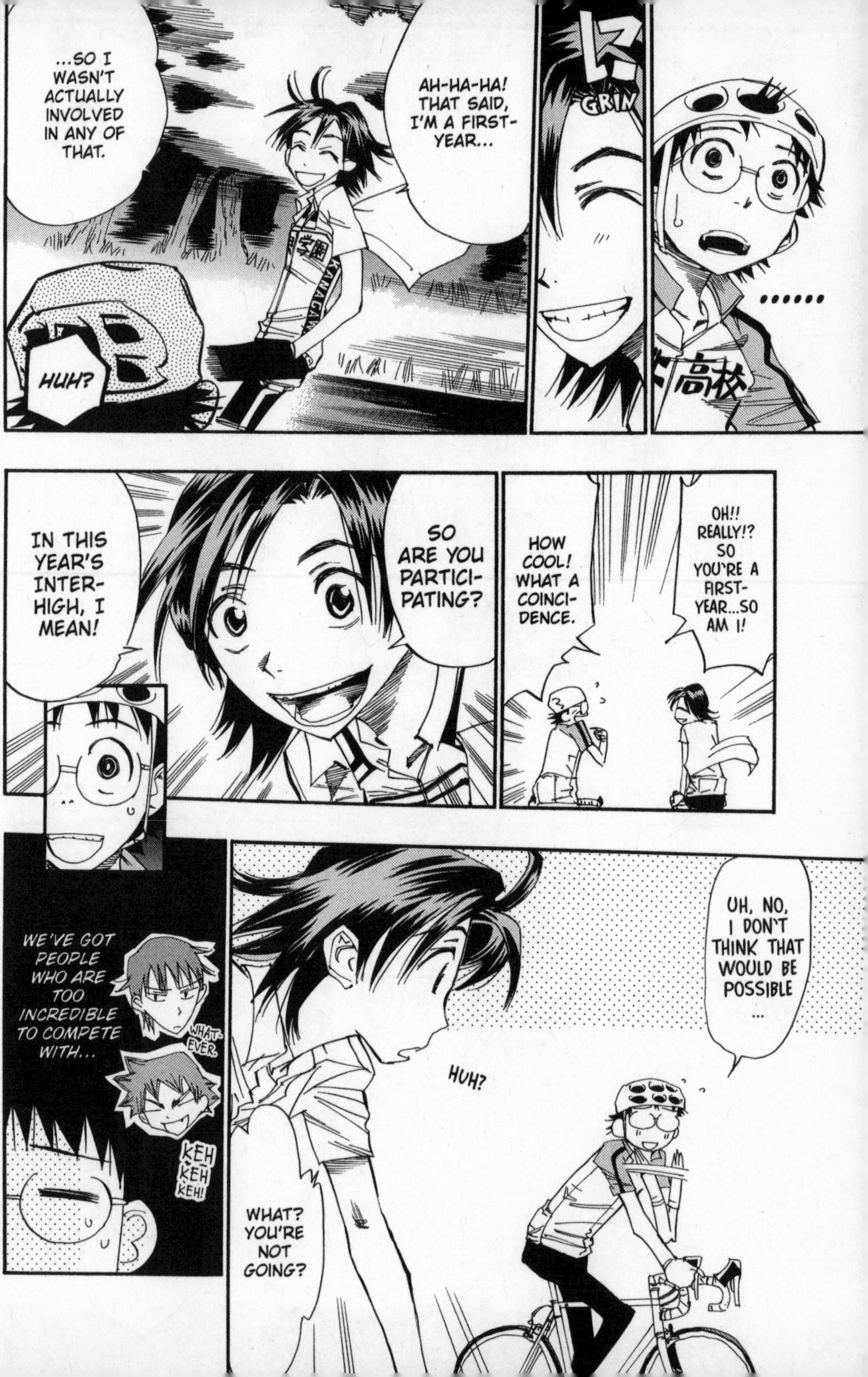
......
GRIN
AH-HA-HA! THAT SAID, I'M A FIRST-YEAR...
...SO I WASN'T ACTUALLY INVOLVED IN ANY OF THAT.
HUH?
OH!! REALLY!? SO YOU'RE A FIRST-YEAR...SO AM I!
HOW COOL! WHAT A COINCIDENCE.
SO ARE YOU PARTICIPATING?
IN THIS YEAR'S INTER-HIGH, I MEAN!
UH, NO, I DON'T THINK THAT WOULD BE POSSIBLE ...
HUH?
WHAT? YOU'RE NOT GOING?
WE'VE GOT PEOPLE WHO ARE TOO INCREDIBLE TO COMPETE WITH...
WHAT-EVER.
KEH KEH KEH!

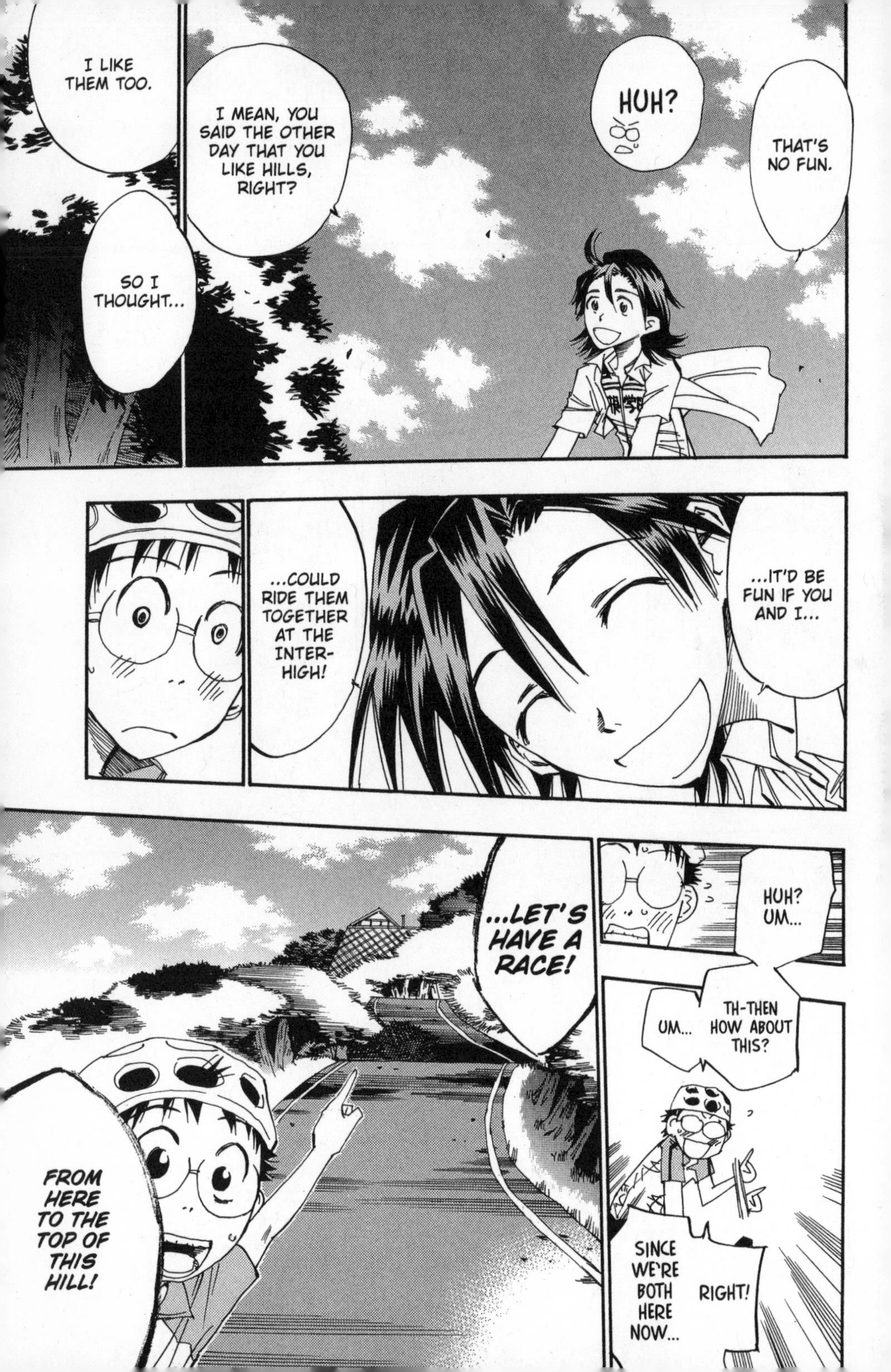
THAT'S NO FUN.
HUH?
I MEAN, YOU SAID THE OTHER DAY THAT YOU LIKE HILLS, RIGHT?
I LIKE THEM TOO.
SO I THOUGHT...
...IT'D BE FUN IF YOU AND I...
...COULD RIDE THEM TOGETHER AT THE INTER-HIGH!
HUH? UM...
TH-THEN HOW ABOUT THIS?
UM...
SINCE WE'RE BOTH HERE NOW...
RIGHT!
...LET'S HAVE A RACE!
FROM HERE TO THE TOP OF THIS HILL!

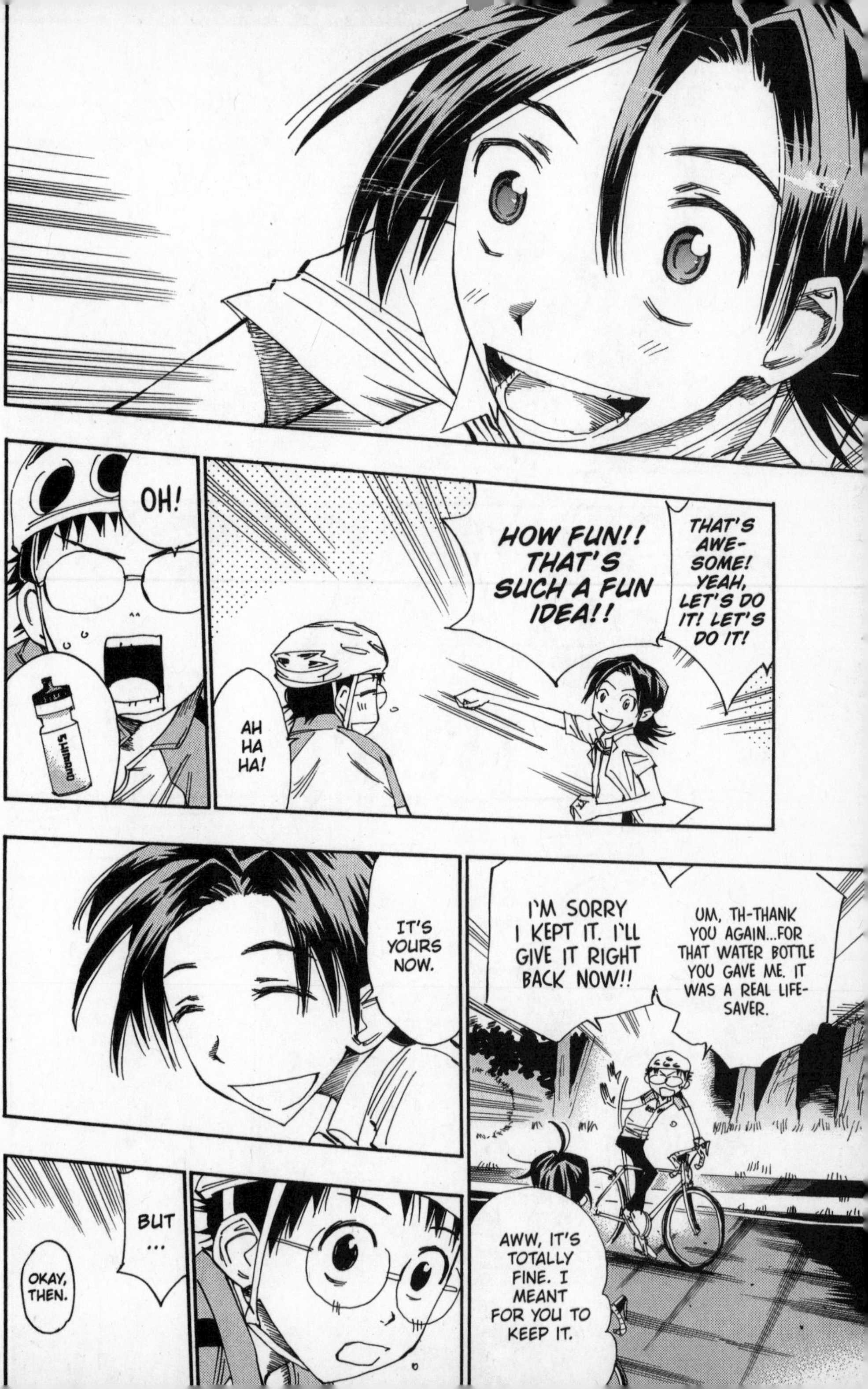
THAT'S AWE-SOME! YEAH, LET'S DO IT! LET'S DO IT!
HOW FUN!! THAT'S SUCH A FUN IDEA!!
AH HA HA!
OH!
SHIMANO
UM, TH-THANK YOU AGAIN...FOR THAT WATER BOTTLE YOU GAVE ME. IT WAS A REAL LIFE-SAVER.
I'M SORRY I KEPT IT. I'LL GIVE IT RIGHT BACK NOW!!
AWW, IT'S TOTALLY FINE. I MEANT FOR YOU TO KEEP IT.
IT'S YOURS NOW.
BUT ...
OKAY, THEN.

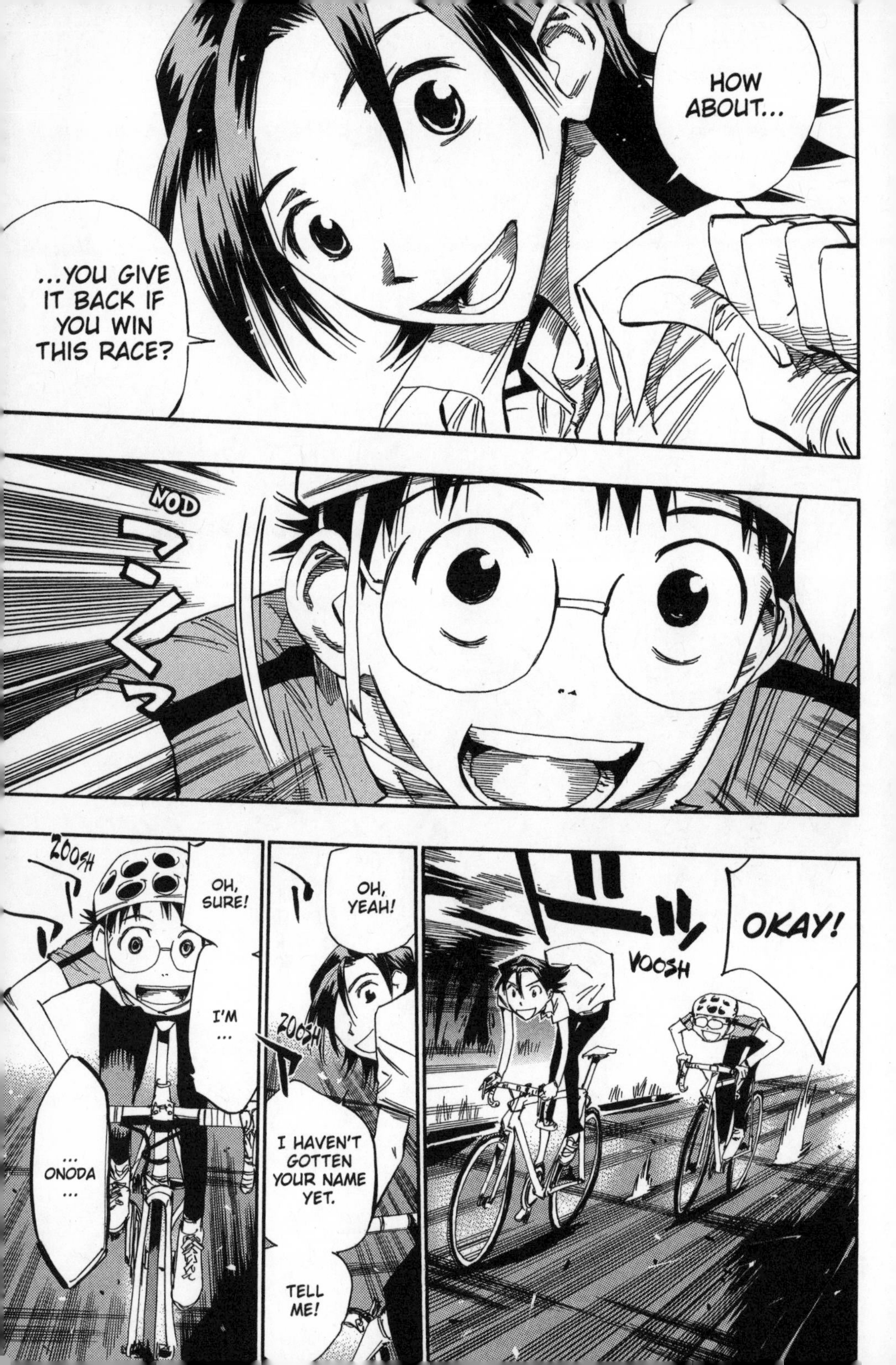
HOW ABOUT...
...YOU GIVE IT BACK IF YOU WIN THIS RACE?
NOD
OKAY!
VOOSH
OH, YEAH!
ZOOSH
I HAVEN'T GOTTEN YOUR NAME YET.
TELL ME!
ZOOSH
OH, SURE!
I'M ...
... ONODA ...

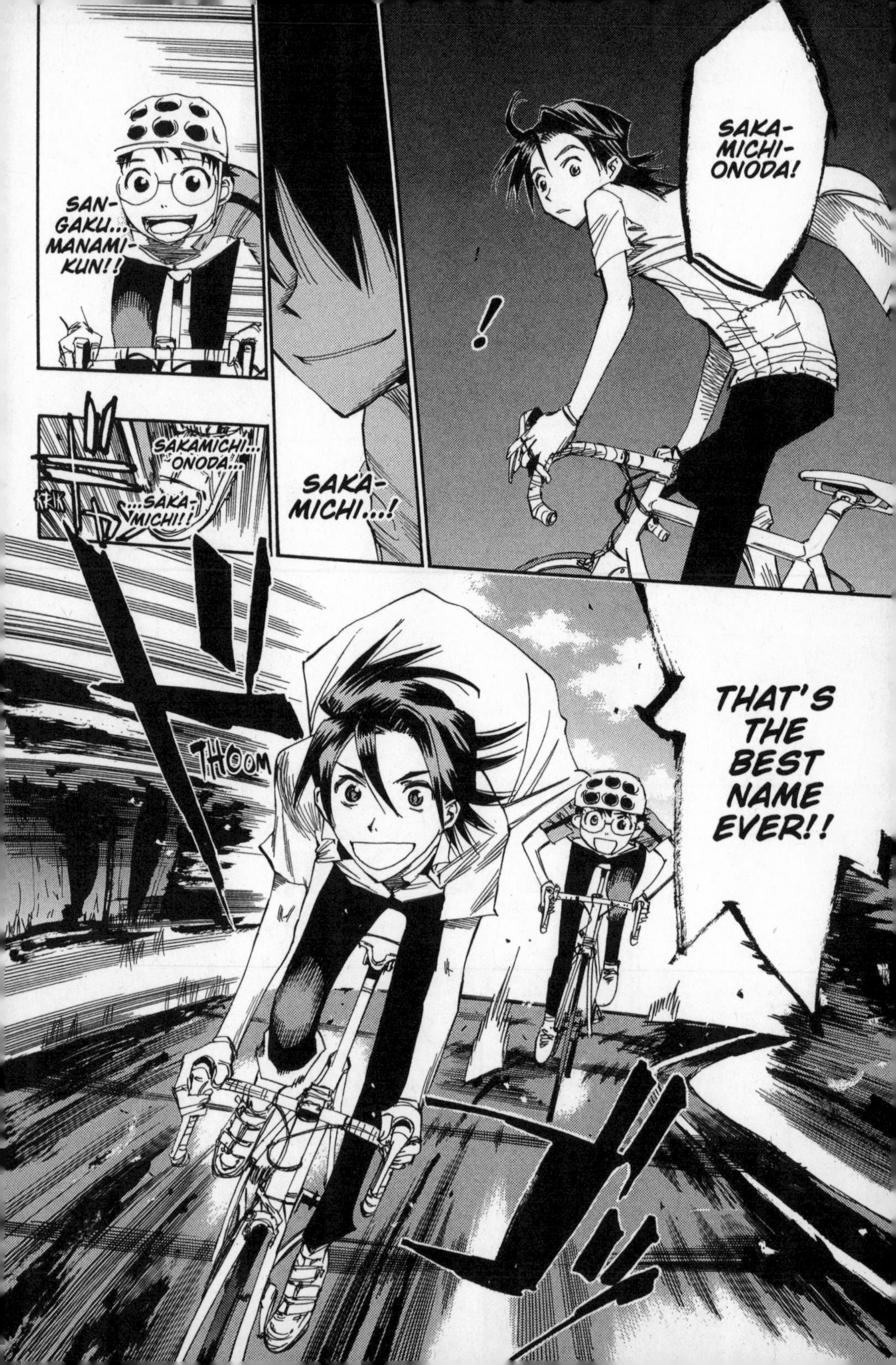
SAKA-MICHI-ONODA!
!
SAKA-MICHI...!
SAN-GAKU... MANAMI-KUN!!
SAKAMICHI... ONODA...
...SAKA-MICHI!!
KRIK
THOOM
THAT'S THE BEST NAME EVER!!

RIDE.47 SANGAKU X SAKAMICHI
[MOUNTAIN] [UPHILL ROAD]

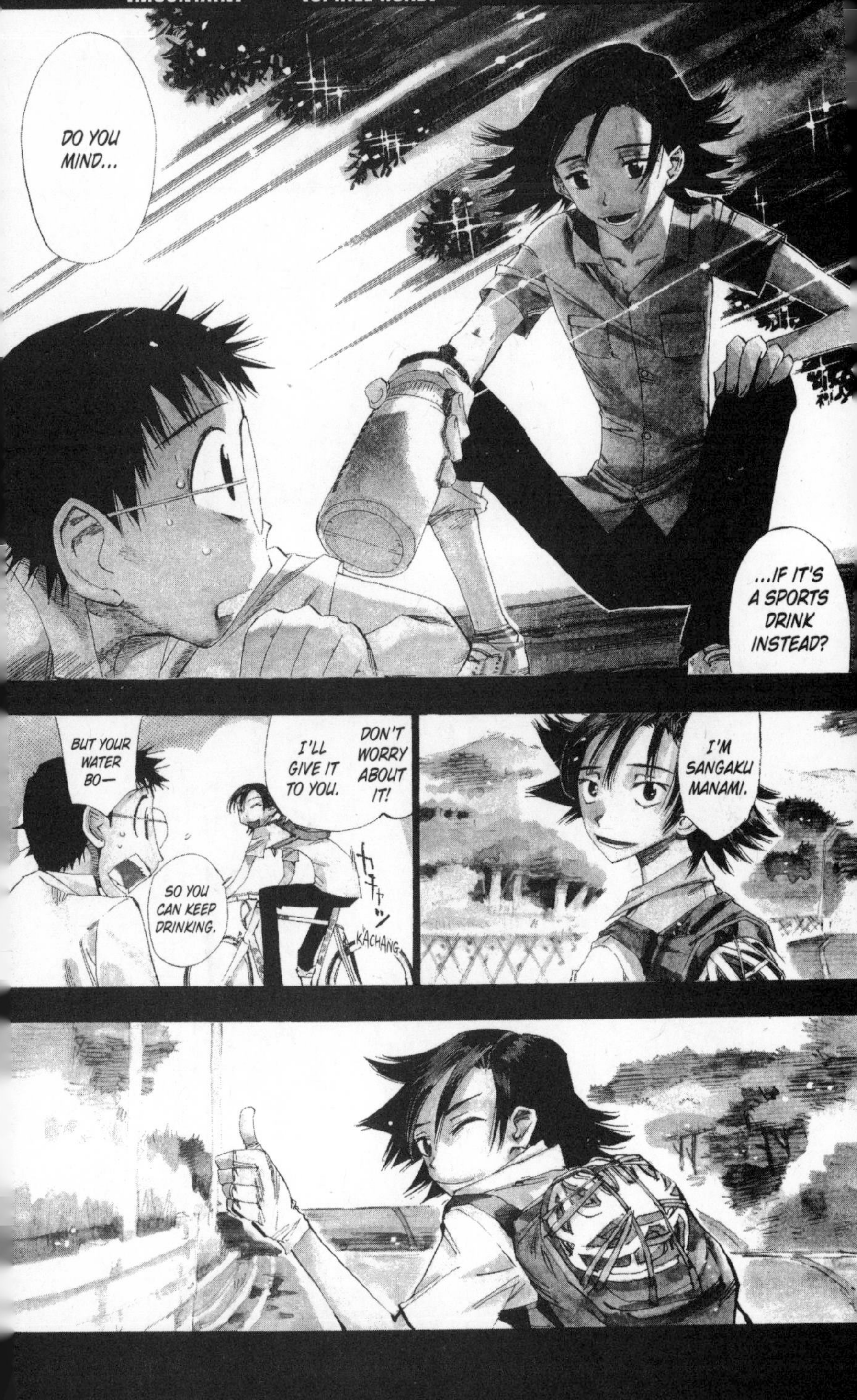
DO YOU MIND...
...IF IT'S A SPORTS DRINK INSTEAD?
I'M SANGAKU MANAMI.
DON'T WORRY ABOUT IT!
I'LL GIVE IT TO YOU.
BUT YOUR WATER BO—
SO YOU CAN KEEP DRINKING.
KACHANG

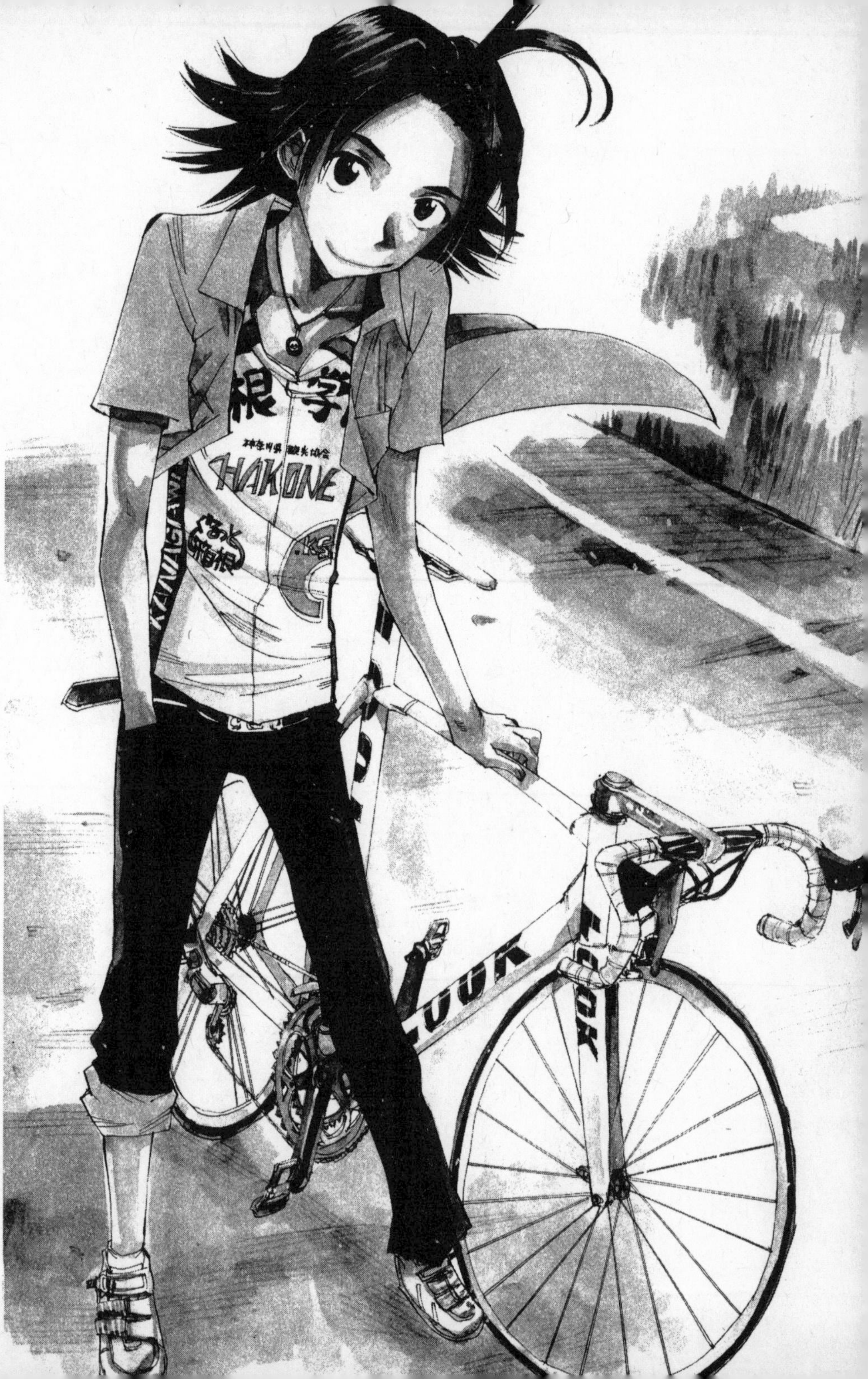
HAKONE
LOOK

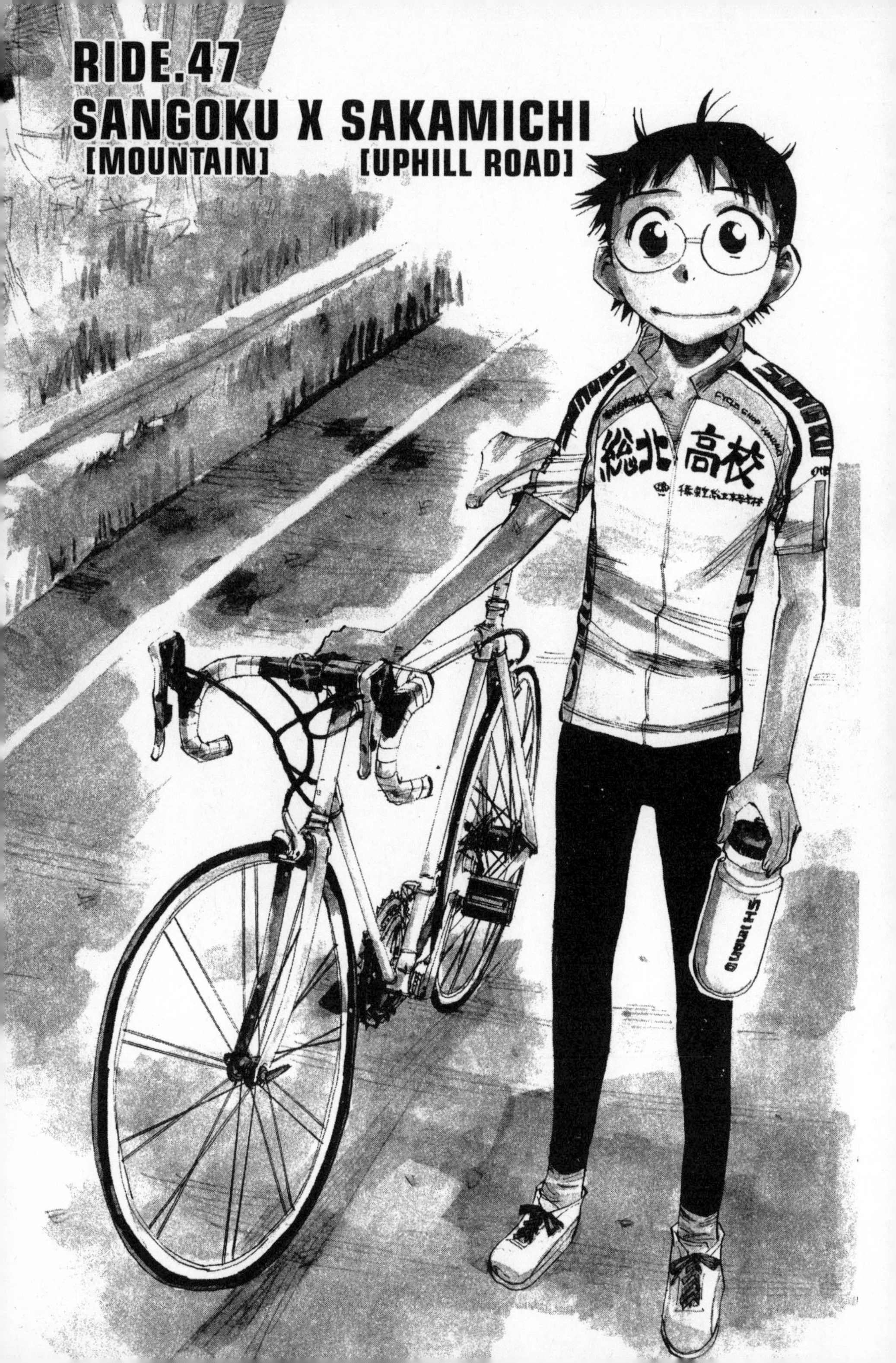
RIDE.47
SANGOKU X SAKAMICHI
[MOUNTAIN]
[UPHILL ROAD]
総北高校

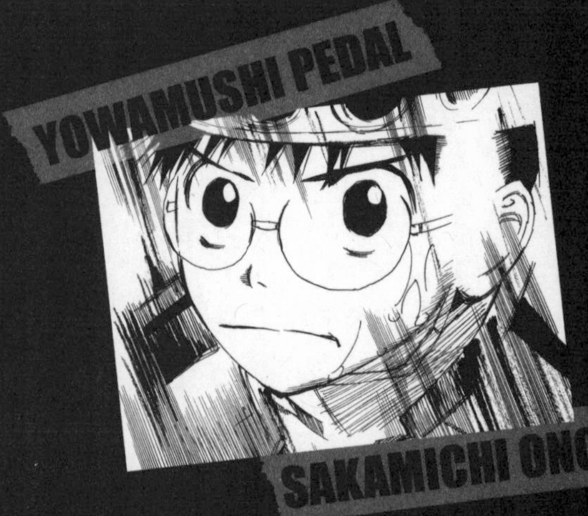
YOWAMUSHI PEDAL
SAKAMICHI ONO

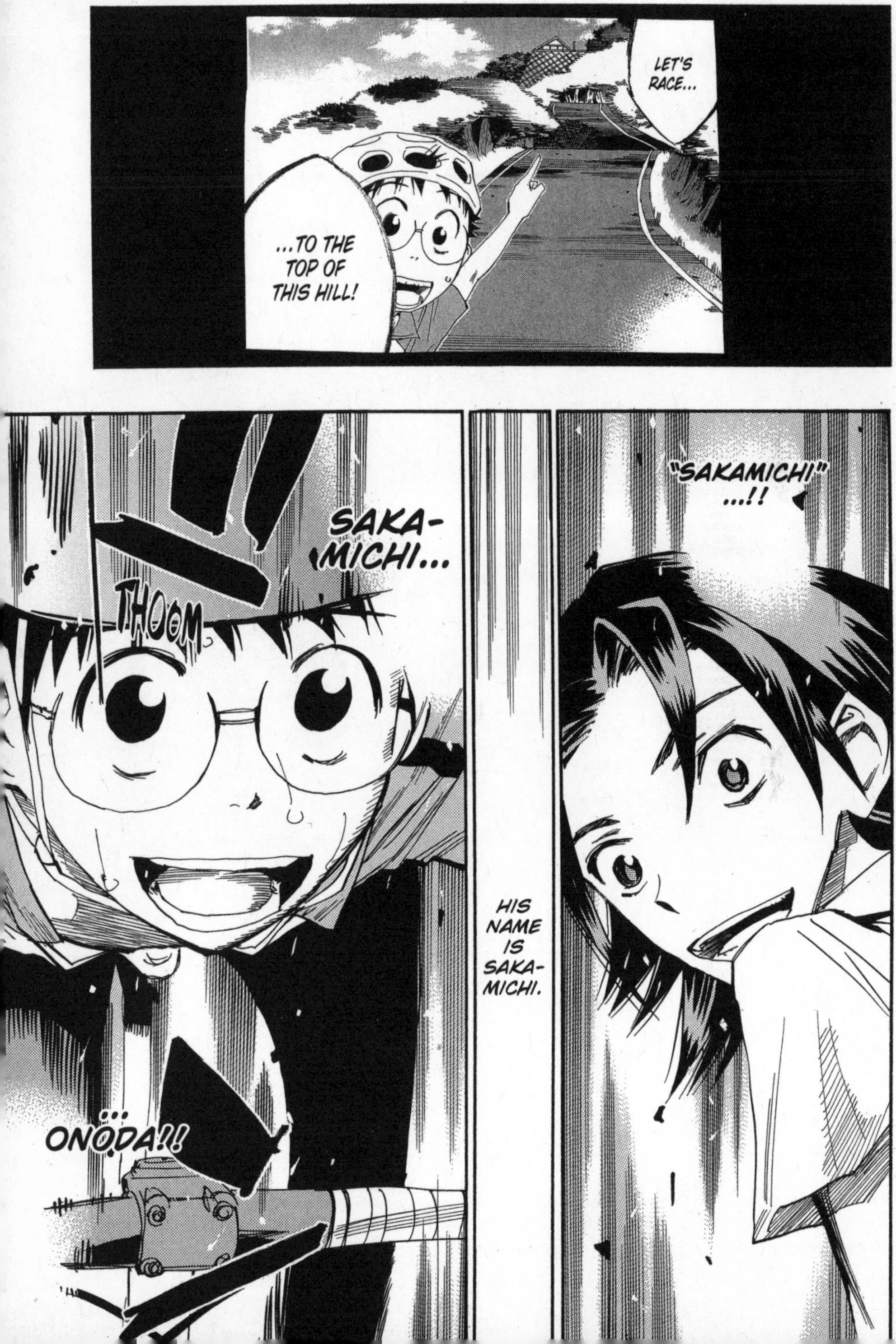
LET'S RACE...
...TO THE TOP OF THIS HILL!
"SAKAMICHI" ...!!
HIS NAME IS SAKAMICHI.
SAKA-MICHI...
THOOM
...ONODA!!

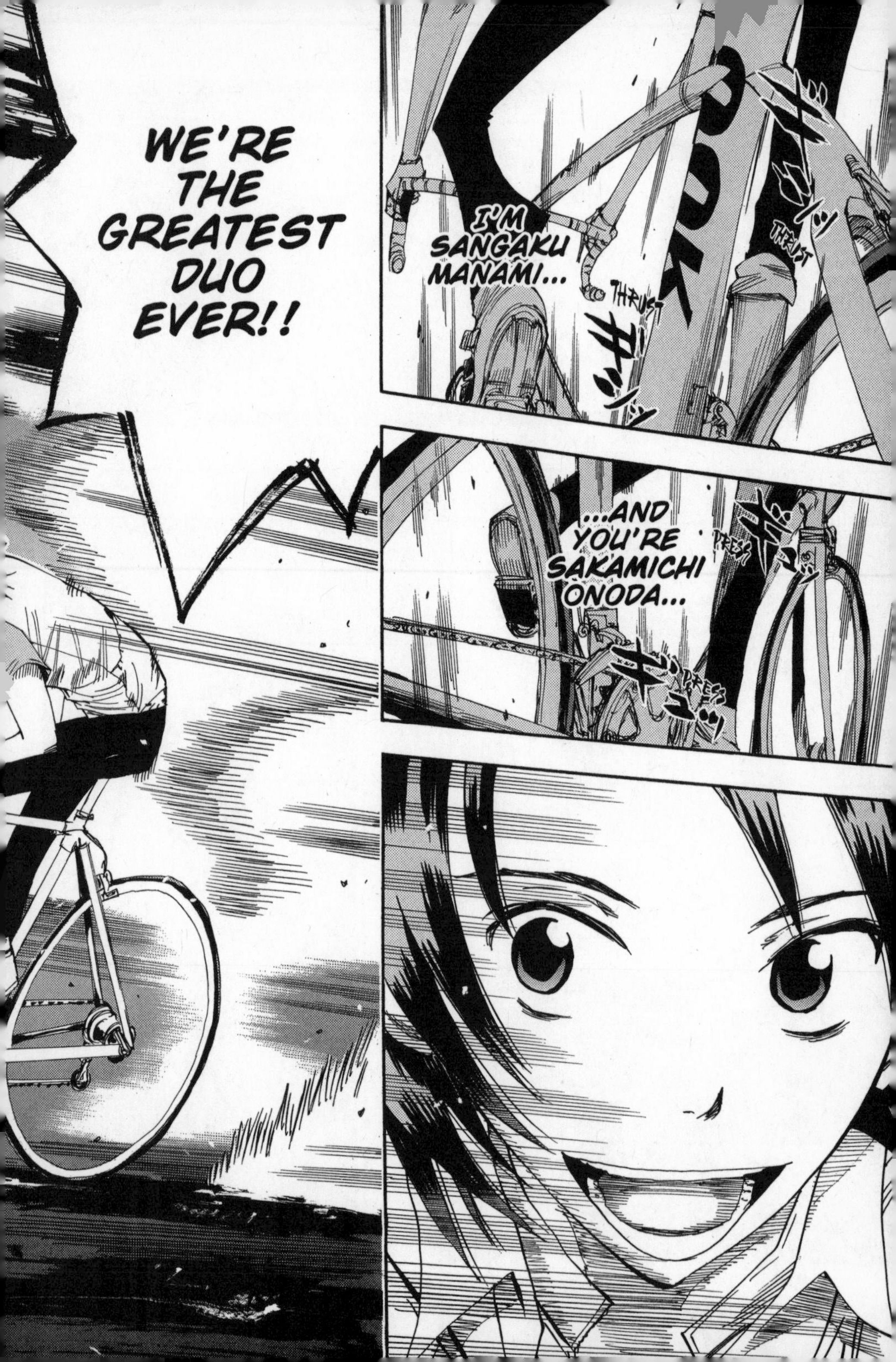
I'M SANGAKU MANAMI...
THRUST
THRUST
...AND YOU'RE SAKAMICHI ONODA...
PRESS
PRESS
WE'RE THE GREATEST DUO EVER!!

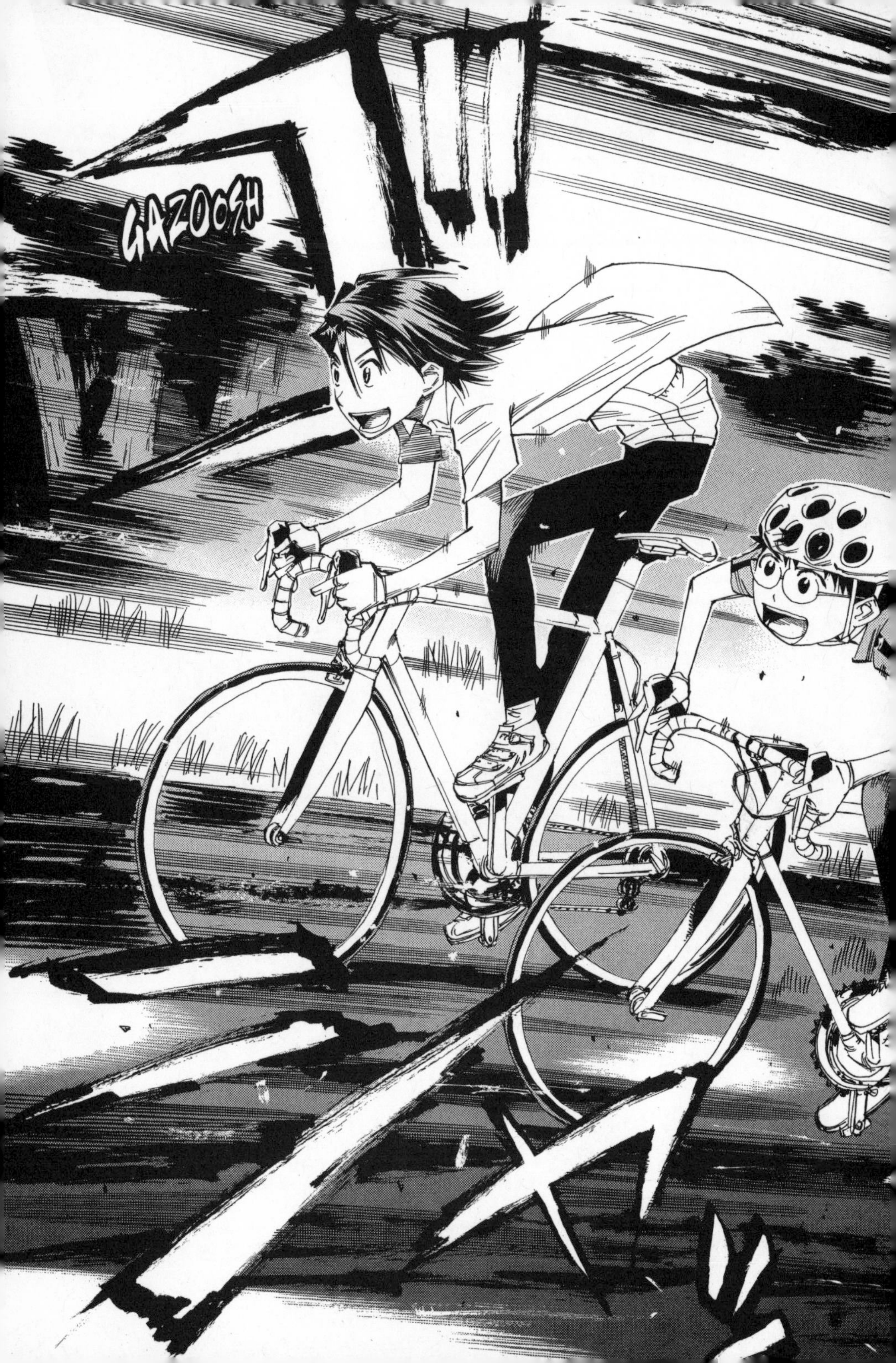
GAZOOSH

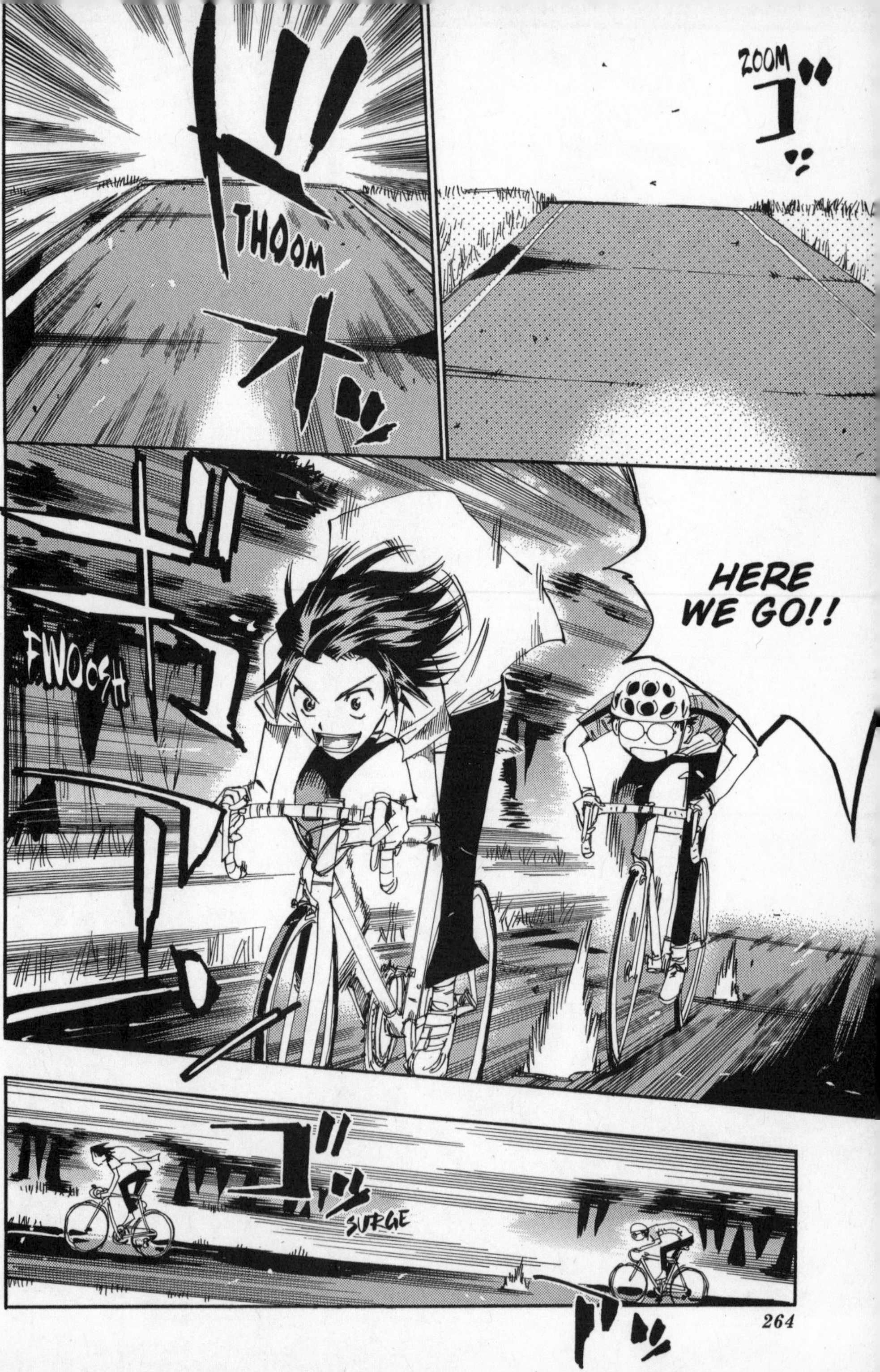
ZOOM
THOOM
HERE WE GO!!
FWOOSH
SURGE

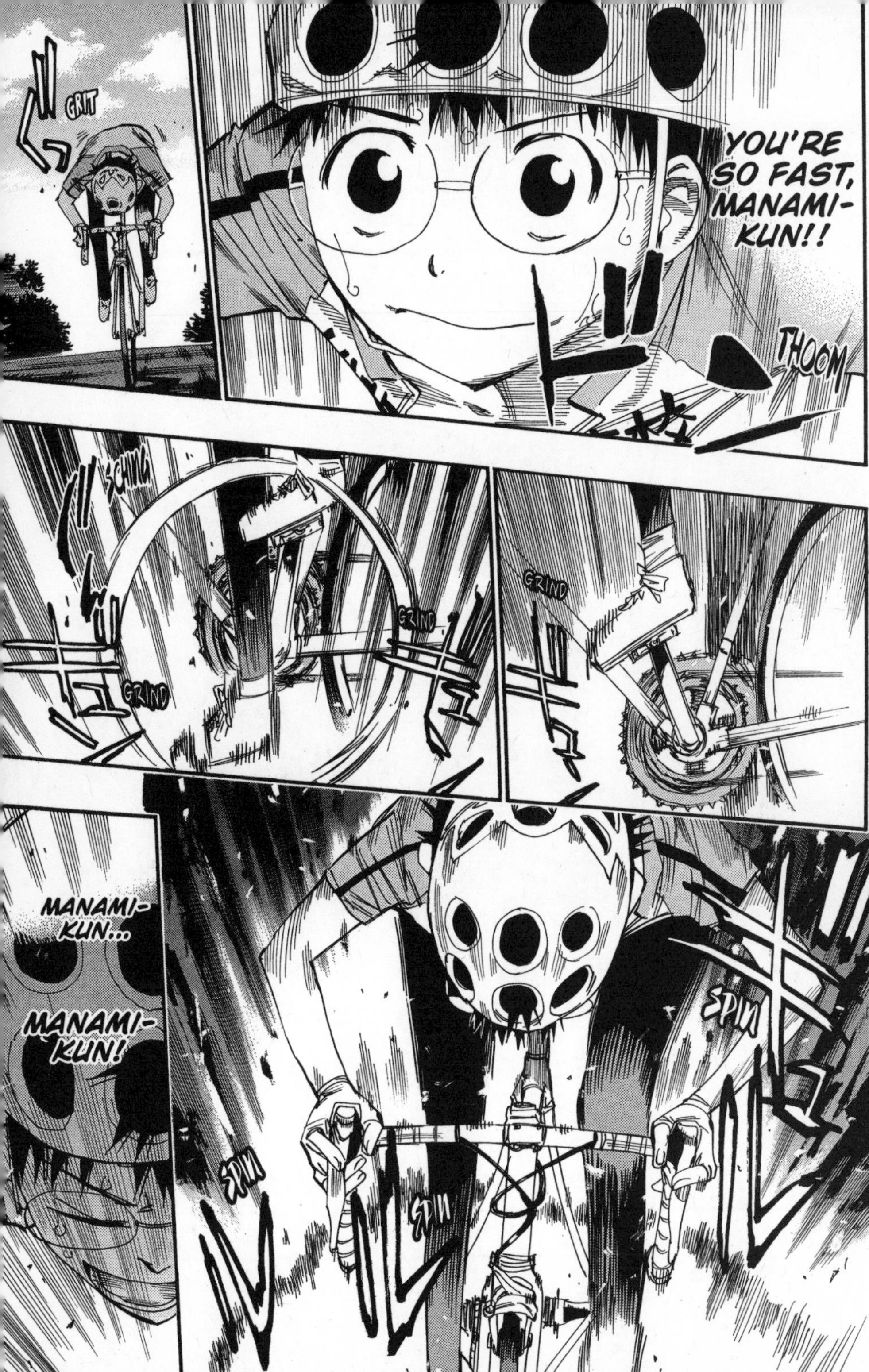
YOU'RE SO FAST, MANAMI-KUN!!
THOOM
GRIT
GRIND
SCHING
GRIND
GRIND
SPIN
SPIN
SPIN
MANAMI-KUN...
MANAMI-KUN!

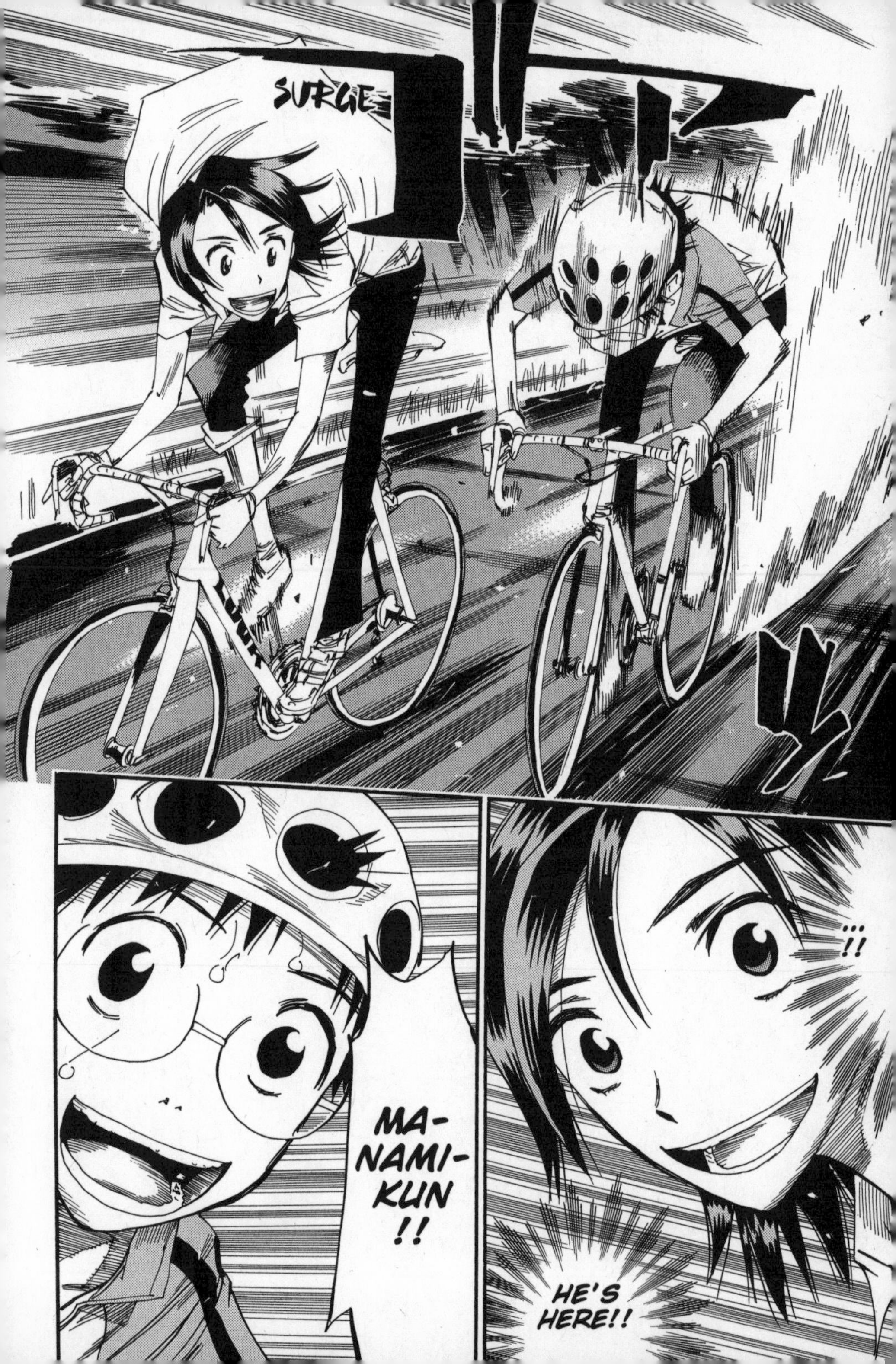
SURGE
...!!
HE'S HERE!!
MA-NAMI-KUN!!

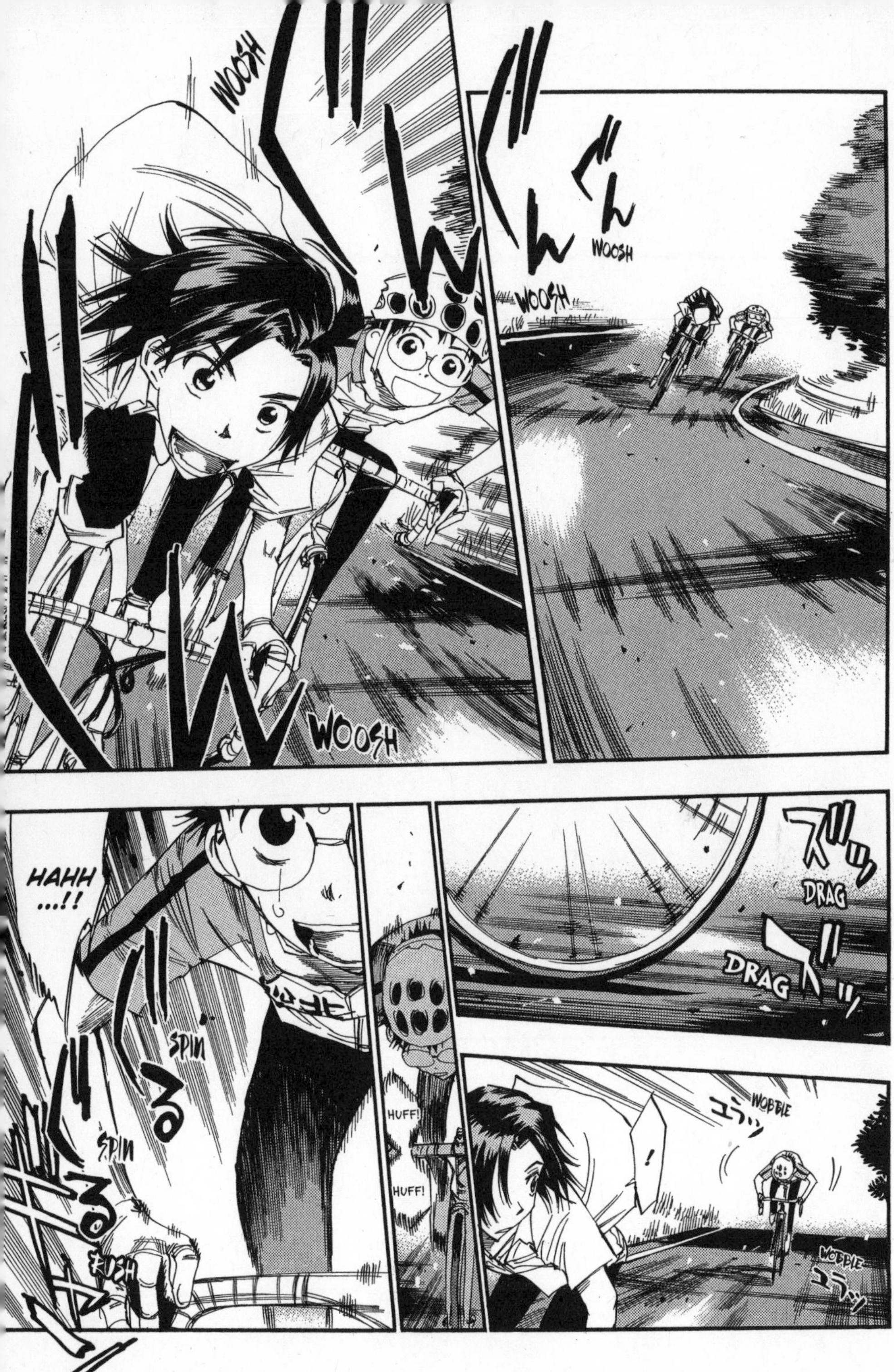

ぐん
WOOSH
WOOSH
WOOSH
WOOSH
ズッ
DRAG
DRAG
ユラッ
WOBBLE
!
WOBBLE
ユラッ
HUFF!
HUFF!
HAHH ...!!
SPIN
る
SPIN
る
RUSH

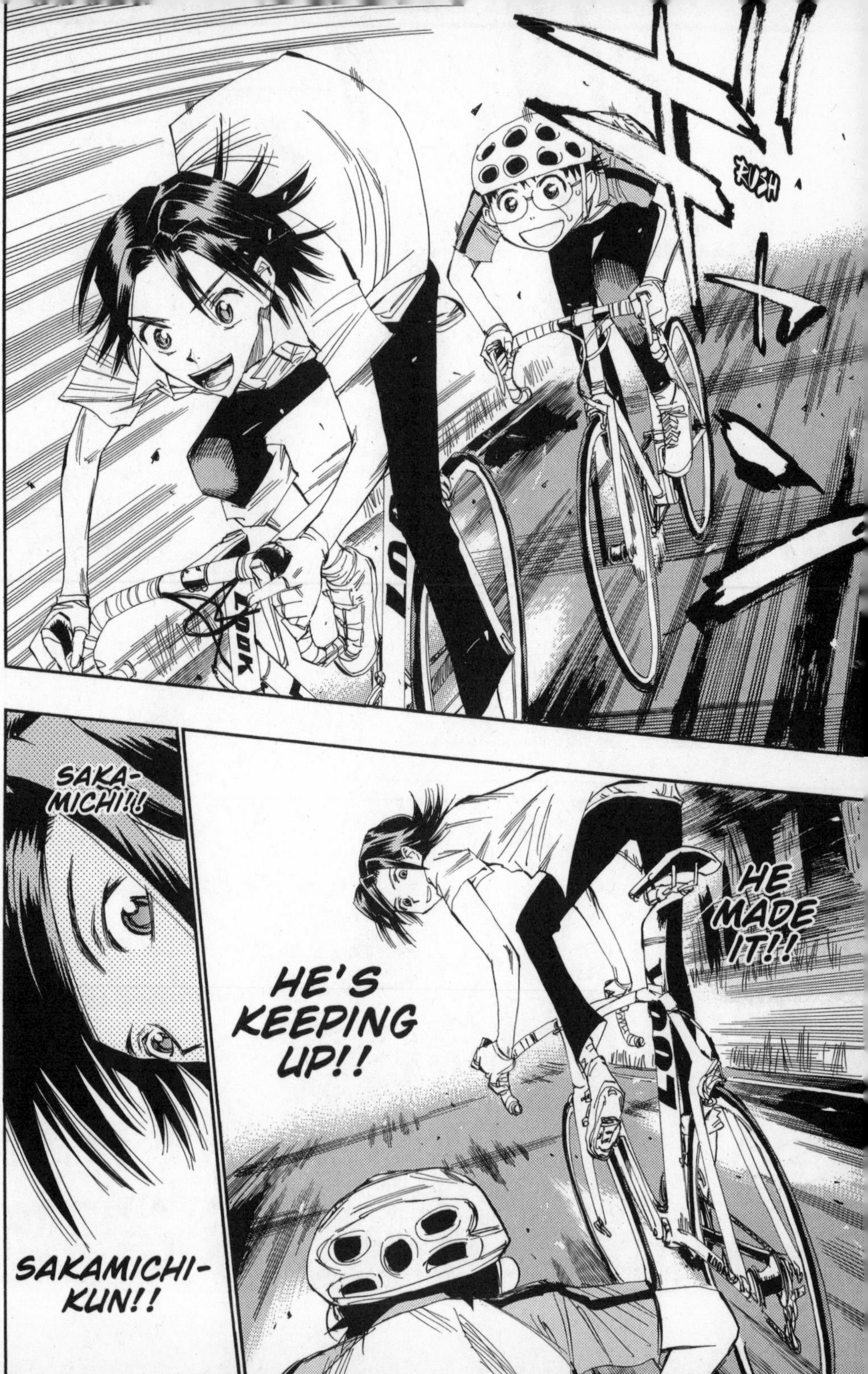
RUSH
HE MADE IT!!
HE'S KEEPING UP!!
SAKA-MICHI!!
SAKAMICHI-KUN!!

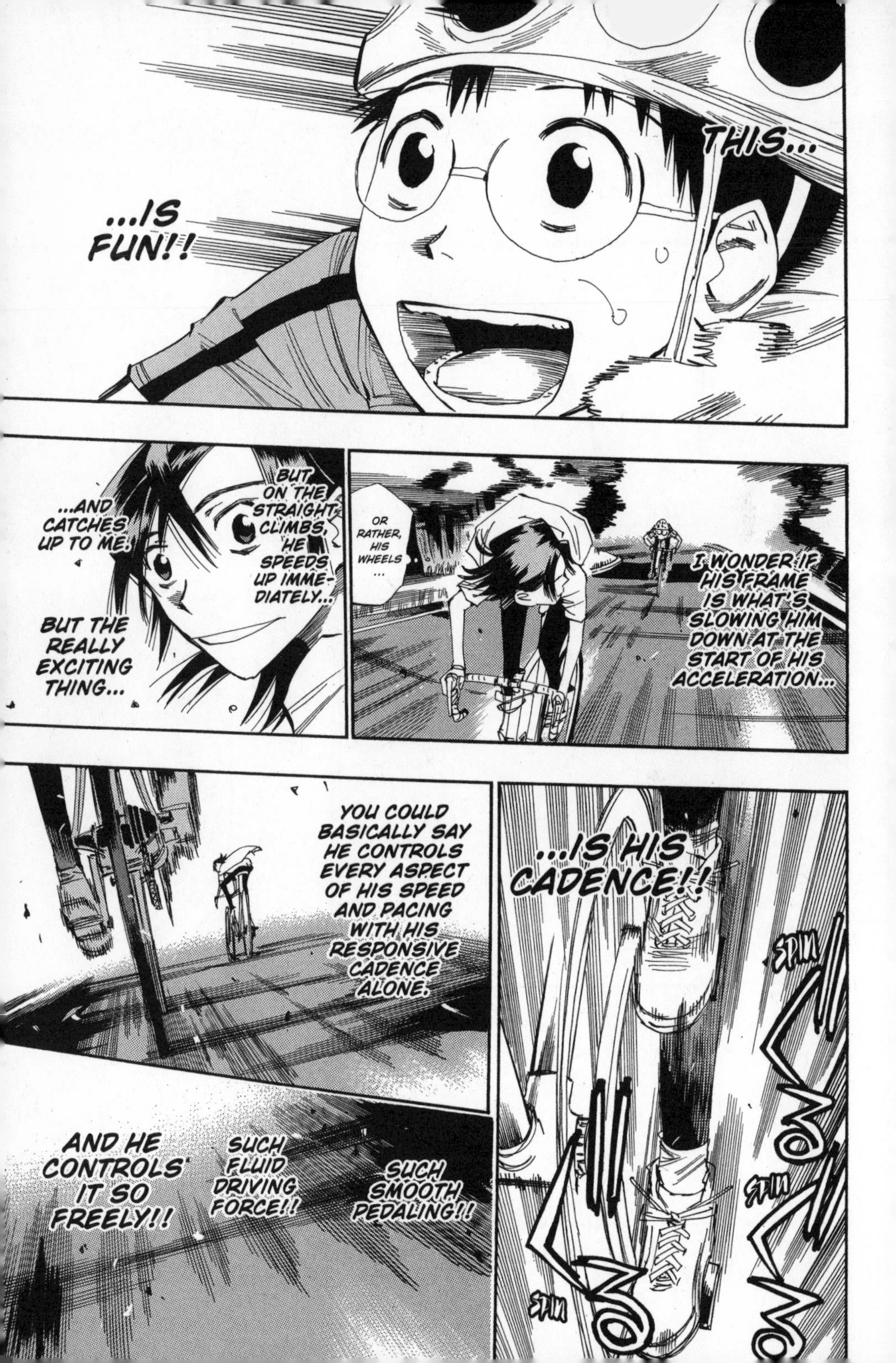
THIS...
...IS FUN!!
I WONDER IF HIS FRAME IS WHAT'S SLOWING HIM DOWN AT THE START OF HIS ACCELERATION...
OR RATHER, HIS WHEELS...
BUT ON THE STRAIGHT CLIMBS, HE SPEEDS UP IMMEDIATELY...
...AND CATCHES UP TO ME.
BUT THE REALLY EXCITING THING...
...IS HIS CADENCE!!
SPIN
SPIN
SPIN
YOU COULD BASICALLY SAY HE CONTROLS EVERY ASPECT OF HIS SPEED AND PACING WITH HIS RESPONSIVE CADENCE ALONE.
SUCH SMOOTH PEDALING!!
SUCH FLUID DRIVING FORCE!!
AND HE CONTROLS IT SO FREELY!!

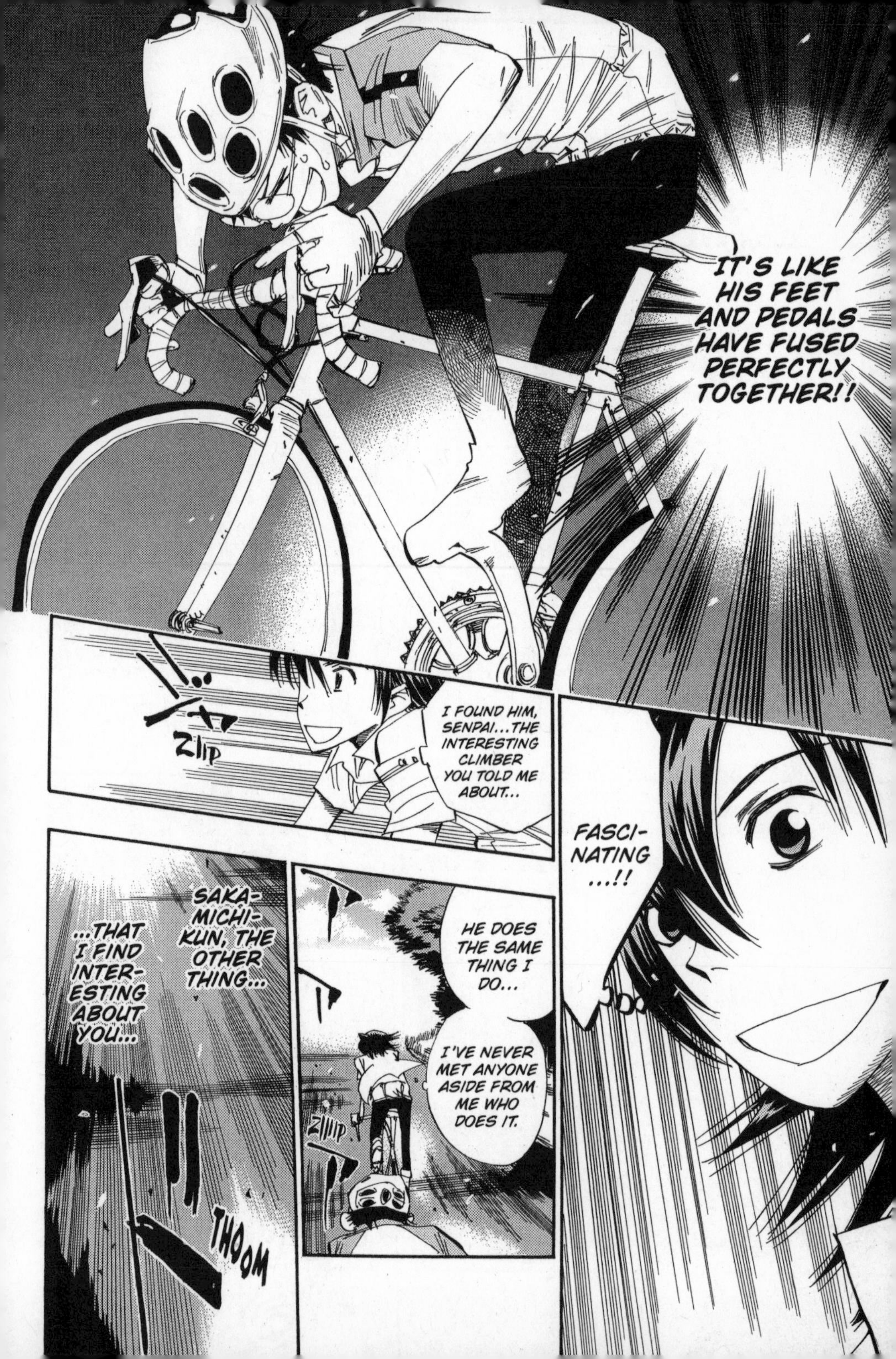
IT'S LIKE HIS FEET AND PEDALS HAVE FUSED PERFECTLY TOGETHER!!
FASCI-NATING ...!!
I FOUND HIM, SENPAI...THE INTERESTING CLIMBER YOU TOLD ME ABOUT...
ZIIP
HE DOES THE SAME THING I DO...
I'VE NEVER MET ANYONE ASIDE FROM ME WHO DOES IT.
ZIIP
SAKA-MICHI-KUN, THE OTHER THING...
...THAT I FIND INTER-ESTING ABOUT YOU...
THOOM

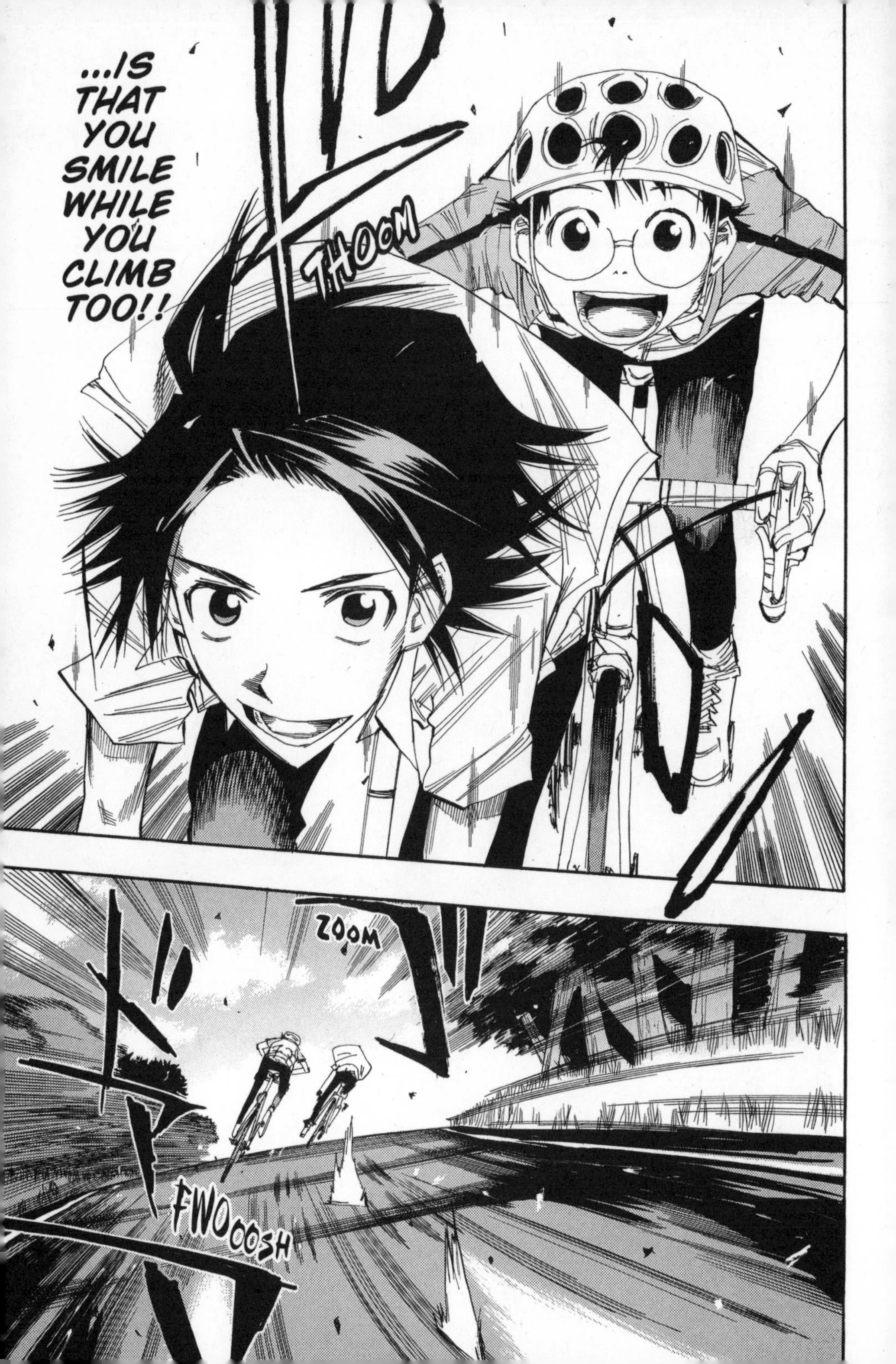
...IS THAT YOU SMILE WHILE YOU CLIMB TOO!!
THOOM
ZOOM
FWOOOSH

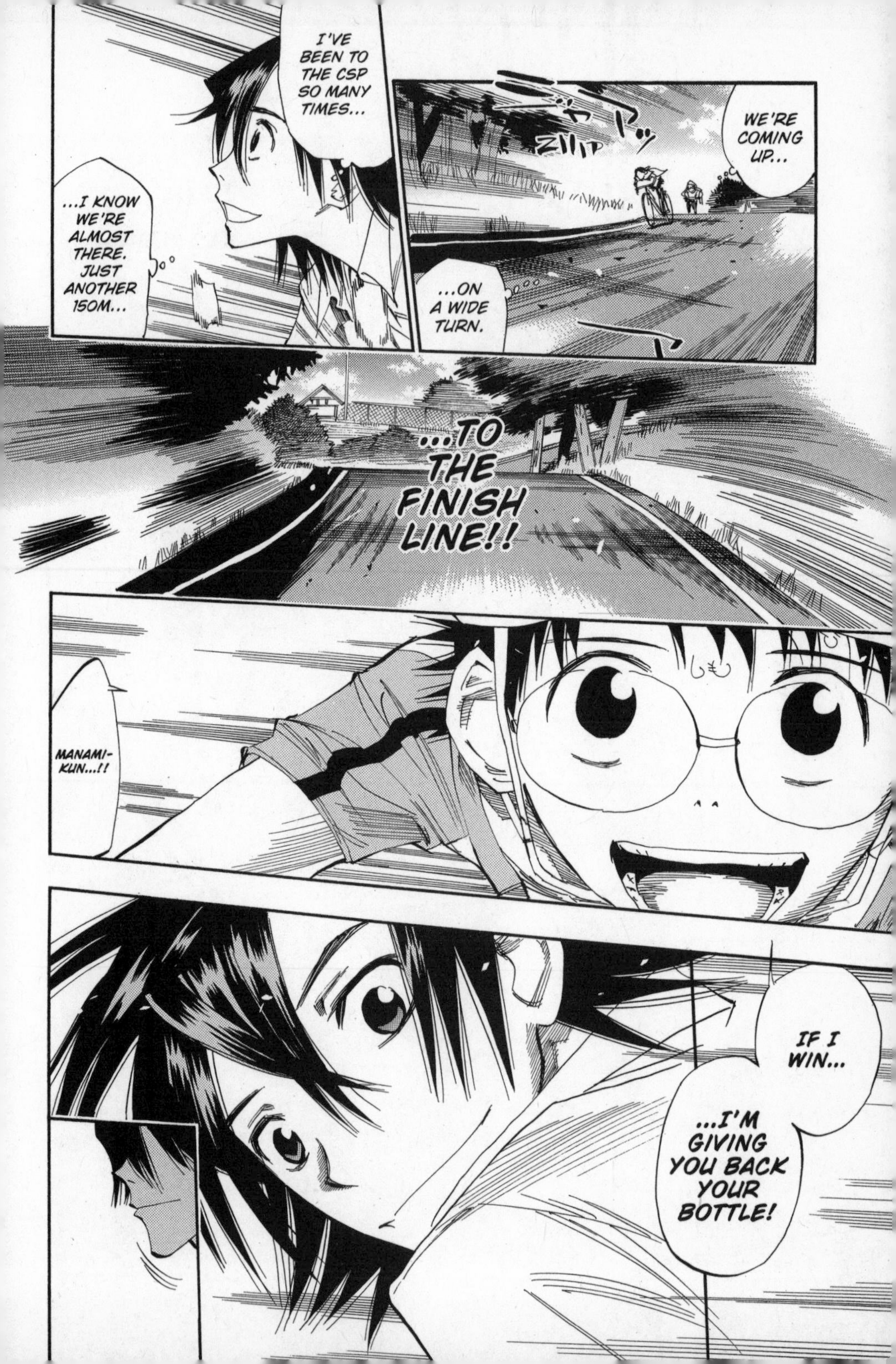
WE'RE COMING UP...
...ON A WIDE TURN.
I'VE BEEN TO THE CSP SO MANY TIMES...
...I KNOW WE'RE ALMOST THERE. JUST ANOTHER 150M...
...TO THE FINISH LINE!!
MANAMI-KUN...!!
IF I WIN...
...I'M GIVING YOU BACK YOUR BOTTLE!

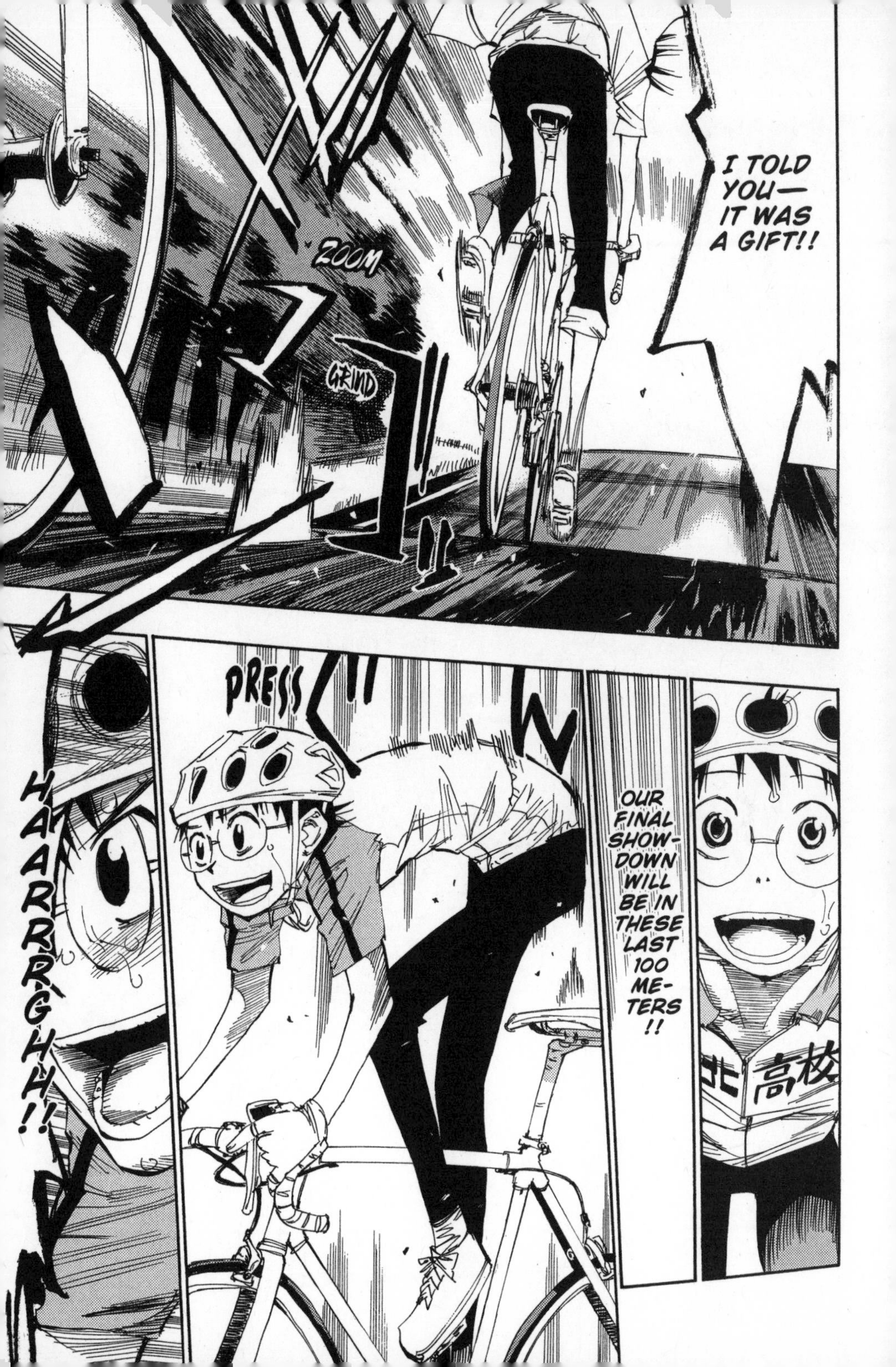
I TOLD YOU— IT WAS A GIFT!!
ZOOM
GRIND
OUR FINAL SHOWDOWN WILL BE IN THESE LAST 100 METERS!!
PRESS
HAARRRGHH!!

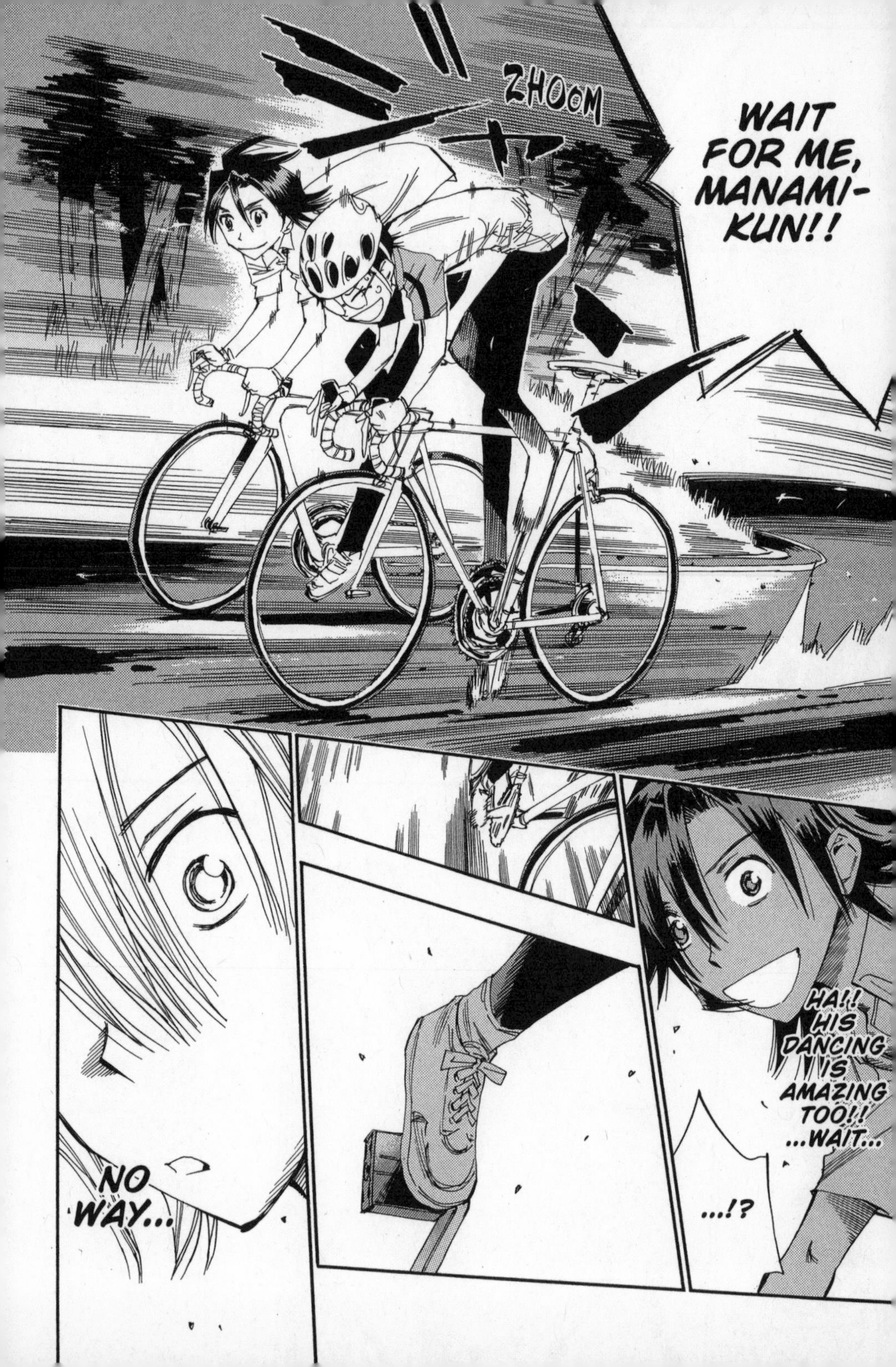
WAIT FOR ME, MANAMI-KUN!!
ZHOOM
HA!! HIS DANCING IS AMAZING TOO!! ...WAIT...
...!?
NO WAY...

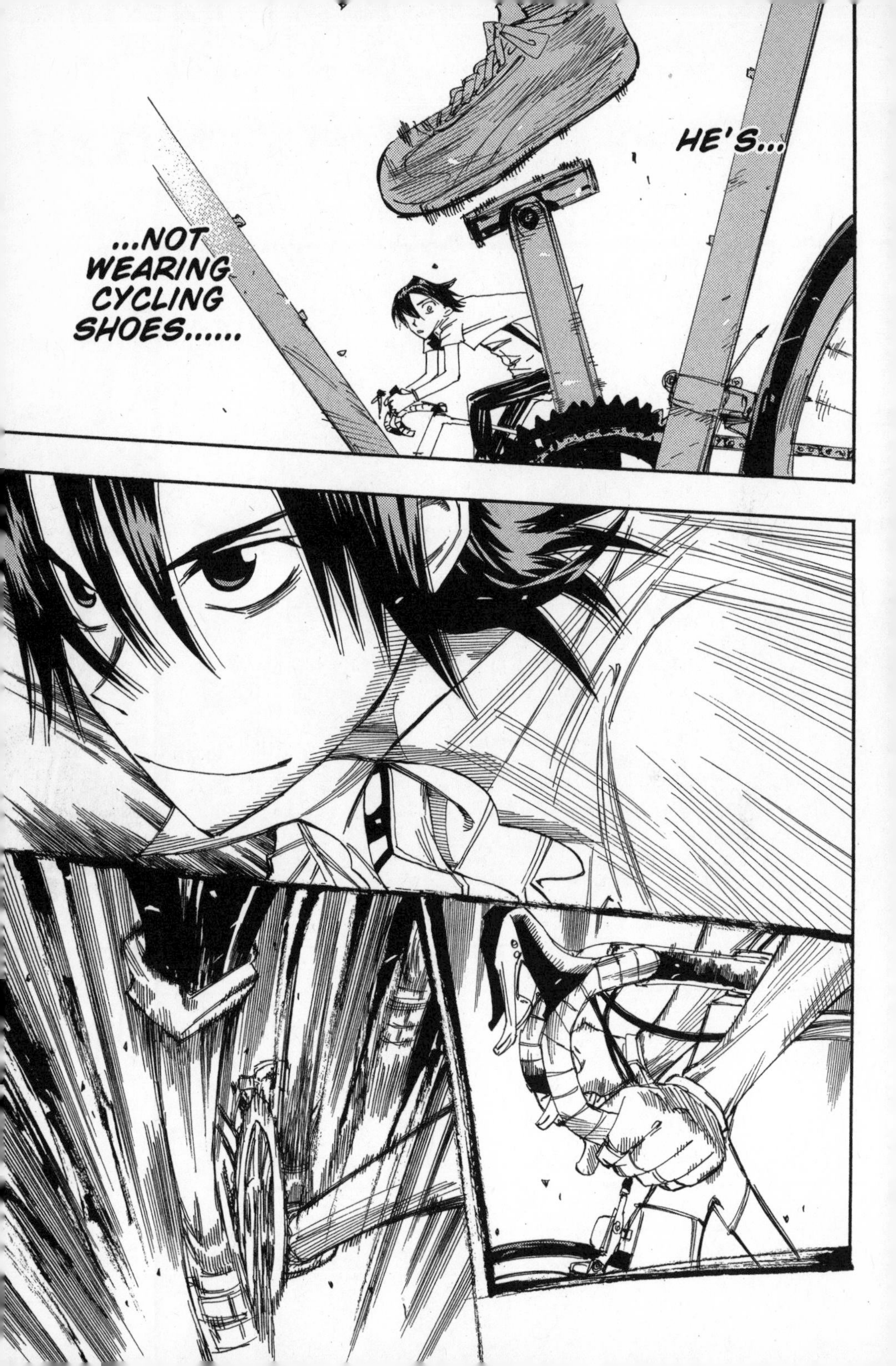
HE'S...
...NOT WEARING CYCLING SHOES......

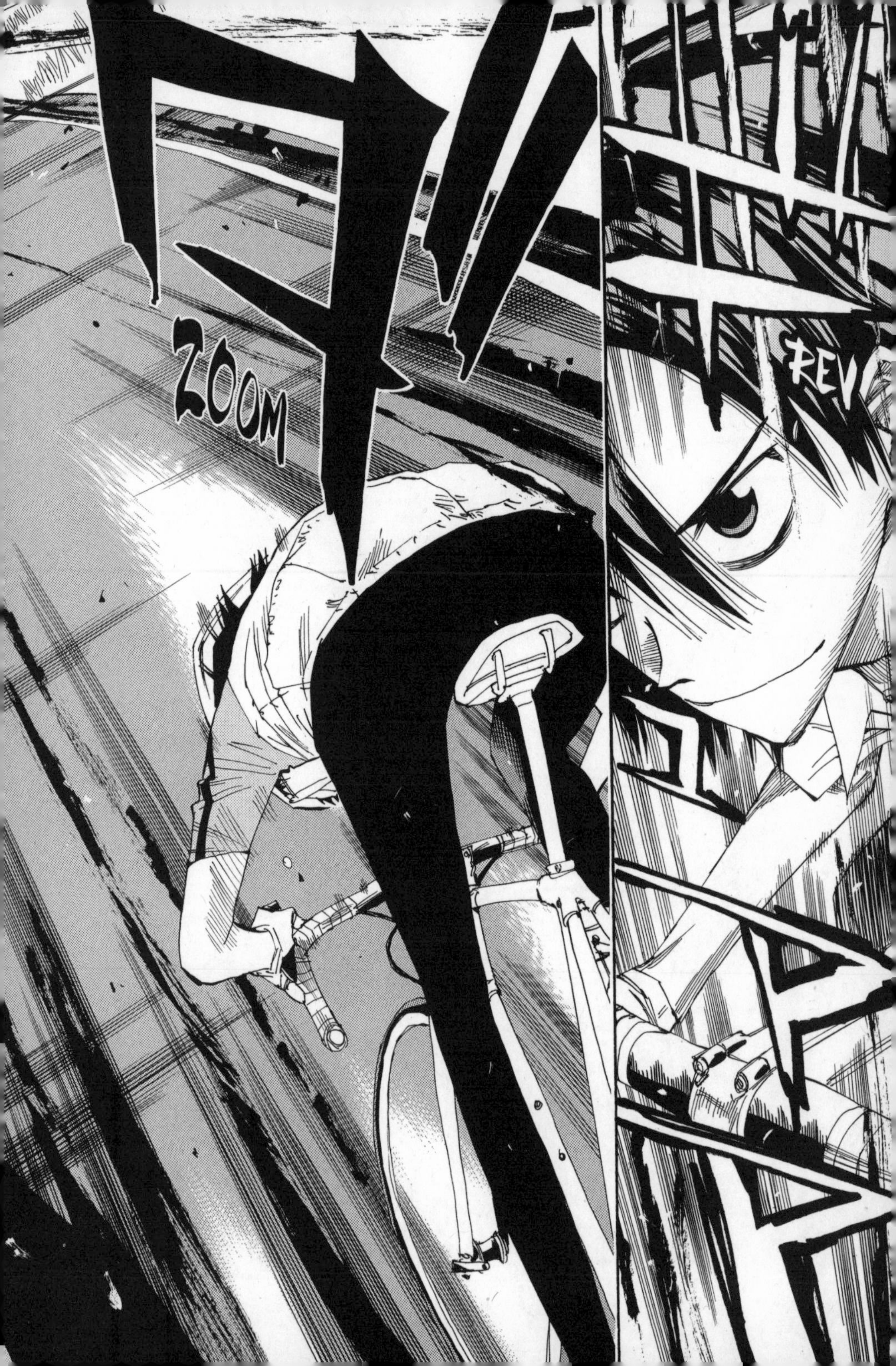
REV
ZOOM

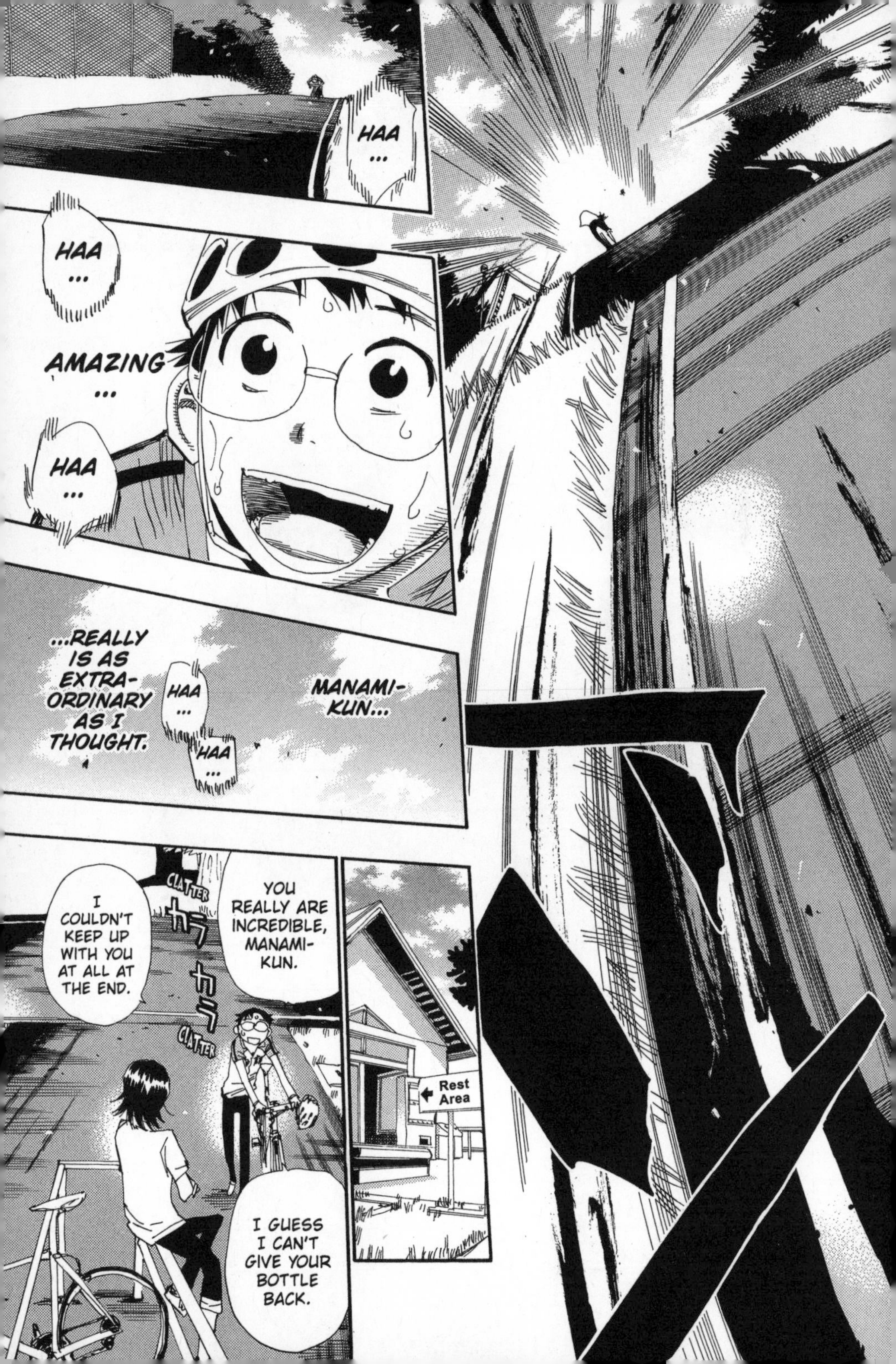

HAA ...
HAA ...
AMAZING ...
HAA ...
MANAMI-KUN...
HAA ...
HAA ...
...REALLY IS AS EXTRA-ORDINARY AS I THOUGHT.
Rest Area
YOU REALLY ARE INCREDIBLE, MANAMI-KUN.
CLATTER カラ
I COULDN'T KEEP UP WITH YOU AT ALL AT THE END.
カラ CLATTER
I GUESS I CAN'T GIVE YOUR BOTTLE BACK.

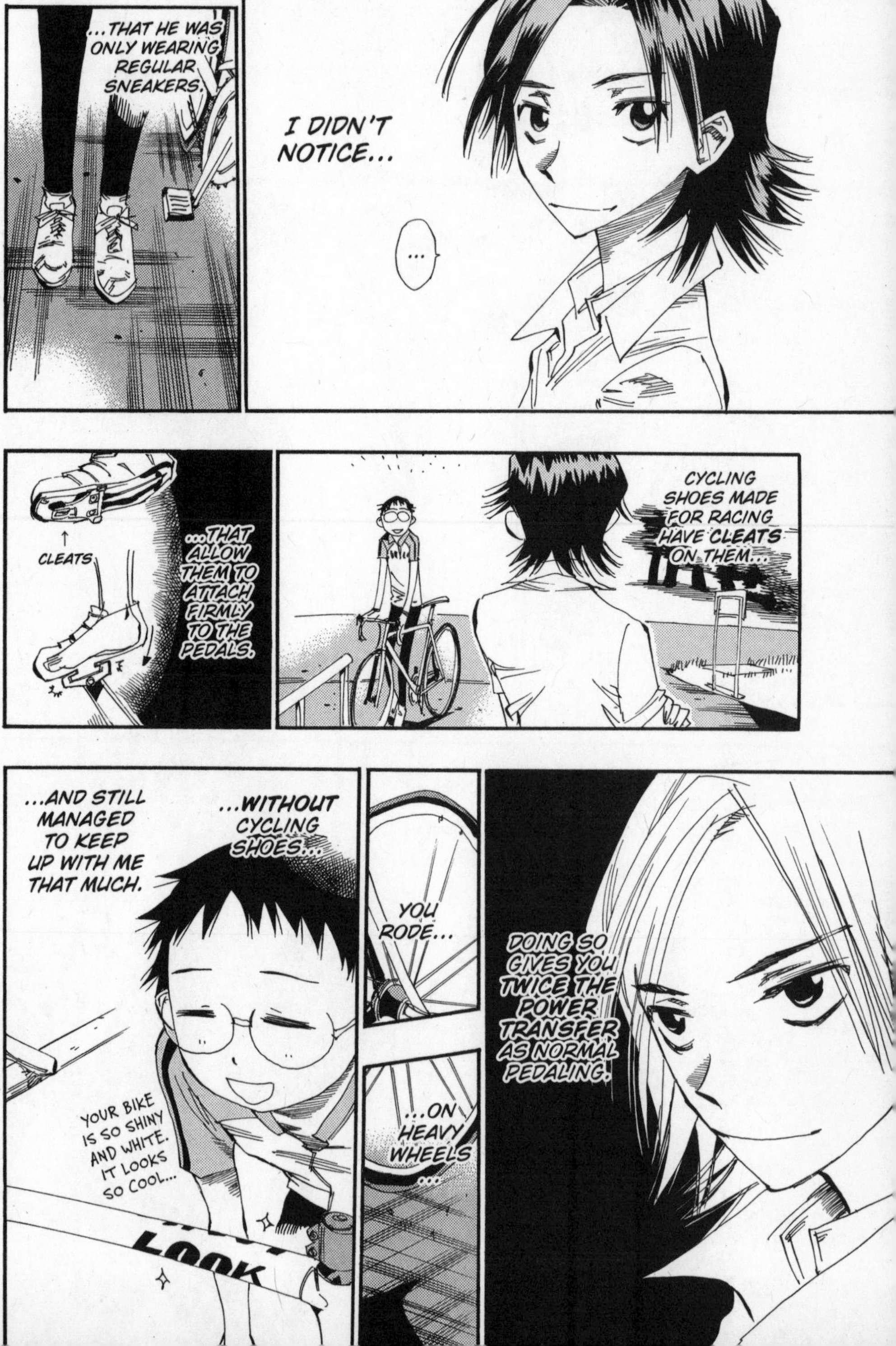
I DIDN'T NOTICE...
...
...THAT HE WAS ONLY WEARING REGULAR SNEAKERS.
CYCLING SHOES MADE FOR RACING HAVE CLEATS ON THEM...
...THAT ALLOW THEM TO ATTACH FIRMLY TO THE PEDALS.
CLEATS
DOING SO GIVES YOU TWICE THE POWER TRANSFER AS NORMAL PEDALING.
YOU RODE...
...ON HEAVY WHEELS...
...WITHOUT CYCLING SHOES...
...AND STILL MANAGED TO KEEP UP WITH ME THAT MUCH.
YOUR BIKE IS SO SHINY AND WHITE. IT LOOKS SO COOL...
LOOK

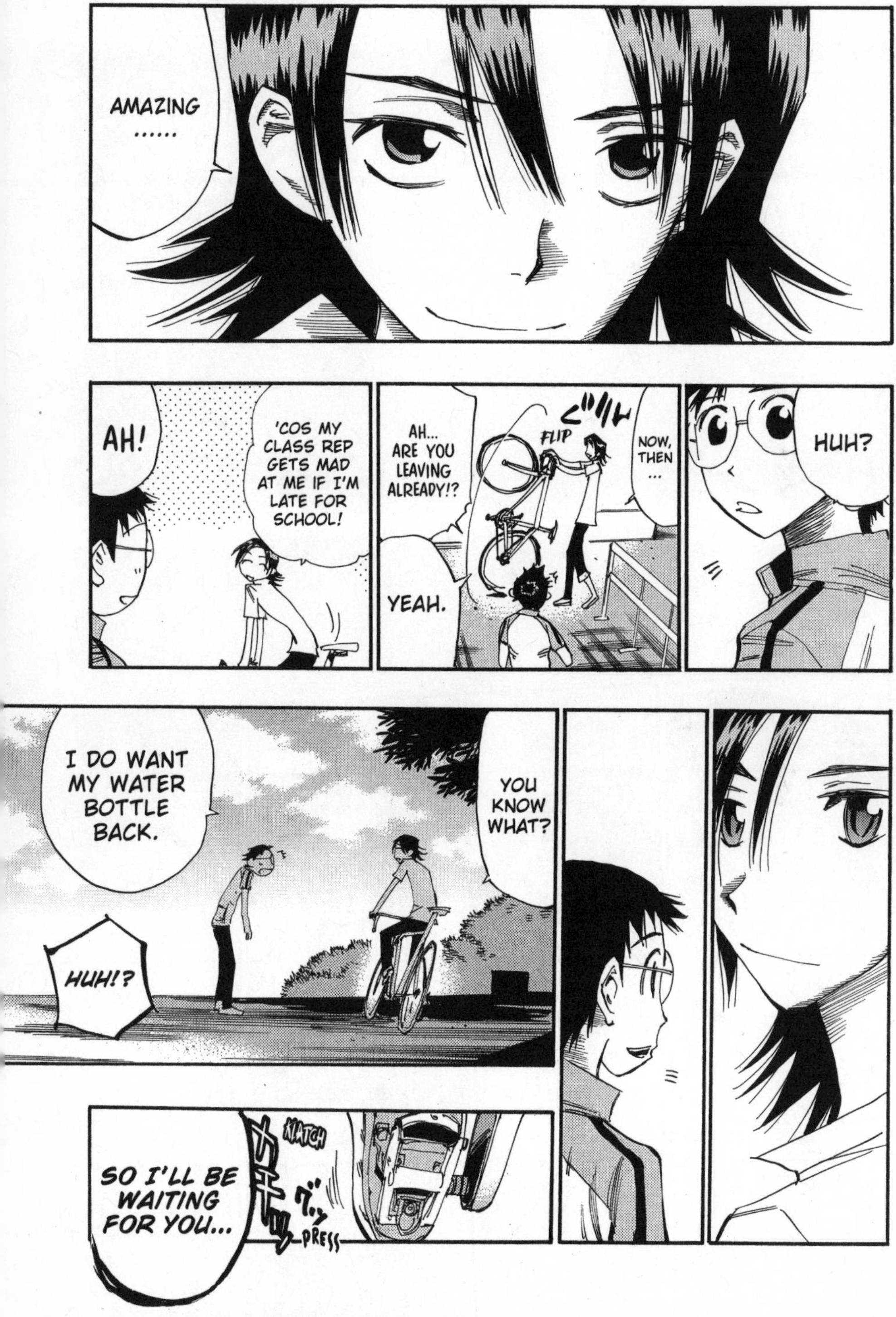
AMAZING ......
HUH?
NOW, THEN ...
FLIP
AH... ARE YOU LEAVING ALREADY!?
YEAH.
'COS MY CLASS REP GETS MAD AT ME IF I'M LATE FOR SCHOOL!
AH!
YOU KNOW WHAT?
I DO WANT MY WATER BOTTLE BACK.
HUH!?
KLATCH
PRESS
SO I'LL BE WAITING FOR YOU...

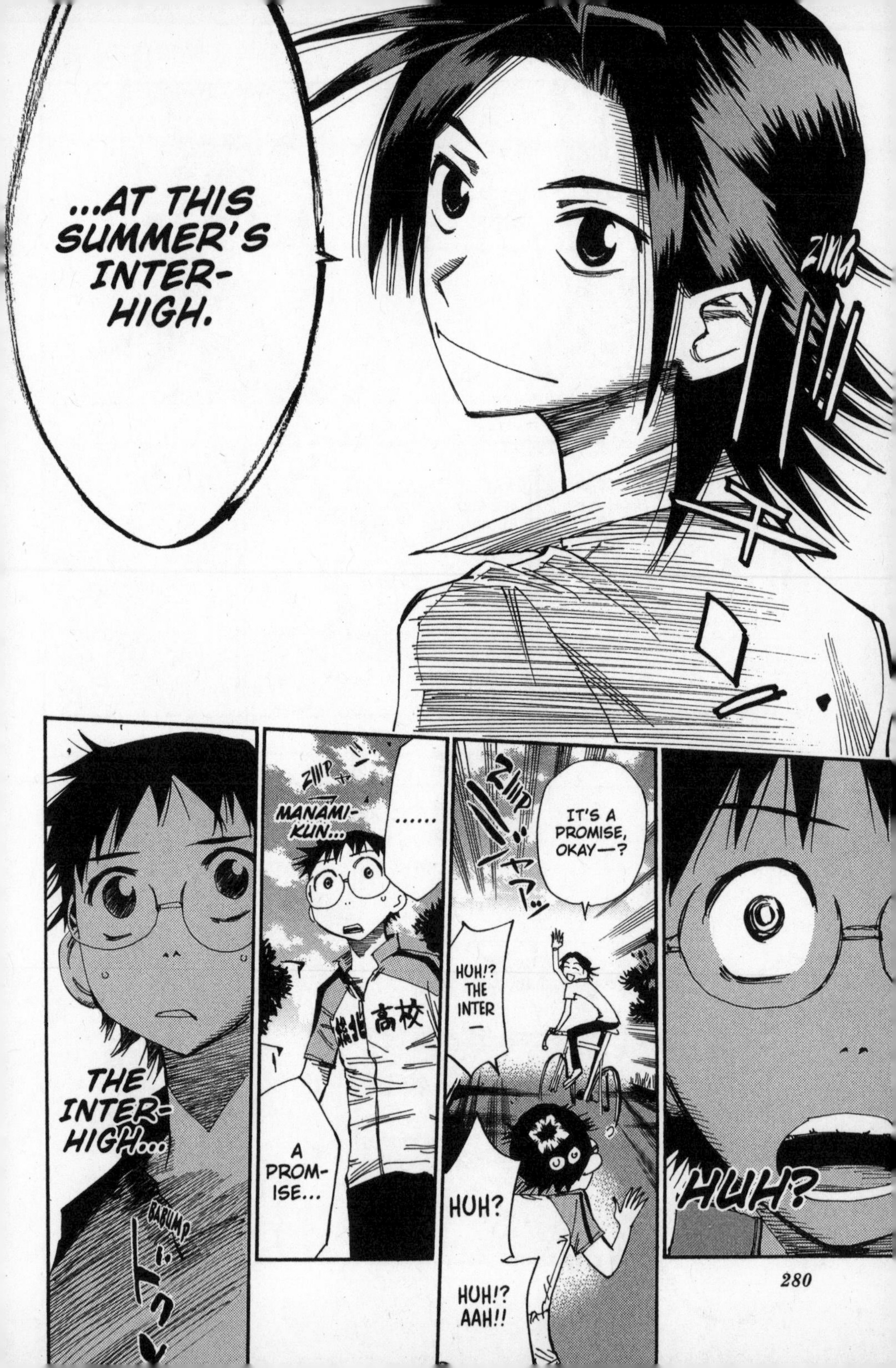
...AT THIS SUMMER'S INTER-HIGH.
ZING
HUH?
ZIIIP
IT'S A PROMISE, OKAY—?
HUH!? THE INTER—
HUH?
HUH!? AAH!!
ZIIIP
MANAMI-KUN...
......
A PROMISE...
THE INTER-HIGH...
BABUMP

RIDE.48 THE INTER-HIGH

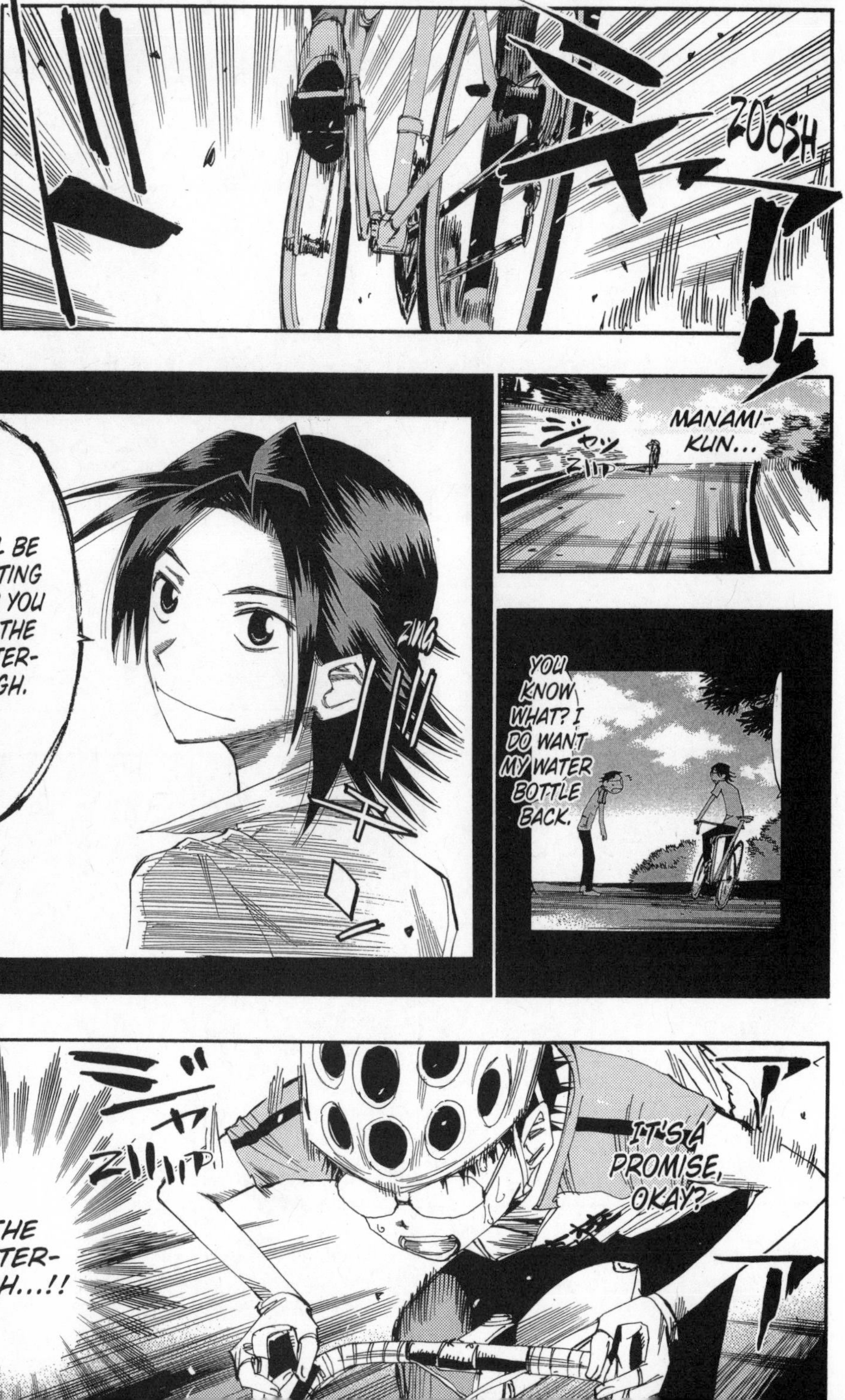
ZOOSH
MANAMI-KUN...
ジャッ
ZIIP
YOU KNOW WHAT? I DO WANT MY WATER BOTTLE BACK.
I'LL BE WAITING FOR YOU AT THE INTER-HIGH.
ZING
IT'S A PROMISE, OKAY?
ジャ
ZIIIIIP
THE INTER-HIGH...!!

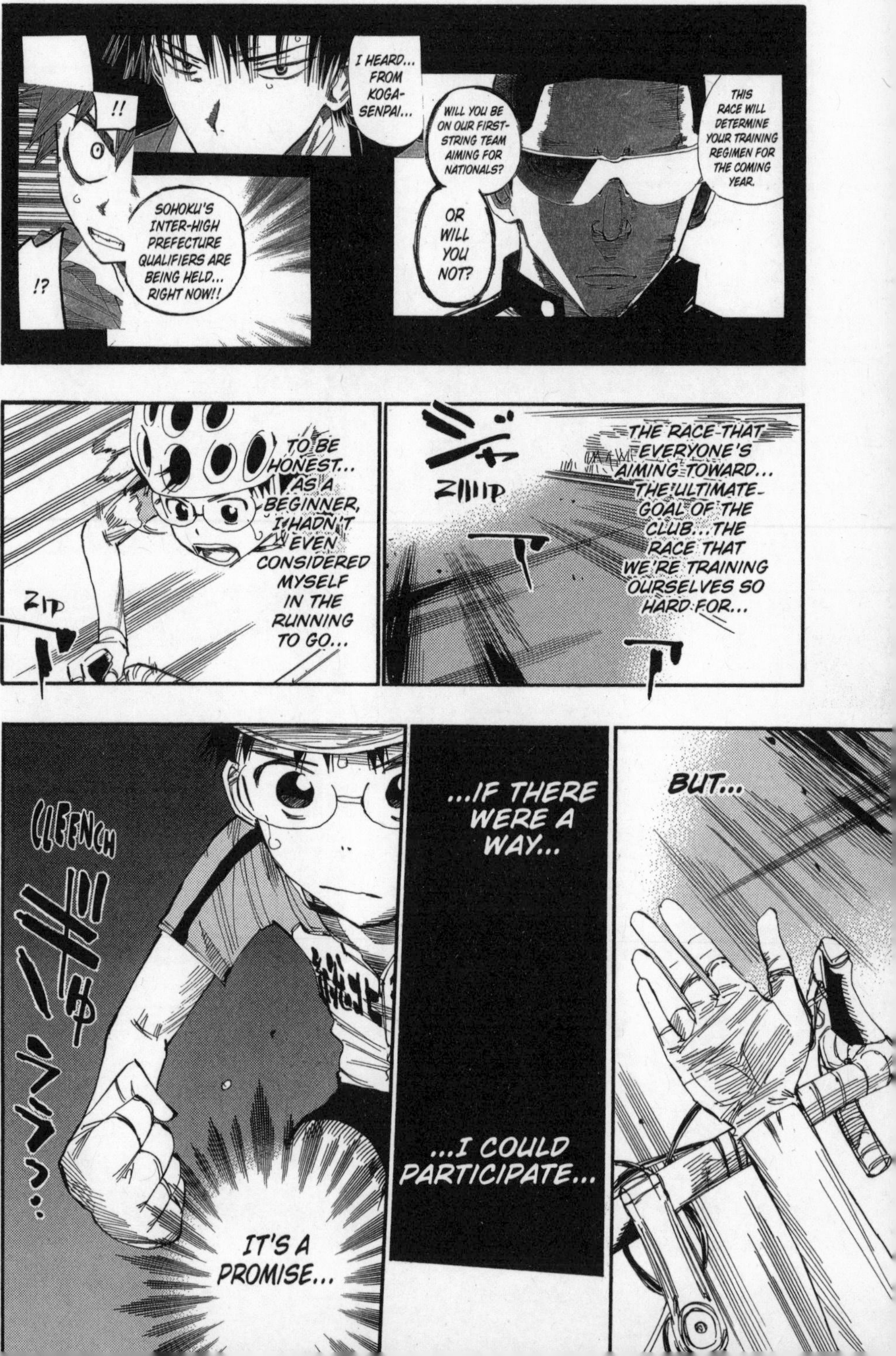
THIS RACE WILL DETERMINE YOUR TRAINING REGIMEN FOR THE COMING YEAR.
WILL YOU BE ON OUR FIRST-STRING TEAM AIMING FOR NATIONALS?
OR WILL YOU NOT?
I HEARD... FROM KOGA-SENPAI...
!!
SOHOKU'S INTER-HIGH PREFECTURE QUALIFIERS ARE BEING HELD... RIGHT NOW!!
!?
ZIIIP
THE RACE THAT EVERYONE'S AIMING TOWARD... THE ULTIMATE GOAL OF THE CLUB... THE RACE THAT WE'RE TRAINING OURSELVES SO HARD FOR...
TO BE HONEST... AS A BEGINNER, I HADN'T EVEN CONSIDERED MYSELF IN THE RUNNING TO GO...
ZIP
BUT...
...IF THERE WERE A WAY...
...I COULD PARTICIPATE...
CLEENCH
IT'S A PROMISE...

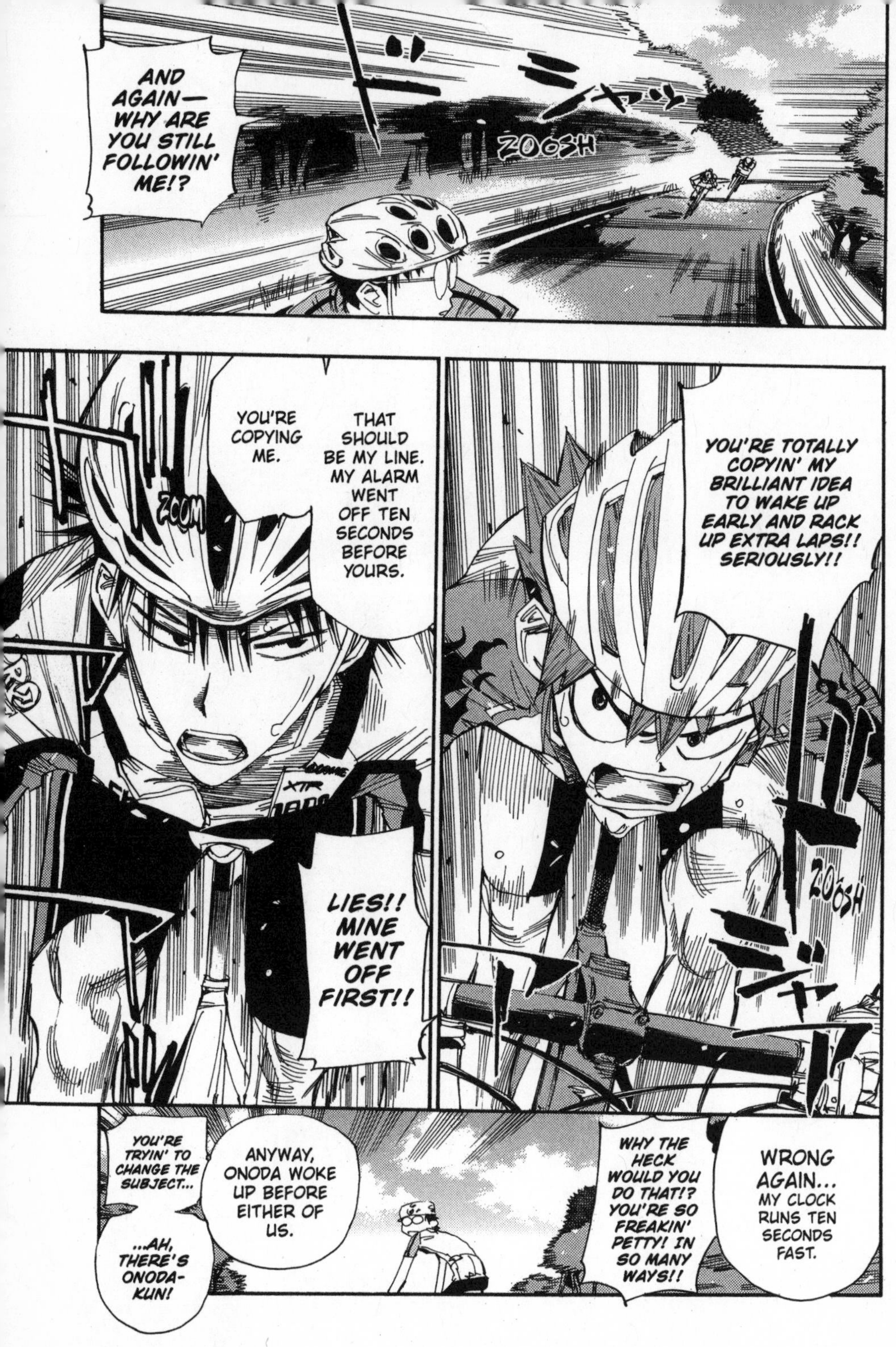
AND AGAIN— WHY ARE YOU STILL FOLLOWIN' ME!?
ZOOSH
YOU'RE TOTALLY COPYIN' MY BRILLIANT IDEA TO WAKE UP EARLY AND RACK UP EXTRA LAPS!! SERIOUSLY!!
ZOOSH
THAT SHOULD BE MY LINE. MY ALARM WENT OFF TEN SECONDS BEFORE YOURS.
YOU'RE COPYING ME.
ZOOM
LIES!! MINE WENT OFF FIRST!!
WRONG AGAIN... MY CLOCK RUNS TEN SECONDS FAST.
WHY THE HECK WOULD YOU DO THAT!? YOU'RE SO FREAKIN' PETTY! IN SO MANY WAYS!!
ANYWAY, ONODA WOKE UP BEFORE EITHER OF US.
YOU'RE TRYIN' TO CHANGE THE SUBJECT...
...AH, THERE'S ONODA-KUN!

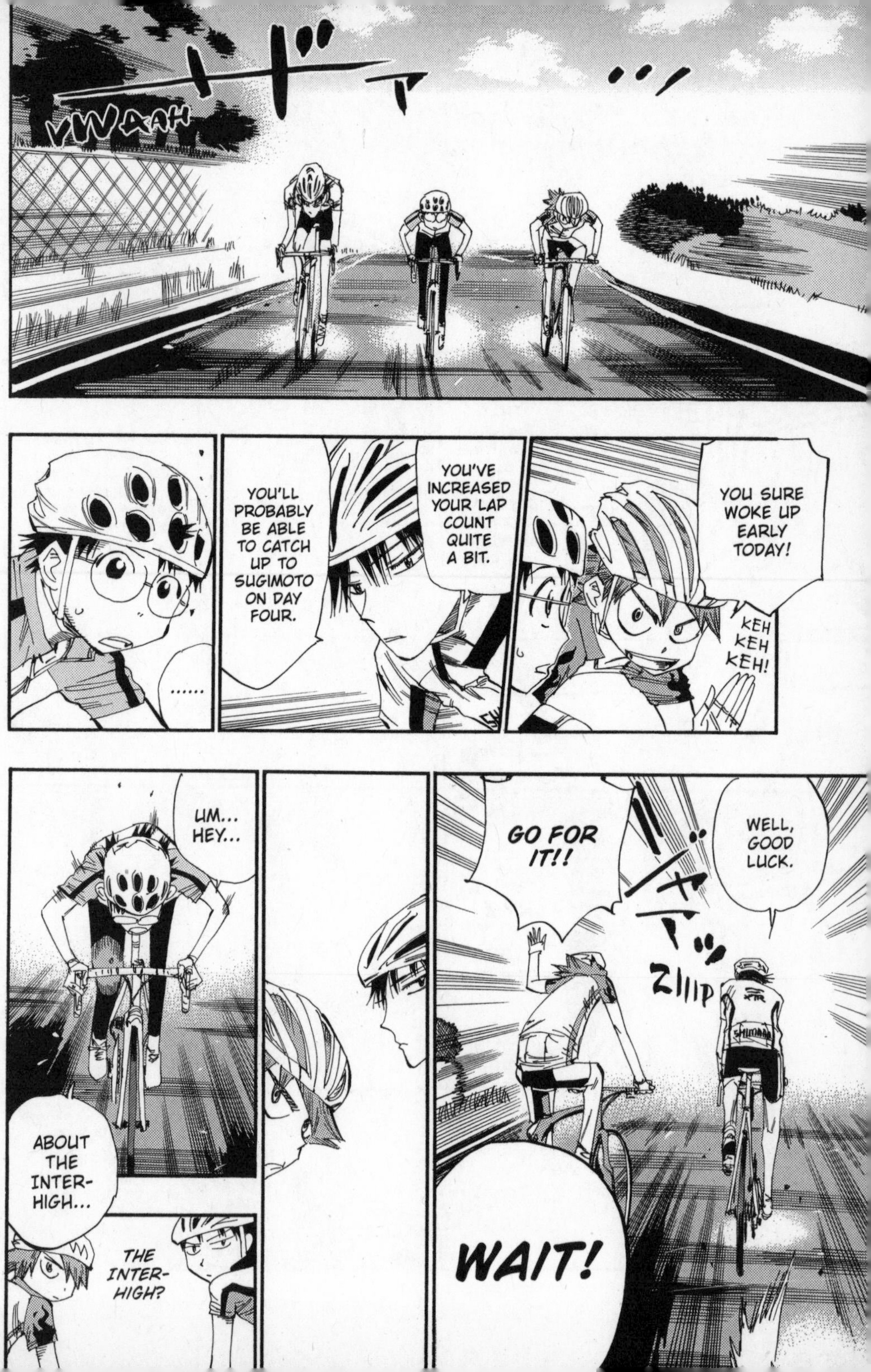
VWAAH
YOU SURE WOKE UP EARLY TODAY!
KEH KEH KEH!
YOU'VE INCREASED YOUR LAP COUNT QUITE A BIT.
YOU'LL PROBABLY BE ABLE TO CATCH UP TO SUGIMOTO ON DAY FOUR.
......
WELL, GOOD LUCK.
GO FOR IT!!
ZIIIP
WAIT!
UM... HEY...
ABOUT THE INTER-HIGH...
THE INTER-HIGH?

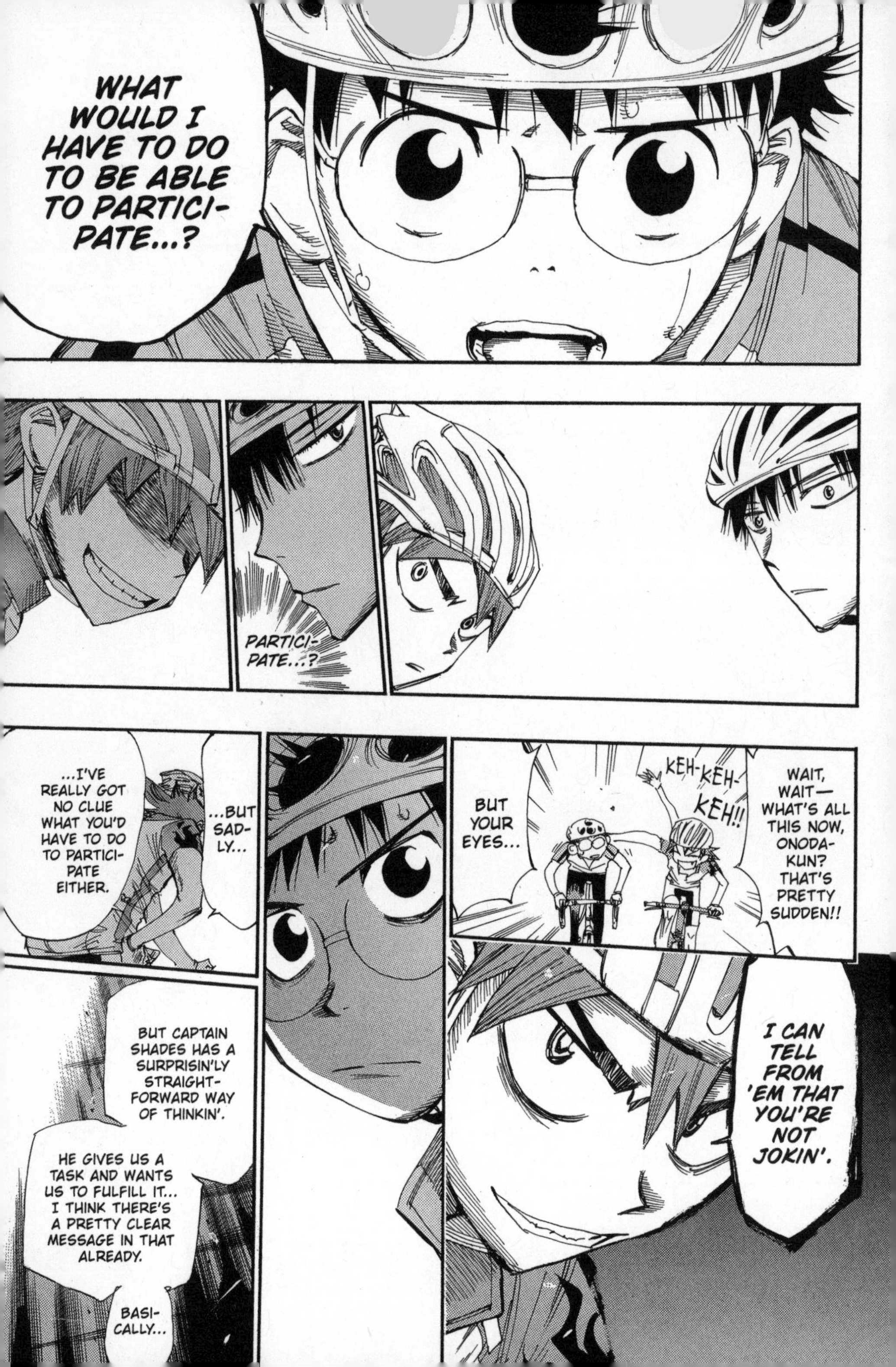
WHAT WOULD I HAVE TO DO TO BE ABLE TO PARTICIPATE...?
PARTICIPATE...?
WAIT, WAIT— WHAT'S ALL THIS NOW, ONODA-KUN? THAT'S PRETTY SUDDEN!!
KEH-KEH-KEH!!
BUT YOUR EYES...
I CAN TELL FROM 'EM THAT YOU'RE NOT JOKIN'.
...BUT SADLY...
...I'VE REALLY GOT NO CLUE WHAT YOU'D HAVE TO DO TO PARTICIPATE EITHER.
BUT CAPTAIN SHADES HAS A SURPRISIN'LY STRAIGHTFORWARD WAY OF THINKIN'.
HE GIVES US A TASK AND WANTS US TO FULFILL IT... I THINK THERE'S A PRETTY CLEAR MESSAGE IN THAT ALREADY.
BASICALLY...

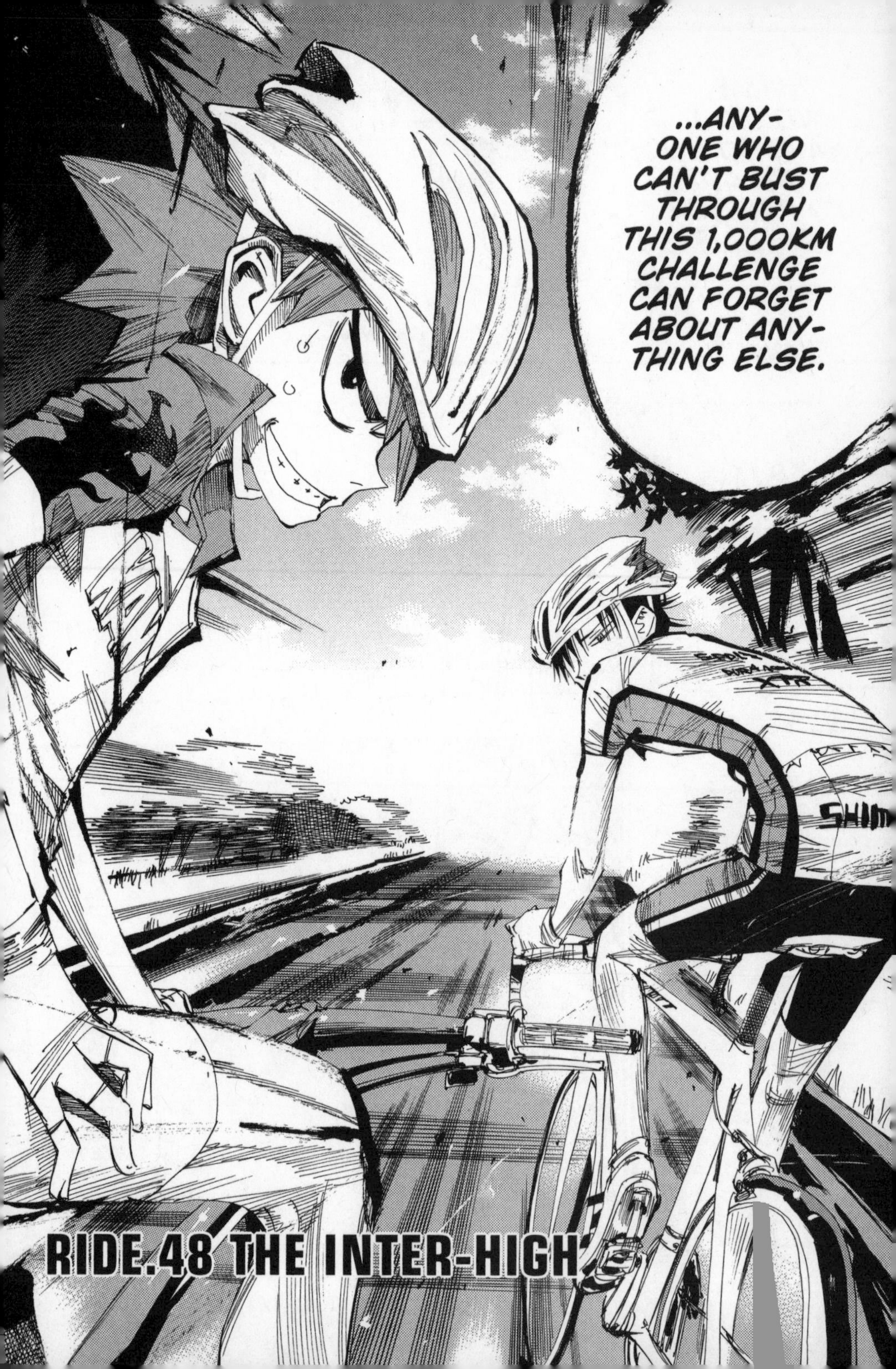
...ANYONE WHO CAN'T BUST THROUGH THIS 1,000KM CHALLENGE CAN FORGET ABOUT ANYTHING ELSE.
RIDE.48 THE INTER-HIGH
SHIM

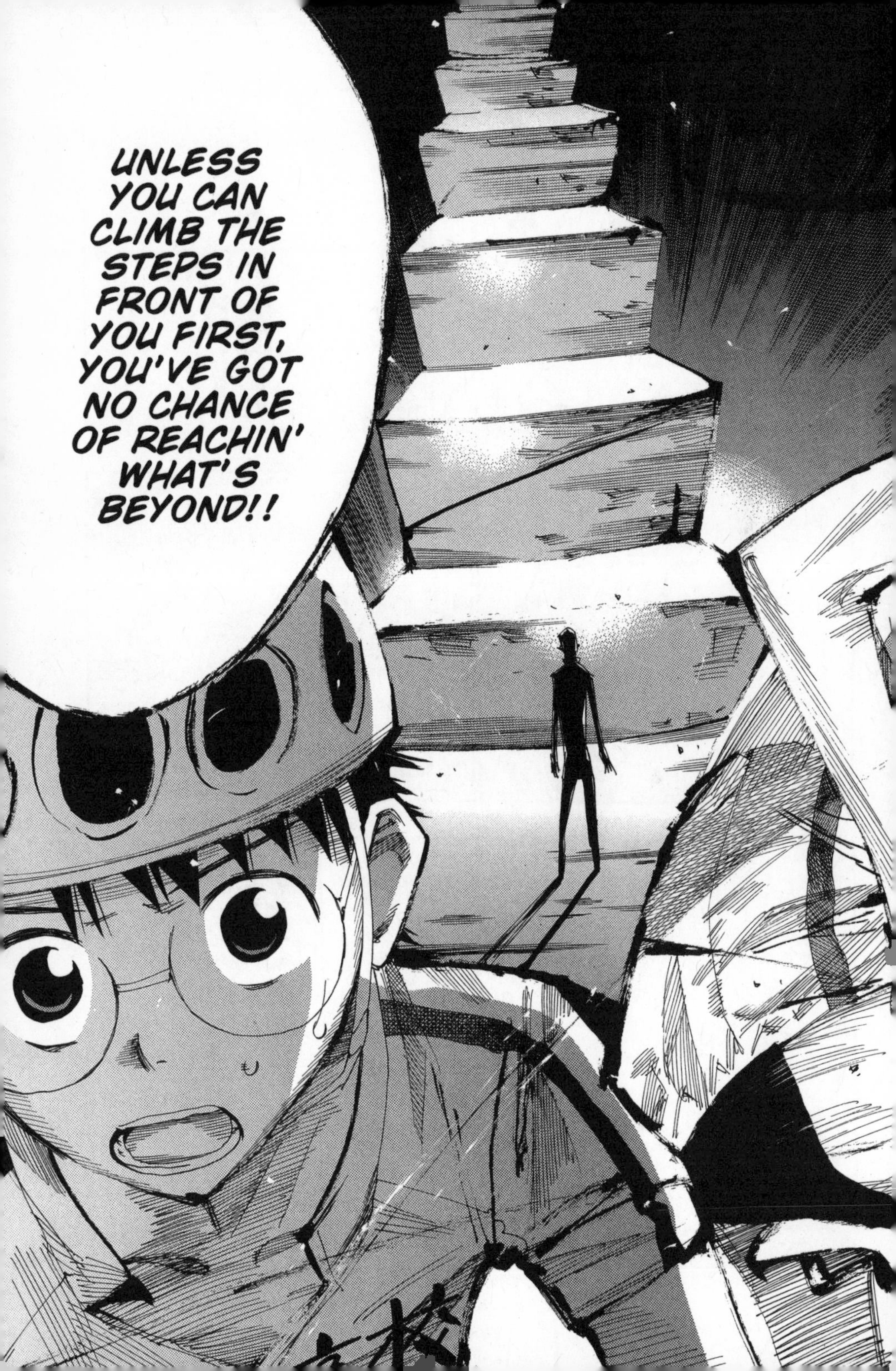
UNLESS YOU CAN CLIMB THE STEPS IN FRONT OF YOU FIRST, YOU'VE GOT NO CHANCE OF REACHIN' WHAT'S BEYOND!!

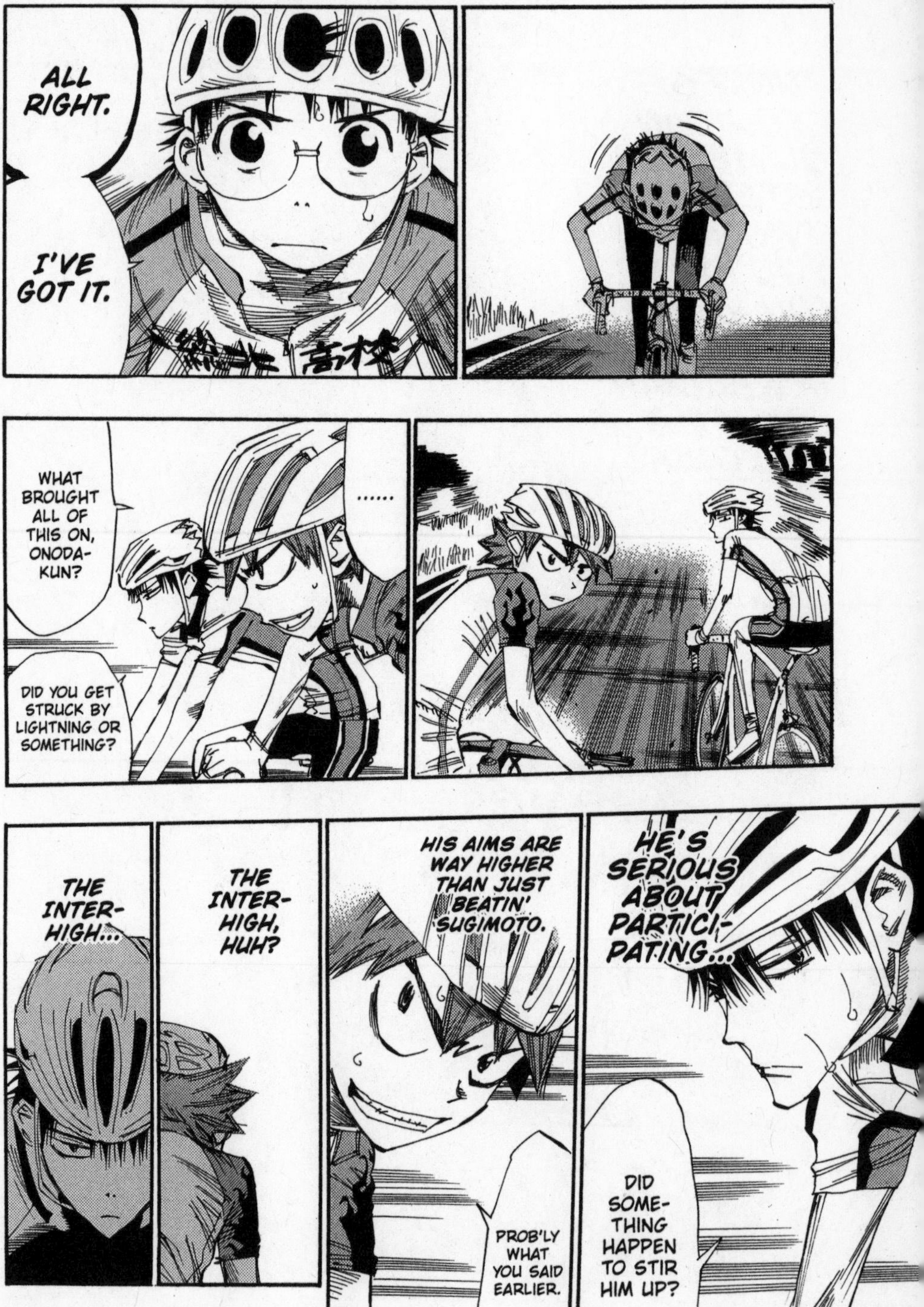
ALL RIGHT.
I'VE GOT IT.
......
WHAT BROUGHT ALL OF THIS ON, ONODA-KUN?
DID YOU GET STRUCK BY LIGHTNING OR SOMETHING?
HE'S SERIOUS ABOUT PARTICIPATING...
DID SOMETHING HAPPEN TO STIR HIM UP?
HIS AIMS ARE WAY HIGHER THAN JUST BEATIN' SUGIMOTO.
PROB'LY WHAT YOU SAID EARLIER.
THE INTER-HIGH, HUH?
THE INTER-HIGH...

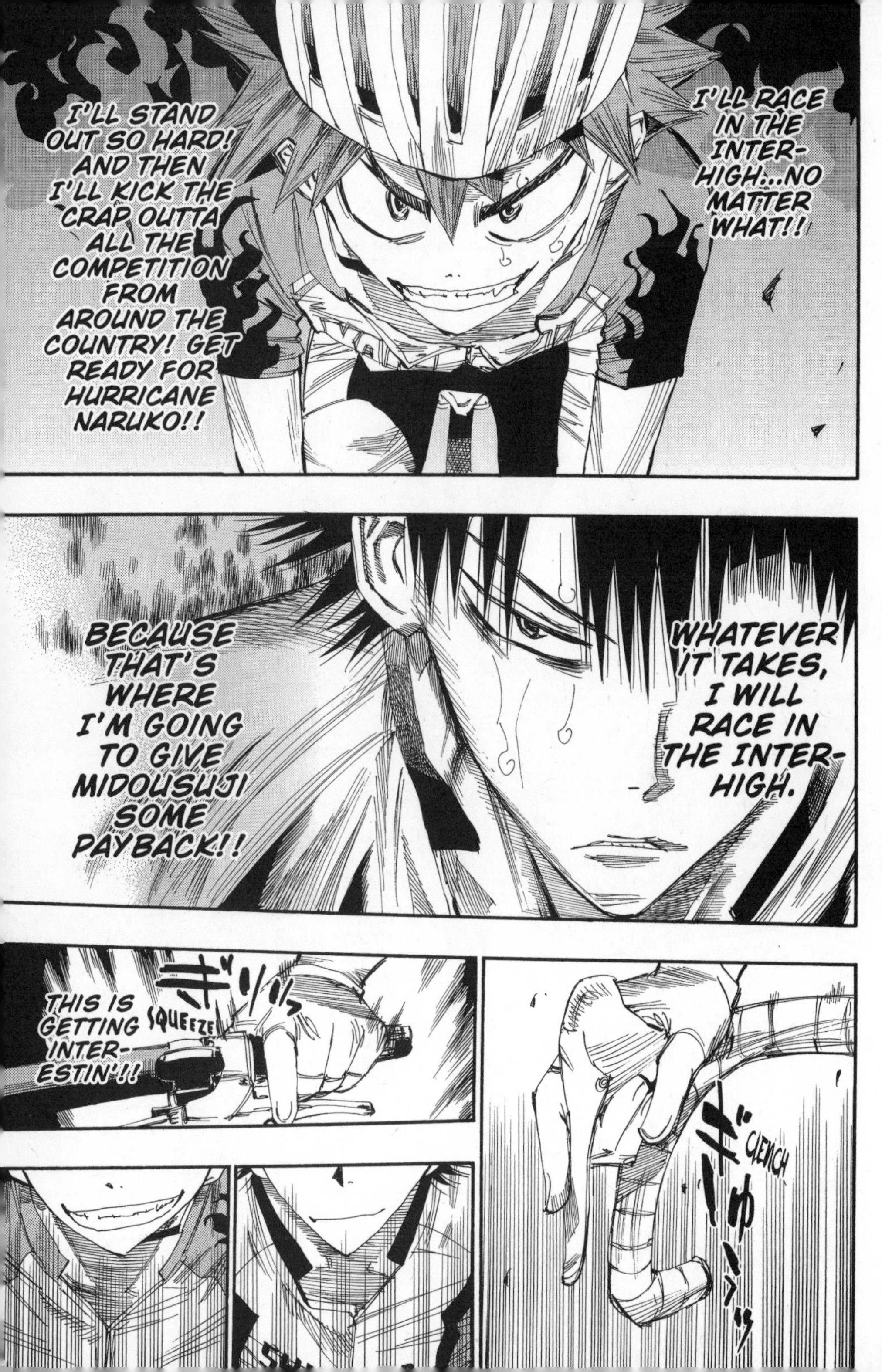
I'LL RACE IN THE INTER-HIGH...NO MATTER WHAT!!
I'LL STAND OUT SO HARD! AND THEN I'LL KICK THE CRAP OUTTA ALL THE COMPETITION FROM AROUND THE COUNTRY! GET READY FOR HURRICANE NARUKO!!
WHATEVER IT TAKES, I WILL RACE IN THE INTER-HIGH.
BECAUSE THAT'S WHERE I'M GOING TO GIVE MIDOUSUJI SOME PAYBACK!!
CLENCH
SQUEEZE
THIS IS GETTING INTER-ESTIN'!!

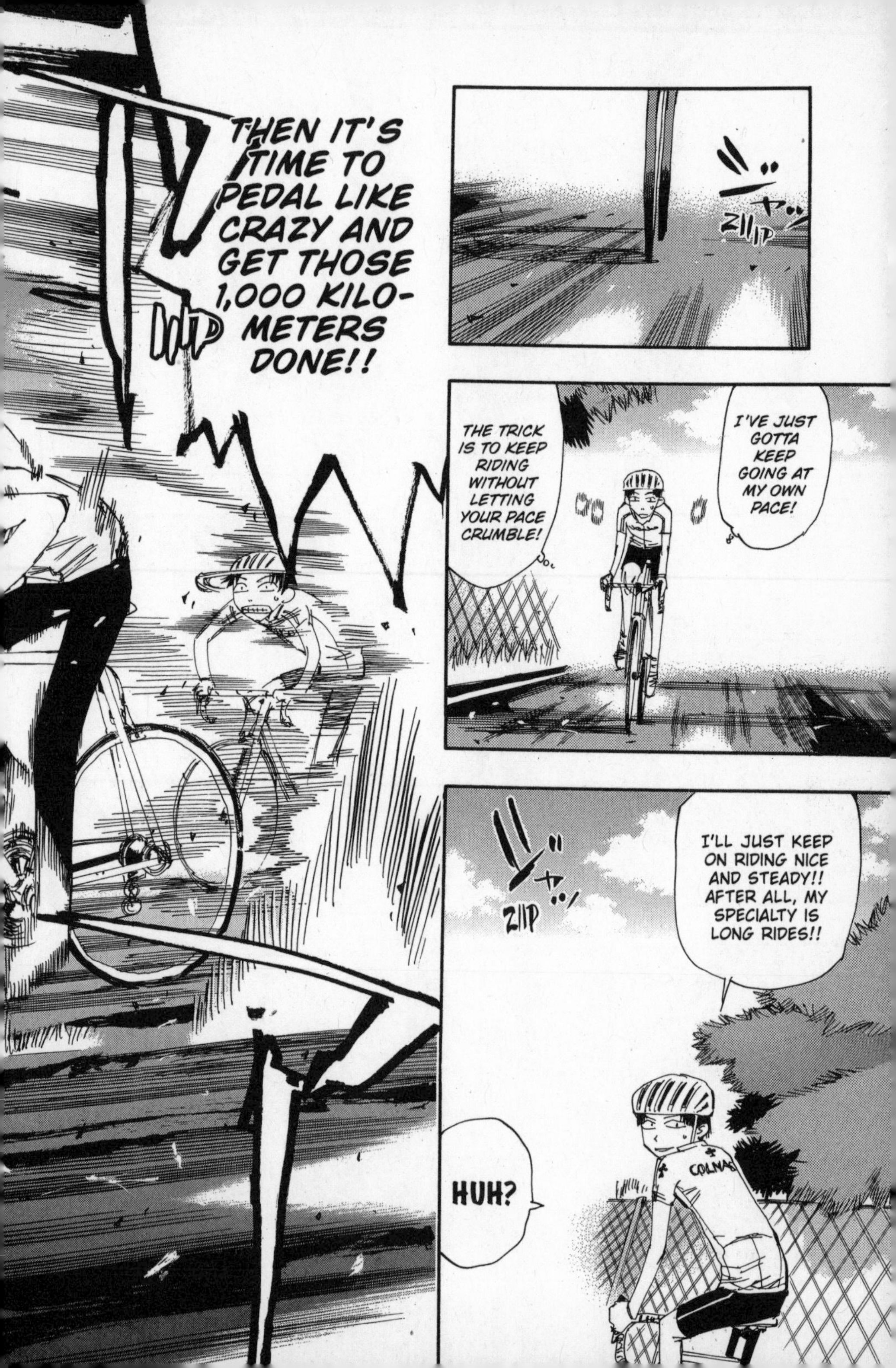
ZIIP
I'VE JUST GOTTA KEEP GOING AT MY OWN PACE!
THE TRICK IS TO KEEP RIDING WITHOUT LETTING YOUR PACE CRUMBLE!
ZIIP
I'LL JUST KEEP ON RIDING NICE AND STEADY!! AFTER ALL, MY SPECIALTY IS LONG RIDES!!
HUH?
COLNAGO
THEN IT'S TIME TO PEDAL LIKE CRAZY AND GET THOSE 1,000 KILOMETERS DONE!!

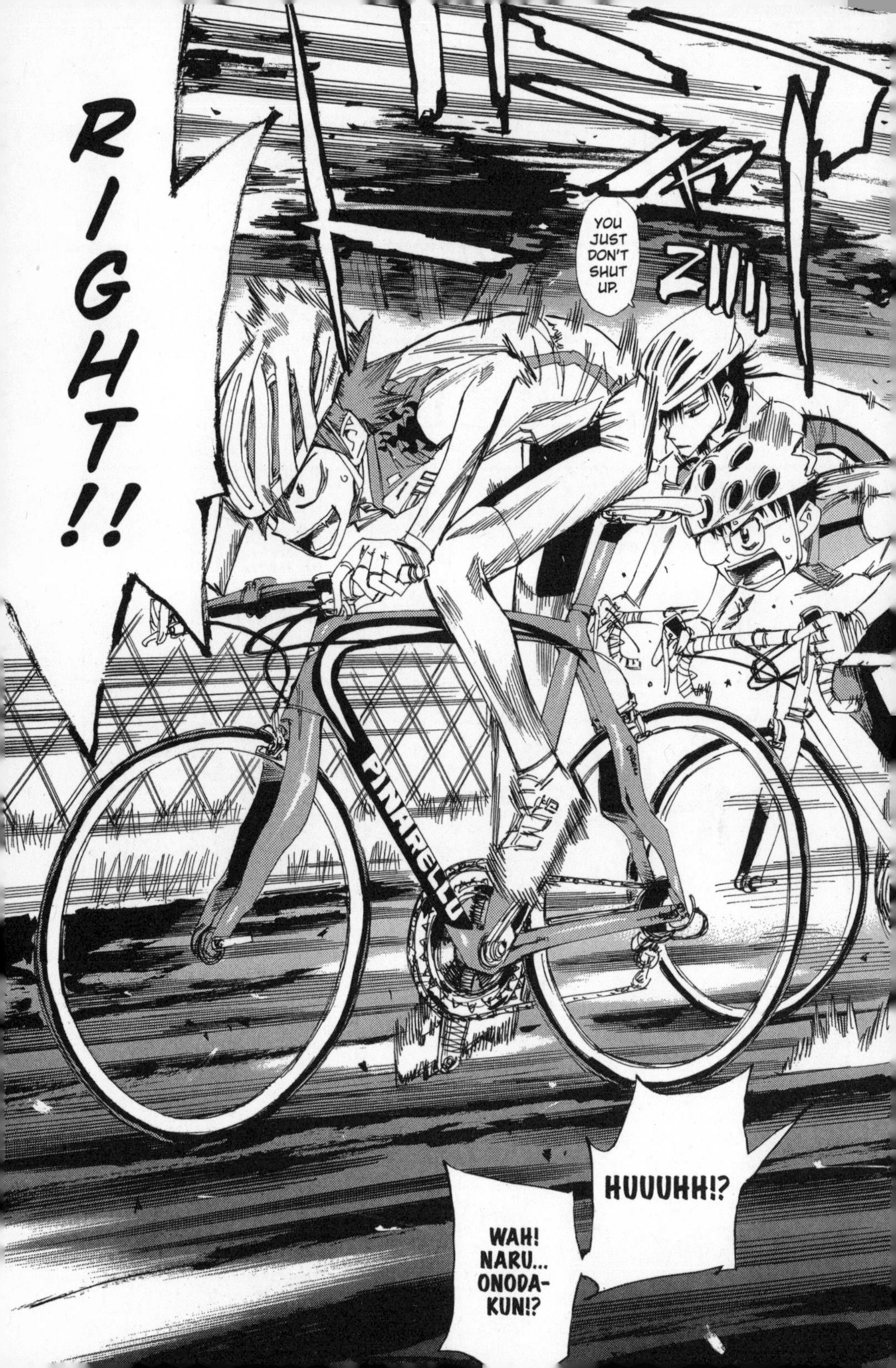
YOU JUST DON'T SHUT UP.
RIGHT!!
HUUUHH!?
WAH! NARU... ONODA-KUN!?

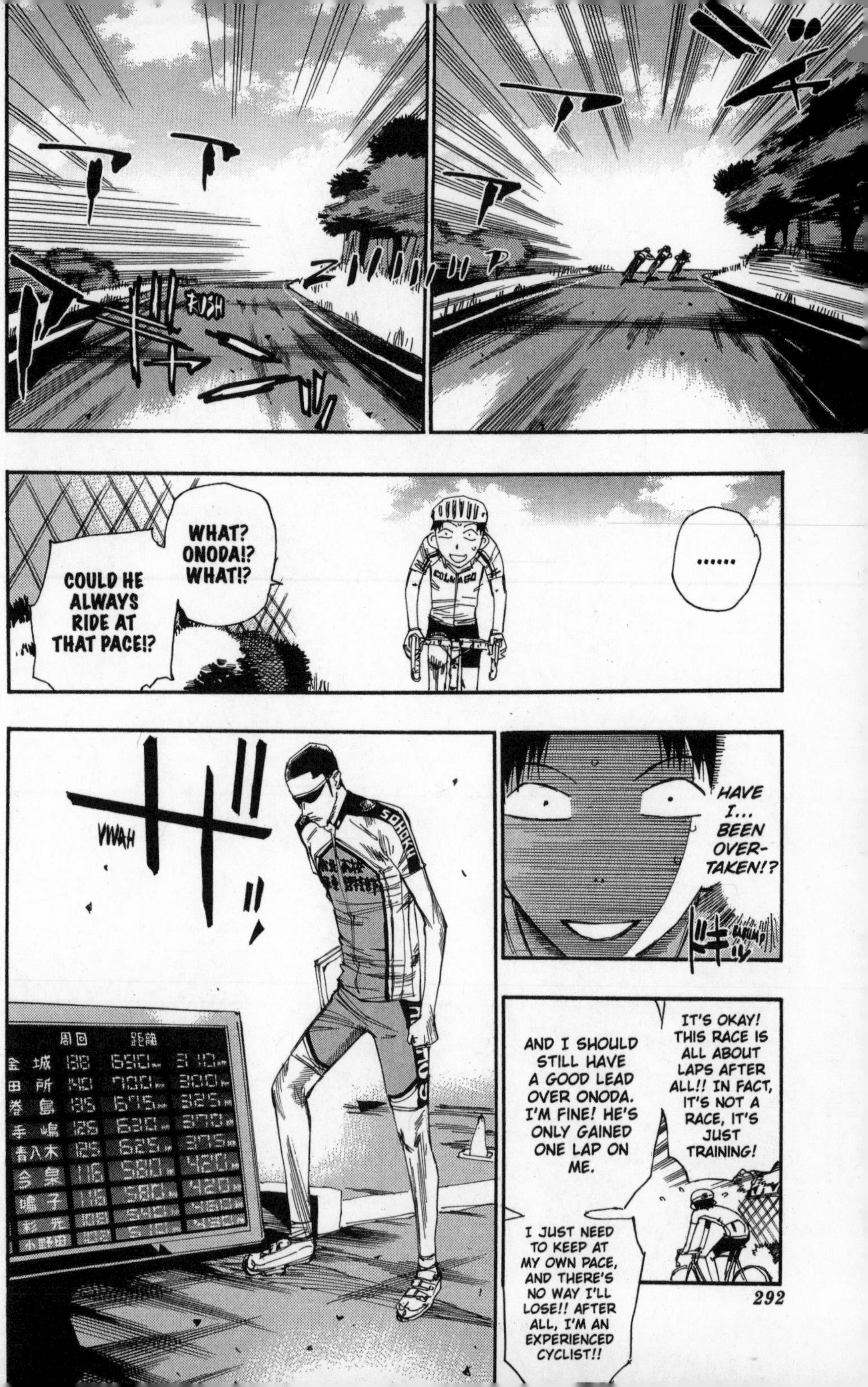
RUSH
......
WHAT? ONODA!? WHAT!?
COULD HE ALWAYS RIDE AT THAT PACE!?
HAVE I... BEEN OVER-TAKEN!?
BABUMP
VWAH
IT'S OKAY! THIS RACE IS ALL ABOUT LAPS AFTER ALL!! IN FACT, IT'S NOT A RACE, IT'S JUST TRAINING!
AND I SHOULD STILL HAVE A GOOD LEAD OVER ONODA. I'M FINE! HE'S ONLY GAINED ONE LAP ON ME.
I JUST NEED TO KEEP AT MY OWN PACE, AND THERE'S NO WAY I'LL LOSE!! AFTER ALL, I'M AN EXPERIENCED CYCLIST!!

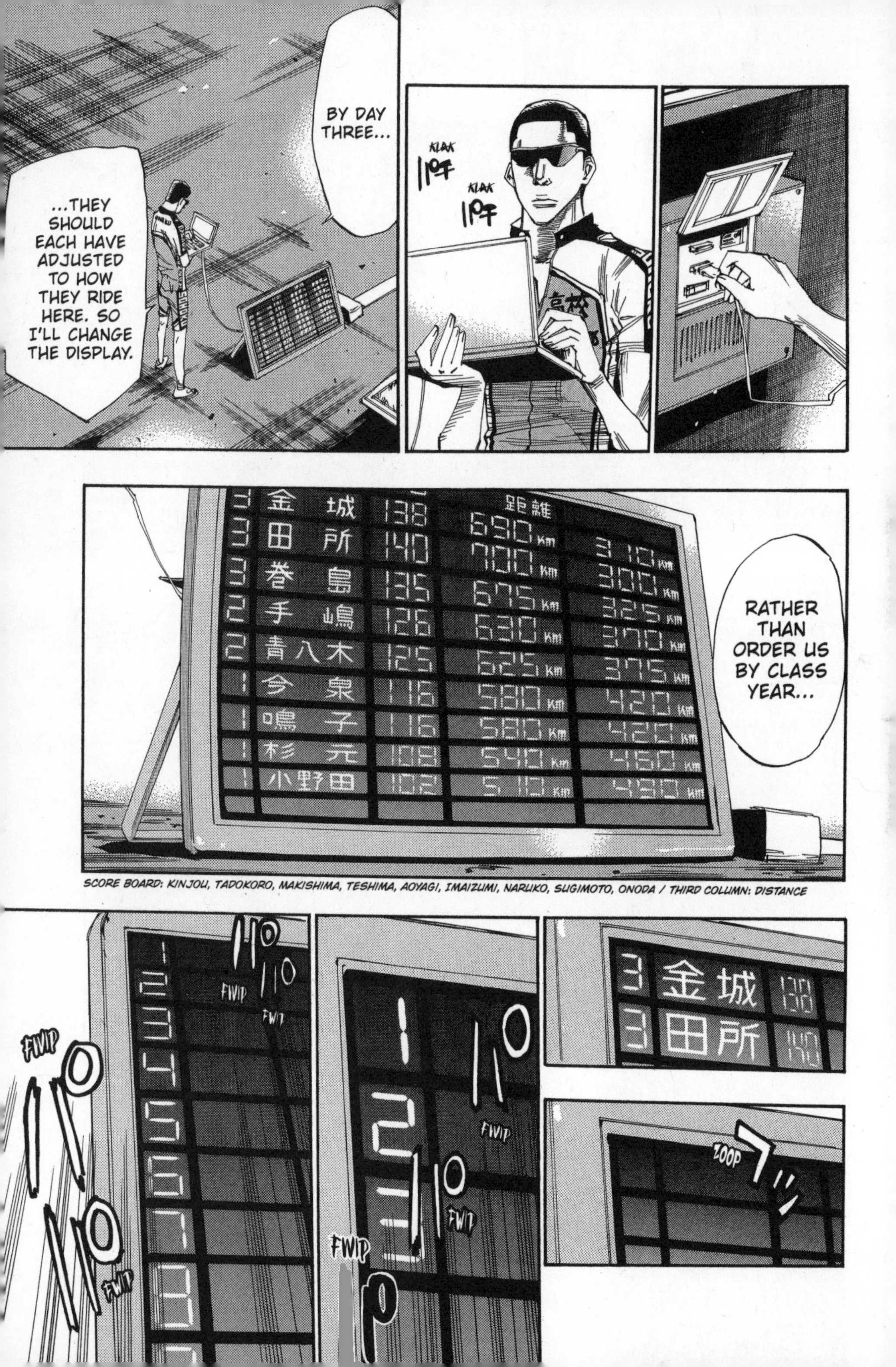
KLAK
KLAK
BY DAY THREE...
...THEY SHOULD EACH HAVE ADJUSTED TO HOW THEY RIDE HERE. SO I'LL CHANGE THE DISPLAY.
RATHER THAN ORDER US BY CLASS YEAR...
距離
3 金城 138 690 km 310 km
3 田所 140 700 km 300 km
3 巻島 135 675 km 325 km
2 手嶋 126 630 km 370 km
2 青八木 125 625 km 375 km
1 今泉 116 580 km 420 km
1 鳴子 116 580 km 420 km
1 杉元 108 540 km 460 km
1 小野田 102 510 km 490 km
3 金城 138
3 田所 140
ZOOP
FWIP
FWIP
FWIP
FWIP
FWIP
FWIP
FWIP
SCORE BOARD: KINJOU, TADOKORO, MAKISHIMA, TESHIMA, AOYAGI, IMAIZUMI, NARUKO, SUGIMOTO, ONODA / THIRD COLUMN: DISTANCE

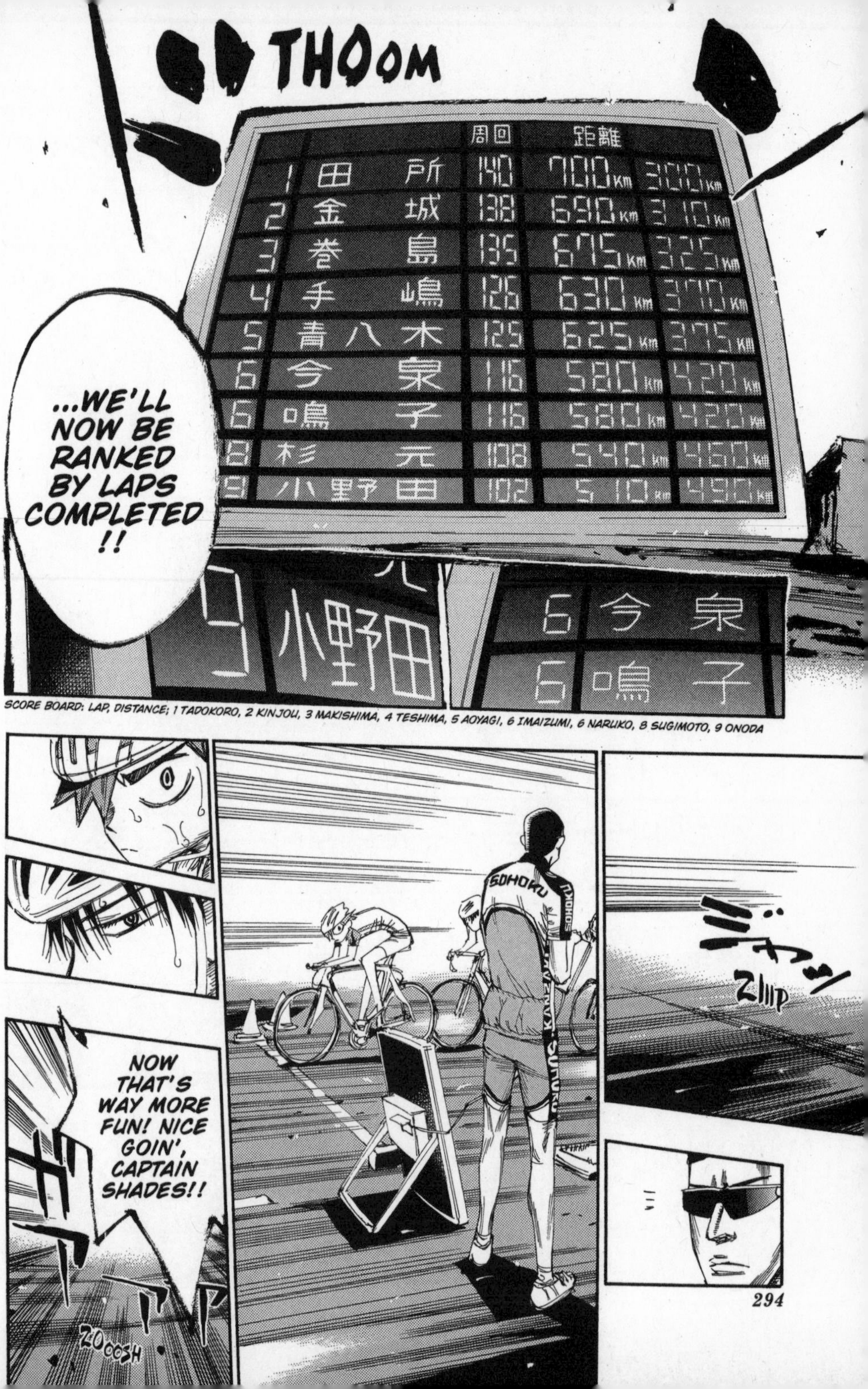
THOOM
周回 距離
1 田所 140 700km 300km
2 金城 138 690km 310km
3 巻島 135 675km 325km
4 手嶋 126 630km 370km
5 青八木 125 625km 375km
6 今泉 116 580km 420km
6 鳴子 116 580km 420km
8 杉元 108 540km 460km
9 小野田 102 510km 490km
...WE'LL NOW BE RANKED BY LAPS COMPLETED!!
9 小野田
6 今泉
6 鳴子
SCORE BOARD: LAP, DISTANCE; 1 TADOKORO, 2 KINJOU, 3 MAKISHIMA, 4 TESHIMA, 5 AOYAGI, 6 IMAIZUMI, 6 NARUKO, 8 SUGIMOTO, 9 ONODA
ジャッ
ZIIP
SOHOKU
NOW THAT'S WAY MORE FUN! NICE GOIN', CAPTAIN SHADES!!
ZOOOSH

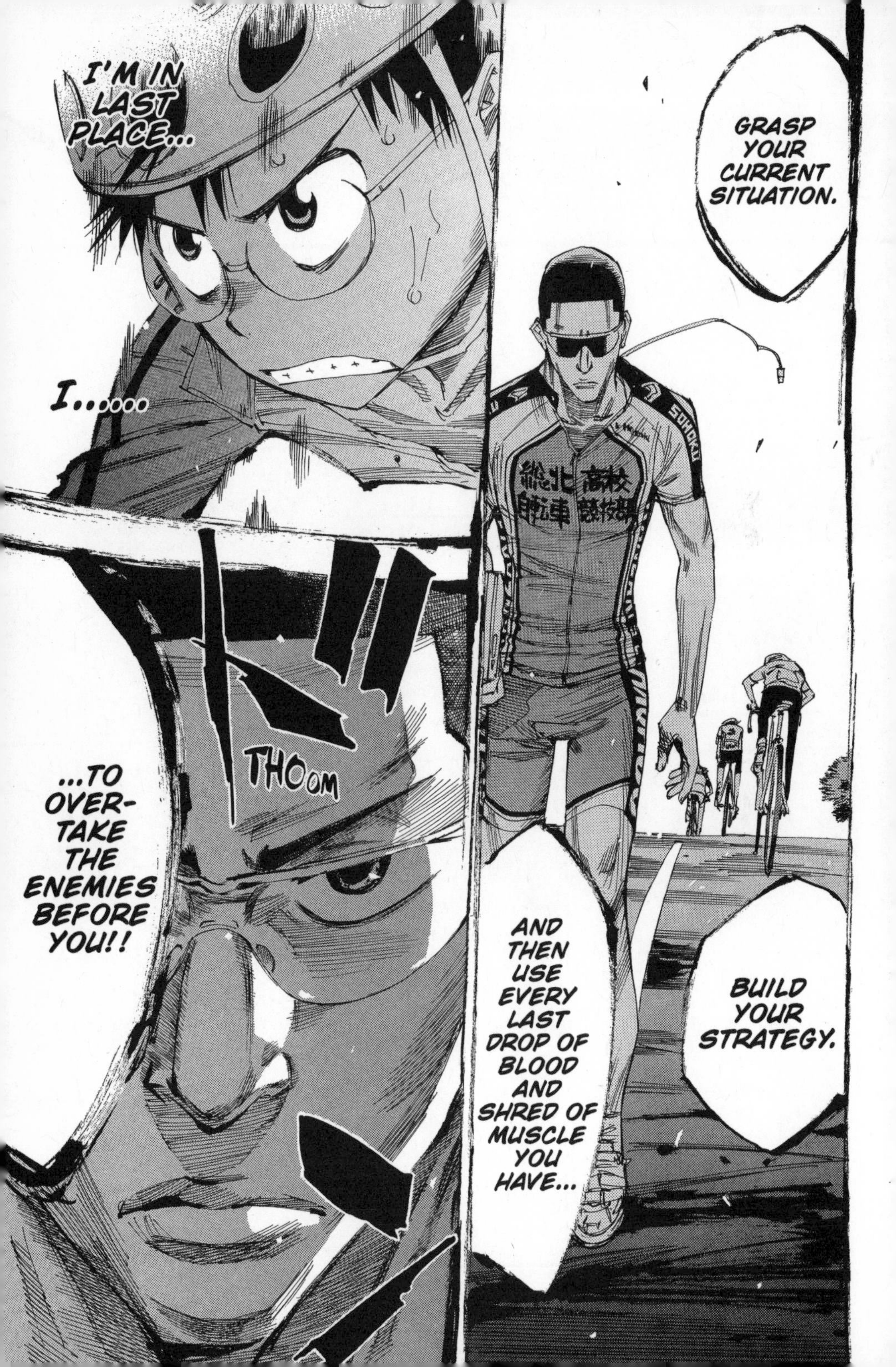
GRASP YOUR CURRENT SITUATION.
総北高校
自転車競技部
SOHOKU
BUILD YOUR STRATEGY.
AND THEN USE EVERY LAST DROP OF BLOOD AND SHRED OF MUSCLE YOU HAVE...
I'M IN LAST PLACE...
I.......
THOOM
...TO OVER-TAKE THE ENEMIES BEFORE YOU!!

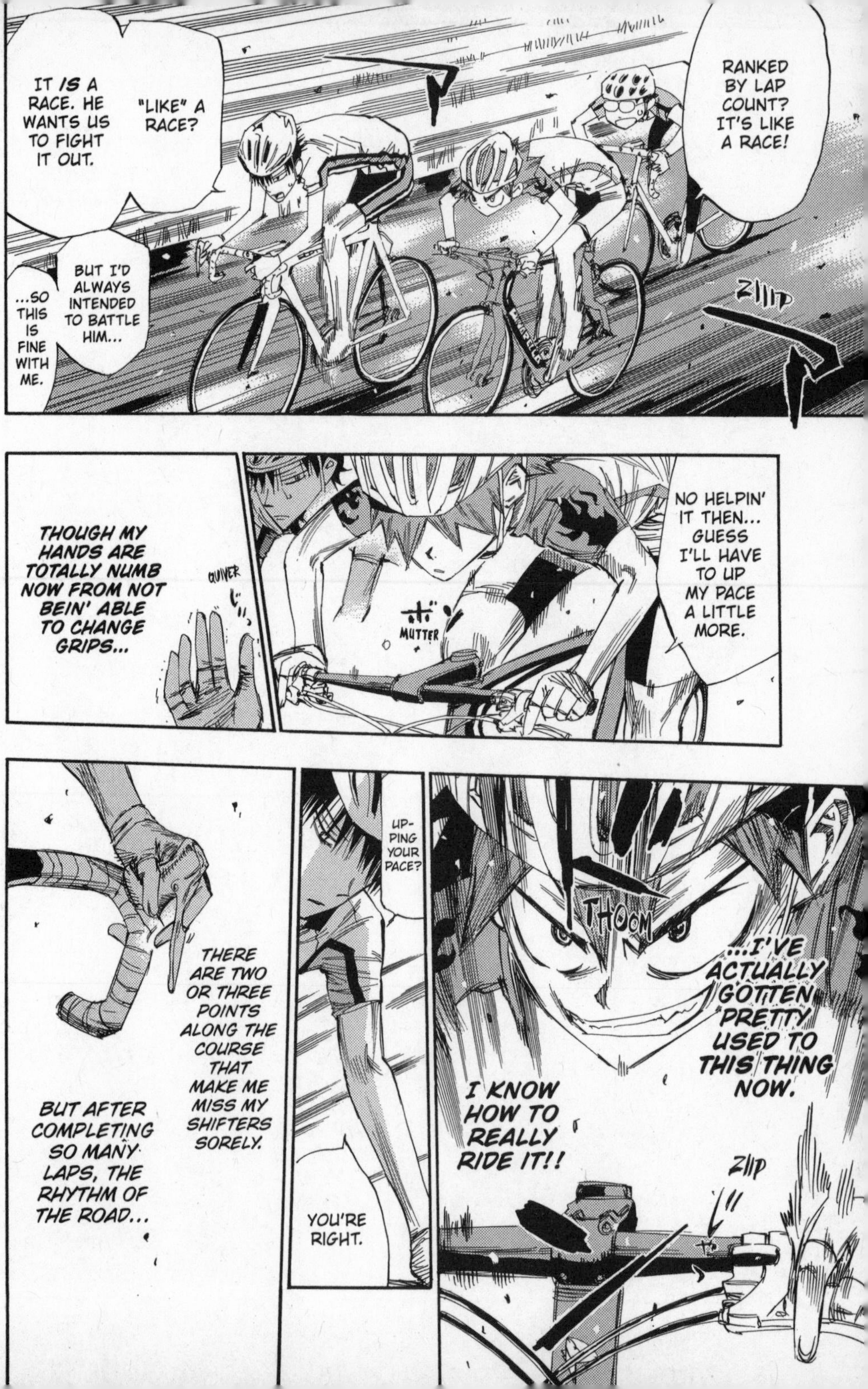
RANKED BY LAP COUNT? IT'S LIKE A RACE!
"LIKE" A RACE?
IT *IS* A RACE. HE WANTS US TO FIGHT IT OUT.
ZIIIP
BUT I'D ALWAYS INTENDED TO BATTLE HIM...
...SO THIS IS FINE WITH ME.
NO HELPIN' IT THEN... GUESS I'LL HAVE TO UP MY PACE A LITTLE MORE.
MUTTER
THOUGH MY HANDS ARE TOTALLY NUMB NOW FROM NOT BEIN' ABLE TO CHANGE GRIPS...
QUIVER
...I'VE ACTUALLY GOTTEN PRETTY USED TO THIS THING NOW.
THOOM
I KNOW HOW TO REALLY RIDE IT!!
ZIIP
UP-PING YOUR PACE?
YOU'RE RIGHT.
THERE ARE TWO OR THREE POINTS ALONG THE COURSE THAT MAKE ME MISS MY SHIFTERS SORELY.
BUT AFTER COMPLETING SO MANY LAPS, THE RHYTHM OF THE ROAD...

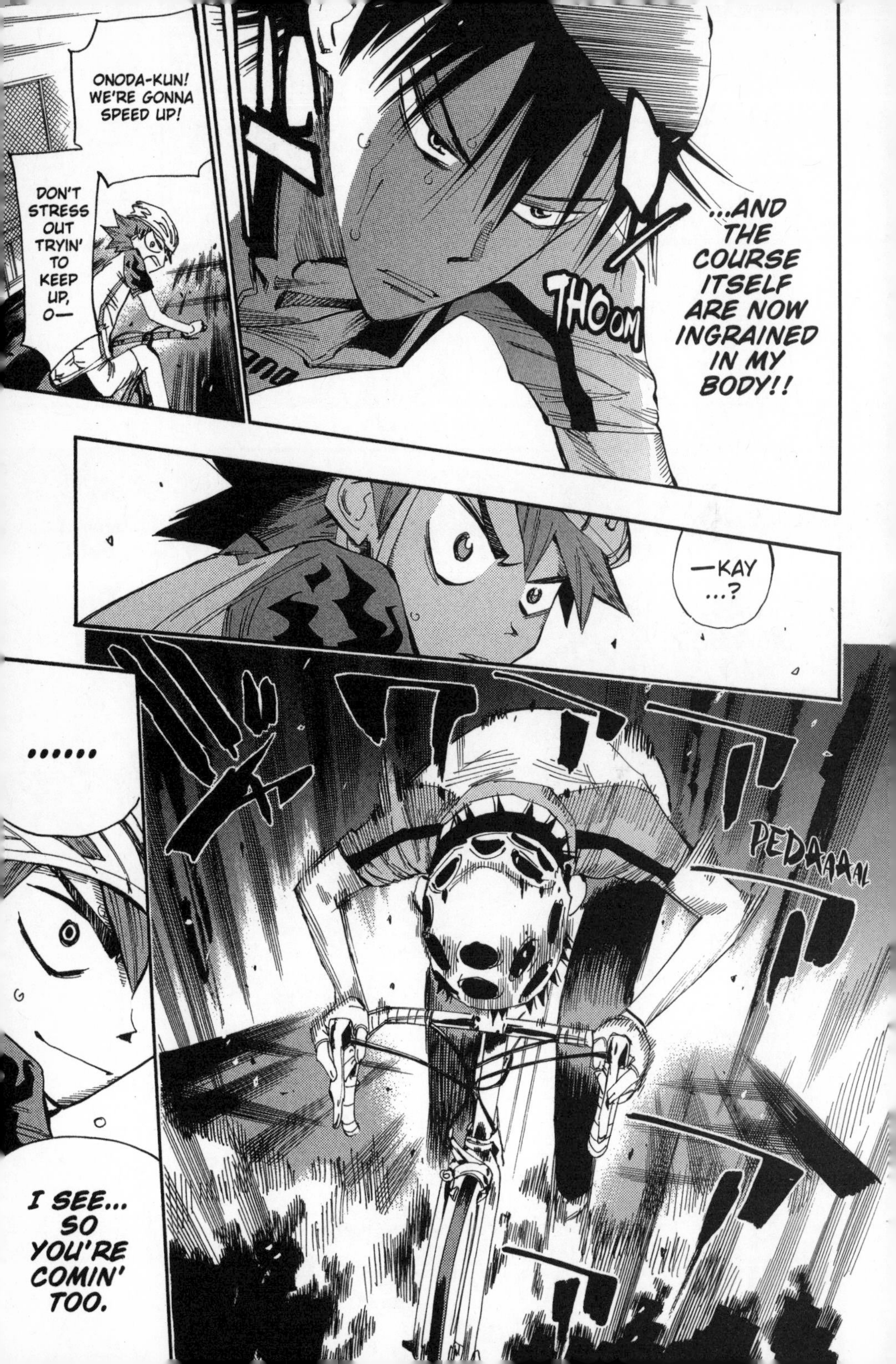
...AND THE COURSE ITSELF ARE NOW INGRAINED IN MY BODY!!
THOOM
ONODA-KUN! WE'RE GONNA SPEED UP!
DON'T STRESS OUT TRYIN' TO KEEP UP, O—
—KAY ...?
PEDAAAAAL
......
I SEE... SO YOU'RE COMIN' TOO.

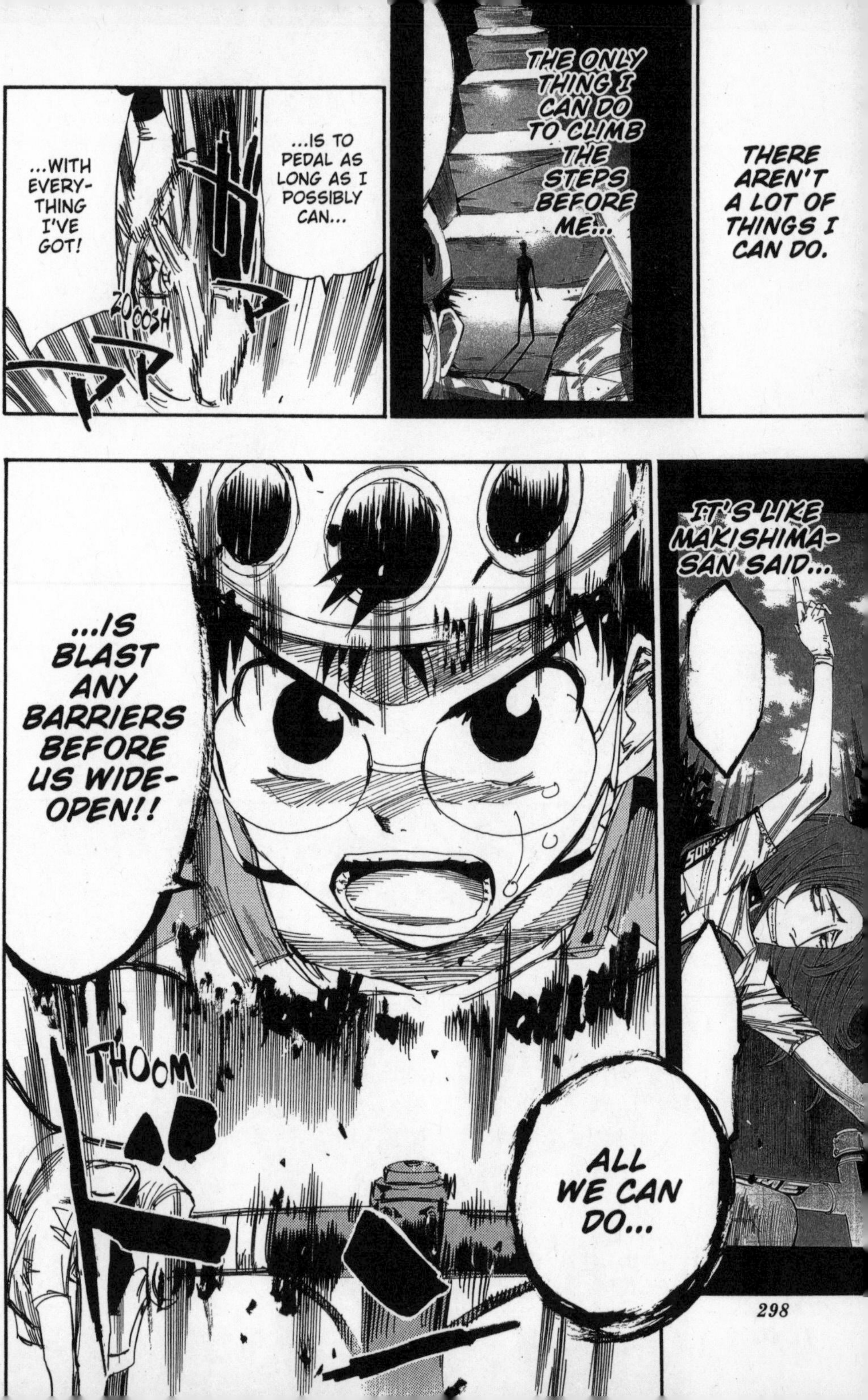
THERE AREN'T A LOT OF THINGS I CAN DO.
THE ONLY THING I CAN DO TO CLIMB THE STEPS BEFORE ME...
...IS TO PEDAL AS LONG AS I POSSIBLY CAN...
...WITH EVERY-THING I'VE GOT!
ZOOOSH
IT'S LIKE MAKISHIMA-SAN SAID...
ALL WE CAN DO...
...IS BLAST ANY BARRIERS BEFORE US WIDE-OPEN!!
THOOM

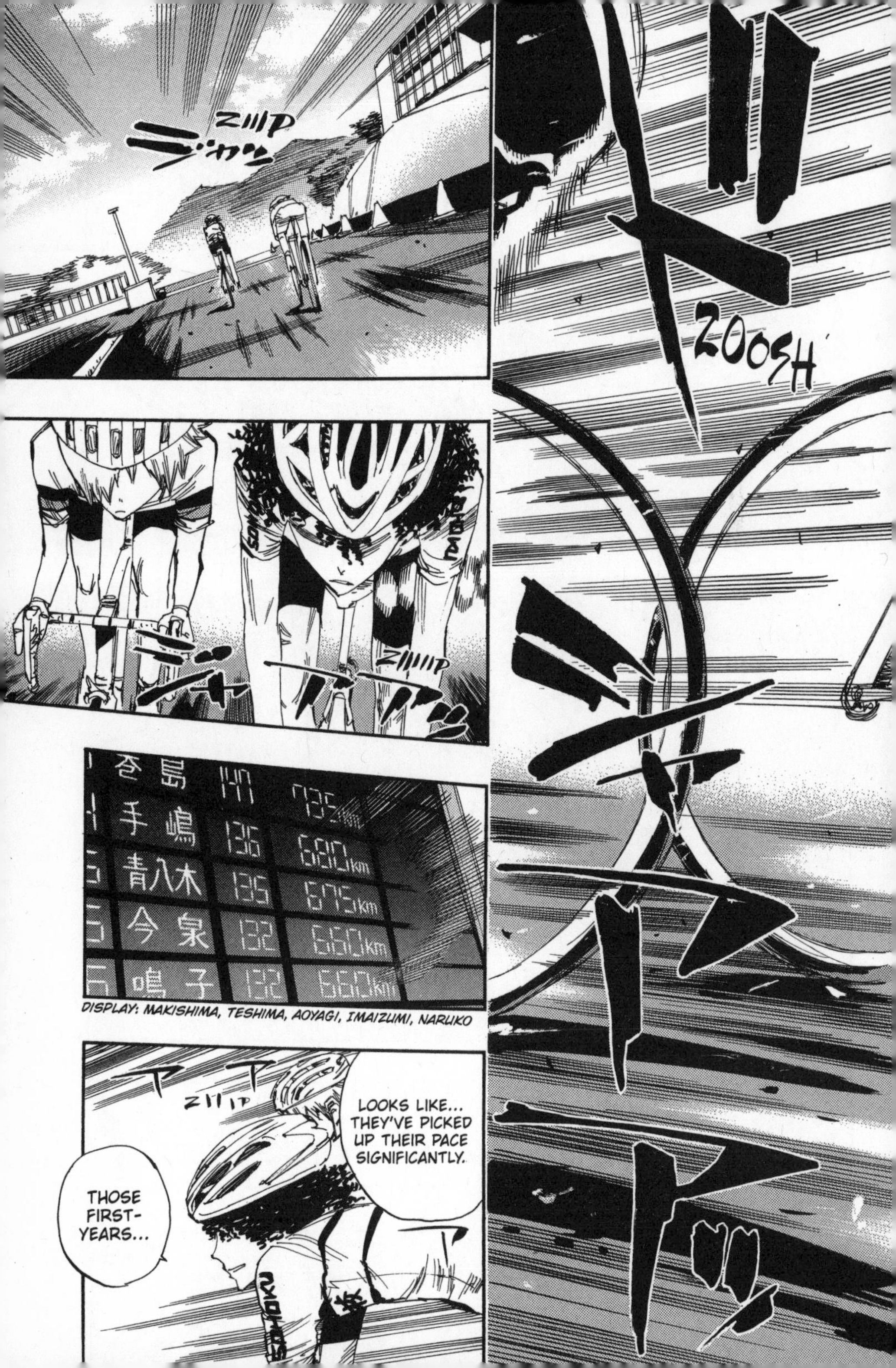
ZOOSH
ZIIIP
ZIIIIP
DISPLAY: MAKISHIMA, TESHIMA, AOYAGI, IMAIZUMI, NARUKO
ZIIIP
LOOKS LIKE... THEY'VE PICKED UP THEIR PACE SIGNIFICANTLY.
THOSE FIRST-YEARS...

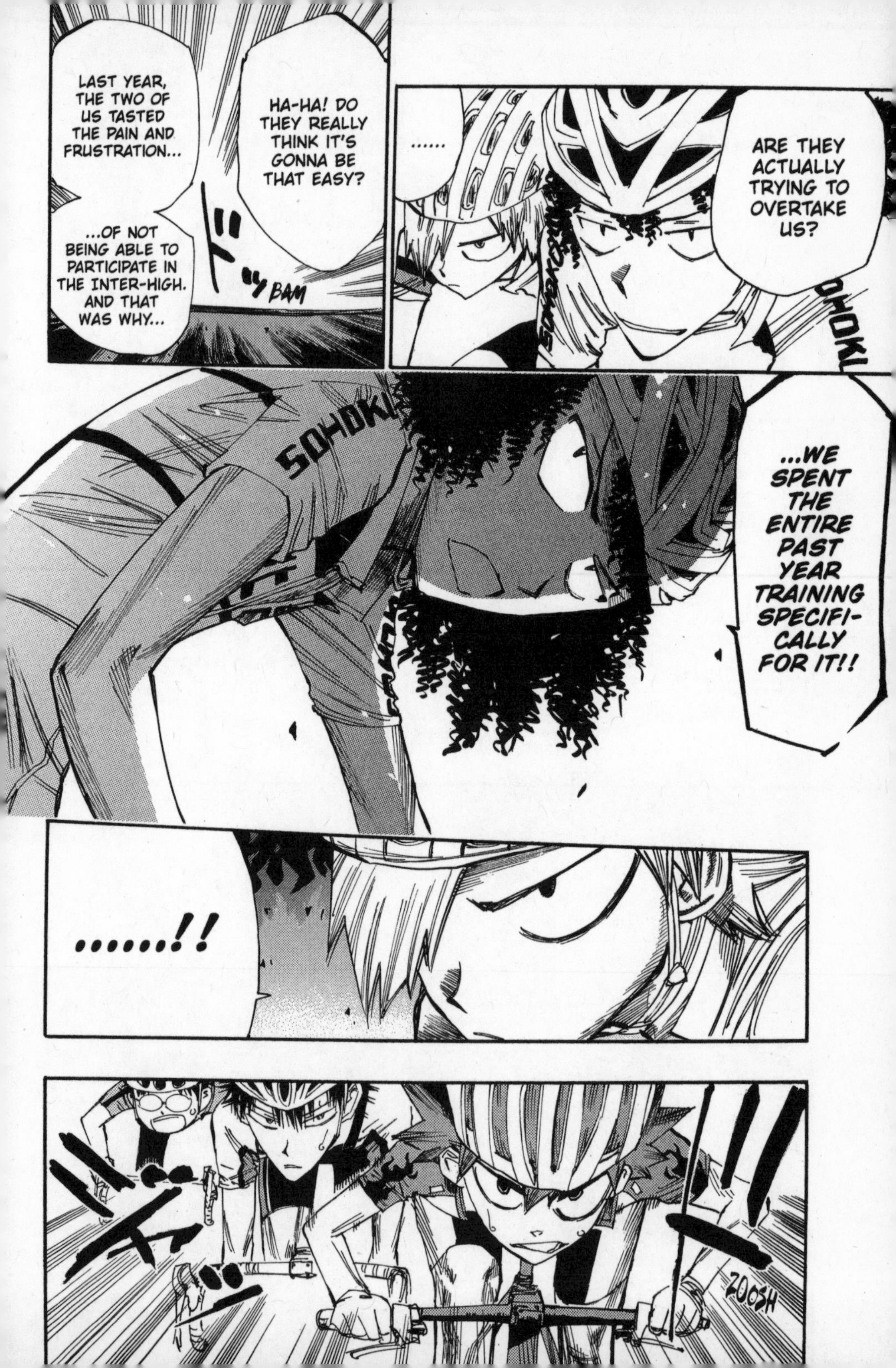

ARE THEY ACTUALLY TRYING TO OVERTAKE US?
......
HA-HA! DO THEY REALLY THINK IT'S GONNA BE THAT EASY?
BAM
LAST YEAR, THE TWO OF US TASTED THE PAIN AND FRUSTRATION...
...OF NOT BEING ABLE TO PARTICIPATE IN THE INTER-HIGH. AND THAT WAS WHY...
...WE SPENT THE ENTIRE PAST YEAR TRAINING SPECIFI-CALLY FOR IT!!
.......!!
ZOOSH

RIDE.49 "740 KILOMETERS"

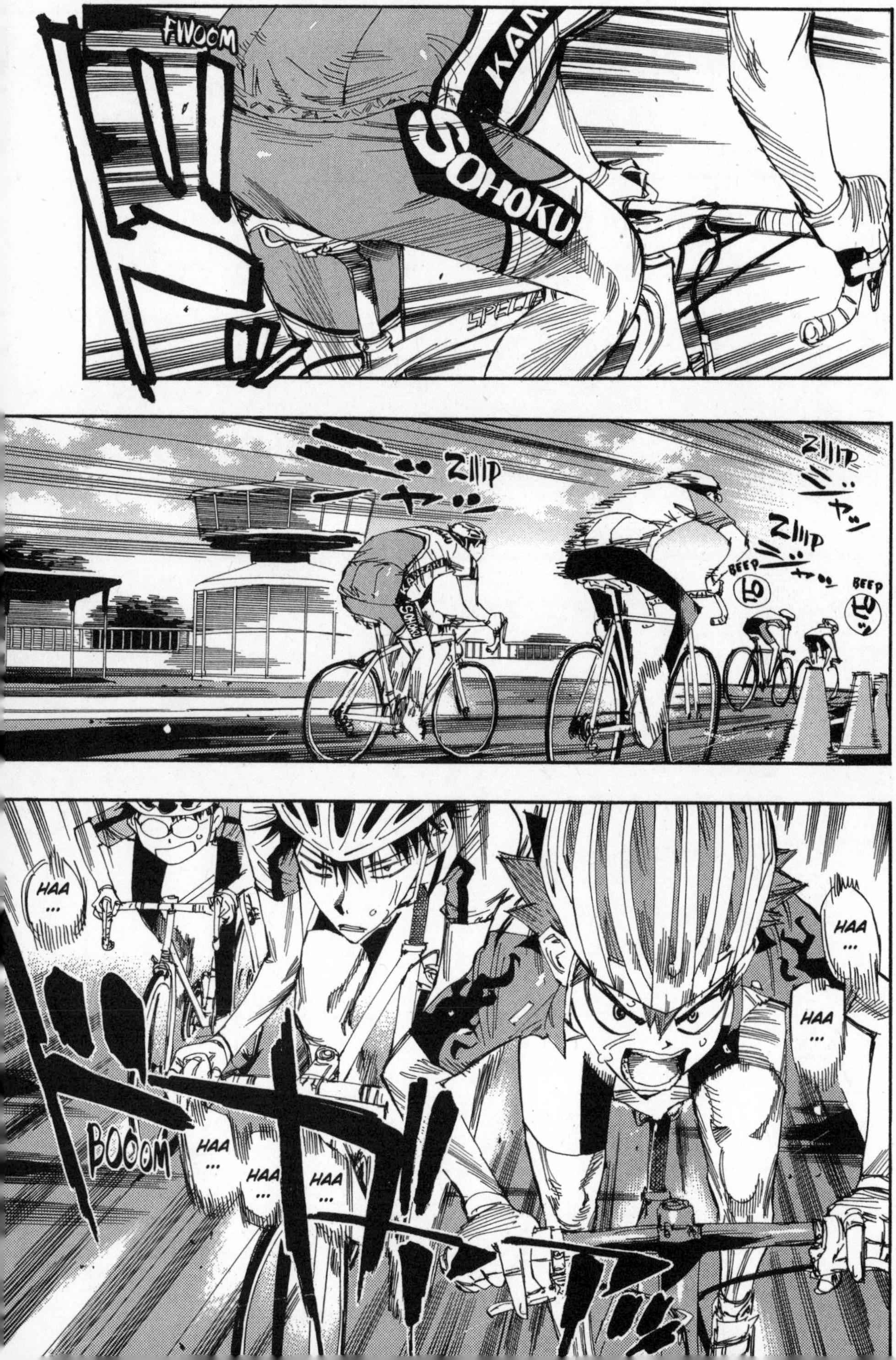
FWOOM
ZIIIP
ZIIIP
BEEP
BEEP
ZIIIP
HAA ...
HAA ...
HAA ...
BOOM
HAA ...
HAA ...
HAA ...

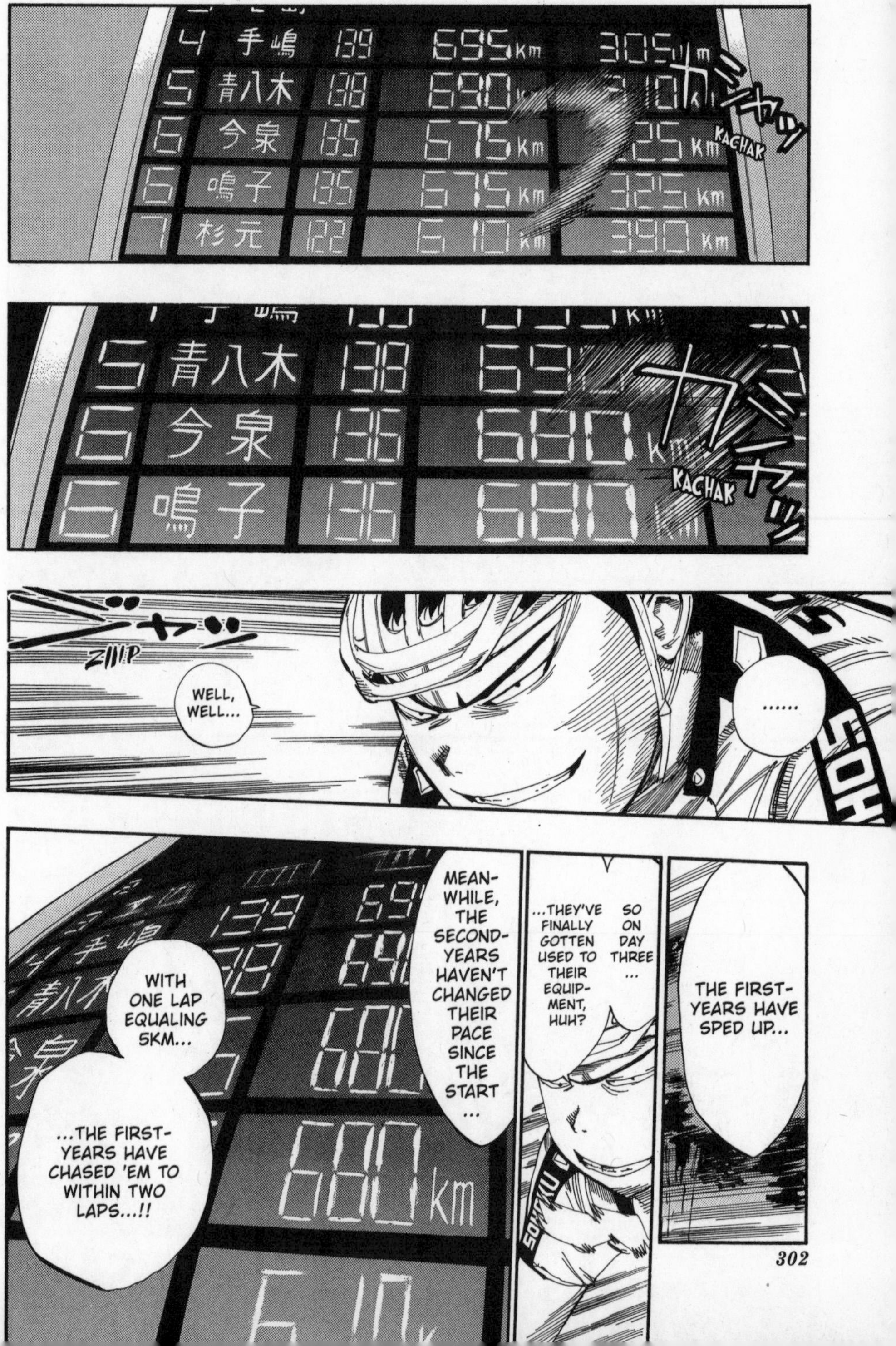
4 手嶋 139 695km 305km
5 青八木 138 690km
6 今泉 135 675km 325km
6 鳴子 135 675km 325km
7 杉元 122 610km 390km
カシャッ
KACHAK
5 青八木 138
6 今泉 136 680km
6 鳴子 136 680
カシャッ
KACHAK
......
WELL, WELL...
ジャッ
ZIIIP
THE FIRST-YEARS HAVE SPED UP...
SO ON DAY THREE...
...THEY'VE FINALLY GOTTEN USED TO THEIR EQUIPMENT, HUH?
MEANWHILE, THE SECOND-YEARS HAVEN'T CHANGED THEIR PACE SINCE THE START...
WITH ONE LAP EQUALING 5KM...
...THE FIRST-YEARS HAVE CHASED 'EM TO WITHIN TWO LAPS...!!

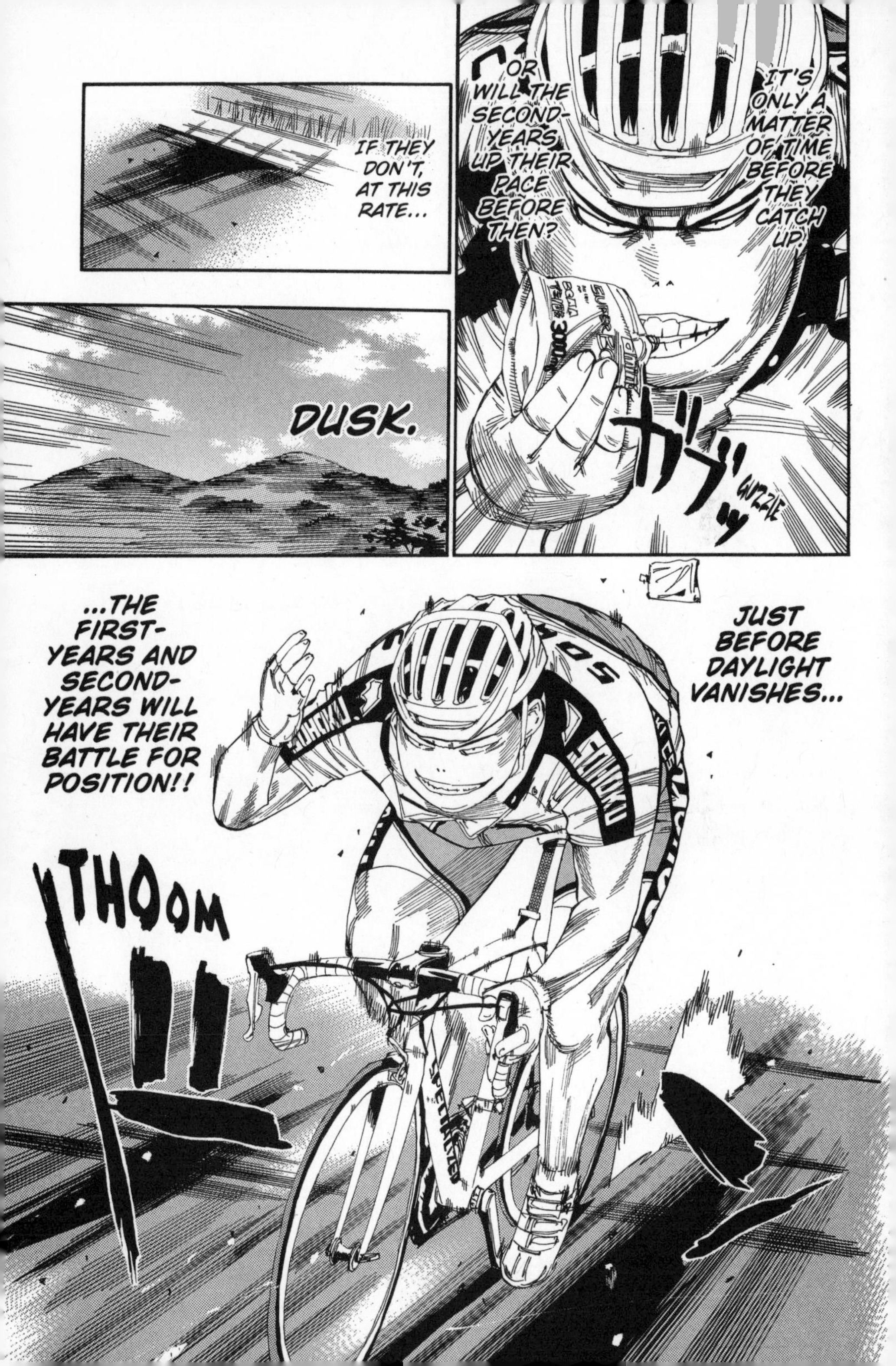
IT'S ONLY A MATTER OF TIME BEFORE THEY CATCH UP.
OR WILL THE SECOND-YEARS UP THEIR PACE BEFORE THEN?
GUZZLE
IF THEY DON'T, AT THIS RATE...
DUSK.
JUST BEFORE DAYLIGHT VANISHES...
...THE FIRST-YEARS AND SECOND-YEARS WILL HAVE THEIR BATTLE FOR POSITION!!
THOOM

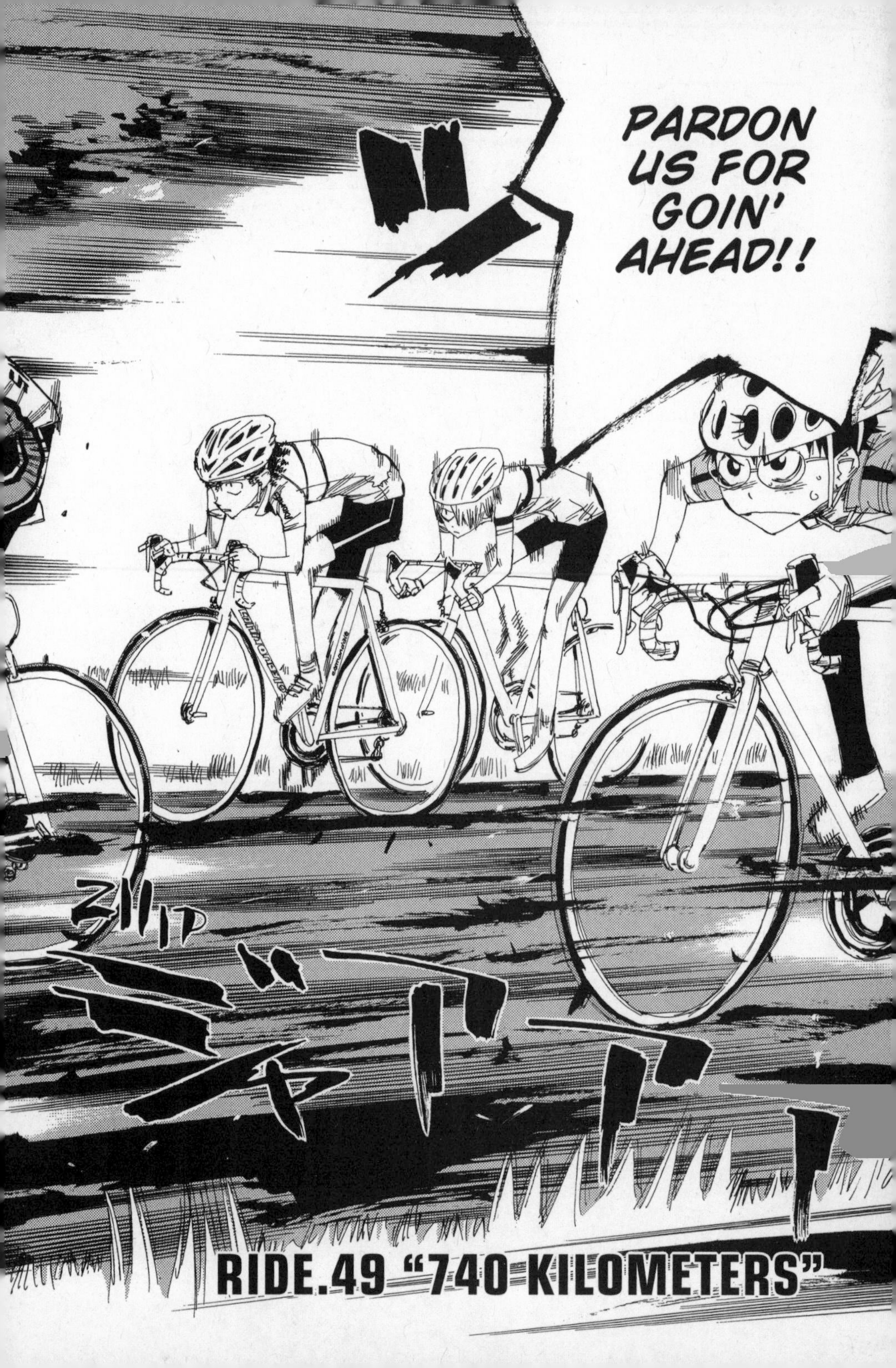
PARDON US FOR GOIN' AHEAD!!
ZWIP
ジャアア
RIDE.49 "740 KILOMETERS"

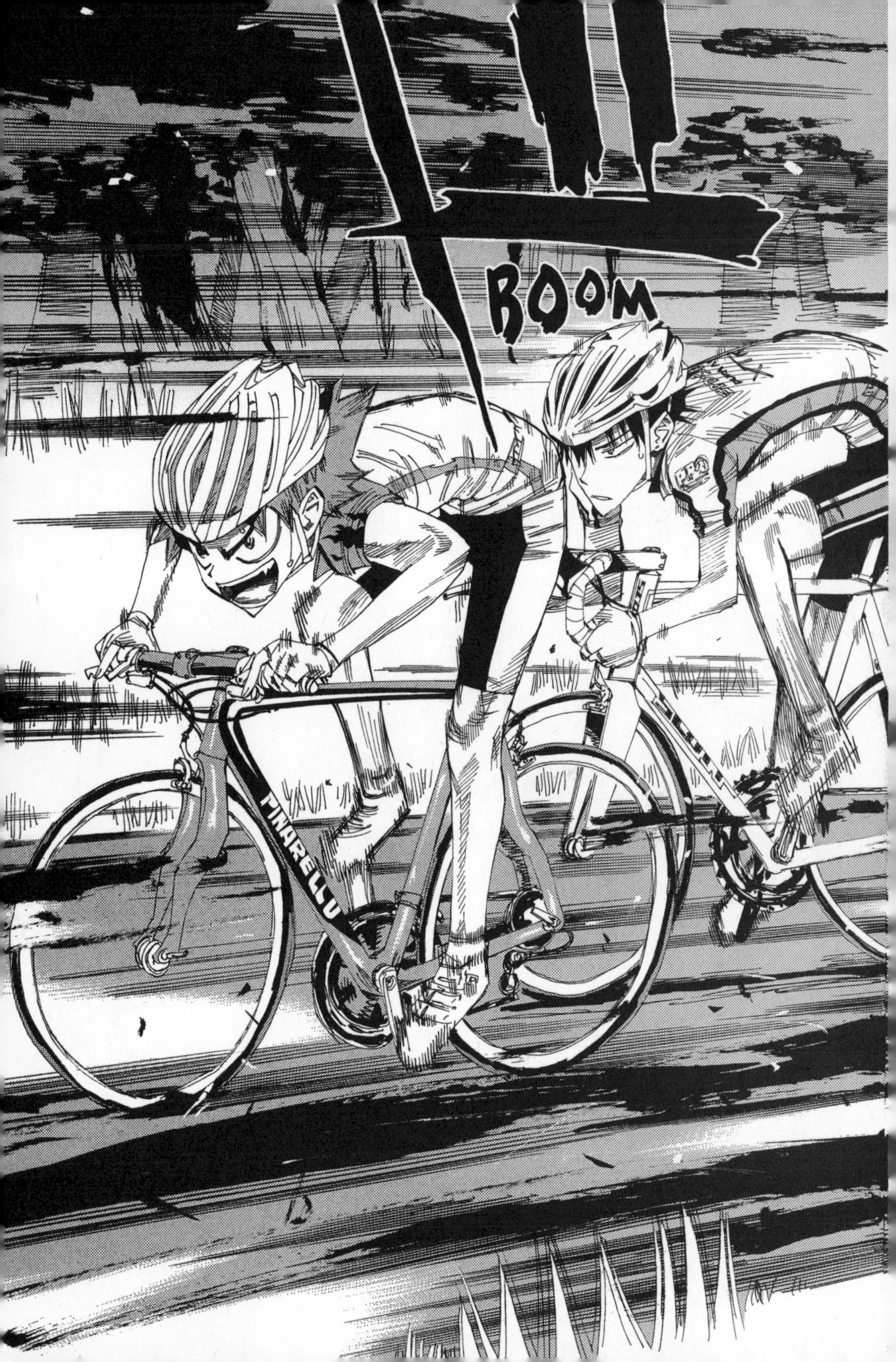
ROOM
PINARELLO

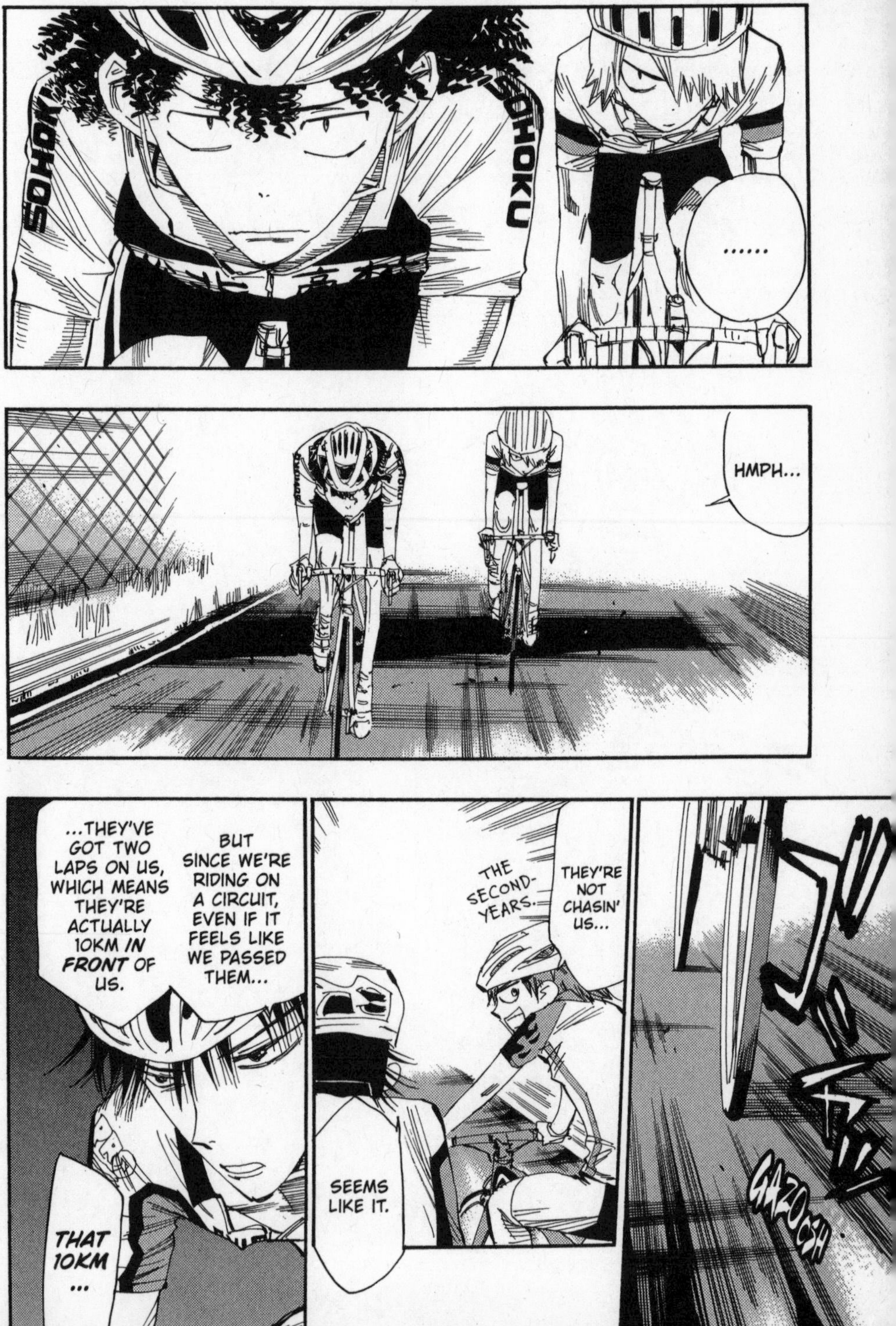
......
HMPH...
THEY'RE NOT CHASIN' US...
THE SECOND-YEARS.
SEEMS LIKE IT.
BUT SINCE WE'RE RIDING ON A CIRCUIT, EVEN IF IT FEELS LIKE WE PASSED THEM...
...THEY'VE GOT TWO LAPS ON US, WHICH MEANS THEY'RE ACTUALLY 10KM *IN FRONT* OF US.
THAT 10KM ...

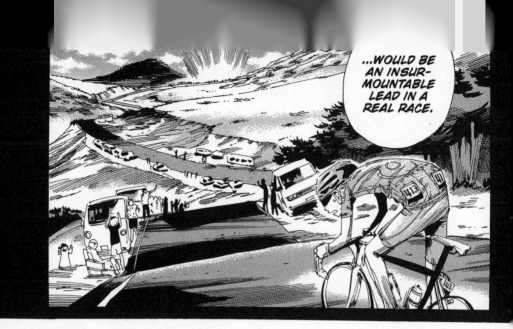

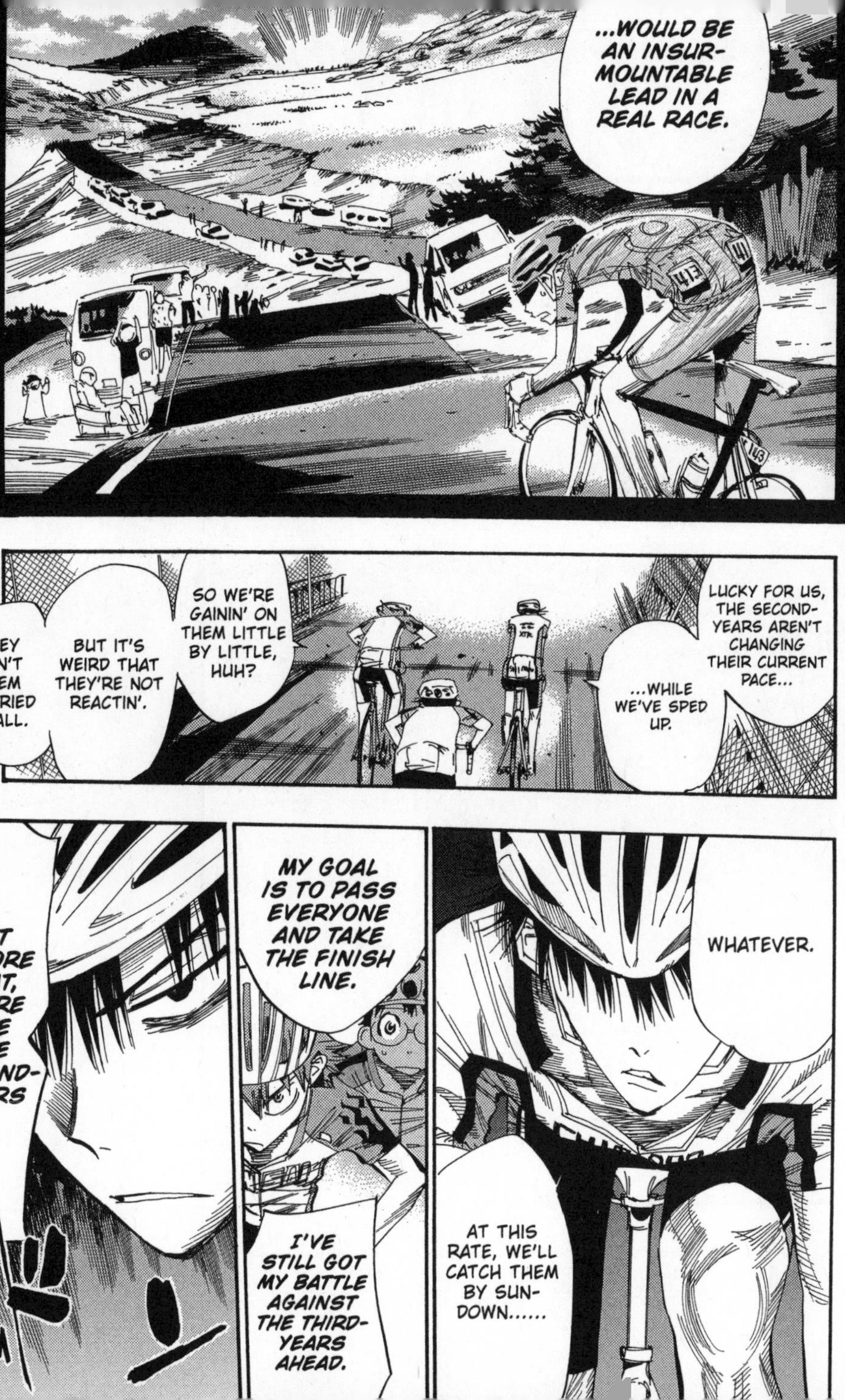
...WOULD BE AN INSURMOUNTABLE LEAD IN A REAL RACE.
LUCKY FOR US, THE SECOND-YEARS AREN'T CHANGING THEIR CURRENT PACE...
...WHILE WE'VE SPED UP.
SO WE'RE GAININ' ON THEM LITTLE BY LITTLE, HUH?
BUT IT'S WEIRD THAT THEY'RE NOT REACTIN'.
THEY DON'T SEEM WORRIED AT ALL.
WHATEVER.
AT THIS RATE, WE'LL CATCH THEM BY SUNDOWN......
MY GOAL IS TO PASS EVERYONE AND TAKE THE FINISH LINE.
I'VE STILL GOT MY BATTLE AGAINST THE THIRD-YEARS AHEAD.
BUT BEFORE THAT, THERE ARE THE SECOND-YEARS...
THOOM

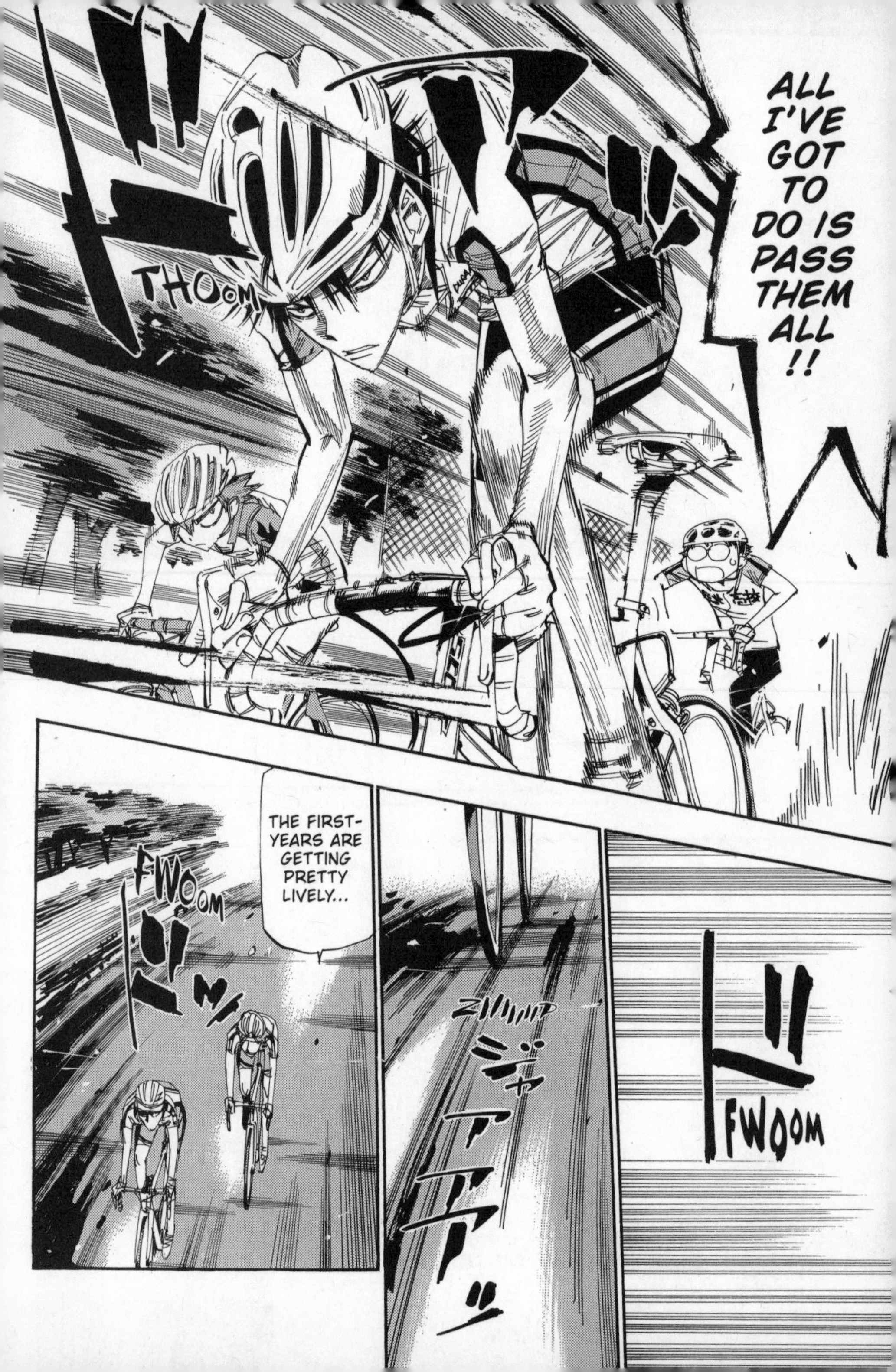
ALL I'VE GOT TO DO IS PASS THEM ALL!!
THOOM
FWOOM
THE FIRST-YEARS ARE GETTING PRETTY LIVELY...
FWOOM

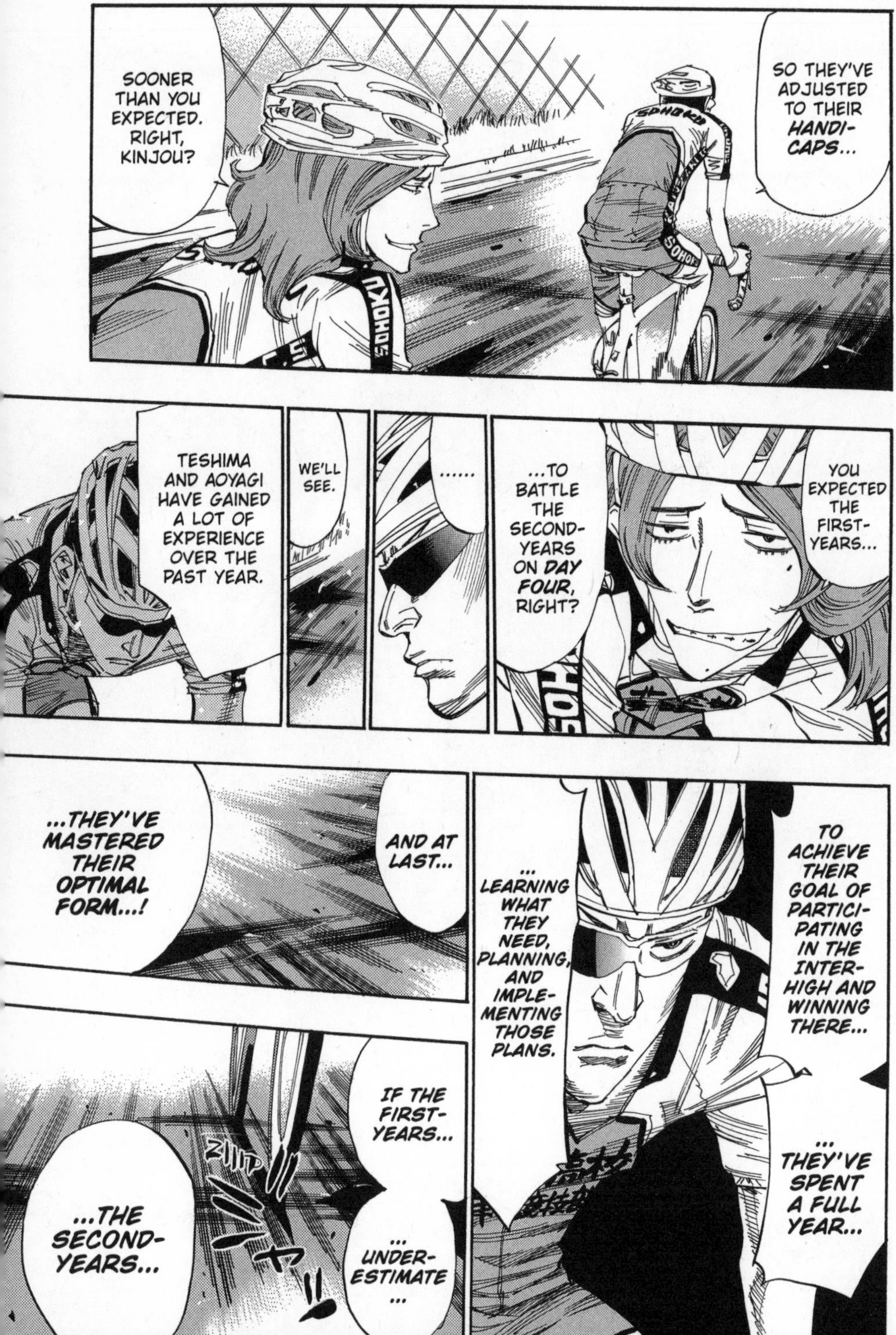
SO THEY'VE ADJUSTED TO THEIR HANDICAPS...
SOONER THAN YOU EXPECTED. RIGHT, KINJOU?
YOU EXPECTED THE FIRST-YEARS...
...TO BATTLE THE SECOND-YEARS ON DAY FOUR, RIGHT?
......
WE'LL SEE.
TESHIMA AND AOYAGI HAVE GAINED A LOT OF EXPERIENCE OVER THE PAST YEAR.
TO ACHIEVE THEIR GOAL OF PARTICIPATING IN THE INTER-HIGH AND WINNING THERE...
...THEY'VE SPENT A FULL YEAR...
...LEARNING WHAT THEY NEED, PLANNING, AND IMPLEMENTING THOSE PLANS.
AND AT LAST...
...THEY'VE MASTERED THEIR OPTIMAL FORM...!
IF THE FIRST-YEARS...
...UNDERESTIMATE...
...THE SECOND-YEARS...
ZIIIP

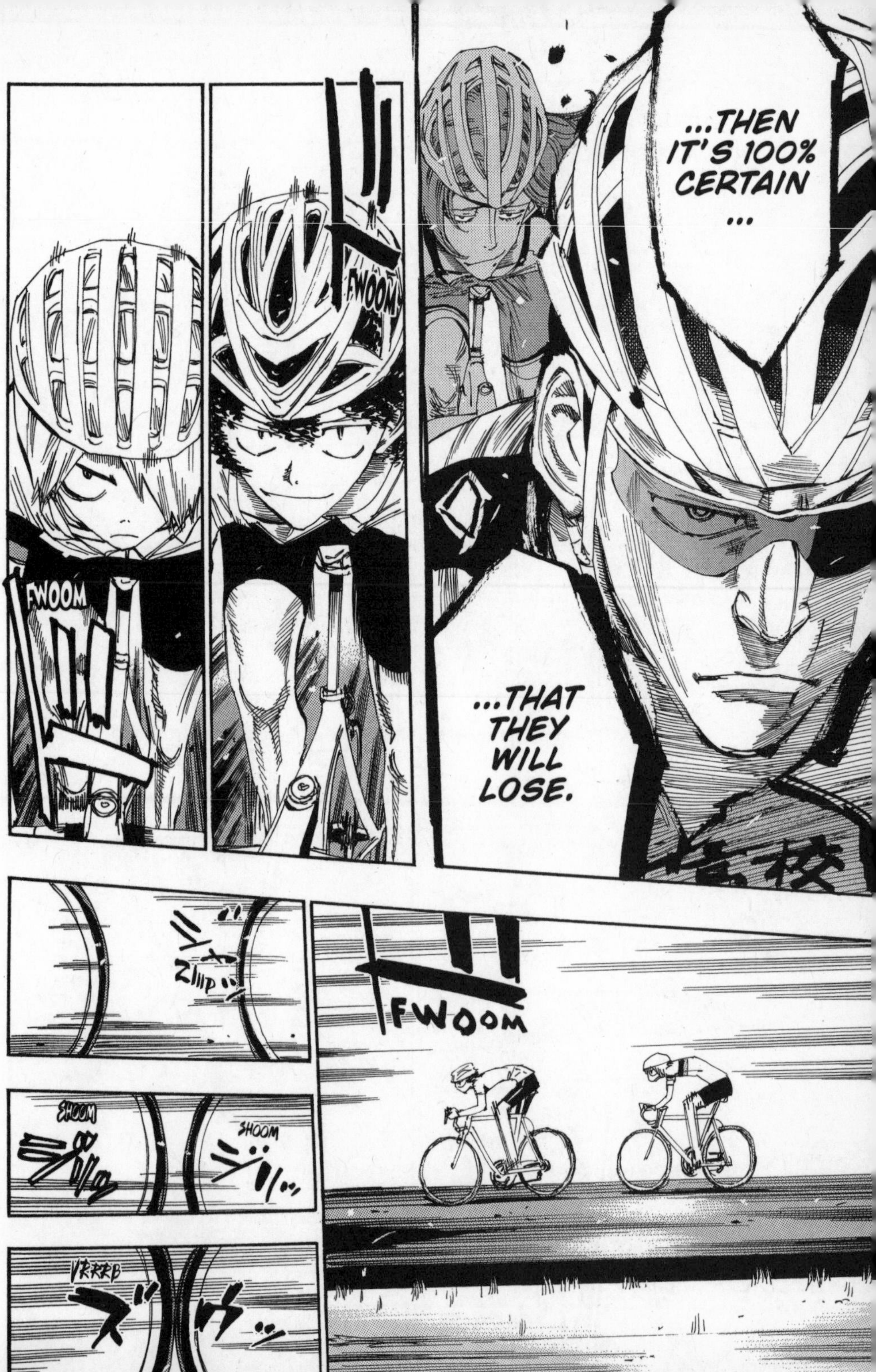
...THEN IT'S 100% CERTAIN ...
...THAT THEY WILL LOSE.
FWOOM
FWOOM
FWOOM
ZIIIP...
SHOOM
SHOOM
VRRRB

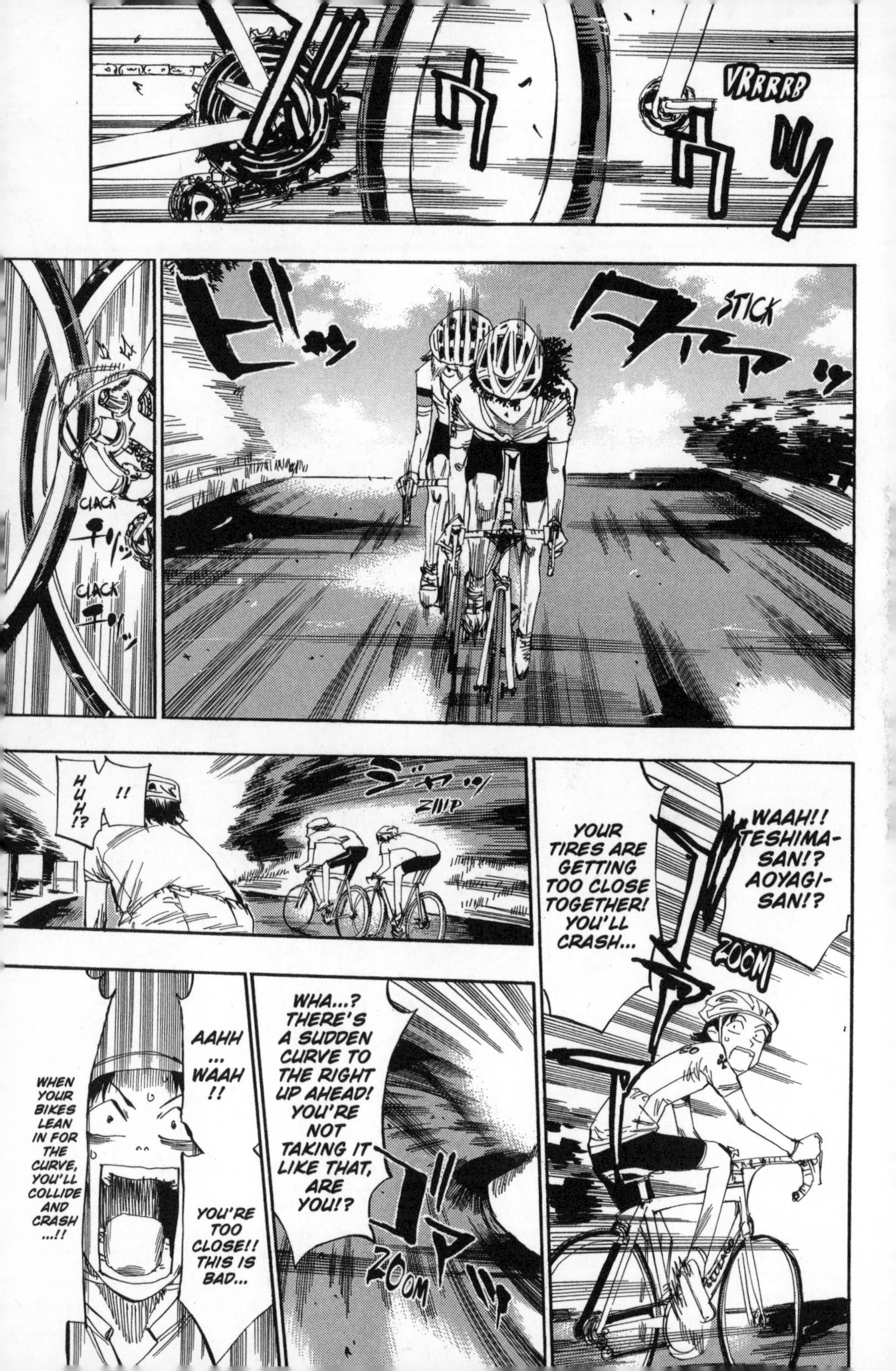
VRRRRB
STICK
CLACK
CLACK
WAAH!! TESHIMA-SAN!? AOYAGI-SAN!?
YOUR TIRES ARE GETTING TOO CLOSE TOGETHER! YOU'LL CRASH...
ZOOM
ZIIIP
!!
HUH!?
WHA...? THERE'S A SUDDEN CURVE TO THE RIGHT UP AHEAD! YOU'RE NOT TAKING IT LIKE THAT, ARE YOU!?
ZOOM
AAHH ... WAAH!!
YOU'RE TOO CLOSE!! THIS IS BAD...
WHEN YOUR BIKES LEAN IN FOR THE CURVE, YOU'LL COLLIDE AND CRASH ...!!

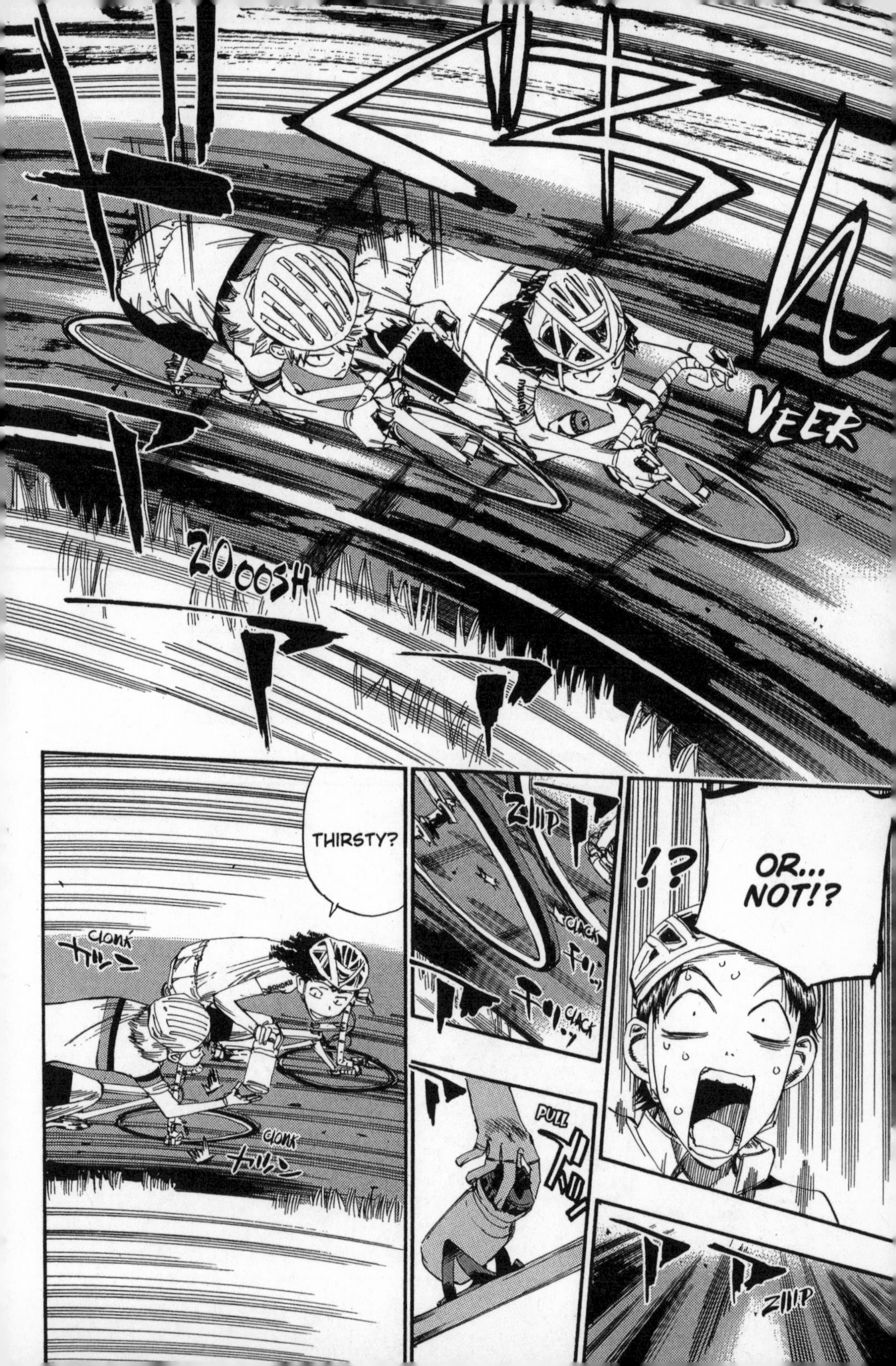
VEER
ZOOOSH
OR... NOT!?
!?
ZIIIP
CLACK
CLACK
THIRSTY?
CLONK
CLONK
PULL
ZIIIP

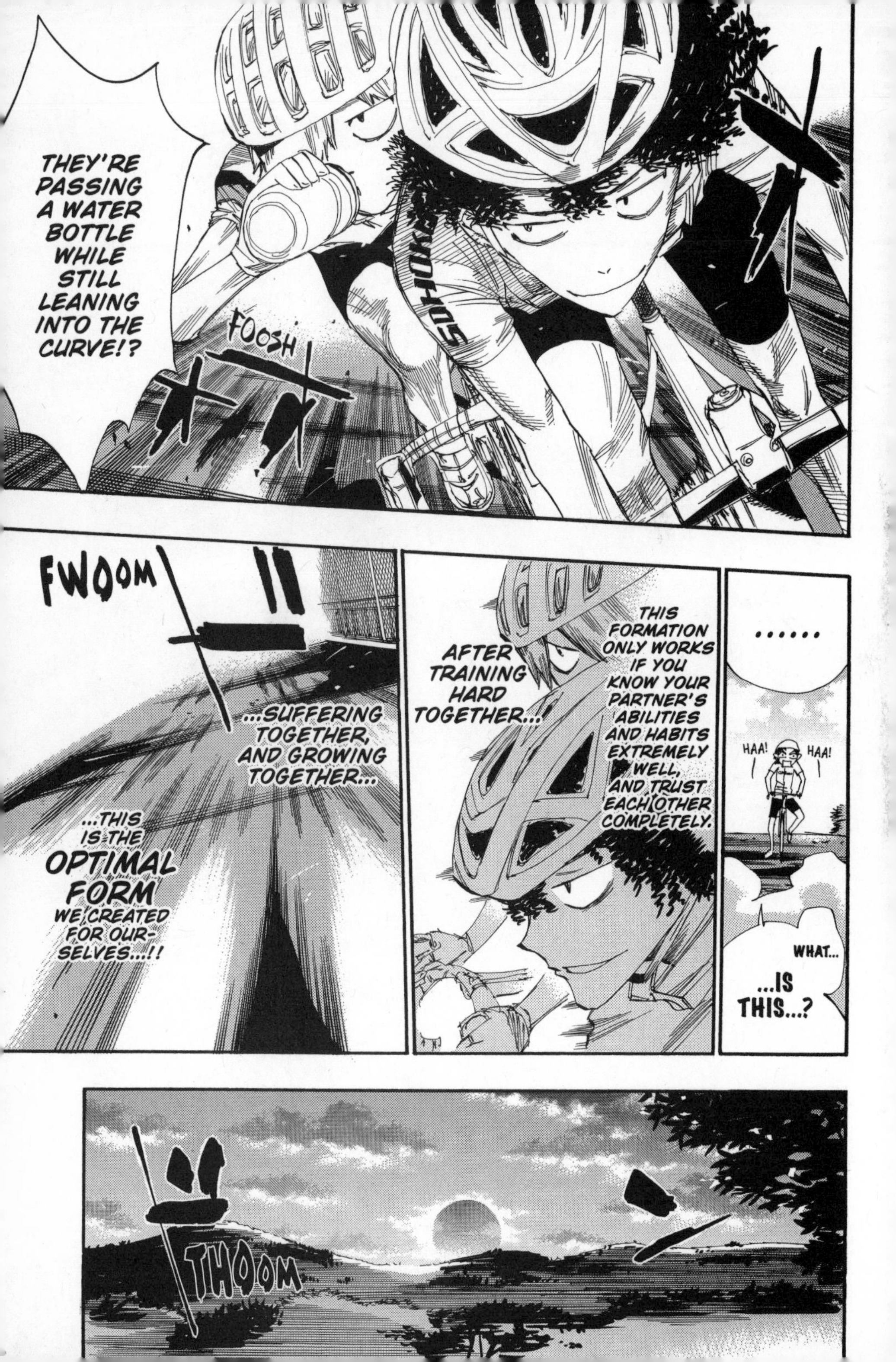
THEY'RE PASSING A WATER BOTTLE WHILE STILL LEANING INTO THE CURVE!?
FOOSH
......
HAA!
HAA!
WHAT...
...IS THIS...?
THIS FORMATION ONLY WORKS IF YOU KNOW YOUR PARTNER'S ABILITIES AND HABITS EXTREMELY WELL, AND TRUST EACH OTHER COMPLETELY.
AFTER TRAINING HARD TOGETHER...
FWOOM
...SUFFERING TOGETHER, AND GROWING TOGETHER...
...THIS IS THE OPTIMAL FORM WE CREATED FOR OUR-SELVES...!!
THOOM

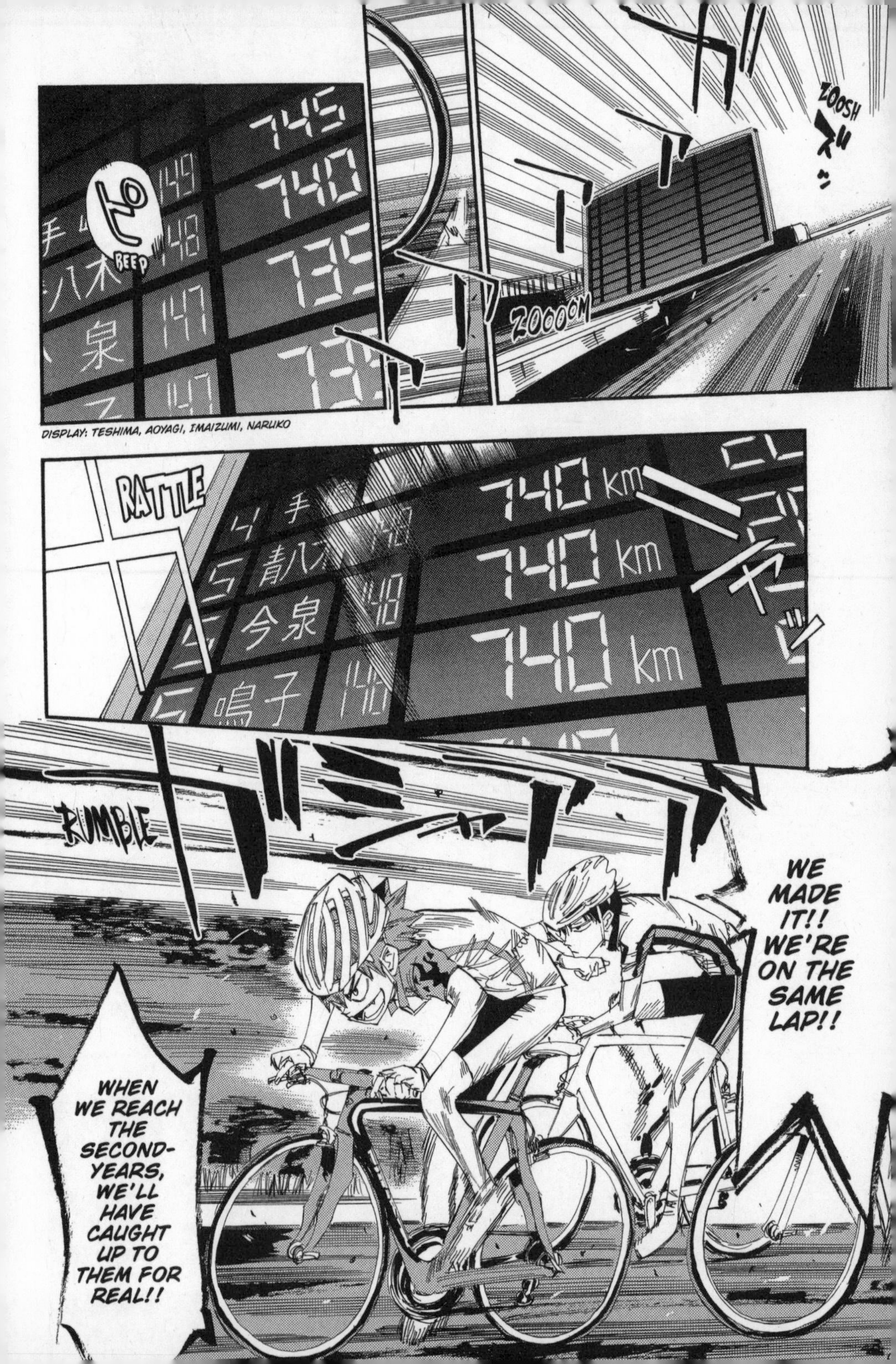
DISPLAY: TESHIMA, AOYAGI, IMAIZUMI, NARUKO
ZOOSH
ZOOOOM
BEEP
745
740
739
RATTLE
740 km
740 km
740 km
今泉
鳴子
RUMBLE
WE MADE IT!! WE'RE ON THE SAME LAP!!
WHEN WE REACH THE SECOND-YEARS, WE'LL HAVE CAUGHT UP TO THEM FOR REAL!!

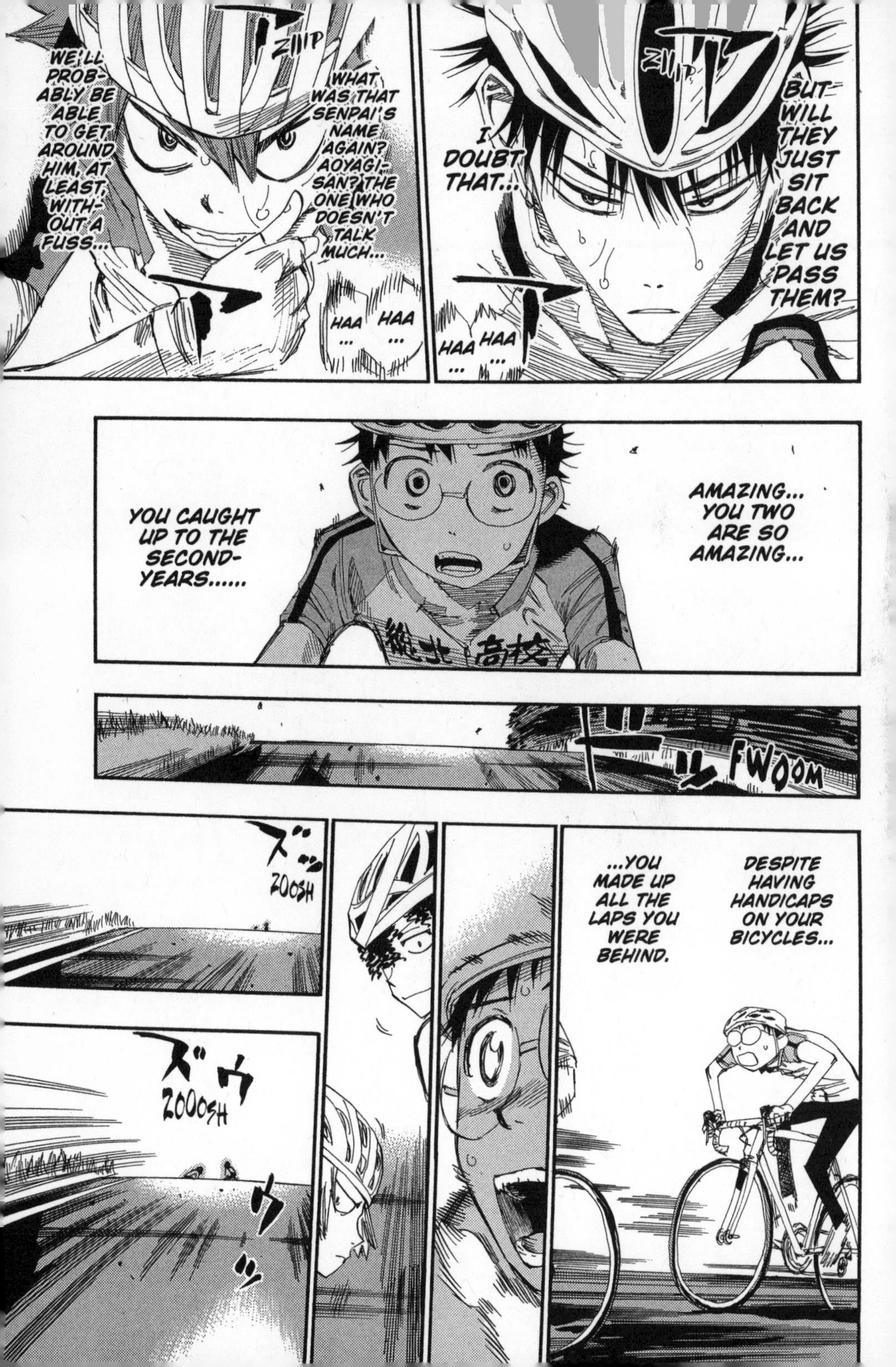
ZIIIP
BUT WILL THEY JUST SIT BACK AND LET US PASS THEM?
I DOUBT THAT...
HAA... HAA...
ZIIIP
WHAT WAS THAT SENPAI'S NAME AGAIN? AOYAGI-SAN? THE ONE WHO DOESN'T TALK MUCH...
WE'LL PROBABLY BE ABLE TO GET AROUND HIM, AT LEAST, WITHOUT A FUSS...
HAA... HAA...
AMAZING... YOU TWO ARE SO AMAZING...
YOU CAUGHT UP TO THE SECOND-YEARS......
FWOOM
DESPITE HAVING HANDICAPS ON YOUR BICYCLES...
...YOU MADE UP ALL THE LAPS YOU WERE BEHIND.
ZOOSH
ZOOOSH

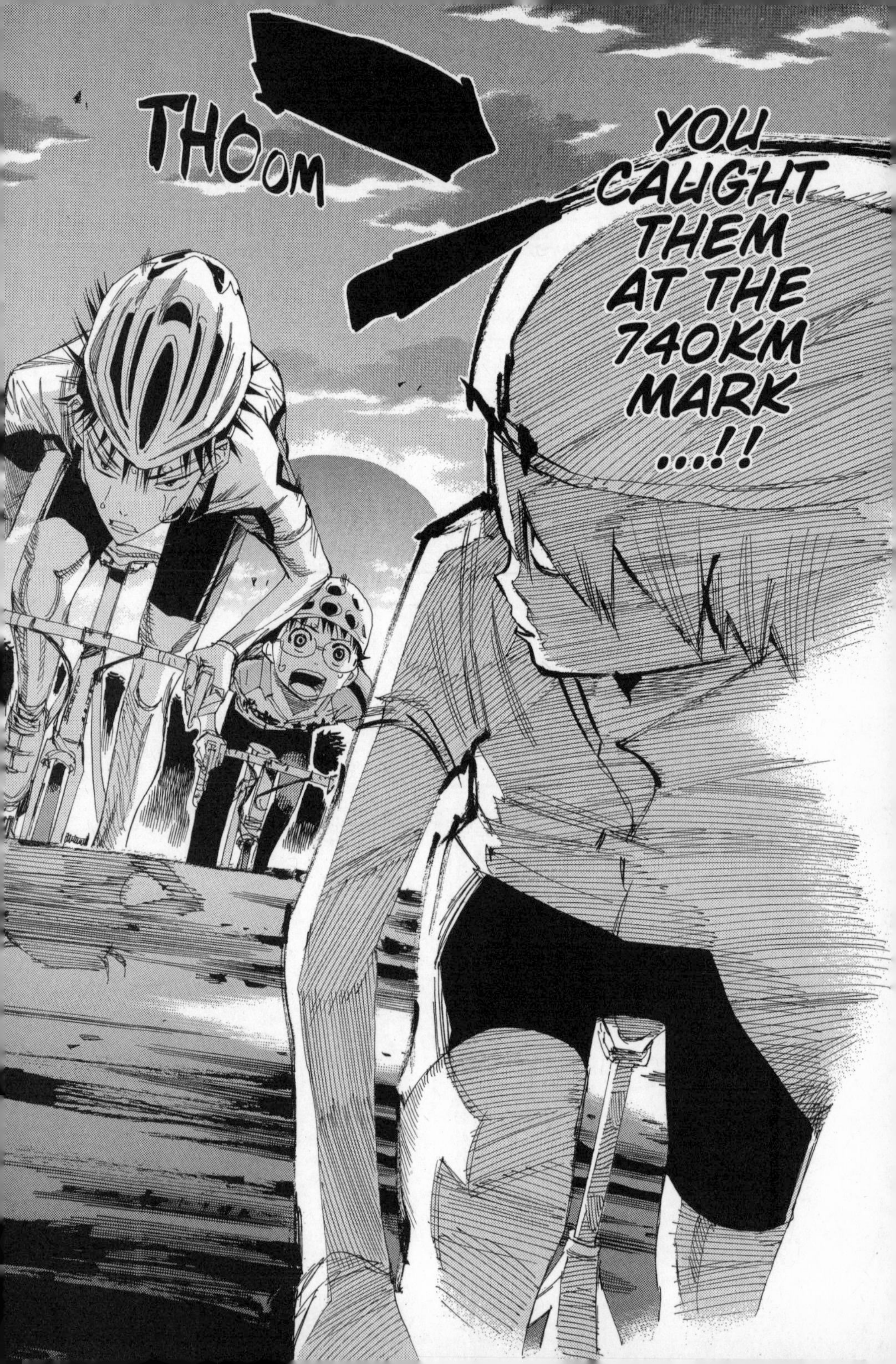

YOU CAUGHT THEM AT THE 740KM MARK ...!!
THOOM

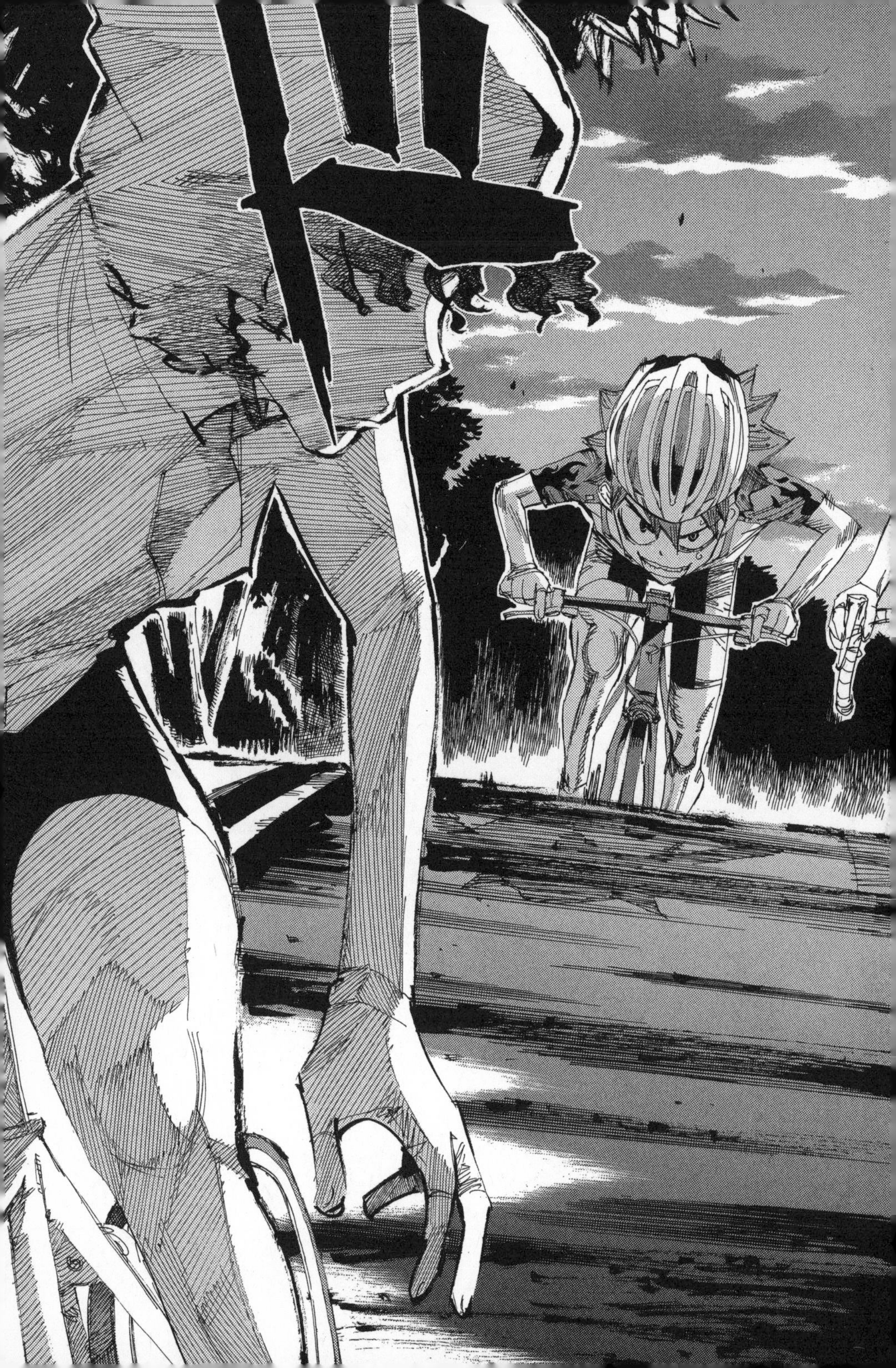

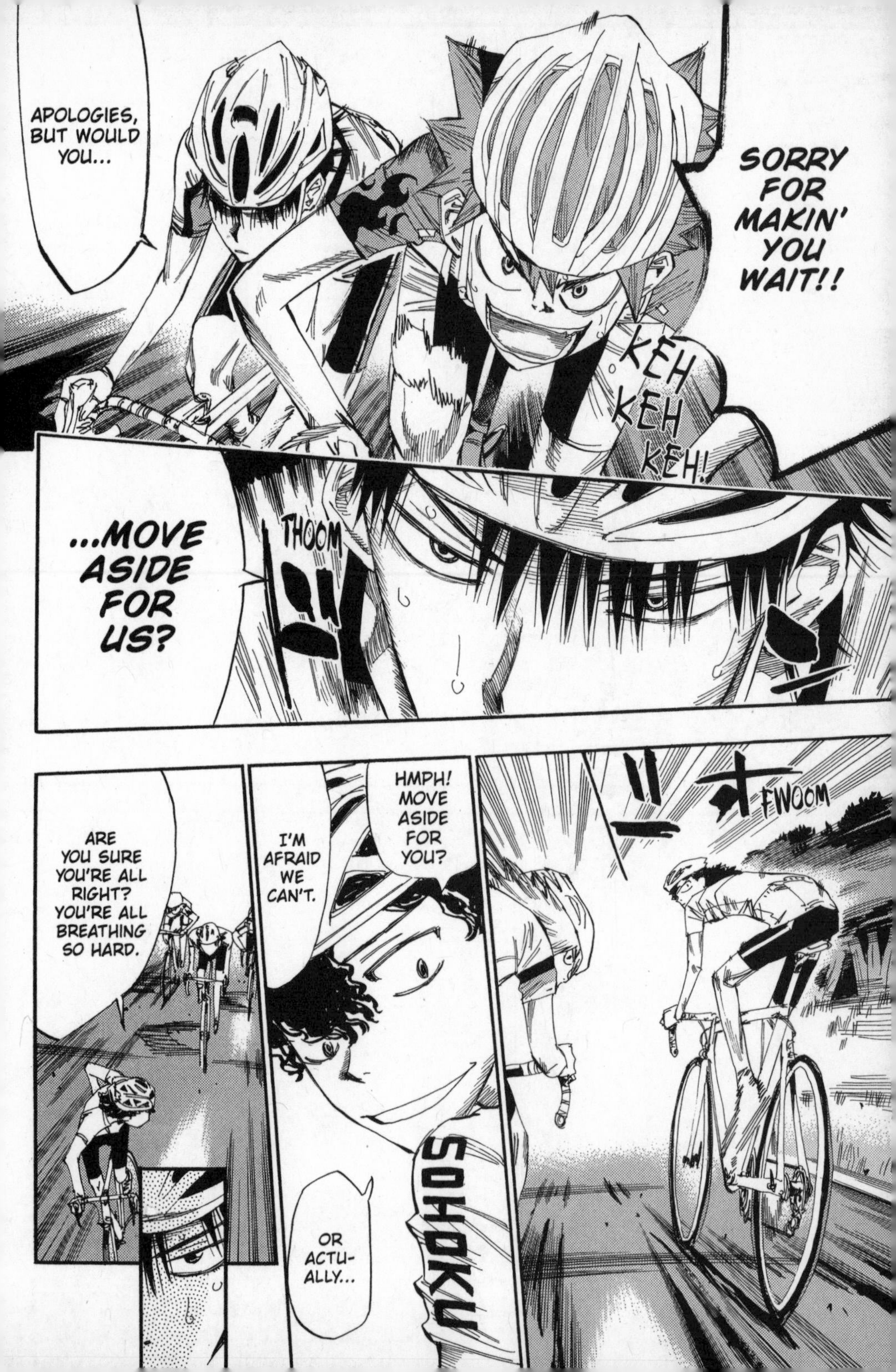
SORRY FOR MAKIN' YOU WAIT!!
KEH KEH KEH!
APOLOGIES, BUT WOULD YOU...
...MOVE ASIDE FOR US?
THOOM
FWOOM
HMPH! MOVE ASIDE FOR YOU?
I'M AFRAID WE CAN'T.
SOHOKU
OR ACTU-ALLY...
ARE YOU SURE YOU'RE ALL RIGHT? YOU'RE ALL BREATHING SO HARD.

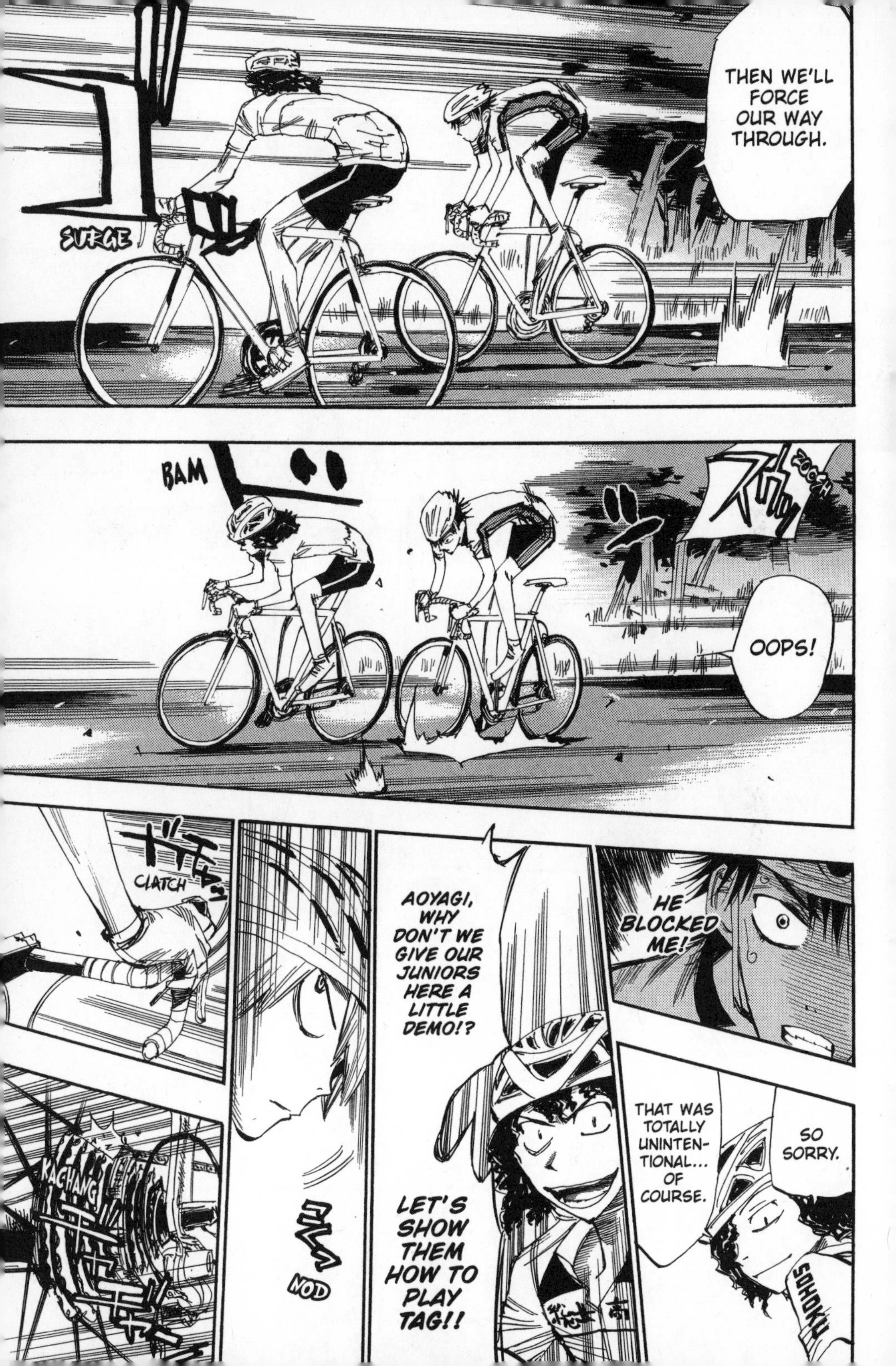
THEN WE'LL FORCE OUR WAY THROUGH.
SURGE
ZOOSH
OOPS!
BAM
HE BLOCKED ME!
SO SORRY.
THAT WAS TOTALLY UNINTEN-TIONAL... OF COURSE.
SOHOKU
AOYAGI, WHY DON'T WE GIVE OUR JUNIORS HERE A LITTLE DEMO!?
LET'S SHOW THEM HOW TO PLAY TAG!!
NOD
CLATCH
KACHANG

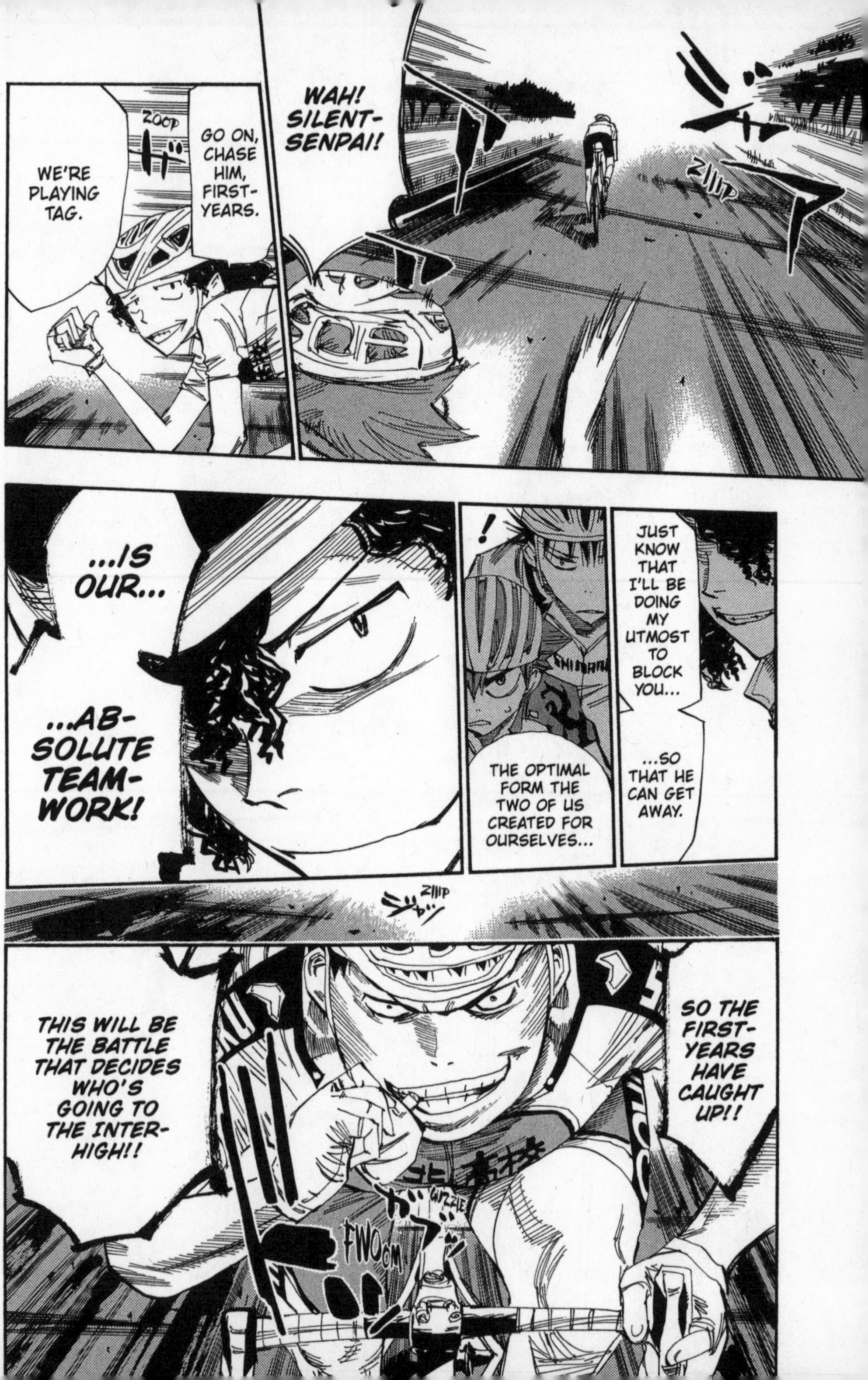
WAH! SILENT-SENPAI!
ZIIIP
ZOOP
GO ON, CHASE HIM, FIRST-YEARS.
WE'RE PLAYING TAG.
JUST KNOW THAT I'LL BE DOING MY UTMOST TO BLOCK YOU...
...SO THAT HE CAN GET AWAY.
!
THE OPTIMAL FORM THE TWO OF US CREATED FOR OURSELVES...
...IS OUR...
...AB-SOLUTE TEAM-WORK!
ZIIIP
SO THE FIRST-YEARS HAVE CAUGHT UP!!
THIS WILL BE THE BATTLE THAT DECIDES WHO'S GOING TO THE INTER-HIGH!!
GUZZLE
FWOOM

RIDE.50 TACTICS

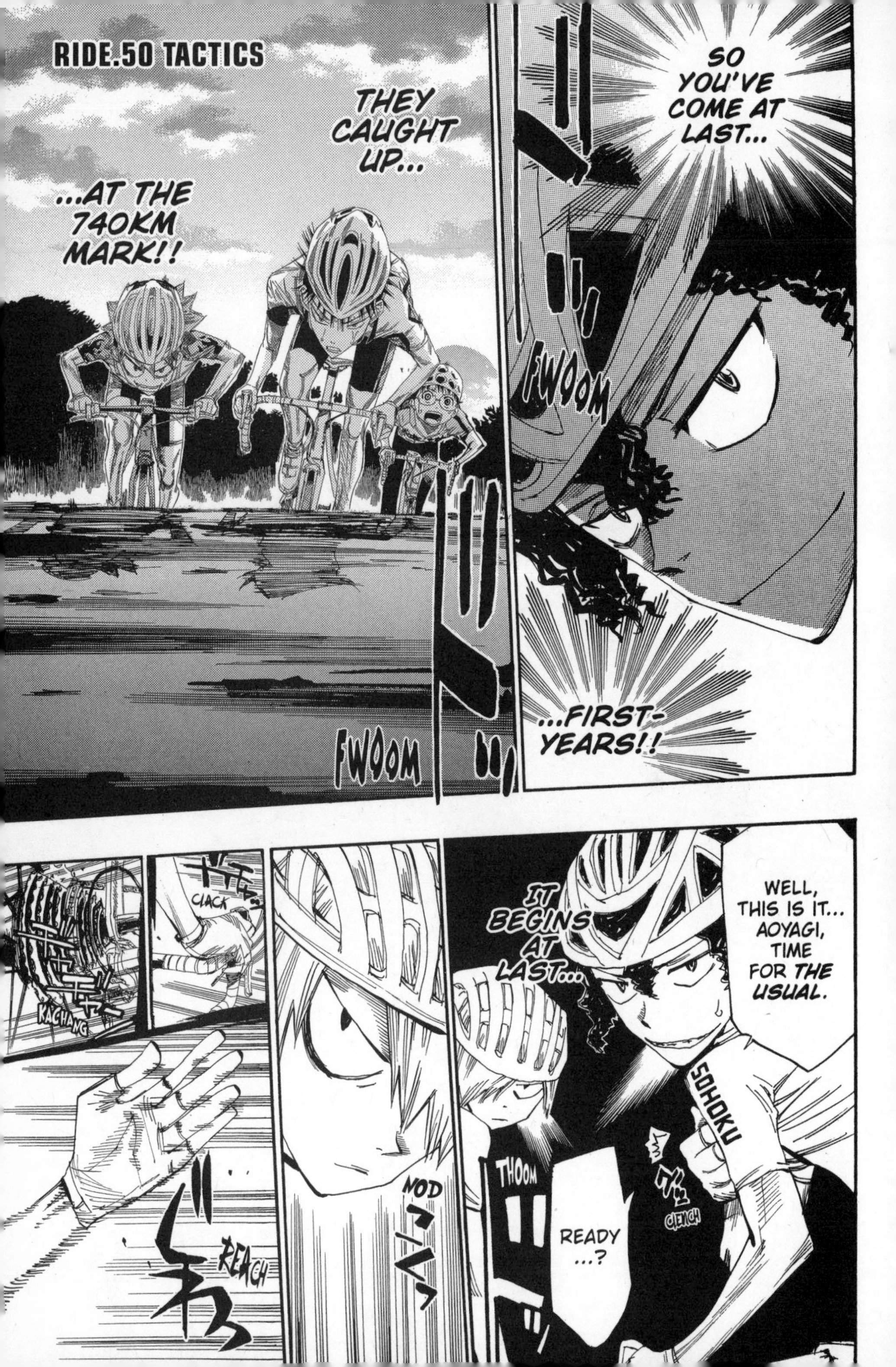

SO YOU'VE COME AT LAST...
FWOOM
...FIRST-YEARS!!
THEY CAUGHT UP...
...AT THE 740KM MARK!!
FWOOM
WELL, THIS IS IT... AOYAGI, TIME FOR THE USUAL.
IT BEGINS AT LAST...
CLENCH
THOOM
READY ...?
NOD
CLACK
KACHANG
REACH

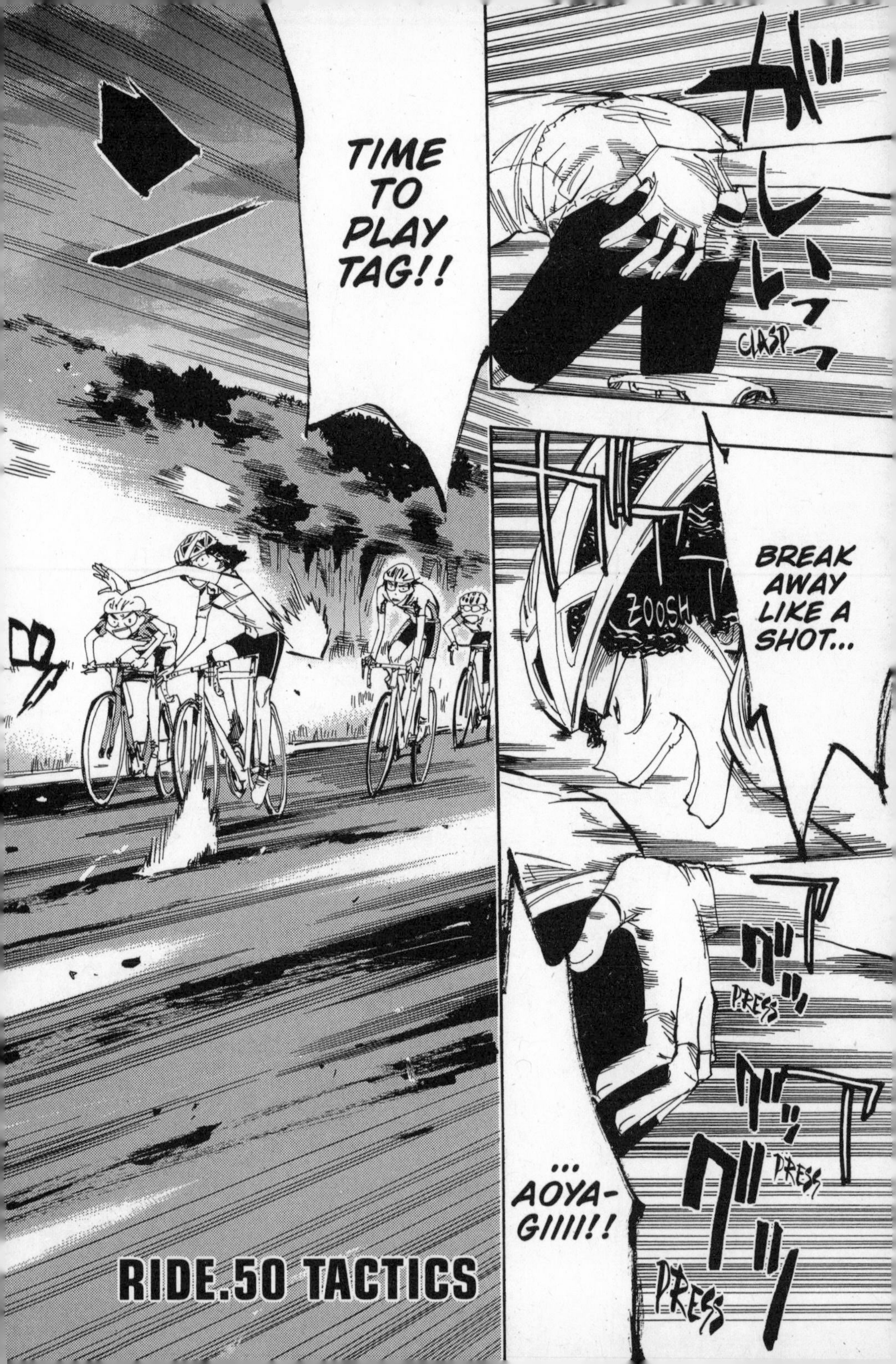
CLASP
ZOOSH
BREAK AWAY LIKE A SHOT...
PRESS
PRESS
...AOYAGIIII!!
PRESS
TIME TO PLAY TAG!!

RIDE.50 TACTICS

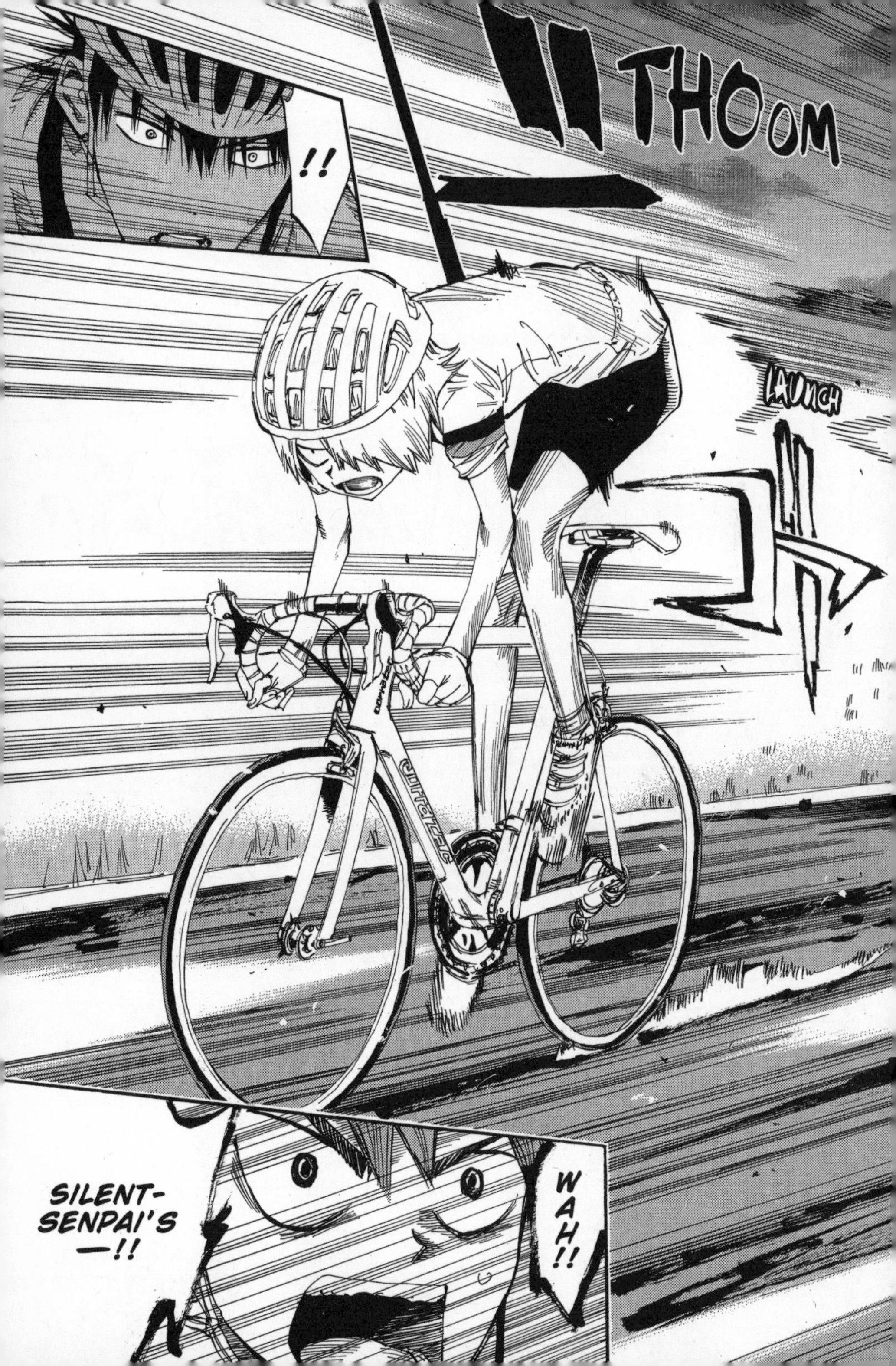
THOOM
!!
LAUNCH
WAH!!
SILENT-SENPAI'S—!!

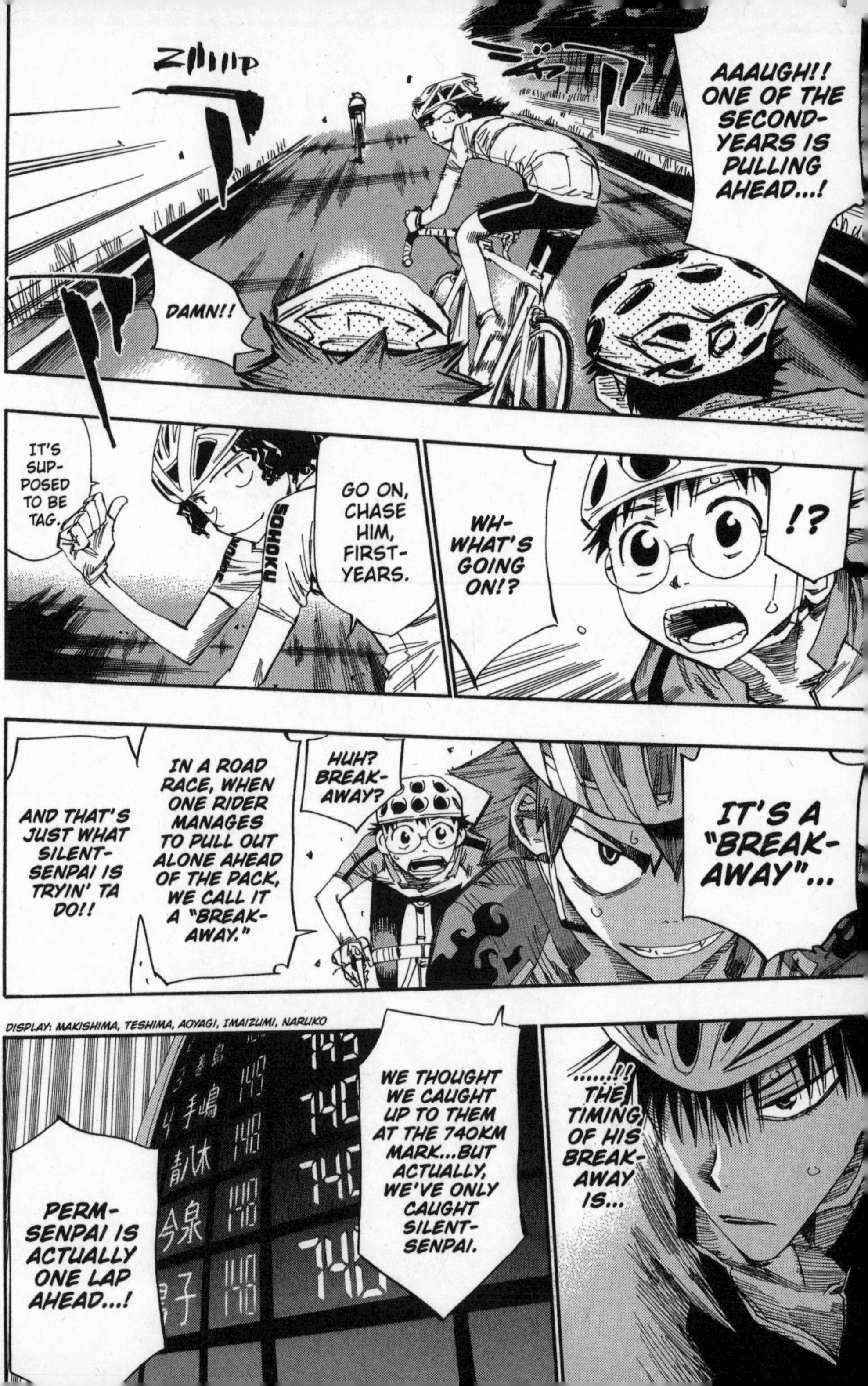

AAAUGH!! ONE OF THE SECOND-YEARS IS PULLING AHEAD...!
ZWIIIP
DAMN!!
!?
WH- WHAT'S GOING ON!?
GO ON, CHASE HIM, FIRST-YEARS.
IT'S SUPPOSED TO BE TAG.
IT'S A "BREAKAWAY"...
HUH? BREAKAWAY?
IN A ROAD RACE, WHEN ONE RIDER MANAGES TO PULL OUT ALONE AHEAD OF THE PACK, WE CALL IT A "BREAKAWAY."
AND THAT'S JUST WHAT SILENT-SENPAI IS TRYIN' TA DO!!
DISPLAY: MAKISHIMA, TESHIMA, AOYAGI, IMAIZUMI, NARUKO
......!! THE TIMING OF HIS BREAKAWAY IS...
WE THOUGHT WE CAUGHT UP TO THEM AT THE 740KM MARK...BUT ACTUALLY, WE'VE ONLY CAUGHT SILENT-SENPAI.
PERM-SENPAI IS ACTUALLY ONE LAP AHEAD...!

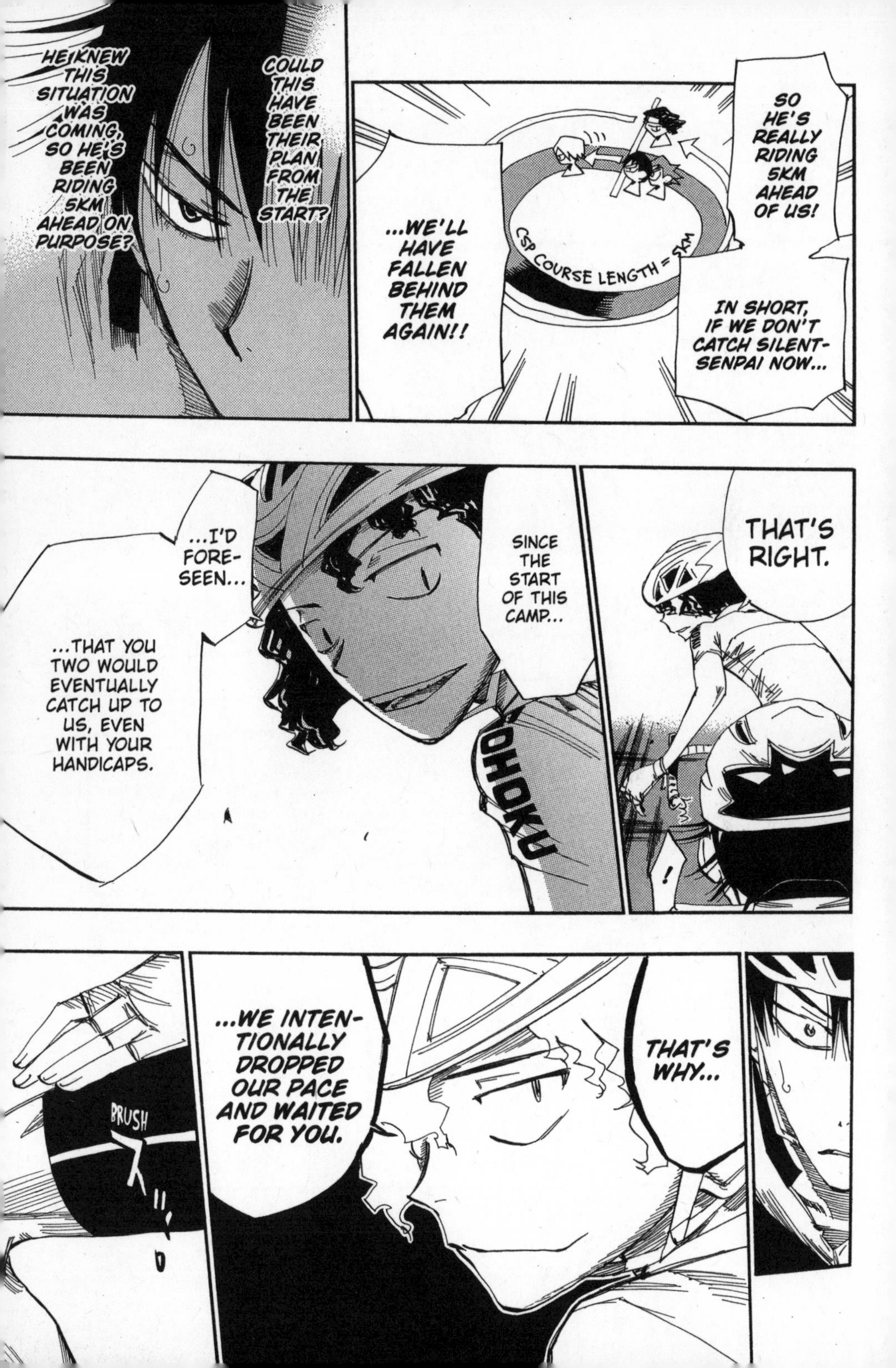
SO HE'S REALLY RIDING 5KM AHEAD OF US!
IN SHORT, IF WE DON'T CATCH SILENT-SENPAI NOW...
...WE'LL HAVE FALLEN BEHIND THEM AGAIN!!
CSP COURSE LENGTH = 5KM
COULD THIS HAVE BEEN THEIR PLAN FROM THE START?
HE KNEW THIS SITUATION WAS COMING, SO HE'S BEEN RIDING 5KM AHEAD ON PURPOSE?
THAT'S RIGHT.
!
SINCE THE START OF THIS CAMP...
...I'D FORESEEN...
...THAT YOU TWO WOULD EVENTUALLY CATCH UP TO US, EVEN WITH YOUR HANDICAPS.
THAT'S WHY...
...WE INTENTIONALLY DROPPED OUR PACE AND WAITED FOR YOU.
BRUSH

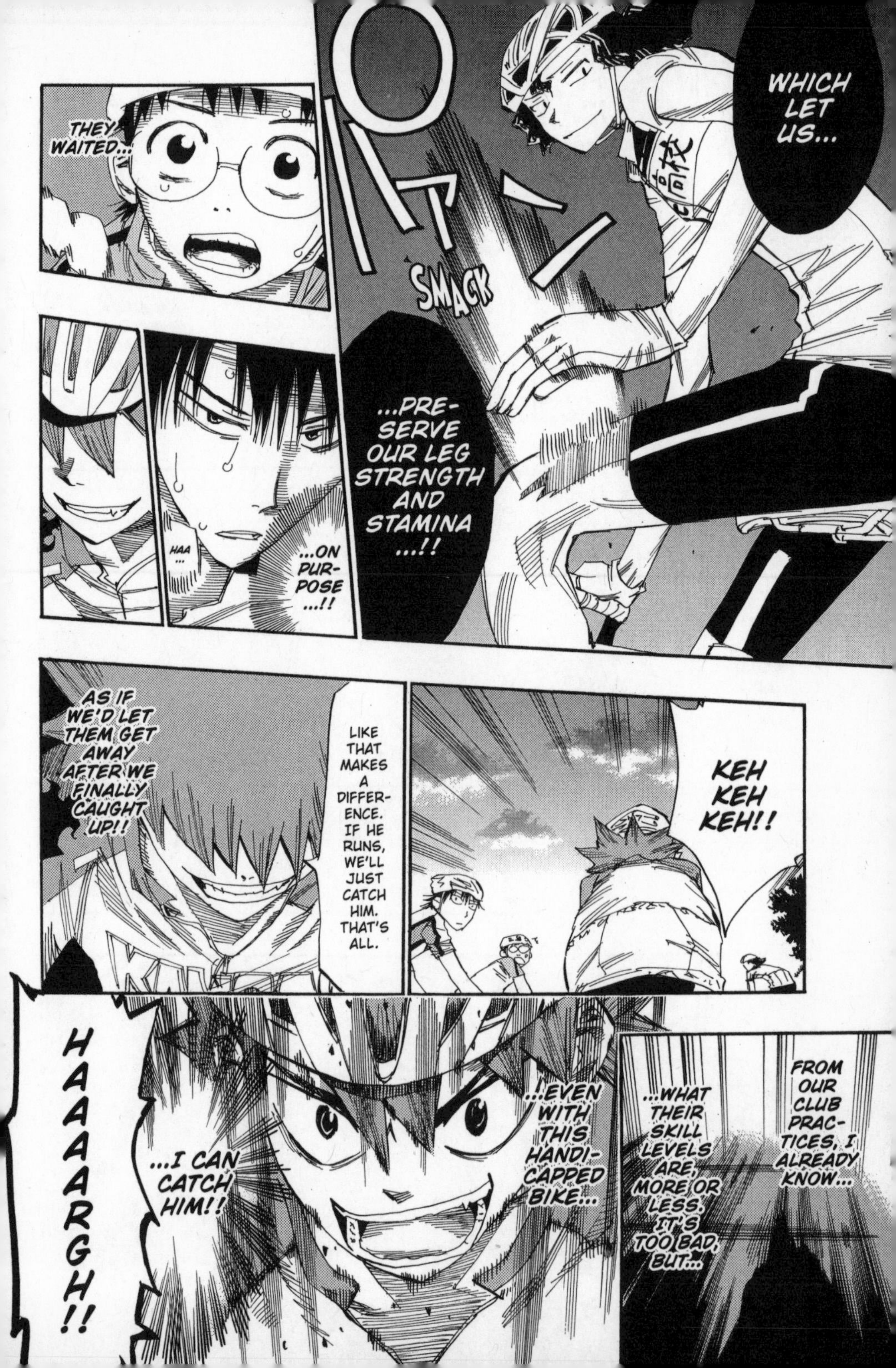
WHICH LET US...
SMACK
...PRE-SERVE OUR LEG STRENGTH AND STAMINA...!!
THEY WAITED...
...ON PURPOSE...!!
HAA...
KEH KEH KEH!!
LIKE THAT MAKES A DIFFERENCE. IF HE RUNS, WE'LL JUST CATCH HIM. THAT'S ALL.
AS IF WE'D LET THEM GET AWAY AFTER WE FINALLY CAUGHT UP!!
FROM OUR CLUB PRACTICES, I ALREADY KNOW...
...WHAT THEIR SKILL LEVELS ARE, MORE OR LESS. IT'S TOO BAD, BUT...
...EVEN WITH THIS HANDICAPPED BIKE...
...I CAN CATCH HIM!!
HAAAAARGH!!

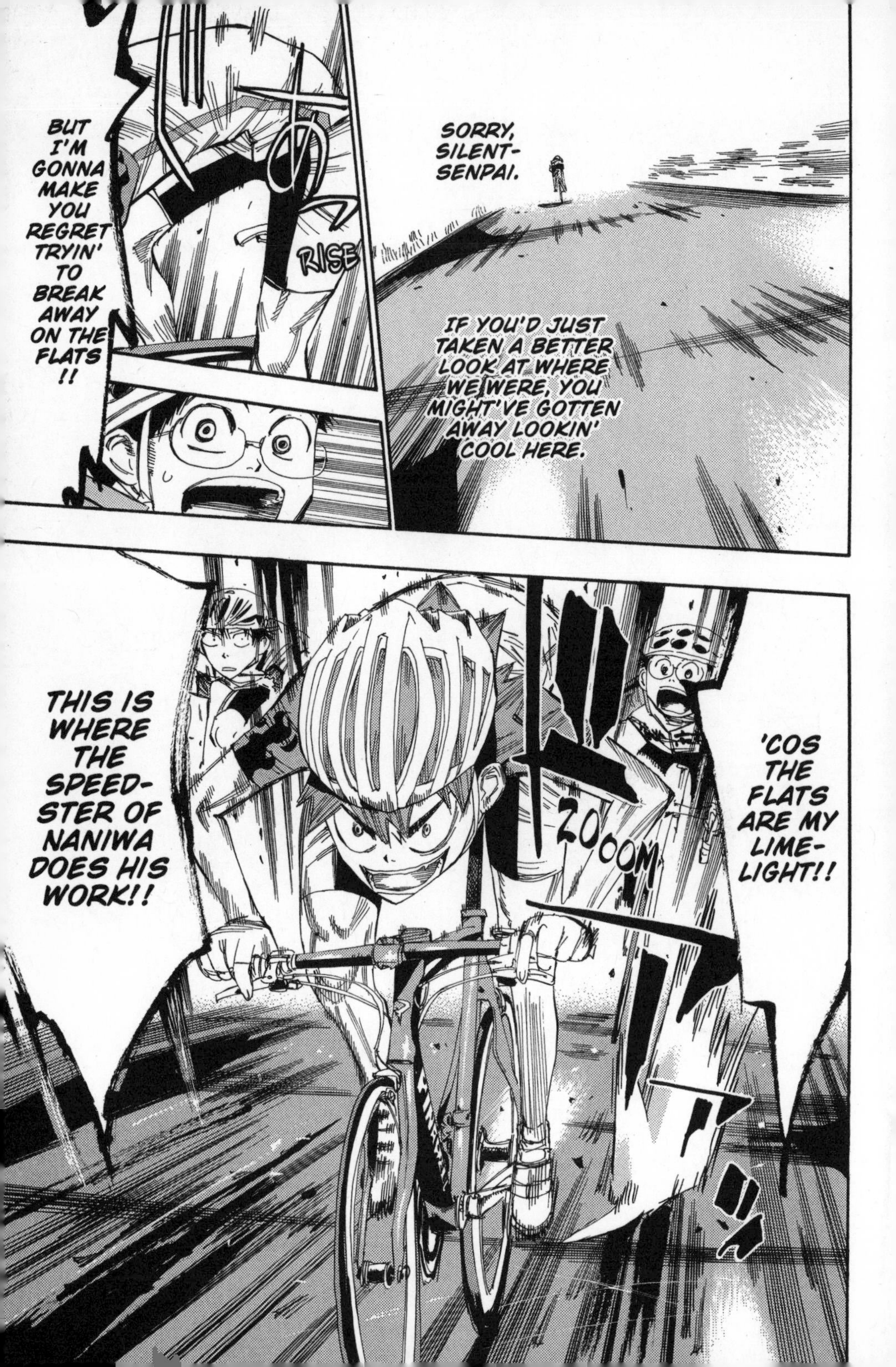
SORRY, SILENT-SENPAI.
IF YOU'D JUST TAKEN A BETTER LOOK AT WHERE WE WERE, YOU MIGHT'VE GOTTEN AWAY LOOKIN' COOL HERE.
BUT I'M GONNA MAKE YOU REGRET TRYIN' TO BREAK AWAY ON THE FLATS !!
RISE
'COS THE FLATS ARE MY LIME-LIGHT!!
ZOOOM
THIS IS WHERE THE SPEED-STER OF NANIWA DOES HIS WORK!!

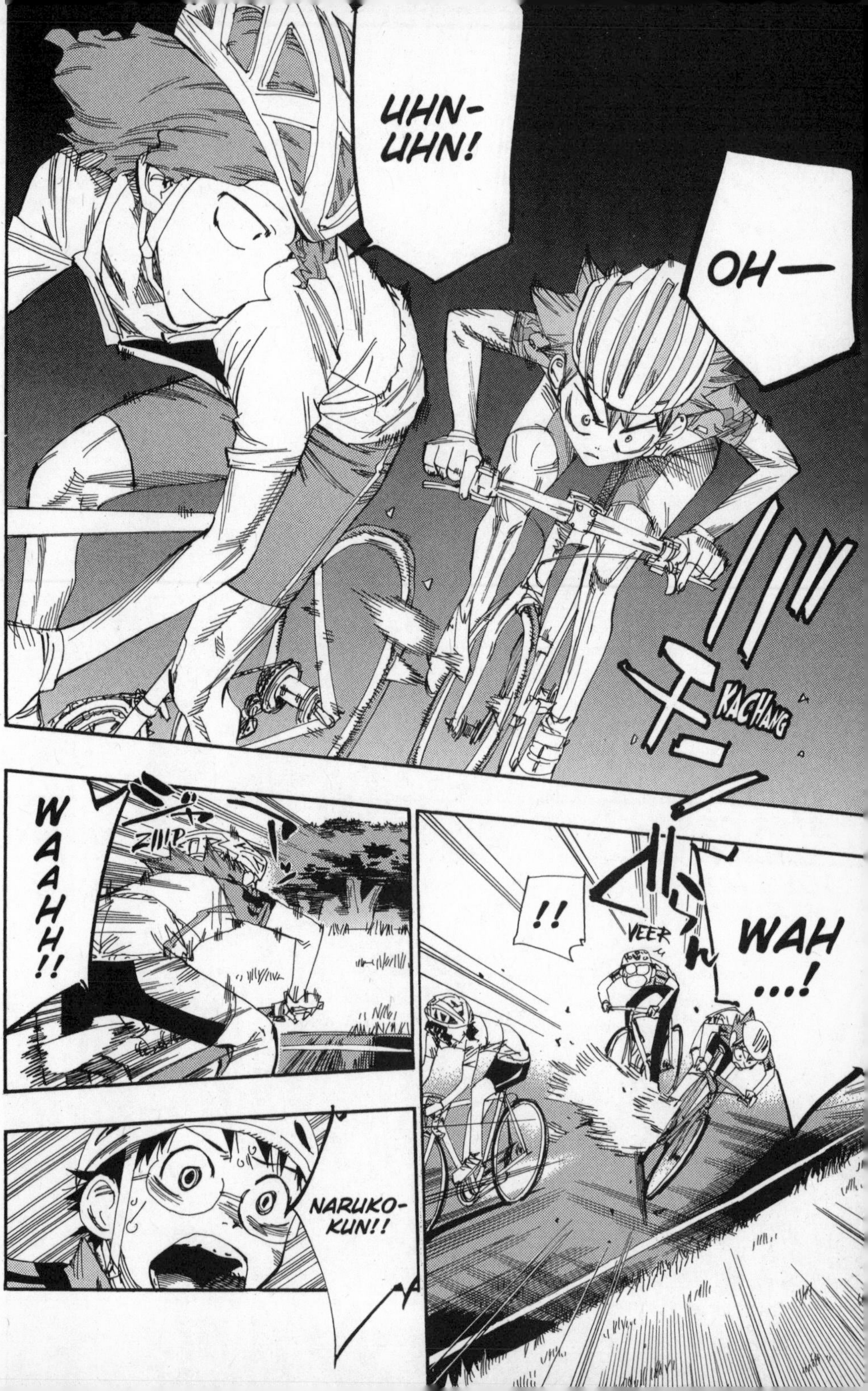
UHN-UHN!
OH—
KACHANG
!!
VEER
WAH...!
ZIIIP
WAAAHH!!
NARUKO-KUN!!

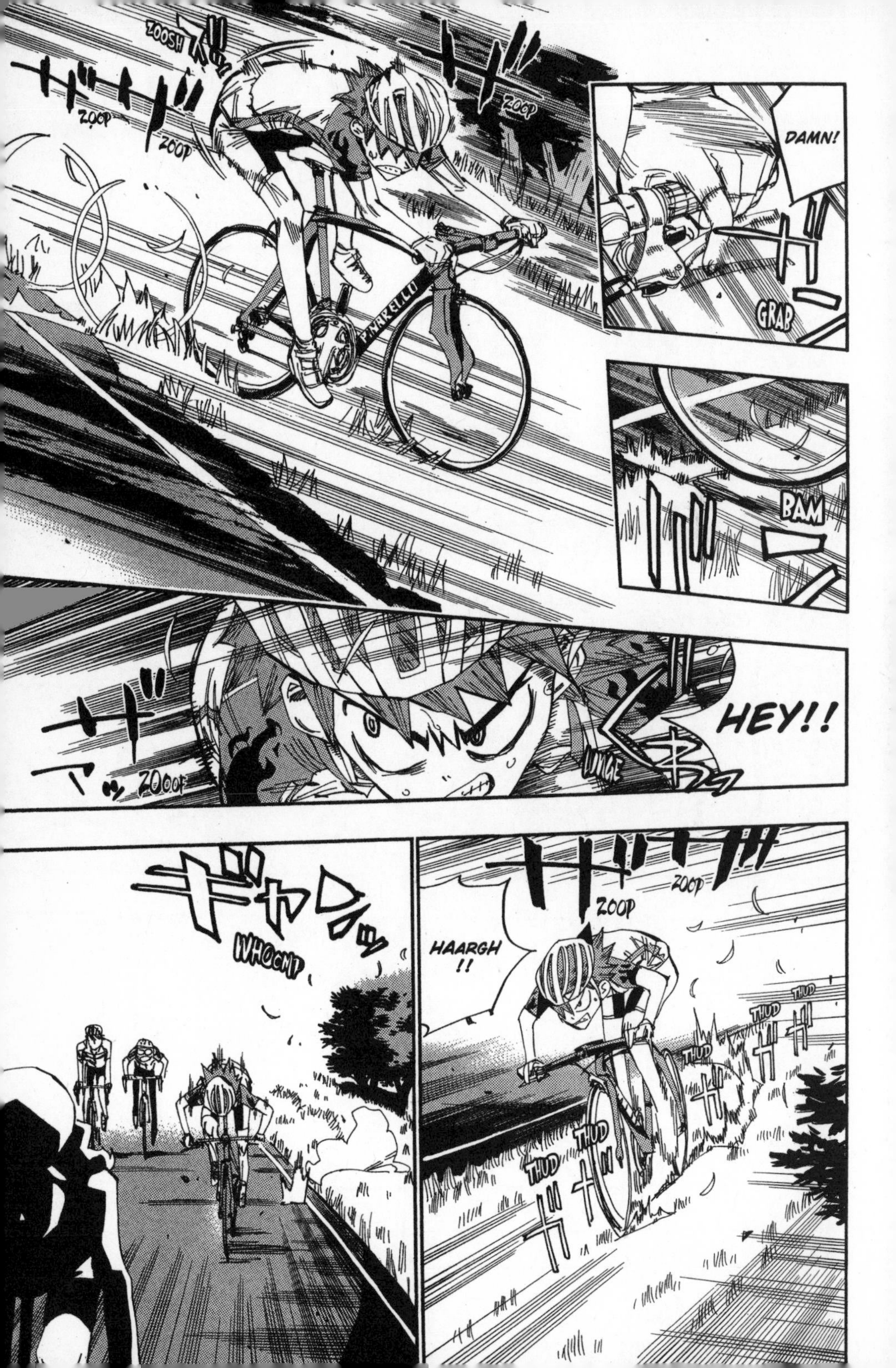

DAMN!
GRAB
BAM
ZOOSH
ZOOP
ZOOP
ZOOP
HEY!!
LUNGE
ZOOOP
ZOOP
ZOOP
HAARGH!!
THUD
THUD
THUD
THUD
THUD
WHOOMP

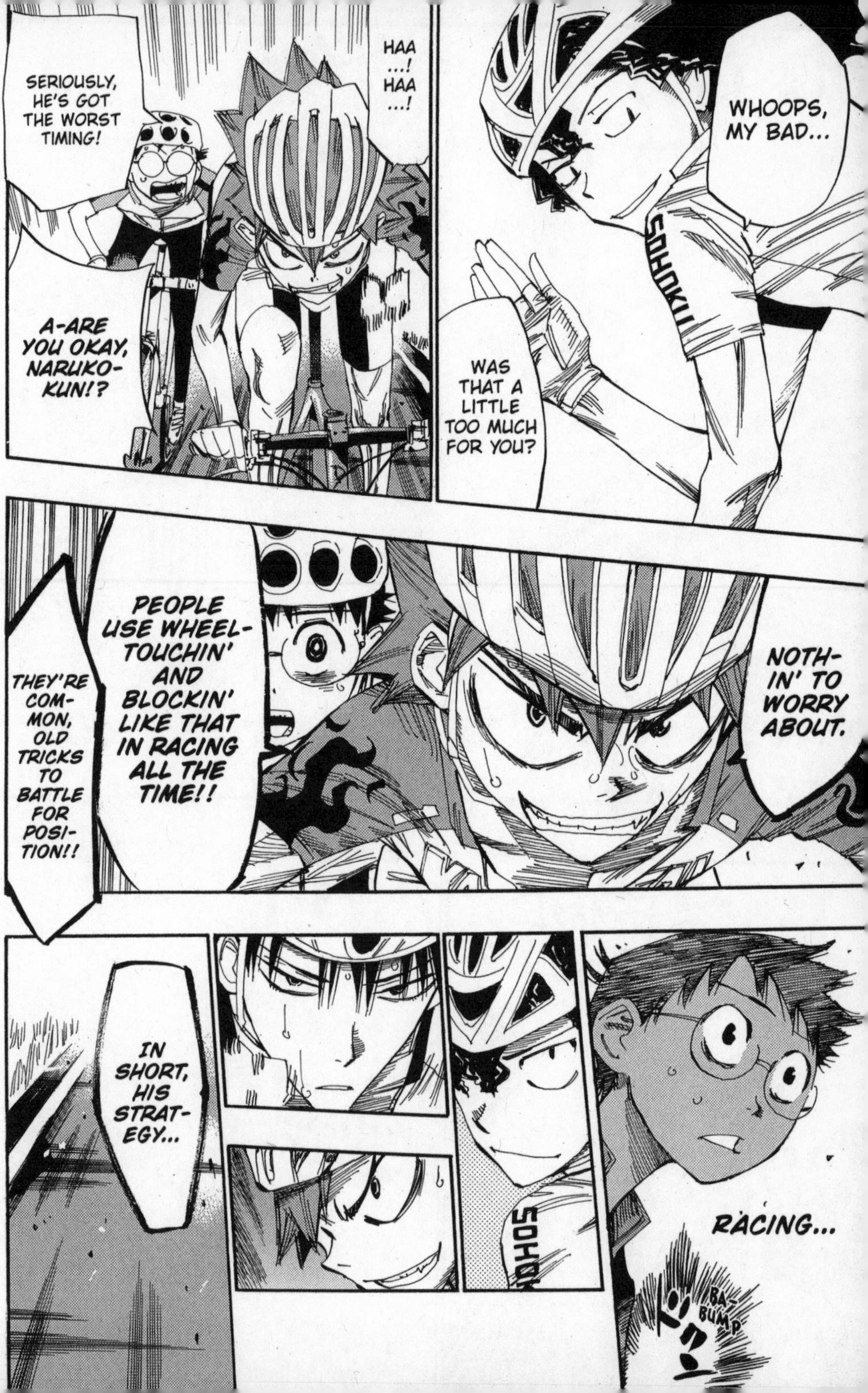
WHOOPS, MY BAD...
WAS THAT A LITTLE TOO MUCH FOR YOU?
HAA...! HAA...!
SERIOUSLY, HE'S GOT THE WORST TIMING!
A-ARE YOU OKAY, NARUKO-KUN!?
NOTHIN' TO WORRY ABOUT.
PEOPLE USE WHEEL-TOUCHIN' AND BLOCKIN' LIKE THAT IN RACING ALL THE TIME!!
THEY'RE COMMON, OLD TRICKS TO BATTLE FOR POSITION!!
RACING...
BA-BUMP
IN SHORT, HIS STRATEGY...

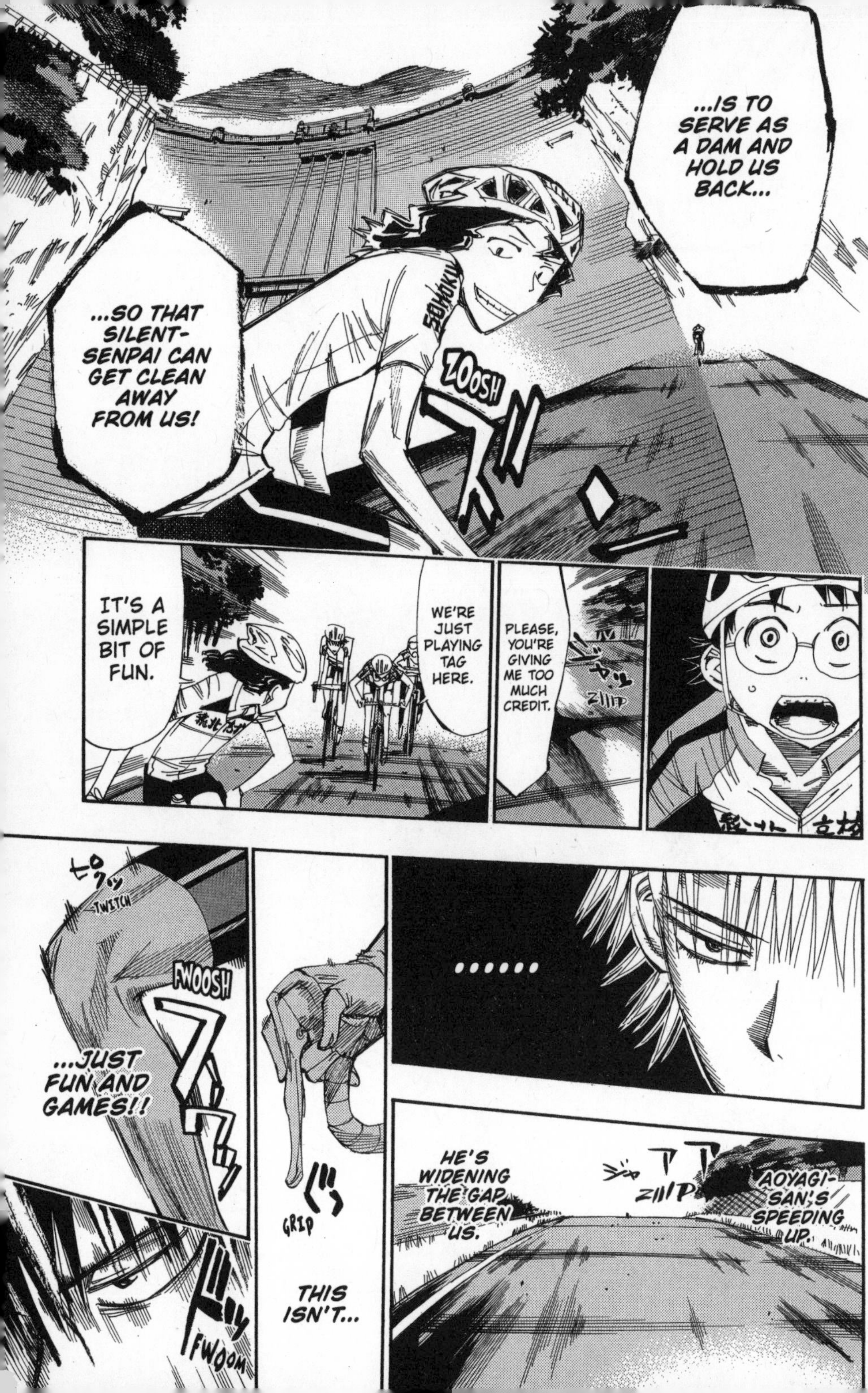
...IS TO SERVE AS A DAM AND HOLD US BACK...
...SO THAT SILENT-SENPAI CAN GET CLEAN AWAY FROM US!
ZOOSH
PLEASE, YOU'RE GIVING ME TOO MUCH CREDIT.
ZIIIP
WE'RE JUST PLAYING TAG HERE.
IT'S A SIMPLE BIT OF FUN.
......
AOYAGI-SAN'S SPEEDING UP.
ZIIIP
HE'S WIDENING THE GAP BETWEEN US.
GRIP
THIS ISN'T...
TWITCH
FWOOSH
...JUST FUN AND GAMES!!
FWOOM

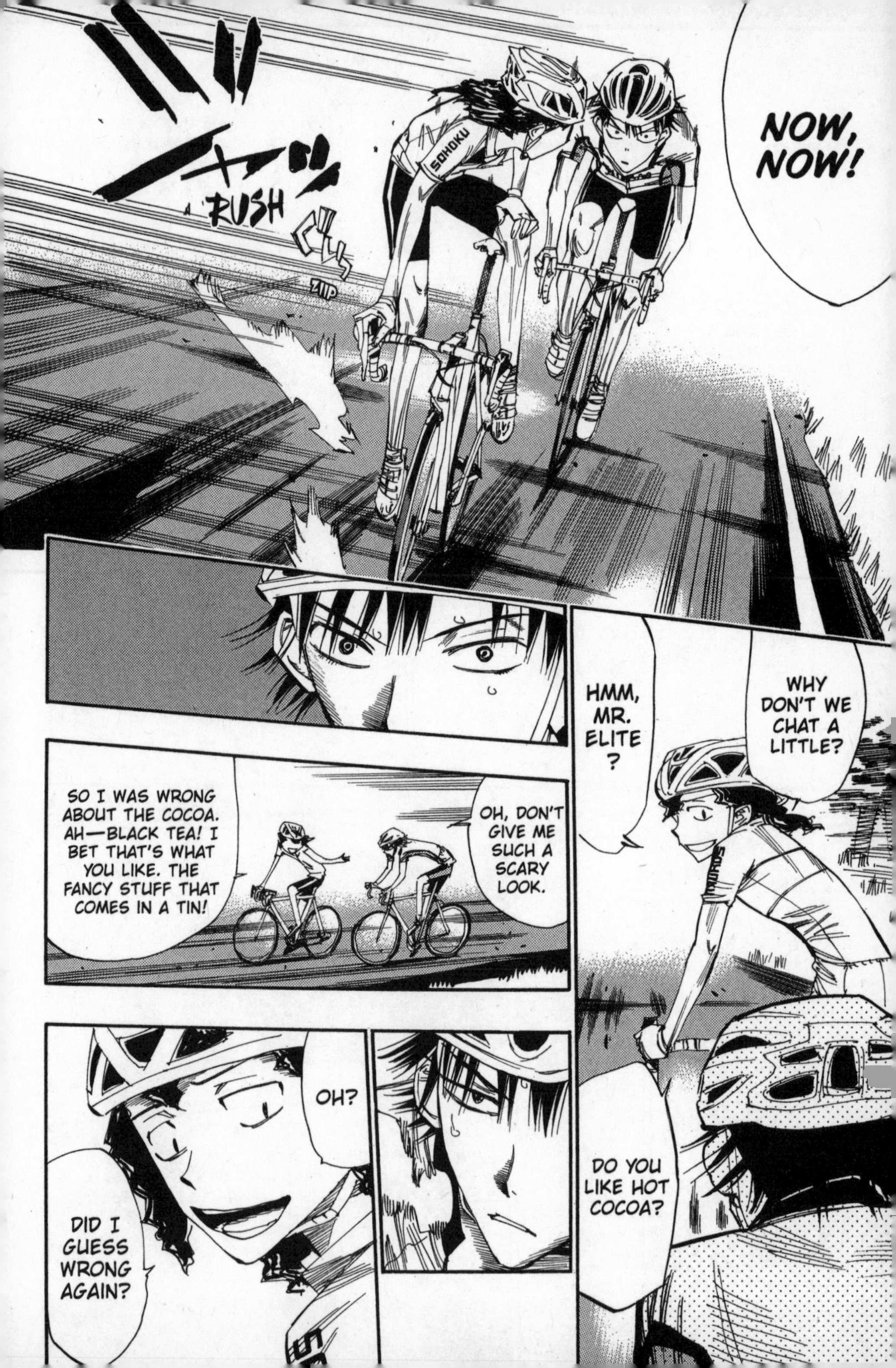
NOW, NOW!
RUSH
ZIP
WHY DON'T WE CHAT A LITTLE?
HMM, MR. ELITE?
DO YOU LIKE HOT COCOA?
OH, DON'T GIVE ME SUCH A SCARY LOOK.
SO I WAS WRONG ABOUT THE COCOA. AH—BLACK TEA! I BET THAT'S WHAT YOU LIKE. THE FANCY STUFF THAT COMES IN A TIN!
OH?
DID I GUESS WRONG AGAIN?

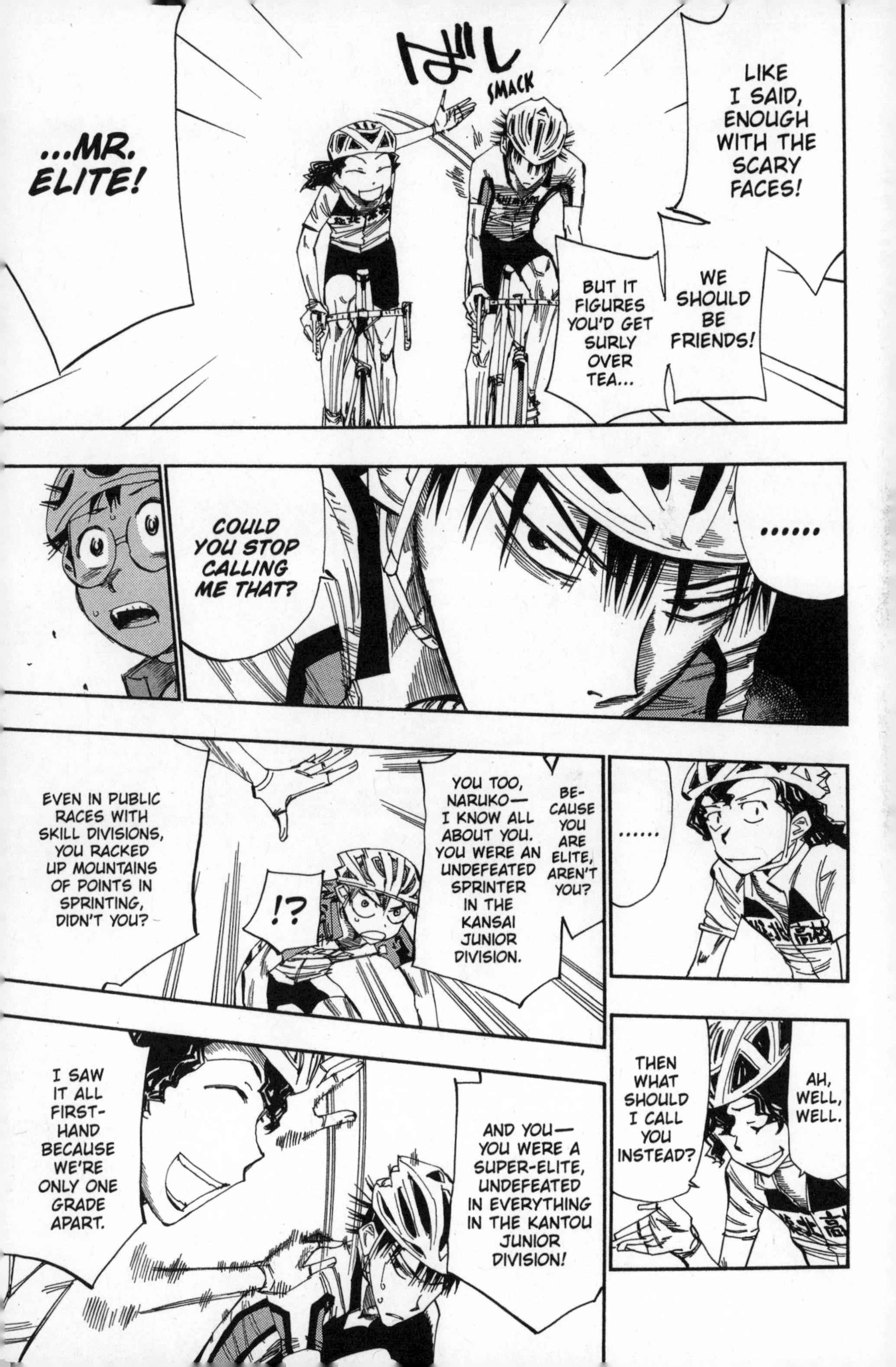

LIKE I SAID, ENOUGH WITH THE SCARY FACES!
WE SHOULD BE FRIENDS!
BUT IT FIGURES YOU'D GET SURLY OVER TEA...
SMACK
...MR. ELITE!
......
COULD YOU STOP CALLING ME THAT?
......
BE-CAUSE YOU ARE ELITE, AREN'T YOU?
YOU TOO, NARUKO— I KNOW ALL ABOUT YOU. YOU WERE AN UNDEFEATED SPRINTER IN THE KANSAI JUNIOR DIVISION.
!?
EVEN IN PUBLIC RACES WITH SKILL DIVISIONS, YOU RACKED UP MOUNTAINS OF POINTS IN SPRINTING, DIDN'T YOU?
AH, WELL, WELL.
THEN WHAT SHOULD I CALL YOU INSTEAD?
AND YOU— YOU WERE A SUPER-ELITE, UNDEFEATED IN EVERYTHING IN THE KANTOU JUNIOR DIVISION!
I SAW IT ALL FIRST-HAND BECAUSE WE'RE ONLY ONE GRADE APART.

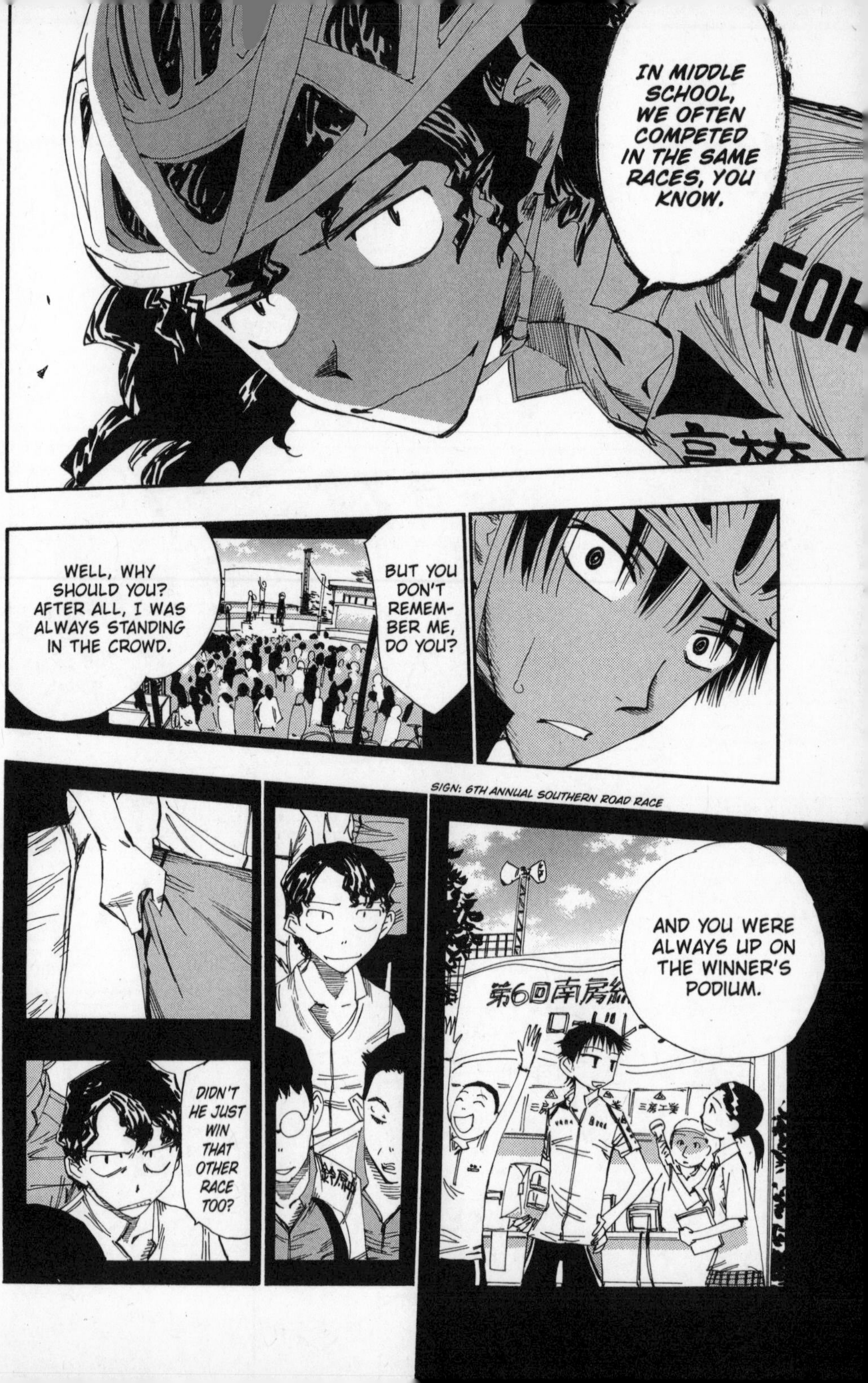
IN MIDDLE SCHOOL, WE OFTEN COMPETED IN THE SAME RACES, YOU KNOW.
BUT YOU DON'T REMEMBER ME, DO YOU?
WELL, WHY SHOULD YOU? AFTER ALL, I WAS ALWAYS STANDING IN THE CROWD.
SIGN: 6TH ANNUAL SOUTHERN ROAD RACE
AND YOU WERE ALWAYS UP ON THE WINNER'S PODIUM.
DIDN'T HE JUST WIN THAT OTHER RACE TOO?

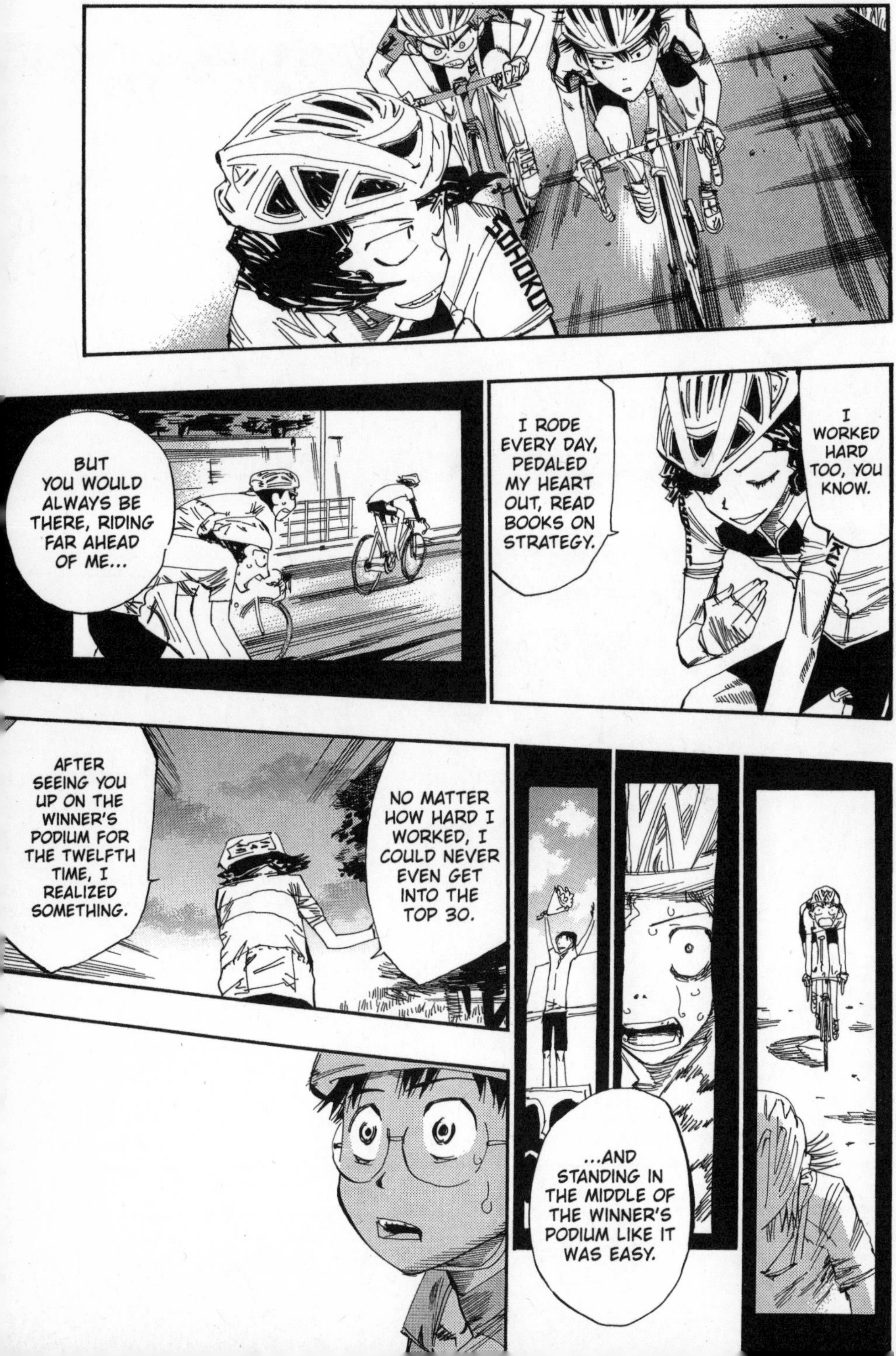
SOHOKU
I WORKED HARD TOO, YOU KNOW.
I RODE EVERY DAY, PEDALED MY HEART OUT, READ BOOKS ON STRATEGY.
BUT YOU WOULD ALWAYS BE THERE, RIDING FAR AHEAD OF ME...
...AND STANDING IN THE MIDDLE OF THE WINNER'S PODIUM LIKE IT WAS EASY.
NO MATTER HOW HARD I WORKED, I COULD NEVER EVEN GET INTO THE TOP 30.
AFTER SEEING YOU UP ON THE WINNER'S PODIUM FOR THE TWELFTH TIME, I REALIZED SOMETHING.

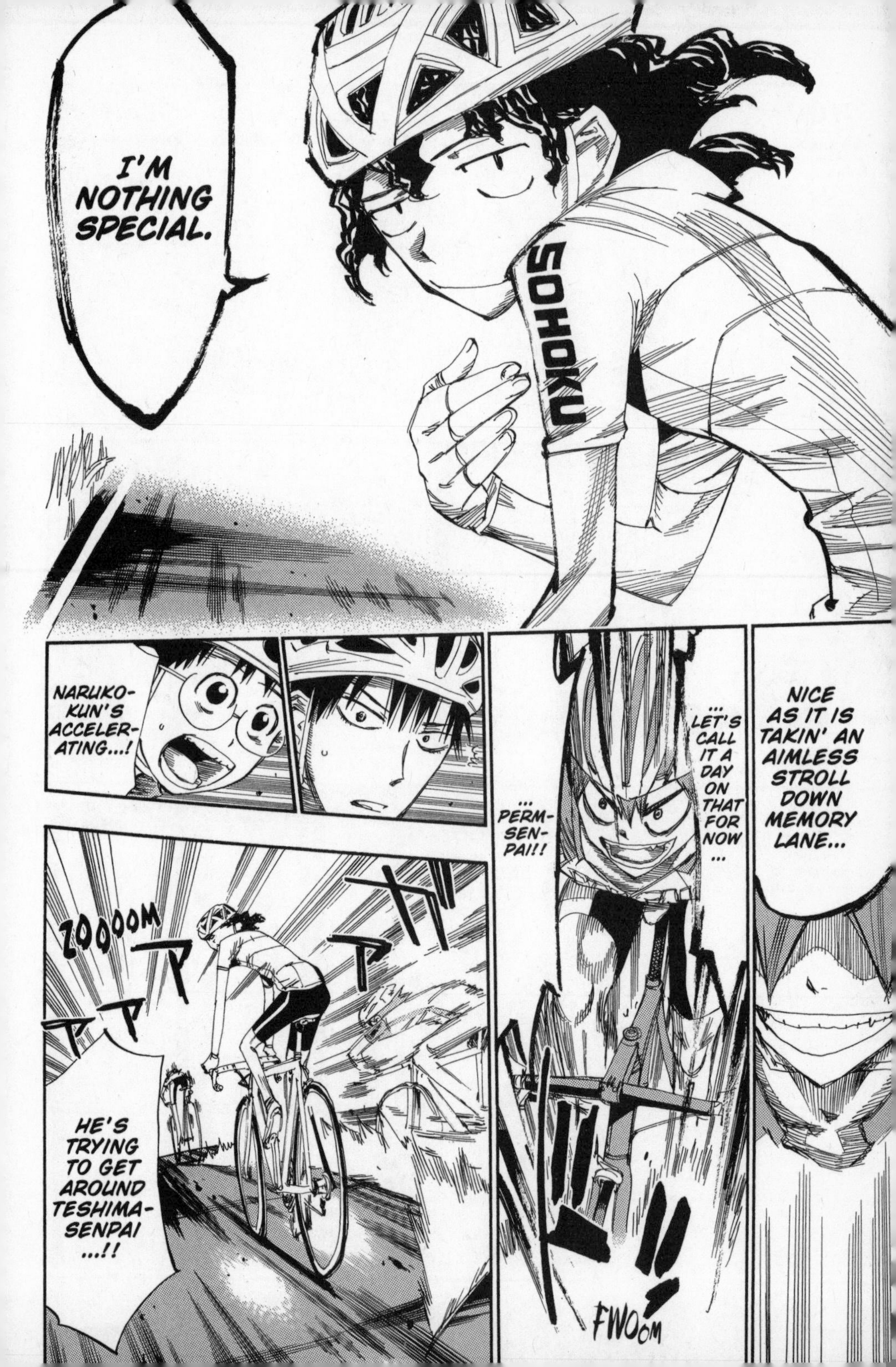
I'M NOTHING SPECIAL.
NICE AS IT IS TAKIN' AN AIMLESS STROLL DOWN MEMORY LANE...
...LET'S CALL IT A DAY ON THAT FOR NOW...
...PERM-SEN-PAI!!
FWOOM
NARUKO-KUN'S ACCELER-ATING...!
ZOOOOM
HE'S TRYING TO GET AROUND TESHIMA-SENPAI...!!

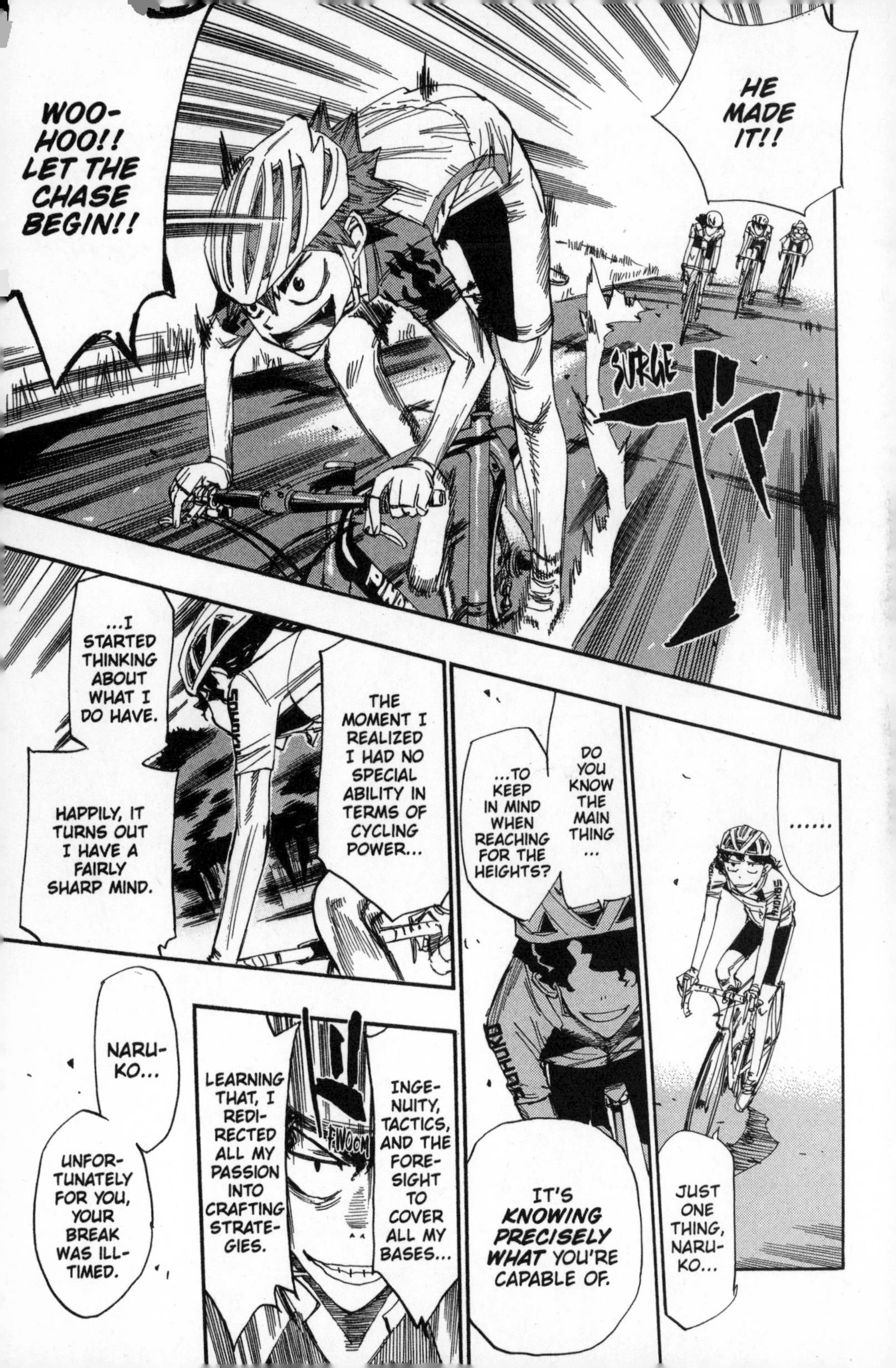
HE MADE IT!!
WOO-HOO!! LET THE CHASE BEGIN!!
SURGE
......
JUST ONE THING, NARUKO...
DO YOU KNOW THE MAIN THING...
...TO KEEP IN MIND WHEN REACHING FOR THE HEIGHTS?
IT'S KNOWING PRECISELY WHAT YOU'RE CAPABLE OF.
THE MOMENT I REALIZED I HAD NO SPECIAL ABILITY IN TERMS OF CYCLING POWER...
...I STARTED THINKING ABOUT WHAT I DO HAVE.
HAPPILY, IT TURNS OUT I HAVE A FAIRLY SHARP MIND.
INGENUITY, TACTICS, AND THE FORESIGHT TO COVER ALL MY BASES...
LEARNING THAT, I REDIRECTED ALL MY PASSION INTO CRAFTING STRATEGIES.
FWOOM
NARUKO...
UNFORTUNATELY FOR YOU, YOUR BREAK WAS ILL-TIMED.

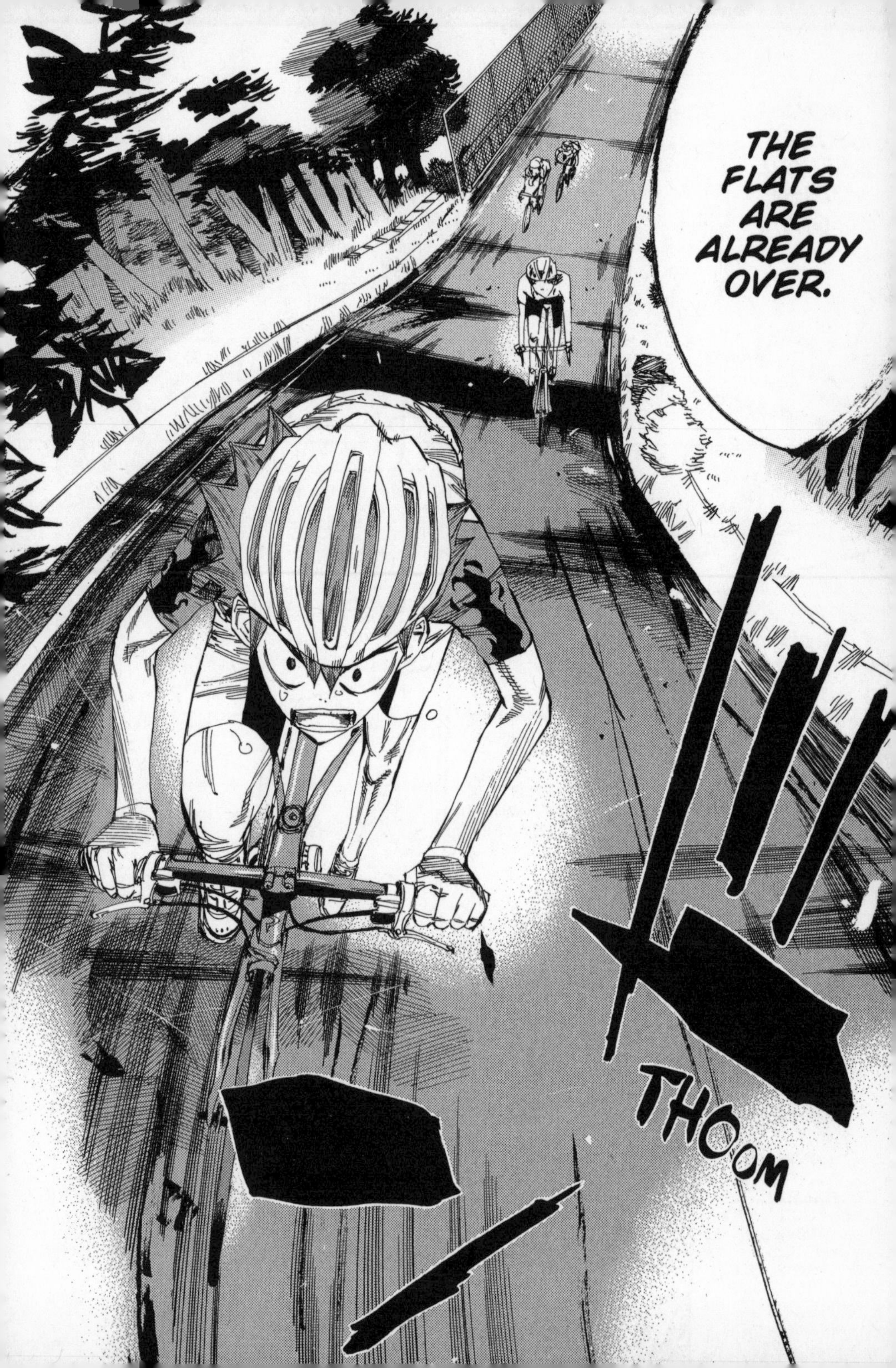
THE FLATS ARE ALREADY OVER.
THOOM

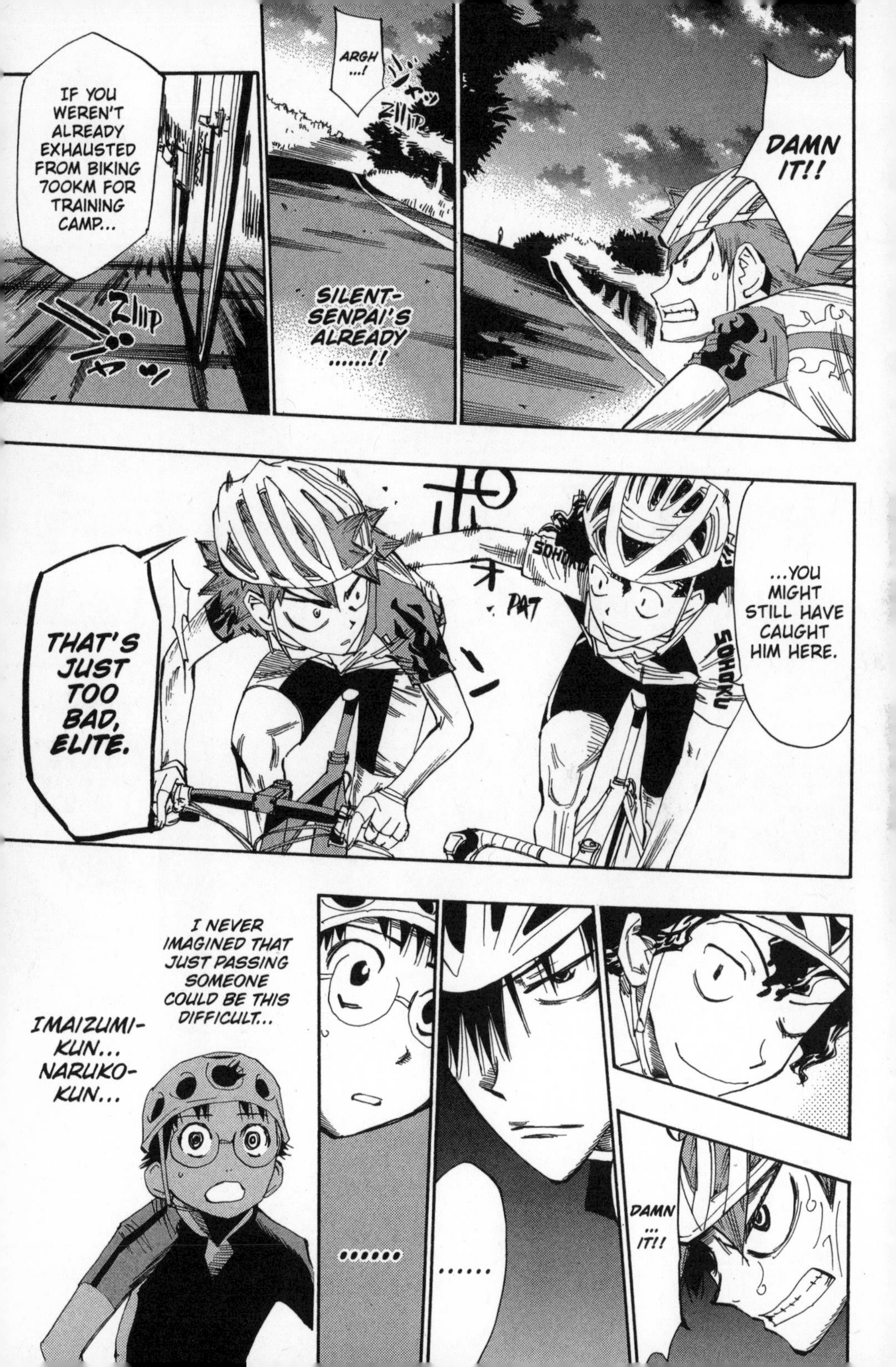
DAMN IT!!
ARGH ...!
ZIIIP
SILENT-SENPAI'S ALREADY ......!!
IF YOU WEREN'T ALREADY EXHAUSTED FROM BIKING 700KM FOR TRAINING CAMP...
ZIIIP
...YOU MIGHT STILL HAVE CAUGHT HIM HERE.
PAT
THAT'S JUST TOO BAD, ELITE.
DAMN ... IT!!
......
......
I NEVER IMAGINED THAT JUST PASSING SOMEONE COULD BE THIS DIFFICULT...
IMAIZUMI-KUN... NARUKO-KUN...

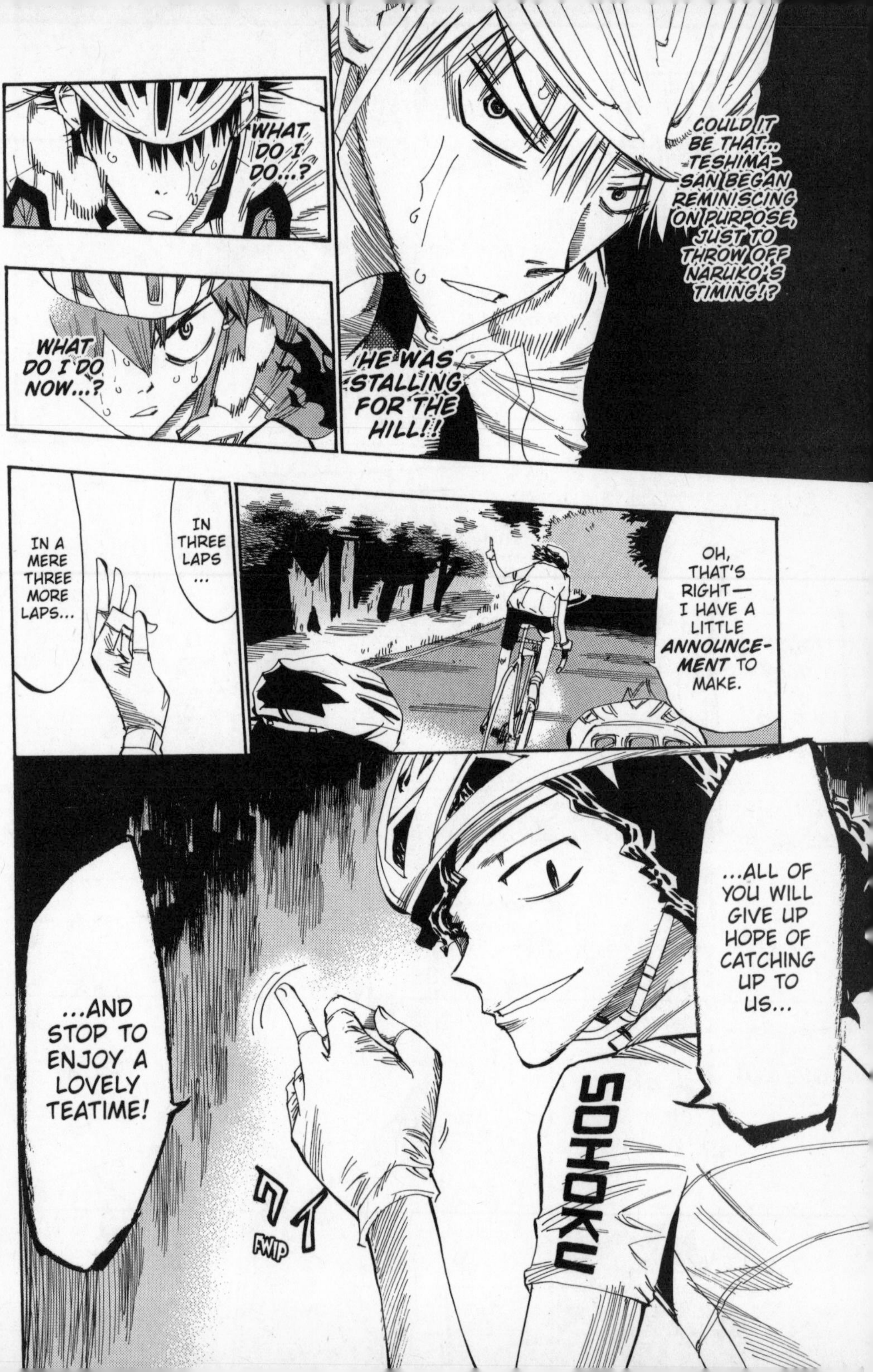
COULD IT BE THAT... TESHIMA-SAN BEGAN REMINISCING ON PURPOSE, JUST TO THROW OFF NARUKO'S TIMING!?
HE WAS STALLING FOR THE HILL!!
WHAT DO I DO...?
WHAT DO I DO NOW...?
OH, THAT'S RIGHT— I HAVE A LITTLE ANNOUNCEMENT TO MAKE.
IN THREE LAPS...
IN A MERE THREE MORE LAPS...
...ALL OF YOU WILL GIVE UP HOPE OF CATCHING UP TO US...
SOHOKU
FWIP
...AND STOP TO ENJOY A LOVELY TEATIME!

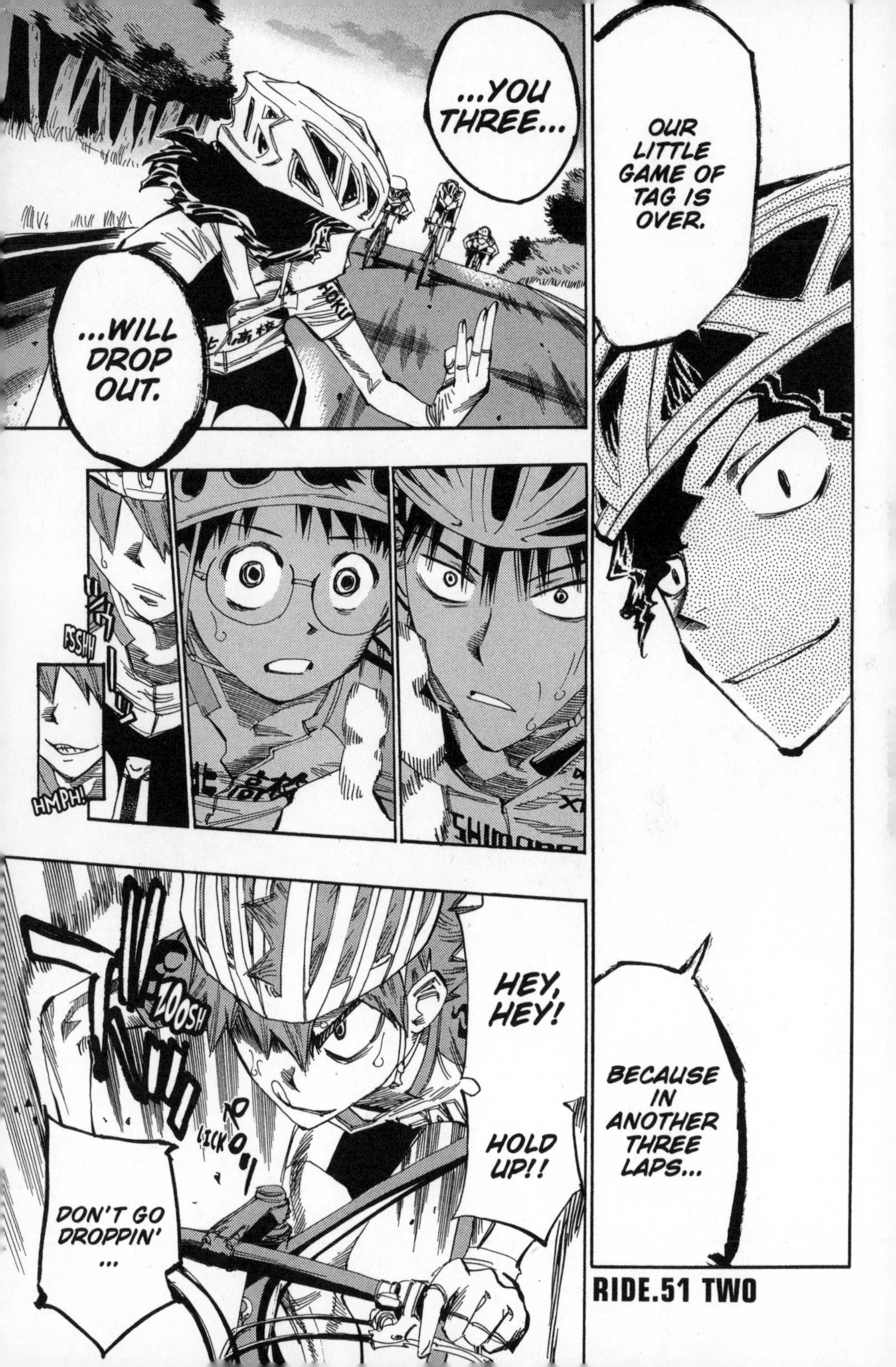
OUR LITTLE GAME OF TAG IS OVER.
BECAUSE IN ANOTHER THREE LAPS...
...YOU THREE...
...WILL DROP OUT.
FSSHH
HMPH!
HEY, HEY!
ZOOSH
LICK
HOLD UP!!
DON'T GO DROPPIN' ...

RIDE.51 TWO

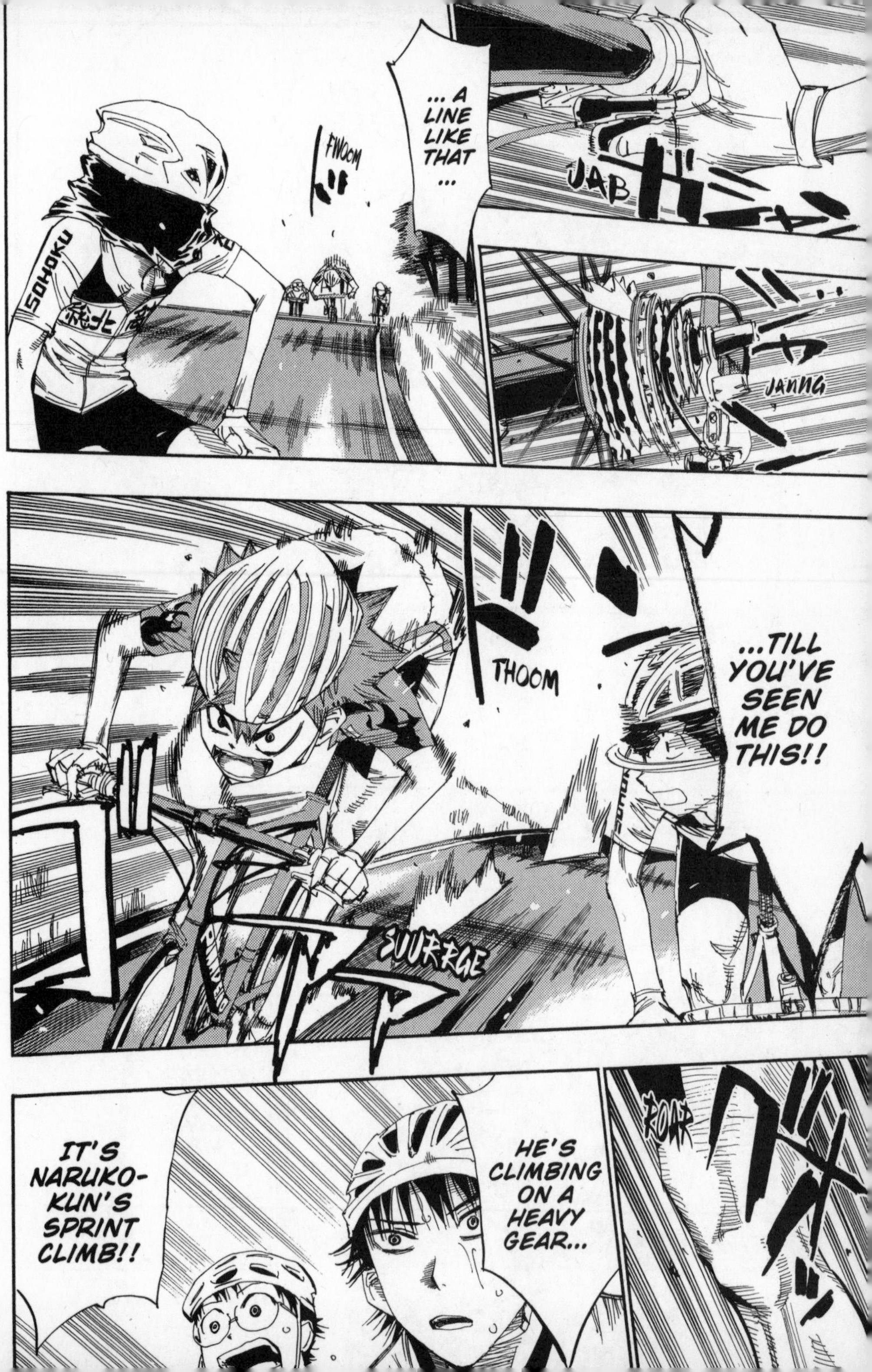
JAB
JANNG
... A LINE LIKE THAT ...
FWOOM
THOOM
...TILL YOU'VE SEEN ME DO THIS!!
SUURRGE
ROAR
HE'S CLIMBING ON A HEAVY GEAR...
IT'S NARUKO-KUN'S SPRINT CLIMB!!

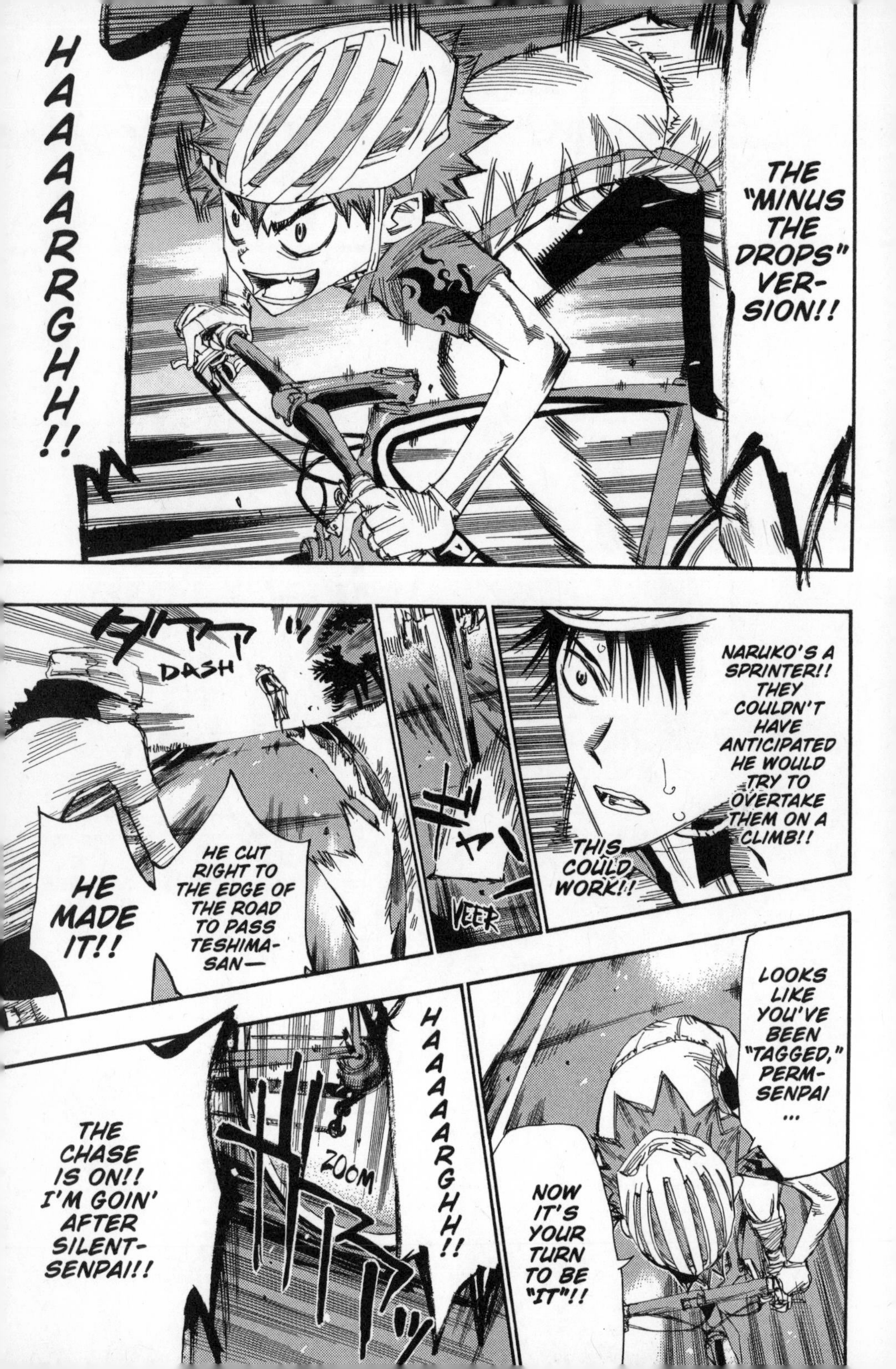

THE "MINUS THE DROPS" VERSION!!
HAAAAARRGHH!!
NARUKO'S A SPRINTER!! THEY COULDN'T HAVE ANTICIPATED HE WOULD TRY TO OVERTAKE THEM ON A CLIMB!!
THIS COULD WORK!!
VEER
DASH
HE CUT RIGHT TO THE EDGE OF THE ROAD TO PASS TESHIMA-SAN—
HE MADE IT!!
LOOKS LIKE YOU'VE BEEN "TAGGED," PERM-SENPAI ...
NOW IT'S YOUR TURN TO BE "IT"!!
HAAAAARGHH!!
ZOOM
THE CHASE IS ON!! I'M GOIN' AFTER SILENT-SENPAI!!

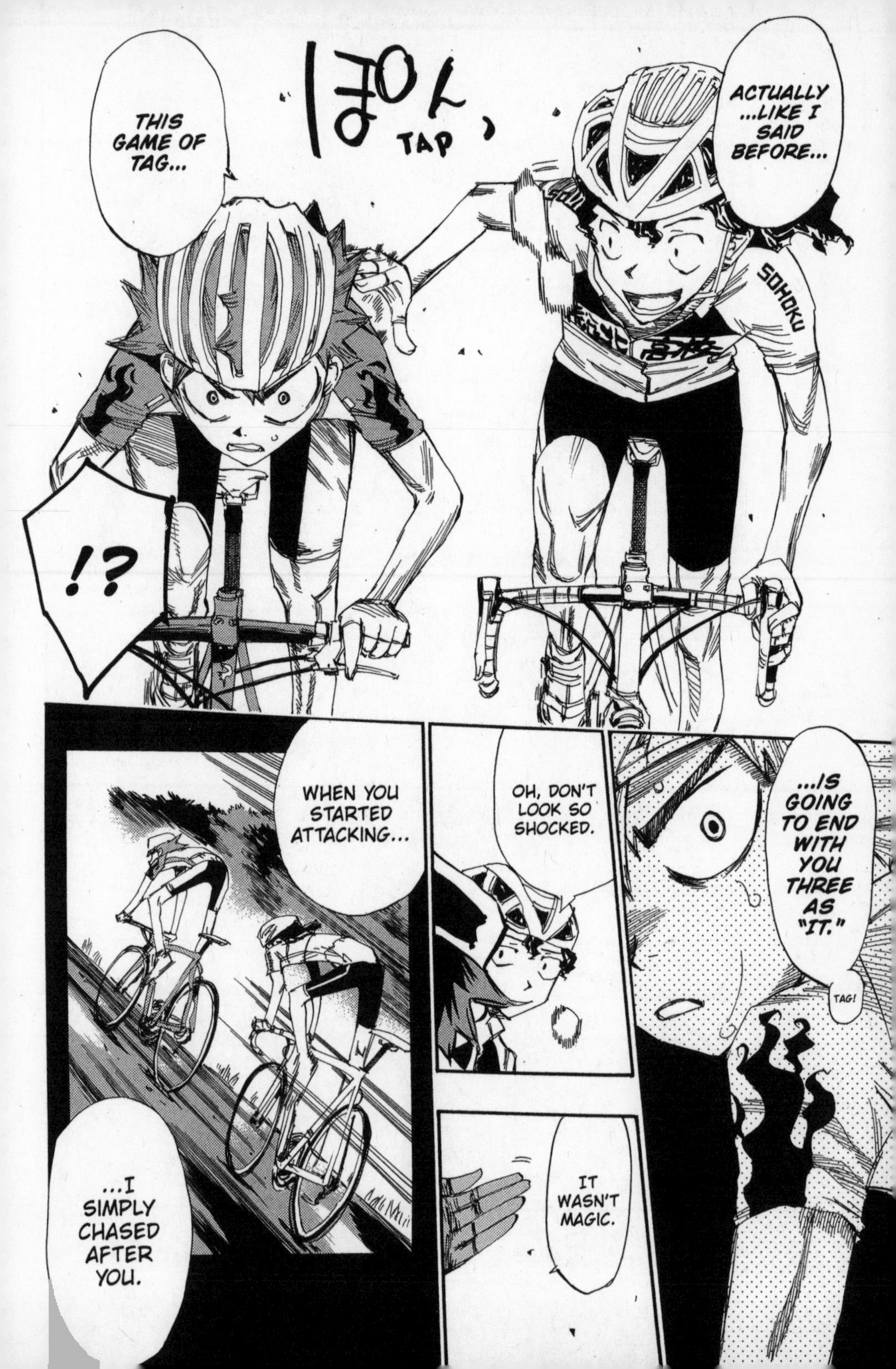
ACTUALLY ...LIKE I SAID BEFORE...
THIS GAME OF TAG...
ぽん
TAP
!?
...IS GOING TO END WITH YOU THREE AS "IT."
TAG!
OH, DON'T LOOK SO SHOCKED.
IT WASN'T MAGIC.
WHEN YOU STARTED ATTACKING...
...I SIMPLY CHASED AFTER YOU.

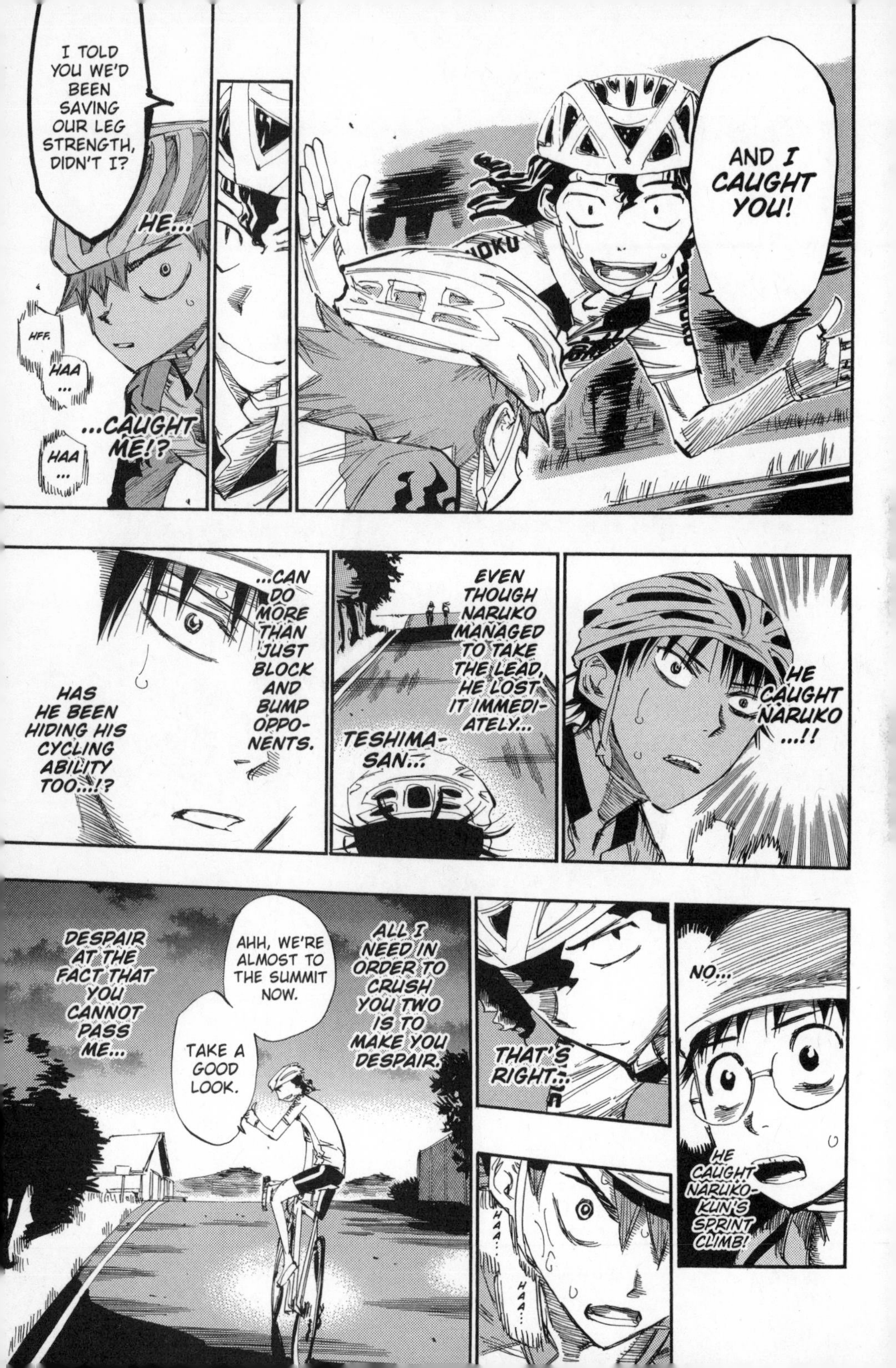
AND I CAUGHT YOU!
I TOLD YOU WE'D BEEN SAVING OUR LEG STRENGTH, DIDN'T I?
HE...
HFF.
HAA...
HAA...
...CAUGHT ME!?
HE CAUGHT NARUKO...!!
EVEN THOUGH NARUKO MANAGED TO TAKE THE LEAD, HE LOST IT IMMEDIATELY...
TESHIMA-SAN...
...CAN DO MORE THAN JUST BLOCK AND BUMP OPPONENTS.
HAS HE BEEN HIDING HIS CYCLING ABILITY TOO...!?
NO...
HE CAUGHT NARUKO-KUN'S SPRINT CLIMB!
THAT'S RIGHT...
HAA...
HAA...
ALL I NEED IN ORDER TO CRUSH YOU TWO IS TO MAKE YOU DESPAIR.
AHH, WE'RE ALMOST TO THE SUMMIT NOW.
DESPAIR AT THE FACT THAT YOU CANNOT PASS ME...
TAKE A GOOD LOOK.

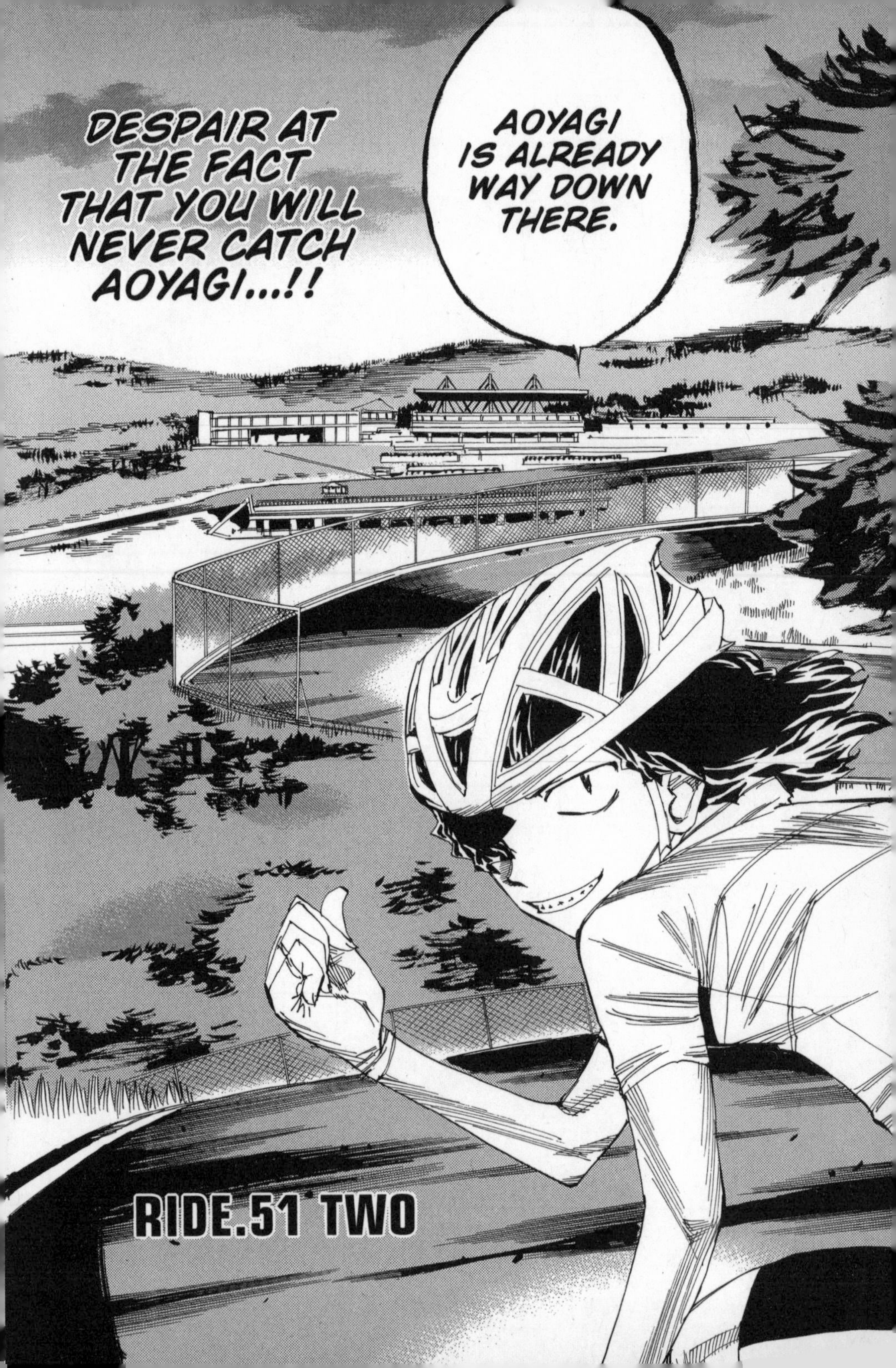
AOYAGI IS ALREADY WAY DOWN THERE.
DESPAIR AT THE FACT THAT YOU WILL NEVER CATCH AOYAGI...!!
RIDE.51 TWO

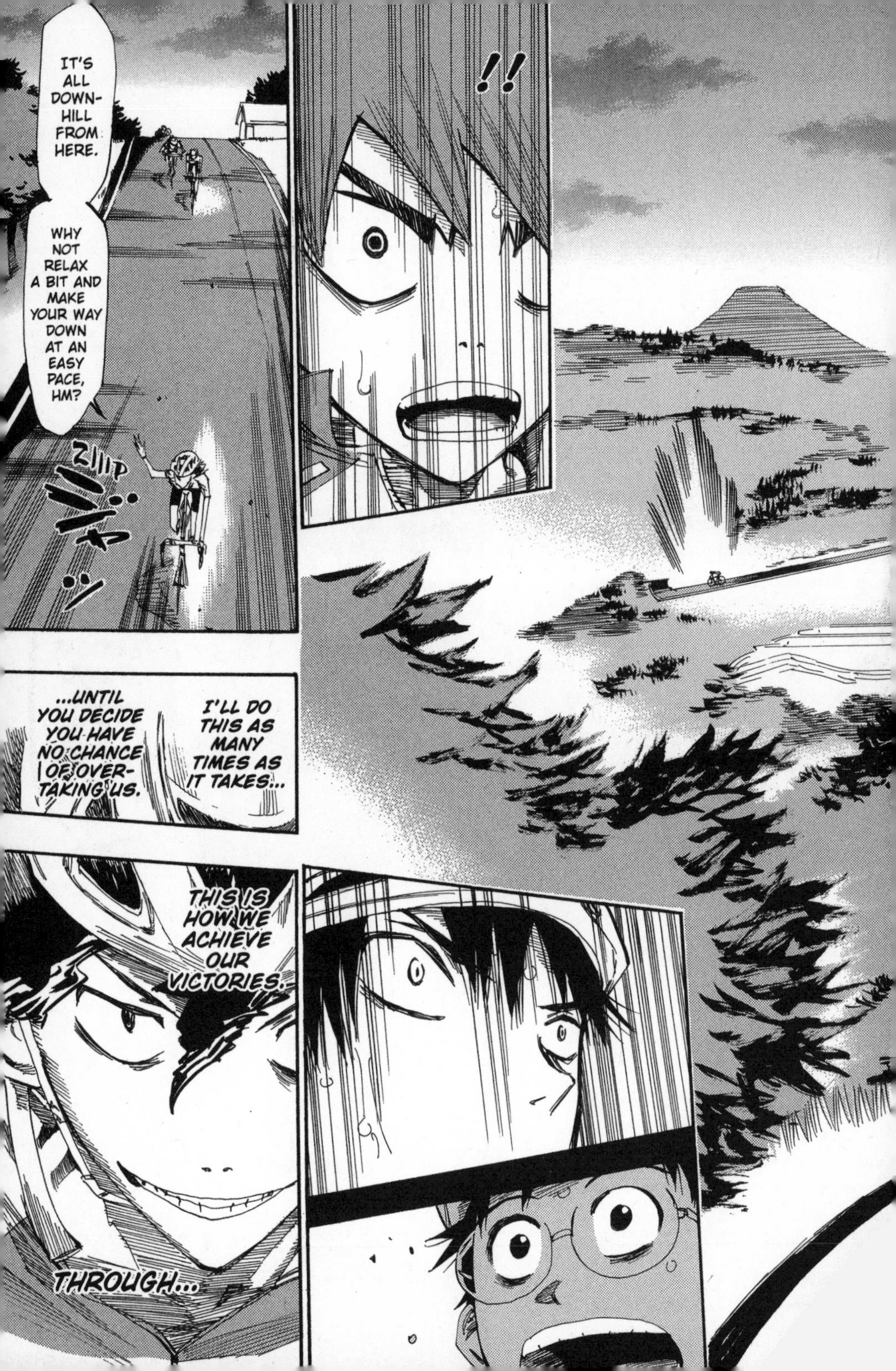
!!
IT'S ALL DOWN-HILL FROM HERE.
WHY NOT RELAX A BIT AND MAKE YOUR WAY DOWN AT AN EASY PACE, HM?
ZIIIP
I'LL DO THIS AS MANY TIMES AS IT TAKES...
...UNTIL YOU DECIDE YOU HAVE NO CHANCE OF OVER-TAKING US.
THIS IS HOW WE ACHIEVE OUR VICTORIES.
THROUGH...

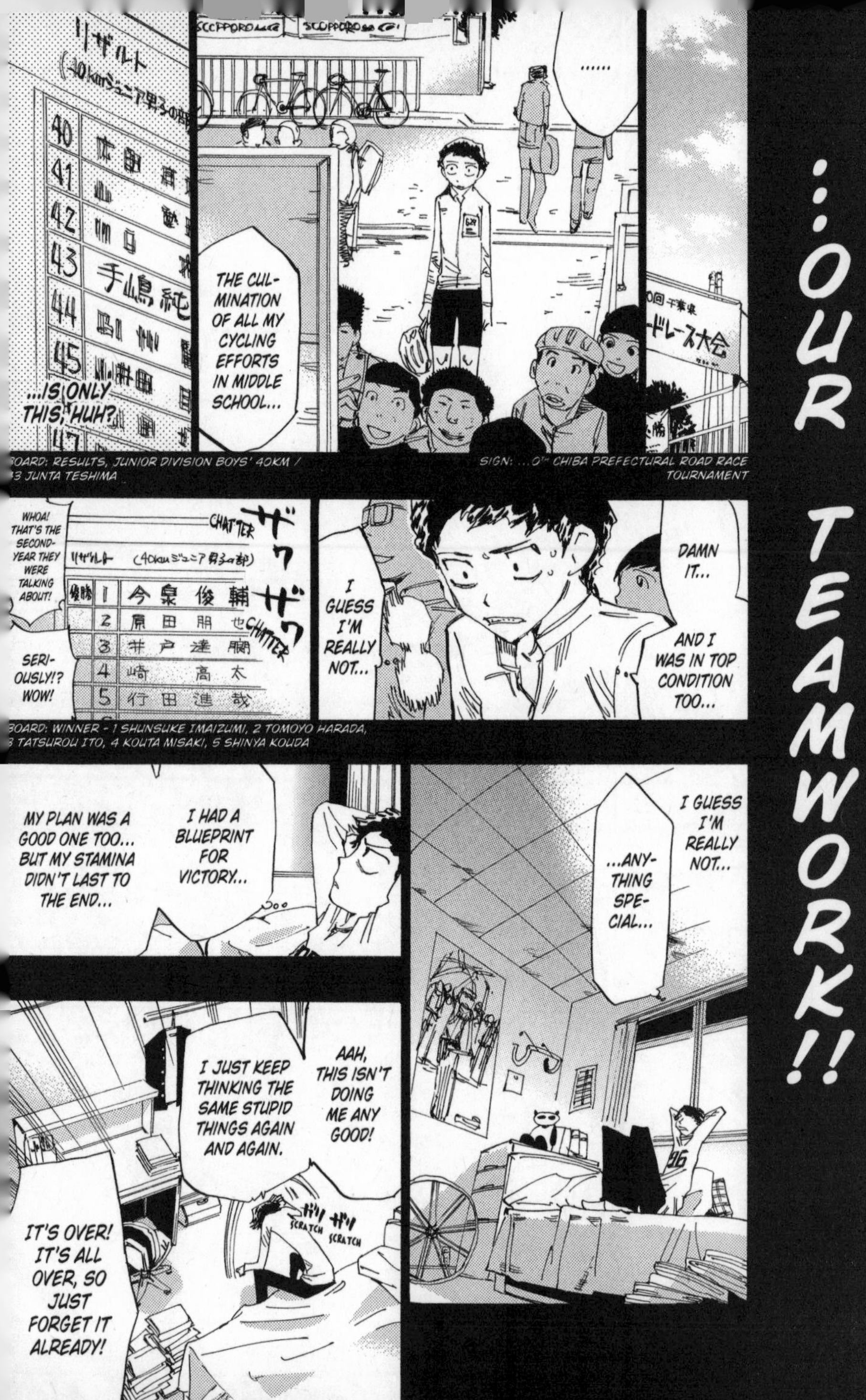

...OUR TEAMWORK!!
......
THE CULMINATION OF ALL MY CYCLING EFFORTS IN MIDDLE SCHOOL...
...IS ONLY THIS, HUH?
SIGN: ...0TH CHIBA PREFECTURAL ROAD RACE TOURNAMENT
BOARD: RESULTS, JUNIOR DIVISION BOYS' 40KM / 43 JUNTA TESHIMA
DAMN IT...
AND I WAS IN TOP CONDITION TOO...
I GUESS I'M REALLY NOT...
CHATTER
CHATTER
WHOA! THAT'S THE SECOND-YEAR THEY WERE TALKING ABOUT!
SERIOUSLY!? WOW!
BOARD: WINNER - 1 SHUNSUKE IMAIZUMI, 2 TOMOYO HARADA, 3 TATSUROU ITO, 4 KOUTA MISAKI, 5 SHINYA KOUDA
I GUESS I'M REALLY NOT...
...ANYTHING SPECIAL...
I HAD A BLUEPRINT FOR VICTORY...
MY PLAN WAS A GOOD ONE TOO... BUT MY STAMINA DIDN'T LAST TO THE END...
AAH, THIS ISN'T DOING ME ANY GOOD!
I JUST KEEP THINKING THE SAME STUPID THINGS AGAIN AND AGAIN.
SCRATCH SCRATCH
IT'S OVER! IT'S ALL OVER, SO JUST FORGET IT ALREADY!

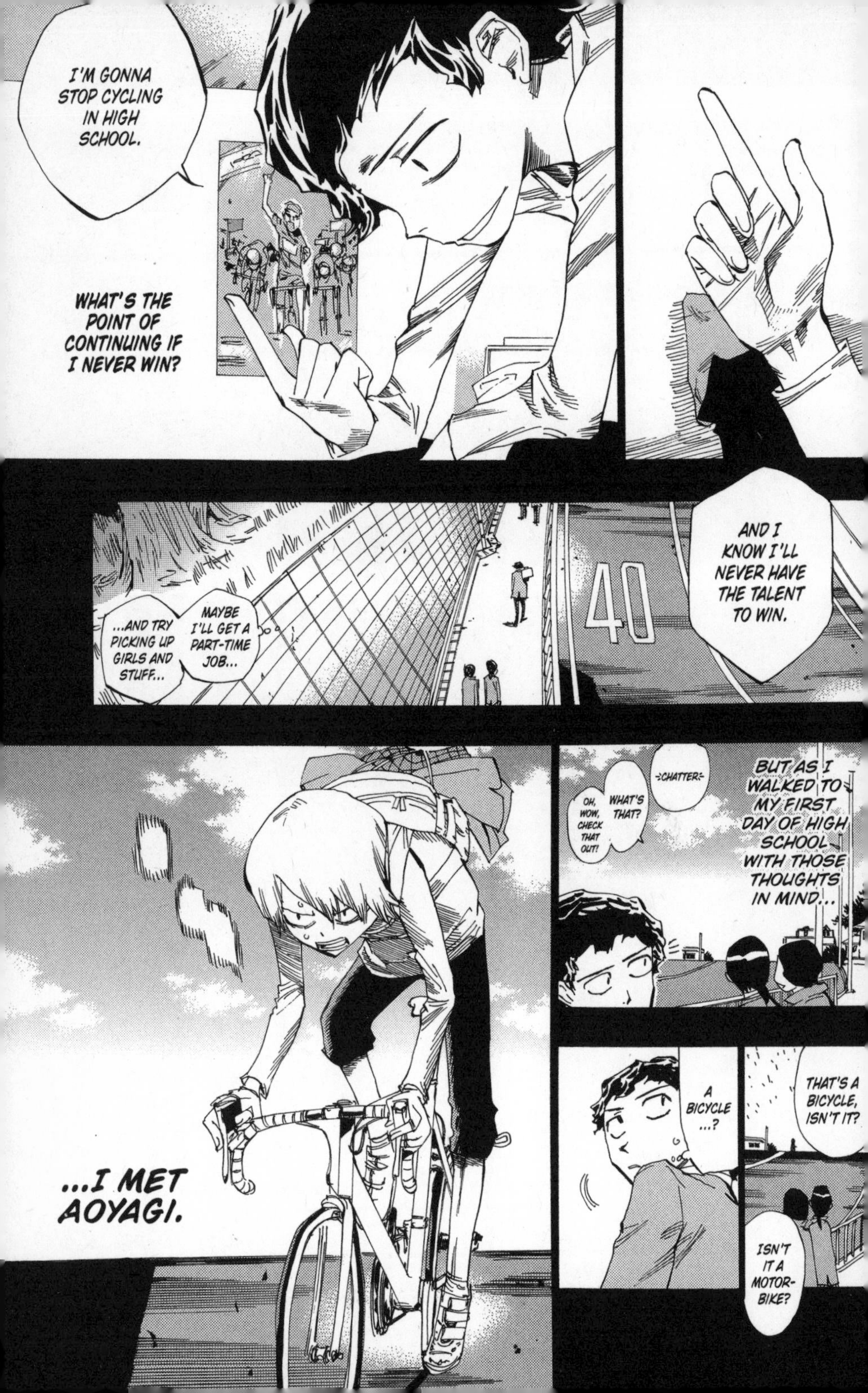
I'M GONNA STOP CYCLING IN HIGH SCHOOL.
WHAT'S THE POINT OF CONTINUING IF I NEVER WIN?
AND I KNOW I'LL NEVER HAVE THE TALENT TO WIN.
MAYBE I'LL GET A PART-TIME JOB...
...AND TRY PICKING UP GIRLS AND STUFF...
BUT AS I WALKED TO MY FIRST DAY OF HIGH SCHOOL WITH THOSE THOUGHTS IN MIND...
CHATTER
WHAT'S THAT?
OH, WOW, CHECK THAT OUT!
THAT'S A BICYCLE, ISN'T IT?
ISN'T IT A MOTOR-BIKE?
A BICYCLE ...?
...I MET AOYAGI.

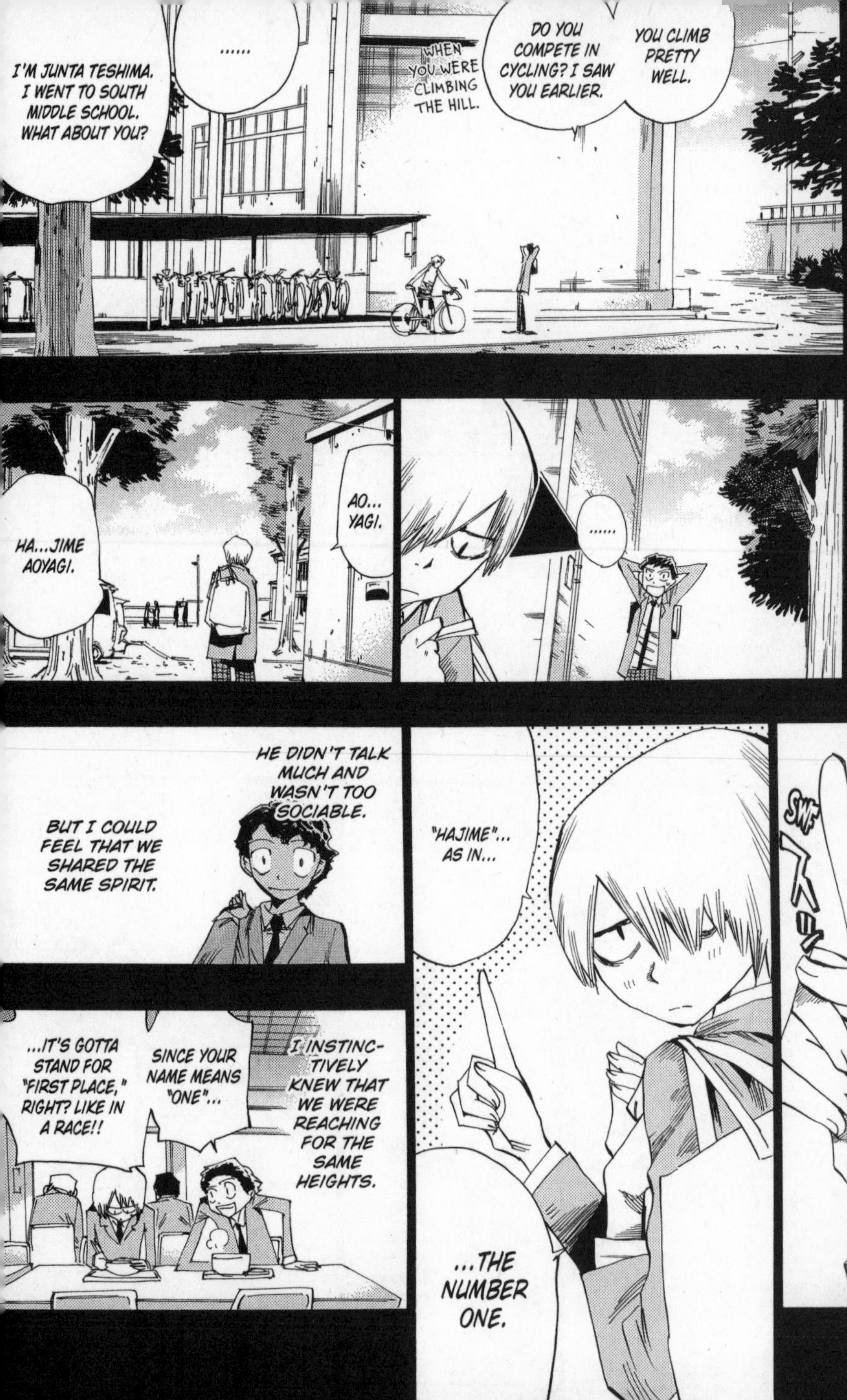
YOU CLIMB PRETTY WELL.
DO YOU COMPETE IN CYCLING? I SAW YOU EARLIER.
WHEN YOU WERE CLIMBING THE HILL.
......
I'M JUNTA TESHIMA. I WENT TO SOUTH MIDDLE SCHOOL. WHAT ABOUT YOU?
......
AO... YAGI.
HA...JIME AOYAGI.
SWF
"HAJIME"... AS IN...
...THE NUMBER ONE.
HE DIDN'T TALK MUCH AND WASN'T TOO SOCIABLE.
BUT I COULD FEEL THAT WE SHARED THE SAME SPIRIT.
I INSTINC-TIVELY KNEW THAT WE WERE REACHING FOR THE SAME HEIGHTS.
SINCE YOUR NAME MEANS "ONE"...
...IT'S GOTTA STAND FOR "FIRST PLACE," RIGHT? LIKE IN A RACE!!

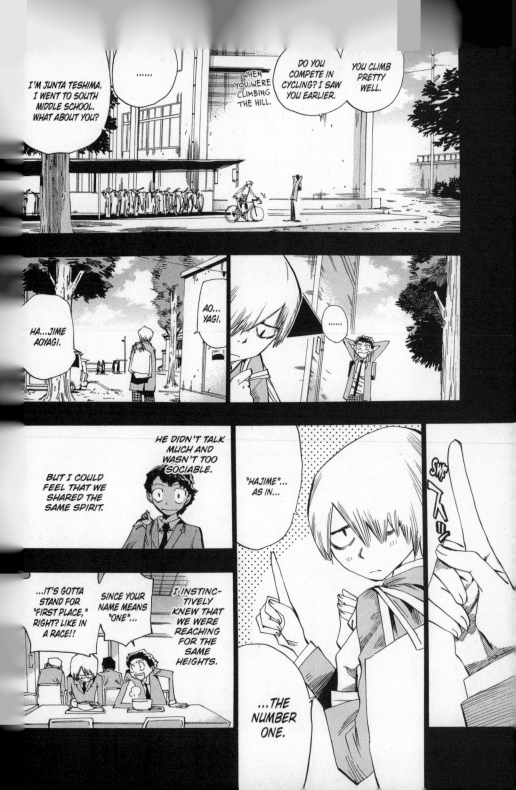

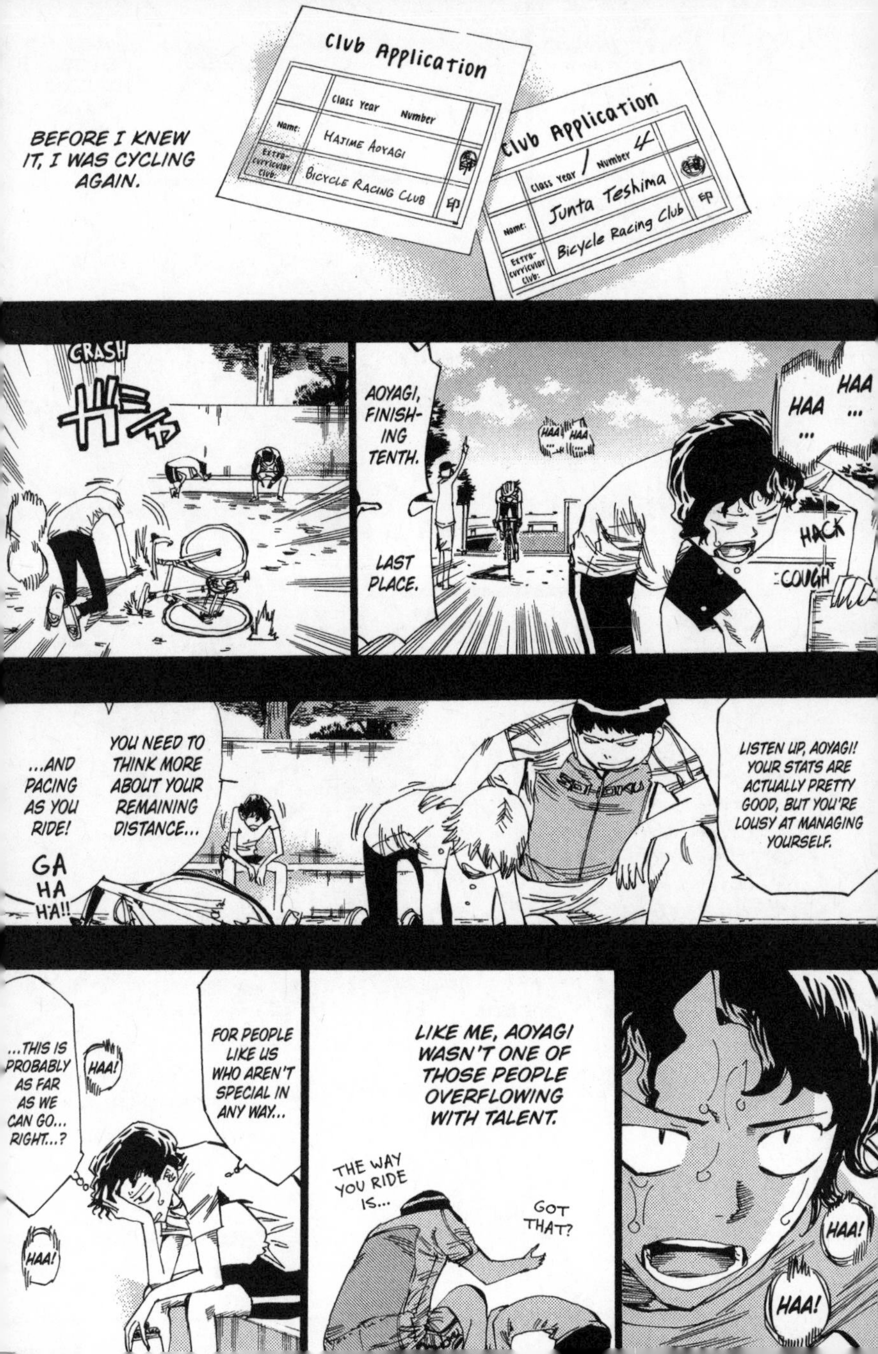
Club Application
Class Year Number
Name: Hajime Aoyagi
Extra-curricular Club: Bicycle Racing Club
Club Application
Class Year 1 Number 4
Name: Junta Teshima
Extra-curricular Club: Bicycle Racing Club
BEFORE I KNEW IT, I WAS CYCLING AGAIN.
HAA ...
HAA ...
AOYAGI, FINISHING TENTH.
HAA HAA
HACK
COUGH
LAST PLACE.
CRASH
LISTEN UP, AOYAGI! YOUR STATS ARE ACTUALLY PRETTY GOOD, BUT YOU'RE LOUSY AT MANAGING YOURSELF.
YOU NEED TO THINK MORE ABOUT YOUR REMAINING DISTANCE...
...AND PACING AS YOU RIDE!
GA HA HA!!
HAA!
HAA!
LIKE ME, AOYAGI WASN'T ONE OF THOSE PEOPLE OVERFLOWING WITH TALENT.
GOT THAT?
THE WAY YOU RIDE IS...
FOR PEOPLE LIKE US WHO AREN'T SPECIAL IN ANY WAY...
...THIS IS PROBABLY AS FAR AS WE CAN GO... RIGHT...?
HAA!
HAA!

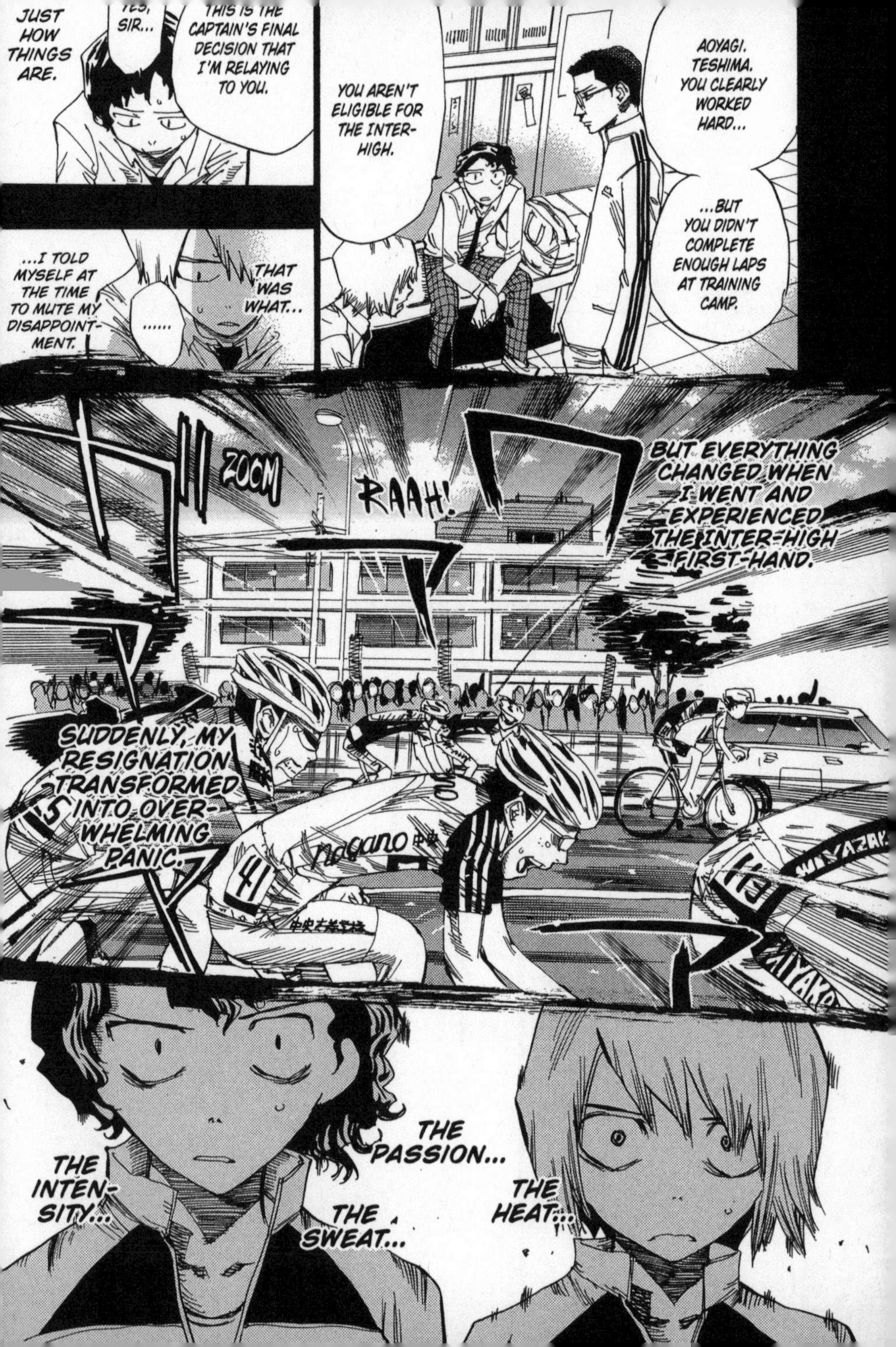
AOYAGI. TESHIMA. YOU CLEARLY WORKED HARD...
...BUT YOU DIDN'T COMPLETE ENOUGH LAPS AT TRAINING CAMP.
YOU AREN'T ELIGIBLE FOR THE INTER-HIGH.
THIS IS THE CAPTAIN'S FINAL DECISION THAT I'M RELAYING TO YOU.
YES, SIR...
JUST HOW THINGS ARE.
THAT WAS WHAT...
......
...I TOLD MYSELF AT THE TIME TO MUTE MY DISAPPOINTMENT.
BUT EVERYTHING CHANGED WHEN I WENT AND EXPERIENCED THE INTER-HIGH FIRST-HAND.
RAAH!
ZOOM
SUDDENLY, MY RESIGNATION TRANSFORMED INTO OVERWHELMING PANIC.
THE HEAT...
THE PASSION...
THE SWEAT...
THE INTENSITY...

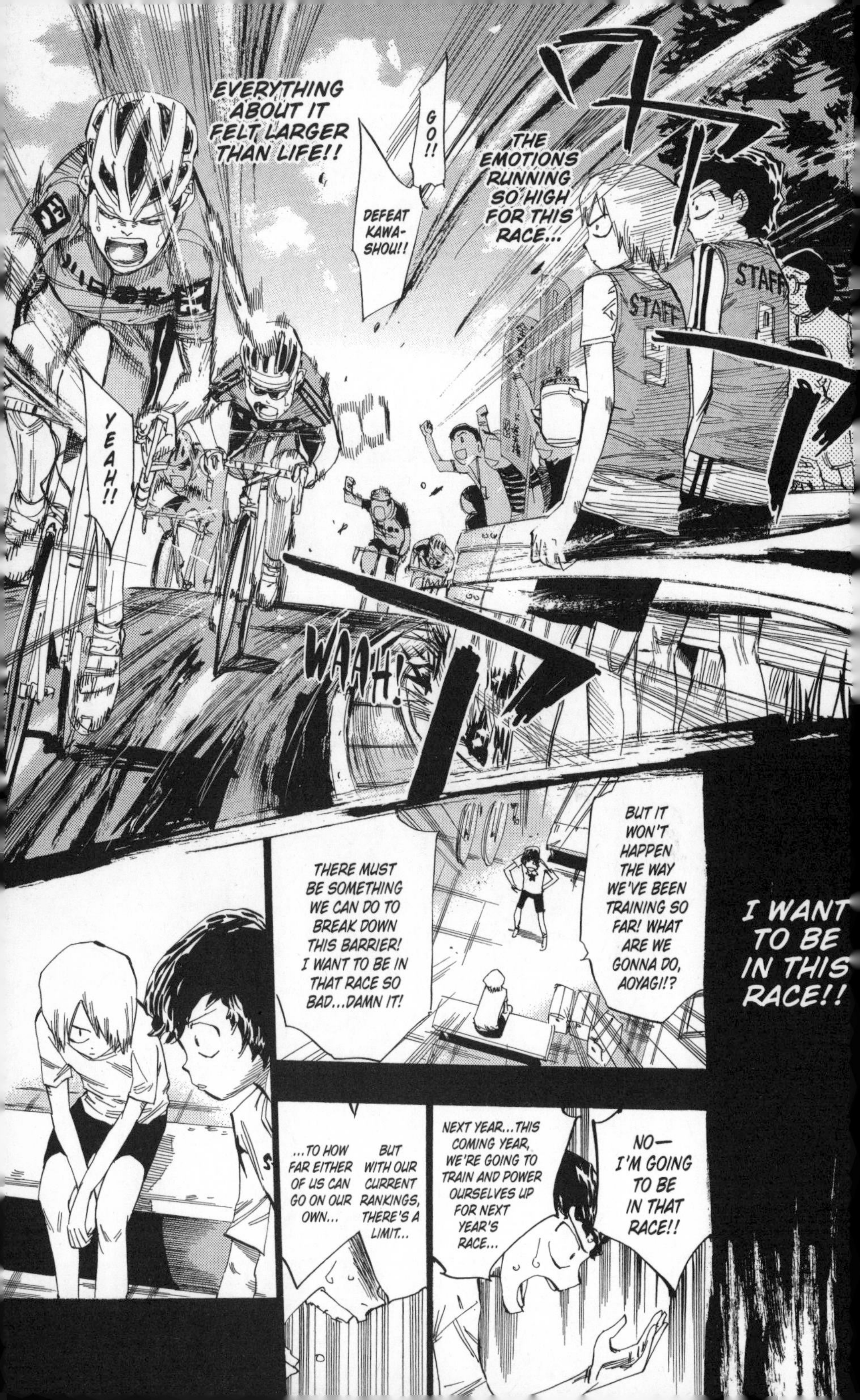
THE EMOTIONS RUNNING SO HIGH FOR THIS RACE...
GO!!
EVERYTHING ABOUT IT FELT LARGER THAN LIFE!!
DEFEAT KAWA-SHOU!!
YEAH!!
WAAH!!
I WANT TO BE IN THIS RACE!!
BUT IT WON'T HAPPEN THE WAY WE'VE BEEN TRAINING SO FAR! WHAT ARE WE GONNA DO, AOYAGI!?
THERE MUST BE SOMETHING WE CAN DO TO BREAK DOWN THIS BARRIER! I WANT TO BE IN THAT RACE SO BAD...DAMN IT!
NO— I'M GOING TO BE IN THAT RACE!!
NEXT YEAR...THIS COMING YEAR, WE'RE GOING TO TRAIN AND POWER OURSELVES UP FOR NEXT YEAR'S RACE...
BUT WITH OUR CURRENT RANKINGS, THERE'S A LIMIT...
...TO HOW FAR EITHER OF US CAN GO ON OUR OWN...

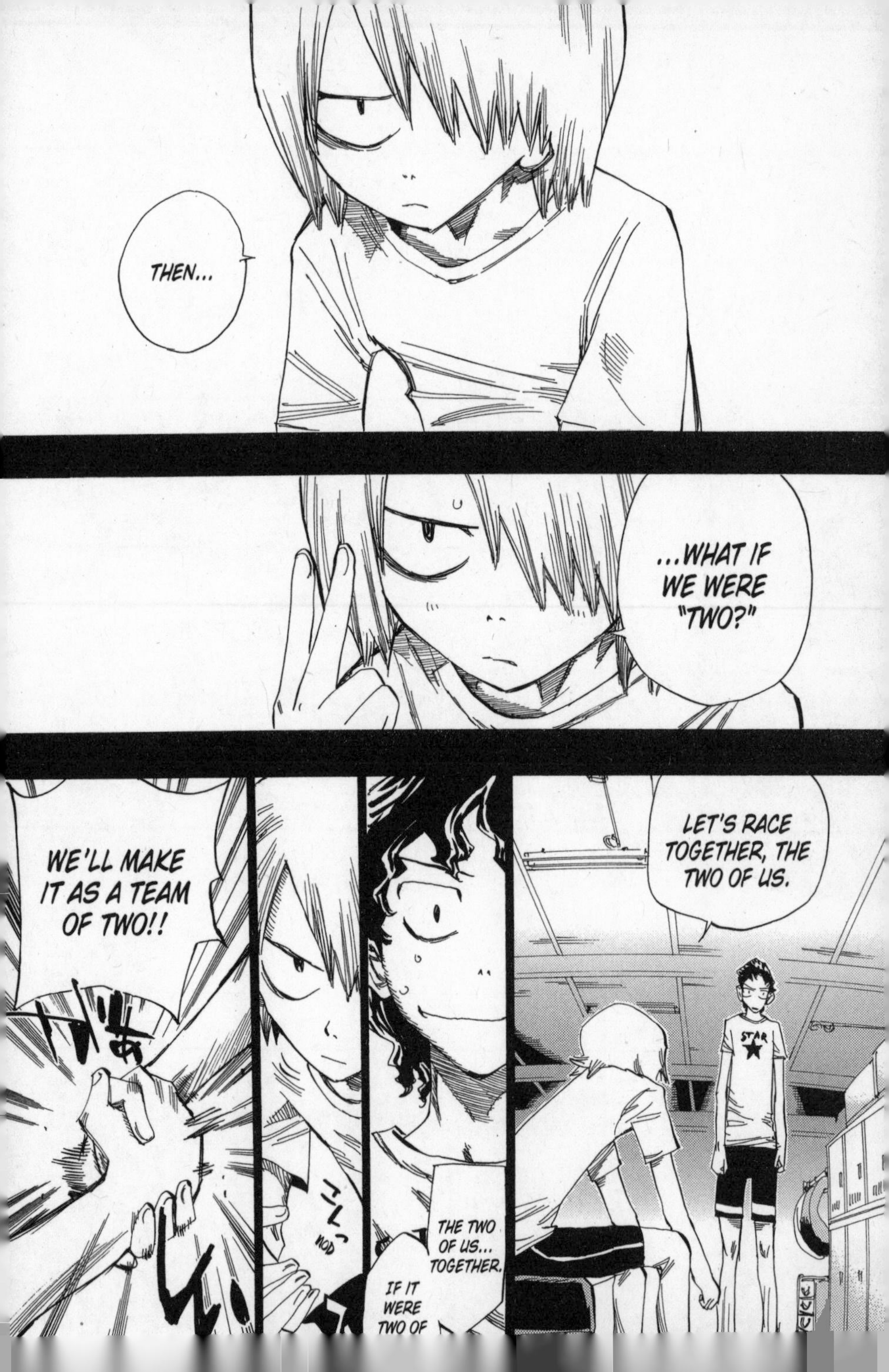
THEN...
...WHAT IF WE WERE "TWO?"
LET'S RACE TOGETHER, THE TWO OF US.
THE TWO OF US... TOGETHER.
IF IT WERE TWO OF
NOD
WE'LL MAKE IT AS A TEAM OF TWO!!

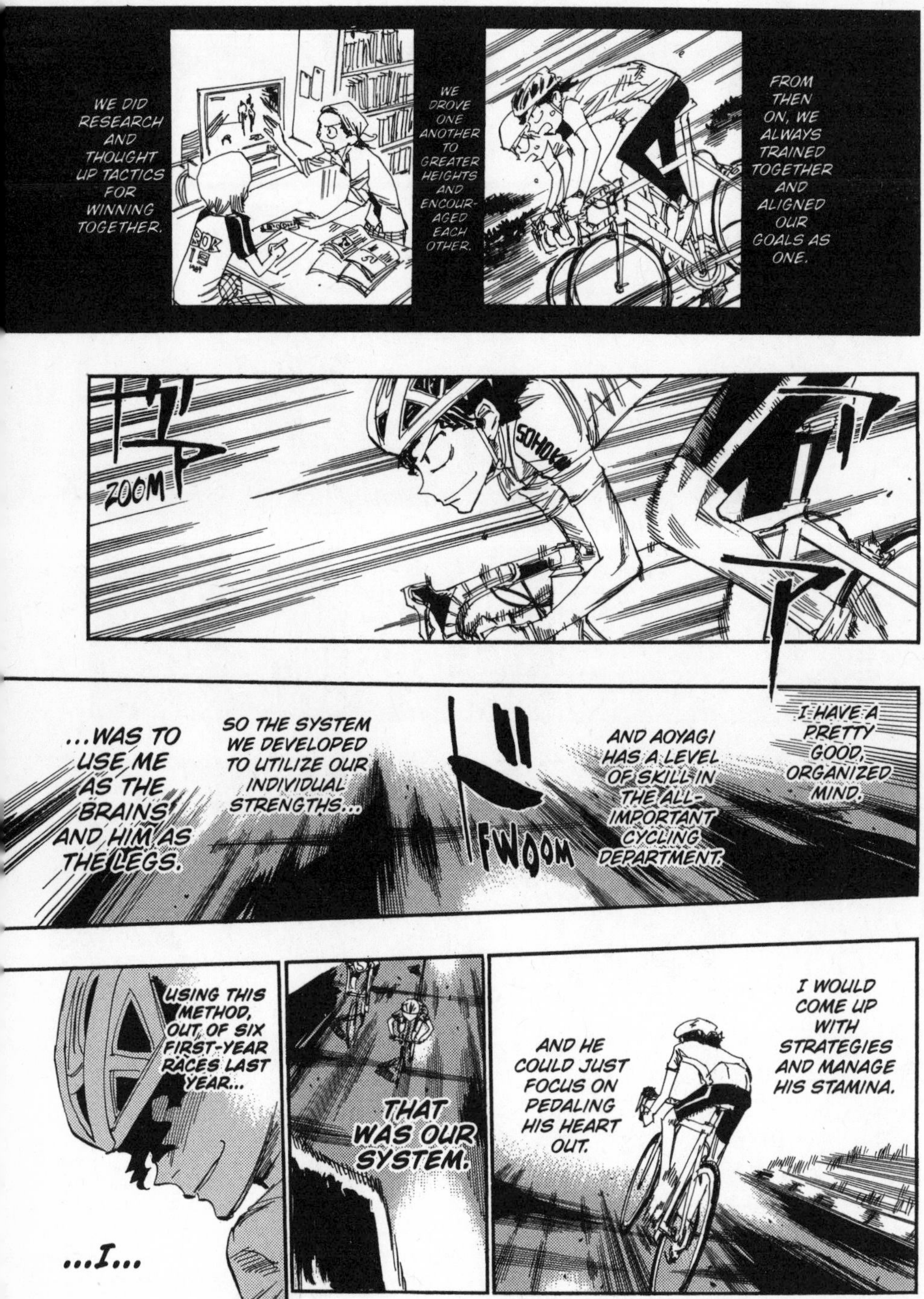
FROM THEN ON, WE ALWAYS TRAINED TOGETHER AND ALIGNED OUR GOALS AS ONE.
WE DROVE ONE ANOTHER TO GREATER HEIGHTS AND ENCOURAGED EACH OTHER.
WE DID RESEARCH AND THOUGHT UP TACTICS FOR WINNING TOGETHER.
SOHOKU
ZOOM
I HAVE A PRETTY GOOD, ORGANIZED MIND.
AND AOYAGI HAS A LEVEL OF SKILL IN THE ALL-IMPORTANT CYCLING DEPARTMENT.
FWOOM
SO THE SYSTEM WE DEVELOPED TO UTILIZE OUR INDIVIDUAL STRENGTHS...
...WAS TO USE ME AS THE BRAINS AND HIM AS THE LEGS.
I WOULD COME UP WITH STRATEGIES AND MANAGE HIS STAMINA.
AND HE COULD JUST FOCUS ON PEDALING HIS HEART OUT.
THAT WAS OUR SYSTEM.
USING THIS METHOD, OUT OF SIX FIRST-YEAR RACES LAST YEAR...
...I...

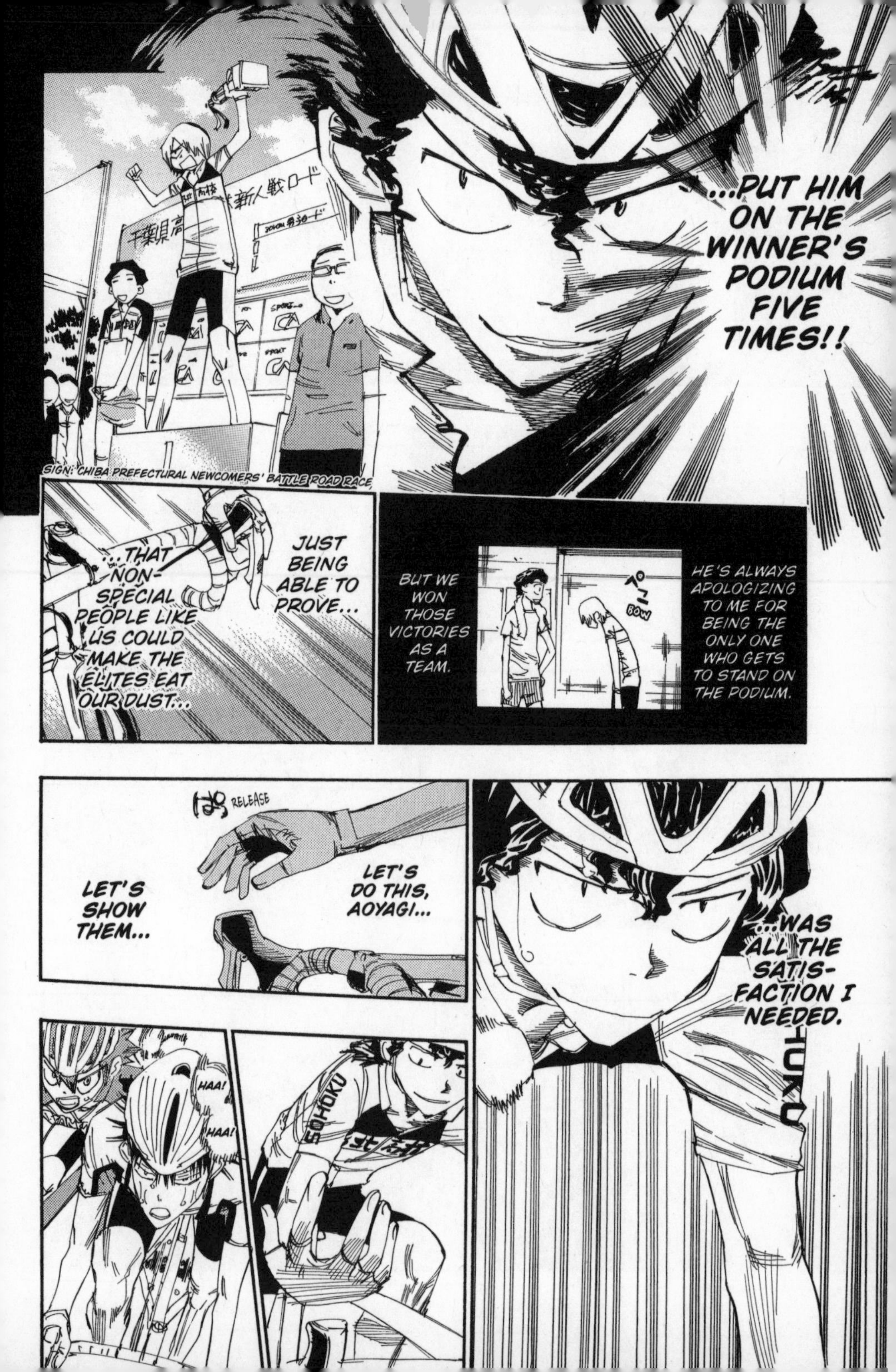

...PUT HIM ON THE WINNER'S PODIUM FIVE TIMES!!
SIGN: CHIBA PREFECTURAL NEWCOMERS' BATTLE ROAD RACE
HE'S ALWAYS APOLOGIZING TO ME FOR BEING THE ONLY ONE WHO GETS TO STAND ON THE PODIUM.
BOW
BUT WE WON THOSE VICTORIES AS A TEAM.
JUST BEING ABLE TO PROVE...
...THAT NON-SPECIAL PEOPLE LIKE US COULD MAKE THE ELITES EAT OUR DUST...
...WAS ALL THE SATIS-FACTION I NEEDED.
RELEASE
LET'S DO THIS, AOYAGI...
LET'S SHOW THEM...
SOHOKU
HAA!
HAA!

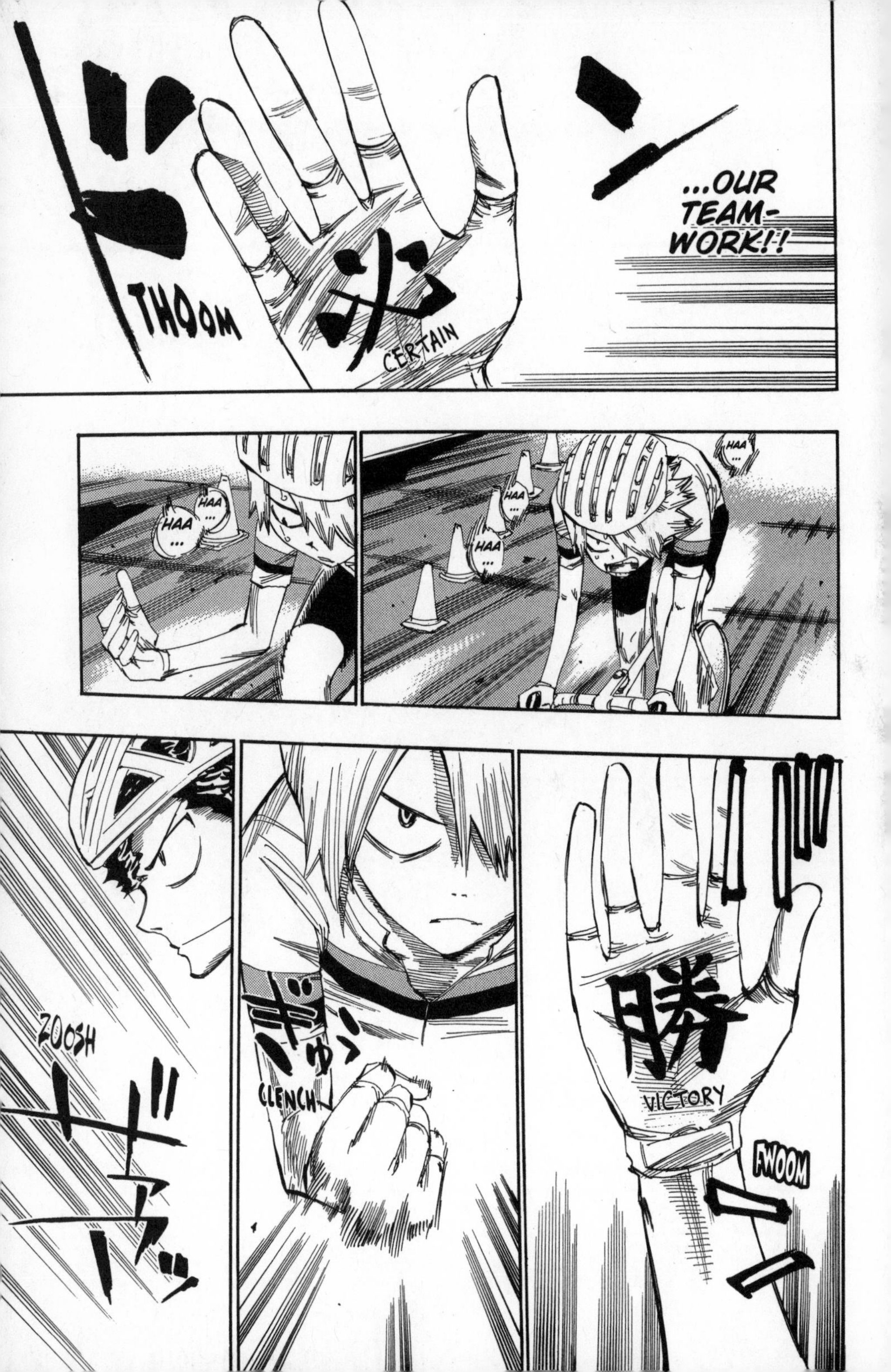

...OUR TEAM-WORK!!
CERTAIN
THOOM
HAA...
HAA...
HAA...
HAA...
HAA...
VICTORY
FWOOM
CLENCH
ZOOSH

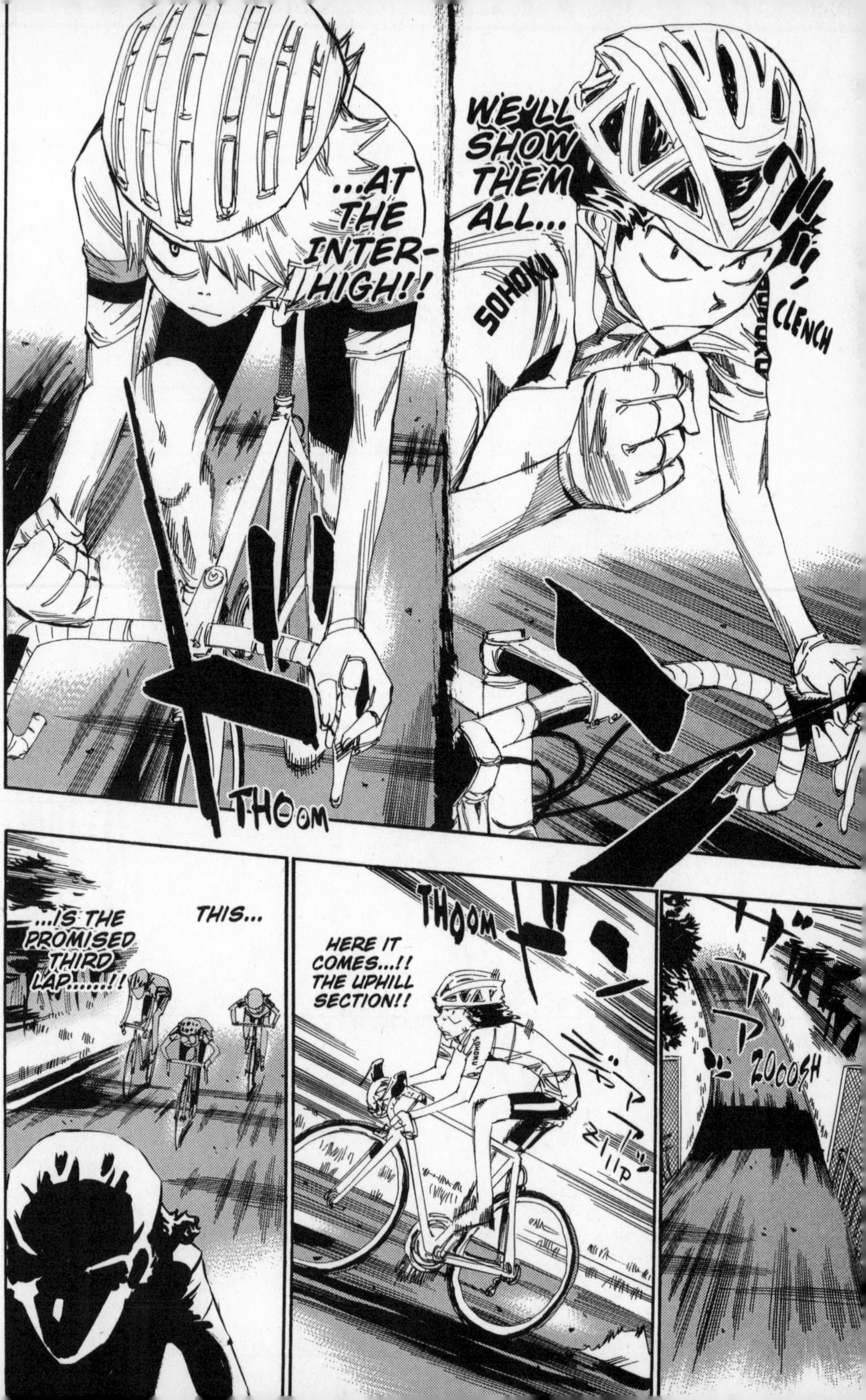
WE'LL SHOW THEM ALL...
SOHOKU
CLENCH
...AT THE INTER-HIGH!!
THOOM
ZOOOSH
THOOM
HERE IT COMES...!! THE UPHILL SECTION!!
ZIIIP
THIS...
...IS THE PROMISED THIRD LAP.......!!

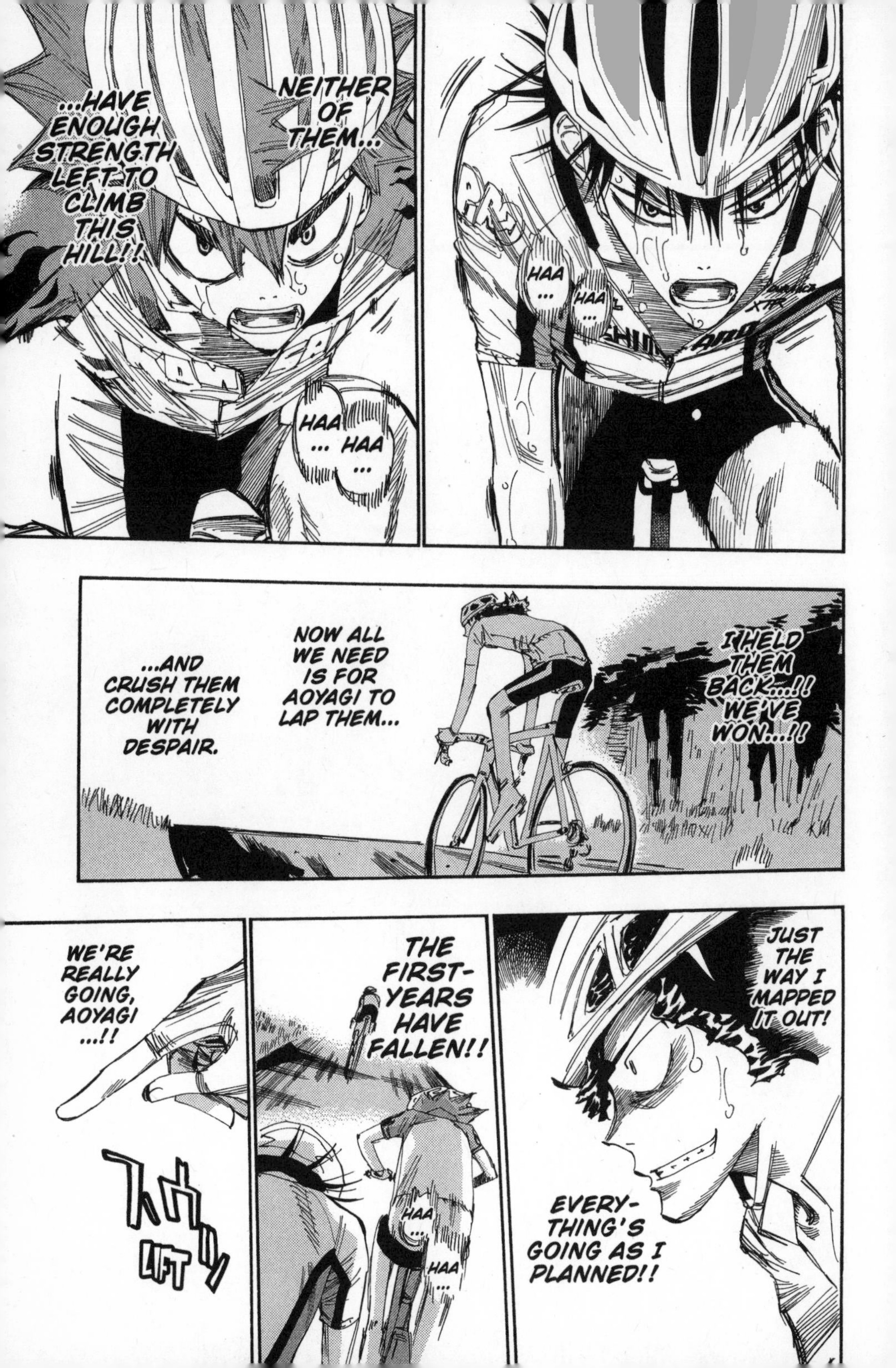
HAA...
HAA...
NEITHER OF THEM...
...HAVE ENOUGH STRENGTH LEFT TO CLIMB THIS HILL!!
HAA... HAA...
I HELD THEM BACK...!! WE'VE WON...!!
NOW ALL WE NEED IS FOR AOYAGI TO LAP THEM...
...AND CRUSH THEM COMPLETELY WITH DESPAIR.
JUST THE WAY I MAPPED IT OUT!
EVERYTHING'S GOING AS I PLANNED!!
THE FIRST-YEARS HAVE FALLEN!!
HAA...
HAA...
WE'RE REALLY GOING, AOYAGI...!!
LIFT

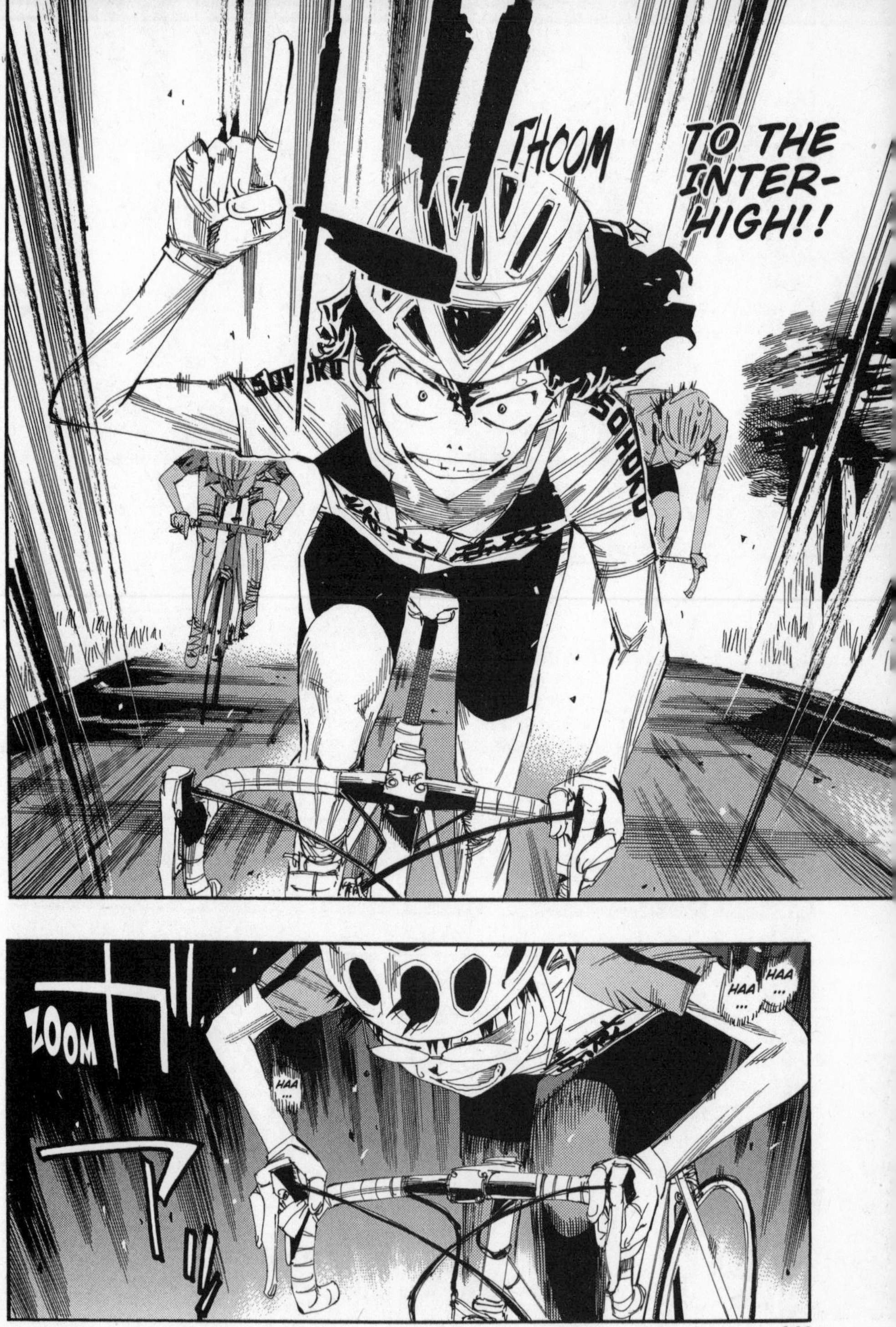
TO THE INTER-HIGH!!
THOOM
HAA ...
HAA ...
HAA ...
ZOOM

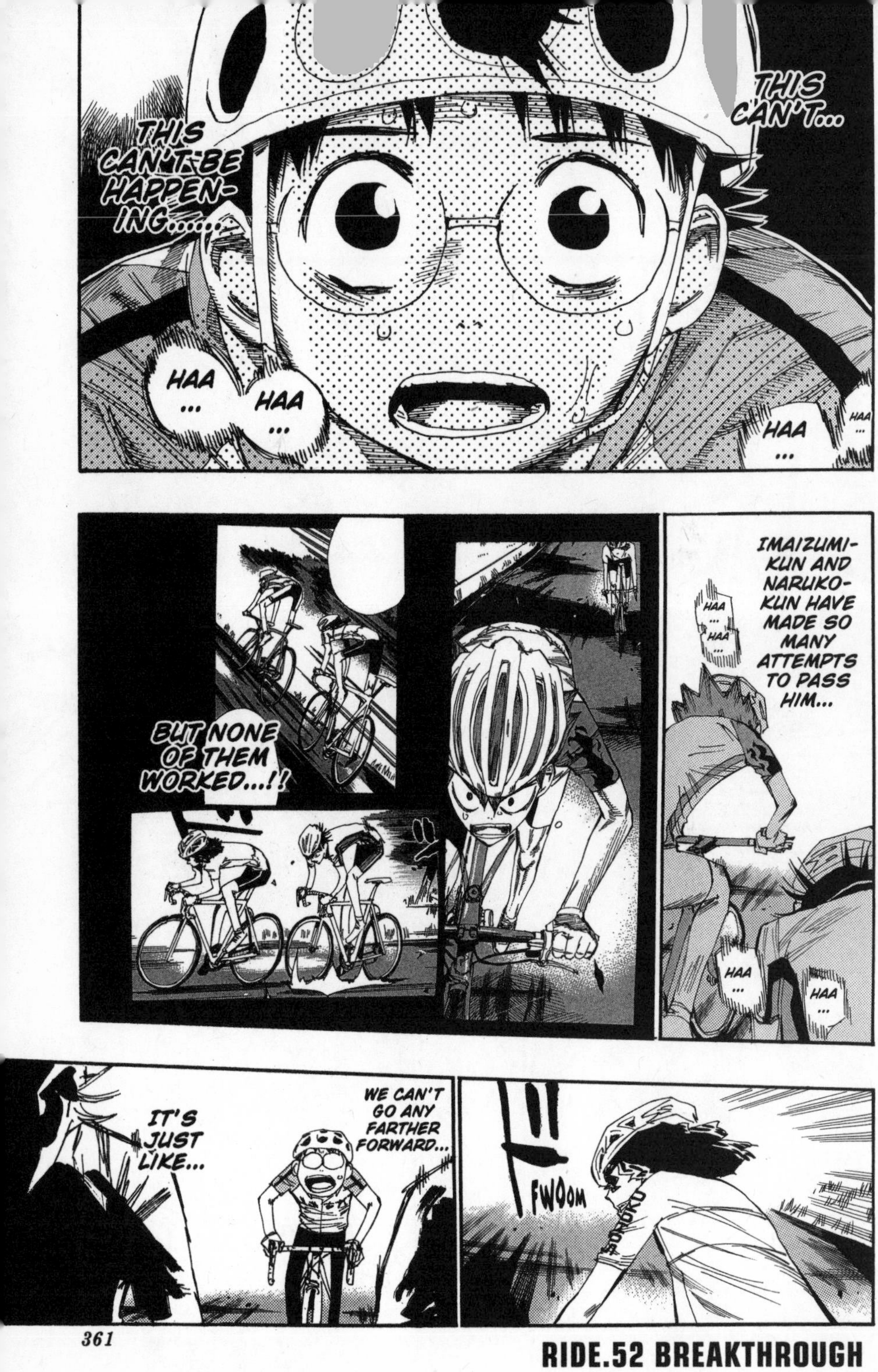

RIDE.52 BREAKTHROUGH

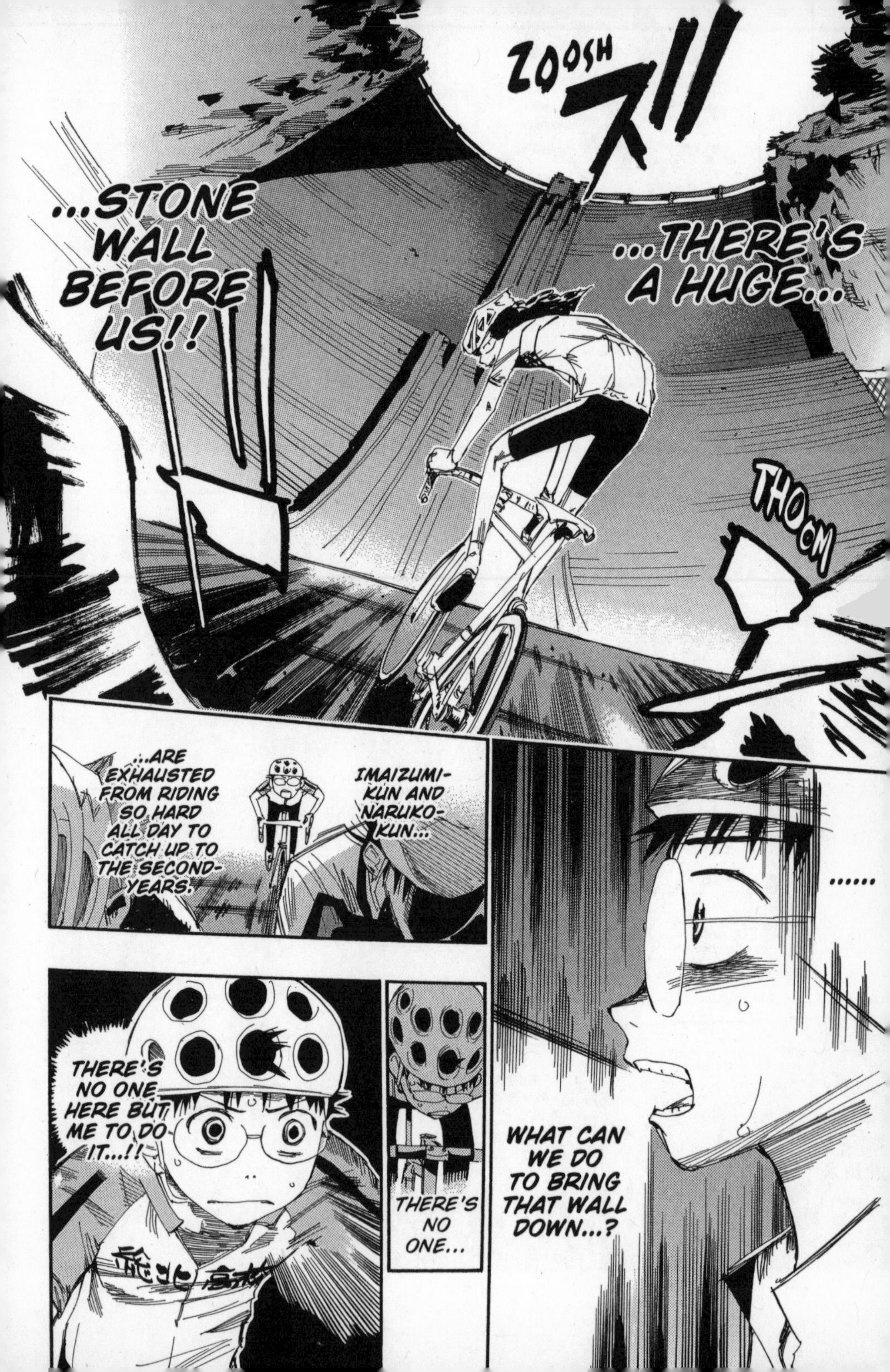
ZOOSH
...THERE'S A HUGE...
...STONE WALL BEFORE US!!
THOOM
......
WHAT CAN WE DO TO BRING THAT WALL DOWN...?
IMAIZUMI-KUN AND NARUKO-KUN...
...ARE EXHAUSTED FROM RIDING SO HARD ALL DAY TO CATCH UP TO THE SECOND-YEARS.
THERE'S NO ONE...
THERE'S NO ONE HERE BUT ME TO DO IT...!!

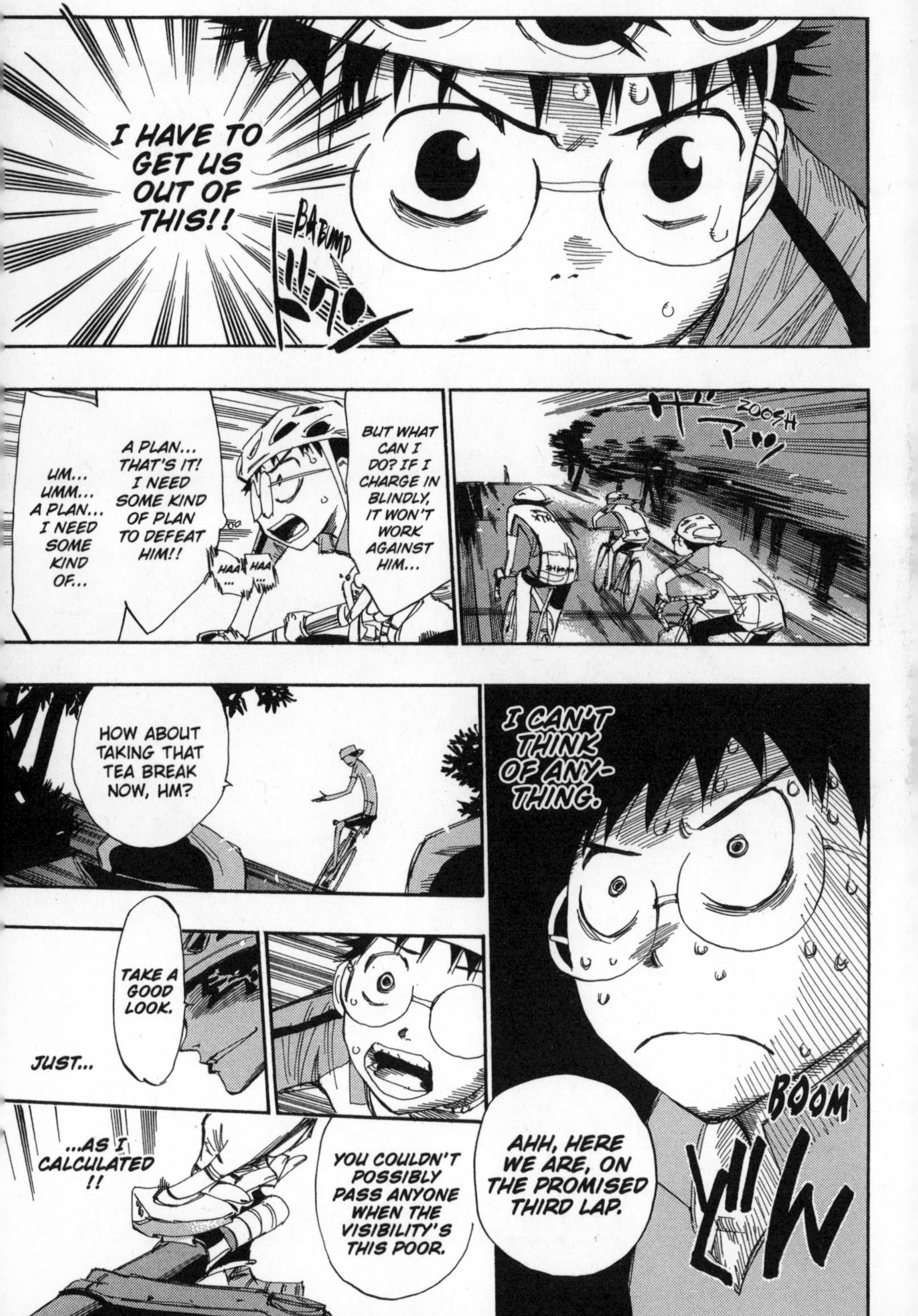
I HAVE TO GET US OUT OF THIS!!
BA-BUMP
ZOOSH
BUT WHAT CAN I DO? IF I CHARGE IN BLINDLY, IT WON'T WORK AGAINST HIM...
A PLAN... THAT'S IT! I NEED SOME KIND OF PLAN TO DEFEAT HIM!!
HAA... HAA...
UM... UMM... A PLAN... I NEED SOME KIND OF...
I CAN'T THINK OF ANYTHING.
BOOM
AHH, HERE WE ARE, ON THE PROMISED THIRD LAP.
HOW ABOUT TAKING THAT TEA BREAK NOW, HM?
TAKE A GOOD LOOK.
JUST...
YOU COULDN'T POSSIBLY PASS ANYONE WHEN THE VISIBILITY'S THIS POOR.
...AS I CALCULATED!!

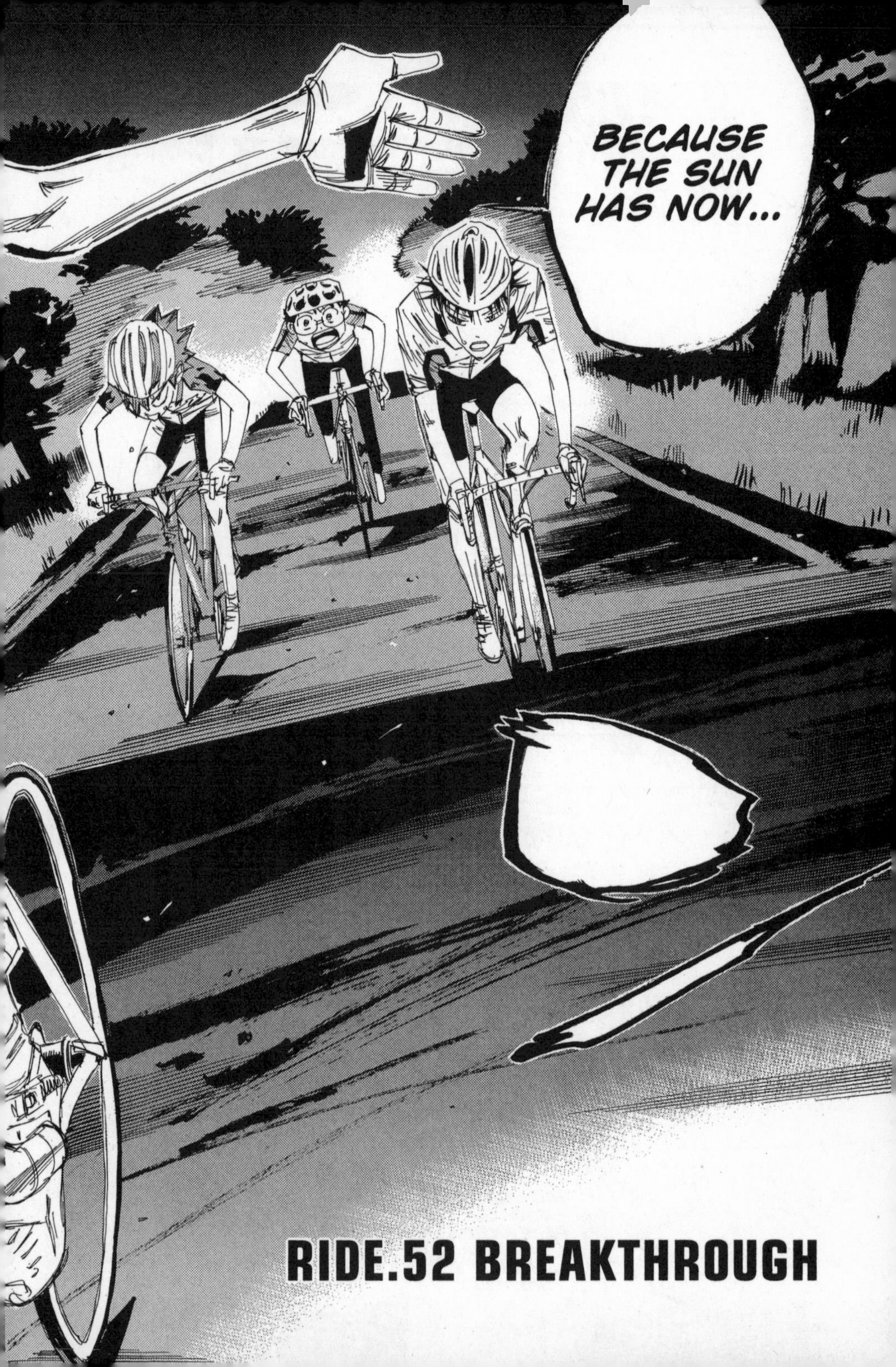
BECAUSE THE SUN HAS NOW...

RIDE.52 BREAKTHROUGH

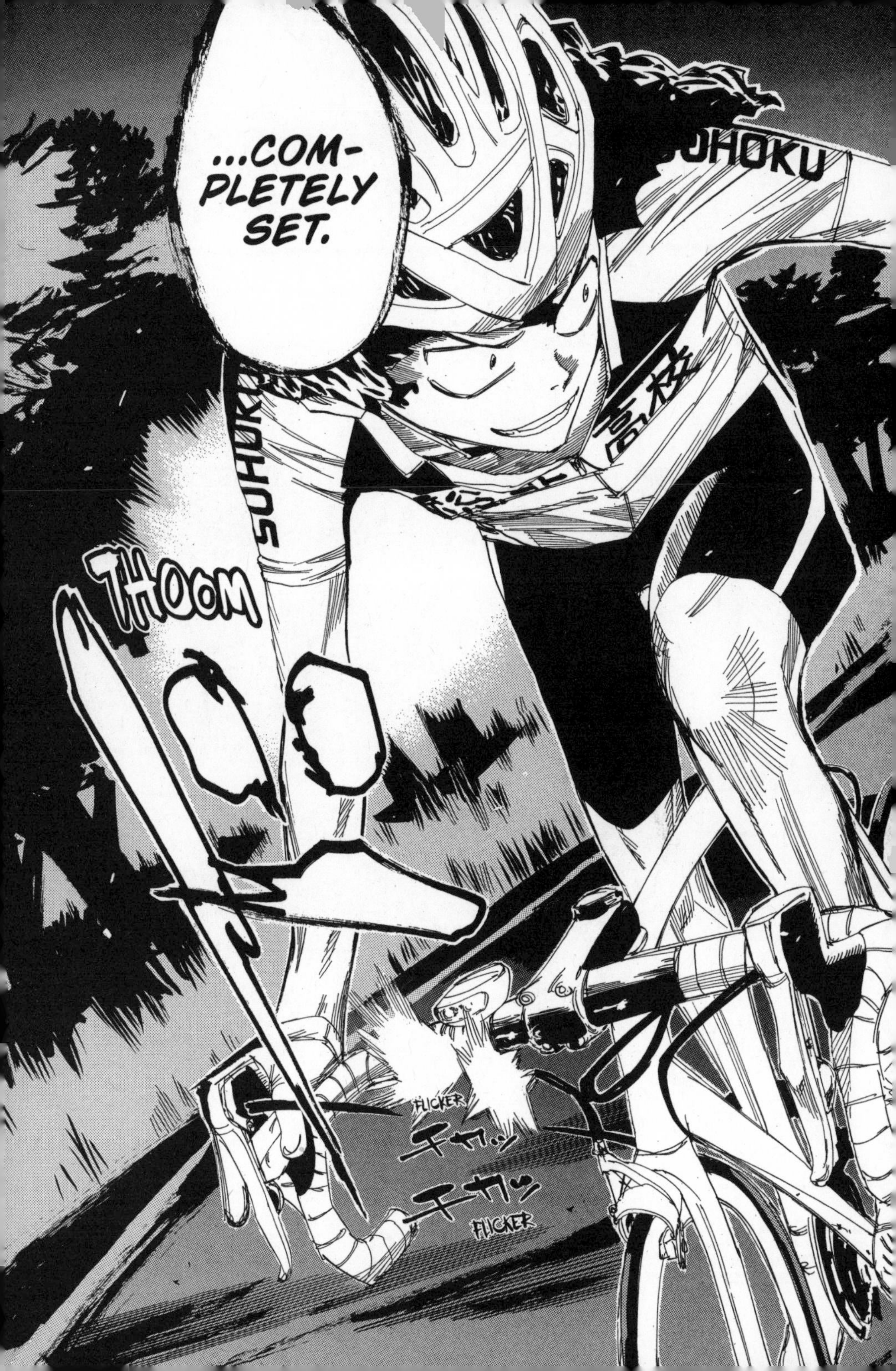
...COM-
PLETELY
SET.
THOOM
FLICKER
チャッ
チャッ
FLICKER

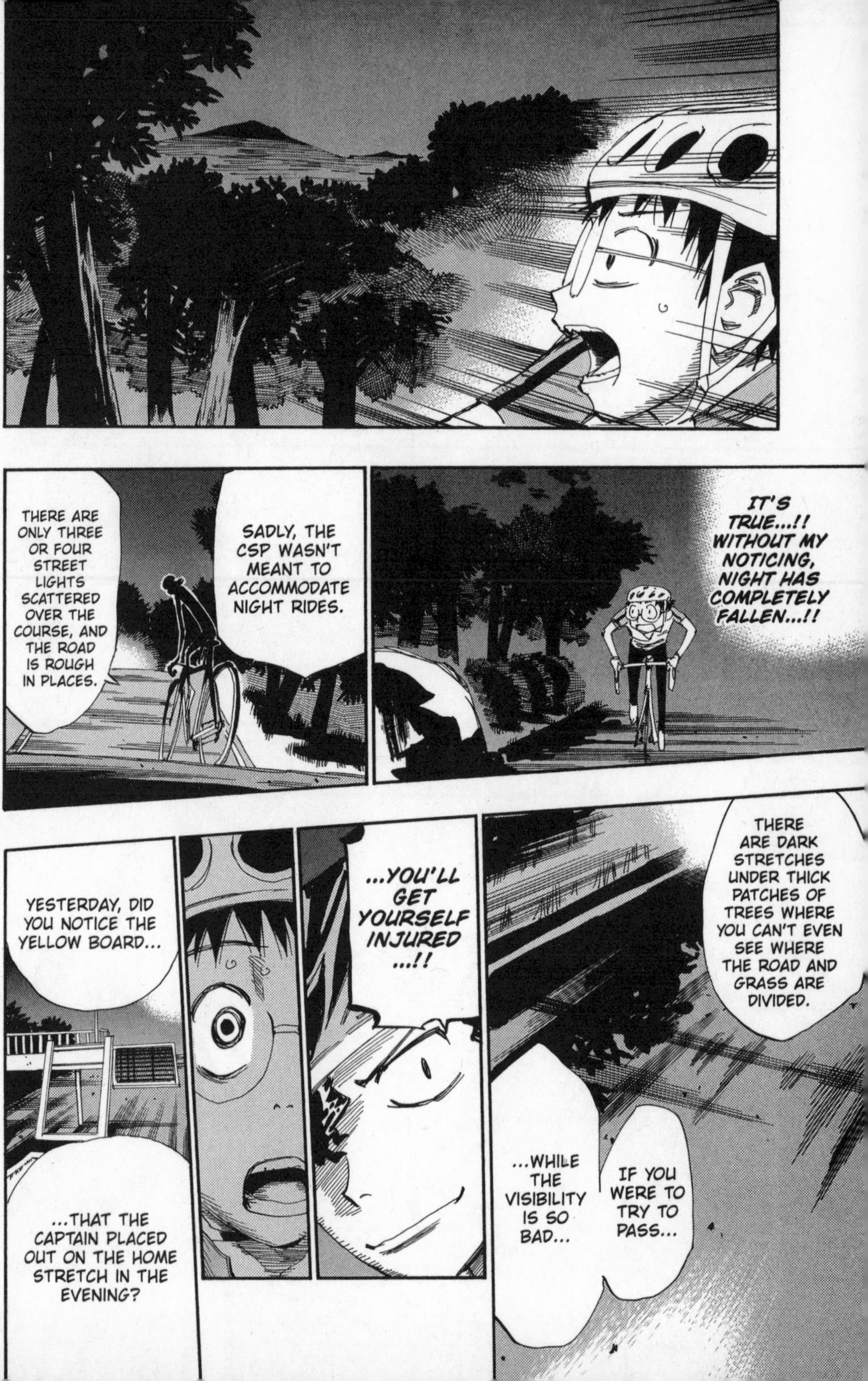
IT'S TRUE...!! WITHOUT MY NOTICING, NIGHT HAS COMPLETELY FALLEN...!!
SADLY, THE CSP WASN'T MEANT TO ACCOMMODATE NIGHT RIDES.
THERE ARE ONLY THREE OR FOUR STREET LIGHTS SCATTERED OVER THE COURSE, AND THE ROAD IS ROUGH IN PLACES.
THERE ARE DARK STRETCHES UNDER THICK PATCHES OF TREES WHERE YOU CAN'T EVEN SEE WHERE THE ROAD AND GRASS ARE DIVIDED.
IF YOU WERE TO TRY TO PASS...
...WHILE THE VISIBILITY IS SO BAD...
...YOU'LL GET YOURSELF INJURED...!!
YESTERDAY, DID YOU NOTICE THE YELLOW BOARD...
...THAT THE CAPTAIN PLACED OUT ON THE HOME STRETCH IN THE EVENING?

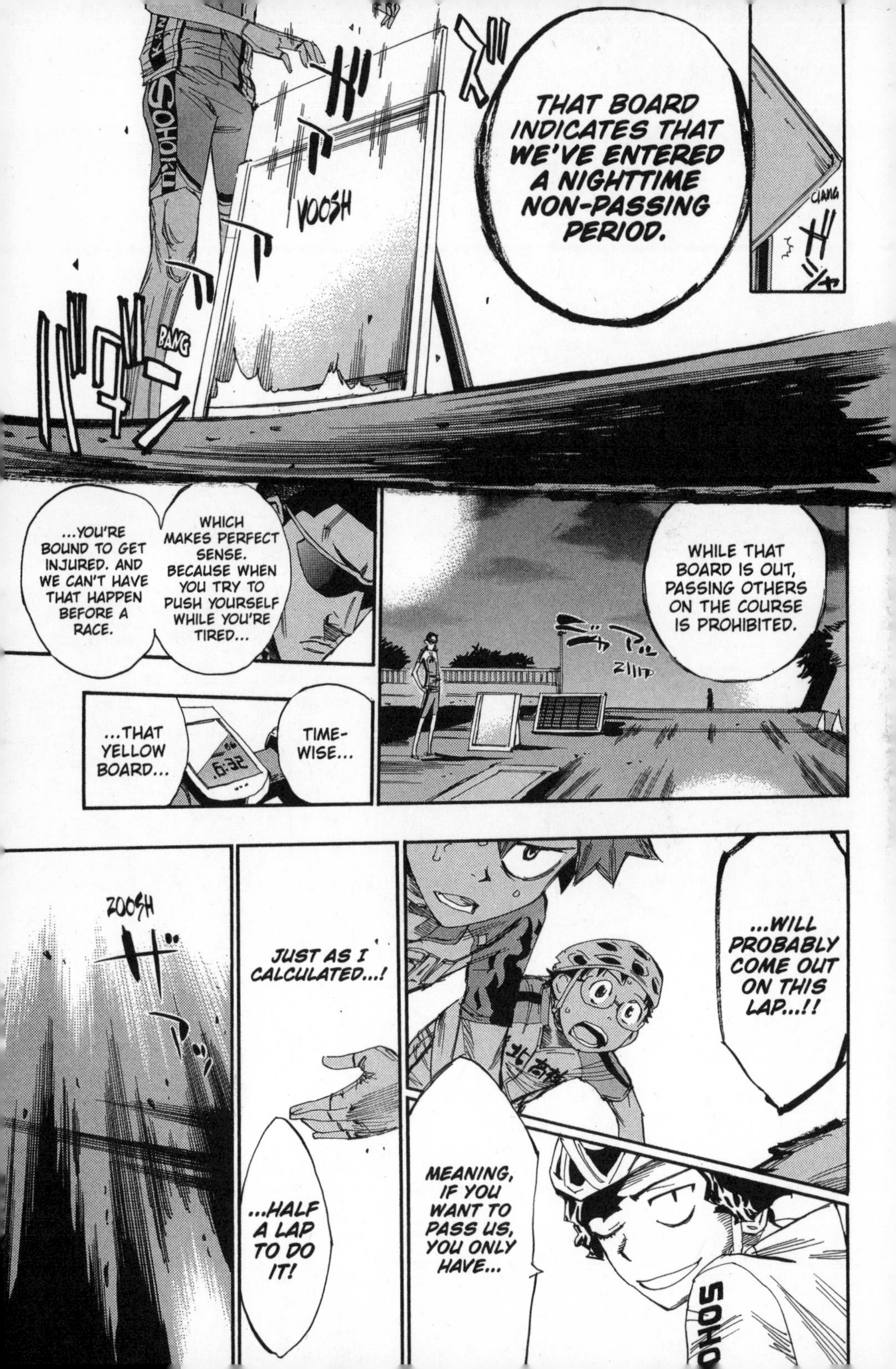

CLANG
THAT BOARD INDICATES THAT WE'VE ENTERED A NIGHTTIME NON-PASSING PERIOD.
VOOSH
BANG
WHILE THAT BOARD IS OUT, PASSING OTHERS ON THE COURSE IS PROHIBITED.
ZIIIP
WHICH MAKES PERFECT SENSE. BECAUSE WHEN YOU TRY TO PUSH YOURSELF WHILE YOU'RE TIRED...
...YOU'RE BOUND TO GET INJURED. AND WE CAN'T HAVE THAT HAPPEN BEFORE A RACE.
TIME-WISE...
...THAT YELLOW BOARD...
...WILL PROBABLY COME OUT ON THIS LAP...!!
MEANING, IF YOU WANT TO PASS US, YOU ONLY HAVE...
JUST AS I CALCULATED...!
...HALF A LAP TO DO IT!
ZOOSH

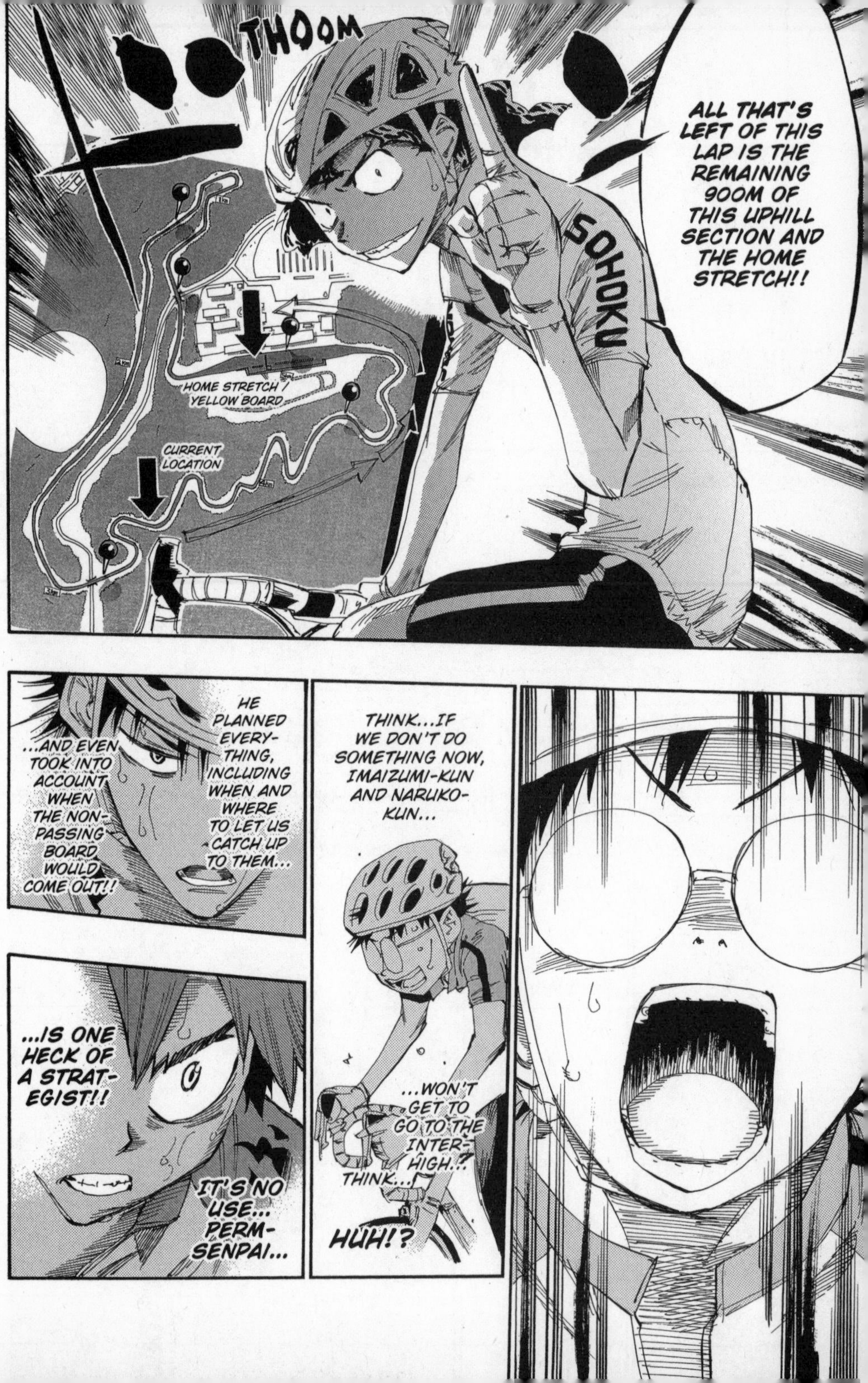
ALL THAT'S LEFT OF THIS LAP IS THE REMAINING 900M OF THIS UPHILL SECTION AND THE HOME STRETCH!!
THOOM
HOME STRETCH / YELLOW BOARD
CURRENT LOCATION
THINK...IF WE DON'T DO SOMETHING NOW, IMAIZUMI-KUN AND NARUKO-KUN...
...WON'T GET TO GO TO THE INTER-HIGH..?
THINK...!
HUH!?
HE PLANNED EVERYTHING, INCLUDING WHEN AND WHERE TO LET US CATCH UP TO THEM...
...AND EVEN TOOK INTO ACCOUNT WHEN THE NON-PASSING BOARD WOULD COME OUT!!
...IS ONE HECK OF A STRATEGIST!!
IT'S NO USE... PERM-SENPAI...

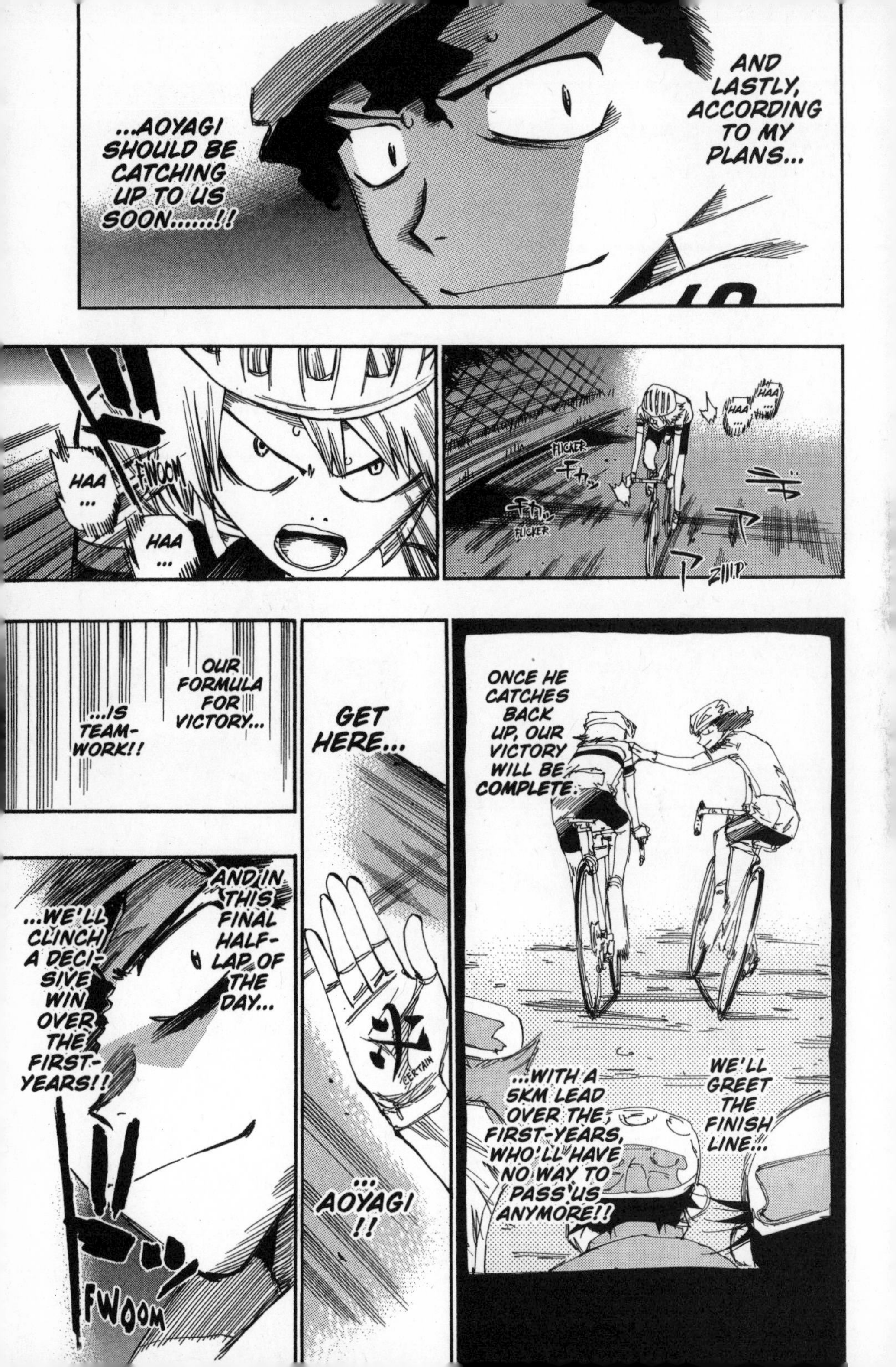
AND LASTLY, ACCORDING TO MY PLANS...
...AOYAGI SHOULD BE CATCHING UP TO US SOON......!!
HAA... HAA...
FLICKER
FLICKER
ZIIIP
HAA...
FWOOM
HAA...
ONCE HE CATCHES BACK UP, OUR VICTORY WILL BE COMPLETE.
WE'LL GREET THE FINISH LINE...
...WITH A 5KM LEAD OVER THE FIRST-YEARS, WHO'LL HAVE NO WAY TO PASS US ANYMORE!!
GET HERE...
CERTAIN
...AOYAGI!!
OUR FORMULA FOR VICTORY...
...IS TEAMWORK!!
AND IN THIS FINAL HALF-LAP OF THE DAY...
...WE'LL CLINCH A DECISIVE WIN OVER THE FIRST-YEARS!!
FWOOM

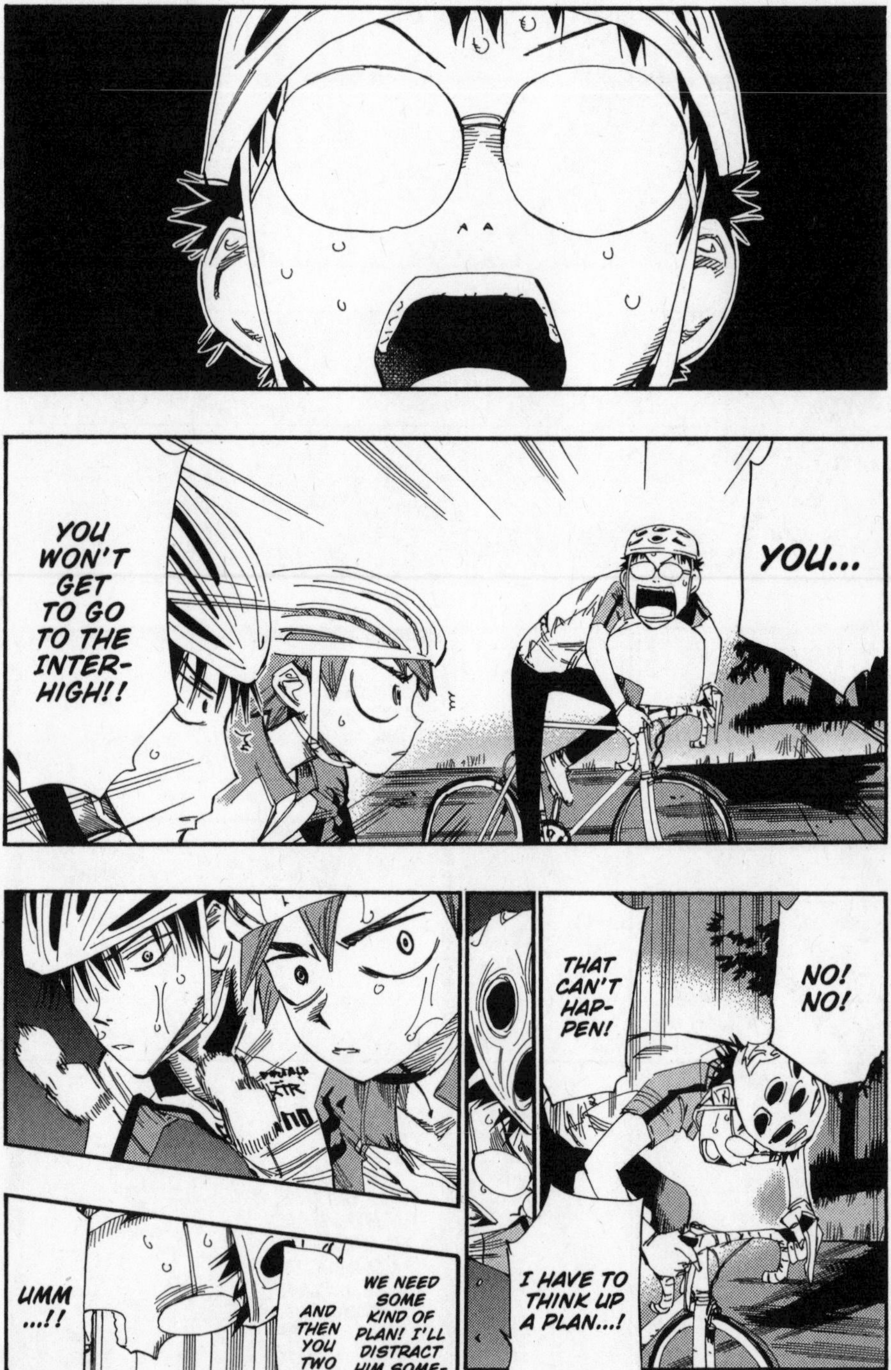
YOU...
YOU WON'T GET TO GO TO THE INTER-HIGH!!
NO! NO!
THAT CAN'T HAP-PEN!
I HAVE TO THINK UP A PLAN...!
WE NEED SOME KIND OF PLAN! I'LL DISTRACT HIM SOME-HOW...
AND THEN YOU TWO CAN... UM...
UMM ...!!

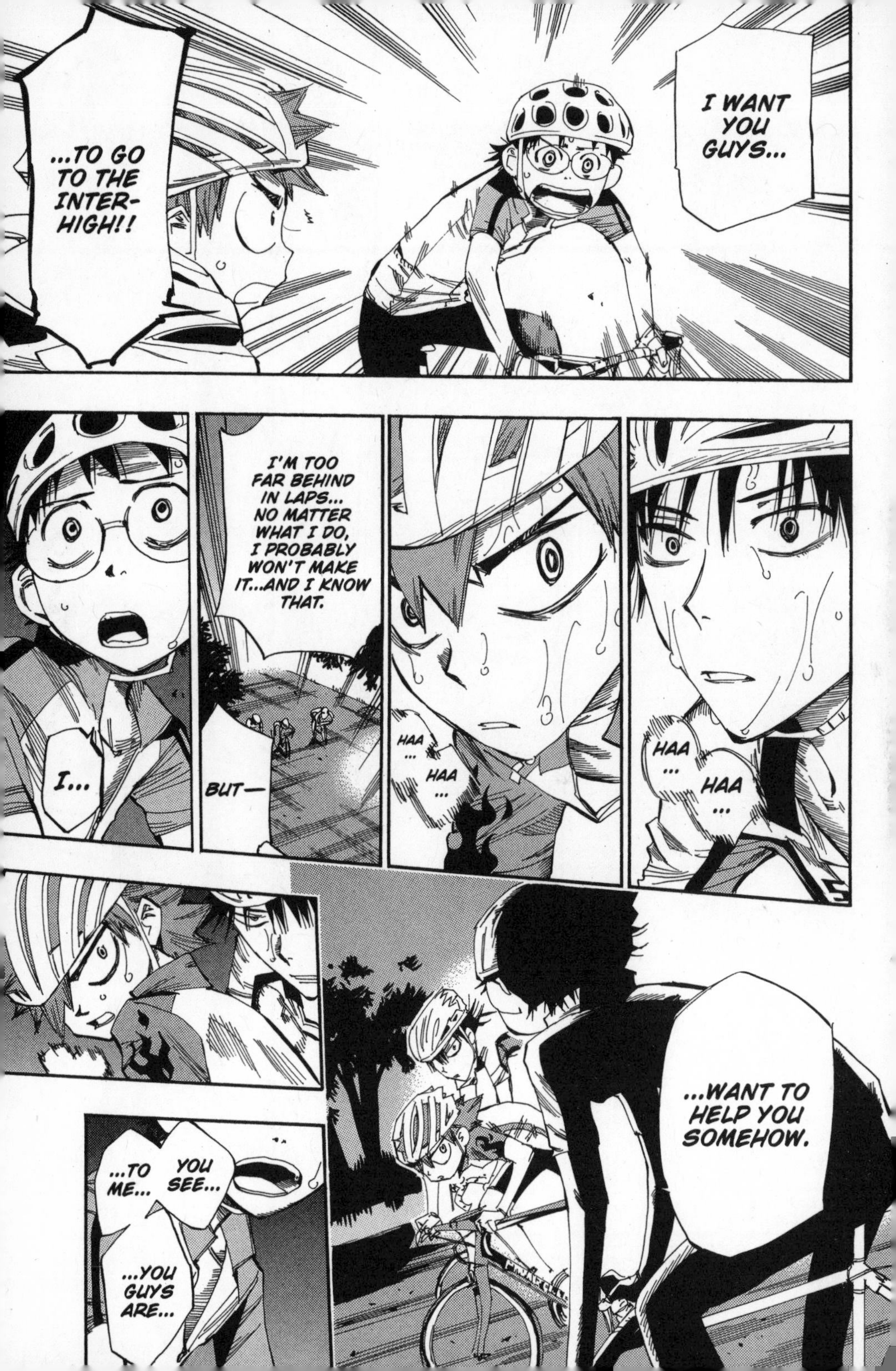

I WANT YOU GUYS...
...TO GO TO THE INTER-HIGH!!
HAA ... HAA ...
HAA ... HAA ...
I'M TOO FAR BEHIND IN LAPS... NO MATTER WHAT I DO, I PROBABLY WON'T MAKE IT...AND I KNOW THAT.
BUT—
I...
...WANT TO HELP YOU SOMEHOW.
YOU SEE...
...TO ME...
...YOU GUYS ARE...

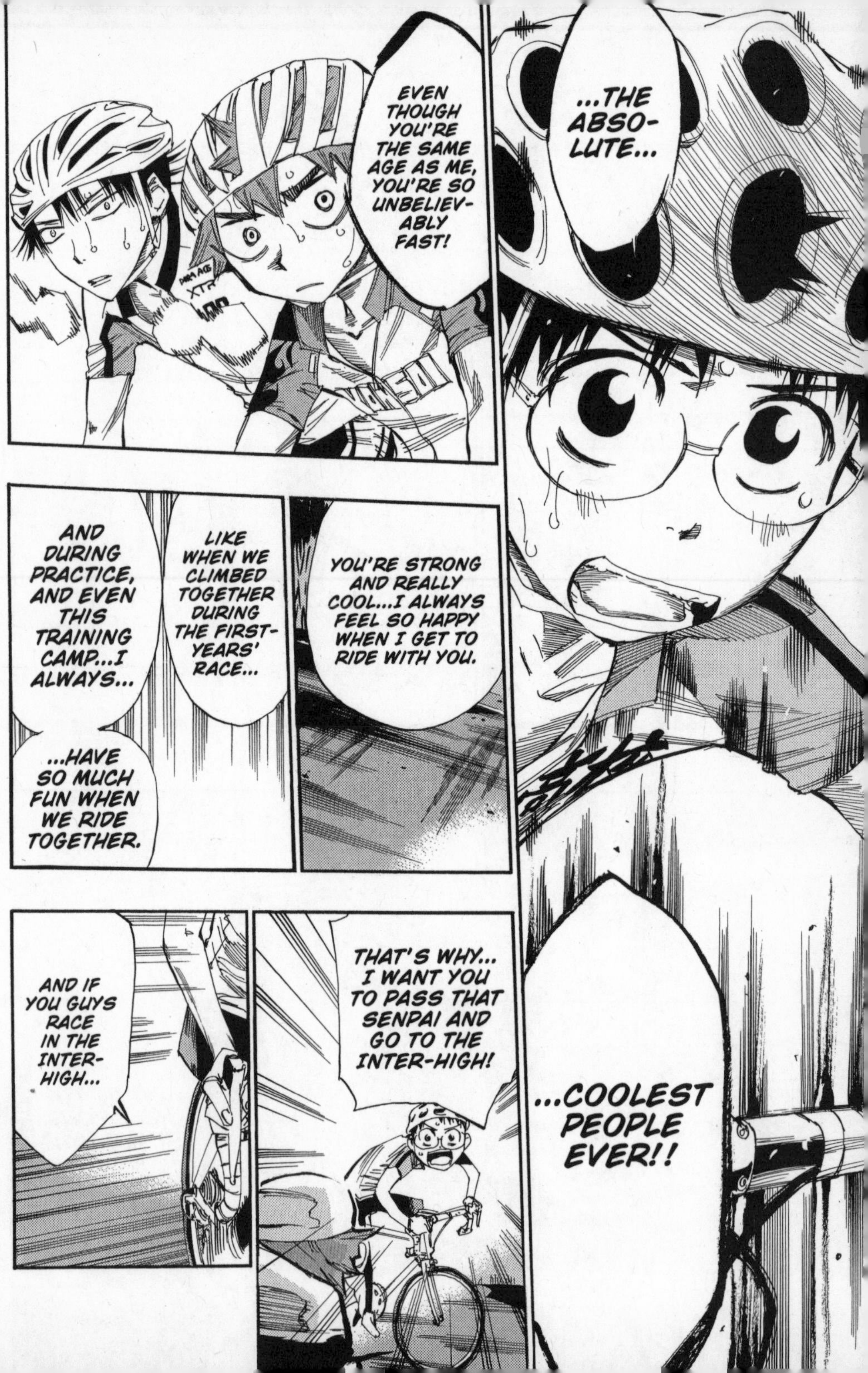
EVEN THOUGH YOU'RE THE SAME AGE AS ME, YOU'RE SO UNBELIEV-ABLY FAST!
YOU'RE STRONG AND REALLY COOL...I ALWAYS FEEL SO HAPPY WHEN I GET TO RIDE WITH YOU.
LIKE WHEN WE CLIMBED TOGETHER DURING THE FIRST-YEARS' RACE...
AND DURING PRACTICE, AND EVEN THIS TRAINING CAMP...I ALWAYS...
...HAVE SO MUCH FUN WHEN WE RIDE TOGETHER.
THAT'S WHY... I WANT YOU TO PASS THAT SENPAI AND GO TO THE INTER-HIGH!
AND IF YOU GUYS RACE IN THE INTER-HIGH...
...THE ABSO-LUTE...
...COOLEST PEOPLE EVER!!

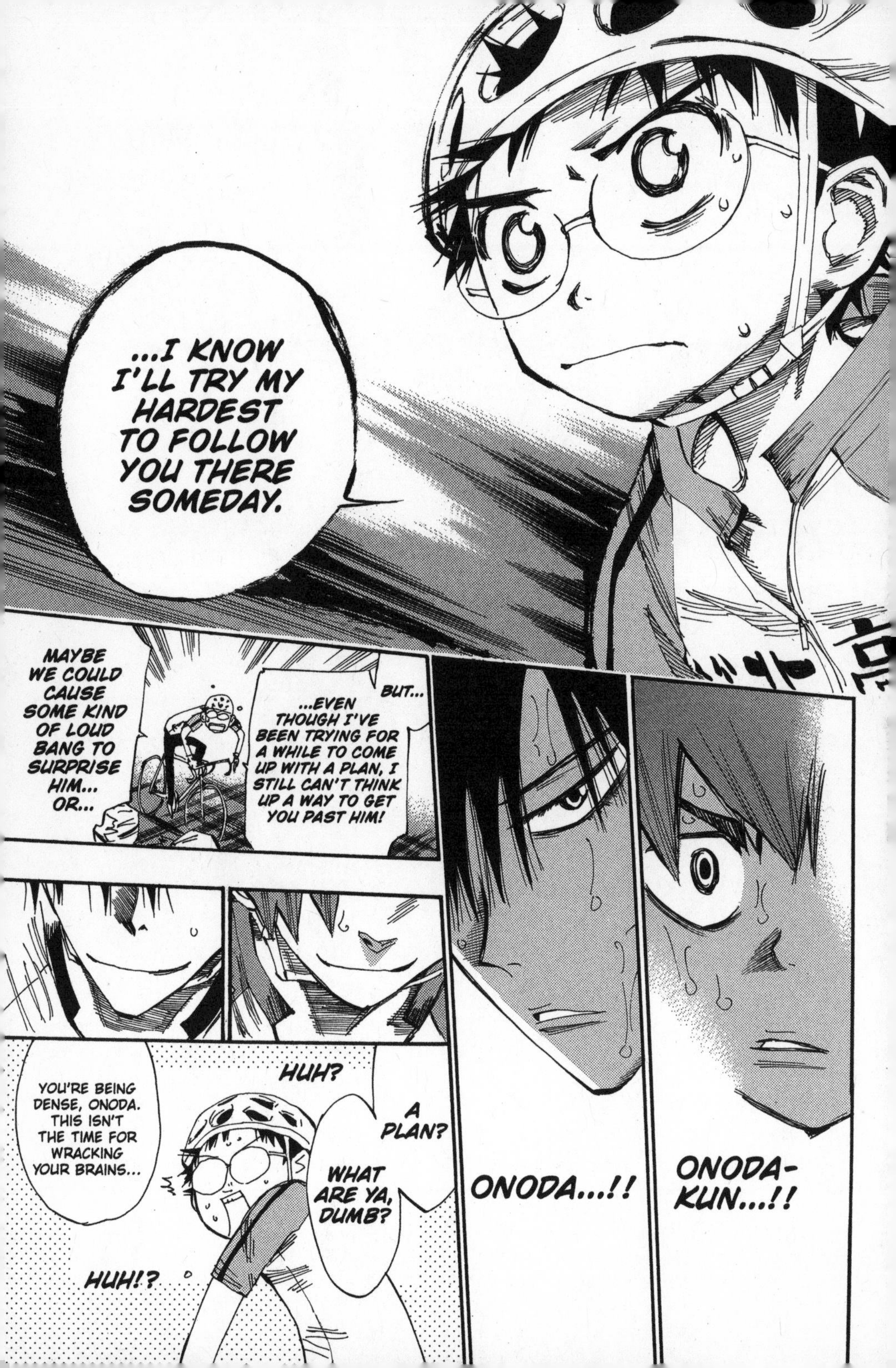
...I KNOW I'LL TRY MY HARDEST TO FOLLOW YOU THERE SOMEDAY.
ONODA-KUN...!!
ONODA...!!
BUT...
...EVEN THOUGH I'VE BEEN TRYING FOR A WHILE TO COME UP WITH A PLAN, I STILL CAN'T THINK UP A WAY TO GET YOU PAST HIM!
MAYBE WE COULD CAUSE SOME KIND OF LOUD BANG TO SURPRISE HIM... OR...
HUH?
A PLAN?
WHAT ARE YA, DUMB?
YOU'RE BEING DENSE, ONODA. THIS ISN'T THE TIME FOR WRACKING YOUR BRAINS...
HUH!?

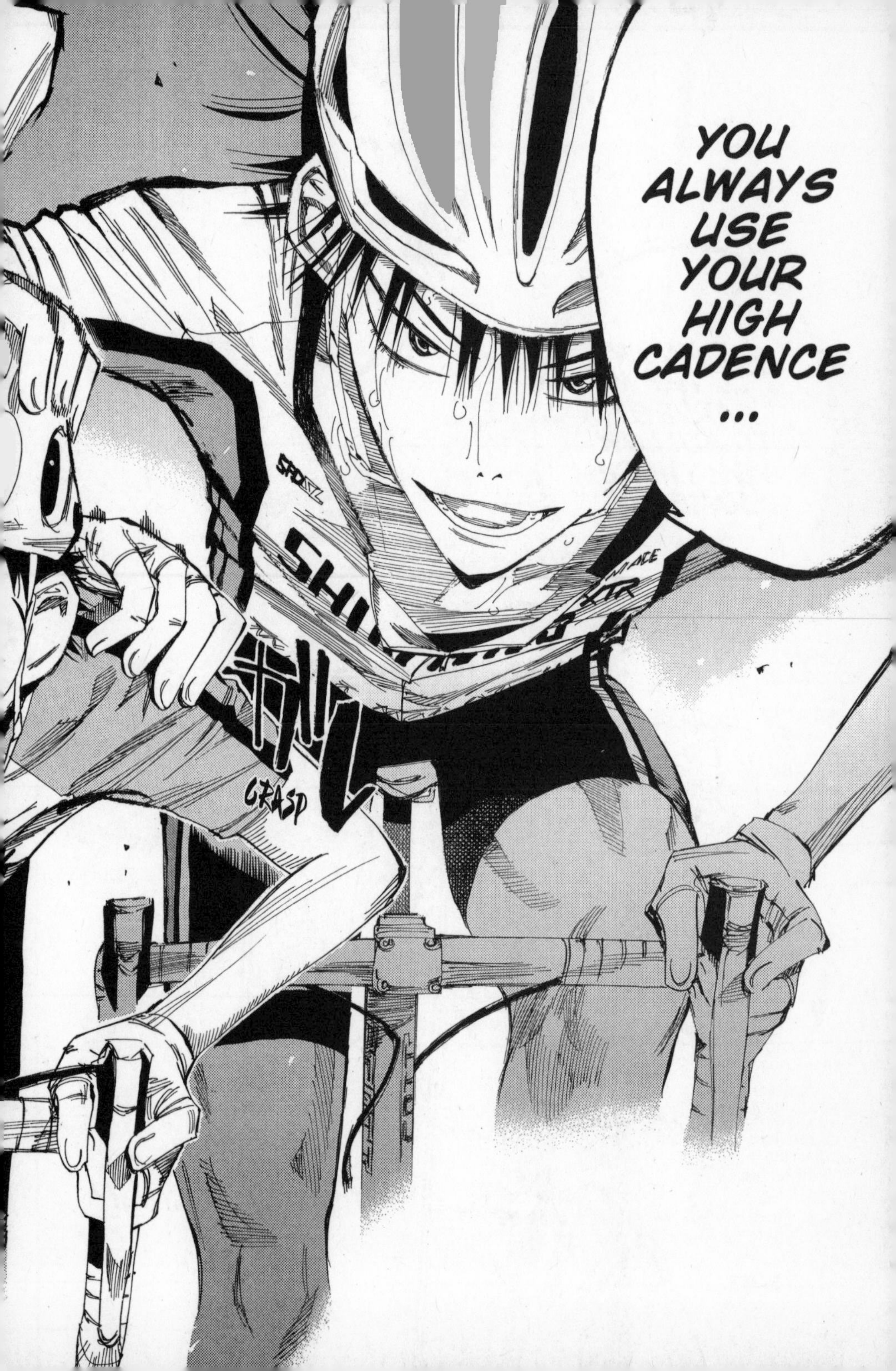
YOU ALWAYS USE YOUR HIGH CADENCE ...
GRASP

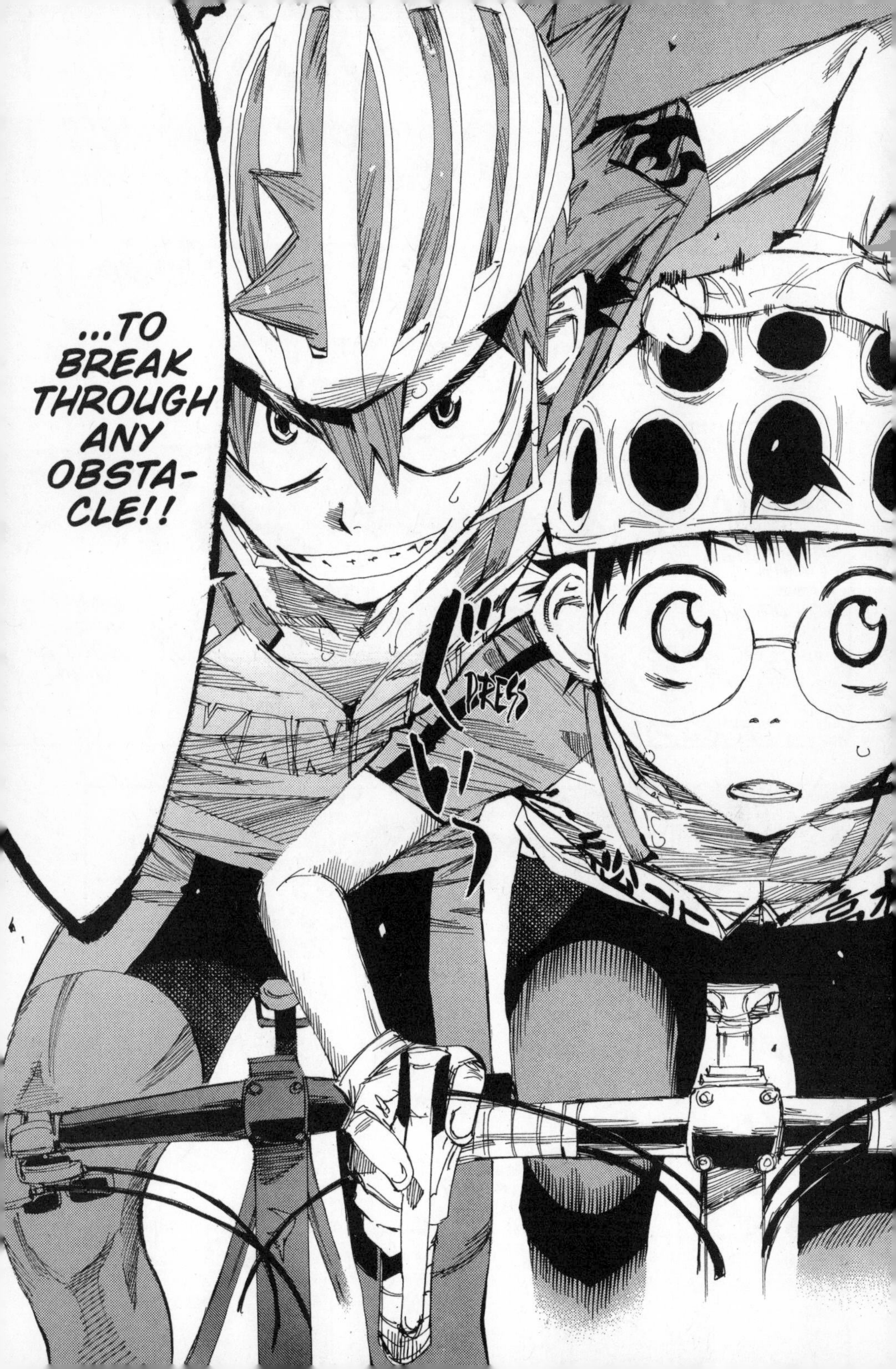
...TO BREAK THROUGH ANY OBSTA-CLE!!
PRESS

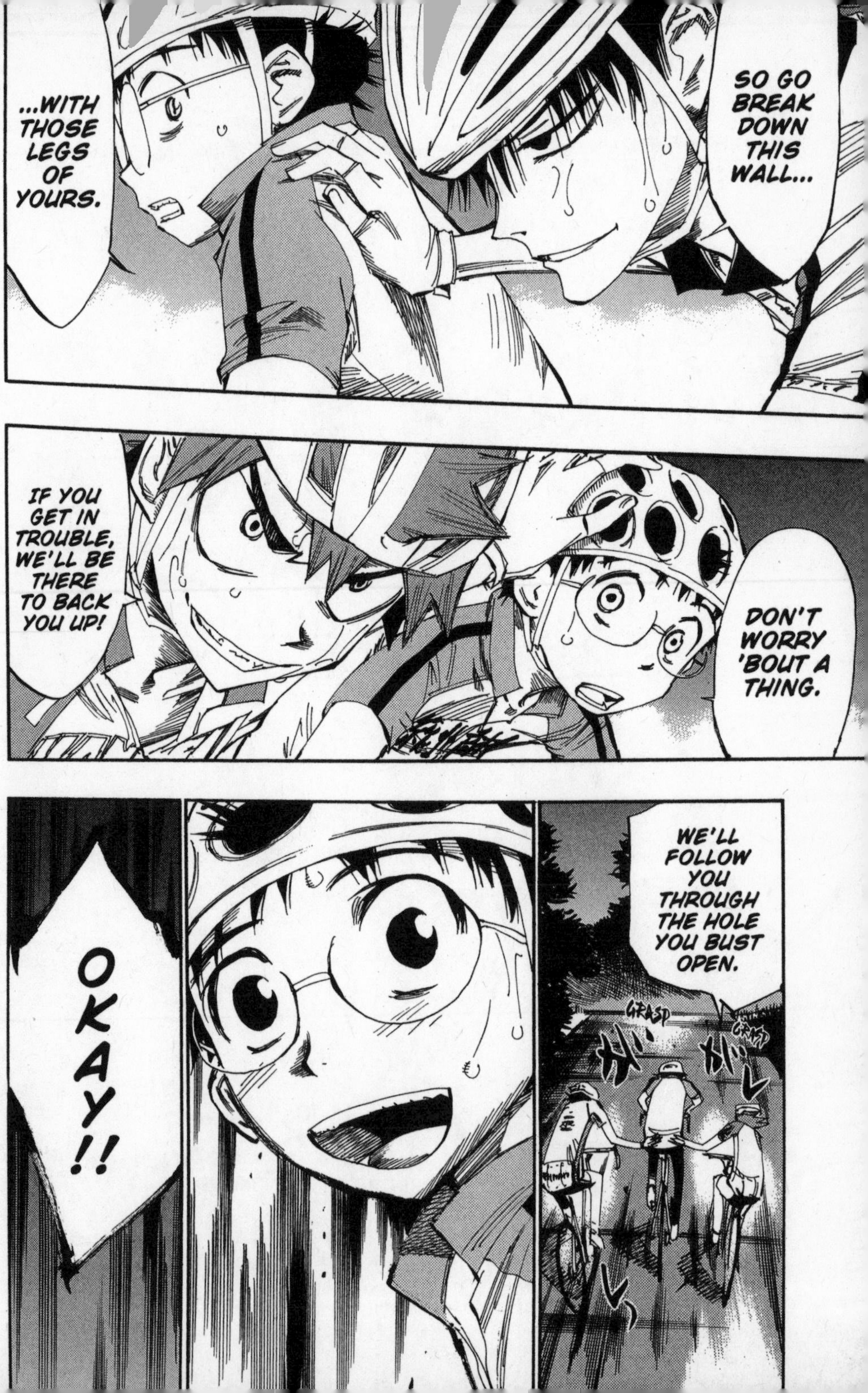

SO GO BREAK DOWN THIS WALL...
...WITH THOSE LEGS OF YOURS.
DON'T WORRY 'BOUT A THING.
IF YOU GET IN TROUBLE, WE'LL BE THERE TO BACK YOU UP!
WE'LL FOLLOW YOU THROUGH THE HOLE YOU BUST OPEN.
GRASP
GRASP
OKAY!!

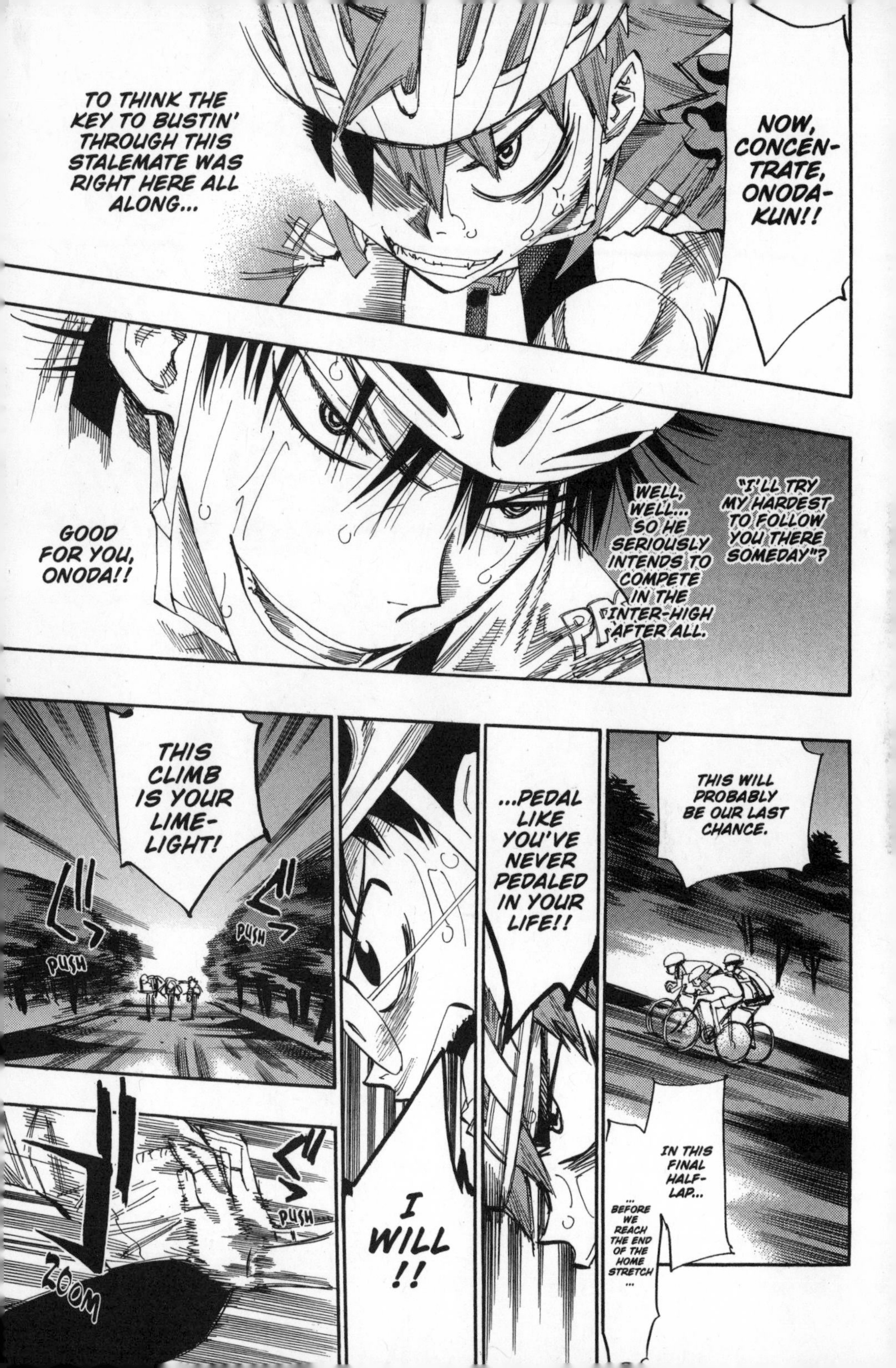
NOW, CONCENTRATE, ONODA-KUN!!
TO THINK THE KEY TO BUSTIN' THROUGH THIS STALEMATE WAS RIGHT HERE ALL ALONG...
"I'LL TRY MY HARDEST TO FOLLOW YOU THERE SOMEDAY"?
WELL, WELL... SO HE SERIOUSLY INTENDS TO COMPETE IN THE INTER-HIGH AFTER ALL.
GOOD FOR YOU, ONODA!!
THIS WILL PROBABLY BE OUR LAST CHANCE.
IN THIS FINAL HALF-LAP...
...BEFORE WE REACH THE END OF THE HOME STRETCH...
...PEDAL LIKE YOU'VE NEVER PEDALED IN YOUR LIFE!!
I WILL!!
THIS CLIMB IS YOUR LIME-LIGHT!
PUSH
PUSH
PUSH
ZOOM

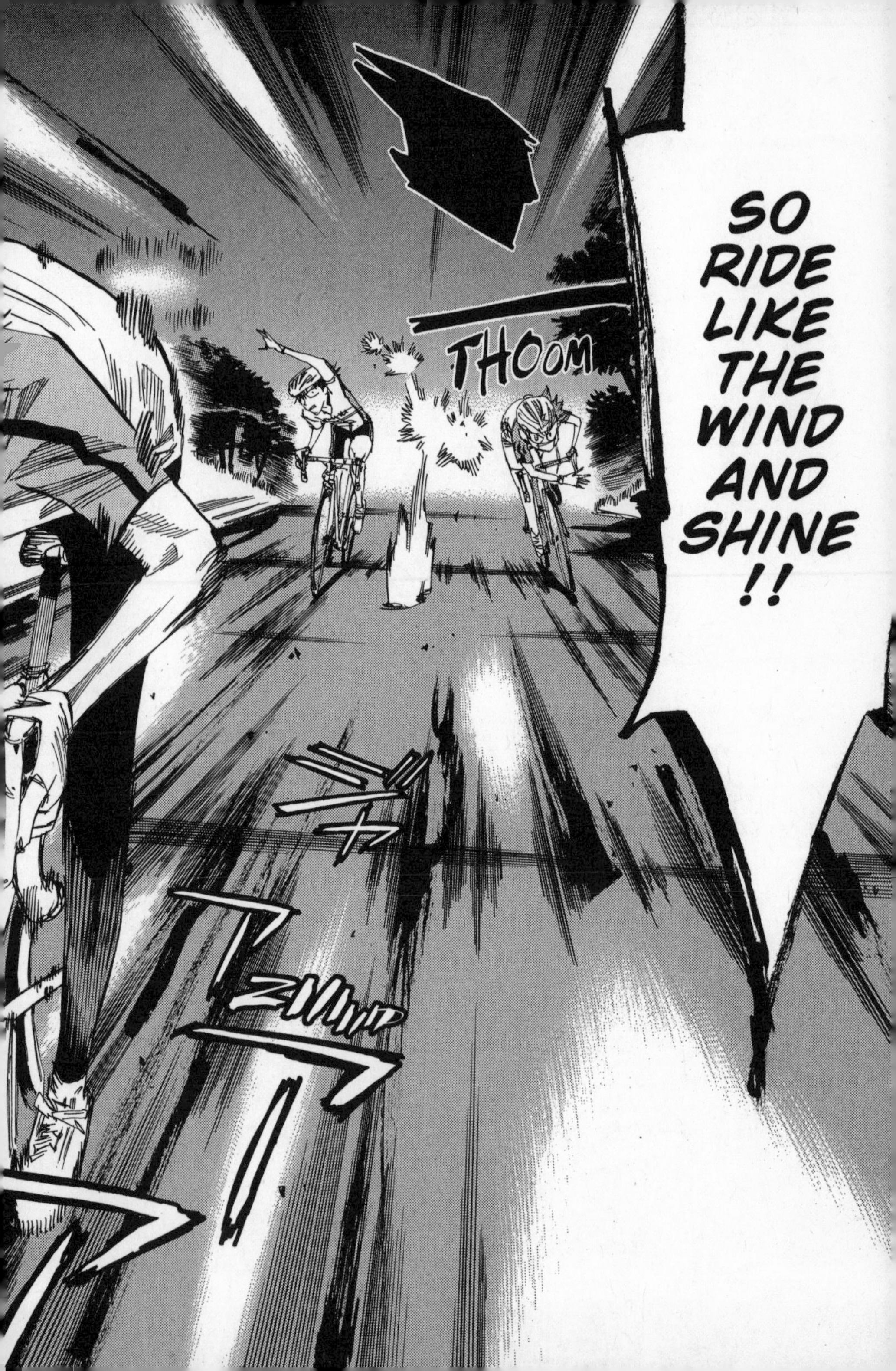
SO RIDE LIKE THE WIND AND SHINE!!
THOOM
ZOOMP

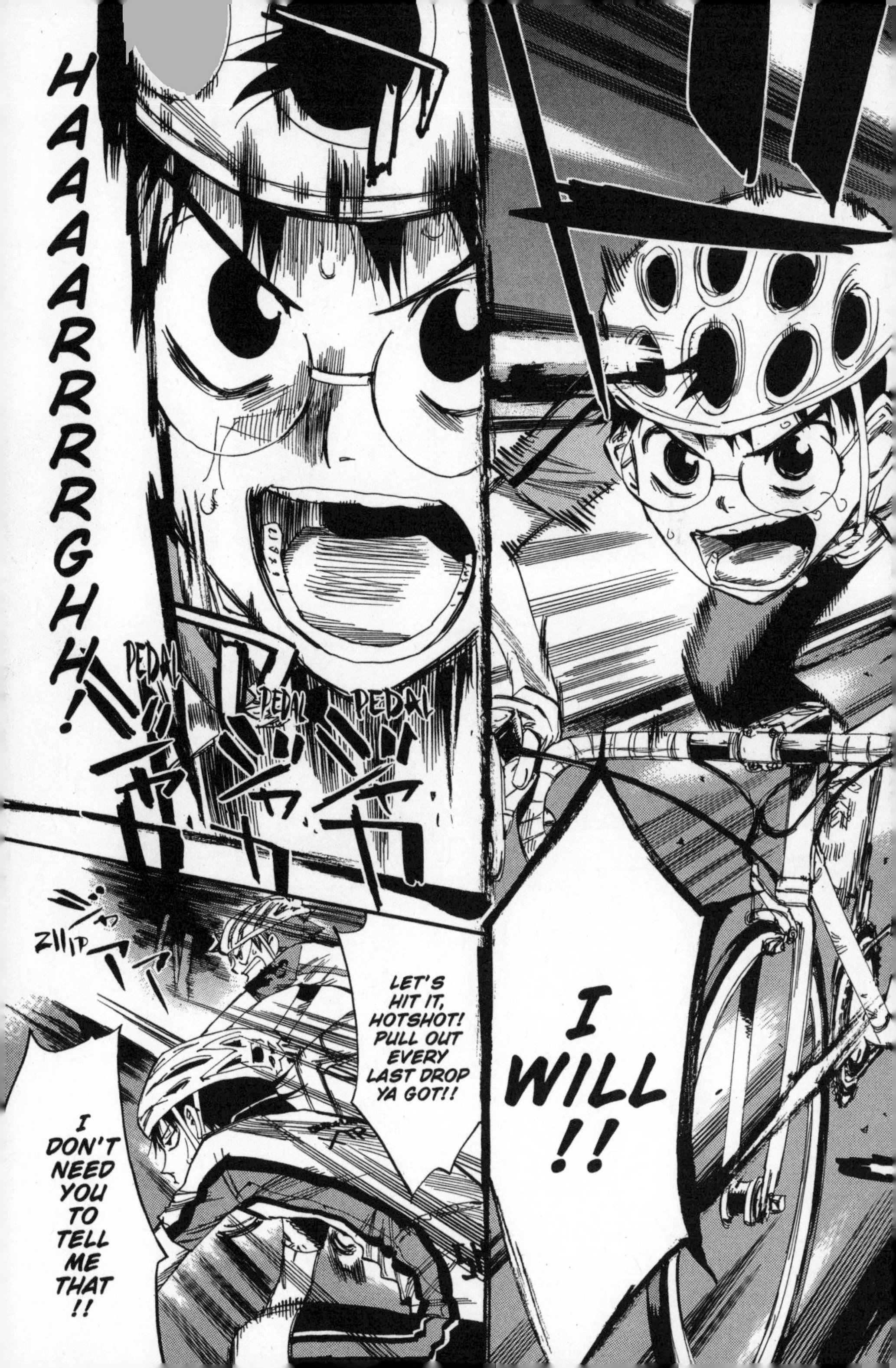
I WILL!!
HAAAARRRRGHH!
PEDAL
PEDAL
PEDAL
ZIIIP
LET'S HIT IT, HOTSHOT! PULL OUT EVERY LAST DROP YA GOT!!
I DON'T NEED YOU TO TELL ME THAT!!

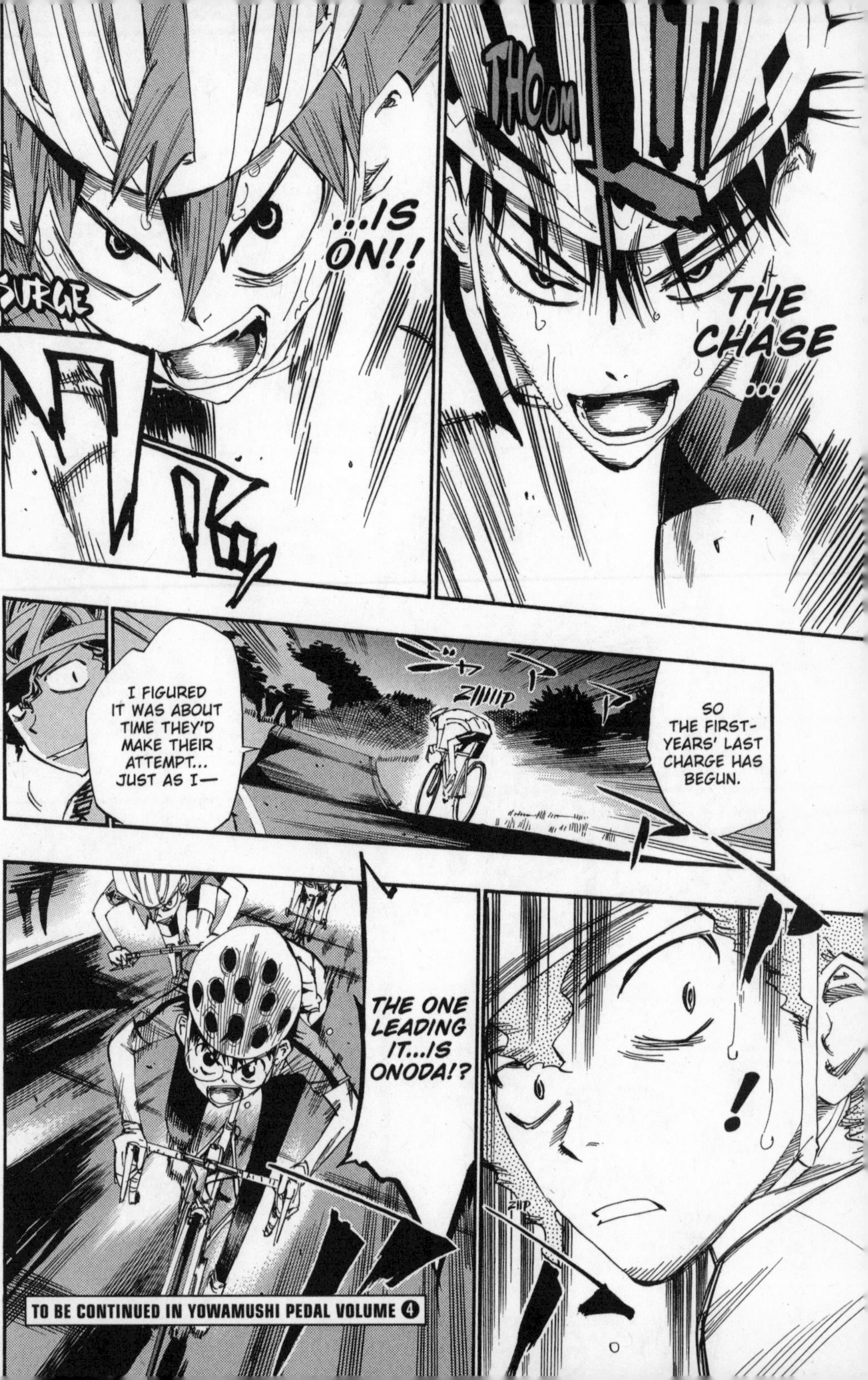
THOOM
THE CHASE...
...IS ON!!
SURGE
SO THE FIRST-YEARS' LAST CHARGE HAS BEGUN.
ZIIIIP
I FIGURED IT WAS ABOUT TIME THEY'D MAKE THEIR ATTEMPT... JUST AS I—
ZIP
THE ONE LEADING IT...IS ONODA!?
TO BE CONTINUED IN YOWAMUSHI PEDAL VOLUME 4

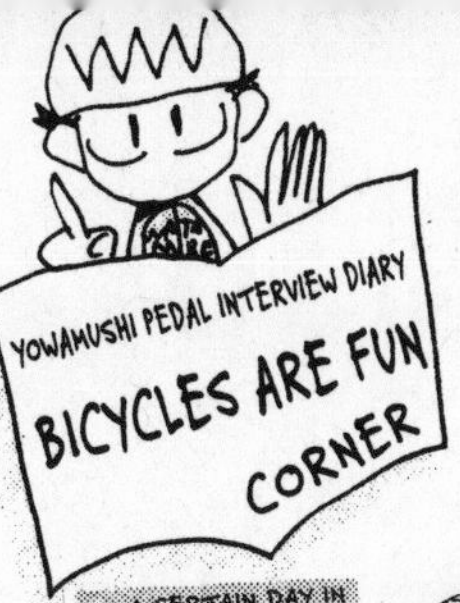
YOWAMUSHI PEDAL INTERVIEW DIARY
BICYCLES ARE FUN CORNER

WHEN I STARTED DRAWING THIS MANGA, I GOT THE OPPORTUNITY TO INTERVIEW A LOT OF DIFFERENT PEOPLE. THIS TIME, I THOUGHT I'D TELL YOU GUYS ABOUT MY MEETING AND INTERVIEW WITH THE SOLE JAPANESE ROAD BICYCLE RACER CURRENTLY COMPETING IN THE GRAND TOUR RACES OF EUROPE, **YUKIYA ARASHIRO**!

(INCIDENTALLY, THERE'S AN ARTICLE ABOUT OUR MEETING IN THE CURRENT ISSUE OF *SHOUNEN CHAMPION* MAGAZINE.)

HE WROTE THE MESSAGE ON THE WRAP-AROUND SLEEVE ON T JAPANESE EDITION OF VOLUME

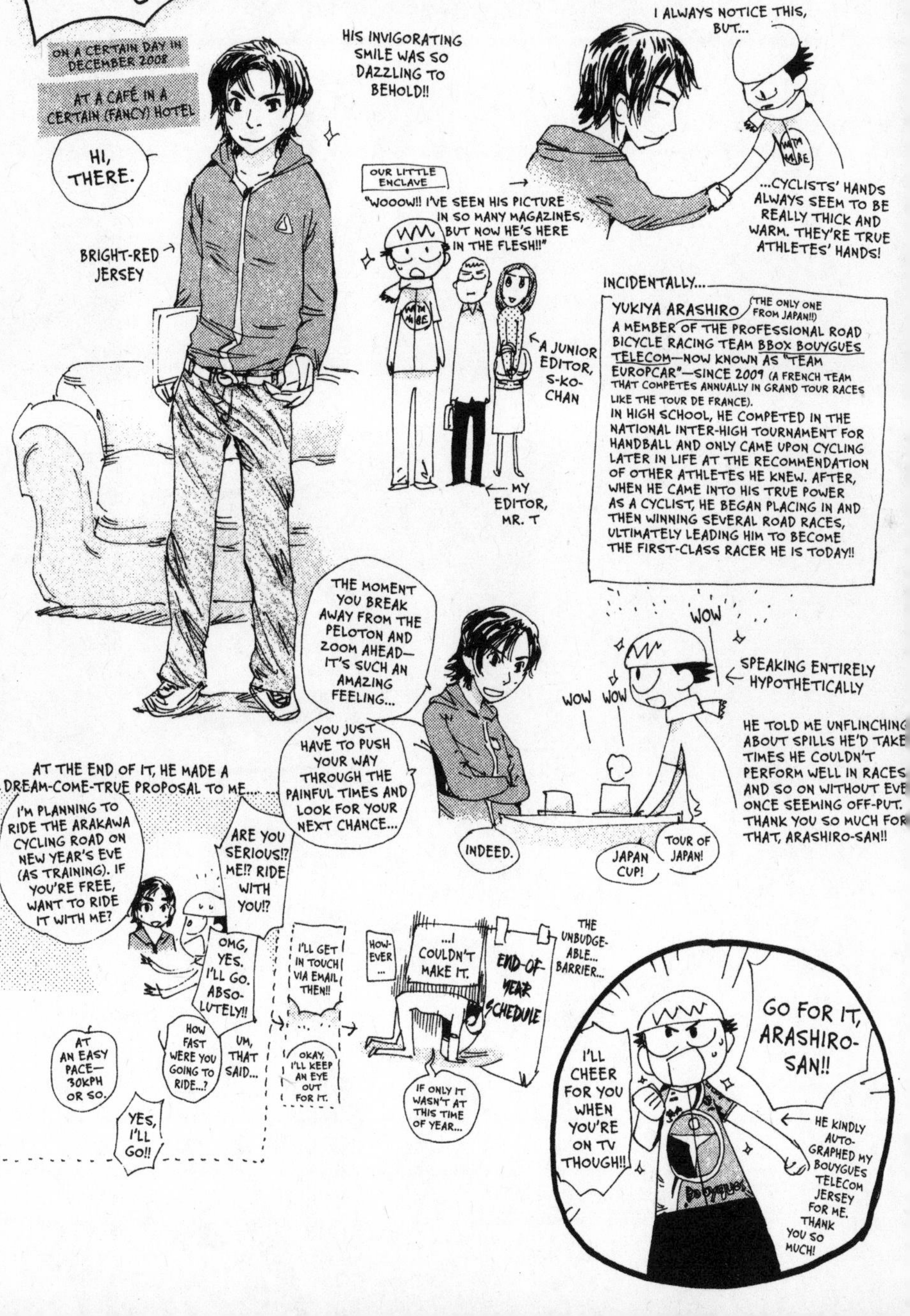
I ALWAYS NOTICE THIS, BUT...
...CYCLISTS' HANDS ALWAYS SEEM TO BE REALLY THICK AND WARM. THEY'RE TRUE ATHLETES' HANDS!
HIS INVIGORATING SMILE WAS SO DAZZLING TO BEHOLD!!
OUR LITTLE ENCLAVE
"WOOOW!! I'VE SEEN HIS PICTURE IN SO MANY MAGAZINES, BUT NOW HE'S HERE IN THE FLESH!!"
A JUNIOR EDITOR, S-KO-CHAN
MY EDITOR, MR. T
ON A CERTAIN DAY IN DECEMBER 2008
AT A CAFÉ IN A CERTAIN (FANCY) HOTEL
HI, THERE.
BRIGHT-RED JERSEY
INCIDENTALLY...
YUKIYA ARASHIRO (THE ONLY ONE FROM JAPAN!!)
A MEMBER OF THE PROFESSIONAL ROAD BICYCLE RACING TEAM BBOX BOUYGUES TELECOM—NOW KNOWN AS "TEAM EUROPCAR"—SINCE 2009 (A FRENCH TEAM THAT COMPETES ANNUALLY IN GRAND TOUR RACES LIKE THE TOUR DE FRANCE).
IN HIGH SCHOOL, HE COMPETED IN THE NATIONAL INTER-HIGH TOURNAMENT FOR HANDBALL AND ONLY CAME UPON CYCLING LATER IN LIFE AT THE RECOMMENDATION OF OTHER ATHLETES HE KNEW. AFTER, WHEN HE CAME INTO HIS TRUE POWER AS A CYCLIST, HE BEGAN PLACING IN AND THEN WINNING SEVERAL ROAD RACES, ULTIMATELY LEADING HIM TO BECOME THE FIRST-CLASS RACER HE IS TODAY!!
WOW
SPEAKING ENTIRELY HYPOTHETICALLY
WOW WOW
HE TOLD ME UNFLINCHING ABOUT SPILLS HE'D TAKE TIMES HE COULDN'T PERFORM WELL IN RACES AND SO ON WITHOUT EVE ONCE SEEMING OFF-PUT. THANK YOU SO MUCH FOR THAT, ARASHIRO-SAN!!
THE MOMENT YOU BREAK AWAY FROM THE PELOTON AND ZOOM AHEAD—IT'S SUCH AN AMAZING FEELING...
YOU JUST HAVE TO PUSH YOUR WAY THROUGH THE PAINFUL TIMES AND LOOK FOR YOUR NEXT CHANCE...
INDEED.
TOUR OF JAPAN!
JAPAN CUP!
AT THE END OF IT, HE MADE A DREAM-COME-TRUE PROPOSAL TO ME...
I'M PLANNING TO RIDE THE ARAKAWA CYCLING ROAD ON NEW YEAR'S EVE (AS TRAINING). IF YOU'RE FREE, WANT TO RIDE IT WITH ME?
ARE YOU SERIOUS!? ME!? RIDE WITH YOU!?
OMG, YES. I'LL GO. ABSOLUTELY!!
HOW FAST WERE YOU GOING TO RIDE...?
AT AN EASY PACE—30KPH OR SO.
UM, THAT SAID...
YES, I'LL GO!!
I'LL GET IN TOUCH VIA EMAIL THEN!!
OKAY, I'LL KEEP AN EYE OUT FOR IT.
HOWEVER...
...I COULDN'T MAKE IT.
THE UNBUDGEABLE... BARRIER...
END-OF-YEAR SCHEDULE
IF ONLY IT WASN'T AT THIS TIME OF YEAR...
GO FOR IT, ARASHIRO-SAN!!
I'LL CHEER FOR YOU WHEN YOU'RE ON TV THOUGH!!
HE KINDLY AUTOGRAPHED MY BOUYGUES TELECOM JERSEY FOR ME. THANK YOU SO MUCH!